FAMILY LAW

Third Edition

D. Kelly Weisberg
Professor of Law
Hastings College of the Law
University of California

The *Emanuel Law Outlines* Series

Wolters Kluwer
Law & Business

AUSTIN BOSTON CHICAGO NEW YORK THE NETHERLANDS

Aspen Publishers
Attn: Permissions Department
76 Ninth Avenue, 7th Floor
New York, NY 10011-5201

To contact Customer Care, e-mail customer.service@aspenpublishers.com, call 1-800-234-1660, fax 1-800-901-9075, or mail correspondence to:

Aspen Publishers
Attn: Order Department
PO Box 990
Frederick, MD 21705

Printed in the United States of America.

1 2 3 4 5 6 7 8 9 0

ISBN 978-0-7355-9776-1

Library of Congress Cataloging-in-Publication Data

Weisberg, D. Kelly.
Family law / D. Kelly Weisberg.—3rd ed.
p. cm.—(The Emanuel law outlines series)
Includes index.
ISBN 978-0-7355-9776-1
1. Domestic relations—United States—Outlines, syllabi, etc. I. Title.

KF505W45 2011
346.7301'5—dc22

2010054041

About Wolters Kluwer Law & Business

Wolters Kluwer Law & Business is a leading provider of research information and workflow solutions in key specialty areas. The strengths of the individual brands of Aspen Publishers, CCH, Kluwer Law International and Loislaw are aligned within Wolters Kluwer Law & Business to provide comprehensive, in-depth solutions and expert-authored content for the legal, professional and education markets.

CCH was founded in 1913 and has served more than four generations of business professionals and their clients. The CCH products in the Wolters Kluwer Law & Business group are highly regarded electronic and print resources for legal, securities, antitrust and trade regulation, government contracting, banking, pension, payroll, employment and labor, and healthcare reimbursement and compliance professionals.

Aspen Publishers is a leading information provider for attorneys, business professionals and law students. Written by preeminent authorities, Aspen products offer analytical and practical information in a range of specialty practice areas from securities law and intellectual property to mergers and acquisitions and pension/benefits. Aspen's trusted legal education resources provide professors and students with high-quality, up-to-date and effective resources for successful instruction and study in all areas of the law.

Kluwer Law International supplies the global business community with comprehensive English-language international legal information. Legal practitioners, corporate counsel and business executives around the world rely on the Kluwer Law International journals, loose-leafs, books and electronic products for authoritative information in many areas of international legal practice.

Loislaw is a premier provider of digitized legal content to small law firm practitioners of various specializations. Loislaw provides attorneys with the ability to quickly and efficiently find the necessary legal information they need, when and where they need it, by facilitating access to primary law as well as state-specific law, records, forms and treatises.

Wolters Kluwer Law & Business, a unit of Wolters Kluwer, is headquartered in New York and Riverwoods, Illinois. Wolters Kluwer is a leading multinational publisher and information services company.

Abbreviations Used in Text

FEDERAL STATUTES

Adoption and Safe Families Act (ASFA)
Adoption Assistance and Child Welfare Act (AACWA)
Americans with Disabilities Act (ADA)
Bankruptcy Abuse Prevention and Consumer Protection Act (BAPCPA)
Bankruptcy Reform Act (BRA)
Child Abuse and Neglect Treatment Act (CAPTA)
Child Support Recovery Act (CSRA)
Deadbeat Parents Punishment Act (DPPA)
Defense of Marriage Act (DOMA)
Employee Retirement Income Security Act (ERISA)
Family and Medical Leave Act (FMLA)
Family Support Act (FSA)
Freedom of Access to Clinic Entrances Act (FACE)
Full Faith and Credit for Child Support Orders Act (FFCSOA)
International Child Abduction Remedies Act (ICARA)
International Parental Kidnapping Crime Act (IPKCA)
Parental Kidnapping Prevention Act (PKPA)
Partial-Birth Abortion Ban Act (PBABA)
Personal Responsibility and Work Opportunity Reconciliation Act (PRWORA)
Pregnancy Discrimination Act (PDA)
Retirement Equity Act (REA or REAct)
Targeted Regulation of Abortion Providers (TRAP)
Unborn Victims of Violence Act (UVVA)
Uniting American Families Act (UAFA)
Violence Against Women Act (VAWA)

UNIFORM ACTS

Revised Uniform Reciprocal Enforcement of Support Act (RURESA)
Uniform Adoption Act (UAA)
Uniform Child Abduction Prevention Act (UCAPA)
Uniform Child Custody Jurisdiction Act (UCCJA)
Uniform Child Custody Jurisdiction and Enforcement Act (UCCJEA)

Uniform Collaborative Law Act (UCLA)
Uniform Interstate Enforcement of Domestic Violence Protection Orders Act (UIEDVPOA)
Uniform Interstate Family Support Act (UIFSA)
Uniform Marital Property Act (UMPA)
Uniform Marriage and Divorce Act (UMDA)
Uniform Parentage Act (UPA)
Uniform Premarital Agreement Act (UPAA)
Uniform Probate Code (UPC)
Uniform Reciprocal Enforcement of Support Act (URESA)
Uniform Services Former Spouses Protection Act (USFSPA)
Uniform Status of Children of Assisted Conception Act (USCACA)

OTHER

American Bar Association (ABA)
American Law Institute (ALI)
American Medical Association (AMA)
In vitro fertilization (IVF)
Qualified domestic relations orders (QDROs)

Summary of Contents

Table of Contents

CHAPTER 3

BEING MARRIED

CHAPTER 4
NONTRADITIONAL FAMILIES

CHAPTER 5

DIVORCE

CHAPTER 6

FINANCIAL CONSEQUENCES OF DISSOLUTION

CHAPTER 7

CHILD CUSTODY

CHAPTER 8

PROCREATION

CHAPTER 9

CHILD ABUSE AND NEGLECT

CHAPTER 10

THE PARENT-CHILD-STATE RELATIONSHIP IN SPECIAL CONTEXTS

Chapter 11
ADOPTION

Preface

Welcome to the exciting and dynamic field of family law!

Family law, also referred to as Domestic Relations, is the body of law that regulates the family and its members. Historically, family law was regulated at the state level. Today, the federal government occupies an increasingly prominent role in family law. This book is designed to help you understand the importance of both state and federal regulation of this fascinating subject area.

This book is not intended as a substitute for class materials or class discussion. Rather, it provides a useful supplement that will help clarify and enhance your understanding of major issues.

Certain special features of this book will help you master this field. These include:

- **Casebook Correlation Chart:** This chart (following this Preface) correlates each section of the *Outline* with the pages covering the same topic in each of the leading family law casebooks.
- **Capsule Summary:** This section summarizes the black-letter law principles of family law.
- **Quiz Yourself:** These short-answer questions, at the end of major sections in each chapter, help you test your knowledge on important concepts in family law.
- **Exam Tips:** These suggestions, at the end of every chapter, alert you to issues that are likely to appear on family law exams to help you focus your studies in preparation for the exam.
- **Glossary:** These definitions of key terms at the end of the book elucidate the meaning of words and phrases that appear in this study guide and in your casebook.

This book will be useful both throughout the semester and during exam preparation. Here are some suggestions about how best to use it:

1. Use this *Emanuel Law Outline* to prepare for each day's class. First, read the assigned material in your casebook. Then, use the *Casebook Correlation Chart* (following this Preface) to locate the corresponding subject matter in the *Outline*. Next, read the material in the *Outline* to help you better understand the casebook assignment. If you want to strengthen your knowledge about a particular case or statute, look up the case name in the Table of Cases or the statute in the Table of Statutes (at the back of this *Outline*), and read the discussion of the case or statute in this book.
2. At the end of each unit in your course, do the *Quiz Yourself* short-answer questions to see if you have grasped the assigned material.
3. At the end of the course, use the material in the *Capsule Summary* to help you structure and supplement your outline (if you choose to prepare a personal outline for the course).
4. When you begin studying for the exam, review the course material by reading the *Capsule Summary*. This overview will aid you in structuring your studying by helping you focus your attention on the areas you need to know for the exam.
5. Review some or all of the *Quiz Yourself* short-answer questions. It is helpful to answer the *Quiz Yourself* questions both orally and in written form. In writing answers, prepare short essays addressing both sides of a question.
6. Review the course material by preparing answers (preferably, under exam conditions) to the full-length *Essay Exam Questions* at the end of this *Outline*. If the *Essay Exam Questions* identify any gaps in your knowledge, refresh your memory by reviewing relevant portions of the *Outline*.

7. On the day before the exam, quickly review the *Capsule Summary* and the *Exam Tips* sections at the end of each chapter.

I hope you will find the numerous study tools provided in this *Emanuel Law Outline* beneficial as you explore family law—an area of law that touches everyone. For research assistance, I would like to thank Kristen Driskell for her invaluable help in the preparation of this manuscript.

Good luck and enjoy family law! If you would like any other publication of Aspen Publishers, you can find it at your bookstore or at *www.AspenLaw.com.*

D. Kelly Weisberg
Professor of Law
Hastings College of the Law
University of California
weisberg@uchastings.edu

Casebook Correlation Chart

(**Note:** General sections of the Outline are omitted for this chart. **NC** = not directly covered by this casebook. For updates to the correlation chart, visit *www.AspenLaw.com.)*

Weisberg: Family Law Emanuel Law Outline (by chapter and section heading)	**Areen & Regan:** ***Family Law: Cases and Materials*** (Fifth Edition, 2006)	**Harris, Carbone & Teitelbaum:** ***Family Law*** (Fourth Edition, 2010)	**Ellman, Kurtz, Weithorn, Bix, Czapanskiy & Eichner:** ***Family Law: Cases, Text, Problems*** (Fifth Edition, 2010)	**Weisberg & Appleton:** ***Modern Family Law: Cases and Materials*** (Fourth Edition, 2010)	**Wadlington & O'Brien:** ***Domestic Relations: Cases and Materials*** (Sixth Edition, 2007)
CHAPTER 1 INTRODUCTION					
I. Generally	2-10	xxix, 3	3-4, 18-19	xxxi-xxxii	v-ix
II. Societal Influences on Family Law	155-172	33-36, 291-292, 865-867	3-24	xxxi-xxxii	NC
III. Contemporary Legal Trends	NC	NC	19-24	xxxii	v
CHAPTER 2 PREPARING TO MARRY					
I. Premarital Controversies	131-132	NC	200-203	108-118	179-192
II. Premarital Agreements	151-154, 201-237	101-102, 691-717	304-305, 810-863	118-130	595-621
III. Restrictions on Entry into Marriage	57-140, 779-782	153-233	58-73, 121-199	130-214	225-265
IV. Annulment	135-141, 407-408	154, 156, 159-160, 174-178	263-264	196	210-225
V. Conflict of Laws: Which Law Governs Marriage Validity?	108-109, 144-145	234-241	175-182	175	265-277
CHAPTER 3 BEING MARRIED					
I. Introduction	155-170	NC	19-24	103-107, 215-222	58-68, 278-281
II. Regulation of Roles and Responsibilities	58-71, 146-238, 345-256	34-109, 179, 144-152	204-227	222-252	281-311, 353-355
III. Parenting	196-201, 216-219, 228-232, 948-954	876-890	NC	252-286	NC
IV. Criminal Law and Tort Law	281-345	109-134	249-254, 495-501	286-337	311-353
CHAPTER 4 NONTRADITIONAL FAMILIES					
I. Introduction	2-10	3-12, 228-233	5-6, 919-924	339	NC
II. Extended Families	1118-1129	112-113	31-39	348-355	NC
III. Communal Family	28-47	18-32	25-31	340-348	NC
IV. Unmarried Couples (Opposite-Sex and Same-Sex Couples)	10-28, 769-782	13-19, 245-287	39-44, 924-1123	355-415	1-11, 20-58, 127-153

Weisberg: Family Law Emanuel Law Outline (by chapter and section heading)	**Areen & Regan:** ***Family Law: Cases and Materials*** (Fifth Edition, 2006)	**Harris, Carbone & Teitelbaum:** ***Family Law*** (Fourth Edition, 2010)	**Ellman, Kurtz, Weithorn, Bix, Czapanskiy & Eichner:** ***Family Law: Cases, Text, Problems*** (Fifth Edition, 2010)	**Weisberg & Appleton:** ***Modern Family Law: Cases and Materials*** (Fourth Edition, 2010)	**Wadlington & O'Brien:** ***Domestic Relations: Cases and Materials*** (Sixth Edition, 2007)
CHAPTER 5 DIVORCE					
I. Background	357-358	291-292	255-264	451-458	356-359
II. Fault-Based Grounds	358-364	292-298	281-282, 302-304, 487-495	458-472	359-376, 378-379
III. Fault-Based Defenses	364-374	298-300	281-282, 487-495	472-479	376-377
IV. No-Fault Divorce	374-408	302-342	264-282	479-504	379-382
V. Access to Divorce	408-420	313-316	273-274, 857-858	505-516	NC
VI. Discrimination on the Basis of Divorce	NC	NC	NC	511-512	NC
VII. Role of Counsel	NC	739-769	NC	518-537	NC
VIII. Divorce Jurisdiction	121-126, 418-420	794-802	304-313, 757-774, 878-883	537-555	383-430
IX. Alternatives to Divorce: Annulments and Separations	135-141, 407-408	159-160, 308-313	263-264, 280-281	512-517	210-214
X. Alternative Dispute Resolution Processes	861-881	769-791	NC	783-785	477-479
CHAPTER 6 FINANCIAL CONSEQUENCES OF DISSOLUTION					
I. Standards for the Initial Award of Property, Spousal Support, and Child Support	697-769, 782-817	343-510	317-466, 503-573	557-617	431-594
II. Modification of Spousal and Child Support Awards	752-758, 798-809	513-542	466-487, 559-573	638-646	569-575
III. Jurisdiction and Enforcement of Child Support Awards	817-861	543-565, 807-824	573-622	646-668	584-595, 648-660
IV. Separation Agreements	846-861	717-737	304-305, 863-915	671-678	660-665
V. Tax Considerations	NC	566-574	NC	617-623	638-648
CHAPTER 7 CHILD CUSTODY					
I. Introduction	429-436	583-584	623-628	679-682	1038
II. Standards for Selecting the Custodial Parent	436-594	584-660	628-693	683-727	1039-1069
III. Standards for Selecting the Noncustodial Parent: Visitation	612-630	660-680	694-703	727-739	1114-1146
IV. Standards: Parent Versus Nonparent Disputes	621-663	584-594, 867-876, 939-972	726-750	739-754	1069-1098
V. Role of Special Participants	554-566	641-643	750-751	754-767	1147-1152

Weisberg: Family Law Emanuel Law Outline (by chapter and section heading)	Areen & Regan: *Family Law: Cases and Materials* (Fifth Edition, 2006)	Harris, Carbone & Teitelbaum: *Family Law* (Fourth Edition, 2010)	Ellman, Kurtz, Weithorn, Bix, Czapanskiy & Eichner: *Family Law: Cases, Text, Problems* (Fifth Edition, 2010)	Weisberg & Appleton: *Modern Family Law: Cases and Materials* (Fourth Edition, 2010)	Wadlington & O'Brien: *Domestic Relations: Cases and Materials* (Sixth Edition, 2007)
VI. Modification	594-612	680-687	703-725	768-778	NC
VII. Jurisdiction and Enforcement	661-695	825-854	774-807	778-781	1153-1178
VIII. Child Abduction	664-682, 685-690	845-861	751-755, 782-784	782-783	1178-1201
IX. Process to Resolve Disputes	864-874, 876-881	781-791	NC	783-793	1099-1113
CHAPTER 8 PROCREATION					
I. Contraception	238-252, 884-890	134-135, 197-200	46-69, 1186-1193	1-20	11-20, 74-84, 732-736
II. Abortion	252-281, 884-899, 907-916, 940-943	135-144	1193-1204	20-92	85-127, 736-737
III. Restrictions on the Rights of Pregnant Women	919-929, 948-954	NC	1238-1244	102, 647-651, 856	902-914
IV. Fetal Homicide Legislation	NC	NC	NC	NC	912-914
V. Alternative Reproductive Technology	954-1016	1013-1041	1403-1443	1003-1045	737-846
CHAPTER 9 CHILD ABUSE AND NEGLECT					
I. Historical Background	1189-1192	775	1204-1205	809-814	1202
II. Threshold Standard for Intervention	1022-1025, 1060-1062, 1189-1192	NC	1204-1224	795-808	1203-1263
III. Defining Child Abuse	1192-1214	652-659	1217-1224	814-857	901-950, 1221
IV. Defining Child Neglect	1214-1236	NC	1224-1238	829-847	889-901, 1221
V. Procedure	1233-1244	NC	1215-1217, 1277-1306	858-874	901-920
VI. Intervention	1244-1303	NC	1244-1277	874-918	1224-1263
CHAPTER 10 THE PARENT-CHILD-STATE RELATIONSHIP IN SPECIAL CONTEXTS					
I. Torts	1130-1137	NC	NC	NC	1023-1033
II. Contracts	1142-1147	NC	NC	NC	NC
III. Property	1147-1154	904-906	1160-1162	918-923	1033-1036
IV. Education	1154-1170	775	1128-1160	15-20, 936-938	847-875
V. Medical Care	1137-1142	36, 144-152	1171-1184	833-836	952-1022
CHAPTER 11 ADOPTION					
I. Introduction	1304-1305	973-976	1307-1310	939-941	1264-1266
II. Selection Standards for Adoptive Parents	1356-1385	992-1005, 1008-1013	1365-1384	954-973	1266-1278, 1306-1326

Weisberg: Family Law Emanuel Law Outline (by chapter and section heading)	**Areen & Regan:** ***Family Law: Cases and Materials*** (Fifth Edition, 2006)	**Harris, Carbone & Teitelbaum:** ***Family Law*** (Fourth Edition, 2010)	**Ellman, Kurtz, Weithorn, Bix, Czapanskiy & Eichner:** ***Family Law: Cases, Text, Problems*** (Fifth Edition, 2010)	**Weisberg & Appleton:** ***Modern Family Law: Cases and Materials*** (Fourth Edition, 2010)	**Wadlington & O'Brien:** ***Domestic Relations: Cases and Materials*** (Sixth Edition, 2007)
III. Consent	638-663, 1306-1317, 1327-1340	976-987	1317-1345	941-953	1278-1306
IV. Placement Procedure	1306-1323, 1351-1356	988-992	1345-1365	973-981	1326-1340
V. Subsidized Adoption	1323-1327	991	1379-1380	885-886, 976-977	1340-1342
VI. International Adoption	NC	1005-1008	1314-1315, 1384-1386	978-980	NC
VII. The Legal Consequences of Adoption	94, 1327-1328, 1346-1351	NC	1399-1400	982-1003	1342-1345
VIII. Open Adoption	1340-1346	984-986	1387, 1393-1399	995-998	1345-1359
IX. Equitable Adoption	1346-1351	976	NC	986	1359-1362
X. Adoptee's Right to Know of Origins	1396-1400	984-986	1387-1392	993-995	1362-1365
XI. Jurisdiction	1385-1388	832-833	NC	977-978	NC
XII. Adult Adoption	NC	NC	NC	985-986	1365-1370
XIII. Adoption Failure: Revocation and Abrogation	1388-1396, 1400-1410	991-992	1400-1403	999-1003	1331-1339

Capsule Summary

This Capsule Summary is useful for a quick review of the course in preparation for the exam. It is not intended as a substitute for mastering the material in the main outline.

CHAPTER 1
INTRODUCTION

I. DEFINITION

Family law explores the legal regulation of the family and its members. [1]

II. SOCIETAL INFLUENCES ON FAMILY LAW

Family law reflects several important societal influences.

A. **Women's movement:** The women's movement led to a change in public policy toward women. [2]

B. **Rising incidence of divorce:** No-fault divorce transformed rules of property distribution, spousal and child support, and custody. [3]

C. **Dissatisfaction with the family and the growth of alternative family forms:** Disillusionment with the nuclear family resulted in a reconceptualization of marriage and the family. Dissatisfaction with traditional means of dispute resolution contributed to the growth of family mediation. [3]

D. **Respect for family autonomy:** Increased dissatisfaction with the adversarial process contributed to the recognition of the ability of the parties to resolve their disputes without judicial intervention. [4]

E. **Children's rights movement:** The civil rights movement and the women's movement contributed to the birth of the children's rights movement, which led to recognition of the child's increased role in decision making. [4]

F. **New reproductive technology:** Developments in reproductive technology have enhanced women's reproductive freedom. [4]

G. **Decreasing influence of morality:** Family law reflects the decreasing influence of ideas of morality. [5]

III. TRENDS

Family law reflects three contemporary trends: (1) *federalization* (increasing congressional role), (2) *constitutionalization* (application of constitutional law), and (3) a movement toward *uniformity* of state law. [5]

CHAPTER 2

PREPARING TO MARRY

I. PREMARITAL CONTROVERSIES

A. Breach of promise to marry

1. **Generally:** A few states permit an action for breach of promise to marry which enables A to recover damages from B, if B terminates the engagement. [10]

2. **Historical background:** The claim of breach of promise to marry has its origins in early English tort and contract law. [10]

3. **Criticisms:** Criticisms have led many states to *abolish* the action. [10]

4. **Judicial and legislative responses to criticisms:** Even in states that continue to recognize the action, courts *circumscribe* recovery. [10]

5. **Damages:** The action is a ***hybrid*** (quasi-contract, quasi-tort), raising questions about the nature of damages, statutes of limitations, and abatement of the action upon death. [11]

6. **Defenses:** Possible defenses include: fraudulent misrepresentation, nondisclosure of previous unchaste conduct, impaired physical or mental health, or the marital status of either party at the time of the engagement. [11]

B. Gifts in contemplation of marriage

1. **Generally:** The ***majority rule*** specifies that, if a ring is given in contemplation of marriage, the *party who breaks* the engagement without justification is *not* entitled to return or retention of the ring. [12]

2. **Legal theories:** Several legal theories support recovery of the engagement ring: *conditional gift*, *fraud*, and *unjust enrichment*. [12]

3. **Modern trend:** The ***modern trend*** is to *minimize the importance of fault* in breaking the engagement. [12]

II. PREMARITAL AGREEMENTS

A. **Traditional view:** Traditionally, premarital contracts that determined financial obligations in the event of dissolution were void, as ***contrary to public policy***. [14]

B. Premarital agreements distinguished from other contracts

1. **Ordinary contracts:** Premarital agreements *differ from ordinary contracts* because the parties are not at arm's length and premarital agreements are executory. [14]

2. **Contracts during marriage:** According to the traditional rule, the parties *during the marriage* may not regulate by private contract their marital rights and responsibilities. [15]

3. **Separation agreements:** Parties enter into a premarital agreement before marriage, and a separation agreement after they have decided to terminate their marriage. [15]

C. Modern approach

1. **Trend:** Courts increasingly recognize premarital agreements. [15]

   a. **Limitation:** Despite increasing recognition of premarital contracts, the parties may *not* enter into an enforceable agreement about *child support* or *child custody*. [15]

   b. **Formalities:** The Statute of Frauds requires that premarital agreements be in *writing* and *signed* by the party to be charged. [16]

   c. **Scope:** The trend is to *broaden the scope* of premarital agreements in terms of what property rights are affected. [16]

2. **Requirements for validity:** A premarital agreement is valid if: (1) it provides full disclosure, (2) it is fair and reasonable, and (3) it is entered into voluntarily by both parties. Some courts reject the requirement that the agreement be reasonable. [16]

   a. **Full disclosure:** Many courts impose an affirmative duty on the prospective spouses to disclose their financial status before execution of a premarital agreement. [16]

   b. **Fair and reasonable**

      i. **Traditional rule:** Traditionally, courts required that the agreement be fair under all the relevant circumstances. [17]

      ii. **Modern trend:** Under the ***modern trend***, *courts will enforce agreements that are unfair* so long as the agreement accords with intent and is entered into voluntarily and with full disclosure. [17]

         (a) **Factors relevant to determination of reasonableness:** Different factors enter into the determination of reasonableness. [18]

         (b) **Time for determination of reasonableness:** Fairness can be evaluated at the time of either *execution* or *enforcement* of the agreement. [18]

   c. **Voluntariness:** Parties must enter a contract without fraud or duress. [18]

3. **Representation:** States generally do not require that the engaged parties be represented by independent counsel. [19]

D. Uniform Premarital Agreement Act: The widely adopted Uniform Premarital Agreement Act (UPAA) and the less widely adopted Uniform Marital Property Act (UMPA) both address premarital agreements. [19]

1. **Policy:** The policy of UPAA is to recognize contractual freedom. [20]

2. **Reform:** The UPAA requires ***a very high standard*** (i.e., "unconscionability") to render a premarital agreement unenforceable. [20]

III. RESTRICTIONS ON ENTRY INTO MARRIAGE

A. **Constitutional limitations on the right to marry:** State restrictions on the right to marry are subject to *strict scrutiny*. To survive constitutional challenge, the restrictions must be *necessary to a compelling state interest.* [21]

   1. **Race:** Racial restrictions on marriage are unconstitutional (*Loving v. Virginia*). [22]

   2. **Poverty:** Restrictions on the right to marry that are based on poverty are unconstitutional (*Zablocki v. Redhail*). [23]

      a. **Some reasonable regulations will be upheld:** Reasonable regulations that do not significantly interfere with decisions to enter into marriage may be upheld (*Zablocki*). [23]

      b. **Direct and substantial requirements:** Only those classifications that *directly* and *substantially* interfere with the right to marry will be reviewed under the strict scrutiny test (*Zablocki*). [23]

B. **Substantive restrictions:** States have substantive restrictions on who may marry. [25]

   1. **Capacity**

      a. **Same sex:** Traditionally, jurisdictions refused to recognize marriages by members of same-sex couples. This attitude is beginning to change. As of early 2011, a small number of states permit same-sex marriage. Several additional states recognize same-sex marriages that were validly performed in other jurisdictions. [25]

         i. **Federal constitutional arguments**

            (a) **Nature of constitutional arguments:** Plaintiffs have raised constitutional challenges to prohibitions on same-sex marriage based on *due process, equal protection, the right of association, and free exercise.* [26]

            (b) **Judicial response:** Plaintiffs' challenges to prohibitions on same-sex marriages have met with a mixed response. [26]

            (c) ***Lawrence v. Texas* and the constitutional right of privacy:** The United States Supreme Court's decision in *Lawrence v. Texas* (which overturned state sodomy laws based on the constitutional right to privacy) had major implications for recognition of same-sex marriage. [27]

         ii. **State constitutional arguments:** Gay and lesbian plaintiffs have argued also that their right to marry is protected by state constitutions on the theory that some state constitutions provide *more expansive protection* for individual rights. Fearing that some favorable judicial opinions would lead to widespread recognition of same-sex marriage (because of the Full Faith and Credit Clause), Congress and many state legislatures acted to limit recognition of same-sex marriages by means of federal and state Defense of Marriage Acts (DOMAs). Same-sex couples in valid marriages have met with mixed success in challenging these federal and state DOMAs. [27]

b. Bigamy: All states refuse to permit marriages that are bigamous or polygamous. [32]

i. Civil restrictions and criminal sanctions: Civil restrictions provide that a person may have only one spouse at a time. Criminal liability for bigamy also exists. [32]

ii. Background: Plural marriage is still practiced by some fundamentalist Mormon sects. [32]

iii. Procedural challenges: Parties have *challenged state restrictions* on bigamy by means of:

- criminal prosecutions;
- challenges to employment terminations;
- child neglect proceedings; and
- custody disputes. [32]

iv. Criminal requirements: Modern courts require *intent* to commit bigamy or polygamy. [32]

v. Effect on validity of successive marriage: If a party is still validly married to a prior spouse, any subsequent marriage is void. This rule is not applied in all cases. [32]

vi. Defenses

(a) Freedom of religion: Religious beliefs are not a valid defense to the crime of bigamy. [32]

(b) Enoch Arden statutes: Some statutes provide defenses to bigamy for spouses who remarry in good faith based on a belief that a prior spouse is dead. [33]

vii. Conflict of laws: Bigamous marriages may present issues of the conflict of laws. [33]

viii. Presumptions: Problems of proof have given rise to a presumption that the *most recent marriage is valid.* [33]

ix. Post-*Lawrence* challenge: Bigamy statutes do not violate the individual's right to privacy protected by *Lawrence v. Texas* because of the state interest in promoting marriage. [34]

c. Incest

i. Civil restrictions: All states have civil restrictions requiring that parties who wish to marry not be related within certain degrees of kinship. [34]

(a) Consanguinity: All states restrict marriages by those related by *blood.* [34]

(b) Affinity: A few states restrict marriages between those parties related by *affinity.* [35]

ii. Criminal sanctions: States also have criminal provisions punishing incest. [36]

iii. Rationale: Common rationale for incest provisions include: genetic, religious, and sociological reasons. [36]

iv. **Post-*Lawrence* challenge:** State incest laws do not violate the constitutional right to privacy (based on *Lawrence v. Texas*) because *Lawrence* has not been interpreted so broadly as to create a fundamental right to engage in all forms of private sexual conduct. [36]

d. **Age:** All state statutes establish *minimum ages* for marriage. Persons below those ages can marry with parental and/or judicial consent, depending on state statute. [36]

i. **Rationale:** The rationale for such restrictions is to promote marriage stability. [37]

ii. **Effect:** At common law, nonage rendered marriage void. Today, *such marriages are voidable*. [37]

iii. **Constitutionality of parental consent requirements:** Courts uphold the constitutionality of parental consent requirements. [37]

iv. **Reforms:** Several states recently raised the minimum age for marriage. [38]

e. **Miscellaneous issues of capacity:** Some statutes provide that certain physical or mental conditions are grounds for annulment. [38]

2. **State of mind:** Fraud and duress furnish grounds for annulment. [39]

a. **Fraud**

i. **Requirements:** Fraud must go to the ***essentials*** (*strictest test*), or be ***material*** (*more liberal test*). [40]

ii. **Significance of consummation:** Some jurisdictions require the essentials test if the marriage has been *consummated*. [41]

iii. **Effect:** The existence of fraud renders a marriage *voidable*, rather than void. [41]

iv. **Immigration fraud:** Congress enacted the Marriage Fraud Amendments Act to curb problems of marriage fraud in immigration. [41]

b. **Duress:** Marriages are *voidable* for reasons of duress. [41]

C. **Procedural restrictions:** States require that the parties *procure a marriage license*. Some states require that the parties *file a health certificate* (including blood tests). All states require *solemnization* of marriage by an authorized person before witnesses. Many states impose a *waiting period*. Failure to comply with these procedural formalities will *not* invalidate the marriage unless the jurisdiction has a statute that expressly provides that issuance of a marriage license is a mandatory requirement for a valid marriage. [43]

D. **Procedural variations and curative devices:** Parties may marry in some jurisdictions by means of ***proxy marriages*** or ***confidential marriages***. Curative devices (*common-law marriage, putative spouse doctrine*) validate a marriage even though some procedural element may be absent. [44-45]

1. **Proxy marriages:** Some jurisdictions recognize proxy marriages in which a *substitute (a proxy) stands in* for an absent bride or groom. [44]

2. **Confidential marriages:** Some states provide that informal "confidential" marriages may be recognized even though they fail to meet all the statutory formalities. [44]

3. **Common-law marriage**

   a. **Generally:** A few states recognize common-law marriage in which the parties presently *agree* to enter into a legal marital relationship, *cohabit*, and *hold themselves out as husband and wife*. [45]

   b. **Elements**

      i. **Present agreement:** Although the parties must agree to enter into a legal marital relationship, *no specific words are required*. [45]

      ii. **Cohabitation:** The couple must cohabit in a jurisdiction that recognizes common-law marriages. [45]

      iii. **Holding out:** The couple must have the reputation in the community of being married. [46]

   c. **Conflict of laws:** Common-law marriages present problems when the parties reside in multiple jurisdictions. [46]

      i. **Initial residence in a common-law jurisdiction:** If the parties first reside in a jurisdiction that recognizes such marriages, but move to a jurisdiction that does not, the latter jurisdiction almost always recognizes the marriage. [46]

      ii. **Initial residence in a non-common-law jurisdiction:** If the parties first reside in a jurisdiction that does not recognize such marriages, but later move to a jurisdiction that does, the latter jurisdiction usually recognizes the marriage. [46]

4. **Putative spouse doctrine: The *putative spouse doctrine*** protects a spouse who has a *good-faith belief* in the validity of the marriage. [46-47]

   a. **Common-law marriage distinguished:** Parties to a common-law marriage are aware that they have not taken part in a marriage ceremony. A putative spouse has a good-faith belief that a valid marriage has occurred [47]

   b. **Conflicting claims:** Occasionally, both a putative spouse and a lawful spouse may assert claims to a benefit stemming from the marriage. [47]

IV. ANNULMENT

An annulment declares a marriage void whereas a divorce declares that a valid marriage has come to an end. [49]

A. **Reasons to seek:** Today, parties may seek an annulment, rather than divorce, for religious or jurisdictional reasons (to avoid longer residency requirements for divorce). [49]

B. **Void/voidable distinction:** An invalid marriage may be characterized as *void or voidable*. [49]

1. **Void:** A void marriage is invalid from inception and may be challenged by the parties themselves or by third parties, and may be collaterally attacked. [49]

2. **Voidable:** A voidable marriage is valid from inception and requires that one of the parties take judicial action to establish its invalidity. It may be attacked only by the parties, and during the lifetime of the marriage, and cannot be collaterally attacked. [49]

C. **Grounds:** Bigamy and incest provide grounds for a void marriage. Fraud, duress, and nonage provide grounds for a voidable marriage. [49]

D. **Relation back doctrine:** The annulment's declaration of invalidity "relates back" to the inception of the void marriage. [49]

E. **Effect of annulment on other's rights:** Some statutes now permit spousal support awards following annulment. At common law, annulment resulted in bastardizing children born during the relationship. Statutes have modified this harsh result. [50]

V. CONFLICT OF LAWS: WHICH LAW GOVERNS MARRIAGE VALIDITY?

A. **Traditional rule: Law of place of celebration:** Under the ***traditional rule***, marriage validity is determined by the law of the state *where the marriage was celebrated.* [51]

B. **Restatement (Second) of Conflicts approach:** The Restatement (Second) of Conflict of Laws §283(1) has modified the general rule, holding that, in absence of statute, the validity of marriage is determined by the state that has the *most significant relationship to the spouses and the marriage*. [51]

C. **Federal DOMA:** Under the federal DOMA, states are not required to recognize same-sex marriages that are validly entered into in another state. Many state legislatures have enacted similar limitations. [52]

CHAPTER 3

BEING MARRIED

I. INTRODUCTION

A. **Historical background: Ecclesiastic versus civil jurisdiction:** In England, ecclesiastic courts maintained exclusive jurisdiction over marriage. [58]

B. **Contract versus status**

1. **Marriage is a contract:** The colonists, rejecting the religious character of marriage, regarded marriage as a contract. [58]

2. **Marriage is a status:** Marriage is also a civil status. [58]

II. REGULATION OF ROLES AND RESPONSIBILITIES

A. **Married women's common-law disabilities:** Under the common-law doctrine of coverture, the husband and wife *became one person* upon marriage (i.e., pursuant to the "fiction of marital unity"). This suspension of the wife's legal identity subjected married women to significant common-law *disabilities*. The Married Women's Property Acts eliminated these disabilities in the mid- to late nineteenth century. [58]

B. Support rights and obligations during marriage

1. **Scope of spousal duty of support:** At common law, the husband had a duty to support his wife. Today, the duty of support is gender neutral. [59]

2. **Limitation on spousal duty of support: Family privacy doctrine:** The spousal duty of support is limited by the doctrine of family privacy: courts are reluctant to interfere in an *ongoing* marriage to settle disputes. [59]

3. **Common-law necessaries doctrine:** A husband had a common-law duty to provide *necessaries* to his wife and children. [59]

   a. **What constitutes a necessary:** Necessaries include: food, clothing, shelter, medical care, and sometimes other items. [59]

   b. **Modern view:** Support obligations that are payable *only by the husband* have been held *unconstitutional*. Some states, either by case law or statute, impose liability for necessaries on both husbands and wives. [59-60]

4. **Criticisms of family privacy doctrine:** Criticisms of the doctrine include the following:

   - The doctrine does not preserve marital harmony.
   - Matters of spousal disagreements are not trivial.
   - Common-law rationales are outdated.
   - The doctrine inappropriately gives preference to third-party rights over those of an injured spouse.
   - The doctrine introduces needless circularity by enabling only creditors to sue. [61]

C. Names

1. **Married woman's name:** At common law, a married woman assumed her husband's surname based on custom. Today, a married woman may retain her birth name so long as she has proven ***consistent and nonfraudulent use***. [61]

   Many states allow a married woman who has adopted her husband's surname either to resume her maiden name or to adopt a name that is different from her husband's. Upon dissolution, many statutes authorize a married woman to resume her maiden name. A few states allow a man to assume his spouse's surname. Some jurisdictions allow same-sex partners to change their surnames. [61-62]

2. **Choice of children's names**

   a. **Generally:** Many modern statutes provide that the parents may choose, as the child's surname, (1) the husband's surname, (2) the wife's maiden name, or (3) a combined surname. [62]

   b. **Standard to resolve disputes:** Courts resolve disputes about *children's* surnames according to the ***best interests of the child standard***. [62-63]

   c. **Constitutional right:** Some cases raise constitutional challenges to statutes restricting parental choice in children's surname. [63]

D. Married woman's domicile

1. **Definition:** ***Domicile*** is important in determining *jurisdiction* for: the validity of a marriage, divorce, custody, legitimacy, and adoption. [64]

2. **Common-law rule:** At common law a married woman lacked the capacity to establish, change, or retain the domicile of her choice. [64]

3. **Reform:** The Restatement (Second) of Conflict of Laws permitted a separate domicile for a wife who was living apart from her husband. Subsequent case law and statutory revisions liberalized the common-law rule to allow either spouse to establish a domicile. [64]

E. Employment: Antinepotism (or no-spousal employment) policies: Antinepotism rules sometimes prevent one spouse from being employed by the other spouse's employer. [64]

1. **Rationale for policies:** Some business rationales support antinepotism policies. [64-65]

2. **Grounds of attack:** Plaintiffs have raised both federal and state challenges to antinepotism policies. Arguments include: antinepotism policies violate the fundamental right to marry and Title VII of the Civil Rights Act of 1964. *Courts are divided as to whether state civil rights statutes apply to no-spouse policies.* [65-66]

F. Health care

1. **Common-law duty to provide medical care:** At common law, a spouse had a duty to provide medical attention to the other spouse. [66]

2. **Spousal right to terminate life support**

   a. **Statutory authorization: Natural death acts:** Some states have enacted ***Natural Death Acts*** that permit a competent person to decide whether life-sustaining procedures shall be utilized. Many statutes confer *priority upon spouses as decision makers.* [67]

   b. **Constitutional right to die:** The United States Supreme Court has not yet determined the scope of a spouse's right to terminate the other spouse's life support. [67]

3. **Property rights to spousal remains:** The prevailing view confers upon the next of kin, including a spouse, a quasi-property right in the disposition of a decedent's body in the event that the decedent fails to exercise that right. [68]

III. PARENTING

A. Mandatory maternity leave policies: Many employers' mandatory maternity leave policies previously required employees to leave employment when they became pregnant. [71]

B. No maternity leave policies: Plaintiffs unsuccessfully challenged, on equal protection grounds and Title VII, those employers' policies permitting disability, but not pregnancy, leave. [71]

C. Pregnancy Discrimination Act

1. **Generally:** Congress responded to dissatisfaction with the lack of maternity leave policies by enacting the ***Pregnancy Discrimination Act (PDA)*** that amended Title VII. [71]

2. **Did the PDA preempt state statutes:** The Supreme Court held that the *PDA did not preempt state statutory schemes* that affirmatively provided for employment-related pregnancy benefits (*Cal. Fed. v. Guerra*). [71-72]

3. **Criticisms:** The PDA treats pregnancy as a "disability" and permits employers to have no policy for pregnancy so long as they have no policy for disability. [72]

4. **Fetal protection policies:** Fetal protection policies violate Title VII (*Johnson Controls*). [72]

5. **Parental and family leave policies: FMLA**
   a. **Constitutional challenges:** In response to constitutional concerns regarding equal protection, Congress liberalized leave policies. Congress enacted the ***Family and Medical Leave Act*** in 1993, requiring certain employers to provide eligible employees with *unpaid* leave. [73-74]

   b. **Criticisms:** The FMLA has been criticized for providing only unpaid leave. [74]

D. **State paid leave legislation:** A few states now offer paid family leave programs. [74]

IV. CRIMINAL LAW AND TORT LAW

In both criminal and tort law, courts and legislatures are abolishing special treatment for spouses. [76]

A. **Crimes involving spouses**

1. **Testimonial privilege**

   a. **Common-law rule:** At common law, a spouse could not testify for or against the other spouse in criminal proceedings. [76]

   b. **Types of communications distinguished:** Adverse spousal testimony may consist of either *confidential marital communications* (made in the presence only of the other spouse) or *communications made to the spouse in the presence of third parties.* [76]

   c. **Different state approaches:** States adopt one of ***four*** approaches to adverse spousal privilege:

      - some adhere to the common-law rule of disqualification;
      - some vest the privilege against adverse spousal testimony in the defendant, or in the husband and wife jointly;
      - some vest the privilege in the witness-spouse; and
      - some abolish the privilege. [76]

   d. **Federal approach:** The Supreme Court vests in the witness-spouse the privilege to *prohibit* testimony about communications made in the presence of third parties, while *leaving intact* the confidential marital communications privilege. [77]

e. ***Crawford v. Washington:*** The United States Supreme Court held (in a case in which a wife refused to testify against her husband based on a state marital privilege and the state therefore sought to introduce her previously recorded statement) that the Sixth Amendment requires actual confrontation when out-of-court *testimonial* statements are at issue. [77]

2. **Wiretapping:** According to the majority approach in the federal appellate courts, Title III of the Omnibus Crime Control Act applies to interspousal electronic surveillance in the marital home. [78]

3. **Marital rape**

a. **Common-law rule:** At common law, a man *could not be guilty* of raping his wife. [78]

b. **Modern trend:** Almost all jurisdictions have ***abolished or limited*** the exemption. [79]

B. Tort actions against third parties

1. **Generally:** At common law, the husband had a right to sue a third party in tort for interference with the marital relationship. [80]

2. **Modern trend:** Many courts and legislatures *abolished* actions for alienation of affections and criminal conversation via *anti-heartbalm legislation*. [80]

3. **Reasons for abolition:** Reasons for abolition include: marital dissolution is not solely attributable to a third party; awards are excessive; damages are difficult to access and inappropriate; the law has no deterrent effect; and spousal affection is not a property right. [80]

4. **Problems posed by abolition:** Problems sometimes arise in imposing civil liability on *psychologists and religious officials who engage in sexual misconduct* in the course of counseling. [80]

5. **Specific tort claims**

a. **Alienation of affections**

i. **Generally:** At common law, a husband might bring an action against a third party for alienation of affections. [80]

ii. **Elements:** A plaintiff must show:

- a valid marriage;
- defendant's wrongful conduct;
- a loss of consortium; and
- a causal connection between defendant's conduct and plaintiff's loss. [80]

iii. **Defenses:** Consent on the part of *plaintiff* is a valid defense. [80]

b. **Criminal conversation**

i. **Generally:** This action was available only to the husband at common law. [81]

ii. **Elements:** A plaintiff had to show:

- a valid marriage; and
- the defendant's sexual intercourse with plaintiff's spouse. [81]

iii. **Defenses:** Criminal conversation was a strict liability offense. [82]

iv. **Alienation of affections distinguished:** A claim for alienation of affections might be brought *without* the need for proof of sexual intercourse. [82]

c. **Loss of consortium**

i. **During marriage:** At common law, a husband could sue a third party for loss of his wife's services, society, companionship, and sexual relations. The action was later expanded from intentional to negligent acts. The ***modern trend*** extends the action to a wife. [82]

ii. **After divorce:** Damages generally are *unavailable* for loss of consortium *following, or contributing to*, dissolution. [83]

C. **Interspousal tort actions**

1. **Interspousal immunity doctrine**

a. **Historical background:** The common-law doctrine of ***interspousal immunity*** barred tort actions between husbands and wives. [83]

b. **Rationale:** Rationales supporting the interspousal immunity doctrine are that the bar:

- promotes marital harmony;
- prevents involving the judiciary in resolution of trivial matters; and
- prevents the spouses from collusion to defraud insurance companies. [83]

c. **Reform:** Currently, the majority of jurisdictions have abolished the doctrine. [83]

2. **Sexual torts:** Interspousal tort liability exists for ***negligent transmission of venereal disease***. [84]

3. **Intimate partner violence:** All states have legislation and case law that address intimate partner violence. Legal policy:

- liberalizes the admission of syndrome evidence;
- provides civil and criminal remedies against the abuser;
- addresses the issue of remedies against law enforcement personnel for failure to protect; and
- permits innovative federal and state reforms. [85]

a. **Admissibility of evidence of battered woman's syndrome:** The ***modern trend*** is to permit admission of evidence of the battered woman's syndrome. The battered woman's syndrome explains why women stay in an abusive relationship. Evidence of the battered woman's syndrome addresses the reasonableness of the perception of imminence and the danger that a woman faces. [85]

b. **State remedies against the batterer:** A batterer may incur criminal liability for assault and/or battery. Most states also have legislation providing for civil protective orders. Some states have mandatory arrest or "no-drop" policies in cases of domestic violence. [86-87]

c. **Remedies against law enforcement for failure to protect**

i. **Federal civil rights action under §1983:** For a time, a few courts recognized a federal civil rights cause of action (under 42 U.S.C. §1983) against law enforcement and/or municipalities for the failure of public officials to protect battered women based on the "special relationship" doctrine (i.e., police assumed an affirmative duty to protect battered spouses who had protective orders). [87]

ii. **Limitation on doctrine:** The United States Supreme Court limited this "special relationship" doctrine in *DeShaney v. Winnebago,* thereby foreclosing claims based on substantive due process against government officials for failure to protect. [87]

iii. **No constitutional entitlement to protection:** The Supreme Court subsequently foreclosed claims based on *procedural* due process against government officials for failure to protect (*Town of Castle Rock v. Gonzales*). [88]

d. **Difficulties for prosecutors:** Problems arise for prosecutors because the Supreme Court limited the admissibility of hearsay evidence in *Crawford v. Washington*. [88-89]

e. **Federal legislative remedies:** The federal legislative approach to battering consists of funding for shelters, the Violence Against Women Act (VAWA), and regulation of firearms by perpetrators of domestic violence. [89]

CHAPTER 4

NONTRADITIONAL FAMILIES

I. INTRODUCTION

The traditional nuclear family is on the decline. Many people now reside in nontraditional families, such as unmarried (opposite-sex or same-sex) couples, communal arrangements, and extended families. The law confers legal recognition on some nontraditional families for some purposes. [95]

II. EXTENDED FAMILIES

A. **Nature of the constitutional protection for the extended family:** To a limited extent, the Constitution protects the freedom of family members to choose to live together as an extended family. [96]

B. **Scope of the constitutional protection for the extended family:** The Constitution does not require a state to provide certain benefits to assist members of extended families to live together. [96]

III. COMMUNAL FAMILY

The Supreme Court *refuses* to provide legal protection, for zoning purposes, to the communal family. *Communal families* receive *more* favorable treatment in *zoning* challenges based on *state* constitutional law. [97]

IV. UNMARRIED COHABITANTS (OPPOSITE-SEX AND SAME-SEX COUPLES)

A. **Criminal sanctions for sexual conduct: Traditional and modern response:** The traditional legal response to unmarried couples is the imposition of ***criminal sanctions***. The United States Supreme Court decision in *Lawrence v. Texas* (which overturned state sodomy laws based on the constitutional right to privacy) signaled a major shift in the legal response to private consensual adult sexual conduct. [98-99]

B. **Zoning: Zoning ordinances and the First Amendment:** A state court *has denied* constitutional protection to *unmarried* couples for *zoning* purposes. [99]

C. **Housing:** States have made much progress in terms of remedying housing discrimination against unmarried couples. [99]

1. **Occupancy rights to a rent-controlled apartment:** A landmark case (*Braschi v. Stahl Assocs.*) recognized the *occupancy rights of same-sex partners* by adopting a broad functional definition of family. [99]

2. **Occupancy rights under state nondiscrimination statutes in the face of a landlord's First Amendment claims:** Landlords' refusals to rent to unmarried couples on religious grounds have met with varying success. [100]

D. **Tort Law:** Courts sometimes deny cohabitants those legal rights in the tort context that are available to members of traditional families. [100]

E. **Contracts: Unmarried couples' rights inter se**

1. **Traditional rule: Refusal to enforce agreements:** Under the ***traditional rule***, courts *refuse to enforce contractual agreements* between members of unmarried couples as *violative of public policy*. A few courts continue to adhere to the traditional rule. [101]

2. **Majority view: Modern judicial approaches**

a. **Express agreements:** Under the ***majority view***, unmarried partners have the *same right as married partners* to enter into express contracts regarding the ownership of property acquired during the relationship, *so long as illicit sexual relations do not form part of the consideration* for the agreement. [101]

b. **Express and implied agreements:** Some courts (following *Marvin v. Marvin*) recognize both express and implied agreements between nonmarital cohabitants. [103]

c. **Criticism of *Marvin:*** Courts and commentators have criticized *Marvin* for its recognition of implied agreements because such agreements are difficult to prove, defy equitable enforcement, and lead to the rebirth of common-law marriage. [105]

3. ***Marvin* and same-sex couples:** Some courts have extended *Marvin* to recognize cohabitation contracts between same-sex couples. However, other states prohibit enforcement of such contracts as violative of public policy. [105]

F. **Employment:** Unmarried cohabitants may face discrimination from employers. Such discrimination may take the form of denial of employment-related health benefits, denial of unemployment compensation, and, sometimes, termination of employment. [106]

G. Modern reform: Domestic partnership ordinances and same-sex marriage: A small number of jurisdictions have enacted *domestic partnership legislation* or allow same-sex marriage, thereby protecting same-sex partners from discrimination. [109]

CHAPTER 5
DIVORCE

I. BACKGROUND

American divorce law traditionally required fault-based grounds. [116]

II. FAULT-BASED GROUNDS

A. Cruelty: Cruelty was the most common ground prior to the adoption of no-fault divorce. [116]

1. **Elements:** To prove cruelty a plaintiff must show:
   - a course of conduct that is so severe as to
   - create an adverse effect on plaintiff's physical or mental well-being. [116]

2. **Physical versus mental cruelty:** Although early courts required physical violence, modern courts recognize mental cruelty. [117]

3. **Short-term versus long-term marriage:** An occasional court has required a higher degree of proof of cruelty for long-term marriages. [117]

B. Adultery

1. **Elements:** To prove adultery a plaintiff must show:
   - ***opportunity*** to commit the offense; and
   - ***disposition*** to commit it. [117]

2. **Criminal versus civil overlap**

   a. **Definition:** Adultery is both a crime and a ground for divorce. For divorce, adultery consists of sexual misconduct with a person other than one's spouse. [118]

   b. **Standard of proof:** The majority of states require a preponderance of evidence. [118]

C. Desertion

1. **Elements:** Desertion requires:
   - ***a voluntary separation;***
   - ***with intent not to resume cohabitation;***
   - ***which is without the partner's consent or without justification***. [118]

2. **Constructive desertion:** Constructive desertion, an alternative ground for divorce and a defense, constitutes conduct that either causes a spouse to leave or justifies the spouse's departure. [118]

III. FAULT-BASED DEFENSES

Fault-based defenses include: *recrimination, connivance, condonation, and collusion.* [119]

A. Recrimination

1. **Rule:** ***Recrimination*** bars a divorce if both spouses are at fault. [119]

2. **Policy rationale and criticism:** Rationales include: clean hands doctrine, access to divorce only for an innocent spouse, preservation of marriage, and the need to provide economic protection to women. Commentators criticize the doctrine for its *harsh consequences.* [120]

3. **Limitation:** The doctrine of ***comparative rectitude*** permits a divorce to the party who was least at fault. [120]

B. Connivance: ***Connivance*** is participation in, or consent to, a spouse's wrongful conduct. [120]

C. Condonation: ***Condonation*** is forgiveness by a spouse, usually implying resumption of sexual relations. [120]

D. Collusion

1. **Rule:** ***Collusion*** occurs when the spouses agree to divorce by means of the commission of a marital offense. [120]

2. **Connivance distinguished:** Connivance is *consent* by one spouse whereas collusion is a spousal *agreement* to commit a marital wrong. [121]

E. Insanity: Insanity is both a ground for divorce and a defense. [121]

IV. NO-FAULT DIVORCE

A. Early no-fault grounds

1. **Living separate and apart**

   a. **Elements:** Most states continue to provide for no-fault divorce based on physical separation. [122]

   b. **Meaning of "separate and apart":** The term ***living separate and apart*** may refer to both physical separation and an intention to dissolve the marriage. [122]

      i. **Physical separation:** Spouses may live separate and apart even though they live in the same house. [122]

      ii. **Intention:** Restrictive jurisdictions require that the spouses *voluntarily* (i.e., *by mutual consent*) live apart for the statutory period. [123]

2. **Incompatibility:** *Incompatibility* was one of the *earliest* no-fault grounds. [123]

B. **Modern no-fault legislation:** All states now have some form of no-fault divorce. No-fault means different things in different jurisdictions. Some states are pure no-fault jurisdictions. Other states merely add no-fault grounds to their fault-based grounds. [123]

1. **California approach:** California (the first jurisdiction to adopt no-fault divorce) permits divorce based on *"irreconcilable differences, which have caused the irremediable breakdown of the marriage."* [124]

2. **UMDA approach:** UMDA permits divorce if the marriage is *"irretrievably broken"* or the parties have *lived separate and apart for six months.* [124]

3. **New York reform:** New York became the last state to adopt a pure no-fault divorce law. The new law permits divorce if a marriage is "irretrievably broken." [124]

4. **Residual relevance of fault:** Some states still consider fault to be relevant in the division of marital property and determination of spousal support. A reform movement has resurrected the role of fault by means of *covenant marriages* that permit dissolution only on fault-based grounds. [125]

V. ACCESS TO DIVORCE

A. **Religious limitations: The "Get":** Under Orthodox Jewish law, a wife whose husband civilly divorces her without granting her a *religious divorce* (***a "Get"***) is unable to remarry. Wives have challenged such denials on tort and contract principles. Religious divorce has constitutional implications. [127]

B. **Financial limitations: Filing fees:** States cannot require an indigent to pay filing fees and court costs prior to filing for divorce (*Boddie v. Connecticut*). [128]

C. **Right to counsel:** Indigent plaintiffs do *not* have a constitutional right to counsel in divorce proceedings. However, some states recognize an indigent's right to counsel in divorce proceedings based on state law. [129-130]

VI. DISCRIMINATION ON THE BASIS OF DIVORCE

Discrimination on the basis of divorce violates the Constitution (*Littlejohn*). [129]

VII. ROLE OF COUNSEL

A. **Dual Representation**

1. **Different approaches:** Many states regard dual or multiple representation in divorce as unethical. A few states permit it subject to restrictions. [130]

2. **Dispelling the aura of dual representation:** An attorney may not give the *impression* of representation of both parties *when one party is unrepresented.* [130]

3. **Confidentiality issues:** An attorney in a dual representation situation *may not reveal confidential information* or use such information to the disadvantage of a client or to the advantage of a third person. [131]

B. Representation of clients in *different* suits involving *substantially related* matters: Representation of clients involved in different lawsuits that deal with "substantially related" matters can also give rise to a prohibited conflict of interest. [131-132]

C. Sexual relations with clients: An increasing number of jurisdictions regulate sexual relations between the attorney and client. [132]

1. **Different approaches:** Some states prohibit all attorney-client sexual relationships. Some states have such a ban but exempt relationships predating the representation. Other states prohibit only those sexual relationships that adversely affect the practice of law. Still other states permit the imposition of sanctions (criminal sanctions or sanctions for violations of state professions codes). [132]

2. **ABA:** An ABA Rule of Professional Conduct bans attorney-client sexual relationships absent a preexisting consensual relationship. [133]

3. **States without express bans:** Even without a specific ban on attorney-client sexual relations, a jurisdiction may nonetheless find that the attorney's conduct violates general conflict of interest rules. [133]

D. Fees: A court may order one spouse in a divorce proceeding to pay the other's fees. Contingent fees in divorce actions are unethical. [133]

VIII. DIVORCE JURISDICTION

A. Subject matter jurisdiction: Traditional rule: Traditionally, a state has jurisdiction to dissolve a marriage based on the petitioner's *domicile* in the forum state. Domicile signifies physical presence plus intention to remain permanently. [134]

B. Restatement view: Divorce without domicile: The Restatement (Second) of Conflict of Laws relaxes the traditional domiciliary requirement. [135]

C. Terminology

1. **Ex parte versus bilateral divorce:** In an ex parte (or unilateral) divorce, the court has personal jurisdiction over only one spouse. In a bilateral divorce, the court has personal jurisdiction over both spouses. [134]

2. **Divisible divorce:** A court in an ex parte divorce has jurisdiction only over the marital status, and may not rule on the support and property rights of the absent spouse. [135]

D. Jurisdiction over the plaintiff

1. **Full Faith and Credit Clause:** The Full Faith and Credit Clause of the Constitution (Article IV, §1) requires that a state give full faith and credit to a decree of a sister state provided that the sister state had personal jurisdiction. This requirement was applied to the divorce context by the United States Supreme Court in *Williams I* and *Williams II*. [136]

2. **Durational residency requirements:** Durational residency requirements, imposed by some states, are constitutional (*Sosna v. Iowa*). [135-136]

3. **The *Williams* cases**

   a. ***Williams I*: Whether to give full faith and credit:** This case held that a state must recognize, under the Full Faith and Credit Clause, a divorce granted to a spouse who is domiciled in a sister state even though the stay-at-home spouse does not appear and is not served with process in the sister state. [136]

   b. ***Williams II*: When to give full faith and credit:** The decree-granting state's finding of domicile may be reexamined to determine the bona fides of a petitioner's domicile. [136]

   c. ***Williams'* limitation to the ex parte situation:** The *Williams* rules operate if the divorce was entered ex parte. The appearance of both parties confers jurisdiction on the court. [137]

E. Personal jurisdiction over the defendant

1. **Notice:** Personal jurisdiction over the defendant is *not* required to terminate a marriage if the plaintiff is domiciled in the forum state. However, *notice* to the defendant in divorce actions *is required* in order to comport with due process. [137]

2. **Transitory presence:** A state may acquire jurisdiction for divorce over a nonresident defendant who is physically present in the state. Minimum contacts are not required. [139]

F. Foreign decrees: Under the ***comity doctrine***, an American jurisdiction *may* recognize a judgment of a foreign nation *provided that* the judgment was rendered after a fair hearing by a court which has personal jurisdiction over one or both of the parties. *Comity* governs the recognition of decrees rendered by the courts of a *foreign country* whereas the *Full Faith and Credit Clause* of the Constitution governs judicial recognition of decrees of *sister states*. [139-140]

G. Domestic relations exception to federal jurisdiction: The United States Supreme Court *limits* the situations in which *federal courts can refuse jurisdiction* to adjudicate cases involving parties in different states who are involved in divorce, alimony, or custody matters (*Ankenbrandt v. Richards*). [141]

H. Same-sex divorce: Jurisdictional issues may arise when the members of a same-sex couple separate.

1. **Termination in the original forum:** A couple may legally terminate their relationship in the original forum where the union was registered. [142]

2. **Termination in another forum:** Jurisdictions disagree about whether a second forum has jurisdiction to dissolve a same-sex relationship that was validly entered into in another jurisdiction. Federal and state DOMAs may prevent recognition of such unions and thereby deprive courts of jurisdiction to terminate them. [142]

3. **Jurisdictional prerequisite:** Proper registration of a domestic partnership is a jurisdictional prerequisite to maintaining an action for termination of that relationship. [143]

IX. ALTERNATIVES TO DIVORCE: ANNULMENTS AND SEPARATIONS

Divorce terminates a valid marriage. An annulment is a judicial declaration that a marriage never took place. A legal separation is a judicial declaration that the parties are separated. A spouse might seek an annulment for religious reasons or to avoid durational residency requirements for divorce. [143]

X. ALTERNATIVE DISPUTE RESOLUTION PROCESSES

A. **Arbitration, conciliation, and mediation distinguished:** Arbitration provisions in separation agreements require the parties to submit future disputes to an arbitrator prior to court action. In arbitration, a neutral third party makes a binding determination. Conciliation is counseling with an eye toward reconciliation. Divorce mediation is a process by which the parties make their own agreements with the mediator serving as a facilitator. [144]

B. **Enforceability of arbitration provisions:** A few states maintain that arbitration of custody and visitation disputes is *violative of public policy*. [144]

C. **Mandatory mediation:** A few states have ***mandatory mediation*** for divorcing parties (e.g., in custody disputes). [145]

D. **Collaborative law procedure:** "Collaborative law" procedure signifies an agreement by the parties and their attorneys to use cooperative techniques without resorting to judicial intervention. Collaborative law's requirement that if the parties are unable to agree then the lawyers must withdraw may pose a potential violation of state rules of professional conduct. [145]

CHAPTER 6

FINANCIAL CONSEQUENCES OF DISSOLUTION

I. STANDARDS FOR AWARDING PROPERTY, SPOUSAL SUPPORT, AND CHILD SUPPORT

At divorce, *absent an agreement*, the court divides the spouses' property and may also award alimony and child support. [149]

A. **Division of property**

1. Marital property regimes defined: Two marital property regimes exist:

- common law, and
- community property. [150]

At ***common law***, all property belonged to the *spouse who acquired it*. On the other hand, ***community property*** gives each spouse the right upon dissolution to an *equal* share of the community property. [150]

2. **Equitable distribution generally:** At dissolution, the majority of states apply the doctrine of equitable distribution. This view attempts to achieve a *fair* distribution of the spouses' property. Equitable distribution takes into account a number of statutory factors. In a jurisdiction that follows equitable distribution, ***both separate and jointly acquired property may be subject to division***. [150]

3. **Traditional rationales:** Different rationales traditionally characterize the distribution of property and spousal support. [152]

   a. **Fault:** The most longstanding principle is to divide the property and award support so as to *punish* the spouse who caused the marital breakdown. [152]

   b. **Need:** The need rationale, which replaces fault, divides property based on *a spouse's need for support*. [152]

   c. **Status:** A court divides property based on the *status* that the parties *enjoyed during the marriage*. [152]

4. **Modern rationale:** A new principle characterizes the distribution of property. According to the contribution theory, a court divides property based on the view that marriage is an economic partnership. Spousal earnings and resulting assets are subject to division. [152]

   a. **Valuation of homemaker services:** Judicial and legislative reforms increasingly provide that homemaker services may be taken into account. [152]

   b. **Community property and the contribution approach:** The community property regime reflects the *contribution* rationale. [153]

   c. **Limited role for fault:** Marital fault continues to play a limited role in equitable distribution. [153]

5. **What is property?**

   a. **Professional licenses and degrees:** Increasingly, courts are asked to determine whether a professional license or degree is an asset subject to distribution upon dissolution. [155]

      i. **Characterization: Majority versus minority approaches:** The majority of states *refuse* to treat professional licenses and degrees as marital property, although some jurisdictions take them into account in awards of spousal support. [155]

      ii. **Criticism of characterization as property:** Courts have difficulty characterizing a license or degree as property because:

         - it lacks the attributes of property;
         - future earning capacity is too difficult and speculative;
         - it is a product of only one spouse's skills; and
         - it would result in indentured servitude. [156]

   b. **Pensions and retirement benefits:** Pension benefits may constitute a significant part of the marital property for many couples. [157]

      i. **Definition:** Vested pension rights are not subject to forfeiture by the employee if the employment terminates. Nonvested pensions are. [158]

ii. **Characterization as marital property:** Under the ***majority rule***, ***both vested and non-vested pensions are marital property*** subject to equitable distribution. Under the ***minority rule***, vested, but *not* nonvested, pensions are marital property subject to equitable distribution. [158]

iii. **Federal pension benefits and federalism principles:** The distribution of federal pension benefits may involve a conflict between federal law versus state equitable distribution or community property law. [158]

6. **Bankruptcy discharge**

a. **Generally:** The Bankruptcy Code permits a debtor-spouse to be discharged from certain divorce-related obligations. [161]

b. **Rule: Nondischargeability from support obligations:** According to the traditional rule, obligations attributable to a *property* division upon divorce are dischargeable but *spousal support and child support obligations are not*. The Bankruptcy Reform Act and the Bankruptcy Abuse Prevention and Consumer Protection Act change the traditional rule to make property obligations nondischargeable in some cases. [162]

c. **Dischargeability of liens:** The Supreme Court has ruled that federal bankruptcy law does not permit a debtor, upon divorce, to defeat (by nullifying a lien) the other spouse's property interest. [163]

B. **Spousal support:** Spousal support consists of the ***award of future payments to one spouse from the future earnings of the other***. The purpose of spousal support has evolved. [165]

1. **Rationale**

a. **Traditional theories**

i. **Need:** At common law, the husband had a duty to support his wife. Because women were economically dependent on men, women "needed" support in the event of a marital breakdown. Courts based awards on the plaintiff's *need* plus the defendant's *ability to pay*. The benchmark for need was the couple's standard of living during the marriage. [166]

ii. **Fault:** In a fault-based regime, only the innocent spouse is awarded spousal support. The guilty spouse is "punished" for his or her transgressions in awards of spousal support (and property). Theories of need and fault have been undermined by the spread of no-fault divorce and the transformation of gender roles brought about by the women's movement. [166]

b. **Modern rationale**

i. **Self-sufficiency:** Many commentators urge that, because the original purposes of alimony awards (fault/need) are no longer relevant, spousal support should be abolished or, alternatively, awarded infrequently and for short periods of time. UMDA was influential in the adoption of self-sufficiency as a rationale for awards of spousal support. [166]

ii. **ALI's loss compensation:** The ALI *Principles* proposes an innovative rationale of "loss compensation" for spousal support by which one spouse makes "compensatory spousal payments" to the other spouse to compensate for certain losses that the second spouse experienced during the marriage. [167]

2. **Spousal support and property division distinguished:** Differences between spousal support and property division include: [167]

   a. **Modifiability:** Unlike property awards, spousal support traditionally was modifiable upon proof of a change of circumstances. [167]

   b. **Terminability:** Spousal support, unlike property payments, was terminable upon remarriage of the recipient-spouse. [167]

   c. **Enforcement by contempt power:** Spousal support obligations, unlike property awards, are enforceable by means of contempt. [167]

   d. **Discharge in bankruptcy:** Spousal support, unlike awards of property, traditionally was not a dischargeable obligation if the payor-spouse declares bankruptcy. Recent reforms limit the dischargeability of property awards in some cases. [167]

   e. **Tax consequences:** Different tax consequences flow from the two awards. [167]

3. **Types:** Permanent alimony is rarely awarded today. Modern forms of spousal support include: rehabilitative alimony and reimbursement alimony. [167]

C. Child support

1. **Liability of both parents:** The ***modern trend*** is to consider *both* parents responsible for the support of their children. [169]

2. **Standards:** Traditionally, vague statutory standards permitted courts to use *considerable discretion* in the award of child support. Modern law now limits judicial discretion. The Child Support Enforcement Amendments requires states to have *guidelines*. The Family Support Act provides that the guidelines should serve as a *rebuttable presumption* and requires states to update their guidelines regularly. [169]

3. **Models of determining support:** States have implemented guidelines based on three different models: income shares model, percentage of income model, and the Melson Formula. [169]

4. **Deviation from guidelines:** A court may order a *deviation* from the statutory guidelines in appropriate cases. [170]

5. **Liability of stepparents:** Modern statutes and case law sometimes impose liability on stepparents. [170]

6. **Postmajority support:** States adopt different approaches to a noncustodial parent's liability for postmajority support. Some states rigidly enforce the statutory age limitation (18 years). Other states, by a variety of legal doctrines, permit continuation of support obligations. [171]

7. **Posthumous support obligations:** According to the traditional view, the obligation to support a child terminates at the obligor's death, absent a written agreement binding the estate. [171]

8. **Support and inheritance rights of nonmarital children**

   a. **Traditional view:** Traditionally, nonmarital children had a right to support and inheritance only from their biological mother. [171]

b. **Modern view:** According to modern statutes, both parents have a duty to support children regardless of legitimacy. The United States Supreme Court has held that some forms of discrimination against nonmarital children are unconstitutional. [171-172]

9. **Support obligations of same-sex parents:** Courts are beginning to recognize the parental rights, as well as the concomitant support obligations, of same-sex parents. [173]

II. MODIFICATION OF SPOUSAL AND CHILD SUPPORT AWARDS

A. **Standard:** The most common standard for modification of spousal and child support is: a ***substantial and material change of circumstances*** since the entry of the decree. UMDA requires that spousal support may be modified only if a change in circumstances has occurred which is ***so substantial and continuing as to make the terms unconscionable.*** [174]

B. **Relevant factors:** Some circumstances may affect a spouse's support obligation. These include: the payor's changed circumstances, the payor's remarriage and subsequent family obligations, the payor's increased resources, the payor's deteriorating health, or the payor's incarceration. The recipient's changed circumstances may also affect the payor-spouse's obligations. Such changed circumstances include remarriage or cohabitation of the recipient. [174]

III. JURISDICTION AND ENFORCEMENT OF CHILD SUPPORT AWARDS

Child support enforcement may be difficult when the parties reside in different states. To make or modify an award of child support or spousal support, a court must have *personal jurisdiction* over the obligor. [177]

A. **Expansion of jurisdiction:** The trend is to expand the traditional methods of acquiring personal jurisdiction over nonresidents for support purposes. Many states authorize the assertion of personal jurisdiction in domestic relations cases by means of special long-arm statutes. This practice must comport with the requisites of due process. [177]

B. **Interstate enforcement: URESA, RURESA, and UIFSA:** The Uniform Reciprocal Enforcement of Support Act (URESA) and the revised RURESA were promulgated to facilitate interstate enforcement of support orders. Problems regarding a lack of uniformity between the states led to the Uniform Interstate Family Support Act (UIFSA). [178]

C. **Federal legislation: Full Faith and Credit for Child Support Orders Act:** To improve interstate enforcement, Congress also enacted legislation (the Full Faith and Credit for Child Support Orders Act). [180]

D. **Enforcement remedies:** State and federal remedies exist to enforce child support obligations. Traditional state remedies include money judgments, criminal nonsupport proceedings, and the contempt power. A number of states are experimenting with such modern remedies as license suspension. The federal government also has enacted some innovative remedies, including wage withholding, tax refund intercepts, and passport revocations. [180-183]

IV. SEPARATION AGREEMENTS

The validity of a separation agreement is determined by *contract law*. Such agreements may be set aside for fraud, duress, or overreaching. Under the traditional rule, *alimony provisions in a settlement agreement generally are not modifiable*; *child support provisions are modifiable* if the child's best interests require it. [185]

V. TAX CONSIDERATIONS

A. Spousal support

1. **Taxable to the recipient:** Spousal support is *taxable* to the recipient. [186]
2. **Deductible by the payor:** Spousal support is *deductible* by the payor. [186]
3. **Choice of different treatment:** The ex-spouses are not obligated to treat spousal support as the Code dictates. [186]

B. Transfers of property to spouse: For transfers of property between spouses, the value of the property is excluded from the recipient's income. [186]

C. Child support: Child support payments are *nontaxable* to the recipient and *nondeductible* by the payor. [186]

D. Other tax considerations

1. **Head of household:** A "head of household" obtains preferential treatment under the Tax Code. [186]
2. **Dependency exemption:** A taxpayer may claim a dependency exemption if she or he provides over one-half of the dependent's support. [187]

CHAPTER 7

CHILD CUSTODY

I. INTRODUCTION

Prior to the nineteenth century, a rule of paternal preference prevailed. However, by the mid-to late nineteenth century, custody law began to reflect a maternal preference. [194]

II. STANDARDS FOR SELECTING THE CUSTODIAL PARENT

A. Presumptions: Some states invoke presumptions to adjudicate custody disputes. Traditional presumptions include the tender years presumption, the primary caretaker presumption, and the nonmarital presumption. Modern presumptions in some jurisdictions operate to deny custody to an abusive parent and to favor custody to a biological parent in custody disputes involving parents and nonparents. [195]

B. Best interests of the child: The prevailing standard for resolution of custody is "the best interests of the child." [196]

1. Constitutional factors

a. Race: The Supreme Court has determined that race may not serve as the *decisive* factor in custody decision making. [196]

b. Religion: The First Amendment serves as a limitation on judicial consideration of religion as a factor in awarding custody. [197]

2. Fitness factors

a. Sexual conduct: According to the modern view, a parent's sexual conduct is only relevant if it has an adverse effect on the child. [198]

b. Careers: Gender bias sometimes results in adverse decisions for mothers who work outside the home. [200]

c. Wealth: The relative wealth of the parties is not determinative *unless* one parent is unable to provide adequately for the child. [200]

d. Domestic violence: Some jurisdictions adopt a presumption against custody to an abusive parent. "Friendly parent" provisions and joint custody disadvantage battered spouses in custody determinations. [200]

e. Disability: Many statutes require consideration of the mental and physical health of the parties when applying the best interest standard. [201]

C. Joint custody: Joint custody allows both parents to share legal responsibility for major childrearing decisions. Joint custody is based on the rationale that children benefit from *continued and frequent contact with both parents*. [202]

1. Different jurisdictions' approaches: Most jurisdictions now provide for joint custody. States adopt one of the following approaches: presumption, preference, or a factor in the best interest determination. Most states follow the third approach. [202]

2. "Joint" custody does not mean equal time: A popular *misconception is that joint custody means equal time* with each parent. [203]

III. STANDARDS FOR SELECTING THE NONCUSTODIAL PARENT: VISITATION

A. Denial of visitation

1. General rule: Courts are reluctant to impose a total denial of visitation. [205]

2. Visitation and support: Independent variables: The right to visitation and the duty of support are not interdependent. [205]

B. Conditions on visitation: Courts sometimes place conditions on visitation in cases of domestic violence, or physical or sexual abuse. A parent's sexual behavior may also lead to conditions on visitation. Sometimes, First Amendment concerns *limit a court's power to settle religious disputes* about visitation. [206]

C. **Interference with visitation rights:** Noncustodial parents may institute proceedings to enforce their visitation rights. Possible remedies for custodial interference include: civil contempt, modification of custody, tort damages, and makeup parenting time. [207]

IV. STANDARDS: PARENT VERSUS NONPARENT DISPUTES

A. **Natural parent presumption:** *A **presumption*** favors ***natural parents*** in *custody disputes* involving parents versus nonparents. [209]

B. **Custody and visitation rights of third parties**

1. **Grandparents:** At common law, grandparents had no right to visitation with their grandchildren. Many states now have visitation statutes that permit visitation to third parties (such as grandparents) in some cases. The United States Supreme Court has held that a grandparent visitation statute infringes on family autonomy when it fails to provide for deference to a fit parent's wishes (*Troxel v. Granville*). [210]

2. **Stepparents:** Some statutes authorize courts to consider stepparents in custody and visitation awards. [211]

3. **Lesbian co-parents:** Courts traditionally have not been receptive to recognition of co-parenting rights after dissolution of a same-sex relationship. However, courts increasingly are willing to recognize the parental rights of the "second parent" (i.e., the nonbiologically related parent) in gay and lesbian families. [211]

V. ROLE OF SPECIAL PARTICIPANTS

A. **Child's preference:** Most states, either by statute or case law, take into account a child's wishes when making custody determinations, but they accord that preference varying weight. [212]

B. **Counsel for the child:** In most states, appointment of a child's legal representative is within the discretion of the court. However, statutory authority exists for the appointment of a guardian ad litem when allegations of abuse are raised in custody hearings. [213]

C. **Expert testimony:** Experts frequently are asked to testify in custody determinations. While a judge may base his decision on expert opinion, the *judge is the ultimate authority*. [213]

VI. MODIFICATION

A. **Standard for modification:** The ***standard*** for custody ***modification*** is ***higher*** than for an initial custody determination. The most commonly accepted standard requires proof of a ***material or substantial change of circumstances***. Some states require ***endangerment***. A few states require only that modification be ***in the best interests*** of the child regardless of any change in circumstances. [214]

B. **Relocation controversies:** Relocation controversies often arise in the postdecree period. Courts employ different standards to resolve such disputes. Some states adopt a presumption favoring the custodial parent's decision. Other states (the modern trend) adopt a balancing test taking into account many factors. [215]

VII. JURISDICTION AND ENFORCEMENT

A. Jurisdiction

1. **Traditional rule:** The traditional rule permitted the assertion of jurisdiction if the *child was domiciled* in the state. Courts later permitted assertions of jurisdiction if another state had a *substantial interest* in the child's welfare. This led frequently to concurrent assertions of jurisdiction. [217]

2. **UCCJEA:** The Uniform Child Custody Jurisdiction and Enforcement Act (UCCJEA) applies to initial custody awards as well as modifications. It was intended to harmonize some of the differences between the Uniform Child Custody Jurisdiction Act (UCCJA) and the Parental Kidnapping Prevention Act (PKPA). The UCCJEA gives priority to home state jurisdiction, eliminates the best interests language, limits the use of emergency jurisdiction, and provides strict requirements for modification. Virtually all states have adopted the UCCJEA. [218]

VIII. CHILD ABDUCTION

Uniform law, federal law, and international treaties address international child abduction. The Uniform Child Abduction Prevention Act (UCAPA) provides for abduction prevention measures. The International Parental Kidnapping Crime Act (IPKCA) makes it a federal crime for a parent wrongfully to remove or retain a child outside the United States. The Hague Convention on the Civil Aspects of International Child Abduction provides for the mandatory return of children to their country of habitual residence and also requires that the new forum refuse to adjudicate the custody dispute. [219]

IX. PROCESS TO RESOLVE DISPUTES

Mediation and collaborative law are modern alternatives to the traditional dispute resolution process by which the parties resolve issues in dispute. Both processes are less expensive and less hostile than the adversarial process. Many statutes permit mediation, although a few states *mandate* it. [220]

CHAPTER 8

PROCREATION

I. CONTRACEPTION

A. Rights of married and unmarried persons: Access to contraception is protected by the constitutional right of privacy and does not depend on marital status (*Eisenstadt v. Baird*). [225]

B. Minors' rights to contraception: The United States Supreme Court extended the constitutional right of privacy to minors' contraceptive choices (*Carey v. Population Services Int'l*). [230]

C. Misrepresentation of contraceptive use

1. **Tort liability:** Courts generally refuse to recognize tort liability for misrepresentation of contraceptive use. [232]

2. **Defense to support obligation:** A father may not avoid his child support obligations based on the mother's misrepresentation about using birth control. [232]

II. ABORTION

A. **Historical background:** Early American proscriptions against abortion date from the 1820s. Reform began in the 1960s when some states adopted the American Law Institute (ALI)'s Model Penal Code abortion provisions liberalizing abortion. The women's movement also contributed to reform. [234]

B. **A woman's right to an abortion**

1. ***Roe v. Wade:*** The Supreme Court holds in *Roe v. Wade* (1973) that a woman has a constitutionally protected right to an abortion. The constitutional source for this right is the right of privacy. *Roe* holds that the right to an abortion is fundamental and requires strict scrutiny. In the first trimester, the woman has an unqualified right to an abortion which may not be infringed by the state. After the first trimester and until the point of viability, the state may regulate abortion in the interest of maternal health. After viability the state's interest in protecting potential life justifies the state in regulating, and even proscribing, abortion. [234-235]

2. **Retrenchment on abortion right: *Planned Parenthood v. Casey:*** In *Planned Parenthood v. Casey*, the Supreme Court retreats from *Roe*'s guarantee of abortion freedom by allowing states to impose regulations provided that those regulations do not place an *undue burden* on the woman's right to an abortion. Rather than continuing to speak of abortion as a fundamental right, the court now refers to it only as a liberty interest. *Casey* weakens *Roe* further by abrogation of the trimester scheme and by the recognition "that there is a substantial state interest in potential life *throughout* pregnancy." [237-238]

C. **The abortion funding cases:** The Supreme Court holds in *Harris v. McRae* that, although a woman has a protected right to an abortion, the government has no obligation to provide funds for that abortion. [239]

D. **Other problems of access: Abortion activists' tactics:** The ***Freedom of Access to Clinic Entrances Act (FACE)*** provides criminal and civil penalties for the use of force, threat of force, or physical obstruction aimed at injuring, intimidating, or interfering with abortion patients or providers. [241]

E. **The husband's rights in the abortion context:** A husband has no constitutionally protected right to influence his wife's abortion decision making (*Planned Parenthood v. Danforth, Planned Parenthood v. Casey*). [241-242]

F. **Minor's right to an abortion**

1. **Parental consent:** In *Bellotti v. Baird*, the Court holds that if a state requires one or both parents' consent, the state must provide an alternative judicial procedure whereby the minor can obtain authorization. [242]

2. **Parental notification:** In *Hodgson v. Minnesota*, the Court invalidates a two-parent notification requirement, but finds that the existence of a judicial bypass procedure mitigates any constitutional defect. [243]

G. Partial-birth abortion bans: Recent federal and state legislation prohibits "partial-birth" (i.e., late-stage) abortions. The Supreme Court upheld the federal Partial-Birth Abortion Ban Act of 2003 despite its lack of a maternal health exception (*Gonzales v. Carhart*). [244]

III. RESTRICTIONS ON THE RIGHTS OF PREGNANT WOMEN

Some states have imposed restrictions on the rights of some pregnant women, e.g., substance abusers, child abusers, or the terminally ill. Most courts are *reluctant to find criminal liability* in cases where a mother uses drugs during pregnancy. A *terminally ill* pregnant woman has the right to determine the course of her medical treatment, including birth procedures, during pregnancy (*In re A.C.*). [245-246]

IV. FETAL HOMICIDE LEGISLATION

State and federal legislation (the Unborn Victims of Violence Act) imposes criminal liability for the killing of a fetus during the commission of a crime as a distinct criminal offense. [248]

V. ALTERNATIVE REPRODUCTIVE TECHNOLOGY

A. Artificial insemination

1. **Definition:** Artificial insemination is a reproductive technique to combat problems of, primarily, male infertility. [250]
2. **Legitimacy of offspring:** Many statutes legitimize the resulting offspring of artificial insemination as the product of the marriage. [250]
3. **Sperm donor's rights:** Many statutes, including the original Uniform Parentage Act, provide that the *sperm donor has no rights* regarding a child born as a result of artificial insemination. A few courts, however, award visitation rights to the sperm donor (especially in the context of lesbian relationships). [250]
4. **Defense to child support:** The husband's *consent* to the artificial insemination of his wife *gives rise to obligations of child support.* [250]
5. **Status of posthumous children:** Children conceived posthumously by artificial insemination may share in a sperm donor's estate if he consented to the insemination and agreed to support the child. [251]
6. **Status of posthumously conceived children:** Posthumously conceived children may be entitled to government benefits as dependents of a deceased insured wage earner. [251]
7. **Access by gay and lesbian partners:** Same-sex partners have been discriminated against in the provision of assisted reproductive technology. [251]

B. Surrogacy

1. **Definition:** Surrogacy is a contractual arrangement whereby a woman agrees to be artificially inseminated with semen, and then to bear and surrender the ensuing child. [252]

2. **Traditional view:** The traditional view toward surrogacy is to treat surrogacy agreements as *void*. Increasingly, however, a few states permit such arrangements subject to state regulation. [252]

3. **Statutory violations:** Opponents contend that surrogacy violates statutory prohibitions on babyselling as well as prohibitions on a mother's ability to give prebirth consent. [255]

4. **Presumption of legitimacy:** The parties to a surrogacy agreement must overcome the *presumption of legitimacy*, i.e., that a married surrogate's husband is presumed to be the natural father of children born during the marriage. [255]

5. **Revised Uniform Parentage Act (UPA):** The recently revised Uniform Parentage Act authorizes gestational agreements provided they are validated by a court. [253]

6. **Surrogacy by same-sex partners:** Surrogacy is increasingly being utilized by same-sex partners. The practice raises such issues as: what role paternity laws (such as the UPA) should play in the establishment of parental rights of children of lesbian couples, and whether states will permit birth certificates to be issued in the names of two parents of the same sex. [253]

7. **Constitutional issues**

   a. **Right to procreate:** Proponents of surrogacy argue that restrictions violate the right of privacy (as recognized by *Griswold*, *Eisenstadt*, and *Roe v. Wade*). [255]

   b. **Equal protection:** Some critics argue that restrictions on surrogacy may violate equal protection by giving rise to differential treatment of infertile women compared to infertile men. [255]

8. **Remedies**

   a. **Breach of contract:** If the surrogate mother refuses to relinquish the child, the contracting father and his wife may sue for breach of contract. However, this remedy does not protect their expectation interest (i.e., their hope for a baby). [256]

   b. **Specific performance:** If the contracting father and his wife sue for specific performance in the event of the surrogate's breach, courts express reluctance to enforce personal services contracts. [256]

9. ***Baby M.*:** The New Jersey Supreme Court ruled that the surrogacy contract is unenforceable as violative of the babyselling law and public policy. The court also ruled that the prospective adoptive parents do not have a constitutionally protected right to procreate by means of surrogacy. Despite holding the surrogacy agreement to be invalid and unenforceable, the court granted custody to the intended parents based on the best-interests-of-the-child standard. [256]

10. **Divorce during the surrogacy process:** The intended parents are responsible for the care and support of a child born via surrogacy even if they divorce during the surrogacy process. [257]

C. **In vitro fertilization:** In vitro fertilization involves the surgical removal of ova which subsequently are placed in a laboratory medium together with sperm where fertilization takes place. The resulting embryo is implanted. The use of frozen embryos (cryopreservation) in conjunction with in vitro fertilization raises potential custody and inheritance issues. [258]

D. **Embryo transfers:** Embryo transfer involves the artificial insemination of an egg, followed by transplantation of the resulting embryo into the uterus of another woman who is to bear the child.

Embryo transfer raises similar legal and social issues to surrogacy, particularly when the birth mother or egg donor is the mother. [258-259]

E. Reproductive material: Ownership and custody: The divorce context raises issues of the ownership, custody, and disposition of genetic material, i.e., whether genetic material is "property" or "persons." [259]

CHAPTER 9
CHILD ABUSE AND NEGLECT

I. HISTORICAL BACKGROUND

Children have been abused and neglected from antiquity due to the low value that society placed on them. [265]

II. THRESHOLD STANDARD FOR INTERVENTION

A. Generally: The state's ability to intervene in the family in cases of abuse and neglect rests on the *parens patriae* power. The state must have a compelling justification in order to intervene in the family. [266]

B. Stages of intervention: Juvenile court proceedings in abuse and neglect cases consist of a *jurisdictional* hearing at which the state asserts jurisdiction followed by a *dispositional* hearing at which the state determines a placement for the child. Emergency jurisdiction also exists for temporary removal of the child from the home prior to a hearing. [267]

III. DEFINING CHILD ABUSE

A. Battering: Successful prosecutions in cases of young children often depend on a court's willingness to admit evidence of "battered child syndrome." [269]

1. Battered child syndrome

a. Generally: Battered child syndrome is a widely accepted description in the medical literature and case law. [269]

b. Definition: Battered child syndrome signifies a child who manifests multiple injuries in various stages of healing. Parental explanations are inconsistent with the nature or severity of injuries. [269]

c. Effect: An expert's testimony that a child is a victim of the battered child syndrome indicates that the child's injuries were intentionally, rather than accidentally, inflicted. [269]

d. Admissibility: Most jurisdictions admit evidence of the battered child syndrome. [269]

B. Abusive discipline

1. Common-law parental privilege to discipline

a. Generally: A common-law ***parental privilege to discipline*** exists. [269]

b. **Limitations on the privilege:** If a child's injury stems from discipline, the force used must be *reasonable* and for purposes of *correction.* [270]

2. **Statutory formulations:** Various statutory formulations codify the common-law parental privilege to discipline. [270]

C. **Religious and/or cultural practices:** Courts have not been receptive to defenses to excuse liability for abuse based on religious or cultural practices. [271]

D. **Psychological or emotional abuse:** Many state statutes subject parents to liability for psychological maltreatment of children. [272]

E. **Sexual abuse**

1. **Generally:** Legal responses to child sexual abuse include civil proceedings (by a juvenile court to assert jurisdiction over an abused child, and lawsuits for damages) as well as criminal proceedings to punish the perpetrator. [272]

2. **Problems of proof:** Since sexual abuse rarely has physical manifestations, evidentiary problems abound. [272]

3. **Sexual abuse allegations in custody disputes:** Sexual abuse allegations in custody proceedings, if proven, may result in conditions on a parent's visitation. [273]

4. **Failure to protect:** Some jurisdictions subject mothers to liability for failure to protect their children from a father's abuse (as a form of child endangerment). A parent's failure to protect the child sometimes may result in termination of that parent's parental rights. [273]

F. **Prenatal abuse:** Jurisdictions have attempted, usually unsuccessfully, to impose criminal liability on female drug abusers for inflicting prenatal harm to their children. [273]

G. **Potential abuse:** A court may determine that a child is abused or neglected based on a finding that other children in the same household have been abused or neglected previously. [274]

IV. DEFINING CHILD NEGLECT

A. **Generally:** Statutes often include broad definitions of parental acts of misconduct or omission. [274]

B. **Parental acts of omission:** A parent has the duty to provide adequate care, including special care warranted by the child's physical or mental condition. [274]

C. **Religious justification for medical neglect:** Some jurisdictions provide that parents who withhold treatment based on religious beliefs are exempt from liability for child abuse. [275]

D. **Emotional neglect:** Emotional neglect, including "failure to thrive," may also be a ground for intervention. [275]

E. **Potential neglect:** Children may be declared neglected even though no parental misconduct or omission has yet occurred. [277]

V. PROCEDURE

A. Reporting laws: All states have reporting laws that require designated individuals to report suspected child abuse and neglect. [278]

1. **Civil and criminal sanctions for failure to report:** Many states impose criminal liability for failure to report child abuse. Some jurisdictions permit a civil cause of action. [279]

2. **Immunity from civil liability for false reports:** Statutes often confer ***immunity*** on reporters. [279]

3. **Central registry:** Many states incorporate into their reporting laws a requirement that a state agency maintain a ***central registry of reported cases***. [279]

B. Evidentiary issues: The primary evidentiary issue in child abuse cases is protection of the victim from the trauma of the judicial process while safeguarding the defendant's constitutional rights. [280]

1. **Competency of child witnesses:** Some states require proof of *competency* before a child witness may testify. [280]

2. **Battered parent profile:** Testimony regarding character, which is introduced to show that the defendant fits the ***battered parent profile***, is generally inadmissible. [280]

3. **Clergy privilege:** Most jurisdictions have a privilege that allows clergy to keep confidential parishioners' communications, such as those involving child abuse. In the wake of the clergy sex abuse scandal, many jurisdictions have abrogated or weakened the privilege. [281]

4. **Child Sexual Abuse Accommodation Syndrome:** The Child Sexual Abuse Accommodation Syndrome (CSAAS) identifies behavioral characteristics of sexually abused children. Many courts hold such evidence inadmissible as proof that the sexual abuse occurred in a given case, but admit the evidence for rehabilitative purposes. [281]

5. **Statutes of limitations and the delayed discovery rule:** Some jurisdictions extend the statutes of limitations by application of the "delayed discovery" rule to toll the statute until the victim knows, or reasonably could have known, of the injury. [281]

6. **The right to confrontation**

   a. **The Sixth Amendment's Confrontation Clause:** The Sixth Amendment provides that an accused shall have the right in criminal prosecutions to confront the witnesses who testify against him or her. Many states enacted special protective testimonial procedures (such as closed circuit television) that apply in criminal prosecutions involving sexual child abuse. Courts have upheld the constitutionality of some of these procedures (*Maryland v. Craig*). However, admission of a child's out-of-court statements, when the defendant does not have the opportunity for cross-examination, may violate the Confrontation Clause (*Crawford v. Washington*). [282-284]

   b. **Hearsay:** ***Hearsay evidence*** (involving a previous out-of-court statement to prove the truth of the matter asserted) is generally *inadmissible* unless it falls within a recognized exception. Many states utilize *traditional hearsay exceptions* to permit a child's previous out-of-court statements. Traditional exceptions include: spontaneous declarations and statements for medical diagnosis and treatment. [283-284]

i. **Spontaneous declarations:** Some states and the Federal Rules of Evidence permit the introduction of hearsay statements termed "spontaneous declarations" if the statements are made *under the influence of a stressful event.* [283]

ii. **Statements for medical diagnosis and treatment:** Some states and the Federal Rules of Evidence permit the introduction of *statements that are made to medical personnel for the purpose of diagnosis and treatment.* [284]

c. **Constitutionality of tender years exemption statutes:** The United States Supreme Court's decision in *Crawford v. Washington* limits the admissibility of a witness's out-of-court statements as hearsay (if the declarant is unavailable at trial and the defendant has no opportunity for cross-examination)—a procedure that was allowed by some states' tender years exemption statutes. [284]

7. **Fifth Amendment privilege against self-incrimination:** A parent *may not invoke the Fifth Amendment* right against self-incrimination to avoid a court order to produce a child (*Baltimore v. Bouknight*). [286]

VI. INTERVENTION

A. **Summary seizure:** Statutes permit the summary removal of a child from the home ex parte when the child is seriously endangered provided that there exists immediate or threatened harm. [287]

B. **Intermediate dispositions**

1. **Foster care**

a. **Generally:** The state places a child in foster care either because the child has been adjudicated abused, neglected, or dependent, or, alternatively, because parents voluntarily place the children in state custody. [287]

b. **Purpose:** Foster care provides a stable environment while preparing the child for return to the biological parents. [288]

c. **Foster parents' rights:** The Supreme Court has *refused to* recognize foster parents' constitutional right to protection of their relationship with their foster children (*Smith v. OFFER*). [288]

2. **Alternatives to foster care:** A juvenile court may order, as an alternative to foster care, that a child be returned to the parent's custody subject to various ***conditions***. [289]

3. **Sanctions for the state's failure to protect**

a. **Duty regarding children not yet removed from the home:** The Supreme Court has ruled that the *state does not owe a duty* for failure to protect a child from abuse *unless the state has taken the child into protective custody* (*DeShaney v. Winnebago*). [289-290]

b. **Duty regarding children placed in foster care**

i. **Adoption Assistance and Child Welfare Act (AACWA):** The ***Adoption Assistance and Child Welfare Act*** provides federal matching funds to states to redress the limbo of foster care by preventing the need for children's removal from the home, facilitating the return of children to their families, or placing them for adoption. To qualify for federal funds, states have to make *reasonable efforts* to prevent the need for placement and to reunify foster children with their families. [290]

ii. Adoption and Safe Families Act: Congress enacted the Adoption and Safe Families Act (ASFA) in 1997 to strengthen the requirements of the AACWA. It eliminates the reasonable efforts requirement in some circumstances and requires states to seek more prompt termination of parental rights for children. [290]

iii. Lawsuits securing compliance with the AACWA: Until 1992, several class action lawsuits brought by foster children against state and local agencies were successful in securing enforcement of the AACWA. The federal courts' willingness to recognize a private right of enforcement of the statutory provisions of the AACWA ended abruptly with the Supreme Court's decision in *Suter v. Artist M.* [291]

iv. Effect of *Suter*: To avoid dismissal under *Suter*, litigants can no longer rely on claims under the AACWA but must utilize other constitutional, federal, or state causes of action. [291]

C. Permanent dispositions: Termination of parental rights

1. **Termination standard:** The state may terminate the parent-child relationship only when the child is subjected to *real physical or emotional harm* and *less drastic measures are unavailing*. [292]

2. **Standard of proof:** The Supreme Court has held that due process requires that the standard of proof for termination of parent rights proceedings must be, at a minimum, clear and convincing evidence (*Santosky v. Kramer*). [292]

3. **Constitutionality:** The constitutionality of termination of parental rights statutes has been challenged on grounds of vagueness. Statutory reforms have resulted in more specific definitions. [292]

4. **Right to counsel:** The *Due Process Clause does not require that an indigent be afforded counsel* prior to the termination of parental rights (*Lassiter v. Dept. of Soc. Servs.*). Despite *Lassiter*, many states hold that an indigent parent has a right to counsel. The child's right to counsel must be distinguished from the parent's right. The *Child Abuse Prevention and Treatment Act* of 1974 requires that, for states to qualify for federal funds, a guardian ad litem shall be appointed to represent the *child*. [292]

5. **State's failure to provide services as a defense:** Some states (following the federal AACWA) require that "reasonable efforts" be made to prevent removal of children from the home and to reunify the family. The state's failure to provide these mandated support services may constitute a defense to a parent in a termination of parental rights proceeding. [293-294]

CAPSULE SUMMARY

CHAPTER 10
THE PARENT-CHILD-STATE RELATIONSHIP IN SPECIAL CONTEXTS

I. TORTS

A. **Traditional rule:** At common law, parents were not liable for children's torts. [299]

1. **Standard of care:** Although children are liable for their torts, they are subject to a different standard of care than for adults. The ***traditional rule*** takes into account the minor's *age and experience*. [299]

2. **Standard of care for contributory negligence**

a. **Majority rule:** The ***majority rule*** adopts an *age-based standard of care* for a child's contributory negligence. [300]

b. **Minority rule:** A ***minority*** of jurisdictions adopt a presumption that children below a certain age cannot be held contributorily negligent. [300]

B. **Exception to rule of liability: Children's conduct of adult activities:** The ***modern trend*** abrogates an age-based standard of care when a minor is performing an adult activity. [300]

C. **Parents' liability for children's torts:** Parents may be liable today for their children's torts by statute, if they employ their child, permit a child to use a dangerous instrumentality, sanction or promote the wrongdoing, or know of their child's violent propensity. [300]

II. CONTRACTS

A. **Common-law rule:** At common law, a minor could ***disaffirm*** a contract, i.e., assert a *defense of infancy*. [302]

B. **Majority rule:** Most jurisdictions still follow the common-law rule. [302]

C. **Policy:** The policy is to protect minors from immaturity and overreaching by adults. [302]

D. **Modern view:** Some courts and legislatures have changed the common-law rule in limited situations (e.g., entertainment contracts). [302]

III. PROPERTY

A. **Earnings**

1. **Common-law rule:** Many modern statutes incorporate the common-law rule that a *parent has the right to a child's services and earnings*. [303]

2. **Emancipation:** ***Emancipation*** permits a child to acquire the right to dispose of his or her own earnings. [303]

B. Inheritance

1. **Traditional rule:** A child may inherit property; however, a guardian may have to be appointed to manage that property. [303]

2. **Guardianship: Definition:** At common law, if a child inherited property or was given property that required active management, a court appointed a ***guardian of the child's estate.*** The term "guardian" actually has two meanings: a guardian of the person or a guardian of the estate (property). [303]

3. **Guardianship: Problems:** Guardianship poses several problems: expense, limited powers, and automatic termination at a statutorily designated age. [303]

4. **Inheritance rights of nonmarital children**

   a. **Traditional rule:** Although both nonmarital and legitimate children could inherit by intestate succession from their mothers at common law, only legitimate children could inherit from their fathers. [304]

   b. **Modern trend:** The modern trend minimizes differences in inheritance between legitimate and nonmarital children (*Trimble v. Gordon, Lalli v. Lalli*). [304]

   c. **Uniform Parentage Act:** States have expanded the inheritance rights of nonmarital children by statute. Many states have adopted the UPA provisions permitting presumptions of paternity, including the presumption based on the father's conduct of "holding out" the child as his child. [304-305]

5. **Capacity to devise property:** Almost all states now define the age for testamentary capacity (e.g., most commonly age 18). [305]

6. **Gifts:** Children may receive property as an inter vivos gift, although the court may appoint a guardian for management purposes. [305]

7. **Trusts:** A minor's property may be held in trust. The ***Uniform Transfers to Minors Act*** (UTMA), permits a minor's property to be registered in the name of a *custodian.* [305]

IV. EDUCATION

A. Parents' right to control the upbringing of their children: A trilogy of Supreme Court cases (*Meyer v. Nebraska, Pierce v. Soc'y of Sisters, Wisconsin v. Yoder*) announces a principle of enormous constitutional significance: Parents have a constitutionally protected right to control the upbringing of their children. The Court's decision in *Troxel v. Granville* affirmed this privilege of family privacy. [306]

B. Minors' First Amendment rights

1. **Political speech:** Students have a right to freedom of expression in terms of political speech, although minors' exercise of that right must not *materially and substantially interfere with school discipline* or *invade the rights of others* (*Tinker v. Des Moines*). [307]

2. **Free speech in the context of school-sponsored activities:** Students' right to freedom of expression is restricted in *school-sponsored* and *school-approved* activities. [307]

C. **Minors' Fourth Amendment rights:** The United States Supreme Court holds that the Fourth Amendment's prohibition against unreasonable searches applies to juveniles. However, the standard for searches of juveniles ("reasonable suspicion") is lower than that for adults ("probable cause"). Thus, the law permits searches of juveniles that would be unconstitutional as applied to adults (e.g., random drug testing but not strip searches). [308-310]

D. **Firearms use by juveniles:** Federal and state legislation restricts juveniles' access to firearms. The United States Supreme Court ruled that Congress exceeded its authority under the Commerce Clause in enacting a prohibition against possession of a firearm in a school zone (*United States v. Lopez*). However, many jurisdictions have enacted similar statutes based on state law. [310-311]

V. MEDICAL CARE

A. **Requirement of parental consent:** At common law, only a parent (not a child) could give consent to medical treatment for the child. [312]

B. **Minor's consent:** Some statutes provide that an unemancipated minor may give consent to medical treatment for himself or herself in limited situations. [312]

C. **Exceptions to parental consent requirements**

1. **Emergency exception:** Under the common-law rule, a doctor may provide medical treatment to a child *without securing parental consent* in the event of an *emergency*. [312]
2. **State-imposed health requirements:** The state may mandate certain health requirements (e.g., newborn screening and testing, compulsory immunizations). [312]
3. **Neglect limitation:** At common law, parents had (and still have) a duty to provide their child with necessary medical care. Parents who refuse may be subject to criminal or civil liability. The state may secure the necessary medical treatment for the child by declaring the child neglected in a juvenile court proceeding. [312]

D. **Baby Doe cases:** A series of cases involving disabled newborns in the 1980s led to a wave of federal and state regulations in an attempt to require medical treatment for these infants. [313-314]

CHAPTER 11
ADOPTION

I. INTRODUCTION

A. **Definition:** Adoption terminates the legal rights and responsibilities of the natural parents and creates new legal rights and responsibilities in the adoptive parents. [319]

B. **Historical background:** Adoption was not recognized by the English common law. As a result, American adoption law is entirely statutory. [319-320]

C. **Voluntary and involuntary termination of parental rights:** Termination of the natural parents' rights prior to adoption may be *voluntary* or *involuntary*. Termination and adoption may take place in the same or separate proceedings. [320]

D. Social reality: Social forces have contributed to a sharp decrease in the number of Caucasian babies available for adoption. [320]

II. SELECTION STANDARDS FOR ADOPTIVE PARENTS

A. Generally: The guiding standard in adoption, as in custody, is the ***best interests of the child***. [320]

B. Relevant factors

1. **Preference for relatives:** Some statutes incorporate a *presumption that adoptive placement with relatives is in the child's best interests*, absent good cause or detriment to the child. [320]

2. **Sexual orientation:** States differ on whether to allow gay or lesbian parents to adopt children. A few states are very restrictive. [320-321]

3. **Race**

   a. **Generally:** Race may be a *relevant, although not determinative*, factor in selecting the adoptive parent. [322]

   b. **Effect of *Palmore v. Sidoti*:** A United States Supreme Court case (*Palmore v. Sidoti*) that addresses race in custody decision making has implications for the consideration of race in adoption: Race may not be a determinative factor. [322]

   c. **Racial matching:** Racial matching is the subject of a highly controversial policy debate. [323]

4. **Religion:** Religion also may be relevant in the selection of adoptive parents. Some states have ***religious matching policies***. [323]

C. Indian Child Welfare Act (ICWA) of 1978: The Indian Child Welfare Act dictates that Native-American origins are relevant in adoption. Some state courts hold that the ICWA does not apply if the Indian child is raised by a non-Indian parent with no tribal contact (the "existing Indian family" exception). [324-325]

III. CONSENT

Statutes generally require parental consent before an adoption. For a nonmarital child (born out of wedlock), courts sometimes may dispense with the father's consent if he has not indicated sufficient ***indicia of parenthood.*** [326]

A. Consent by the unmarried father

1. **Ramifications of *Stanley v. Illinois*:** A statutory presumption that denies a father a fitness hearing before removal of his children violates procedural due process (*Stanley v. Illinois*). [326]

2. **Indicia of parenthood:** The Supreme Court has held, in a trilogy of cases (*Lehr v. Robertson, Caban v. Mohammed, Quilloin v. Walcott*), that an unmarried father is entitled to constitutional protection of his parental rights so long as he manifests certain "indicia of parenthood." [327]

3. **Consent requirement where father never has opportunity to develop a relationship:** The most difficult cases occur when a father *never has an opportunity to develop a relationship* with his child. [328]

B. **Divorced noncustodial parent's consent in the face of a stepparent adoption:** Some statutes facilitate stepparent adoptions by dispensing with a noncustodial parent's consent. [328]

IV. PLACEMENT PROCEDURE

A biological parent (or parents) may relinquish a child to a licensed public or private *agency* or arrange for an *independent adoption* by which an intermediary facilitates the adoption. [330]

A. **Agency's role: Disclosure requirements:** An agency that discloses information to prospective adoptive parents about the natural parents or medical history of the child or parents has a *duty not to mislead.* [330]

B. **Independent placement: Intermediary's role:** Some statutes limit or prohibit the participation of independent agents in the placement process. [330]

V. SUBSIDIZED ADOPTION

All states provide ***subsidized adoption programs*** to *facilitate adoption of those children who are difficult to place* for reasons of age, physical or mental disability, or racial or ethnic background. [331]

VI. INTERNATIONAL ADOPTION

International adoption has generated controversy similar to that of transracial adoption, i.e., the concern that adopted children will lose their cultural heritage. The Hague Convention on Protection of Children and Cooperation in Respect of Intercountry Adoption facilitates international adoptions by requiring determinations that adoption serves the child's best interests. The legislation applies only when both countries involved are signatories to the Convention. [331]

VII. THE LEGAL CONSEQUENCES OF ADOPTION

A. **Marriage limitations:** Whether two people related by adoption may marry depends on statute. [332]

B. **Inheritance:** Adoption into an adoptive family generally results in the child's losing the right to inherit from a biological parent. Some jurisdictions correct this result by statute. [333]

VIII. OPEN ADOPTION

Open adoption, i.e., the continuation of contact between the biological parents and adopted child, is growing in popularity. [334]

IX. EQUITABLE ADOPTION

Equitable adoption is an equitable device whereby courts effectuate an adoption (or effectuate the consequences of an adoption) in cases in which a legal adoption never occurred. [335]

X. ADOPTEE'S RIGHT TO KNOW OF ORIGINS

A. **Traditional rule:** State adoption statutes traditionally required strict confidentiality. [336]

B. **Modern view:** The trend facilitates the exchange of information between an adopted child and the natural parents. [337]

XI. JURISDICTION

Some jurisdictions hold that the statutes governing multijurisdictional custody disputes also are controlling in proceedings involving termination of parental rights and adoptions. [337]

XII. ADULT ADOPTION

A. **General rule:** Most states allow the adoption of an adult. However, some states have limitations on the practice. [338]

B. **Limitations:** Some jurisdictions inquire into the purpose of the adult adoption. [338]

C. **Adoptions involving gays and lesbians:** Some states refuse to permit adult adoption involving same-sex partners. [338-339]

XII. ADOPTION FAILURE: REVOCATION AND ABROGATION

Adoptions may fail either because of the actions of a *natural parent who revokes her consent* or because of the desires of an *adoptive parent or parents to abrogate* the adoption. [339]

A. **Revocation of consent:** Statutes confer the right on a biological parent to revoke consent on grounds of fraud, duress, or coercion. Most jurisdictions now limit the time period during which the birth mother may withdraw consent. [339]

B. **Abrogation:** States allow abrogation (i.e., annulment of an adoption) by the adoptive parents in limited circumstances. [340]

CHAPTER 1

INTRODUCTION

ChapterScope

This chapter provides an introduction to family law. First, it presents a definition of the field. Second, it examines societal influences that have contributed to dramatic changes in the field. Third, it explores important contemporary legal trends that characterize family law. Here are a few of the key principles covered in this chapter:

- **Definition:** Family law explores the legal regulation of the family and its members.
- **Societal influences:** Family law reflects several important societal influences that have effectuated dramatic changes in the field, including:
  - the women's movement;
  - the rising incidence of divorce;
  - dissatisfaction with the traditional family and the growth of alternative family forms;
  - dissatisfaction with traditional dispute resolution processes;
  - the children's rights movement;
  - the decreasing influence of morality; and
  - the new reproductive technology.
- **Family law reflects three contemporary legal trends:** federalization, constitutionalization, and a movement toward uniformity of state law.
  - ***Federalization:*** The federal government occupies an increasingly prominent role in the regulation of the family.
  - ***Constitutionalization:*** A considerable body of federal constitutional law now applies to the family, family relationships, and family members.
  - ***Uniformity:*** Family law reflects a movement toward uniformity in the variety of state laws that apply to the family and its members.

I. GENERALLY

A. **Definition:** Family law explores the legal regulation of the family and its members. These members include: husband and wife, parent and child, as well as members of nontraditional families.

B. **Central theme:** Family law is characterized by a conflict between individual and social interests. The individual interest is the desire to give consideration to a family member's decisional autonomy in private matters. On the other hand, the state has various interests that precipitate its intervention in the family, including interests in the protection of family members and the promotion of marriage as an institution, among others.

C. **Dynamic nature of field:** Family law is a field in *transition*. This transformation is apparent even in nomenclature (for example, family law formerly was called the "law of domestic relations"). Change is apparent especially in terms of the roles and responsibilities of family members, the definition of a ***family***, and the nature of legal regulation of the family and its members. This dynamic nature of the field is due, in part, to societal influences.

II. SOCIETAL INFLUENCES ON FAMILY LAW

Family law reflects several important societal influences (social developments and social movements) that have effectuated dramatic changes in the field over the past several decades.

A. **Women's movement:** In the early 1960s, the civil rights movement and the publication of Betty Friedan's *The Feminine Mystique* (1963) triggered the contemporary women's movement. The women's movement led to a change in public policy toward women by both Congress and the courts. Congress prohibited sexual discrimination in employment by the Equal Pay Act in 1963 and Title VII of the Civil Rights Act of 1964. These pieces of legislation precipitated a change from a policy of paternalism toward women (e.g., the era of protective labor legislation) to a policy reflecting equality of opportunity. Women, and especially married women, flocked to the workplace as employment barriers came down.

During the same period, the United States Supreme Court significantly expanded women's legal protection by holding that sex discrimination is a violation of equal protection. In *Reed v. Reed*, 404 U.S. 71 (1971), the Court held that an Idaho statute was unconstitutional, and without a rational basis, for giving priority to men in the administration of estates. The Court followed with *Craig v. Boren*, 429 U.S. 190 (1976), ruling unconstitutional an Oklahoma law that permitted the sale of 3.2 beer to women over age 18, but to men only over age 21. *Craig v. Boren* requires that laws and practices discriminating on the basis of gender must meet the more exacting intermediate scrutiny test: A regulation or practice must be "substantially related to an important governmental interest." *Id.* at 204.

The Supreme Court subsequently subtly heightened the level of scrutiny applicable to gender-based classifications. In *United States v. Virginia*, 518 U.S. 515 (1996), the Court held that a policy restricting admission to only men by a public military academy violated equal protection. Justice Ruth Bader Ginsburg thereby announced a revised standard of review for gender discrimination: The parties seeking to defend the classification must demonstrate "an exceedingly persuasive justification." Justice Scalia in a strongly worded dissent criticized that the Court was covertly applying "strict scrutiny."

Historically, some states have been more sympathetic than the Supreme Court to challenges regarding gender-based classifications. States, such as California, apply a higher level of scrutiny (i.e., strict scrutiny), thereby equating sex-based classifications to racial discrimination. *See, e.g., Sail'er Inn v. Kirby*, 485 P.2d 529 (Cal. 1971) (finding unconstitutional a statute that prohibited women from working as bartenders). The strict scrutiny test requires that the regulation or practice be necessary to a compelling state interest.

Women's entry into the public arena was accompanied by an evolution in gender roles. Women were no longer completely dependent upon men financially. Nor were women entirely relegated to the private world of the family, with men in the public world of work. As women took on the role of providers, they called upon men to shoulder increasing responsibilities for child care and housework.

Family law reflects the ensuing degenderization of family roles. For example, the diminution in women's status as child caretaker leads to the demise of the maternal presumption in awards of custody. The rise in men's participation in child care and housework leads to the joint custody doctrine. Women's enhanced financial position contributes to both men and women being financially responsible for child support, as well as to divorced women being regarded as less needy of spousal support. Some feminist commentators (e.g., Professors Martha Fineman, Mary Becker, Deborah Rhode, and Martha Minow) charge that the adoption of this "equal treatment approach" has led to a diminution of women's rights.

B. Rising incidence of divorce: Until the nineteenth century, marriage tended to be a permanent commitment. Divorce was difficult and costly to obtain, and stigmatizing for the parties. Courts and legislators permitted divorce infrequently and only upon proof of serious marital misconduct.

California's enactment of "no-fault divorce" in 1968 eliminated the need to obtain fault-based grounds there. Rather than marital misconduct, the parties needed only show that "irreconcilable differences" caused the breakdown of the marriage. Further, no longer was the "guilty" spouse punished by means of deprivation of property or the denial of spousal support. A few years later, in 1974, the National Conference of Commissioners on Uniform State Laws (NCCUSL) ratified the Uniform Marriage and Divorce Act (UMDA), which also permitted no-fault divorce (UMDA §§302 and 305 permit dissolution of marriages based on "irretrievable breakdown" or a six-month separation). Under UMDA, marital misconduct is irrelevant to issues of spousal support, property distribution, or custody.

Since then, many states have followed California's or UMDA's lead by adopting a no-fault system — either in whole (by replacing completely their fault-based systems with no-fault regimes) or in part (by superimposing no-fault onto fault-based grounds).

No-fault divorce transformed rules of property distribution, spousal support, and custody. The no-fault divorce doctrine reflects the evolution in women's status brought about by women's increased economic opportunities. The legal treatment of spousal support provides one example. The gender-based concept of "alimony" has been replaced with the more neutral terms "spousal support" or "maintenance." Although support is now available theoretically to either spouse after divorce, fewer courts today award spousal support than in the past and such awards tend to be limited in duration. This transformation has been accompanied by unanticipated adverse economic consequences for divorced women and their children. As sociologist Lenore Weitzman points out in *The Divorce Revolution* (1985), the standard of living for divorced women decreases after divorce while men's standard of living increases. *Id.* at 382.

C. Dissatisfaction with the family and the growth of alternative family forms: The 1960s witnessed increasing disillusionment with the nuclear family. In particular, radical psychiatrists (e.g., R.D. Laing) as well as radical feminists (e.g., Shulamith Firestone, Kate Millett) highlighted the ills of the private nuclear family. Feminists, for example, challenged several beliefs: the nuclear family as a biological given with its sexual division of labor, the hierarchy of family relationships with women being subordinate to men, women's primary commitment to the home and children, and procreation as the central purpose of the family.

These criticisms contributed to a gradual reconceptualization of marriage and the family. Marriage came to be perceived as a means of personal fulfillment and a source of companionship. Rather than the concept of marriage as forever, a new idea took hold: When marriage failed to meet the parties' expectations, the parties could and should seek fulfillment elsewhere.

Further, criticisms of the traditional family contributed to a growing awareness of, and acceptance of, the diversity of family forms (such as unmarried opposite-sex couples as well as same-sex couples). Nontraditional, as well as traditional, families provide intimacy and companionship. These criticisms contributed to a fundamental challenge to the definition of the family.

Illustrative of this reconceptualization of the family is the social movement toward marriage equality. In recent years, society has witnessed the legalization of same-sex marriage in several states. Other jurisdictions have enacted legislation recognizing a range of legal protections for same-sex couples (relationships that are referred to as "domestic partnerships" or "civil unions" or "reciprocal beneficiaries").

D. **Dissatisfaction with traditional dispute resolution processes: The emergence of private ordering:** The 1960s also witnessed increased dissatisfaction with traditional means of dispute resolution. Lawyers, judges, and scholars criticized the legal system and manifested a new interest in alternate dispute resolution. Critics recognized that the law was unwieldy and intrusive, especially in the resolution of private disputes. This movement increasingly recognized "private ordering" — i.e., the ability of the parties to resolve their disputes without judicial intervention. We witness this development in the judicial recognition of premarital agreements, the growth of mediation of family disputes, and the development of the collaborative law movement.

E. **Children's rights movement:** Children now occupy a more central role in the family and society. Unlike in past centuries, families no longer value children solely for their economic contributions. Childhood has been reconceptualized as a prolonged period of economic and social dependency.

In the 1960s, the civil rights movement and the women's movement contributed to the birth of the children's rights movement. Family law began to reflect the idea of children having legally enforceable rights, including the right to a voice (although limited) in decision making that affected them. Thus, we speak of the child's role in child custody decisions, as well as the child's role in abortion decision making.

F. **New reproductive technology:** Major developments in reproductive technology have enhanced women's reproductive freedom. The discovery of the birth control pill led to a decreased concern with the means to prevent reproduction. New concerns subsequently surfaced regarding the means to facilitate reproduction. Medical technology made possible several new methods of addressing infertility (e.g., in vitro fertilization, embryo transplants, and surrogate motherhood).

Several social conditions contributed to the development and use of these technologies, including an increase in infertility resulting from delayed childbearing, harmful contraceptive methods, and pelvic inflammatory disease, as well as the shortage of infants for adoption. Family law is now grappling with the delineation of the rights and responsibilities that flow from the development and utilization of the new reproductive technology (especially, for example, new definitions of parenthood).

G. Decreasing influence of morality: Beginning in the 1960s, family law reflected the decreasing influence of ideas about morality. The women's movement and the birth control movement liberalized sexual mores. Control over conception significantly decreased the number of illegitimate (now called "nonmarital") children. The women's movement cast negative light on the sexual double standard that permitted premarital and extramarital sexual relationships for men but not for women.

The gay rights movement also was rooted in the late 1960s. The Stonewall Riot at a Greenwich Village bar in New York City in 1969 led to a national outcry against discrimination directed at gays and lesbians. The gay rights movement contributed to the liberalization of views about the legal recognition of the rights of same-sex partners.

The waning of morality is reflected in family law in several ways. For example, no-fault divorce signifies the increasing acceptance of the termination of the marital relationship. Nonmarital children are no longer stigmatized and have enhanced legal rights. Fault-based notions no longer play a significant role in determinations of spousal support, property, and custody. The law is conferring increasing legal rights on same-sex couples (for example, in the areas of marriage, divorce, domestic violence, child support, child custody, and adoption, to name a few).

The waning of morality is also reflected in family law terminology. To eliminate strains of stigma, for example, we now speak of "dissolution" (rather than "divorce"), "spousal support" or "maintenance" (rather than "alimony"), "nonmarital children" (rather than "illegitimate" or "out-of-wedlock" children), and "unmarried couples" (rather than "persons living in sin" or persons involved in "meretricious" relationships).

III. CONTEMPORARY LEGAL TRENDS

Family law reflects three contemporary legal trends: (1) *federalization* (i.e., an increasing congressional role in family policy), (2) *constitutionalization* (i.e., the growing recognition of the constitutional dimensions of the regulation of intimate relationships), and (3) a movement toward *uniformity* of state law.

A. Federalization of family law: Increasing congressional role: The federal government occupies an increasingly prominent role in the regulation of family law. Formerly, family law was exclusively the domain of state regulation. However, in the past several decades, Congress has enacted considerable legislation on many issues of family life.

Federal legislation now addresses adoption, child support, child custody, child abuse and neglect, domestic violence, foster care, marriage validity, paternity establishment, and parental leaves. The ever-increasing number of federal statutes includes (among others):

- Adoption and Safe Families Act (ASFA) (promoting adoption of children with special needs and those in foster care), and Adoption Assistance and Child Welfare Act (AACWA) (addressing foster care reform);
- Child Abuse Prevention and Treatment Act (CAPTA) (providing state programs and procedures to address the prevention and treatment of child abuse and neglect);
- Child Support Enforcement Amendments (requiring states participating in the federal child support program to have procedures to establish paternity, to obtain child support awards, and to enforce child support obligations);

- Defense of Marriage Act (DOMA) (providing a heterosexual definition of marriage for purposes of federal legislation);
- Family Support Act (FSA) (requiring states to adopt numerical guidelines); and the subsequent Full Faith and Credit for Child Support Orders Act (FFCCSOA) (requiring states to adopt procedures regarding recognition of other states' decrees of child support);
- Family and Medical Leave Act (FMLA) (granting unpaid leave for birth, adoption, and illnesses of family members);
- Foster Care Independence Act (FCIA) (helping youth who "age out of" foster care to achieve independent living skills) and Fostering Connection to Success and Increasing Adoptions Act (FCSIAA) (extending benefits to older foster youth and facilitating kinship guardianship assistance payments);
- Indian Child Welfare Act (ICWA) (providing that the tribe has exclusive jurisdiction as against any state concerning child custody, adoption, and foster care placements involving Indian children);
- Parental Kidnapping Prevention Act (PKPA) (addressing parental abduction and jurisdictional conflicts between state courts regarding child custody);
- Partial-Birth Abortion Ban Act (PBABA) (prohibiting a form of late-term abortion);
- Pregnancy Discrimination Act (PDA) of Title VII of the Civil Rights Act (specifying that "sex discrimination" includes discrimination "on the basis of pregnancy" for purposes of employment discrimination);
- Unborn Victims of Violence Act (UVVA) (recognizing unborn children as victims when they are injured or killed during the commission of federal crimes of violence); and
- Violence Against Women Act (VAWA) (providing federal remedies for harm to a spouse or intimate partner and providing for interstate enforcement of protection orders).

These federal regulations usurp state supremacy over many issues of family law that were regulated previously by the states.

B. Constitutionalization of family law: Beginning in the 1960s, the United States Supreme Court handed down a number of rulings on family issues. Before that time, the Court only occasionally regulated the family. A considerable body of federal constitutional law now applies to the family and supplements state regulation of family relationships. The Court's application of principles of due process and equal protection have transformed family law.

For example, the Court expanded rights in the areas of (among others): abortion (*Roe v. Wade, Planned Parenthood v. Danforth*); contraception (*Griswold v. Conn.*, *Eisenstadt v. Baird*); sexual conduct between consenting adults in the home (*Lawrence v. Texas*); the right to marry (*Loving v. Virginia, Zablocki v. Redhail*); the right to divorce (*Boddie v. Conn.*); parental rights (*Wisconsin v. Yoder*, *Santosky v. Kramer*); the rights of women (*Reed v. Reed*, *Craig v. Boren*); and the rights of members of nonmarital families (*Stanley v. Illinois*, *Caban v. Mohammed*) (all discussed *infra*). At the same time, the Court developed notions of marital privacy and family privacy based on liberal interpretations of the Fourteenth Amendment.

C. Movement toward uniform state laws: Family law, formerly, was a matter of state law and reflected state supremacy. That is, matters of marriage, divorce, custody, support, etc. were considered matters for exclusive state jurisdiction — matters regulated by the states and enforced by state courts. This resulted in considerable *variation* in the legal regulations applicable to the family and family members.

In an effort to impose some uniformity on family law, the National Conference of Commissioners on Uniform State Laws in the past several decades has promulgated important model statutes. These include (among others):

- the Uniform Adoption Act (UAA) (revised) (regulating adoption);
- the Uniform Child Abduction Prevention Act (addressing measures to prevent child abduction);
- the Uniform Child Custody Jurisdiction and Enforcement Act (UCCJEA) (addressing interstate enforcement of custody decrees);
- the Uniform Collaborative Law Act (UCLA) (regulating the use of collaborate law as a form of alternative dispute resolution);
- the Uniform Interstate Enforcement of Domestic Violence Protection Orders Act (UIEDVPOA) (establishing uniform procedures to enable courts to enforce domestic violence protection orders issued in other jurisdictions);
- the Uniform Interstate Family Support Act (UIFSA) (concerning the establishment, enforcement, and modification of child support obligations);
- the Uniform Marriage and Divorce Act (UMDA) (addressing marriage, divorce, and custody);
- the Uniform Marital Property Act (UMPA) (addressing marital property and premarital agreements);
- the Uniform Parentage Act (revised) (dealing with paternity establishment);
- the Uniform Premarital Agreement Act (UPAA) (regarding premarital agreements); and
- the Uniform Representation of Children in Abuse, Neglect, and Custody Proceedings Act (addressing issues regarding counsel for children in various contexts).

In addition, the ***American Law Institute (ALI)*** completed a decade-long project that promotes uniformity in family law. (The American Law Institute is an influential group of lawyers, law professors, and judges who engage in law reform.) The product of that project is titled *Principles of the Law of Family Dissolution: Analysis and Recommendations* (2002) [hereinafter ALI *Principles*]. These *Principles* attempt to reform family law by clarifying its underlying principles and making policy recommendations for implementation by courts and legislatures. The *Principles* cover such issues as: the allocation of custodial and decision-making responsibilities for children, child support, distribution of marital property, compensatory payments to former spouses, resolution of the economic claims of domestic partners, and the legal effect of various agreements between the parties. (Note that the work is titled "*Principles*" rather than the more traditional formulation "*Restatement*" because of its emphasis on the clarification of fundamental assumptions about the best interests of children, fairness to divorcing spouses, and the legitimacy of claims of unmarried partners.)

CHAPTER 2

PREPARING TO MARRY

ChapterScope

This chapter explores the law that governs the individual's *decision to marry*. First, the chapter examines the resolution of premarital controversies and the validity of premarital agreements. Second, it examines restrictions on entry into marriage. Third, it explores initial problems of marriage validity, such as annulment and conflict of laws. Here are a few of the key principles covered in this chapter:

- **Premarital controversies:** The two primary types of premarital controversies include (1) ***actions for breach of promise to marry*** and (2) ***actions for the return of gifts in contemplation of marriage.***
  - A few states allow an action for a ***breach of a promise to marry***, permitting A to recover damages from B, if B ends the engagement. However, the ***modern trend*** is toward ***abolition*** of the action.
  - ***Gifts in contemplation of marriage*** are gifts that are conditioned on the occurrence of a marriage. Pursuant to the ***majority rule***, the party who is at fault in breaking the engagement is not entitled to the return or retention of the ring. According to the ***modern trend***, the gift is recoverable without regard to fault.
- **Premarital agreements:** Under the ***traditional view***, agreements between prospective spouses were void as contrary to public policy. Under the ***modern view***, courts permit parties to regulate the financial aspects of the marriage. To be valid, such agreements must meet tests for procedural and/or substantive fairness.
- **Restrictions on entry into marriage:** Various restrictions exist concerning entry into marriage. Such restrictions consist of: (1) ***constitutional limitations***, (2) ***substantive restrictions***, and (3) ***procedural restrictions***.
  - The United States Supreme Court has held that restrictions on marriage that are based on ***race*** and ***poverty*** are unconstitutional.
  - State substantive restrictions refer to ***capacity*** to marry and ***state of mind***.
  - State procedural restrictions regulate the ***marriage procedure***.
- **Annulment:** An annulment declares a marriage ***void ab initio***. In contrast, a divorce terminates a valid marriage. Grounds for annulment include fraud, duress, and nonage.
- **Conflict of laws:** Issues of conflict of laws concern which law governs marriage validity. Under the ***traditional rule***, marriage validity is determined by the law of the place where the marriage was celebrated. Under the ***Restatement (Second) of Conflict of Laws***, the validity of marriage is determined by the state that has the "most significant relationship to the spouses and the marriage."

I. PREMARITAL CONTROVERSIES

A. Breach of promise to marry

1. **Generally:** A few states permit an action for breach of promise to marry. Under this cause of action, A can recover damages from B, if B breaches a promise to marry A (i.e., if B terminates the engagement).

2. **Historical background:** The claim of breach of promise to marry has its origins in early English common law. Although early cases resembled tort actions, the action gradually began to resemble contract claims.

   Recovery was premised on a view of marriage as a property transaction, and the belief that a woman is "sullied" by the broken engagement (i.e., stigmatized by the possible loss of virginity). The action came to be called a "heart balm" suit because damages (i.e., the balm) soothed a plaintiff's broken heart.

3. **Criticisms:** Criticisms led most states to abolish the action via "anti-heartbalm legislation" (sometimes, confusingly, called "Heart Balm Acts"). These criticisms include:

   - the action is a form of blackmail;
   - persons should be permitted to break engagements without fear of legal damages;
   - juries are unfairly biased in favor of the "wronged" woman;
   - the action is based on sexist and archaic stereotypes of women; and
   - damages are based on an outdated view of marriage as a property transaction (by compensating women for loss of social and economic position).

   Sometimes, plaintiffs try to recharacterize the action to avoid the application of anti-heartbalm statutes. Such strategies have met with limited success.

   Example: Plaintiff claims that her boyfriend (who was married at the time to another person) promised her that, in exchange for his gift of $75,000 and her obtaining an abortion, he would obtain a divorce from his wife, marry Plaintiff, and have children with her. When he subsequently refuses to do so, Plaintiff sues for emotional distress, battery, fraud, and misrepresentation. The court of appeals rejects her claims, concluding that each tort claim is premised on the abolished cause of action of breach of promise to marry. *M.N. v. D.S.*, 616 N.W.2d 284 (Minn. Ct. App. 2000).

4. **Judicial and legislative responses to criticisms:** Even in the few states that continue to recognize the action, some courts circumscribe recovery either by limiting damages or by strict adherence to statutory requirements.

   Example: A Chicago attorney agrees to marry an Oregon cattle rancher. They purchase rings and set a wedding date. After several weeks, the rancher has doubts. Subsequently, he breaks off the engagement. Plaintiff sues under the Illinois Breach of Promise Act, seeking damages for medical bills for her depression, lost income, and pain and suffering. The jury returns a verdict for $178,000. Defendant appeals. The court of appeals reverses, holding that Plaintiff's letter informing her fiancé of her intention to sue did not comply with the notice requirements of the Illinois statute (i.e., she failed to include the date they became engaged and did not comply with the statutory requirement that notice be given within three months after the breach). *Wildey v. Springs*, 47 F.3d 1475 (7th Cir. 1995).

5. **Damages:** The breach-of-promise suit is a hybrid action (quasi-contract, quasi-tort). Its hybrid nature raises issues about the proper measure of damages, the applicability of the Statute of Limitations for contract or tort (many courts apply the longer statute), and the abatement of the action upon the death of either party (most courts hold that the action does abate in this event).

   Example: Plaintiff and Defendant agree to marry. Defendant promises Plaintiff that she can quit her job after their marriage, they will travel, and he will support her two sons and her mother. Defendant breaks off the engagement. Plaintiff sues Defendant for damages to compensate for her loss of expected financial security. The court recognizes Plaintiff's claim but determines that recovery should be limited to foreseeable special and general damages (including economic loss and mental anguish); however, damages for loss of expected financial and social position should no longer be recoverable for the reason that such damages are premised on outdated views of marriage. *Stanard v. Bolin*, *supra*. (The Washington Supreme Court affirmed the limitation on damages in *Bell v. Leppard*, 2006 WL 2468760 (Wash. Ct. App. 2006) (rejecting a woman's claim, nonetheless, based on insufficient evidence).)

6. **Defenses:** Traditional defenses include:
   - plaintiff's fraudulent misrepresentation;
   - nondisclosure of prior sexual conduct with a third party;
   - impaired physical or mental health;
   - the fact that either party was married at the time of the engagement;
   - plaintiff's lack of love for the defendant; and
   - mutuality of the decision to terminate the engagement.

7. **Conflict of laws:** Recovery for breach of promise to marry may present difficulties if the "promise" occurs in a jurisdiction that recognizes the cause of action but the "breach" occurs in a jurisdiction that does not.

   Example: Brian and Dana meet through an Internet dating service. Brian, who represents himself as divorced, proposes marriage while the couple is visiting South Carolina. Subsequently, they live together in Brian's New York apartment. Dana breaks up when she suspects that Brian is dating other women. When he files suit in New York for the return of the engagement ring or its value, she counterclaims for breach of promise to marry (recognized by South Carolina but not New York). The New York court dismisses her counterclaim, based on the state statute banning suits for breach of promise to marry "whether such action arose within or without the state." N.Y. Civ. Rights L. §81 (McKinney 2004). The court also rules that, because Brian was already married when he proposed, the agreement to marry was void as against public policy. *Callahan v. Parker*, 824 N.Y.S.2d 768 (Sup. Ct. 2006).

B. Gifts in contemplation of marriage

1. **Generally:** During an engagement, the parties may give gifts to each other. Commonly, for example, the man gives an engagement ring to the woman. If the engagement is broken, whether a party must return the gift may depend on who was responsible (at *fault*) for terminating the engagement.

According to the majority rule, if a ring is given in contemplation of marriage, the party who breaks the engagement without justification is not entitled to either the return or retention of the ring.

Example: Plaintiff and Defendant date for five months. A few days before Christmas, Plaintiff gives Defendant an engagement ring worth $13,500. Six weeks later, Plaintiff breaks off the relationship based on his belief that Defendant is not the "right" person and because his family opposes the match. He files suit for return of the ring or its value. Defendant argues that the ring was a Christmas gift or, alternatively, a conditional gift that she could retain because Plaintiff terminated the engagement. The court holds that the gift was an engagement present rather than a Christmas gift and that, in accordance with the state's fault-based approach, Defendant was entitled to keep the engagement ring (that the court characterizes as a conditional gift in contemplation of marriage) because her fiancé broke off the engagement through no fault of hers. *Clippard v. Pfefferkorn*, 168 S.W.3d 616 (Mo. Ct. App. 2005).

2. **Legal theories:** Several legal theories support the recovery of the engagement ring, including: conditional gift, fraud, and unjust enrichment.

   a. **Conditional gift:** Under this widespread theory, A's gift to B of an engagement ring is conditioned on B's performance of an act (getting married). If the condition (the marriage) is not fulfilled, then A may recover the gift.

   b. **Fraud:** Under this theory, if B obtains a ring fraudulently (i.e., if B had no intention of marrying A), then the ring is recoverable under equitable principles.

   c. **Unjust enrichment:** Under this theory, B has received a benefit (the ring) under circumstances such that it would be inequitable for B to retain the benefit without payment. B must disgorge the benefit by making restitution to A of the ring or its value.

3. **Modern trend:** Under the minority rule (which is also the modern trend), the ring is recoverable without regard to fault (i.e., regardless of who broke the engagement).

   Example: Robert Fowler and Sue Perry live together and have a child. Sometime after Robert gives Sue an engagement ring, she moves out of the state. Robert intends to follow after he finishes college. But, prior to his graduation, Sue breaks off their relationship. She never returns the ring, which is later stolen, and she retains the insurance money. Robert sues for return of the ring or its value. The appellate court holds that Robert is entitled to recover the ring or its value because the ring was a conditional gift. In addition, the court adopts the no-fault approach to support Robert's recovery, reasoning that the no-fault approach is consistent with the jurisdiction's policy of no-fault divorce and also would avoid the need to have a court evaluate each party's reproaches. *Fowler v. Perry*, 830 N.E.2d 97 (Ind. Ct. App. 2005).

4. **Other gifts:** Engaged parties may give each other various other tokens of affection in addition to an engagement ring. Whether these gifts must be returned depends on whether the gift is conditioned on the marriage.

   Example: Layne proposes marriage to Jody and gives her an engagement ring. During their engagement, Jody asks Layne to pay for trips to Alaska and France, to buy a car for her son, and to have a vasectomy. Jody then breaks off the engagement and returns the ring. Layne sells the ring for half its purchase price. He then brings suit under theories of conditional gift and unjust enrichment, seeking reimbursement of $25,000 for the cost of the travel, car, vasectomy and a reversal procedure, and the difference between the ring's purchase and sale price.

Rejecting his claims, the court holds that simply because the gifts were made during the engagement does not mean that they were conditioned on the marriage. *Hess v. Johnson*, 163 P.3d 747 (Utah Ct. App. 2007).

5. **Effect of abolition of heartbalm suits on the recovery of engagement gifts:** In some jurisdictions that have abolished heartbalm suits (e.g., breach of promise to marry), the question arises as to the effect of the statutory abolition. That is, do such statutes similarly abolish the cause of action for return of an engagement ring?

   Example: Dennis gives Terry a ring when they become engaged. Three months later the engagement ends. Dennis sues Terry for return of the ring. Both allege that the other terminated the engagement. Dennis appeals from the dismissal of his claim for return of the engagement ring. He argues that the trial court erred in holding that recovery was barred by the statutory abolition of actions for breach of promise to marry. The appellate court holds that abolition of breach of promise suits does *not* preclude suits for recovery of engagement rings, based on strict statutory construction (i.e., the statute contemplates abolition of "awards of damages for breach of contract to marry" and not restitutionary damages, such as return of the ring). *Brown v. Thomas*, 379 N.W.2d 868 (Wis. Ct. App. 1985).

Quiz Yourself on *PREMARITAL CONTROVERSIES*

1. Sally and Tom have been living together for several years. On Sally's birthday, Tom asks her to marry him, and she accepts. Three months later, after a fight, Tom breaks off the engagement. Can Sally recover from Tom for breach of promise to marry? ____________________

2. Alice and Bob have been living together for several years. During this time, Alice has never secured a divorce from her husband Carl. Bob asks Alice to marry him. She accepts, indicating that she would marry him after she divorces Carl. Several months later, Bob breaks off the engagement. In a jurisdiction that recognizes a cause of action for breach of promise to marry, can Alice recover from Bob? ____________________

3. During his engagement to Linda, Martin purchases a number of items for Linda, including a diamond engagement ring, a car, a computer, and several horses. He also pays off her car loan and makes various improvements to her house. After a disagreement, Martin moves out of their apartment and breaks off the engagement. He then brings an action, seeking reimbursement for all of his gifts. Will his suit be successful? ____________________

4. Same basic facts as above. Linda alleges that Martin is not entitled to the return of the engagement ring because he unjustifiably broke the engagement. Will her argument prevail? ____________________

5. Frank brings an action against his ex-fiancée, Frances, seeking recovery of his $20,000 engagement ring. The jurisdiction has an "anti-heartbalm" statute that bars all actions in contract law that arise from breaches of a promise to marry. Frances claims that Frank's action to recover the engagement ring is barred by the statute. Is his action barred? ____________________

Answers

1. It depends on the jurisdiction. A few jurisdictions still permit this cause of action.
2. No. Courts have held that the fact that either party was ***still married*** at the time of the engagement ***precludes recovery*** for breach of promise to marry. Some courts theorize that the party who is still married ***lacks capacity*** to enter into a subsequent marriage.
3. Yes, Martin's suit probably will be successful, but only for recovery of the engagement ring. The court will probably hold that the engagement ring is a conditional gift given in contemplation of marriage but the other items were irrevocable inter vivos gifts that were not expressly conditioned on the subsequent marriage.
4. No, probably not. According to the modern trend, the ring is recoverable by the donor without regard to fault (i.e., without regard to who broke the engagement).
5. No, probably not. A court would probably find that the anti-heartbalm statute is limited to precluding breach-of-promise suits and does not bar an action for return of an engagement ring.

II. PREMARITAL AGREEMENTS

Premarital agreements (sometimes termed "antenuptial agreements" or "prenuptial agreements") are agreements between prospective spouses made in contemplation of the marriage. Such agreements typically require a party to limit or relinquish certain rights (e.g., property rights, spousal support, inheritance rights) that the party would have acquired by reason of the marriage.

A. Traditional view: Traditionally, premarital contracts that determined financial obligations in the event of *dissolution* were void, as contrary to public policy. Such agreements were disfavored because it was thought they facilitated divorce by providing inducements to end the marriage and denigrating the status of marriage. However, premarital contracts that determined financial consequences upon *death* were permitted.

B. Premarital agreements distinguished from other contracts

1. Ordinary contracts: Premarital agreements differ from ordinary contracts in several ways:

- The parties in ordinary commercial contracts are "at arm's length," i.e., the parties are bound without regard to whether they understand the terms or whether those terms are reasonable. Because of the state's heightened interest in marriage, premarital contracts traditionally have been governed by stricter requirements. Thus, for example, courts frequently inquire into the fairness of the premarital agreement, whereas courts expect the parties to ordinary contracts to look after their own interests.
- Further, because premarital agreements are executory (performed in the future), the possibility is more likely that future circumstances may make them unwise or unfair. Thus, a greater need arises for equitable intervention.

2. **Contracts *during* marriage**

   a. **Traditional rule:** According to the traditional rule, the parties are not able to regulate, by means of their private contracts, state-imposed rights and responsibilities of the marriage (e.g., husband's duty of support, wife's duty to provide services).

   Example: During their marriage, Margrethe agrees to pay Sidney $300 per month. In return, Sidney agrees to accompany Margrethe on her travels. Upon their divorce, Sidney sues to enforce the agreement. The court holds that because the agreement alters the essential obligations of the marriage contract (wife must follow husband's choice of domicile and husband has duty of support), it is void as contrary to public policy. *Graham v. Graham*, 33 F. Supp. 936 (E.D. Mich. 1940).

   b. **Modern view:** Under the modern view, courts are more willing to permit the parties to regulate the financial aspects of the marriage. Public policy favors individuals' ordering of their interests through contractual arrangements.

   Note: Community property jurisdictions have always permitted the spouses to enter into contracts that *transmute* (i.e., change the character of) separate property into community property or vice versa.

3. **Separation agreements:** Both separation agreements and premarital agreements address the financial consequences of dissolution. However, the parties enter into a premarital agreement before marriage, whereas they enter into a separation agreement (or a "settlement agreement") *after* they decide to terminate their marriage.

C. Modern approach

1. **Trend:** Courts, increasingly, are recognizing premarital agreements. This change has resulted from the rising incidence of divorce and remarriage, the decreasing influence of morality, changing gender roles, and an enhanced respect for decisional autonomy ("private ordering").

   Example: A 53-year-old lawyer marries a 33-year-old journalist. Both have been previously married. They decide to marry in order to legitimize their nonmarital child. A few days before the wedding, the bridegroom insists that the bride sign a prenuptial agreement that he has prepared. The agreement, rather than state community property law, would control the disposition of the couple's marital property upon divorce. After eight years of marriage, Husband files for divorce. Wife alleges that the agreement is unenforceable. The court holds that the agreement is valid. "[I]n keeping with the trend to apply traditional contract analysis to issues involving premarital agreements, there is a trend toward allowing the agreement to stand, even if one party has given up all his or her rights in the property of the other." *Lebeck v. Lebeck*, 881 P.2d 727, 734 (N.M. Ct. App. 1994).

2. **Limitation:** Despite increasing recognition of premarital contracts, the parties may not enter into an enforceable agreement about child support or child custody. This results from the state's countervailing interest in child welfare. *See, e.g.,* Uniform Premarital Agreement Act (UPAA) §3(b), 9B U.L.A. 369 (1983) ("the right of a child to support may not be adversely affected by a premarital agreement"). (The Uniform Marital Property Act (UMPA) also precludes spousal agreements about child support.)

3. **Formalities**

   a. **Writing:** The Statute of Frauds requires that premarital agreements be in writing and signed by the party to be charged.

   b. **Consideration:** UPAA §2 provides that consideration is *not* required ("A premarital agreement must be in writing and signed by both parties. It is enforceable without consideration.").

4. **Scope:** The trend is to broaden the scope of premarital agreements in terms of the property rights that are affected. For example, UPAA §3(a), which permits considerable latitude regarding contractual freedom, permits the parties to contract regarding the property of either or both spouses and "whenever and wherever acquired or located," management and control of property, spousal support, making of a will or a trust, death benefits in life insurance policies, choice of law, and "any other matter, including their personal rights and obligations not in violation of public policy or a statute imposing a criminal penalty."

   Most states permit a waiver of alimony in a prenuptial agreement, provided that the waiver is explicit. But cf. Cal. Fam. Code §1612(c) (West 2004) (providing that prenuptial waivers of spousal support are not enforceable if the party against whom enforcement is sought was not represented by counsel or if the waiver is unconscionable at the time of enforcement).

   Example: Husband, an attorney, marries Wife, an antique dealer. Before the marriage, Husband drafts, and Wife signs, a premarital agreement in which she waives her spousal property rights. Specifically, Wife agrees to "Waive and Renounce any and all Rights that, and to which, [she] would otherwise be entitled to because of such marriage, whether present or future rights, to any and all property which [plaintiff] has now, or which he may acquire in the future, whether the same be real, personal, [or] mixed property, or of any kind or nature and wherever situated." When Husband initiates divorce proceedings, he claims that the prenuptial agreement precludes equitable distribution of his assets. The court rules that the prenuptial agreement effected a waiver only of Wife's right to distribution of property either then owned or later acquired, but did not result in a waiver of Husband's maintenance or support obligations because the waiver was not sufficiently explicit. *Bloomfield v. Bloomfield*, 764 N.E.2d 650 (N.Y. 2001).

5. **Application to same-sex marriages:** It is not yet known whether laws on premarital agreements will apply to same-sex marriages. The UPAA limits its application to "prospective spouses," and thereby excludes agreements between cohabitants. However, a few states have modified their versions of the UPAA to extend it to partners in same-sex relationships. *See, e.g.,* N.J. Stat. §§37:2-32 to 37:2-34 (West 2007) (civil unions).

D. **Requirements for validity:** A premarital agreement is valid if: (1) it provides full disclosure; (2) it is fair and reasonable; and (3) it is entered into voluntarily by both parties. Procedural fairness refers to disclosure and the voluntariness with which each party enters into the agreement. Substantive fairness refers to the fairness of the substantive terms of the agreement.

   Note: Some courts do not require all of the preceding elements. That is, some courts enforce an unfair agreement provided that a party executed it voluntarily and with full disclosure.

   1. **Full disclosure:** A valid premarital agreement requires full disclosure. However, full disclosure does not require *detailed* disclosure. Moreover, a spouse's independent knowledge of the other spouse's financial status can serve as a substitute for disclosure.

Example: At divorce, Wife contends that Husband's failure to disclose his income at the time of the parties' premarital agreement renders the agreement unenforceable. The court rejects her argument. The court concludes that, although Husband's financial statement did not list his income, it did include the value of his CPA practice, investment accounts, home, and lake house. In short, it revealed that he was wealthy and had "significant income-producing assets." That disclosure, together with the fact that Wife lived with him for four years before marriage, supports the trial court ruling that the absence of Husband's income did not constitute nondisclosure of a material fact that would make the premarital agreement unenforceable. *Dove v. Dove*, 680 S.E.2d 839 (Ga. 2009).

Example: Teresa, a court reporter and bookkeeper, agrees to marry Randall, a personal injury attorney. Randall desires a premarital agreement to preserve his assets for the children of his prior marriage. He drafts the premarital agreement, to which he attaches a list of each party's assets. When the marriage ends, Teresa challenges the agreement as unconscionable, arguing that Randall failed to provide full and fair disclosure. The court rejects her claim, concluding that, because Teresa served as Randall's paralegal and secretary, she was sufficiently knowledgeable about his finances to satisfy the disclosure requirement. *In re Marriage of Shanks*, 758 N.W.2d 506 (Iowa 2008).

Note that a majority of jurisdictions now regard the engaged parties as being involved in a confidential relationship (thereby imposing heightened duties to each other). *Friezo v. Friezo*, 914 A.2d 533, 549 (Conn. 2007).

2. **Fair and reasonable:** Courts differ in their determination of the substantive fairness of the agreement.

   a. **Traditional rule:** Traditionally, courts required that the agreement be fair under all the relevant circumstances.

   b. **Modern trend:** Under the modern trend that reflects increasing respect for decisional autonomy and changing gender roles, some courts enforce agreements that are unfair so long as the agreement accords with intent, and also is entered into voluntarily and with full disclosure. This development renders premarital agreements more similar to ordinary contracts.

   Example: A 23-year-old unemployed nurse marries a 39-year-old neurosurgeon. Their prenuptial agreement limits her right to spousal support to $200 a week, subject to a maximum of $25,000. At divorce, she argues that the payments are not reasonable. The court upholds the agreement despite its unfairness because "there is no longer validity in the implicit assumption . . . that spouses are of unequal status [and] women are not knowledgeable enough to understand the nature of contracts. . . ." *Simeone v. Simeone*, 581 A.2d 162 (Pa. 1990).

   Example: A prospective bridegroom demands that his fiancée execute a premarital agreement. She signs an agreement that, upon divorce, precludes spousal support, a share in the marital home (which was the man's separate property), any portion of the man's retirement and investment assets, and attorney's fees. When the parties divorce 17 years later, the wife challenges the agreement as unconscionable based on the substantial increase in the husband's assets (i.e., appreciation due to his stock options and the value of the marital home). The court disagrees, finding that these financial circumstances were reasonably within the contemplation of the parties. *Crews v. Crews*, 989 A.2d 1060 (Conn. 2010).

i. **Factors relevant to determination of reasonableness:** The following factors may enter into the judicial determination of reasonableness:

- the parties' respective wealth;
- respective ages;
- respective intelligence, literacy, and business acumen; and
- prior family ties.

ii. **Time for determination of reasonableness:** Some courts determine fairness at the time of *execution* of the agreement. An increasing number of states evaluate fairness at the time of execution of the agreement and also at the time of *enforcement* (at divorce). The former policy emphasizes contractual freedom; the latter, equitable principles.

Note: UPAA §6 (a)(2) requires *unconscionability* at the time of *execution*. The ALI *Principles* §7.05 assess fairness (requiring "substantial injustice" rather than unconscionability) at the time of *enforcement*.

3. **Voluntariness:** The parties must enter the contract voluntarily, i.e., without fraud or duress.

a. **Meaning:** Although courts are not in accord about what constitutes duress, they tend to agree that a party's insistence on the premarital agreement as a condition of the marriage is not duress. In addition, courts increasingly hold that the presence of independent counsel militates against a finding of duress.

Example: Wife argues that she signed a premarital agreement under duress because she discovered that she was pregnant and that Husband refused to marry her unless she signed. Although this situation presented Wife with "a difficult choice" according to the court, it is not sufficient to "divest[] the wife of her free will and judgment," especially considering that she was presented with the agreement one week before the wedding and had time to obtain the advice of counsel (that she rejected). The court adds that other jurisdictions reach the same result based on similar facts. *Biliouris v. Biliouris*, 852 N.E.2d 687 (Mass. App. Ct. 2006).

b. **Timing of Execution of Agreement:** Some plaintiffs challenge premarital agreements by arguing that presentation of the agreement in close proximity to the day of the wedding constitutes duress. However, most courts reject this view.

Example: On the night before the wedding, the bridegroom presents the bride with a premarital agreement that precludes her right to alimony and that treats all property acquired during the marriage as separate property. She signs after the bridegroom threatens that he would not marry her otherwise. At divorce, she challenges the agreement on the ground of duress. The court holds that the bridegroom's threat did not constitute legally sufficient duress. *Howell v. Landry*, 386 S.E.2d 610 (N.C. Ct. App. 1989), *aff'd*, 392 S.E.2d 90 (N.C. 1990).

Example: Three days before the wedding, Albert (a lawyer) presents Bonnie with a premarital agreement that he drafted. He insists that she sign it as a condition of their marriage. The agreement requires her to forgo her rights under state law regarding the disposition of community property upon divorce. They marry to legitimize their nonmarital child. After eight years of marriage, Albert files for divorce. Bonnie claims the agreement is invalid on grounds of duress. The court holds that Albert's request three days before the wedding and his insistence on the agreement as a condition of the marriage did not constitute duress, especially because he made full disclosure and because she signed voluntarily after consulting an attorney of her choice. *Lebeck v. Lebeck*, 881 P.2d 727 (N.M. Ct. App. 1994).

Some state statutes address the problem of timing by requiring a designated amount of time between execution of the agreement and the marriage. See also the ALI *Principles* discussed *infra.*

E. **Representation:** States generally do not require that the engaged parties be represented by independent counsel. Some states specify that the parties must have an *opportunity* to consult counsel, but do not require that they *actually do so*, in order for the agreement to be valid.

Rationale: A requirement of representation would be paternalistic and an interference with contractual freedom.

Example: When baseball player Barry Bonds marries Sun at the beginning of his career, he insists that she sign a prenuptial agreement providing that each party's earnings and acquisitions remain separate property. When they separate, he is earning $8 million annually. She alleges that the agreement was not executed voluntarily because she did not understand it and was not represented by counsel. The California Supreme Court upholds the agreement, ruling that representation by counsel is only one of several factors to be considered and that substantial evidence supported the view that Sun understood the agreement and executed it voluntarily. *In re Marriage of Bonds*, 99 Cal. Rptr. 2d 252 (Cal. 2000).

F. **Spousal Support:** Some case law and state statutes reflect a distaste for those premarital agreements that preclude the possibility of spousal support.

Example: Appellant, 29-year-old Wife with a high school education, works as a hotel night desk clerk, earning $19,000 a year when she marries a 26-year-old stockbroker earning $166,000 per year. The parties' premarital agreement waives her right to spousal support, and provides that the separate property of each party remains separate. During the marriage, Wife is a homemaker and primary caregiver for their two children. When the marriage ends nine years later, Husband earns approximately $1 million annually and is a partner in a brokerage firm. Wife challenges the validity of the premarital agreement. The state supreme court upholds the premarital agreement but rules that the waiver of spousal support is unconscionable. The court reasons that, at the time of the marriage, both parties were in their twenties (i.e., implying they are not "legally sophisticated" products of previous divorces); the wife quit her job to care for the children while the husband's career advanced rapidly; the disparity in the parties' incomes grew exponentially because the husband was able to concentrate on his career; and the parties maintained an affluent lifestyle. *Lane v. Lane*, 202 S.W.3d 577 (Ky. 2006).

See also Cal. Fam. Code §1612(c) (West 2004) (providing that a provision in a premarital agreement regarding spousal support (including a waiver thereof) is not enforceable if the party against whom enforcement is sought was not represented by independent counsel or if the provision was unconscionable at the time of enforcement).

G. **Uniform Premarital Agreement Act:** The National Conference of Commissioners on Uniform State Laws approved the Uniform Premarital Agreements Act (UPAA), 9B U.L.A. 369, in 1983. Currently, more than half of the states have adopted UPAA or some version thereof.

UPAA is one of two uniform acts that address premarital agreements. (The other is the Uniform Marital Property Act (UMPA), 9A U.L.A. 97 (1987), that was drafted with the much broader purpose of encouraging support for a system of shared property during the marriage.) UPAA is more widely followed.

1. **Policy:** The policy behind UPAA is to recognize considerable contractual freedom so long as the ensuing agreements do not violate public policy.

2. **Reform:** UPAA requires a higher standard than previously in order to find an antenuptial agreement unenforceable. A party either must have executed the agreement involuntarily *or* the agreement must be "unconscionable." UPAA borrows the term "unconscionability" from commercial settings, thereby requiring more than mere lack of fairness.

   To constitute unconscionability, the agreement must have been unconscionable at the time of execution and, in addition, the party must not have been provided "fair and reasonable disclosure," not waived the right to disclosure, and did not have (or could not have had) adequate knowledge of the other's property.

   Thus, UPAA requires proof of both substantive fairness (termed "unconscionability") and procedural fairness (disclosure and voluntary execution).

H. ALI *Principles:* The ALI *Principles* require that premarital agreements must meet standards of substantive fairness as well as procedural fairness (i.e., informed consent and disclosure). A rebuttable presumption arises that the agreement satisfies the informed consent requirement if (1) it was executed at least 30 days prior to the marriage; (2) both parties had, or were advised to obtain, counsel and had the opportunity to do so; and (3) if one of the parties did not have counsel, the agreement contained understandable information about the parties' rights and the adverse nature of their interests. ALI *Principles* §7.04(e)(a)(b) and (c).

Quiz Yourself on PREMARITAL AGREEMENTS

6. Jane and Paul enter into a premarital agreement under which each waives any future right to the property of the other. Appended to the agreement is a general list of assets (e.g., "All shares of X Company," "All existing accounts at Bank of Blackacre in Husband's name") without valuations. At the divorce, Jane alleges that the agreement is invalid because it fails to provide full and fair disclosure of Paul's assets. Will her argument prevail? ____________________

7. Edmund and Charissa execute a premarital agreement that is motivated by a clause in Edmund's divorce agreement from his first wife that restricted his visitation with his son from the prior marriage. Edmund and Charissa's premarital agreement provides that, in the event of divorce, any children shall spend equal residential time with both parents. When Charissa challenges the agreement, will she prevail? ____________________

8. At the time that Wendy and John are contemplating marriage, bankruptcy proceedings are pending against Wendy and her former husband. Several weeks before the wedding, John asks Wendy to execute a premarital agreement because of his concern that creditors in the bankruptcy proceeding

will go after his assets once he and Wendy marry. They execute a premarital agreement specifying that each party retains sole title to any property acquired prior to and during the marriage and that any debts incurred prior to and during the marriage would remain the debt of the party who incurred the debt. Additionally, the parties waive rights to alimony and property. When Wendy files for divorce, she alleges that the premarital agreement is invalid because she was not represented by counsel. Will her argument be successful? ____________________

9. The day before their wedding, Mark tells his fiancée Fran that they are going to get a marriage license but drives her instead to his lawyer's office where he insists that she sign a premarital agreement as a condition of the marriage. Mark's attorney tells her that she has a right to obtain counsel. She has the opportunity to review the document but looks at it only briefly before she signs. Upon divorce, she claims that the premarital agreement is invalid because of fraud and duress. Will her argument be successful? ____________________

Answers

6. No. Although courts require full and fair disclosure in premarital agreements, they do not require detailed disclosure. It is sufficient if the prospective wife knows that the prospective husband is worth considerable money and that she is relinquishing certain rights.

7. Yes. The parties may not enter into an enforceable premarital agreement that concerns child custody, stemming from the state's interest in child welfare.

8. No. Legal representation is not a prerequisite to the validity of a premarital agreement. Wendy never sought independent legal advice even though she had ample time to do so. She was not coerced into signing the agreement. Furthermore, when she executed the agreement, she had knowledge of the importance of independent legal advice because she had been a party to prior legal proceedings (bankruptcy and a prior divorce).

9. No. The pressure tactics will not negate the knowing and voluntary nature of the execution because Fran had the opportunity to review the document and also to retain counsel but she chose to do neither. However, if the jurisdiction follows the ALI *Principles*, the agreement should have been signed at least 30 days before the marriage to raise a rebuttable presumption that the agreement satisfies the informed consent requirement. (Additional requirements to raise the presumption are that both parties had, or were advised to obtain, counsel and had the opportunity to do so; and, if one of the parties did not have counsel, the agreement contained understandable information about the parties' rights and the adverse nature of their interests.)

III. RESTRICTIONS ON ENTRY INTO MARRIAGE

A. Constitutional limitations on regulation of the right to marry: All states have restrictions on who may marry. Beginning in 1967, the Supreme Court invalidated several state restrictions on marriage.

The Supreme Court established that the right to marry is a *fundamental right*. As a result, state restrictions on the right to marry are subject to *strict scrutiny* (the highest level of protection for the individual's freedom to marry).

Three different tests exist for scrutinizing the constitutionality of state statutes, regulations, practices, or policies:

- Under the lowest level of scrutiny (the rational basis test), the restriction merely must be "reasonably related to a legitimate state objective."
- The intermediate level of scrutiny requires that the restriction must be "substantially related to an important governmental objective."
- In contrast, the strict scrutiny test mandates that the restriction be "necessary to a compelling state interest" in order to survive constitutional challenge.

Note that the Supreme Court treats the right to marry as part of substantive due process ("liberty") and also as part of the "fundamental rights" branch of equal protection. That is, classifications that infringe upon fundamental rights trigger strict scrutiny in the same manner as do suspect classifications. A violation of equal protection occurs when the state or federal government treats similar groups of persons differently. Under traditional equal protection analysis, classifications based on gender or illegitimacy trigger intermediate scrutiny. Strict scrutiny applies to suspect classifications based on race, alienage, and national origin.

Example: A U.S. citizen and an undocumented alien from Mexico live together for two years, during which time they have a son. They request an application for a marriage license from the county registrar. Although the undocumented alien presents his birth certificate, Mexican passport, and documents from an immigration proceeding, he is denied the application, according to local policy, because he lacks either a "green card" or a foreign passport with a visa. The couple file a civil rights suit under 42 U.S.C. §1983, alleging that the registrar violated their rights to equal protection and due process. A federal district court rules that the policy, requiring an alien seeking to marry a U.S. citizen to produce certain forms of identification, violates the parties' fundamental right to marry because, based on strict scrutiny review, the policy significantly interferes with the right to marry by placing a direct legal obstacle in their path. *Buck v. Stankovic*, 485 F. Supp.2d 576 (M.D. Pa. 2007).

1. **Race:** The United States Supreme Court has held that racial restrictions on marriage are unconstitutional.

   Example: Mildred Jeter, an African-American, marries Richard Loving, a white man, in June 1958 in the District of Columbia. The Lovings are forced to go to the District of Columbia (i.e., leaving their state of Virginia) in order to marry because Virginia is one of 16 states that prohibits interracial marriage (by means of an "anti-miscegenation" statute). After their marriage, the Lovings return to Virginia. Subsequently, they are convicted of violating the statutory ban, and given a suspended sentence of 25 years provided that they leave Virginia. They appeal their convictions, arguing that the statutory ban prohibiting marriage on the basis of racial classifications violates the Equal Protection Clause and the Due Process Clause. The United States Supreme Court holds that the state statute restricting the right to marry on the basis of racial classifications violates both the Equal Protection Clause and the Due Process Clause. *Loving v. Virginia*, 388 U.S. 1 (1967).

Note: Rule of lex loci. Under the rule of "lex loci," a marriage valid where performed is valid everywhere. Thus, the Lovings' marriage should have been valid in Virginia. This rule is subject to the exception that a jurisdiction need not recognize the marriage if contrary to public policy. On this basis, Virginia argues that it did not have to recognize the Lovings' marriage. The Supreme Court, in effect, holds that such a racially motivated public policy is unconstitutional.

2. **Poverty:** The Supreme Court also has invalidated a restriction on the right to marry based on poverty.

Example: A Wisconsin statute provides that certain Wisconsin residents (i.e., noncustodial parents with court-ordered support obligations) may not marry without a court order. To obtain the court's permission, the applicant (Redhail) has to prove that his children are not public charges and are unlikely to be in the future and that he is current in his support obligation. Redhail requests the Milwaukee county clerk to issue him a marriage license. The clerk refuses because Redhail fathered a nonmarital child two years earlier (when he was a high school student), and has outstanding child support payments. His child has been a public charge since birth. Redhail argues that the statute violates his right to marry, and challenges the constitutionality of the statute on both equal protection and due process grounds.

The Court reaffirms that the right to marry is a fundamental right protected by the Fourteenth Amendment Due Process Clause. The Court states this holding more explicitly than it did in *Loving*. It also holds that the restriction violates equal protection. Applying the strict scrutiny test, the Court concedes that the asserted state interests (i.e., counseling the individual regarding support obligations and protecting children's welfare) are sufficiently important. However, the Court finds that the state's chosen means are not closely tailored to achieve those interests because the statute does not compel counseling nor does it guarantee that money would be delivered to the applicant's children. The Court reasons that less drastic means are available to compel compliance with support obligations without impinging on the right to marry. *Zablocki v. Redhail*, 434 U.S. 374 (1978).

a. **Some reasonable regulations will be upheld:** The *Zablocki* Court reaffirms that restrictions on the right to marry are subject to strict scrutiny. However, the Court states that *not all* state restrictions on the right to marry are to receive heightened scrutiny.

   Rather, "*reasonable regulations that do not significantly interfere with decisions to enter into the marital relationship may legitimately be imposed.*" *Zablocki*, 434 U.S. at 386.

   The Court elaborates that only those classifications that *directly* and *substantially* interfere with the right to marry will be reviewed under the strict scrutiny test. *Id.*

b. **Direct and substantial requirements:** The *Zablocki* Court provides a clue to the meaning of "direct" and "substantially" by distinguishing *Zablocki* from *Califano v. Jobst*, 434 U.S. 47 (1977), in which the Court upheld the constitutionality of a Social Security provision that penalized marriage by the loss of benefits. According to *Zablocki*, a legal obstacle constitutes the element of "directness," in contrast to a statutory penalty that results in the individual's loss of public benefits because of the marriage (*Jobst*). Further, the ban in *Zablocki* was total (satisfying the element of "substantiality") because only the state can confer the legal status of marriage, whereas the loss in *Jobst* was merely $20 per month.

3. **Special context: Prisons:** The Supreme Court has upheld the right to marry in such special contexts as prisons. Further, any governmental policy that refuses to permit prisoners to marry must be reasonably related to legitimate penological goals.

   Example: A Missouri Division of Corrections regulation permits a prison inmate to marry only with the superintendent's permission and, then, only when compelling reasons exist. Although "compelling" is not defined in the regulation, prison officials interpret it to permit marriages only in cases of pregnancy or the birth of nonmarital children. Inmates who desire permission to marry challenge the rule as a violation of their constitutionally protected right to marry. Prison officials, although conceding that the right to marry is fundamental, argue that the right does not apply in the prison context. They assert that the state's interests in prison security (i.e., prevention of "love triangles") and rehabilitation (i.e., marriage would detract from prisoners' developing necessary skills of self-reliance) support the prohibition. The Court holds that the prison regulation is unconstitutional because it fails to satisfy even the rational basis test, i.e., it is not reasonably related to the stated goals. *Turner v. Safley*, 482 U.S. 78 (1987).

   Turner is significant for its affirmation that the right to marry applies even in those special contexts (e.g., prisons) that traditionally have been subject to considerable state regulation.

   Note: In *Turner*, the Supreme Court affirms its prior holding in *Butler v. Wilson*, 415 U.S. 953 (1974), that a prohibition on marriage for *life* inmates is constitutional as punishment for crime.

Quiz Yourself on CONSTITUTIONAL LIMITATIONS ON REGULATION OF THE RIGHT TO MARRY

10. Nancy, a probation officer for the state Department of Corrections, falls in love with Mitch, one of her clients who is serving a sentence for a property offense. They plan to marry. When Nancy's supervisor learns of her romantic relationship, he informs her that she must either give up Mitch or her job, pursuant to a departmental regulation that forbids probation officers from becoming involved socially with their clients in or out of jail. When Nancy refuses to stop seeing Mitch, she is terminated. She brings an action alleging that the departmental regulation forbidding employees from becoming socially involved with clients violates her due process right to marry. Will her argument be successful? ____________________

11. Patricia is convicted of harboring her fugitive husband Charlie and being an accessory after the fact. Charlie is wanted for $177,000 in unpaid child support to his former wife Victoria. Knowing that Charlie is wanted for a violation of federal criminal law, Patricia helps Charlie flee to Mexico, provides him funds, and refuses to divulge his whereabouts. She appeals her conviction, alleging that the harboring and accessory statutes impermissibly infringe upon her right to marry. Will Patricia's argument be successful? ____________________

12. Prisoner and his fiancée sue state officials alleging that the prison's policy (i.e., the prison's refusal to facilitate the ability of *both* parties to appear at the probate court to request a marriage license, as required by statute) violates their fundamental right to marry. Will their argument be successful? ____________________

Answers

10. No. The departmental regulation did not violate Nancy's due process right because it did not forbid Nancy from marrying in general or from marrying Mitch. It merely made it more costly for her to marry Mitch—the cost being the loss of her job. The regulation burdened her right to marry but did not impermissibly preclude her from marrying.

11. No. The fact that a statute affects the marriage relationship does not mean that the statute infringes on the right to marry. *Loving* involved normal spousal conduct, whereas the harboring and accessory statutes punish conduct that demonstrates an intent to frustrate law enforcement. Also, there is a significant difference between the importance of the government interests involved. The purpose of the statute in *Loving* was to prevent interracial marriage, whereas the harboring and accessory statutes advance the orderly operation of essential government functions of apprehending criminals.

12. Yes. The prison's policy (refusing to allow the prisoner to go to the probate court to apply for a marriage license) completely frustrates the couple's right to marry and, therefore, violates the parties' due process rights. Prison officials must prove that the policy is reasonably related to legitimate penological objectives (such as safety concerns). The prison would have a difficult time making such a showing because it would be possible to permit the inmate to travel to the probate court (e.g., accompanied by an escort) without endangering the safety of other inmates or that of the community.

B. Substantive restrictions: Capacity: All states have substantive restrictions on who may marry. These refer to regulations regarding capacity to marry and state of mind. ***Capacity*** traditionally required that the parties (1) be of opposite sexes, (2) be married to only one spouse at a time, (3) not be related, and (4) be above the statutorily defined age. State of mind restrictions (discussed *infra*) require that the parties marry (1) voluntarily, (2) without fraud, and (3) without duress.

1. Same sex

a. Traditional rule: Under the traditional rule, jurisdictions refuse to recognize same-sex marriage. Most jurisdictions have explicit statutory definitions of marriage as "the union of a man and a woman." The absence of an express statutory prohibition in a few states, however, provided an opportunity for constitutional attack.

b. Rationale for traditional rule: States have provided various rationales for their restrictions on same-sex marriages, including:

- marriage is for the propagation of the species;
- marriage protects the health and welfare of children;
- children need two parents of the opposite sex for children's well-being; and

- the state has an interest in fostering and facilitating traditional notions of marriage and the family.

c. Challenges based on the federal constitution: Beginning in the 1970s, plaintiffs raised a variety of constitutional challenges to state marriage bans on both federal and state grounds. Cases often arose when couples were denied a marriage license for the reason that they lack "capacity" to marry.

i. Nature of constitutional arguments: Plaintiffs argued that state restrictions violate their federal constitutional rights to marry under the Due Process Clause, Equal Protection Clause, right of association, right to free exercise of religion, and the Ninth Amendment.

ii. Judicial response: Until quite recently, courts rejected these arguments.

iii. Obstacle based on constitutional right of privacy: *Bowers v. Hardwick* and *Lawrence v. Texas* (discussed *infra*): A significant obstacle to gay and lesbian plaintiffs' success was *Bowers v. Hardwick*, 478 U.S. 186 (1986), upholding the constitutionality of a Georgia sodomy statute applied to consensual same-sex sodomy, finding that the statute did not violate a fundamental right. According to *Bowers*, the right of privacy under the federal Constitution does not protect the choice of same-sex sexual partners.

Note: However, in *Lawrence v. Texas*, 539 U.S. 558 (2003), the United States Supreme Court declared a state sodomy statute unconstitutional, thereby overturning *Bowers*. *Lawrence* is discussed *infra*.

d. Challenges based on state constitutions

i. Nature of state constitutional arguments: Beginning in the 1990s, gay and lesbian plaintiffs again raised arguments that their right to marry was protected by certain state constitutional guarantees (particularly, state equal rights amendments, and state protections of the right to privacy and equal protection).

ii. Judicial responses: The provisions of some state constitutions provide more expansive protection for individual rights than does the federal constitution. Beginning with *Baehr v. Lewin* (*infra*), plaintiffs initially witnessed some success on this basis.

e. Modern developments: The beginning of change (*Baehr v. Lewin*): *Baehr v. Lewin*, 852 P.2d 44 (Haw. 1993) (finding that the state ban implicates the Equal Protection Clause of the state constitution), marked the beginning of the change. Plaintiffs also prevailed in Alaska and Vermont. See *Brause v. Bureau of Vital Statistics*, 1998 WL 88743 (Alaska Super. Ct. 1998) (holding that a gender-neutral marriage statute violates plaintiffs' right to privacy under the state constitution); *Baker v. Nelson*, 744 A.2d 864 (Vt. 1999) (ruling that the exclusion of same-sex couples from marriage violates the Common Benefits Clause of the state constitution). However, legislatures in these states (as well as Congress) reacted to these favorable judicial decisions by limiting the legal protections available to same-sex couples.

In Hawaii, the legislature enacted the Reciprocal Beneficiaries Act (Haw. Rev. Stat. Ann. §§572C-1 to 572C-7) (2006) entitling members of same-sex couples to such limited benefits as survivorship rights, health-related benefits, benefits relating to jointly held property, legal status relating to wrongful death, victims' rights, and protection from domestic violence. In Alaska, the legislature proposed and voters passed a constitutional amendment recognizing only marriages between a man and a woman. And, finally, the Vermont legislature enacted legislation (Vt. Stat. Ann. tit. 15, §§1201-1207 (2005)) recognizing "civil unions" that confer on same-sex couples the rights and benefits of traditional marriage but not the name "marriage." (Vermont later legalized same-sex marriage, discussed *infra*.)

f. State and federal responses to *Baehr*: The question arose (after *Baehr* raised the possibility of state recognition of same-sex marriage) whether one state must recognize a same-sex marriage that is validly contracted in another state. Two doctrines would appear to dictate an affirmative answer: the Full Faith and Credit Clause of the Constitution, Art. IV, §1 (i.e., the requirement that a state shall give full faith and credit to "the public acts, records and judicial proceedings" of other states) and the rule of "lex loci" (i.e., a marriage valid where performed is valid everywhere).

However, the federal Defense of Marriage Act (DOMA) (discussed *infra*) permits states to exercise discretion not to recognize same-sex marriages. And a public policy exception exists to the rule of lex loci (i.e., a marriage contracted in one state is valid in any other state unless recognition of that marriage would be contrary to public policy).

Following *Baehr*, states and the federal government responded to stymie efforts to legalize same-sex marriage.

i. State responses: Many state legislatures enacted statutes or state constitutional amendments expressly providing that marriage is a relationship between "a man and a woman." These enactments are sometimes referred to as "Baby DOMAs" patterned on the federal Defense of Marriage Act (*infra*).

ii. Federal response: The Defense of Marriage Act: Congress responded to the possibility that a state might uphold same-sex marriage by enacting the Defense of Marriage Act, 28 U.S.C. §1738(c), in 1996. The Act does the following:

- it creates a federal definition of marriage as a union between a man and a woman (for purposes of federal law regarding immigration, government benefits, etc.) (Section 3), and
- it leaves recognition of same-sex marriage to state discretion (Section 2).

Challenges to the federal DOMA (discussed *infra*) have met with mixed results.

iii. *Lawrence v. Texas*: The United States Supreme Court decision in *Lawrence v. Texas,* 539 U.S. 558 (2003), had major ramifications for recognition of same-sex marriages.

In *Lawrence v. Texas*, John Lawrence and Tyron Garner are convicted of engaging in same-sex sexual conduct in violation of a Texas sodomy statute (criminalizing "deviate sexual intercourse" with an individual of the same sex). They appeal, raising state and federal due process claims. The United States Supreme Court, overruling its decision in *Bowers v. Hardwick*, holds that the state sodomy statute violates defendants' substantive due process rights. The Court chooses a broad due process rationale, protecting the individual's *liberty to engage in intimate personal relationships*, rather than more narrow equal protection grounds. The Court reasons that moral disapproval cannot justify criminal sanctions for private consensual sexual conduct. "Our obligation is to define the liberty of all, not to mandate our own moral code." *Id.* at 571.

In his dissent, Justice Scalia predicts that *Lawrence* calls into question state laws against "bigamy, same-sex marriage, adult incest, prostitution, masturbation, adultery, fornication, bestiality, and obscenity." *Id.* at 590 (Scalia, J., dissenting). Subsequent developments confirm that prediction regarding same-sex marriage laws. (The influence of *Lawrence* on other state laws is discussed *infra.*)

iv. **Post-*Lawrence* challenges to state laws:** Several cases in the post-*Lawrence* era (discussed below) challenged, with varying degrees of success, state restrictions against same-sex marriage.

v. **Goodridge v. Department of Public Health:** Massachusetts was the first state to permit same-sex marriage.

Example: Seven same-sex couples are denied a marriage license by town clerks on the ground that Massachusetts state law does not recognize same-sex marriage. Plaintiffs file an action for a declaratory judgment, alleging that the Department of Public Health's policy violates the state constitution. (The ban was departmental "policy" because state law did not explicitly specify that being of the same sex constitutes an impediment to marriage.) The Supreme Judicial Court holds that the marriage licensing statutes are not susceptible of an interpretation that permits same-sex couples to obtain marriage licenses (because of the common-law definition of marriage and legislative intent not to permit licensing of same-sex unions) but that the restriction on marriage to opposite sexes lacks a rational basis and violates equal protection under the state constitution. *Goodridge v. Dept. of Public Health*, 798 N.E.2d 941 (Mass. 2003).

Subsequent to *Goodridge*, opponents of same-sex marriage unsuccessfully attempted to overturn the decision there via judicial and legislative means. Although same-sex marriage in Massachusetts originally was restricted to state residents (because of the state's enactment of the Uniform Marriage Evasion Act (UMEA)), the Massachusetts legislature subsequently repealed these statutes. (Massachusetts formerly was one of only a few states that enacted the UMEA, which invalidates the marriages of persons who marry outside their home state in an attempt to evade their home state's marriage restrictions.)

vi. **Setbacks to marriage equality after *Goodridge*:** Following *Goodridge*, several state supreme courts *upheld* their respective bans on same-sex marriage. *See, e.g., Conaway v. Deane*, 932 A.2d 571 (Md. 2007); *Lewis v. Harris*, 908 A.2d 196 (N.J. 2006); *Hernandez v. Robles*, 821 N.Y.S.2d 770 (N.Y. 2006); *Andersen v. King County*, 138 P.3d 963 (Wash. 2006).

vii. **Trend toward marriage equality:** Recent case law reveals a more favorable attitude toward marriage equality. *See, e.g., In re Marriage Cases*, 183 P.2d 384 (Cal. 2008) (holding that differential treatment accorded same-sex couples by the state domestic partnership law violates the right to privacy and equal protection under the state constitution); *Kerrigan v. Commissioner of Public Health*, 957 A.2d 407 (Conn. 2008) (holding that the state ban differentiating between same-sex civil unions and opposite-sex marriage fails to survive intermediate scrutiny and violates substantive due process and equal protection under the state constitution); *Varnum v. Brien*, 763 N.W.2d 862 (Iowa 2009) (holding that, based on intermediate scrutiny review, the state ban on same-sex marriage violates that state constitution's Due Process and Equal Protection Clauses). However, California voters passed a state constitutional amendment (Proposition 8) that abrogated that state supreme court decision. Subsequently, in *Perry v. Schwarzenegger*, 704 F. Supp.2d 921 (N.D. Cal. 2010), a federal district court ruled that Proposition 8 violates the Due Process and Equal Protection Clauses of the *federal* Constitution. The Ninth Circuit Court of Appeals responded by asking the California Supreme Court for clarity regarding whether the proponents of Proposition 8 have standing (in light of the fact that state officials refused to defend the Proposition).

Same-sex marriage is also finding legitimacy through some state legislatures. For example, New Hampshire, Vermont, and the District of Columbia all recognize same-sex marriage by statute. In New Hampshire, same-sex marriages are valid if: (1) religious groups and religious officials are not required to hold religious ceremonies for same-sex couples, and (2) church-related organizations that serve charitable or educational purposes are exempt from having to provide benefits to same-sex spouses of employees. See N.H. Rev. Stat. §§457:1-a, 457:37 (2009). See also Vt. Stat. Ann. tit. 15 §8 (2009). The Maine legislature also legalized same-sex marriage, but voters there subsequently repealed that law.

viii. **Limited interstate recognition:** Some states confer recognition on same-sex marriages that were validly entered into in *other* jurisdictions (even if the former states preclude same-sex partners from marrying in their own forums). For example, Maryland, New Mexico, New York, and Rhode Island recognize same-sex marriages that were validly performed elsewhere.

ix. **Domestic partnership legislation:** Several jurisdictions have enacted a *range* of legal protections for domestic partners. A few states (i.e., California, Maine, Oregon, and Washington) have legislation conferring rights on, specifically, "domestic partners." Other states (i.e., Illinois, New Jersey) have legislation protecting "civil unions." In those particular jurisdictions that formerly recognized civil unions or domestic partnerships but that subsequently permitted same-sex marriage (i.e., Connecticut, District of Columbia, New Hampshire, and Vermont), all former civil unions and domestic partnerships will be phased out or converted to marriages.

x. **Challenges to federal DOMA:** Same-sex couples in valid marriages have had mixed success in raising constitutional challenges to DOMA. For example, in *Smelt v. County of Orange*, 447 F.3d 673 (9th Cir. 2006), the Ninth Circuit rejected plaintiffs' claims that the federal DOMA violates the Full Faith and Credit Clause, holding that plaintiffs lacked standing. However, in *Gill v. Office of Personnel Management*, 699 F. Supp.2d 374 (D. Mass. 2010), a federal district court held DOMA's Section 3 (restricting federal benefits to persons in opposite-sex marriages) was unconstitutional as a violation of the Equal Protection requirement of the Fifth Amendment Due Process Clause. The case was brought by same-sex partners who were married in Massachusetts and who were denied certain federal benefits (i.e., tax benefits, government health insurance, Social Security survivors' benefits) that were available to similarly situated opposite-sex couples. *Gill* is one of several pending cases that challenge the federal DOMA and state DOMAs. *See* Julie Bolcer, Two New Lawsuits Challenge DOMA, *The Advocate*, Nov. 9, 2010 (discussing *Windsor v. USA* and also *Pedersen et al. v. Office of Personnel Management*), available at http://advocate.com/News/Daily_News/2010/11/09/Two_New_Lawsuits_Challenge_DOMA/. See also *Bishop v. Oklahoma*, 2009 WL 1566802 (10th Cir. Okla. 2009).

xi. **International developments:** Currently, several countries (including Belgium, Canada, the Netherlands, Norway, South Africa, Spain, and Sweden) permit same-sex couples to marry.

xii. **Effect on immigration status:** Although a foreign citizen who is married to a U.S. citizen normally receives preferential treatment in the issuance of permanent residence status, the federal DOMA prevents partners in same-sex relationships from benefiting from such treatment. Several congressional attempts to enact remedial legislation (i.e., the Uniting American Families Act) have been unsuccessful.

g. **Transgender persons' right to marry:** Occasional cases concern the validity of the marriage of a transgender person (i.e., a person who experiences a discrepancy between physical anatomy and psychological identity). Hormone treatment and sex reassignment surgery can alter anatomy to enable the person's biological sex to conform to the psychological gender.

Some courts determine the validity of such marriages by reference to *anatomy*. (Under this theory, a postoperative male-to-female transgender person would be considered female.) Other courts hold that sexual identity is determined by *birth and chromosomes*.

Example: After his father dies intestate, a son petitions for letters of administration, naming himself as sole heir, and claiming that the marriage between his father and a postoperative male-to-female transgender person was void. The Kansas Supreme Court holds that a postoperative male-to-female transgender person is not a woman within the meaning of the statutes recognizing marriage, and that the marriage was void as against public policy (thereby following the chromosome approach). *In re Estate of Gardiner*, 42 P.2d 120 (Kan. 2002).

Quiz Yourself on *SUBSTANTIVE RESTRICTIONS: SAME SEX*

13. Jane and Jill, who have been in a committed relationship for eight years, decide to get married. Because their jurisdiction of Whiteacre does not permit same-sex marriage, they decide to go to the neighboring jurisdiction of Blackacre where such marriages are allowed. When they return home to Whiteacre, Jane submits a request to her state employer, requesting health benefits for her new "spouse." Is Jane's employer required to grant such benefits? ____________________

14. Same basic facts as above. Aware that their home state does not permit same-sex marriage, Jane and Jill decide to go to Canada, where such marriages are legal. They take a vacation to Toronto, get married there, and return to their home state in the United States. Then, Jane submits a request to her state employer, requesting health benefits for her new "spouse." Is Jane's employer required to grant such benefits? ____________________

15. A woman "Jo" is married to Tom. One day, Jo is arrested for a traffic violation in the state of Blackacre. In the course of a routine motor vehicle check, the police determine that "Jo" is really biologically male (a man named "Joe"). The police notify the marriage board in Blackacre (where same-sex marriage is prohibited). As a result, the marriage board invalidates "Jo" and Tom's marriage. "Jo" and Tom appeal, arguing that "Jo" identifies as female so that the marriage is valid. Will the couple's argument be successful? ____________________

16. John and Jerry are married in the jurisdiction of Whiteacre, which allows same-sex marriage. John is a resident of Whiteacre; Jerry is a national of Ireland. After their marriage, Jerry asserts that, as John's "spouse," he is entitled to preferential status for immigration purposes. Will Jerry's argument be successful? ____________________

Answers

13. No. Jane could argue that Whiteacre has to recognize her marriage in Blackacre based on the Full Faith and Credit Clause of the Constitution or the rule of lex loci. The Full Faith and Credit Clause requires that a state confer full faith and credit to public acts, records, and judicial proceedings of sister states. The rule of lex loci provides that a marriage valid where celebrated (here, Blackacre) is valid everywhere. However, the federal Defense of Marriage Act (DOMA) would permit Whiteacre to refuse to recognize a same-sex marriage that was contracted in another state. And most courts have upheld the constitutionality of the federal DOMA. Moreover, Whiteacre might refuse to recognize Jane's marriage under the rule of lex loci based on a public policy exception. It is also possible that Whiteacre has a "baby DOMA" (either a state statute or constitutional amendment) that prohibits recognition of same-sex marriages contracted in another state. As a result, Jane's employer most likely does not have to honor Jane's request. However, Jane's employer might recognize Jane's marriage if Whiteacre is one of the few jurisdictions that confer recognition on same-sex marriages that were validly entered into in *other* jurisdictions (even if Whiteacre's law would preclude same-sex partners from marrying there).

14. No. Even though same-sex couples who are U.S. citizens may go to Canada to marry (provided they fulfill Canadian marriage requirements), when Jane and Jill return to the United States, they will discover that such marriages of same-sex partners are not legally recognized in all states. The Full Faith and Credit Clause is inapplicable because it applies only to public acts, records, and judicial proceedings of *sister states*. Jane's employer does not have to honor Jane's request unless Whiteacre is one of the few states that confer limited recognition on same-sex marriages that are validly entered into in other states or other countries.

15. No. A court most likely would uphold the Blackacre marriage board's decision, finding that "Jo" (who was born male and has not undergone sex reassignment surgery) entered into an invalid same-sex marriage in Blackacre. Note that the couple's marriage would be invalid under either theory that has been applied to validate marriages of transgender persons because "Jo" is male by virtue of both chromosomes and current anatomy.

16. No. Federal law governs immigration. The federal Defense of Marriage Act (DOMA) provides a heterosexual definition of marriage for purposes of federal law, such as immigration. DOMA would preclude Jerry from qualifying as John's spouse for immigration purposes.

2. **Bigamy:** All states refuse to permit marriages that are bigamous (i.e., having two spouses at the same time) or polygamous (i.e., having more than two spouses at the same time).

   a. **Civil restrictions and criminal sanctions:** Civil restrictions provide that a person may have only one spouse at a time. States also make bigamy and polygamy criminal offenses.

   b. **Background:** Plural marriage is still practiced by some fundamentalist Mormon sects in accordance with the dictates of the Church of Jesus Christ of Latter Day Saints' founder, Joseph Smith. In a famous incident, Arizona law enforcement officials raided the small polygamous community of Short Creek in 1953. The raid resulted in criminal convictions of husbands, and the removal of children from their homes and their placement in foster care. This costly venture failed to eradicate polygamy.

   Note: A similar raid by law enforcement and Child Protective Services took place in 2008 at the Yearning for Zion Ranch, a rural polygamous community in Eldorado, Texas. This raid also resulted in the removal of a large number of children from their homes. The Texas Supreme Court subsequently ordered that these children be returned to their families, concluding that the culture of polygamy did not warrant the grant of emergency custody of all the children to the state social welfare department. *In re Texas Dept. of Family and Protective Services*, 255 S.W.3d 613 (Tex. 2008). (The case is discussed in Chapter 9 *infra*.)

   c. **Procedural challenges:** Procedurally, parties have challenged state restrictions on bigamy and polygamy in the context of:

   - criminal prosecutions such as for bigamy;
   - violations of the Mann Act;
   - termination of employment based on an employee's practice of polygamy;
   - adjudication of child neglect involving children of polygamous parents; and
   - custody disputes between parties of a former polygamous union.

   d. **Criminal requirements:** Modern courts require intent, i.e., that the defendant enter into a second marriage with the knowledge that the first marriage is still valid. Some jurisdictions, however, penalize a defendant despite the defendant's bona fide belief that the first marriage has ended.

   e. **Effect on validity of successive marriage:** If a party to a marriage is still validly married to a prior living spouse, then the subsequent marriage is void. This rule is not applied in all cases; for example, it is subject to a presumption (discussed *infra*) that is applicable in limited circumstances.

   f. **Defenses:** Parties have asserted two defenses to criminal liability for bigamy/polygamy, one based on constitutional grounds and one based on state grounds.

      i. **Freedom of religion:** Sometimes, a defendant claims that plural marriage is required by the defendant's religious beliefs and that the defendant's choice is thereby protected by the First Amendment. Courts have held that such religious beliefs are not a valid defense to the crime of bigamy.

      Example: George Reynolds appeals from his conviction for bigamy. He defends by saying that his fundamentalist Mormon church requires its members to practice polygamy. The court holds that the defendant's practice of plural marriage is a *religious practice* rather than a religious belief. Although the First Amendment dictates that government cannot interfere with religious beliefs, religious practices do not merit the same constitutional protection. *Reynolds v. United States*, 98 U.S. 145 (1878).

ii. Enoch Arden statutes: Some statutes, following English law, provide defenses to bigamy for spouses who remarry in good faith based on a belief that a prior spouse is dead. These "Enoch Arden" statutes, although not validating the subsequent marriage, permit a spouse to remarry without criminal liability after a specified time period. The statutes are named after a protagonist in a Tennyson poem who was shipwrecked and returns after a long absence to find that his wife, who believed him dead, has remarried.

g. Conflict of laws: Bigamous marriages may present conflict-of-laws issues. Recognition of a bigamous marriage (for example, a bigamous marriage that is permitted in another country) by an American jurisdiction may depend on the purpose of the litigation. That is, a jurisdiction may recognize the marriage only for the purposes of legitimacy of children or inheritance.

Example: A native of India dies intestate (without a will) in California. When his estate is probated, two residents of India each allege that they are entitled to share his estate as his lawful widows according to Indian law that permits plural marriage. The court holds that the wives may share equally because no public policy is violated when neither wife contests the other's claim. Further, they are the only interested parties, and the purpose is inheritance. *In re Dalip Singh Bir's Estate*, 188 P.2d 499 (Cal. Ct. App. 1948).

h. Presumptions and the burden of proof: Problems of proof have given rise to a presumption that may operate in doubtful cases. Under this presumption, the most recent marriage is valid. The party asserting the invalidity of the second marriage has the burden of rebutting the presumption by conclusive evidence.

This presumption prevails over another presumption that a valid marriage exists until proof of its end by death or divorce. Courts are especially likely to apply the presumption of validity to the most recent marriage if the second marriage is longstanding, has produced children, and the challenge is by an employer or governmental entity (i.e., for benefits purposes).

Example: Hattie and Gertrude Gordon both claim to be the widow of Samuel Gordon. Both seek widow's annuity benefits under the Railroad Retirement Act. Each has proof of her marriage. Hattie's marriage to Samuel preceded Gertrude's. Gertrude and Samuel are living together at Samuel's death. During the latter 13-year marriage, they had one child. The court holds that the second wife, Gertrude, prevails based on the presumption of validity of the most recent marriage. *Gordon v. Railroad Retirement Bd.*, 696 F.2d 131 (D.C. Cir. 1983).

Example: Jerry Lee Sumners divorces Patricia O'Neil. Their Nebraska decree orders the parties to refrain from remarrying for six months. Three months later in Iowa, Jerry marries Sharon who is then pregnant with his child. When Sharon subsequently petitions for dissolution, Jerry challenges the court's jurisdiction. He argues that his marriage to Sharon, occurring before the termination of his prior marriage to Patricia, was bigamous and void. Based on the presumption of validity of the most recent marriage (a presumption that the court determines Jerry failed to rebut), the court holds that Jerry's marriage to Sharon is valid and should have been dissolved by the lower court. *In re Marriage of Sumners*, 645 S.W.2d 205 (Mo. Ct. App. 1983).

i. **Child bigamy laws:** Among the state interests underlying polygamy prohibitions is the interest in preventing child sexual exploitation that is often associated with polygamous practices. To address this problem, the Utah legislature enacted legislation that increases the penalty for bigamy involving teenage brides (Utah Code Ann. §76-7-101.5 (2008)).

j. **Modern developments: Post-*Lawrence* challenges to state and federal bigamy laws:** In *Lawrence v. Texas*, Justice Scalia suggested, in his dissent, that *Lawrence* would call into question state laws against same-sex marriage and bigamy (as well as "adult incest, prostitution, masturbation, adultery, fornication, bestiality, and obscenity") (539 U.S. at 590). Post-*Lawrence*, plaintiffs have raised challenges to state and federal bigamy laws on this basis.

Example: Rodney Holm, a fundamentalist Mormon police officer, is legally married to Suzie Stubbs. Subsequently, he participates in a religious marriage ceremony with two other women, one of whom is 16-year-old Ruth Stubbs (who is Suzie's sister). Holm is convicted of bigamy and sexual contact with a minor. He challenges the constitutionality of the bigamy statute and alleges that his conduct is protected as a fundamental liberty interest based on *Lawrence v. Texas.* The Utah Supreme Court upholds the constitutionality of the bigamy statute, saying it does not violate defendant's right to freedom of association, it is not unconstitutionally vague as applied, and also that the prohibition against sexual contact with a minor does not violate equal protection by distinguishing between married and unmarried persons. The court distinguishes *Lawrence* by saying that (1) the present case implicates the institution of marriage (rather than mere private consensual conduct) because the state has an interest in preventing the formation of marital forms it deems harmful, and (2) the present case involves a minor, and sexual conduct involving minors is outside the scope of *Lawrence*. *State v. Holm*, 137 P.3d 726 (Utah 2006).

3. **Incest:** All states regulate the degrees of kinship within which persons may marry. Marriages between persons who are related within prohibited degrees of kinship are void.

a. **Civil restrictions:** States have *civil* restrictions requiring that prospective spouses may not be granted marriage licenses if the parties are related to each other within certain prohibited degrees of kinship.

i. **Consanguinity:** All states restrict marriages by *consanguinity* (i.e., blood relationships, such as those between parent and child, brother and sister, uncle and niece, aunt and nephew). Some states also prohibit first-cousin marriages.

Example: A man marries his niece in Italy. Because the parties obtain a dispensation, the marriage is legal there. The newlyweds return to Connecticut where they reside until the husband's death. The widow petitions the probate court for a widow's allowance pursuant to state law, claiming that she is his lawful spouse. The court holds that although the marriage was valid in Italy, a marriage between an uncle and niece contravenes public policy in Connecticut. Therefore, the woman is not the decedent's legal spouse and is not entitled to a widow's allowance. *Catalano v. Catalano*, 170 A.2d 726 (Conn. 1961).

Occasionally, a question of statutory interpretation arises, for example, as to whether consanguinity restrictions prohibit marriage among half-blood relatives.

Example: An uncle and niece by the half blood (the wife's mother is the husband's half-sister) marry in Connecticut. Based on the advice of counsel that their marriage is incestuous and void, the parties seek an annulment in Connecticut. Four years later, they remarry in California where such marriages are not proscribed. Thereafter, in Connecticut, they seek to set aside the annulment. The court holds that the marriage is void. Based on strict statutory interpretation (the common meaning of "uncle" and "niece"), the court holds that marital restrictions based on consanguinity extend to relationships of the half blood as well as whole blood. *Singh v. Singh*, 569 A.2d 1112 (Conn. 1990).

ii. Affinity: Some states also restrict marriages between parties related by *affinity* (i.e., relationships established by law, such as marriage with in-laws, step relatives, or relatives by adoption).

Example: Martin and Tammy Israel, brother and sister who are related by adoption, desire to marry. (Martin's father married Tammy's mother when Martin was 18 and Tammy was 13.) The parties are denied a license because of Colorado's express statutory prohibition on marriages between brother and sister whether "by the half or the whole blood or by adoption." The parties argue that the statute is unconstitutional as violative of equal protection. The court holds that the provision is unconstitutional, having no rational basis (i.e., it fails to further any state interest in family harmony). *Israel v. Allen*, 577 P.2d 762 (Colo. 1978). (But cf. UMDA §207 prohibiting marriage between a brother and sister of the whole blood or who are related by adoption.)

Example: Mr. and Mrs. X adopt a daughter who is referred to as M. The adoptive parents divorce when M is 22 years old, although the parents separated several years prior to that time. Shortly after the divorce, M gives birth to a son whose father is M's adoptive father. M and her adoptive father now desire to marry. M seeks to vacate her adoption by her adoptive father (Mr. X) so that she can marry him. Under New Jersey law, an adoption may be vacated upon a showing of "truly exceptional circumstances" when it is in the best interest of the child and adoptive parents. The court determines that the facts constitute truly exceptional circumstances in order to eradicate the legal impediment to M's marriage to her adoptive father and to legitimize the infant. *In re Adoption of M*, 722 A.2d 615 (N.J. Super. Ct. Ch. Div. 1998).

iii. End of affinity relationship for marriage purposes: Occasionally, a question arises as to when a relationship of affinity ends so as to permit a subsequent marriage with a relative by affinity.

Example: William Back marries a widow who has a daughter by her former marriage. Four years after his divorce from the widow, he marries his former wife's daughter. Two years later, his first wife dies. William and his second wife have four children. After William's death, his second wife petitions the probate court for a widow's allowance. A family member challenges her claim, arguing that the marriage is incestuous and therefore void. The court follows the majority rule, declaring that the marriage is valid because the relationship by affinity ceased upon termination of William's marriage to his first wife. *Back v. Back*, 124 N.W. 1109 (Iowa 1910).

b. **Criminal sanctions:** In addition to civil restrictions, states also have *criminal* provisions punishing incest.

i. **Definition:** Incest is defined, for purposes of the criminal law, as marriage *or* sexual intercourse between persons who are related within the prohibited degrees of kinship.

Note: Beginning in the 1960s, public attention to the problem of child abuse caused some forms of sexual misconduct between adults and minors (formerly labeled "incest") to be redefined as "sexual abuse."

ii. **Rationale:** Common rationale for legal regulation of incest (both criminal and civil aspects) include the following:

- genetic (inbreeding results in transmission of harmful genetic traits);
- religious (based on biblical proscriptions);
- sociobiological (need to encourage the formation of new families);
- sexual (necessity to eliminate intrafamilial sexual competition); and
- psychological (prevention of exploitation of vulnerable family members).

Some of the rationales have been called into question in regard to some of the prohibited relationships. For example, the genetic concern is absent in step and adoptive relationships.

c. **Modern development: Post-*Lawrence* challenges and state incest laws:** Some courts have held that state incest prohibitions do not violate the constitutional right to privacy after *Lawrence v. Texas.*

Example: Allen Muth marries his younger sister Patricia. The couple has three children. After the couple abandons their disabled child, Wisconsin officials terminate their parental rights based on their incestuous parenthood and then charge them with criminal liability for incest. In the husband's petition for a writ of habeas corpus, he argues that the state incest statute is unconstitutional because it criminalizes a sexual relationship between consenting adults in violation of *Lawrence v. Texas*. The U.S. Court of Appeals refuses to read *Lawrence* so broadly as to create a fundamental right to engage in all forms of private sexual intimacy, reasoning that *Lawrence* had a limited focus on same-sex sodomy and also that *Lawrence* failed to apply strict scrutiny review. *Muth v. Frank*, 412 F.3d 808 (7th Cir. 2005).

4. **Age**

a. **Generally:** All states establish minimum ages for marriage. Currently, most states establish 18 years as the requisite minimum age at which an individual can validly consent to marriage. (See UMDA §§203, 208.)

Persons who are under the age of consent may still marry. However, minors must secure parental consent. The permission of one parent is sufficient in many states. Some states provide that judicial consent *plus* parental consent is required for very young minors or for those minors in exceptional circumstances (i.e., pregnancy).

Several states permit courts to override parental refusal.

b. Historical rule: At common law, a valid marriage could be contracted by a boy at age 14 and a girl at age 12. Today, statutory provisions are gender neutral.

c. Rationale: The rationale for marital age restrictions is that maturity is necessary to promote marriage stability.

d. Effect of noncompliance: At common law, nonage was a civil disability which rendered *void* any marriage involving a minor under age seven. Marriages involving older, but still under-age, parties were *voidable* at the request of the under-age minor until the youth reached the age of capacity.

Today, defects of nonage or lack of consent render a marriage *voidable* upon the initiative of the under-age party. If the party fails to disaffirm, the marriage is validated when that party reaches the age of consent.

Some states permit annulment actions to be brought by the parent of the minor. However, absent statutory authority, a parent cannot initiate annulment proceedings for nonage or lack of consent.

e. Constitutionality of parental consent requirements: Courts have upheld the constitutionality of parental consent requirements against attacks based on the children's right to due process.

Example: Raoul Roe, 18 years old, desires to marry 15-year-old Maria Moe, who is the mother of his child. According to New York law, males between 16 and 18 years old and females between 14 and 18 must obtain parental consent. Maria's mother, a widow, refuses consent, allegedly because she desires to continue to receive Maria's welfare benefits. Plaintiffs Maria Moe and Raoul Roe institute a class action on behalf of all under-age persons who wish to marry but cannot because such persons cannot obtain either a marriage license or judicial approval for the reason that they lack parental consent. They charge that the provision is an unconstitutional deprivation of their liberty under the Due Process Clause. Plaintiffs contend that the statute is arbitrary, denies them the opportunity to make an individualized showing of maturity, and denies them the only means to legitimize their child. The court upholds the constitutionality of the parental consent requirement. Although prior cases recognize the constitutionally protected right of privacy, the state's interest in the protection of minors dictates use of a rational basis standard. The court finds that the statute is rationally related to the state's interests in protecting minors from immature decision making and unstable marriages, and supporting the parent's right to act in the child's best interests. Moreover, the statute results not in total deprivation of plaintiffs' rights, but only a delay. *Moe v. Dinkins*, 533 F. Supp. 623 (S.D.N.Y. 1981), *aff'd*, 669 F.2d 67 (2d Cir. 1982), *cert. denied*, 459 U.S. 827 (1982).

Note: Plaintiffs did not challenge the differential age requirements for young men and women. Such differences, however, appear to be of questionable constitutionality (as a violation of equal protection). *See, e.g.*, *Stanton v. Stanton*, 421 U.S. 7 (1975) (holding unconstitutional a statute establishing different gender-based age requirements for parental support purposes).

Courts also have upheld state age-based marriage laws based on a challenge that the statutes violate the *parent's* due process to raise a child as the parent sees fit.

Example: A father and mother have joint custody of their daughter following their divorce. The mother and daughter relocate to New Mexico, where the 15-year-old daughter expresses her wish to marry her 48-year-old piano teacher. Because New Mexico law does not permit under-age marriages, the couple goes to Las Vegas where they obtain judicial authorization (with the mother's consent). The father, who was not notified of the judicial proceeding, petitions to vacate the order authorizing the marriage and to annul the marriage. The Nevada Supreme Court holds that a statute allowing judicial authorization of a marriage of an under-age person does not violate the substantive or procedural due process rights of a nonconsenting parent and that the father lacked standing to annul the marriage. The court reasons that a parent's constitutional right to raise his child as he sees fit is not absolute and must be weighed against the child's fundamental right to marry. *Kirkpatrick v. The Eighth Judicial District Court*, 64 P.3d 1056 (Nev. 2003).

f. **Recent reform:** Several states raised the minimum age for marriage in the past few years.

Example: A 15-year-old girl enters a common-law marriage with a felon. The Department of Human Services files a petition challenging the validity of the marriage of the girl who is subject to a dependency and neglect proceeding. (The marriage had been entered into without parental consent.) The court of appeals holds that, because the common-law age of consent applies to common-law marriages, the 15-year-old female was competent to consent to a common-law marriage. *In re Marriage of J.M.H. and Rouse*, 143 P.3d 1116 (Colo. Ct. App. 2006).

Note: In response, the legislature raises the minimum age for common-law marriage to 18, or 16 with parental and judicial approval—the same ages as for marriage generally in the state.

g. **International perspectives:** More than 30 countries allow marriages involving children below the age of 15. The reasons for child marriages are largely economic (i.e., early marriage relieves parents of economic burdens) as well as the desire to control female sexuality.

5. **Miscellaneous issues of capacity:** Some statutes also provide that certain physical conditions (e.g., impotence) or mental incompetence provide grounds for annulment. For mental competence, courts require that a person have sufficient capacity to understand the nature of the marriage contract, its obligations, and responsibilities.

Example: Harold Edmunds, a 59-year-old mentally retarded man marries Inez Edwards, a mentally retarded woman who is a resident of the same institution. Two years later his guardian seeks to annul the marriage, alleging that Harold lacked mental capacity to enter the marriage. Based on evidence that Harold understood the nature of the marriage contract and wanted to be married, the court holds that the marriage is valid. *Edmunds v. Edwards*, 287 N.W.2d 420 (Neb. 1980).

Quiz Yourself on ***SUBSTANTIVE RESTRICTIONS: INCEST, BIGAMY, AGE***

17. Sandra marries Tom. Tom had been previously married to Nancy. Unbeknownst to Sandra, Tom's divorce was not final when they married. Therefore, her marriage to Tom is not valid. Can Sandra be prosecuted for bigamy? ____________________

18. John, a Utah police officer, is terminated by his employer after his employer learns that he practices plural marriage. He seeks declaratory and injunctive relief to determine that Utah's laws prohibiting plural marriage are invalid and to enjoin their enforcement. He alleges that the discharge violates his constitutional rights. Will he be successful? ____________________

19. Alison is 14 years old and a freshman in high school. She and her 21-year-old boyfriend Bobby wish to marry. However, Alison and Bobby know that Alison's parents will never consent because they believe that Alison is too young to marry. Alison decides to go to court to obtain judicial consent to marry, in hopes that she will not have to obtain her parents' consent. Is her strategy likely to be successful? ____________________

Answers

17. No. Bigamy consists of the crime of entering into marriage when one of the parties is married to a third person who was then still living. Modern courts generally require intent to commit bigamy, i.e., that the defendant enter into a second marriage with the knowledge that the first marriage is still valid. Sandra did not have the requisite intent.

18. Probably not. Plaintiff's First Amendment argument would not prevail based on *Reynolds v. United States*. According to *Reynolds*, although the First Amendment dictates that government cannot interfere with religious beliefs, religious practices (such as bigamy/polygamy) do not merit the same constitutional protection. Also, Plaintiff's argument that the discharge violates his constitutional right to privacy will fail because bigamy is distinguishable from the monogamous relationship protected by *Lawrence v. Texas*. The state could argue that it is justified, by a compelling interest, in upholding the discharge to protect monogamy that is rooted in history and tradition.

19. Probably not. Generally, minors must secure parental consent to marry, according to state law. However, several states provide that for very young minors (such as Alison), *both* judicial consent and parental consent are required. If Alison resides in such a jurisdiction, judicial consent would not be sufficient. Either Alison would need to secure parental consent or wait until she obtains her majority.

C. Substantive restrictions: State of mind: A majority of states provide that fraud and duress are grounds to annul a marriage. The existence of fraud or duress vitiates consent and makes the marriage voidable at the request of the injured party. Today, annulment is less important than in the past because no-fault divorce makes dissolution more easily obtainable.

1. Fraud

a. Requirements: Judges have adopted different tests to annul a marriage based on fraud.

i. Strict test: Under the strictest test to annul a marriage, the fraud must go to the "essentials" of the marriage. Case law interprets "essentials" as referring to sexual intercourse or procreation.

Example: When Judith files for divorce from her husband James, James counterclaims by seeking an annulment on the ground of fraud. He alleges that Judith misrepresented that her prior husband was dead. He, a practicing Roman Catholic, claims that he would not have married Judith had he known of the misrepresentation. The court holds that the defendant is entitled to an annulment because the plaintiff's fraud goes to the essentials of the marital relationship (i.e., the defendant's knowledge makes it impossible for him to perform his marital duties and obligations). *Wolfe v. Wolfe*, 389 N.E.2d 1143 (Ill. 1979).

Example: Plaintiff marries Defendant based on his representation that he is a practicing Orthodox Jew. The marriage is consummated. When Plaintiff discovers Defendant's fraudulent misrepresentation, she seeks an annulment. The court holds that Defendant's fraud goes to the essentials of the marriage because Plaintiff could not perform her duties as wife and mother, following her religion, without believing that her husband shared her religious beliefs. *Bilowit v. Dolitsky*, 304 A.2d 774 (N.J. Super. Ct. Ch. Div. 1973).

ii. Materiality test: Other jurisdictions adopt a "material" or "but for" test (similar to the materiality standard for ordinary contracts), requiring that the plaintiff would not have married the defendant had the plaintiff known of the misrepresentation. Generally, misrepresentations of health, wealth, and status are not legally sufficient grounds for annulment.

Example: Husband appeals from a judgment denying his petition for annulment, claiming that he would not have married Wife but for her representations related to the son's paternity. The appellate court affirms, finding sufficient evidence supporting the trial court's determination that Husband would have married Wife regardless of the representation as to the son's paternity. Husband admits that, during their two-year courtship, he fell in love with Wife. Prior to the marriage, the couple had a daughter. Further, both parties admit that Husband had questions about the son's paternity prior to the marriage, but that he married her anyway, and that he subsequently adopted both children. Husband's testimony therefore fails to establish that he relied upon the representations regarding the son's paternity in deciding whether to marry Wife, only that it played a part in his decision to begin a relationship with her. *Blair v. Blair,* 147 S.W.3d 882 (Mo. Ct. App. 2004).

b. Standard of proof: Fraud must be proven by clear and convincing evidence.

Example: Beatriz and Gilbert meet through a pen pal service when she is living in the Philippines. They exchange love letters and telephone calls for ten years. He visits her twice. After the first visit, she tells him that she miscarried his child. Gilbert eventually obtains approval for her to immigrate, and they marry. A few months later, she is diagnosed with tuberculosis. Beatriz does not conceive, despite the couple's efforts. Stemming from his concern about the contagiousness of the disease, Gilbert asks Beatriz to move out. He files for an annulment, alleging that his consent to marry was induced by her misrepresentation that she wanted to conceive his child. Adopting a clear-and-convincing-evidence standard of proof, the state supreme court denies Gilbert an annulment, reasoning that he failed to satisfy his burden of proof because (1) the wife never told him that she was infertile, (2) he testified that even if she was infertile, he still would have married her, and (3) he testified that having a child with her was not his primary reason for marrying her. *Irving v. Irving*, 134 P.3d 718 (Nev. 2006).

c. **Significance of consummation:** Some jurisdictions require the higher standard of fraud (that the fraud go to the "essentials") if the marriage has been consummated. This judicial reluctance to annul such marriages stems from the fear that invalidation in these cases would work a hardship on the woman (i.e., because she is no longer a virgin and thereby is "tainted goods").

d. **Effect:** The existence of fraud renders a marriage voidable (rather than void) at the request of the injured party.

e. **Immigration fraud:** Marriage to a U.S. citizen exempts an alien from the quota restrictions of the Immigration and Nationality Act (INA), 8 U.S.C. §1151(a), (b) (2006). Some immigrants may contract marriage fraudulently with a U.S. citizen in an effort to obtain preferential entry status. To curb such fraud, Congress enacted the Marriage Fraud Amendments Act, 8 U.S.C. §§1154(h), 1255(e), in 1986, granting permanent resident status (following conditional status) if an applicant has remained married for two years. This rule imposed a hardship on some women who were forced to remain in abusive relationships in order to obtain permanent resident status. As a result, Congress amended the Violence Against Women Act (VAWA) to permit self-petitions by battered spouses and establish a special visa for battered spouses ineligible for self-petition. Illegal Immigration Reform and Immigration Responsibility Act of 1996 §204(a)(1), 8 U.S.C. §1154(A)(iii)(1) (2006); 8 U.S.C. §1254(a)(3) (2006).

i. **Limited purpose marriages:** Cases of immigration fraud are sometimes considered "marriages for a limited purpose" or "sham" marriages. That is, consent is given for a limited purpose (to enable a person to qualify for immigration entry status) or, alternatively, the marriage is considered a sham. In such cases, the government is the party challenging the marriage.

ii. **Same-sex couples and immigration fraud:** Sham marriages also occur among same-sex couples. A foreign same-sex partner (even one who is a legal spouse, domestic partner, or member of a civil union) is not permitted to obtain permanent resident status in the same manner as a spouse of a U.S. citizen or a lawful permanent resident, based on the federal Defense of Marriage Act.

Legislation has been introduced in Congress (the Uniting American Families Act) to amend the Immigration and Nationality Act to allow an American to sponsor a same-sex "permanent partner" for legal residency and to penalize immigration fraud in connection with permanent domestic partnerships. Currently, many countries allow their citizens to sponsor same-sex partners for immigration purposes.

2. **Duress:** Marriages are voidable and may be annulled if a party enters the marriage because of duress. Traditionally, courts required that physical force or the threat of such force (the

"shotgun" marriage) be sufficient to overcome the plaintiff's will (a subjective test) as opposed to a reasonable person's will (an objective test). Courts have held that threats of criminal prosecution will not suffice. Mental distress may suffice but must make a party unable to act as a free agent in entering the marriage.

Example: A Pakistani man, Shahid, has been living in Scotland with his Scottish woman friend and their child for four years. His parents wish him to marry his cousin who lives in Pakistan. He refuses repeatedly. After his father expresses a dying wish that he marry the cousin and his parents constantly remind him of the shame he causes them by his refusal, Shahid agrees and marries his cousin. Later he petitions for annulment. The Scottish court holds that the parental pressure overcame his will and constitutes legally sufficient duress to vitiate his consent. *Mahmud v. Mahmud*, 1994 S.L.T. 599.

Quiz Yourself on *SUBSTANTIVE RESTRICTIONS: STATE OF MIND*

20. Jim meets Paula through an Internet chat room. They discuss many things—their backgrounds, religions, finances, etc. At the time, Jim has more financial resources than does Paula. A few months later, they marry. After several months, they break up. Jim contends that the marriage was procured by Paula's fraud in being untruthful regarding her financial situation. He alleges that she wanted to marry him in order to access his finances and solve her financial difficulties. Will his argument regarding her alleged fraud be successful? ____________________

21. When Anne and Donald marry, he draws up a document that explains that the marriage is taking place against Donald's wishes and only because of Anne's threats against him (that she will blacken his name at his place of employment) and her threats against herself (that she will commit suicide). The document adds that Anne is marrying him because she is desirous of reestablishing herself in the good graces of her relatives and also because she cannot bear to continue to live with her sister. When Anne and Donald separate after a 10-year marriage, Donald argues that the marriage is invalid on grounds of duress. Will his argument be successful? ____________________

22. Barbara, a national of Poland, is living in Washington State with David when she meets and marries Anthony. She informs Anthony that she is looking for a husband so that she can remain in the United States. He asks her to marry him based on his affection for her, and she agrees. After a brief marriage to Anthony, Barbara files a petition for divorce. Anthony files a counterpetition alleging the invalidity of the marriage based on fraud. He alleges that Barbara continued her relationship with David after her marriage to Anthony. Anthony contends that Barbara lied about her relationship with David so that Anthony would marry her in order to enable her to get permanent residency status in the United States. Will Anthony's allegation of fraud be successful? ____________________

Answers

20. No. Jim's argument regarding Paula's alleged fraud about her financial situation is not of a nature sufficient to entitle him to an annulment based on fraud. False representations as to wealth (like those regarding health, character, etc.) are not legally sufficient grounds for annulment.

21. No. Donald's allegations of duress are not legally sufficient to invalidate the marriage. Here, the duress was mental (rather than physical). To succeed, Donald would have had to prove that Anne's duress (threats and persuasion) rendered him unable to act as a free agent in entering the marriage. These allegations of duress do not approach that standard. Donald could have refused to marry Anne.

22. Probably not. A finding of fraud serves to vitiate consent to marry. Many courts hold that fraud (for annulment purposes) must go to the "essentials" of the marriage (generally pertaining to sexual intercourse or childbearing). Barbara's deception to Anthony consisted of a false representation of her affection for him. Courts have held that such misrepresentations do not go to the essentials of the marriage. Barbara's second alleged misrepresentation concerned her desire to obtain status for immigration purposes. Courts generally hold that concealment of the fact that one party married the other for the sole purpose of obtaining status for immigration purposes is sufficient misrepresentation to go to the essence in an action for annulment. However, Anthony's assertion that he would not have married Barbara had he known that she was marrying him to obtain permanent residency status is contradicted by the record. Hence, he cannot prove that she misrepresented the truth or that he relied on such "misrepresentation."

D. Procedural restrictions: All states regulate marriage procedure. Such regulation is intended to promote the stability of marriage and to facilitate the collection of vital statistics.

1. **Licensure:** States require that the parties procure a marriage license, often by applying to a county clerk. The clerk may refuse to issue the license if the information provided by the parties reveals that they are ineligible to marry. Some states provide that a portion of marriage license fees shall support domestic violence programs.

2. **Physical examination and blood tests:** Many states require that before the clerk issues the license, the parties file a health certificate, signed by a physician, stating the applicants have undergone a physical examination (including blood tests) and are free from communicable venereal disease.

   A few states require testing for rubella. The tests are for informational purposes. That is, lack of immunity does not preclude a party from marrying (whereas the presence of venereal disease does).

   At one time, a few states (Illinois, Louisiana) required mandatory AIDS testing. These statutes since have been repealed. See also *T.E.P. v. Leavitt*, 840 F. Supp. 110 (D. Utah 1993) (holding Utah statute, which voids marriages in which either party is infected with AIDS, violates Americans with Disability Act).

   Some states have substituted the requirement for blood tests with a provision for the distribution of a brochure that furnishes applicants with information about the statutory requirements for licenses, including information about testing for and treatment of genetic and sexually transmissible diseases (e.g., Cal. Fam. Code §358 (West 2004 & Supp. 2010)).

3. **Solemnization:** All states require solemnization of marriage by an authorized person before witnesses (subject to some exceptions, discussed *infra*). However, no specific form of ceremony is prescribed.

4. **Waiting period:** Many states impose a waiting period (often three to five days) between the time of the parties' application for the license and the issuance thereof in order to deter hasty marriages. For example, UMDA §204 requires a three-day waiting period.

5. **Recordation:** The person solemnizing the marriage must sign the marriage certificate and submit it to the county clerk. The clerk then registers the marriage so that it becomes part of the public record.

6. **Failure to comply with the procedural formalities:** Failure to comply with these procedural formalities will not invalidate a marriage. This rule operates unless the jurisdiction has a statute expressly making a marriage invalid without a license.

   Example: Plaintiff and Defendant are married by a priest in a Roman Catholic ceremony, although they fail to obtain a marriage license. They live together for 25 years and raise 4 children. When Wife petitions for divorce, Husband alleges that the marriage is void because of their noncompliance with the statutory licensure requirement. The court holds that in the absence of a statute invalidating an unlicensed marriage, a ceremonial marriage contracted without a marriage license is not void on public policy grounds (i.e., no useful purpose is served by nullifying a longstanding marriage). *Carabetta v. Carabetta*, 438 A.2d 109 (Conn. 1980).

   Example: Jack Harris and Derrel DePasse live together for several years. DePasse becomes terminally ill and is hospitalized. The day before she dies, the hospital chaplain performs a marriage ceremony for the couple. Although aware that a marriage license was required, the parties do not obtain a license because of her imminent death. After her death, Jack claims an interest in her estate as her surviving spouse. Her executor challenges his petition on the ground that the marriage was not valid because the parties failed to obtain a marriage license. The court finds that, based on the statutes governing marriage, the issuance of a marriage license is a mandatory requirement for a valid marriage in California and therefore denies his petition to qualify as a surviving spouse. *Estate of DePasse*, 118 Cal. Rptr. 2d 143 (Ct. App. 2002).

E. **Procedural variations:** Parties may marry by resort to procedures that differ from the traditional marriage ceremony. Such procedures include: proxy marriages and confidential marriages.

1. **Proxy marriages:** Some jurisdictions recognize proxy marriages in which a substitute or "proxy" stands in for an absent bride or groom (subject to the latter's authorization). Parties may resort to such marriages in times of war or other international conflict. If the proxy marriage is valid where performed, other jurisdictions will recognize it. UMDA §206(b) permits recognition of such marriages if the proxy acts with written authorization.

2. **Confidential marriages:** Some states provide for recognition of certain types of marriages that fail to meet all the statutory formalities. For example, California recognizes "confidential marriages" that require a ceremony but dispense with the requirements of licenses and health certificates for an unmarried man and woman who are of marriageable age, not minors, and are living together. Cal. Fam. Code §500 (West 2004). Although the marriage must be recorded,

the records are not open to public inspection except upon a showing of "good cause." Cal. Fam. Code §511 (West 2004 & Supp. 2010). The purpose of recognition of these marriages is to encourage legalization of the relationship without subjecting the couple to potentially embarrassing publicity.

F. Curative procedural doctrines: Some doctrines protect the parties to a marriage who fail to observe the requisite *procedural formalities* (i.e., common-law marriage), or the party who is unaware of an *impediment* to the marriage (i.e., putative spouse doctrine).

1. Common-law marriage

a. Generally: Approximately a dozen states recognize common-law marriage. Many cases arise on the dissolution of the relationship or on death when the survivor attempts to claim inheritance or health insurance benefits, workers' compensation, or Social Security survivor benefits. For common-law marriage, no ceremony is required. Rather, the parties presently *agree* to enter into a legal marital relationship, *cohabit*, and *hold themselves out* as husband and wife in the community. Such a relationship constitutes a valid marriage and can only be terminated by death or dissolution.

b. Elements

i. Present agreement: No specific words are required. However, words or conduct must indicate a present agreement; words of futurity are insufficient. Also, the present agreement must take place when neither party is under a legal impediment (such as from a prior marriage). Many states require a new present agreement after removal of any legal impediment.

Example: Elizabeth and Harold marry and have a daughter. Several years later, Harold leaves Elizabeth and moves in with Mildred. He remains with Mildred until his death 20 years later. Six years before his death, he finally divorces Elizabeth. When he shows Mildred the decree, he says, "Now, we're legally married." She replies, "It's about time!" After his death, Mildred argues that she is entitled to an intestate share of his estate as his legal spouse. The court holds that Mildred was Harold's common-law wife from the date Harold was divorced from his first wife. The parties' words, upon their seeing the decree, constituted a present agreement to marry. *Estate of Garges*, 378 A.2d 307 (Pa. 1977).

ii. Cohabitation: The couple must cohabit in a jurisdiction that recognizes common-law marriages. Statute and case law fail to require a specific period of cohabitation. In fact, the couple's duration in the common-law jurisdiction may be brief, although some courts require that visits be longer than a day or two.

Example: Lena and Bruce obtain a marriage license in California. Bruce misrepresents that he is divorced from a prior spouse. They "marry" in California and travel to Arizona. They reside together in Arizona and represent that they are husband and wife. When they relocate to Virginia, they drive through Texas and Oklahoma (both common-law states) and stop there overnight. Lena subsequently seeks a divorce. Bruce challenges the validity of the marriage. The court holds that the parties did not establish a common-law marriage under either Oklahoma or Texas law that would be recognized by Virginia merely by their brief overnight stays in common-law states during the cross-country relocation trip. *Kelderhaus v. Kelderhaus*, 467 S.E.2d 303 (Va. Ct. App. 1996).

iii. **Holding out:** The couple must have the reputation in the community of being married. This "holding out" requirement establishes evidence of the couple's reputation as married and prevents fraud. It can be accomplished by using "Mr. and Mrs.," wearing wedding rings, etc.

Example: Sandra begins dating Dave, a California baseball player. The couple spends time in California, New Jersey, and Texas. (Only Texas recognizes common-law marriage.) After Sandra becomes pregnant, Dave tells her he wants to have a private ceremony. She makes a reservation at a hotel and they stay in the "honeymoon suite." Subsequently, she informs her mother that they are married. They rent a condo with the name "Winfield" on the mailbox. Sandra continues to use her surname. She signs the baby's birth certificate with her surname. She does not wear a wedding ring. She files income tax returns and health insurance forms as single. Sandra files for divorce, claiming that she is Dave's common-law wife. The court holds that they have failed to establish the requisite element of "holding out." *Winfield v. Renfro*, 821 S.W.2d 640 (Tex. Ct. App. 1991).

c. **Conflict of laws:** Common-law marriages present problems when the couple resides at various times in multiple jurisdictions, i.e., both a jurisdiction that does not recognize common-law marriage as well as one that does.

i. **Initial residence in a common-law jurisdiction:** If the parties meet the requirements for a common-law marriage and first reside in a jurisdiction that recognizes such marriages, but later move to a jurisdiction that does not, the latter jurisdiction almost always recognizes the marriage.

ii. **Initial residence in a non-common-law jurisdiction:** If the parties meet the requirements for a common-law marriage but first reside in a jurisdiction that does not recognize such marriages, but later move to a jurisdiction that does, the latter jurisdiction usually recognizes the marriage.

If the parties meet the requirements for a common-law marriage and reside in a jurisdiction that does not recognize such marriage, but later *visit* a jurisdiction that does, and then return to the former jurisdiction (that does not recognize such marriages), many courts in the home state will hold that a valid common-law marriage took place in the jurisdiction that the couple visited.

Note: In general, courts appear to be more sympathetic to a finding of a common-law marriage in cases of lengthy relationships and in claims against defendants who are governmental entities.

d. **Criticism:** A criticism of the common-law marriage doctrine is that it imposes governmental regulation on parties who, specifically, have chosen this intimate relationship because they desire to eschew governmental regulation.

2. **Putative spouse doctrine:** Another curative doctrine to protect the interests of a marital party is the "putative spouse doctrine."

a. Definition: The putative spouse doctrine protects a spouse who has a good-faith belief in the validity of the marriage.

Example: Wife marries Husband, believing that he is divorced. Unbeknownst to Wife, Husband's prior marriage was not yet terminated. When Husband and Wife divorce six years later, Wife obtains an annulment based on Husband's bigamy. Husband then seeks equitable division of the assets based on his status as a "putative spouse." Rejecting his claim, the court finds that Husband did not have a reasonable good-faith belief in the validity of his second marriage, because he filed a petition to dissolve his first marriage on the day *after* he married his second wife. Further, the court explains, the doctrine is intended to protect innocent parties (i.e., second Wife here, and not Husband). *In re Marriage of Guo*, 12 Cal. Rptr. 3d 906 (Ct. App. 2010).

b. Purpose: The doctrine is often relied upon in claims to confer benefits upon an "innocent" spouse at death (e.g., for inheritance purposes, state or federal death benefits, to establish standing to sue for wrongful death) or dissolution (e.g., to establish rights to marital property or spousal support).

c. Common-law marriage distinguished: In a common-law marriage, the parties are aware that they have not taken part in a marriage ceremony. In contrast, under the putative spouse doctrine, the parties have undergone a marriage ceremony and at least one party has a good-faith belief that a valid marriage has occurred.

In addition, a common-law marriage may be terminated only by death or dissolution. Dissolution is not necessary to terminate a putative marriage.

d. Conflicting claims: Occasionally, both a putative spouse and lawful spouse may assert claims to a benefit stemming from the marriage.

Example: Juan marries Mildred in 1929. They have three children and live together until his death in 1969. Josephine meets Juan in 1942. He informs her that he is divorced. She marries him in 1945 and has four children with him. He lives a double life, maintaining homes with *both* women until 1969. Upon his death in an auto accident, both wives claim an intestate share of his estate as his legal spouse. The court holds that, although Josephine's marriage was void because Juan was still married to Mildred, Josephine acquired the status as a putative spouse based on her good-faith belief that she was validly married. As such, she is entitled to share equally in his estate with his lawful spouse Mildred. *Estate of Vargas*, 111 Cal. Rptr. 779 (Ct. App. 1974).

Quiz Yourself on PROCEDURAL VARIATIONS AND CURATIVE PROCEDURAL DOCTRINES

23. Daniel and Laverne are married while he is hospitalized with an inoperable malignant brain tumor. The clerk issues a marriage license but Daniel never signs the application or appears before the clerk. At the ceremony, Daniel is unable to respond. A third party acknowledges the marriage vows for

Daniel. When Daniel dies four days later, Laverne files a petition for letters of administration alleging her status as the decedent's wife. She contends that she married Daniel by proxy. Daniel's children from a prior marriage argue that the proxy marriage was invalid. Will their argument be successful? ____________________

24. Anna and Dickie apply for, and are issued, a marriage license. They participate in a marriage ceremony, at which the minister signs their marriage license. However, the parties never file the license. They live together for a month after the ceremony. Anna contends that they married because of Dickie's concern with his family members' belief that he would go to hell because of his sinful relationship. She claims Dickie proposed a fake ceremony and represented that the marriage would not be valid. After the ceremony, Anna burns the license, allegedly with the knowledge and consent of Dickie. When Dickie files for divorce, Anna denies the existence of the marriage based on a failure to comply with the requisite formalities. Will her argument be successful? ____________________

25. Julian marries Bernice, separates from her, and finally divorces her many years after their separation (in 2008). He lives with Louisa in California and Nevada during his separation from Bernice and until his death in Nevada in 2011. Although Julian and Louisa never celebrate a marriage ceremony, Louisa uses the name "Mrs. Orr." They hold themselves out to their friends as husband and wife. In 2009, Julian and Louise visit Texas several times, the longest trip being two weeks, to visit Louisa's relatives. Although neither California nor Nevada recognizes common-law marriages, Texas does. At Julian's death, Louisa claims Social Security survivor benefits as his legal spouse. Will she be successful? ____________________

26. After several months of dating, Gary asks Lillie to marry him. She declines, saying she is not yet ready to marry. Several times over the next ten years of dating, Lillie asks Gary to marry her, but he does not do so. Instead, he occasionally promises to marry her some time in the future. Gary stays at Lillie's house several nights each week. Each maintains a separate residence and separate bank accounts. They sometimes take vacations together. Gary never represents that he and Lillie are married. When they break up, Lillie alleges that they had a common-law marriage. Will her argument be successful? ____________________

Answers

23. Yes. Even if this state legislature authorizes marriage by proxy, this ceremony does not satisfy the necessary requirements. There was no evidence of a written proxy authorizing a representative to obtain the license and acknowledge the vows. This case is not analogous to proxy marriage during war time. Instead, it raises the possibility that others might take advantage of the infirm.

24. No. Failure to comply with the procedural formalities (i.e., filing the license) will not invalidate the marriage. Courts generally interpret compliance with the procedural formalities as a directory, ministerial act rather than as a mandatory requirement (absent a state statute that expressly provides that the issuance of a marriage license is a mandatory requirement for a valid marriage).

25. Yes. Louisa is entitled to benefits as the decedent's common-law spouse. A valid common-law marriage came into existence after 2008 (when Julian divorces Bernice) based on Louisa and Julian's visits to Texas. The couple cohabited and held themselves out as husband and wife (implying that their conduct indicated that they had a present agreement to marry).

26. No. Lillie failed to establish that a common-law marriage existed. She and Gary never agreed to live together as husband and wife. (Lillie rejected Gary's sole proposal.) They did not cohabit because each maintained a separate residence throughout the relationship. Gary never represented that they were married. Even if Gary intended to marry Lillie at some future point, an agreement to marry in the future is insufficient to establish the requisite agreement to establish a common-law marriage.

IV. ANNULMENT

An annulment declares a marriage *void ab initio*, i.e., the marriage never occurred. This contrasts with a divorce, which declares that a marriage that was once valid has come to an end (as of the date of the dissolution decree).

A. Reasons to seek: Annulments, historically, enjoyed great popularity prior to no-fault when divorce was difficult to obtain. Today, parties may resort to annulment, rather than divorce, for religious reasons. Or, parties may seek an annulment for jurisdictional reasons to avoid longer residency requirements for divorce or to reinstate a benefit that was lost upon marriage.

B. Void/voidable distinction: A marriage may be characterized as void or voidable. Several features differentiate a void from a voidable marriage.

1. **Void:** A void marriage is invalid from inception. No legal action is required to declare its invalidity. It may be challenged by the parties themselves or by third parties, and may be collaterally attacked (in actions other than annulment) even after the death of one of the parties. A void marriage offends a strong state policy.

2. **Voidable:** A voidable marriage is valid from inception and requires that one of the parties take judicial action to establish its invalidity. If neither party acts to disaffirm the marriage, the marriage remains valid. A voidable marriage may be attacked only by the parties (although some statutes permit parents of a minor to attack a marriage). A voidable marriage cannot be collaterally attacked (i.e., in actions other than annulment). Such a marriage offends public policy less than does a void marriage.

3. **Grounds:** Bigamy and incest provide grounds for a void marriage. Fraud, duress, and nonage provide grounds for a voidable marriage.

   Example: Elizabeth seeks to annul the marriage of her deceased father, comedian Richard Pryor. Pryor remarried Jennifer while she was caring for him during his last illness. (He had previously been married to Jennifer briefly 20 years earlier.) After Pryor's death, his daughter discovers the later marriage and petitions to annul it on the ground of fraud, alleging that her father's name was forged on the marriage license. Finding that she lacks standing, the court reasons that Pryor's marriage was voidable and not subject to collateral attack. Thus, only Pryor could have commenced the annulment proceeding. *Pryor v. Pryor*, 99 Cal. Rptr. 3d 853 (Ct. App. 2009).

4. **Relation back doctrine:** Under this doctrine, a marriage that has been annulled is considered as void from inception. The doctrine is useful in some circumstances (such as the reinstatement of an employment benefit that was lost because of the marital relationship). Note that judicial discretion is involved in the application of the doctrine.

Example: Wife marries Husband #1 but never divorces him. She later marries Husband #2. When they separate, she sues Husband #2 for spousal support. After discovering that Wife's prior marriage was never terminated, Husband seeks to void their marriage on the ground of bigamy. Wife obtains an annulment of her first marriage and seeks to assert it as a defense to Husband #2's claim of bigamy. The court rules that an annulment that declares a prior marriage *void ab initio* does not *relate back* so as to give validity to a subsequent marriage that was bigamous when the annulment was granted based on the state's strong public policy against bigamy. *Lukich v. Lukich*, 666 S.E.2d 906 (S.C. 2008).

5. Effect of annulment on other's rights

a. Spousal rights: Traditionally, courts awarded alimony upon divorce, not upon annulment. Some statutes now permit spousal support awards following an annulment.

A question sometimes arises whether annulment of a second marriage results in reinstatement of spousal support from a prior marriage. Most courts do not reinstate spousal support based on a policy of protecting the first spouse's expectations.

b. Children's rights: At common law, annulment resulted in bastardizing any children born during the relationship (as a result of the application of the relation back doctrine). Statutes have modified this harsh result. See UMDA §207(c) providing that children who are born to a void marriage are legitimate.

Quiz Yourself on ANNULMENT

27. At the time of the marriage between Leslie and Mitchell, Leslie is working as an attorney for the state Department of Corrections. Prior to and during their marriage, Mitchell conceals from Leslie the fact that he had been convicted of a second-degree felony (theft of property) in another state. Leslie's employer discovers Mitchell's criminal record and informs her that because of her marriage to a convicted felon, her employer has determined that there is a conflict of interest and her employment would terminate. Leslie and Mitchell separate, and she requests an annulment on grounds of fraud. Is Leslie entitled to the annulment? If so, will the annulment enable her to continue her employment? ____________________

28. Martha begins work as a housekeeper for widower Otto and his children. Some time later, Martha accepts Otto's proposal of marriage; however, they never take part in a marriage ceremony. They cohabit and attend social events together. On various occasions, she registers as single (for a hospitalization), as does he (executing a mortgage), and they file tax returns as single persons. After Otto's death, Martha claims a dower interest as Otto's common-law widow. Otto's children contend that Martha is not entitled to a dower interest because there was no common-law marriage between their father and Martha. Will their argument succeed? ____________________

Answers

27. Yes on both counts. Courts grant annulments where one spouse has concealed from the other a criminal background because it goes to the essentials of the marriage. Mitchell's misrepresentations violated the essential purpose of the marriage (sexual intercourse and procreation). (Leslie wanted a husband and prospective father to her children of whom she could be proud.) The annulment will be held to "relate back" to the date of the marriage, and thereby, eliminate Leslie's conflict of interest.

28. Yes. Although Martha and Otto had a present agreement to marry and cohabited, Martha and Otto failed to establish the required "holding out" as married. Thus, Martha is not the decedent's common-law wife.

V. CONFLICT OF LAWS: WHICH LAW GOVERNS MARRIAGE VALIDITY?

A. Generally: Sometimes it is necessary for a court to make a determination regarding which state's law shall govern the validity of a marriage. This involves an issue regarding the conflict of laws (or choice-of-law problem).

B. Traditional rule: Law of place of celebration: Under the traditional rule, marriage validity is determined by the law of the state where the marriage was celebrated. (Recall that under the rule of ***lex loci***, a marriage valid where celebrated is valid everywhere unless recognition of the marriage would be violative of public policy.) UMDA §210 takes this approach.

Example: Wife and Husband are first cousins who marry in their native Iran. When Wife later files for divorce in Louisiana, the trial court dismisses her petition based on its refusal to extend comity to a first-cousin marriage. Reversing, the appellate court rules that, because the marriage was valid in Iran where it was contracted, the marriage should be recognized as valid in Louisiana, absent a violation of strong public policy. Finding no such public policy exists because first-cousin marriages are not prohibited by Louisiana incest law, the court holds that the marriage was valid and reverses the dismissal of Wife's divorce petition. *Ghassemi v. Ghassemi*, 998 So.2d 731 (La. Ct. App. 2008).

C. Restatement (Second) of Conflicts approach: Restatement (Second) of Conflict of Laws §283(1) (1971) has modified the general rule, holding that, in the absence of a statutory directive as to choice of law, the validity of marriage is determined by the state which has the "most significant relationship to the spouses and the marriage." Relevant factors in the application of this rule include: the policy of the forum state and the protection of the parties' expectations.

Thus, the state's interest depends on the purpose to be achieved by the rule and the relation of the state to the marriage and the parties.

D. Uniform Marriage Evasion Act: In contrast to the above approaches, the Uniform Marriage Evasion Act (1912) declared void all marriages entered into by parties who married in another state for the purpose of evading their home state restrictions on marriage. Although the Act was not widely adopted and has been withdrawn, some states have similar statutes.

E. **Federal DOMA.** Under the federal DOMA, states are not required to recognize same-sex marriages that are validly entered into in another state. Many states have enacted similar limitations by means of constitutional or statutory "baby DOMAs."

Exam Tips on *PREPARING TO MARRY*

Premarital Controversies

- **Identifying the controversy:** First determine the type of premarital controversy: *breach of promise to marry* or a *gift in contemplation of marriage.*

- **Breach of promise to marry:** First address the issue whether the jurisdiction still recognizes breach of promise to marry. Only a few jurisdictions still do. However, in any case, be sure to continue to discuss the elements, defenses, and damages.

  - Be sure to check whether there has been an ***actual promise*** by A to marry B. Under this cause of action, A can recover damages from B if B breaches a promise to marry. (Note that the issue of who broke the engagement may become important subsequently in actions for recovery of gifts in contemplation of marriage.)

  - **Defenses:** Check whether A may exert any defenses (such as B's fraudulent misrepresentation, B's nondisclosure of prior sexual conduct with a third party, B's impaired health, B's lack of love for A, the fact that either A or B was married at the time of the engagement, and mutuality of the decision to end the engagement).

  - **Damages:** Determine A's damages. A can recover the monetary and social value of the marriage (expectation damages) as well as expenses incurred in preparation for marriage (reliance damages). Damages for mental anguish and humiliation may also be recoverable; punitive damages sometimes are permitted. Note that some jurisdictions limit damages to economic loss.

  - Be sure to mention the existence of heartbalm legislation and the rationale therefor, the abolition movement, and the modern trend. Look out for exam questions that involve both types of premarital controversies (breach of promise to marry and gifts in contemplation of marriage). In such cross-over questions, be sure to determine who was "at fault" (if anyone) in breaking the engagement because it becomes relevant in recovery or retention of an engagement ring.

- **Gifts in contemplation of marriage:** The usual gift that is given in contemplation of marriage is an engagement ring. Here, the important issue is the existence of fault. Be sure to determine if either party is at fault. Discuss the role of fault and the modern trend.

  - Remember that there are two views about fault. At common law, fault (breaking the engagement) barred recovery or retention of the engagement ring. However, under the modern rule, fault is irrelevant, meaning that the donor can recover the ring regardless of who broke the engagement or if the termination of the engagement was mutual.

- ☞ Make sure whether the suit involves recovery of only an engagement ring or other objects as well. If the latter, determine whether a given object was actually given in contemplation of (conditional on) the marriage. Many objects that are given typically during intimate relationships are irrevocable gifts (i.e., they are completed transfers that are not recoverable).
- ☞ Consider the interaction of abolition of actions for breach of promise on actions for recovery of gifts given in contemplation of marriage. Many courts that have abolished the former action still permit the latter action.

☛ **Premarital contracts:** Verify whether this was an agreement between prospective spouses made in contemplation of the marriage. Determine what rights are being limited or relinquished (property rights during the marriage or after death, spousal support, etc.).

- ☞ **Different views:** Be sure to point out the traditional and modern views about the validity of premarital contracts.
- ☞ **Limitations:** Check for possible invalid limitations on child support or child custody.
- ☞ **Formalities:** Mention the requirement of a writing and that consideration is not normally required.

☛ **Validity requirements:** Check to see if the ***substantive*** and ***procedural*** fairness requirements have been satisfied.

- ☞ For substantive requirements, recall that there are two ***views on fairness***. Some courts require that the agreement be fair under the circumstances whereas other courts will enforce unfair agreements (if entered into voluntarily and with full disclosure). For procedural fairness, courts require that the parties entered the agreement voluntarily, and with full and fair disclosure. Recall that full disclosure does not require detailed disclosure.
- ☞ Another aspect of procedural fairness is the presence of ***independent counsel***. Determine whether the party against whom enforcement is sought (usually the woman) was represented. If not, was she informed of her right to counsel and given the opportunity to consult? Recall that courts do not require her to be represented.
- ☞ **Special rules for spousal support waivers:** Remember that some courts have a different rule for premarital agreements that concern spousal support. Many courts permit the prospective spouses to execute agreements regarding spousal support. However, some courts have special rules regarding such agreements (they deny enforcement if support provisions leave a spouse destitute or require representation for agreements that incorporate waivers of spousal support).
- ☞ Two final points: Recall that the UPAA requires a ***higher standard*** for unfairness (unconscionability). Also, be sure to check the ***time*** of the fairness determination: whether the appropriate assessment of fairness is at the time of execution of the contract or the time of enforcement (dependent on the relevant statute or case law). If fairness is determined at the time of enforcement, then ascertain whether any event has occurred (e.g., spouse's illness) that would make the agreement unfair even though it was fair at the time of execution.

Restrictions on Entry into Marriage: Constitutional, Substantive, Procedural

Constitutional Limitations on Regulation of the Right to Marry: Race, Poverty

- ☛ In discussing constitutional rights, be sure to identify the constitutional ***status*** of the right (i.e., is it a fundamental right), the constitutional ***source*** of the right, and the appropriate level of ***scrutiny***. Determine whether the restriction is a limitation on the right to marry and the nature of that limitation (for example, does it ***preclude marriage*** or merely make marriage more ***costly***?). Remember that infringements on the right to marry can violate substantive due process as well as the fundamental rights branch of equal protection.

- ☛ ***Identify the correct level of scrutiny***. Recall that different tests exist for scrutinizing the constitutionality of state statutes, regulations, practices, or policies. Begin with the presumption that the lowest level of scrutiny (rational basis) applies, but determine if a more rigorous level of scrutiny (intermediate or strict scrutiny) should apply. Remember that suspect classifications and infringements of fundamental rights (such as racial classifications and infringements on the right to marry) trigger strict scrutiny. Classifications by sex or illegitimacy trigger intermediate scrutiny.

  - ☞ In applying the correct level of scrutiny, remember that each test has a ***means*** (fit) and an ***end*** (goal or objective) component. That is, for the rational basis test, is the restriction "reasonably related" (is the "means" reasonable) to a "legitimate state objective" (is the "end" legitimate)? For the intermediate level of scrutiny, is the restriction "substantially related" (the means) to "an important governmental objective" (is the end sufficiently important)? Finally, for the strict scrutiny test, is the restriction "necessary" (the means) to a "compelling state interest" (the "end" must be so important that it is "compelling") to survive constitutional challenge?

  - ☞ Remember that *Zablocki* states that *not all* state restrictions on the right to marry receive strict scrutiny and that "*reasonable regulations that do not significantly interfere with decisions to enter into the marital relationship may legitimately be imposed*." Therefore, you need to determine if the restriction "significantly interferes" (i.e., whether it *directly* and *substantially* interferes) with the right to marry in order for strict scrutiny to apply.

  - ☞ Be aware that exam questions sometimes raise cross-over constitutional issues related to the right to privacy (contraception, abortion) as well as the right to enter the marital relationship.

Substantive Limitations

- ☛ Identify and discuss any substantive restrictions on marriage. Remember that substantive restrictions on marriage refer both to ***capacity to marry*** and ***state of mind***. Capacity includes: opposite sex, one spouse at one time, not related, above a statutorily defined age. Sometimes questions involve one or more issues of capacity. State of mind restrictions are fraud and duress.

  - ☞ Be sure to note that substantive restrictions involve both ***civil*** restrictions (preclusions of the right to marry) as well as ***criminal*** sanctions (bigamy, incest). Remember that *Lawrence v. Texas* invalidated state sodomy laws. When the discussion involves same-sex marriage, be sure to look for constitutional issues (due process, equal protection, and the application of *Lawrence*) as well as jurisdictional issues (the validity of a marriage contracted in a different jurisdiction than the home state). Discuss full faith and credit, lex loci, and state and federal DOMAs.

  - ☞ For issues of bigamy and incest, be sure to mention the potential impact of ***Lawrence***. By recognizing a constitutionally protected right to engage in consensual intimate sexual relationships in the home, *Lawrence* may foreshadow broader recognition of bigamy and incest (unless courts distinguish the latter acts from same-sex sexual conduct).

- ***State of mind restrictions*** involve fraud and duress. For fraud, discuss the different standards (i.e., essentials, materiality). For duress, ascertain whether the coercion is physical or mental. If mental, apply both subjective and objective standards.

Procedural Limitations

- Procedural restrictions refer to the procedural formalities associated with marriage (licensure, solemnization, blood tests, filing the license, etc.). If you find an issue regarding substantive or procedural restrictions, be sure to discuss the effect of failure to comply with these restrictions on marriage validity. Mention the void-voidable distinction and the consequences thereof, as well as potential criminal liability (bigamy, incest).
  - **Annulment:** If a question raises annulment, be sure to identify the appropriate grounds therefor. Discuss why the plaintiff might be seeking an annulment rather than a divorce (e.g., jurisdictional, avoidance of financial implications of divorce). Discuss the traditional versus modern rule for spousal support and children's rights following annulments. Determine if the relation back doctrine applies and discuss the consequences of applying the doctrine.

Procedural Variations and Curative Procedural Devices

- If there are issues of marriage validity, explore the presence of procedural **variations** (i.e., ***proxy marriages, confidential marriages***). Determine if any ***curative devices*** (i.e., ***common-law marriage*** or the ***putative spouse doctrine***) apply to protect a party or parties. Identify and discuss the requirements for application of each doctrine. If you establish the existence of a common-law marriage, check the chronology carefully to ensure that no ***impediment*** exists (such as a prior marriage) that would prevent formation of the common-law marriage. Make sure that the parties "hold themselves out" as husband and wife. Identify the aspects of ***holding out*** (use of joint names on documents, referring to each other as spouses, etc.). Remember that no special amount of time is necessary to establish a common-law marriage.

Conflict of Laws

- For questions involving marriage validity, always be on the lookout for conflict-of-laws issues. Analyze the applicability of the rule of ***lex loci*** and the ***Full Faith and Credit Clause of the Constitution***. Remember that the Full Faith and Credit Clause applies to public acts, records, and judicial proceedings of ***sister states***.
  - For choice-of-law issues, be sure to discuss the applicable law in all relevant jurisdictions. Do not assume that discussion of the law in one jurisdiction will obviate the need to discuss the applicable law in other jurisdictions.

CHAPTER 3

BEING MARRIED

ChapterScope

This chapter addresses the legal regulation of marital roles and responsibilities. It explores the rights and duties of the parties at common law, under various statutory regimes, and based on constitutional doctrine. Here are a few of the key principles covered in this chapter.

- **Marriage — Contract or status:** Marriage is both a ***contract*** (an agreement between two parties) and a ***civil status*** (regulated by the state).
- **Support rights and obligations during marriage:** At common law, a husband had a duty to support his wife, and the wife had a correlative duty to render services. Modern statutes make the duty of support gender neutral. A limitation on the spousal duty of support is the ***family privacy doctrine*** (courts are reluctant to interfere in an ongoing marriage).
- **Regulation of roles and responsibilities**
  - **Names:** Today, a ***married woman*** may retain her birth name. Parental disputes regarding ***children's surnames*** are resolved by resorting to the best-interests-of-the-child standard.
  - **Domicile:** At common law, a married woman lacked the capacity to establish her domicile. Today, both women and men may acquire a domicile of choice.
  - **Employment:** ***Antinepotism rules*** prevent one spouse from being employed by the other spouse's employer. Federal and state challenges to such policies have been raised.
  - **Parenting:** Formerly, ***mandatory maternity leave policies*** required female employees to leave employment when they became pregnant. Congress has responded with the ***Pregnancy Discrimination Act*** and the ***Family and Medical Leave Act***.
- **Criminal law and tort:** In both criminal law and tort law, courts and legislatures are abolishing special treatment for marital parties.
  - **Testimonial privilege:** At common law, a spouse could not testify for or against the other spouse in criminal proceedings. The Supreme Court has held that a spouse may testify against the other in criminal proceedings in limited circumstances.
  - **Marital rape:** Modern jurisdictions are abolishing or limiting the ***common-law marital rape exemption*** under which a husband could not be guilty of raping his wife.
  - **Alienation of affections:** Most jurisdictions have ***abolished*** tort actions for alienation of affections (tort actions against a third party for interfering in the marital relationship).
  - **Interspousal immunity doctrine:** Jurisdictions have ***abolished*** the common-law doctrine of interspousal immunity that barred tort actions between husbands and wives.

I. INTRODUCTION

The law regulates marital roles and responsibilities. The women's movement and the ensuing transformation of gender roles has altered traditional marital roles and responsibilities.

A. Historical background: Ecclesiastic versus civil jurisdiction: In England, ecclesiastic courts maintained exclusive jurisdiction over marriage from the Norman Conquest until the mid-nineteenth century. In contrast, in the American colonies, marriage was a civil matter. Today, civil courts continue to have jurisdiction over marriage, but vestiges of canon law and practice remain (marriage procedure, grounds for annulment and divorce, etc.).

B. Contract versus status

1. **Marriage is a contract:** Marriage is an agreement between two people. The American colonists, rejecting the religious character of marriage, regarded marriage as a civil contract. Similar to other contracts, marriage involves parties who are legally capable of consent, rests on consideration consisting of the exchange of mutual promises, and imposes rights and obligations. It differs from other contracts because the state is also a party (imposing obligations), and because it cannot be modified as easily as other contracts.

2. **Marriage is a status:** Marriage is also a civil status. The classic view of the dual nature of marriage as a status and contract was declared in *Maynard v. Hill*, 125 U.S. 190 (1888) (upholding the constitutionality of a state's assertion of broad power over regulation of marital status):

> [Marriage] is something more than a mere contract. The consent of the parties is of course essential to its existence, but when the contract to marry is executed by the marriage, a relation between the parties is created which they cannot change. . . . The relation once formed, the law steps in and holds the parties to various obligations and liabilities. . . .

Id. at 210-211.

II. REGULATION OF ROLES AND RESPONSIBILITIES

A. Background: Married women's common-law disabilities: Under the common-law doctrine of ***coverture***, the husband and wife became one person upon marriage — and, as Blackstone stated, the husband was *that* one. This was sometimes called the doctrine of "marital unity" or "merger." This suspension of the wife's legal identity subjected married women to significant common-law disabilities.

Absent her husband's consent, a wife was unable to:

- sue or be sued;
- enter into contracts;
- alienate real property;
- make a will; or
- retain or control her own earnings and property.

The husband was liable for her premarital and marital debts and torts. Special rules of procedure required joinder of the husband and wife in claims against the wife.

Although equity mitigated these harsh rules somewhat, it was not until the Married Women's Property Acts (enacted during the mid- and late nineteenth century) that these disabilities were largely eliminated.

B. Support rights and obligations during marriage

1. **Scope of spousal duty of support:** At common law, the husband had a duty to support his wife. The wife had a correlative duty to render services to her husband. Modern statutes make the duty of support gender neutral.

2. **Limitation on spousal duty of support — family privacy doctrine:** The spousal duty of support was limited by the doctrine of family privacy in cases of intact marriages. Under this common-law ***doctrine of nonintervention***, courts are reluctant to interfere in an *ongoing* marriage to settle disputes between the parties. Rationales include: (1) a desire to preserve marital harmony, (2) a judicial reluctance to adjudicate trivial matters, (3) adherence to the view that the husband, as head of the family, should determine family expenditures, and (4) the existence of the wife's common-law disability to sue her husband.

   Example: During a 33-year marriage, Wife cooks, cleans, and performs household chores. Despite his substantial assets, Husband fails to provide wife with clothes, furniture, household necessities (e.g., indoor bathroom, kitchen sink, or working furnace), or entertainment. Wife brings an action against Husband to recover support. The court denies Wife recovery. Because the parties are not separated, the court will not intervene to order spousal support. For public policy reasons, a married couple's disputes are not a matter for judicial resolution. *McGuire v. McGuire*, 59 N.W.2d 336 (Neb. 1953).

3. **Common-law necessaries doctrine:** A husband had a common-law duty to provide ***necessaries*** (i.e., necessary goods and services) to his wife and children. (The necessaries doctrine was designed to protect married women who surrendered their property to their husbands.) At common law, courts permitted indirect enforcement of the husband's duty of support. That is, notwithstanding the doctrine of nonintervention, courts allowed third parties (i.e., creditors) to sue the husband to enforce his duty to provide a wife or children with necessaries.

   a. **What constitutes a necessary:** Necessaries generally include food, clothing, shelter, and medical care. (Courts sometimes include other items.)

   b. **Constitutional challenges:** Support obligations that are payable only by the husband have been held unconstitutional.

      Example: Hospital sues Husband for services rendered to Wife, based on Virginia's statutory codification of the common-law duty of the husband to provide necessaries. Husband defends by challenging the statute as unconstitutional. The court holds that the statute which imposes financial obligations only on the husband constitutes gender-based discrimination under the Virginia constitution as well as the Equal Protection Clause. *Schilling v. Bedford Cty. Mem. Hosp.*, 303 S.E.2d 905 (Va. 1983). *But cf. Marshfield Clinic v. Discher*, 314 N.W.2d 326 (Wis. 1982) (holding that a rule whereby husbands are primarily liable for spousal debts satisfies equal protection doctrine in a society in which women earn less than men).

   c. **Modern view:** By requiring the husband but not the wife to be financially responsible for necessaries, the doctrine constitutes gender-based discrimination. States take a variety of approaches, by case law or statute, to the necessaries doctrine in order to avoid equal protection problems. These approaches include:

- abolition of the doctrine;
- expansion of liability to both spouses;
- primary liability on the serviced spouse (i.e., make the creditor seek payment first from that spouse, and, if unable to collect, then from the other).

The emerging trend is the gender-neutral imposition of primary liability on the serviced spouse but if that spouse is unable to pay, then on the other spouse (the last alternative above).

Example: Hospital sues Wife (and Husband's estate) for services rendered to Husband during his last illness. Plaintiff contends that the common-law rule requiring Husband to pay for Wife's necessaries should extend to Wife, based on modern notions of women's increased independence, marriage as a partnership, and equal treatment. The court holds that both spouses are liable for the necessary expenses incurred by either. However, in the absence of spousal agreement to undertake the debt, creditors should first attach the assets of the spouse incurring the debt; only if those assets are insufficient should the creditor be permitted to reach the other spouse's assets. (***Note*:** The court did not apply the rule retroactively since both parties relied on prior law.) *Jersey Shore Med. Ctr. v. Estate of Baum*, 417 A.2d 1003 (N.J. 1980). See also *Cheshire Med. Ctr. v. Holbrook*, 663 A.2d 1344 (N.H. 1995).

d. **Same-sex unions:** Statutes that expand liability to spouses but not to members of same-sex unions have been challenged on equal protection grounds.

Example: A hospital seeks to impose liability on a patient's wife when the patient fails to pay for medical services. Wife's defense is that the statute's imposition of joint liability on spouses for marital debts violates equal protection because it fails to impose liability on similarly situated members of civil unions. To cure the equal protection problem, the court extends liability to members of civil unions. *Bristol Hosp. Inc. v. Smith*, 2007 WL 1470326 (Conn. Super. Ct. 2007).

4. **Child's necessaries:** Modern statutes and case law make gender neutral the parent's common-law duty to furnish necessaries to a child.

5. **Statutory support obligations:** State legislation (supplementing and sometimes codifying the common-law necessaries doctrine) also imposes support obligations. Many ***Family Expense Acts*** (originally enacted to protect creditors) now require both spouses to provide support for the expenses of the family.

Example: Patrick Suiter is charged with a felony for altering a canal for the purpose of benefiting his wife's real property. He appeals his conviction, arguing that the court erred when it denied his request for court-appointed counsel because of his indigency. The appellate court rules that, because of the mutual obligation of support owed by one spouse to another, the district court properly included the separate property of Patrick's wife when it determined that Patrick was not indigent and not entitled to court-appointed counsel. The court reasons that, based on the common-law doctrine of necessaries, a spouse's duty of support includes the duty to finance the legal defense of a spouse who faces criminal charges. *State v. Suiter*, 67 P.3d 1274 (Idaho Ct. App. 2003).

6. **Criticisms of family privacy doctrine:** Criticisms of the doctrine include the following:

- The doctrine does not preserve marital harmony. Because support obligations may be adjudicated only upon separation or dissolution, the doctrine encourages the parties to terminate their relationship.
- Matters of spousal disagreements are not trivial. The doctrine leaves a more vulnerable spouse without remedy.
- Common-law rationales for the doctrine (husband as decision maker, wife's disability to sue) are outdated.
- The doctrine inappropriately gives preference to third-party rights over those of an injured spouse (by permitting third-party suits but not interspousal suits).
- Further, the doctrine introduces needless circularity to judicial resolution of intrafamilial disputes (by enabling only creditors to sue).

C. **Names:** A person may change his or her name in two ways: (1) the common-law method (without legal proceedings) by adopting another name and using it consistently and without fraudulent intent; and (2) adherence to a statutorily designated procedure. The statutory method does not repeal or displace the common-law ability to change one's name. The statutory method has the advantage of establishing the name change more easily and reliably. Opinion No. 00-205, 83 Ops. Cal. Atty. Gen. 136 (2000).

1. **Married woman's name:** At common law, a married woman assumed her husband's surname based on custom, not operation of law.

a. **Retention of "maiden" name**

i. **Generally:** Today, a married woman may retain her birth name so long as she has proven consistent and nonfraudulent use of that name. (Fraudulent use, for example, would involve an attempt to mislead creditors.) This follows from the common-law right of *any* person to adopt any name absent fraudulent intent.

Example: Mary Emily Stuart marries Samuel Austell. Before the marriage, they orally agree that she shall retain her birth name. She registers to vote using that name, but indicates that she is now married. Defendant-voter registrar notifies her that her voter registration will be canceled unless she assumes her husband's name. Defendant cancels her voter registration when Plaintiff fails to re-register. She challenges Defendant's action. The court holds that Plaintiff is entitled to continue to retain her birth name, following her marriage, if she shows that she consistently and nonfraudulently used that name. *Stuart v. Bd. of Supervisors of Elections*, 295 A.2d 223 (Md. Ct. App. 1972).

ii. **No constitutional right to retain "maiden" name:** The Supreme Court has not recognized a constitutional right to the retention of a woman's maiden name.

Example: Plaintiff challenges, on due process and equal protection grounds, an Alabama statute that requires a married woman to use her husband's surname to obtain a driver's license. Upholding the constitutionality of the statute, the district court holds that the statute was rationally related to the legitimate state interests of administrative convenience and maintenance of custom. The Supreme Court affirms without opinion. *Forbush v. Wallace*, 341 F. Supp. 217 (M.D. Ala. 1971), *aff'd per curiam* 405 U.S. 970 (1972).

b. Resumption of maiden name

i. During marriage: Many states allow a married woman who has adopted her husband's surname either to resume her maiden name or to adopt a name that is different from her husband's, absent fraudulent intent.

Example: Judith marries Daniel Natale, a school administrator. Husband does not wish to list his home phone. Attorney-wife desires to do so. She requests a judicial name change to Judith Natale Montague (*not* her surname prior to marriage). The trial court denies the petition based on possible detriment to third parties. Wife appeals. The court holds that Plaintiff may change her name since no evidence was presented of harm to third parties (i.e., Husband consented, possible harm to future offspring is too speculative, and no harm to state was shown). *In re Natale*, 527 S.W.2d 402 (Mo. Ct. App. 1975).

ii. Upon divorce: Statutes frequently authorize a married woman to resume her maiden name upon dissolution. Formerly, absent a statute, some trial courts expressly refused such a resumption, voicing concerns about the need for a husband's consent or fear of possible harmful consequences for the children. However, appellate decisions rejected such reasoning. *See, e.g., Miller v. Miller*, 670 S.W.2d 591 (Mo. Ct. App. 1984).

2. **Men's right to change their names upon marriage:** A few state statutes expressly provide for a man to assume his spouse's surname.

3. **Same-sex partners' name change:** Some jurisdictions now permit members of same-sex couples to change their surnames to that of their partner or to choose a hyphenated name combining both surnames.

4. **Transgender person's name change:** Some states grant a name change to a transgender person only upon medical proof of sex reassignment surgery.

5. **Victims of domestic violence:** Victims of domestic violence who seek to change their names to escape their abusers face difficulties with open public records and publication requirements. Some states address this problem by providing that records of a name change may be sealed and any publication waived where there is a threat to safety.

6. **Choice of children's names:**

a. Generally: Under common law, custom dictated that a child born in wedlock adopted the father's surname. Out-of-wedlock children (now termed ***nonmarital children***) adopted the mother's name. Many modern statutes provide that parents may choose the father's surname, the mother's surname, or a hyphenated surname combining the two.

b. Standard to resolve disputes: Courts resolve parental disputes about children's surnames according to the ***"best interests of the child"*** standard. Relevant factors include:

- the child's preference;
- the effect of a name change on child-parent relationships; and

- parental motives.

Example: Jessica Spero and David Heath have a nonmarital child Ella. Before Ella's birth, the parents' relationship ends, and Jessica tells David that he is not Ella's father. Jessica gives Ella her surname. After a paternity test confirms that Ella is David's child, David files a petition to change Ella's surname from Jessica's to his. The Virginia Supreme Court determines that the name change is not in the child's best interests because the father failed to satisfy the requisite burden of proof (under prior case law): that is, he failed to prove that the mother had abandoned the child or engaged in misconduct sufficient to embarrass the child by the continued use of the mother's surname, the child would suffer detriment by bearing the mother's surname, or the child is sufficiently mature to choose her own surname. *Spero ex rel. Spero v. Heath*, 593 S.E.2d 239 (Va. 2004).

Example: The father of a nonmarital child is a successful businessman in a small Texas town; he objects to the mother's petition to change the daughter's surname to his surname and argues that the name change would embarrass members of his marital family by exposing his affair. The appellate court rejects the father's arguments, ruling that the best interests test focuses on the welfare of the child and not the "self-seeking interests" of the noncustodial parent. *Scoggins v. Trevino*, 200 S.W.3d 832, 840 (Tex. App. 2006).

7. Third-party rights: Courts have held that the preferences of grandparents are *not* influential in disputes over surname changes of a child.

Example: A toddler's paternal grandparents obtain visitation after the death of the child's father (their son) in an automobile accident. When the mother remarries three years later, her new husband petitions to adopt the child. The mother and her new husband also petition to change the child's surname to that of the new husband in order for all family members to share the same surname. The grandparents object to the surname change. The trial court rejects the grandparents' claim, emphasizing that the applicable adoption statutes (1) afford no discretion to the trial court to reject a proposed name change (unlike name-change statutes), (2) expressly contemplate the change of the child's surname incident to an adoption, and (3) do not provide for a right to object to a proposed name change during an adoption by persons (such as the grandparents here) who merely are entitled to notice of the adoption proceeding. *In re Adoption of Jon L.*, 625 S.E.2d 251 (W.Va. 2005).

a. Constitutional challenges to restrictions: Some cases raise constitutional challenges to statutes restricting parental choice in the selection of children's surnames.

Example: Debra Henne, wife of Robert Henne, bears a child fathered by Gary Brinton. She wishes to name the child Alica Renee Brinton. Another plaintiff, unmarried Linda Spidell, wishes to give her daughter the same surname ("McKenzie") as that of her two other children. (Spidell chose a surname with which her child had no connection because Spidell liked it.) A Nebraska statute restricts the choice of children's surnames, for married women, to: (1) the husband's surname; (2) the mother's surname; (3) the mother's birth name; or (4) a fused surname. Unmarried women may choose (a) the father's or mother's surname, or (b) a fused surname. Plaintiffs argue that the statute is unconstitutional as a violation of their right of privacy. The court holds that parents have no fundamental constitutional right of privacy to confer a surname with which the child has no legally recognized connection. The statute is rationally related to legitimate state interests in promoting the welfare of children, recordkeeping, and insuring that names are not appropriated for improper purposes. *Henne v. Wright*, 904 F.2d 1208 (8th Cir. 1990).

b. **International perspective:** Several countries regulate children's surnames more strictly. For instance, parents in some countries must secure governmental approval for their choice of a child's name.

D. Married woman's domicile

1. **Definition:** Domicile, a legal concept defining a person's legal relationship to the state, is important in determining jurisdiction for such family matters as the validity of a marriage, the award of divorce and custody, the establishment of legitimacy, and adoption.

2. **Common-law rule:** At common law, a married woman lacked the capacity to establish, change, or retain the domicile of her choice. Instead, the law assigned to her the legal domicile of her husband.

3. **Reform:** The traditional rule began to change when the ***Restatement (Second) of Conflict of Laws*** permitted a "special circumstances" exception to the assignment of the husband's domicile and permitted a separate domicile for a wife who was living apart from her husband. *Restatement (Second) of Conflict of Laws* §21(1) (1971).

   Subsequent case law and statutory revisions liberalized the common-law rule. See *Restatement (Second) of Conflict of Laws* §21 (Supp. 1988) (permitting unmarried and married women, as well as men, to acquire a domicile of choice).

E. Employment

1. **Common-law disability:** At common law, married women's civil disabilities prevented them from being employed in some professions.

   Example: Myra Bradwell, a married woman, seeks admission to the Illinois bar. The Illinois Supreme Court denies her request based on a married woman's common-law disability to enter into contracts. The United States Supreme Court affirms, and extends the prohibition to single women as well. A concurring opinion (by Justice Bradley) rests on the ***doctrine of separate spheres*** (women belong in the private sphere of the family whereas men belong in the public sphere). *Bradwell v. Illinois*, 83 U.S. (16 Wall.) 130 (1873).

2. **Antinepotism (or no-spousal employment) policies:** Antinepotism rules, which were formulated historically to prevent public officials from hiring unqualified relatives, may serve to prevent one spouse from being employed by the other spouse's employer.

   These rules often affect married women more than men. This result occurs because women are more likely to be the "last hired" as they enter the labor market later than men (e.g., due to childbearing or the custom of marrying older men).

   a. **Rationale for policies**

      i. **Business rationale:** Common rationales in support of antinepotism policies include arguments that employment of married persons in the workplace leads to:

      - increasing incidence of quarrels at work;
      - favoritism;

- scheduling conflicts (e.g., vacations, holidays); and
- dual absenteeism.

ii. Conflicts of interest: Some employers have no-spousal policies to prohibit employment of certain professionals, such as lawyers and judges. Rationales include: the avoidance of actual or potential conflicts of interests, and the appearance of impropriety.

Example: Judge's wife seeks relaxation of a state supreme court rule barring a judge's spouse from running for public office. Court upholds its policy and Wife requests reconsideration. Recognizing Wife's First Amendment right to engage in political activity, the court holds that the justifications for the prohibition no longer exist. Women's common-law disabilities have disappeared (husband and wife are no longer regarded as one entity). However, the court does establish guidelines restricting use of marital assets and marital home for political purposes and advises against a judge accompanying the spouse to political gatherings. *In re Gaulkin*, 351 A.2d 740 (N.J. 1976).

Example: Wife retains Ms. Zimmerman to represent her in a divorce proceeding. Husband retains Ms. Zimmerman's husband, Mr. Bond. Bond and Zimmerman negotiate a settlement for custody and alimony. At the request of Wife, Zimmerman's law firm files a motion to disqualify Bond, alleging a conflict of interest based on his marriage. The trial court grants the motion to disqualify Bond. The state supreme court reverses, holding that disqualification was improper because no evidence existed of actual impropriety on the part of either attorney. The court thereby rejects the idea of a per se appearance of impropriety or a conflict of interest based merely on the marital status of opposing counsel. *Jones v. Jones*, 369 S.E.2d 478 (Ga. 1988).

b. Grounds of attack: Plaintiffs raise both federal and state challenges to antinepotism policies.

i. Constitutional challenges: Antinepotism policies have been challenged as a violation of the ***fundamental right to marry*** under *Loving v. Virginia*, 388 U.S. 1 (1967), and *Zablocki v. Redhail*, 434 U.S. 374 (1978).

Example: Husband is a special education teacher at an elementary school. Wife is appointed principal of that school. School board has a no-spousal employment policy that leads to Husband's transfer. He files a grievance challenging the policy, alleging, in part, that the policy violates his freedom to marry. His claim is denied. The court reasons that the Board's policy does not deny Husband the right to marry, but only denies him the right to be supervised by his wife. *Townshend v. Bd. of Educ.*, 396 S.E.2d 185 (W. Va. 1990).

Example: Two employees of a power company, Jennifer and Keith, get married. When they are terminated because of their employer's antinepotism rule, they allege that the terminations violate their constitutional rights. The court concludes that the employer's policy does not merit strict scrutiny review because it does not place a "direct and substantial" burden on the right of marriage. Based on rational basis review, the court finds that the policy advances a legitimate governmental interest (regarding fostering loyalty and discipline). The court also finds that a fact question existed on the retaliatory discharge claim (thereby precluding summary judgment) regarding whether the termination was a consequence of the employee's speech (his unwillingness to "fully agree" with the employer's rule) protected by the First Amendment and whether the termination therefore was an attempt to chill his First Amendment rights. *Vaughn v. Lawrenceburg Power System*, 269 F.3d 703 (6th Cir. 2001).

ii. Title VII: Title VII of the Civil Rights Act of 1964, 42 U.S.C. §2000e-2(a)(1) (2006), may provide another vehicle to attack antinepotism policies. (Title VII prohibits discrimination based on race, color, religion, sex, or national origin.) Because Title VII does not prohibit discrimination based on marital status, most antinepotism challenges under Title VII raise "disparate impact" claims: Although the policies are facially neutral (saying "no spouses" may be employed), the policies adversely affect a particular class of employees (women).

Example: Employers defend disparate impact actions by alleging that antinepotism policies are justified by ***business necessity***. *See, e.g., EEOC v. Rath Packing Co.*, 787 F.2d 318 (8th Cir. 1986) (invalidating no-spousal policy under Title VII, reasoning that alleged business necessity did not justify discriminatory policy).

iii. State civil rights statutes: Most often, plaintiffs challenge antinepotism policies based on state civil rights statutes that prohibit discrimination on the basis of marital status. Courts are split as to whether such statutes apply to no-spousal employment policies. Some courts have invalidated such policies based on state civil rights laws. However, other courts narrowly interpret the statutes to bar only discrimination based on marital *status* (i.e., whether a person is single, married, divorced) and not to bar discrimination that is based on the fact of marriage to a particular individual (i.e., another employee).

iv. Public policy: In states without civil rights statutes, plaintiffs have challenged antinepotism policies based on public policy arguments (but generally without success).

Example: Karen, a dispatch operator with the police department, marries George, a police officer. George dies shortly thereafter. After George's death, the department terminates Karen's employment based on her violation of the city's antinepotism policy. Karen sues for wrongful discharge, claiming that the antinepotism policy violates the state's public policy favoring the institution of marriage. The court finds the city is immune pursuant to the governmental tort liability act. *Roberts-Deckard v. City of Sevierville*, 2009 WL 1409981 (Tenn. Ct. App. 2009).

F. Health care

1. **Common-law duty to provide medical care:** At common law, a spouse had a duty to provide medical attention to the other spouse. This requirement was based on the duty to provide necessaries.

Breach of this spousal duty of care may result in criminal liability, especially if the injured or vulnerable spouse is unable to summon aid.

Example: Husband and Wife spend the day in town drinking. That evening outside the house, in snow that is two to three feet deep, Wife passes out. Husband allows Wife to lie outside unconscious all night, knowing that she is not warmly dressed, even though she was within easy distance of the house and even though he had a hired man who lived with them who could help carry her inside. When they brought Wife into the house the next morning, Husband made no effort to secure medical care for her (she was barely conscious). Court affirms his conviction for manslaughter. The court adds that Husband's drunkenness does not excuse him from the discharge of his duty to his spouse. *Territory v. Manton*, 19 P. 387 (Mont. 1888).

However, case law holds that a spouse does not incur liability for failure to provide medical care *if* the omission is in good faith and at the request of a competent spouse.

Example: Wife requires daily medication to control epilepsy and diabetes. Husband and Wife are "born-again" Christians. After a religious meeting, Wife believes that she is healed and resolves to discontinue medication. When she suffers ensuing seizures, Husband fails to summon aid. He is indicted for criminally negligent homicide. The court holds that because Wife, a competent adult, made a rational decision and exercised her free will to refuse medical assistance, Husband is not criminally liable. *People v. Robbins*, 443 N.Y.S.2d 1016 (App. Div. 1981).

2. **Spousal right to terminate life support — Natural death acts:** Some states have enacted ***natural death acts*** that permit a competent person to decide (via "a living will") whether life-sustaining procedures shall be utilized if the person becomes incompetent. Many statutes confer priority upon spouses to serve as designated decision makers if the patient has not executed such a document.

3. **Constitutional right to die:** Although the United States Supreme Court has not yet determined the scope of a spouse's right to terminate the other's life support, the Court has provided some general guidance.

   Example: Nancy Cruzan sustains brain damage as a result of an automobile accident and lapses into a coma (a "persistent vegetative state"). Surgeons implant a feeding and hydration tube to facilitate feeding. Because she has no hope of recovery, her parents request the hospital to terminate life support. When the hospital refuses to do so without judicial approval, her parents seek such approval. Missouri requires that an incompetent person's wishes to withdraw life support be proved by clear and convincing evidence. The state trial court authorizes termination, but the Missouri Supreme Court reverses. The parents appeal. The United States Supreme Court holds, on the assumption that a competent person has a constitutionally protected liberty interest under the Due Process Clause to refuse life-sustaining procedures, that the Constitution does not forbid a state's adoption of a heightened evidentiary requirement to determine an *incompetent's* wishes for withdrawal of life support. The state has an interest in the preservation of human life and the protection of family members against abuse. The Court finds that the Missouri Supreme Court's determination that the evidence did not reach the requisite standard was not in error. *Cruzan v. Director, Mo. Dept. of Health*, 497 U.S. 261 (1990).

   Epilogue: The family then seeks a new trial and presents newly discovered evidence of statements by Cruzan's friends as to her wishes. The probate court rules that these statements constitute clear and convincing evidence of her wishes to terminate life support and authorizes her parents to do so. Cruzan dies after her life support is disconnected.

   Note: In subsequent cases, the Supreme Court holds that *Cruzan* does not establish a constitutionally protected right to commit suicide. *See, e.g., Washington v. Glucksberg*, 521 U.S. 702 (1997) (rejecting a due process challenge to state ban on assisted suicide); *Vacco v. Quill*, 521 U.S. 793 (1997) (rejecting an equal protection challenge to state ban based on the difference in consequences of terminating treatment as compared to rendering assistance in hastening death).

4. **Property rights in spousal remains:** At common law there were no property rights in a dead body. Therefore, neither a person nor the person's spouse could make a disposition of a body by will. The prevailing American and English view now confers upon the next of kin (including a spouse) a "quasi-property" right in the disposition of the decedent's body for burial and other dispositive purposes.

   Example: The next of kin of deceased persons bring a federal civil rights action (pursuant to 42 U.S.C. §1983), alleging that the county violated the procedural due process rights of the next of kin by removing the corneas or eyeballs of their recently deceased relatives. (The relatives' bodies were the object of autopsies by the county hospital.) The federal district court dismisses the action, and the next of kin appeal. The appellate court reverses, holding that the next of kin have a constitutionally protected property interest in the bodies of their deceased relatives. *Whaley v. County of Tuscola*, 58 F.3d 1111 (6th Cir. 1995).

Quiz Yourself on REGULATION OF ROLES AND RESPONSIBILITIES

29. Husband is admitted to the hospital for treatment for the final stages of colon cancer. Wife gives her authorization for Husband's medical treatment, although only Husband promises to pay for all medical services to be rendered to him. Upon Husband's death, the hospital sues Wife for Husband's medical care. The hospital argues that the state's codification of the common-law duty of a husband to provide necessaries is unconstitutional and that liability should extend to the wife based on the modern view of marriage as a partnership. Is Wife liable? ____________________

30. Stuart Morgan calls 911 and reports that his wife Beth is unconscious. The operator tells Stuart how to start CPR (cardiopulmonary resuscitation). When paramedics and police arrive promptly, they find Beth unconscious on the floor. Stuart maintains that he has done CPR for 20 minutes, but the police notice that Stuart's hair is dripping wet and that the bathtub and shower walls are wet. Beth, who was without oxygen for more than 5 minutes, is placed on life support but subsequently dies. Bruising on her arms indicates drug use and that Stuart injected her with cocaine. Stuart is charged and convicted of manslaughter. He appeals. Will the conviction be upheld? ____________________

31. When Debbie and William Jones divorce, they are awarded joint legal custody of their four children. A few months later, one of the children dies. In the midst of a dispute about child support obligations, Debbie files a petition alleging (among other claims) that she should be reimbursed by William for one-half of the medical expenses and burial expenses she had incurred with respect to the deceased child. Will Debbie prevail? ____________________

32. Mary Smith marries John Jones. After their marriage, they orally agree that Mary shall take on the new hyphenated surname "Mary Smith-Jones." Mary begins to use that surname on all formal and informal documents. However, after the couple marries, John's relatives refuse to recognize Mary as "Mary Smith-Jones," and persist in calling her "Mary Jones." The relatives inform Mary that her common-law name change is invalid. Are they correct? ____________________

33. When Jane divorces Peter, Peter insists that Jane stop using his surname. However, Jane refuses. She desires to continue using Peter's surname in order that she and their children will continue to share the same last name. Does Peter have standing to force Jane to stop using his surname after the divorce? ____________________

34. Rhonda and Ronald marry. Rhonda becomes pregnant. Marital difficulties lead to a divorce during which Rhonda is given primary residential custody of James (their unborn child). During the divorce, Rhonda changes her surname to "Acosta," the name of the man she plans to marry soon. Rhonda is pregnant during the divorce proceedings. When James is born, prior to entry of the divorce decree, Rhonda gives him the surname Acosta. During the divorce proceedings, Ronald challenges the refusal of the trial court to change James's surname to Ronald's and argues that custom dictates the father's choice of surname. Will Ronald succeed? ____________________

35. Lillian and Jack live in a rent-subsidized apartment in New York. They purchase a condo in Florida and divide their time equally between New York and Florida each year. While they are absent from New York, their apartment remains furnished and is not sublet. Jack has a Florida driver's license and has moved his assets there. Lillian, although she has no driver's license because she does not drive, does maintain personal and financial ties to New York. They file federal income tax returns listing Florida as their residence and claim a Florida homestead exemption. They have bank accounts in both states and vote in New York. Their New York landlord seeks to evict them, contending that they have forfeited their rent-subsidized apartment by acquiring a new domicile in Florida. Jack and Lillian respond that Jack's primary residence is in Florida but Lillian's domicile remains in New York. Will the couple's argument be successful? ____________________

36. After Sue Smith, who is secretary to the police chief, marries a police officer, Sue is transferred to a clerk typist position in another city department. Her boss claims that he transferred her because he was afraid that her marriage would interfere with her ability to maintain the confidentiality required by his office. What constitutional arguments would you make on Sue's behalf to challenge the transfer? What counterarguments would you expect? ____________________

37. After Husband is pronounced dead, the hospital asks Wife to make an anatomical gift of his remains. Hospital documents Wife's refusal, based on Husband's previously expressed wishes, in the hospital records. Pursuant to established state procedures, the coroner (who fails to inquire as to the existence of objections and follows standard policy by not inspecting medical records) removes Husband's corneas. Wife institutes suit for deprivation of property (i.e., her property interest in her husband's corneas) under color of state law, alleging a violation of due process. Will she prevail? ____________________

Answers

29. Probably. Wife may be held liable for Husband's necessary medical expenses. At common law, the husband had a duty to pay for the wife's necessaries, including medical care. Because of successful constitutional challenges to this doctrine (based on the equal protection doctrine), states now adopt a variety of approaches, either by case law or statute, to avoid this form of gender-based discrimination. Some states have abolished the doctrine; others expand liability to both spouses. The emerging trend is to impose primary liability on the serviced spouse (i.e., to make the creditor seek payment first from the serviced spouse's estate, and, if unable to collect, then from the other spouse).

Depending on the approach that this jurisdiction follows, Wife may incur liability. If the jurisdiction follows the emerging trend, the hospital may recover from Wife if the hospital unsuccessfully sought payment from Husband's estate.

30. Yes. The husband's violation of the duty to provide medical care to his wife and the duty to summon aid for someone he helped place in danger amounted to recklessness. His actions provided a sufficient basis on which to rest a manslaughter conviction.

31. Yes. The necessaries doctrine requires that both parents (even divorced parents) are jointly and severally liable for the medical and funeral expenses of their minor children. Although some states have statutes so providing, other states have determined that such a duty exists at common law. On this basis, Debbie has a good argument that William should have to reimburse her for one-half of the deceased child's medical and burial expenses.

32. No. A person may change his or her name at common law without legal proceedings by adopting another name and using it consistently and absent fraudulent intent. A common-law name change is valid despite the failure or refusal of others to recognize and rely on the new name. The validity of the name change does not require that it be recognized or accepted by anyone other than the person who assumes the new name.

33. No. A person has no standing to seek a name change for another person. A husband cannot insist in a divorce proceeding that the court "restore" the ex-wife's maiden name if she chooses not to institute such a request.

34. No. Courts generally resolve parental disputes about children's surnames according to the best-interests-of-the-child standard. In this case, a court would weigh Rhonda's versus Ronald's reasons for the name change. Rhonda would argue that James should take the name "Acosta" because James will be physically present in her home and will bear the same surname as his mother and new stepfather. On the other hand, Ronald would argue that James should have Ronald's surname because Ronald has an interest in the preservation of his parental relationship, which could be weakened if James does not bear his surname. A court might find that the best interests of James dictate that he should be permitted to retain the surname "Acosta." Ronald's concerns might be addressed by having him strengthen the father-child bond in other ways during the exercise of his visitation rights.

35. Yes. A wife now has the same capacity to acquire a domicile of choice as does her husband. A husband's domicile no longer is deemed to be the domicile of the wife. Each spouse may have a separate domicile. Jack may choose Florida as his domicile, and Lillian may choose New York.

36. Sue would argue that the governmental action burdens her constitutional right to marry. Therefore, she would argue that the policy is subject to strict scrutiny and cannot be shown to be narrowly tailored to serve a compelling government interest. The police chief would counter that the policy did not deny her right to marry and that the transfer was necessary to serve a compelling government interest in the effective functioning of the police department (by preserving confidentiality in such matters as discipline and access to private information).

37. Yes. Wife has a legitimate claim of entitlement in Husband's body that is protected by due process. The coroner's policy fails to provide adequate procedures for deprivation of that property interest.

III. PARENTING

The entrance into the workplace of more women with children as well as an increasing number of women of childbearing age has prompted calls for enhanced protection against employment discrimination.

A. **Mandatory maternity leave policies:** Many employers' mandatory maternity leave policies formerly required employees to leave their employment when they became pregnant. Plaintiffs challenged these rules on constitutional grounds.

Example: School board requires pregnant teachers to take maternity leave without pay beginning five months before birth, and requires them to wait until their child is three months old before the mother returns to work. Another school district's policy requires their pregnant teachers to give six months' notice and to leave work four months prior to birth. Plaintiffs challenge the policies as violations of due process and equal protection. The United States Supreme Court holds that these regulations violate plaintiffs' due process rights by their conclusive presumption that pregnant employees are unable to work; the rationale of administrative convenience fails to justify the constitutional defect. *Cleveland Bd. of Educ. v. LaFleur*, 414 U.S. 632 (1974).

B. **No maternity "leave" policies:** Some employers failed to provide pregnancy leaves, although they did have leave policies for other disabilities. Their policies were permitted by some state statutes that created disability policies providing wage replacement for all forms of disability except pregnancy.

Prior to 1978, plaintiffs unsuccessfully challenged these statutes on equal protection grounds and under Title VII. *See Geduldig v. Aiello*, 417 U.S. 484 (1974) (finding that California's state disability plan did not violate equal protection since the exclusion was rationally related to legitimate objective of cost containment); *General Electric v. Gilbert*, 429 U.S. 125 (1976) (finding that private employer's disability insurance plan did not violate Title VII).

Considerable dissatisfaction with the Supreme Court's holding that pregnancy discrimination did not constitute sex discrimination led to enactment of the Pregnancy Discrimination Act.

C. **Pregnancy Discrimination Act**

1. **Generally:** Congress enacted the Pregnancy Discrimination Act (PDA), 42 U.S.C. §2000e(k) (2006), in 1978. The PDA is an amendment to Title VII of the Civil Rights Act of 1964 that prohibits discrimination in employment. The PDA has two prongs:

   - it amends the definitional section of Title VII to provide that employment discrimination on the "basis of pregnancy, childbirth and related medical conditions" is sex discrimination for purposes of the Act (thus overruling prior Supreme Court cases); and
   - it provides that women affected by pregnancy, childbirth, or related medical conditions shall be treated the same for employment purposes as other persons who are disabled from work.

2. **PDA's preemption of state statutes:** Following enactment of the PDA, a question arose as to the effect of the PDA on those particular state statutes that affirmatively provided for employment-related pregnancy benefits.

   Example: California statute requires employers to provide four months maternity leave and to provide a qualified right to reinstatement (unless business necessity renders employee's former job not available). Bank policy permits employees to take unpaid leaves for pregnancy, but does not mandate employee's reinstatement. When receptionist Lillian Garland desires to return to work after her maternity leave, the bank tells her that her job has been filled and that no similar positions are available. She charges the bank with a violation of state statute. Employer defends on ground that state statute is invalid because it is preempted by Title VII. The United States Supreme Court holds that the California statute is not invalid as preempted by Title VII because it is not inconsistent with the purposes of Title VII. Congress intended PDA to be a "floor" below which maternity benefits could not drop and not a "ceiling" (i.e., a state can provide more expansive benefits if it wishes). *California Federal Savings & Loan Assn. ("Cal. Fed.") v. Guerra*, 479 U.S. 272 (1987)

3. **Discrimination after the PDA:** Despite the PDA, employees continue to report acts of discrimination in the workplace. Such acts sometimes take the form of "family responsibilities discrimination," that is, adverse employment decisions based on caretaking duties (discussed *infra*).

4. **Criticisms of the PDA:** The PDA treats pregnancy as a "disability," rather than as a normal stage of a woman's life. In addition, by mandating employers to provide the *same* benefits for pregnancy as for persons with other disabilities, the PDA permits employers to have *no* policy for pregnancy if they have no policy for disability generally. The PDA has also been criticized for covering only discrimination arising from pregnancy and not addressing other issues necessary to secure equality for women in the workplace, such as adequate child care and breastfeeding.

D. Fetal protection policies: Some employers prohibited women from working in certain types of employment that might present occupational exposure to health risks for the fetus. Plaintiffs successfully challenged these fetal protection policies as gender-based discrimination.

Example: Employer-battery manufacturer excludes females of childbearing age from employment that involves exposure to lead (because of health risks to a fetus). Employees' union sues employer alleging sex discrimination in violation of Title VII. Employer raises defense that sterility is bona fide occupation qualification (BFOQ), arguing that the policy was based on permissible safety concerns. The Supreme Court holds that Title VII, as amended by the PDA, forbids gender-based fetal protection policies. Employer's safety concerns about offspring do not establish female sterility as a BFOQ because offspring are neither customers nor third parties whose safety is essential to the employer. Employer may not discriminate because of a woman's childbearing potential unless actual pregnancy impedes her ability to perform her job. Conception decisions and decisions regarding child welfare should be left to parents. An employer will not incur tort liability if it informs employee of risk. *Int'l Union, UAW v. Johnson Controls*, 499 U.S. 187 (1991).

E. Unemployment benefits: Unemployment benefits often were unavailable to employees who were out of work because of pregnancy-related reasons. State unemployment compensation statutes typically regarded terminations for pregnancy as permissible (i.e., "for good cause"). Plaintiffs challenged the constitutionality of exclusions of pregnancy from state unemployment compensation schemes.

Example: An employee of J.C. Penney Company requests, and is granted, pregnancy leave, which is without guaranteed reinstatement according to company policy. When employee desires to return, employer informs her that no positions are available. She files for unemployment benefits. State statute disqualifies claimants who leave "voluntarily without good cause [for reasons] attributable to the work or employer." The State Division of Employment Security denies her claim. She appeals, alleging that administration of state statute violates federal standards, i.e., Federal Unemployment Tax Act that prohibits denying claims on the basis of pregnancy. The United States Supreme Court holds that federal standards do not prohibit a state from denying unemployment compensation to claimants who leave their job because of pregnancy, if a state imposes similar treatment on all claimants who leave employment for reasons not connected to their work or employer. *Wimberly v. Labor & Indus. Relations Comm'n*, 479 U.S. 511 (1987).

F. Parental and family leave policies

1. **Generally:** In the 1970s many persons began advocating for a federal leave policy, claiming that the United States was one of few industrialized countries without such a policy. Some commentators (e.g., Professor Wendy Williams) urged that the proposed policy should adopt an "equal treatment" approach (i.e., gender-neutral parental leaves), rather than a "special treatment" approach (i.e., gender-based maternity leaves).

   At the same time, fathers began demanding that courts recognize fathers' roles in child rearing. In response to fathers' constitutional concerns, some employers liberalized sex-specific leave policies.

2. **Judicial challenges:** Parents initiated judicial challenges on constitutional grounds to gender-based leave policies.

   Example: Husband and Wife are university teachers. When Wife becomes pregnant, couple agrees that Wife will continue working and Husband will care for Child. Husband requests, but is denied, "parental leave of absence." Such leaves are routinely granted to women. He charges that the denial is a violation of equal protection. The court holds that Husband may have a colorable claim and may proceed to trial (court denies employer's motion for summary judgment). (The case never went to trial because the Board of Education amended its policy to include fathers.) *Danielson v. Bd. of Higher Educ.*, 358 F. Supp. 22 (S.D.N.Y. 1972).

3. **Legislative reform: The Family and Medical Leave Act:** Legislative reform was more successful, although advocates labored for decades to convince Congress to enact legislation.

   a. **Generally:** Congress enacted the Family and Medical Leave Act (FMLA), 29 U.S.C. §§2601 et seq., in 1993. The Act requires:

      - employers of 50 or more;
      - to provide eligible employees (those who are employed for at least one year);
      - with unpaid leave for up to three months;
      - because of birth, adoption, or to care for a family member with a serious health condition.

      The FMLA also provides for reinstatement to the same or an equivalent position. However, it does not entitle the employee to the accrual of seniority benefits.

      Example: Caldwell, a single mother, sues her employer, alleging that the latter terminated her employment in violation of the Family and Medical Leave Act after she took time off work in order to care for her three-year-old son who suffered from a serious ear infection. Caldwell's son required constant care for more than three days and he required two postoperative doctor visits. The trial court grants the employer's motion for summary judgment, holding that Caldwell's son did not suffer a "serious health condition" under the FMLA. The appellate court reverses, holding that Caldwell presented sufficient evidence to raise a question of fact as to whether her son's ear infection incapacitated him for more than three days and whether he received subsequent treatment for his condition. *Caldwell v. Holland of Texas, Inc.*, 208 F.3d 671 (8th Cir. 2000).

b. Criticisms: The FMLA has been criticized for the following reasons, among others:

- FMLA provides only unpaid leave (i.e., many women cannot afford to take unpaid leave);
- other countries provide for paid leaves;
- FMLA contains a traditional definition of a parent as biological or adoptive and, thereby, fails to provide adequately for nontraditional family members such as same-sex co-parents;
- FMLA allows employers to contact health care providers to verify information about leaves, thereby raising privacy concerns for employees.

c. Recent reform: The U.S. Department of Labor liberalized the definition of *parent* in the FMLA in 2010 by allowing persons to take family and medical leave to care for the newborn or sick child of their same-sex partner even in the absence of a legal adoption of that child.

G. Work-family conflict and accommodating family needs in the workplace: Courts are now being called upon to resolve issues presented by the work-family conflict (i.e., workplace problems experienced by mothers who struggle to accommodate family needs).

Example: Employee (full-time accounts payable clerk) is absent frequently because of her baby's illnesses. After giving Employee written warnings, the employer discharges the mother for excessive absenteeism. Employee applies for unemployment compensation, which is denied. She appeals the determination that she was discharged for "misconduct," by arguing that she could not find affordable child care compatible with her work schedule (6:30 AM to 3 PM). The court holds that Employee is entitled to unemployment benefits. Employee's inability to find child care does not constitute "misconduct" within the meaning of the statute in light of her good-faith efforts to remedy the problem. *McCourtney v. Imprimis Technology, Inc.*, 465 N.W.2d 721 (Minn. Ct. App. 1991).

Example: A kindergarten teacher arranges to breastfeed her baby during lunch period. Her husband or babysitter brings the baby to her and she nurses in a private room. After three months, Principal notifies her that she is violating a directive against employees' bringing children onto school property (intended to avoid disruption of teachers' duties and harm to their children). Teacher arranges for infant to have formula during the day. Baby develops an allergy to the formula and refuses to take a bottle. Teacher requests permission to resume breastfeeding during off-duty time off campus. School board refuses, based on rule prohibiting teachers from leaving school premises during work day. Teacher is compelled to take unpaid leave. She sues school board alleging that its policy violates her constitutional right to breastfeed. The court holds that a woman has a protected liberty interest in breastfeeding. The Constitution protects excessive interference with that interest (court remands to determine whether school board's asserted interests are sufficiently important and narrowly tailored to justify the policy). *Dike v. School Bd.*, 650 F.2d 783 (5th Cir. 1981).

Family responsibilities discrimination (FRD): FRD is a recently identified form of discrimination against workers based on their caregiving responsibilities for children, elderly parents, or ill spouses and partners. FRD includes not only pregnancy discrimination and the "maternal wall" that blocks women's advancement when they become mothers, but also discrimination against men who seek to take on a larger family caregiving role for young children, elderly parents, or ill spouses than traditional gender stereotypes of men envision. Examples of FRD include assigning a mother to less important "mommy track" work based on the assumption that she will be less committed to work or retaliating against a male employee who takes time off to care for his elderly parent or ill wife. *See* Joan C. Williams, *Reshaping the Work-Family Debate: Why Men and Class Matter* (2008).

H. State paid leave legislation: A few states (e.g., California, Washington) offer paid family leave programs financed through the use of unemployment insurance programs, temporary disability insurance, or tax incentives.

I. International perspectives: Until the FMLA, the United States was one of two industrialized countries (with South Africa) without national family leave. However, even after the FMLA, other countries generally provide better parental leave policies.

Quiz Yourself on *PARENTING*

38. Speedy-Clean, the employer of a small dry cleaning establishment (with 15 employees), has no medical leave policy for pregnancy or other disabilities. Speedy-Clean defends the lack of a policy by arguing that the business is not profitable enough to enable them to provide such a policy. Pauline, a pregnant employee, challenges the employer's lack of a maternity leave policy under the Pregnancy Discrimination Act. Will she prevail? ____________________

39. Same basic facts as above. Pauline also challenges the employer's lack of a maternity leave policy under the Family and Medical Leave Act. Will she prevail? ____________________

Answers

38. No. Pauline will not be successful on her PDA claim. The PDA requires that employers treat pregnant employees the same as other disabled employees. Because Speedy-Clean has no policy for pregnancy, and has no policy for other disabilities, the employer is treating all employees alike and, therefore, will not be liable.

39. No. Pauline will not be successful on her FMLA claim. The FMLA only requires employers of 50 or more employees to provide unpaid leave. Therefore, the FMLA would not apply to Speedy-Clean, an employer with only 15 employees.

IV. CRIMINAL LAW AND TORT LAW

In both criminal and tort law, courts and legislatures are abolishing the special evidentiary privileges for marital partners that were mandated by the common law.

A. Crimes involving spouses

1. Testimonial privileges

a. **Common-law rules:** At common law, evidentiary rules concerned the competence of spousal witnesses and the privacy of communications between the spouses.

i. **Competence: Rule of spousal disqualification:** At common law, the spouse of a party was not considered a competent witness. A common-law rule of disqualification prevented a spouse from testifying for or against the other spouse in criminal or civil proceedings. The rule was based on the legal fiction of marital unity, the possibility of bias, and the judicial desire to foster harmony and to promote the sanctity of marriage.

ii. **Privacy of marital communications:** At common law, a special privilege applied to a certain type of testimony, i.e., marital communications. The marital communications privilege enabled a defendant to assert a privilege to prevent his or her spouse from testifying as to any confidential communications between husband and wife. Adverse spousal testimony is a broad term that includes (among other types of testimony): *confidential marital communications* (made in the presence of only the other spouse) and also *communications made to the spouse in the presence of third parties*. Today, different rules apply in the federal courts to these two different types of marital communications (see *infra*).

b. **Modern approach**

i. **Competence:** A majority of jurisdictions now regard a spouse as a competent witness to testify for or against the other in *civil* proceedings. Most permit the defendant's spouse to testify *for* the defendant in *criminal* cases as well. The jurisdictions are divided, however, concerning *adverse* spousal testimony in *criminal* cases.

ii. **Adverse spousal testimony: Different state approaches:** The case of *Trammel v. United States*, 445 U.S. 40 (1980) (discussed *infra*), determined the rule regarding adverse spousal testimony that is applicable in criminal proceedings in the federal courts.

Prior to *Trammel*, states adopted one of four approaches:

- some adhered to the common-law rule of disqualification;
- some vested the privilege against adverse spousal testimony in the defendant, or in the husband and wife jointly;
- some states vested the privilege in the witness-spouse; and
- some states abolished the privilege.

c. **Federal approach:** The Supreme Court in *Trammel* adopts the approach of vesting in the witness-spouse the privilege to testify about communications made in the presence of third parties. (*Trammel* leaves intact the confidential marital communications privilege.) This approach is adopted only by the federal courts.

Example: Husband and Wife (and two other men) are arrested for importing heroin. Husband is indicted. The indictment also names Wife as an unindicted co-conspirator. Wife agrees to testify against Husband under a grant of immunity and a promise of lenient treatment. Husband asserts a defense of marital privilege to prevent Wife from testifying against him. The district court and court of appeals rule that Wife can testify as to communications made in the presence of third parties, but not as to confidential marital communications. The United States Supreme Court affirms. As to communications made in the presence of third parties, the Court vests the privilege in the witness-spouse. She has the privilege to refuse to testify adversely. Thus, if she chooses to give adverse testimony, she may do so. The Court reasons that this modification of the spousal disqualification rule furthers the interest in marital harmony without unduly impeding legitimate law enforcement objectives. *Trammel v. United States*, 445 U.S. 40 (1980).

d. **Exceptions to *Trammel:*** A number of exceptions exist to the *Trammel* rule.

- if the spouses have jointly participated in the crime;
- if the spouses are permanently separated at the time of the communication; and
- if the underlying offense was committed against a spouse or a child of either spouse (a "familial offense").

Note: *Trammel* is applicable only in federal courts; states are free to adopt whatever rule they choose.

e. ***Crawford v. Washington:*** The United States Supreme Court subsequently addressed a case (summarized below) that involved the marital communications privilege. In a criminal prosecution, the state sought to introduce evidence that was barred by the marital communications privilege, i.e., by means of the admission of a wife's recorded out-of-court statement implicating her husband. The case has broad implications for the prosecution of child abuse cases (discussed in Chapter 7).

Example: Husband is tried for assault and attempted murder. During the police investigation, Wife makes a recorded statement that contradicts Husband's claim of self-defense. At his trial, the state seeks to introduce her recorded statement because Wife refuses to testify based on Washington state's marital privilege that prohibits spouses from testifying against each other. The trial court admits the Wife's recorded statement in the face of Wife's unavailability, as an exception to the hearsay rule (i.e., an out-of-court statement bearing sufficient indicia of reliability). The United States Supreme Court reverses the conviction, holding that the use of Wife's recorded statement violates Husband's rights under the Confrontation Clause because, where *out-of-court testimonial statements* are at issue, the Sixth Amendment requires actual confrontation. *Crawford v. Washington*, 541 U.S. 36 (2004).

Note: The marital communications privilege does not apply to exclude a witness-spouse's *observations*.

2. **Wiretapping:** The question of liability for interspousal wiretapping has divided federal courts.

   a. **Interspousal wiretaps and federal rule:** Title III of the Omnibus Crime Control Act, 18 U.S.C. §§2510-2520 (2006), provides for civil and criminal liability for willfully intercepting another's communications. The Act permits actual damages of $100 per day for each day of violation or $1,000 (whichever is higher), punitive damages, plus attorneys' fees and other litigation costs.

   According to the majority rule (i.e., Fourth, Sixth, Eighth, Tenth, Eleventh Circuits), federal courts impose liability for *spousal* wiretapping in the home under Title III.

   Example: After being married 19 years, James Glazner filed for divorce against his wife, Elisabeth. During the divorce proceedings, James put a recording device on the home telephone. The device recorded conversations between Elisabeth and third parties without the consent of any party to the conversations. When Elisabeth discovered the device, she filed a complaint for damages in federal district court alleging that James violated the federal wiretapping statute. The Eleventh Circuit Court of Appeals held that no implied exception in Title III existed for interspousal wiretapping within the marital home (thereby overruling prior law in that circuit) and added that the new rule abolishing the interspousal wiretapping exception applied retroactively in order to further the rule's operation by compensating past victims of illegal interspousal wiretapping and, at the same time, deterring those persons who were either currently wiretapping their spouses or planning to do so in the future. *Glazner v. Glazner,* 347 F.3d 1212 (11th Cir. 2003).

   b. **Interspousal wiretaps and state legislation:** States have enacted wiretapping statutes similar to the federal law. Most of these states refuse to recognize an interspousal exception to a state wiretap law. *See, e.g., Dommer v. Dommer*, 829 N.E.2d 125 (Ind. Ct. App. 2005) (joining the majority of states that refuse to recognize such an exception based on legislative intent).

   c. **Parental liability for wiretapping a child:** *Consent* to the interception of a communication precludes the imposition of liability under the federal Wiretap Act. Courts have wrestled with the issue whether a parent can vicariously consent to the recording of a minor child's phone calls.

   Example: A man, appealing his conviction for sexual assault of a minor, seeks to exclude a recording of a telephone conversation between the 12-year-old female victim and himself, which was recorded by the victim's mother. He argues that the victim did not consent to the wiretap, and that therefore the conversation is inadmissible under federal wiretap laws. The court disagrees, citing the parent-child vicarious-consent defense, which allows a parent to consent to the wiretap of his or her child. *Alameda v. State*, 235 S.W.2d 218 (Tex. Crim. App. 2007).

3. **Marital rape**

   a. **Common-law rule:** A common-law rule provided for a marital exemption from rape. Under this rule, a married man could not be guilty of raping his wife. The rule is based on the wife's implied consent to intercourse, the idea of the wife as property, the fiction of marital unity, and the doctrine of family privacy (i.e., the judicial reluctance to disturb marital harmony).

b. **Modern trend:** Currently, many jurisdictions have abolished or limited the exemption either by statute or case law. States that limit the exemption take one of the following approaches:

- some states preclude the husband's resort to the exemption if the parties are living apart;
- other states preclude resort to the exemption if one party has initiated legal proceedings; and
- still other states require both that the parties are living apart *and* one party has initiated legal proceedings.

Several states now make their rape statutes gender neutral.

Note, however, that the marital rape exemption is not dead and buried. Some states still provide preferential treatment to spousal rapists (e.g., by making marital rape a lesser, separate offense to rape). Other states manifest a countertrend: They extend immunity from prosecution to nonmarital cohabitants.

Example: Husband, while separated from Wife because of physical abuse, calls Wife to request if he can visit Son. Wife agrees, and also agrees to return to his motel provided that a friend will be present. At the motel, the friend leaves. Husband forcibly rapes and sodomizes Wife in front of two-year-old son. Husband, although unable to resort to marital rape exemption because of the legal separation order, attempts to defend by contending that the exemption violates equal protection by its application to married men. Reasoning that no rational basis exists for distinguishing between marital rape and nonmarital rape, the court rules that the marital rape exemption violates equal protection. The court rejects the following rationales: prosecutions will lead to fabricated complaints by vindictive wives, disrupt marital privacy, and impede reconciliation; and marital rape is not as serious as other rapes. Disagreeing that the exemption protects against governmental intrusion in marital privacy, the court reasons that only consensual acts are protected by the privacy doctrine. Although finding that the exemption is unconstitutional, the court does not reverse Husband's conviction. *People v. Liberta*, 474 N.E.2d 567 (N.Y. 1984).

4. **Crimes against spousal property:** At common law, a spouse could not be liable for a criminal act involving the other spouse's property based on the fiction of marital unity (husband and wife constitute a single legal entity). Modern case law rejects this common-law rule.

   Example: Husband and Wife are informally (i.e., not judicially) separated. Wife moves into her own apartment. Husband has no ownership or possessory interest in her apartment, nor has he ever resided there. Husband breaks into Wife's locked apartment on two occasions. He is charged with burglary. He defends by arguing that since the victim was his wife, he was able to enter her apartment as a matter of law. The court holds that where the premises are in sole possession of Wife, Husband is guilty of burglary. *Cladd v. State*, 398 So.2d 442 (Fla. 1981).

5. **Other crimes:** At common law, the marital parties could not be criminally liable as co-conspirators. Nor did wives face criminal liability for the commission of a criminal act in their husband's presence (i.e., based on the presumption that they acted upon their husband's duress). The trend is to abolish these common-law rules.

B. Tort actions against third parties

1. **Generally:** At common law, the husband had a right to sue a third party in tort for interference with the marital relationship. Each spouse had a legally cognizable interest in ***consortium***, i.e., the services, companionship, and affection of the other spouse, as well as the sexual relationship.

   A third party's tortious interference with the husband-wife relationship might precipitate a legal action for:

   - ***alienation of affections,***
   - ***criminal conversation***, and/or
   - ***loss of consortium.***

2. **Modern trend:** Courts and legislatures in the 1930s began abolishing actions for alienation of affections and criminal conversation via anti-heartbalm legislation (sometimes, confusingly, referred to as "heartbalm statutes") — the same legislation that eliminated actions for breach of promise to marry.

3. **Reasons for abolition:** Reasons for abolition include: (1) the modern view that marital dissolution is never solely attributable to a third party's intervention, (2) the excessive nature of awards, (3) the difficulty of assessing damages, (4) the inappropriateness of awarding monetary damages as compensation for dissolution, (5) the lack of deterrent effect, and (6) a reluctance to equate spousal affection with a property right.

4. **Problems posed by abolition:** The abolition of such actions creates problems for plaintiffs who seek to impose civil liability on psychologists and religious officials who engage in sexual misconduct while in the course of marital counseling. Often, such suits must proceed on other grounds (negligence, infliction of emotional distress, etc.).

5. **Specific tort claims**

   a. **Alienation of affections**

      i. **Generally:** At common law, a husband might bring an action against a third party for alienation of affections. Gradually, the suit was also made available to the wife.

      ii. **Elements:** To prevail, a plaintiff must show:

      - plaintiff's valid marriage,
      - defendant's wrongful conduct with plaintiff's spouse,
      - an ensuing loss of consortium, and
      - a causal connection between defendant's conduct and plaintiff's loss.

      In assessing damages, a court may take into account the quality and duration of the relationship. Further, punitive damages may be awarded if a defendant's conduct is malicious, and the defendant has the ability to pay.

      iii. **Defenses:** A defendant may defend by showing consent on the part of *plaintiff* (**note:** not plaintiff's spouse).

iv. **Modern trend:** the modern trend is to abolish the cause of action. Most states have abolished the tort either by statute or case law.

Example: Shortly after Katherine and David divorce, Katherine files suit against David's lover for alienation of affections, alleging that the lover intentionally interfered with the marriage. After a jury verdict in Katherine's favor, David files a post-trial motion to abolish the tort of alienation of affections. Agreeing, the Missouri Supreme Court reasons that the tort of alienation of affections is premised upon antiquated property concepts (in a spouse) and faulty assumptions (that it preserves marriages), and is inconsistent with precedent (abolition in Missouri of the tort of criminal conversation). *Helsel v. Noellsch*, 107 S.W.3d 231 (Mo. 2003).

Example: James and his wife, Paris, undergo marital counseling with their church pastor (Bailey). Bailey initiates an affair with Paris. After James and Paris divorce, James sues Bailey, asserting that he negligently and wantonly performed his pastoral duties thereby causing the husband extreme mental anguish. Bailey appeals the jury verdict, contending that the husband's suit constitutes a claim for alienation of affections and therefore is barred by Alabama law. The appellate court reduces the jury's punitive damages award but otherwise affirms the verdict. The state supreme court, however, holds that the former husband's claim of "negligent marital counseling" is barred by the statutory abolition of amatory torts. *Bailey v. Faulkner*, 940 So.2d 247 (Ala. 2006).

v. **Jurisdictional issues:** In states that continue to recognize the action, jurisdictional issues may arise when the alleged acts of sexual misconduct occur *outside* the forum state.

Example: Mary Beth sues her husband's paramour, Tracy, for interfering with Mary Beth's marital relationship (with husband, Skip). Defendant moves to dismiss for lack of jurisdiction, alleging that she had insufficient contacts with the forum because she never had sexual relations with the husband *in North Carolina* or did anything to avail herself of the laws and privileges *of North Carolina*. Her contacts with the husband allegedly consisted of numerous telephone conversations and email messages while she resided in Georgia and he resided in North Carolina (although the husband disputes her claim that they never had sex while in North Carolina). The appellate court rules that the exercise of personal jurisdiction over Defendant, based on the aforementioned contacts, does not violate her due process rights, because there was a direct link between Defendant's contacts with the state and the plaintiff's injuries. *Fox v. Gibson*, 626 S.E.2d 841 (N.C. Ct. App. 2006).

b. Criminal conversation

i. **Generally:** This action was available only to the husband at common law. The rationale was to prevent the husband from having to support illegitimate children. Damages were for the plaintiff's humiliation, loss of reputation, and loss of consortium.

ii. **Elements:** To prevail, a plaintiff had to show:

- proof of a valid marriage; and
- the defendant had sexual intercourse with the plaintiff's spouse.

The law presumed a resultant loss of affection.

Example: Patricia and Frank are married and have two children. Patricia meets a supervisor in her real estate office. Suspecting that Patricia is having an affair with the supervisor, Frank hires detectives who substantiate Patricia's presence in the supervisor's apartment on two occasions. Frank sues the supervisor for criminal conversation. The supervisor appeals the jury's award of punitive damages ($28,000 actual damages and $270,000 punitive damages). The court finds the defendant liable for criminal conversation (based on the circumstantial evidence), but concludes that the punitive damage award is unsupported by the evidence (i.e., defendant's conduct was not malicious, nor did defendant have sufficient assets to pay such an award). *Albertini v. Veal*, 357 S.E.2d 716 (S.C. Ct. App. 1987).

iii. Defenses: Criminal conversation was considered a strict liability offense, because the defendant could not defend by showing that the plaintiff's wife consented, nor that the spouses were living apart.

iv. Alienation of affections distinguished: Whereas criminal conversation requires evidence of sexual intercourse between the defendant and the plaintiff's spouse, a claim for alienation of affection may be brought without the need for proof of such conduct.

c. Applicable statutes of limitations: Courts disagree about the application of the statute of limitations for alienation of affections and criminal conversation if an innocent spouse discovers the affair *long after* the affair ceases.

Example: Wife has an affair after ten years of marriage. The marriage continues (and produces two additional children) for three years after the end of the affair until Husband learns of it and sues Wife's paramour for alienation of affections. The court of appeals remands the case for a determination of when the cause of action accrued for purposes of the statute of limitations (i.e., when the affair terminated or when the husband learned of it). The court states that the relevant focus should be on *when the wife's affections* (and not the husband's) were alienated. *Hancock v. Watson*, 962 So.2d 627 (Miss. Ct. App. 2007).

Example: Husband sues Wife's paramour for criminal conversation based on the paramour's affair with Wife. The appellate court reverses the judgment on the jury's verdict in favor of Husband, reasoning that the discovery rule did not apply to toll the three-year limitations period governing a suit for criminal conversation. Husband appeals. The state supreme court reverses, holding that the statute of limitations in a criminal conversation action runs from the time that the Husband *discovers* the adultery and not when it was committed. *Misenheimer v. Burris*, 637 S.E.2d 173 (N.C. 2006).

d. Loss of consortium

i. During marriage: At common law, a husband could sue a third party for causing the loss of his wife's services, society, companionship, and sexual relations. Although the action originally was limited to intentional acts, it was later expanded to include negligent acts. The modern trend is to extend the action to permit a wife also to recover.

Example: Husband suffers serious work-related spinal cord injury. Wife gives up her secretarial job to care for him. In addition to a suit for Husband's physical injuries, Wife files suit for injuries to her ("loss of consortium") caused by employer's negligence. Prior case law held that a wife was not entitled to recover for loss of consortium. Court recognizes Wife's cause of action, based on the rationales that Wife's injury is not too indirect (because harm to her was foreseeable), damages are not too speculative, and recovery would not result in liability to too many other classes of litigants. *Rodriguez v. Bethlehem Steel Corp.*, 525 P.2d 669 (Cal. 1974).

ii. **After divorce:** Sometimes, injuries to a spouse may contribute to the divorce. A possible question is whether damages for loss of consortium are available if divorce results.

Example: Wife sues Defendant for loss of consortium and for the novel tort of "wrongful divorce." Wife alleges that Defendant's negligent operation of automobile led to Husband's sustaining injuries that resulted in the dissolution of their marriage. The court holds that an action for loss of consortium is not available when a marriage terminates, based on public policy considerations. The court, similarly, refuses to recognize "wrongful divorce" based on the difficulty of determining the extent to which a single factor contributed to the dissolution. *Prill v. Hampton*, 453 N.W.2d 909 (Wis. Ct. App. 1990).

C. Interspousal tort actions

1. Interspousal immunity doctrine

a. **Historical background:** The common-law doctrine of interspousal immunity, based on the legal fiction of marital unity, barred tort actions between husbands and wives. Thus, a wife could not sue her husband (or vice versa) at common law for either negligence or an intentional tort (assault, etc.).

b. **Rationale:** Traditional rationales for the interspousal immunity doctrine are that the bar:

- promotes marital harmony;
- prevents involvement of the judiciary in trivial matters;
- prevents the spouses from collusion to defraud insurance companies;
- prevents rewarding the defendant for his or her own wrong (because the plaintiff-spouse would share any recovery with the wrongdoer); and
- is necessary because alternative remedies exist and are adequate (e.g., criminal sanctions or divorce).

c. **Reform:** The Married Women's Property Acts in the mid- to late nineteenth century liberalized the rule to permit a wife to sue a husband for torts concerning her property. Gradually, case law and statutory law abolished the common-law rule and permitted recovery, first, for negligent torts and, subsequently, for intentional torts. A majority of courts have either abolished or limited the doctrine. (Those that limit the doctrine will preclude recovery only for negligent torts.)

Some jurisdictions attempted to mitigate the harshness of the rule by providing for exceptions for premarital torts, or for suits by a party who was divorced at the time of the suit.

Example: Husband and Wife die in the crash of an airplane that was owned and operated by Husband. Executor of Wife's estate brings a wrongful death action against estate of

Husband, alleging that Wife's death was caused by Husband's negligence. Husband's executor defends by asserting that the interspousal immunity doctrine bars recovery. District court concurs; Wife's executor appeals. The court abrogates the doctrine in regard to negligent torts and extends abolition to intentional torts as well, reasoning that denial of access to the courts would not further marital harmony, and that insurance companies and the justice system can guard against the possibility of fraud. *Shook v. Crabb*, 281 N.W.2d 616 (Iowa 1979).

d. **Family exclusion clauses:** Insurance companies have responded to the abolition of the interspousal immunity doctrine by the insertion into policies (i.e., automobile, homeowners') of "family exclusion clauses" that exclude coresident family members from coverage. Courts are split on whether such clauses violate public policy.

2. **Sexual torts:** Interspousal tort liability also exists for negligent transmission of venereal disease. Whereas some courts formerly barred recovery based on the interspousal tort immunity doctrine, many states now impose liability.

a. **Duty to disclose:** The Restatement of Torts postulates that a spouse has a duty to disclose physical conditions that make cohabitation dangerous. Restatement (Second) of Torts §554 (1977).

b. **Liability for constructive knowledge:** A majority of courts holds that liability for negligent transmission of venereal disease extends to situations in which the defendant has *constructive*, not merely actual, knowledge that he or she is infected.

Example: Wife sues Husband for infecting her with HIV (human immunodeficiency virus), claiming intentional and negligent infliction of emotional distress, fraud, and negligence. An issue arose as to whether spouses have a duty to disclose to each other their HIV-related status. The California Supreme Court holds that, in the balance of the husband's state constitutional right to privacy against the wife's right to discover relevant facts, the husband's medical records and sexual history (extending to six months prior to his negative HIV test) are discoverable. Further, the court holds that liability for negligent transmission of HIV extends to situations when a person had reason to know of the infection (constructive knowledge). *John B. v. Superior Court*, 137 P.3d 153 (Cal. 2006).

c. **Disclosure by third parties:** Courts are reluctant to extend liability to third parties to require them to disclose a family member's exposure to the innocent spouse or sexual partner.

Example: A woman files suit against her fiancé's parents, alleging fraudulent and negligent misrepresentation, for their informing her that their son's medical condition was metal poisoning and Lyme disease when he actually was HIV positive and had been diagnosed with AIDS (acquired immunodeficiency syndrome). The appellate court holds that the parents' failure to disclose is not actionable for negligent misrepresentation because the state law prohibits disclosure of his HIV testing or status. The court also holds that Plaintiff's reliance was not justifiable because she should have directed her concerns about her own health to medical professionals. *Doe v. Dilling*, 861 N.E.2d 1052 (Ill. App. Ct. 2006).

3. **Intentional infliction of emotional distress:** Although some courts recognize the interspousal tort of intentional infliction of emotional distress to enable a spouse to recover damages for acts of extreme cruelty by the other, there is a split among jurisdictions regarding recognition of such suits in the divorce context. Among courts that permit such actions, some prohibit joinder, others mandate joinder, and some adopt a permissive policy of joinder. A majority of jurisdictions adopt a permissive approach, i.e., permitting but not mandating joinder. *Chen v. Fisher*, 843 N.E.2d 723, 726 (N.Y. 2005). Some critics charge that recognition of this tort re-introduces notions of fault into the divorce process.

   a. **Statute of limitations:** Statutes of limitations may prevent recovery for tortious acts that occurred early in the marriage. Victims sometimes wait years after the occurrence of physical abuse before they file for divorce. Some courts resolve this problem by ruling that in tort actions involving a continuing or repeated injury (such as domestic violence), the limitations period does not begin to run until the date of the last injury or the date the tortious acts cease.

   b. **Claim preclusion:** Courts also are split regarding whether a battered spouse's claim is barred in a separate post-divorce tort action because of the res judicata effect of the divorce decree.

4. **Intimate partner violence**

   a. **Traditional rule:** At common law, a husband had the right of "moderate chastisement" of his wife (according to Blackstone). Moreover, a wife was barred by the interspousal immunity doctrine from suing her husband for intentional torts (e.g., assault, battery).

   b. **Modern view:** The women's movement focused public attention on intimate partner violence and contributed to legal policy on this problem. Currently, all states have legislation and case law that address domestic violence. Legal policy takes several forms:

      - rules liberalizing the admission of battered woman's syndrome evidence;
      - remedies (civil and criminal) against the abuser;
      - remedies against law enforcement personnel; and
      - federal reforms.

   c. **Battered woman's syndrome**

      i. **Admissibility of evidence of battered woman's syndrome:** Commentators and criminal defense attorneys have urged admission of evidence of the ***battered woman's syndrome*** to enable battered women to receive more humane treatment by the criminal justice system. Although courts initially were reluctant to admit such evidence, the trend is to liberalize rules and permit admission of such evidence.

      ii. **Definition of battered woman's syndrome:** The battered woman's syndrome is a theory of behavior, based on the work of psychologist Lenore Walker, that explains: the cycle of violence (i.e., abuse occurs within a gradual escalation of tension during a relationship); and the concept of "learned helplessness" (i.e., women stay in an abusive relationship because they become so depressed by the abuse that they lose the motivation to respond).

iii. Rationale for admission of evidence: Expert testimony on the battered woman's syndrome has been used to support a battered woman's claims of self-defense in cases of homicide (i.e., when a battered woman kills her abuser). To rely on the doctrine of self-defense, a defendant must prove that she reasonably feared that she was in imminent danger of serious bodily harm. Evidence of the battered woman's syndrome addresses the reasonableness of the perception of imminence and the danger that a woman faces.

iv. Requirements for admission of evidence: To admit evidence of the battered woman's syndrome, courts generally require that the evidence be *relevant* to the woman's claim of self-defense and also that the evidence meet the *scientific acceptance test.*

Federal courts traditionally evaluated the admissibility of novel scientific evidence based on the *Frye* standard (*Frye v. United States*, 293 F. 1013 (D.C. Cir. 1923)), permitting the admission of evidence if it has become generally accepted by scientists in the relevant field of study. That standard was replaced by a new standard in *Daubert v. Merrell Dow Pharmaceuticals*, 509 U.S. 579 (1993), that adopted Federal Rule of Evidence 702 (holding that evidence may be admitted if it is helpful to the trier of fact and if the methodology is scientifically valid).

Note: Whereas *Daubert* technically applies to the federal courts, many state courts follow it also.

Example: Husband, when drunk, frequently assaults wife during seven-year marriage. In the midst of one argument, Wife stabs Husband to death with a pair of scissors. At trial, she claims self-defense stemming from her fear that he was going to kill her. To establish the requisite state of mind for self-defense, Wife calls an expert witness to testify about the battered woman's syndrome. The trial court rules the evidence inadmissible. The appellate court reverses Wife's conviction. The court states that the admissibility of evidence of the battered woman's syndrome depends on (1) whether the evidence is relevant to the defendant's claim of self-defense, and (2) whether the standards for admission of expert testimony (general acceptability in the scientific community) are met. The court concludes that the testimony was relevant to support Wife's testimony that she honestly believed she was in imminent danger of death. However, the court remands for a new trial on the issue of the acceptability of the syndrome evidence in the scientific community. *State v. Kelly*, 478 A.2d 364 (N.J. 1984).

d. Remedies against the batterer: All states have criminal and civil statutes addressing intimate partner violence.

i. Criminal: A batterer may incur criminal liability for assault and/or battery. Historically, police departments have been reluctant to treat wife-beating as seriously as other assaults. Legal policy addresses this reluctance by means of case law (i.e., federal civil rights actions against municipalities and police departments, discussed *infra*) as well as statutory law (i.e., statutes that eliminate police discretion by requiring mandatory arrests of batterers).

ii. Civil: Most states also have legislation providing for civil protective orders. Such temporary orders are issued *ex parte* (without notice to the batterer or an opportunity for a full adversary hearing). Restraining orders restrain a batterer from entering a dwelling or committing further acts of abuse. Orders of protection also permit awards of temporary custody and support of children, and spousal support. Following a full hearing, temporary orders may be made permanent. Although a few cases have challenged these civil protection orders as a violation of due process, appellate courts have upheld their constitutionality.

e. **Remedies against law enforcement for failure to protect:**

i. **Federal civil rights action under §1983:** A few courts have recognized a federal civil rights cause of action against law enforcement and/or municipalities for the failure to protect battered women. Claims are based on 42 U.S.C. §1983 that imposes liability on governmental officials for deprivation of a constitutional right (e.g., due process or equal protection) under color of law. Generally, no right to police protection exists for private acts of violence. Thus, a cause of action arises only if the state discriminates in providing protection to the public in violation of the Equal Protection Clause or if the state has a "special relationship" to an individual such that the state has an affirmative duty to act.

ii. **Special relationship requirement:** For a limited time, courts applied the "special relationship doctrine" to enable battered women to recover in suits against law enforcement agencies. Under the general rule, a cause of action will not arise for failure to provide a specific individual with police protection (because the police owe a duty to the public at large) unless a "special relationship" exists between the governmental agency and the individual.

To establish a special relationship, the governmental agency must:

- assume an affirmative duty to act on behalf of the injured party;
- have knowledge of the consequences of inaction;
- have direct contact with the injured party; and
- incur the injured party's justifiable reliance on the municipality's affirmative undertaking.

iii. **Limitation on doctrine: *DeShaney v. Winnebago*:** The Supreme Court subsequently limited the "special relationship" exception in a child abuse case that has significant implications for battered women. In *DeShaney v. Winnebago*, 489 U.S. 189 (1989), the Court holds that no special relationship exists between a child protective service agency and an abused child even though the agency was investigating the family and was aware of the continuing abuse. Absent a special relationship, the state has no constitutional duty to protect its citizens against deprivation of life, liberty, or property committed by private individuals. The Court reasons that a special relationship might arise, however, if the agency placed the child in custody or in a worse position than he would have occupied in the absence of state intervention.

Courts have applied *DeShaney* in the context of spousal abuse to foreclose claims by battered women.

Although *DeShaney* may have foreclosed claims on *substantive* due process grounds, the equal protection doctrine may still be a possible route to recovery by plaintiffs alleging inadequate governmental responses to domestic violence.

iv. No constitutional right to protection: The Supreme Court addressed the question left unanswered by *Deshaney*, i.e., whether the state violates *procedural* due process rights by failing to provide procedural safeguards. The Court in *Town of Castle Rock v. Gonzales*, 545 U.S. 748 (2005), held that a constitutional claim for failure to protect does not lie under procedural due process.

Example: Jessica Gonzales alleges that city officials in Castle Rock, Colorado, violated her due process rights and those of her children (pursuant to 42 U.S.C. §1983) by police officers' failure to enforce her restraining order against her former husband, specifically by their failure to respond to her repeated reports over a day's period that her ex-husband had abducted the couple's three daughters. In the early morning hours after the abduction, the father arrived at the police station and committed "suicide by cop." In the ensuing gun battle, the police killed the father and later discovered the bodies of the three children in the back of his truck (and concluded that he murdered the children earlier). The U.S. Supreme Court holds that the Due Process Clause does not entitle the mother to a property interest in the enforcement of the restraining order against the father. The Court reasons that, although the restraining order statute provided that police "shall use" every reasonable means to enforce a restraining order, the language did not make the enforcement of restraining orders mandatory but rather discretionary, especially because arrest was not always possible or practical; the statute provided for an alternative to immediate enforcement (initiation of an arrest warrant and the right to initiate contempt proceedings) but did not expressly give a protected person a right to demand an arrest. *Town of Castle Rock v. Gonzales*, 545 U.S. 748 (2005).

Epilogue: Jessica Gonzales subsequently filed a petition with the Inter-American Commission on Human Rights (IACHR) alleging that the actions of the police and the decision of the Supreme Court violated her human rights. The case is still pending.

f. Difficulties for prosecutors: Problems arise for prosecutors because corroboration of battering may be difficult (as the act takes place in private), and victims may not be able to testify (e.g., due to fear, unwillingness, or death). The admissibility of hearsay evidence, which was fairly commonplace before 2004, was restricted by the United States Supreme Court in *Crawford v. Washington*, 541 U.S. 36 (2004) (discussed *supra*), which has implications for prosecutions of domestic violence. In *Crawford*, during investigation of a stabbing, the suspect's wife made a recorded statement that contradicted her husband's claim of self-defense. The state sought to admit her statement that was barred by the husband's assertion of the marital privilege. The U.S. Supreme Court reversed the husband's conviction, holding that the use of the wife's statement violated the Confrontation Clause because the Sixth Amendment requires witness unavailability *and* a prior opportunity for cross-examination when out-of-court testimonial statements are at issue.

i. Implications of *Crawford*: *Crawford* severely limits the opportunity for admission of victims' and witnesses' out-of-court statements if these persons are "unavailable" for trial (e.g., afraid to testify), and if their out-of-court statements are deemed "testimonial" (i.e., made for the purpose of prosecution).

ii. Meaning of testimonial hearsay: The Supreme Court clarified the meaning of testimonial hearsay in two post-*Crawford* domestic violence cases. In *Davis v. Washington*, 547 U.S. 813 (2006), the Court held that statements to 911 operators are not testimonial and therefore admissible because they are elicited to resolve an ongoing emergency. However, in the consolidated case of *Hammon v. Indiana,* the Court held that admission of a victim's statement to a responding police officer violates the right to confrontation (absent the opportunity for cross-examination) because the officer was investigating a possible crime.

iii. **Exception to *Crawford:*** An exception has developed to the *Crawford* rule that bars the use of "testimonial" statements, as a violation of the Confrontation Clause, in cases of witness unavailability. The "forfeiture by wrongdoing" exception (based on the public policy of deterring wrongdoing threatening the legal process) holds that one who obtains the absence of a witness by wrongdoing, in order to prevent the witness from testifying, forfeits his or her constitutional right to confrontation. In the case of battered spouses, a wrongdoer might make a witness "unavailable" at trial by any number of means, ranging from killing the witness (in an intimate partner homicide) to using coercion to prevent the witness from testifying. *See Giles v. California,* 128 S. Ct. 2678 (U.S. 2008).

g. **Mandatory arrest:** Over half of the states require mandatory arrest for misdemeanor domestic-violence offenses. The benefits and detriments of mandatory arrest remain contested. Advocates argue that mandatory arrest protects victims more effectively by immediate relief. Opponents question whether such policy is an effective deterrent to abusive behavior and suggest that mandatory arrest contributes to the escalation of domestic violence.

h. **No-drop policies:** No-drop policies also dispense with discretion, requiring the state to prosecute batterers even if the victim does not wish to pursue the matter. No-drop policies present controversial policy issues of ensuring the victim's protection versus diminishing the victim's autonomy.

i. **Federal legislative reforms:** The federal approach to battering consists of: funding for shelters, the Violence Against Women Act (VAWA), and regulation of firearms by perpetrators of domestic violence.

i. **Shelters:** Federal legislation began providing funding for battered women's shelters in 1984. The shelters provide a battered woman and her children with refuge from the batterer and also provide counseling and other services.

ii. **Violence Against Women Act:** In 1994, Congress enacted the Violence Against Women Act (VAWA), 42 U.S.C. §§14014 et seq. (2006). VAWA has several purposes, including: (1) the authorization of grants for purposes of funding battered women's shelters, implementing of mandatory arrest policies, and providing education about domestic violence generally; (2) the imposition of federal criminal liability upon an individual who crosses a state line with intent to injure or harass a current or former spouse or intimate partner; (3) the provision of full faith and credit for protection orders; and (4) the provision of a federal cause of action for victims of crimes of violence motivated by gender.

Several federal courts examined the constitutionality of VAWA. In *United States v. Morrison*, 529 U.S. 598 (2000), the Supreme Court held that Congress exceeded its power under the Commerce Clause in creating the specific VAWA provision that authorized a private cause of action for victims of gender-motivated crimes. The Court reasoned that such gender-motivated crimes are not analogous to economic activity so as to evoke regulation of interstate commerce. *But cf. United States v. Al-Zubaidy*, 283 F.3d 804 (6th Cir. 2002) (holding that Congress did not exceed its powers under the Commerce Clause in enacting 18 U.S.C. §2261(a)(1) punishing interstate stalking).

Congress reauthorized VAWA several times. The Violence Against Women and Department of Justice Reauthorization Act of 2005 (Pub. L. No. 109-162, known as VAWA 2005) renews and increases funding for law enforcement and civil legal assistance; increases criminal penalties for repeat domestic violence offenders; incorporates GPS technology; and requires DNA fingerprinting for federal offenders. The next reauthorization is scheduled for 2011.

iii. Firearm restrictions: Federal legislation also punishes firearm possession by any person convicted of crimes of domestic violence or subject to protective orders (restraining orders). Such legislation was brought into question after the U.S. Supreme Court struck down a statutory ban on handguns as a violation of the Second Amendment right to keep firearms for private use in the home. *District of Columbia v. Heller*, 128 S. Ct. 2783 (2008). However, following *Heller*, several courts have upheld the constitutionality of federal restrictions on handgun ownership for persons subject to domestic violence restraining orders or those convicted of misdemeanor crimes of domestic violence. *See, e.g., U.S. v. Skoien*, 614 F.3d 638 (7th Cir. 2010); *United States v. Knight*, 574 F. Supp.2d 224 (D. Me. 2008).

Quiz Yourself on
CRIMINAL LAW AND TORT LAW

40. Donna separates from Cedric. Before their divorce becomes final, Cedric visits their daughter at Donna's residence. He comes across documents there that indicate that Donna filed the false loan applications for which she is eventually convicted. At the request of the FBI, Cedric agrees to tape a conversation with Donna at which she makes incriminating statements. When the taped conversation is admitted into evidence, Donna objects based on the marital communications privilege. Will her argument be successful? ____________________

41. Husband is charged with drug offenses. The prosecution wishes to introduce testimony of the Wife regarding statements of the Husband concerning his drug use that were made in the presence of third parties and also in private. Wife and Husband are separated, but have not yet filed for divorce. Wife asserts the privilege against adverse spousal testimony and confidential marital communications. Will she prevail? ____________________

42. Husband moves out of home in response to marital difficulties. Without Wife's knowledge or consent, Husband attaches a recording device to the home phone. He tapes conversations between Wife and third parties. Wife secures a divorce and brings a federal wiretapping action against Husband. Husband defends by saying that he did not know that wiretapping was illegal and also that his main concern was his children's welfare. Will Husband's arguments regarding federal wiretapping be successful? ____________________

43. After Katherine and Bill have a child, Katherine tells Bill that he should quitclaim a half interest in his home to her in order to protect their child if Bill should die. Trusting Katherine because she is an attorney, Bill quitclaims his interest, only later to discover that she lied about the law. Katherine also opens numerous credit cards by forging Bill's name and makes false allegations that cause him to be investigated for embezzlement. Bill and Katherine divorce. Bill sues Katherine for fraud, breach of fiduciary duty, defamation, and malicious abuse of process. Katherine argues that interspousal immunity bars these claims. Will she prevail? ____________________

44. Wife and Husband have been married for 20 years and have three children. They have grown apart and have not had intercourse for several years. Wife decides to attend art classes at a nearby college. She takes an apartment there to allow her more time to study. She considers this a "trial" separation. She establishes a relationship with Winston, a wealthy insurance salesman, telling him that she is divorced. When Husband discovers the relationship, he sues Winston for alienation of affections. Is Husband likely to be successful? ____________________

Answers

40. No. The marital communications privilege applies to communications made between the spouses. However, these spouses, although still technically married, were living separate lives with no reasonable expectation of reconciliation (in other words, the couple was "permanently separated"), so there was no marital harmony to promote.

41. Probably. Because the privilege against adverse spousal testimony vests in the Wife, and the privilege as to confidential marital communications vests in either spouse, Wife will likely prevail as to both assertions. In addition, courts have held that the privileges apply so long as the Husband and Wife are still married, even if a divorce is pending.

42. No. According to the majority approach among the federal courts, Husband will be liable for damages to Wife for violating the federal wiretapping statute Title III. His defenses do not absolve him from liability under the federal statute.

43. No. Katherine's claim of interspousal immunity will be rejected because most jurisdictions have abolished the doctrine. The doctrine also probably would be inapplicable because the tort claims here, although arising in the marriage, were not related to the marital relationship itself — unlike claims of unfaithfulness or intentional infliction of emotional distress. Nor will the court be concerned with the policy of preservation of marital harmony (where the couple is now divorced and the claims do not rely on the nature of the marital relationship).

44. No. To recover for alienation of affections, Husband must prove: a valid marriage, defendant's wrongful conduct, an ensuing loss of consortium, and a causal connection between defendant's conduct and plaintiff's loss. Although Husband can prove the validity of the marriage, he will have difficulty establishing the other elements. Winston had no intention to alienate Wife's affections because he believed she was divorced. Husband's loss of consortium, as well as the loss of Wife's affections, predated Winston's relationship with Wife and was not attributable to Winston's actions.

Further, most courts have abolished this cause of action because it is based on outdated views of marriage and divorce.

Exam Tips on BEING MARRIED

Regulation of Roles and Responsibilities

- **Identifying the marital role or responsibility at issue:** First determine the nature of the controversy: support, names, employment, health care, or parenting. Does the issue involve civil or criminal law?

- **Duty of support:** First determine if the question involves support rights and obligations ***during*** marriage. If so, you will need to discuss the ***family privacy doctrine***, i.e., the common-law doctrine of nonintervention in an ongoing marriage.

  - Check if the disputed item involves ***necessaries***. Define necessaries. If necessaries are at issue, you will need to discuss the common-law necessaries doctrine. Determine ***who*** is initiating the suit — a spouse or third party (such as a creditor) — and on whose behalf (spouse, child).

  - Be on the lookout for any ***constitutional issues*** (gender-based obligations that might violate equal protection doctrine). Be sure to discuss modern responses to equal protection problems (i.e., expansion of liability, or the imposition of primary liability on the serviced spouse and secondarily, from the other spouse).

- **Names:** Identify the naming dispute. Does it involve a ***married woman's name***, a dispute over a ***domestic partner's surname***, or a dispute over a ***child's surname***? Clarify ***who*** is initiating suit (i.e., a married woman, a governmental entity, the other parent of a child). Determine whether the suit involves ***retention*** or ***resumption*** of a surname or the ***adoption of a new surname***. Discuss the two ***methods*** of name change (common-law and statutory). If the question involves a divorced woman, discuss the special statutes that authorize divorced women to restore their former surnames.

  - If the dispute concerns a child's surname, discuss the ***prevailing standard*** to resolve the dispute (the best interests of the child). Take into account all relevant factors in determining which surname would be in the child's best interests. **Tip**: Be sure to look for any ***constitutional challenges*** to naming restrictions, such as the right of the state to restrict parental choice in children's surname selection. Discuss the judicial views on whether parents have a ***fundamental right*** of privacy to confer a surname on a child and also discuss ***equal protection*** issues in cases favoring one parent's right to name a child.

- **Domicile:** Be sure to look for any "lurking" issues regarding the domicile of the parties. If the question involves the domicile of a married woman, explain the ***common-law*** rule, the ***Restatement (Second) of Conflict of Laws*** view, and the ***modern view*** that now permits a man or woman to acquire a domicile of choice.

- **Employment:** Look for issues of a ***married woman's common-law disability*** and ***antinepotism policies***. If you spot an issue regarding an antinepotism policy, be sure to explain the nature of the policy (does it prevent one spouse from being employed by the other spouse's employer, or is it broader and prevents employment of any "relative"?). Identify the ***business rationale*** for such policies. Be sure to determine if the common business rationale is applicable to the facts at hand.
    - If an antinepotism policy is being challenged, discuss all possible grounds of attack: ***federal*** (constitutional and Title VII) and ***state***. In terms of federal constitutional issues, be sure to discuss the ***fundamental right to marry***. For ***Title VII***, be sure to explain that Title VII does not prohibit discrimination based on marital status; therefore plaintiffs must raise claims under "disparate impact" analysis. In the latter cases, discuss the usual employers' defense of business necessity. For state issues, be sure to discuss ***state civil rights statutes*** prohibiting discrimination on the basis of marital status. Mention the ***split of opinion*** as to whether such statutes apply to no-spousal employment policies: Some states apply such statutes but other states narrowly interpret the statutes to bar only discrimination based on the status of being single, married, or divorced (and not to bar discrimination based on marriage to a particular individual).
- **Health care:** Determine if there is an issue regarding the ***duty to provide medical care to a spouse*** or if the issue concerns the ***termination of life support*** (by a spouse or other family member). If the former, discuss the spouse's ***common-law duty*** to provide medical care to the other. Determine if the injured spouse requested the other spouse not to provide care (because in such cases, the latter does not incur liability for the failure to provide care). If the issue is the termination of life support, discuss the applicability of state ***natural death legislation***. Be on the lookout for any constitutional issues (such as the right to die).
- **Parenting:** The primary issues here concern ***mandatory leave policies***, ***parental and family leave policies***, and the ***work-family conflict***.
    - Be sure to check for the applicability of federal legislation (Pregnancy Discrimination Act, the Family and Medical Leave Act, Title VII). Recall that the PDA does not provide affirmative protection for pregnant women, but only guarantees equal treatment between pregnant women and other disabled workers. Recall, too, that the FMLA has its limitations: unpaid leave, traditional definitions of family members (only recently liberalized).
- **Criminal and tort law:** Identify whether the question concerns issues of criminal and/or tort law. For crimes involving spouses, look for issues of ***testimonial privileges***, ***wiretapping***, ***marital rape***, and ***property offenses***.
    - If the question involves testimonial privileges, be sure to mention that ***two*** possible privileges exist (confidential marital communications and spousal communications made in the presence of third parties).
    - Identify which privilege is at issue because different rules apply. Discuss the impact of the United States Supreme Court's ***Trammel decision*** on the privilege regarding spousal communications in the presence of third parties (leaving intact the confidential marital communications privilege). Remember that *Trammel* applies to criminal proceedings in federal courts (although the case has influenced state court proceedings).

- ☞ If the question involves wiretapping, be sure to point out the ***source of wiretapping liability*** (Title III of the Omnibus Crime Control Act) that provides for civil and criminal liability. Note the ***modern trend*** in federal courts to impose liability for spousal wiretapping in the home.

- ☞ Determine whether the question involves marital rape. Explain the ***marital rape exemption*** (exempting husbands from the crime of rape of their wives). Discuss the ***transition*** from the common-law rule to the modern trend (to abolish or limit the exemption). Point out that the marital rape exemption is not defunct.

☛ **Tort issues:** Identify all possible tort issues. Are there tort actions against ***third parties*** or ***interspousal*** actions? If the claims are against third parties, are there legal actions for ***alienation of affections***, ***criminal conversation***, and/or ***loss of consortium***? Be sure to discuss the ***elements*** of each claim and determine if they apply to the facts. Explore whether the defendant has any defenses. Be sure to point out the difference between criminal conversation and alienation of affections (the former requires that the defendant have sexual intercourse with the plaintiff's spouse). For loss of consortium, determine the time of the injury. Be sure that it occurred during the marriage (i.e., there may be problems with recovery if the injuries occurred pre- or post-marriage).

- ☞ If the action is an interspousal tort claim, determine whether the interspousal immunity doctrine applies. Be sure to explain the doctrine (as barring tort actions between husbands and wives), its rationale, and jurisdictions' early attempts to mitigate its harshness.

☛ **Domestic violence:** Determine if the claims involve ***civil*** and/or ***criminal*** actions. Note the ***common-law rule*** of moderate chastisement and point out the ***family privacy*** doctrine that led to a policy of judicial nonintervention in an ongoing marriage.

- ☞ If there is an issue of a battered wife who killed her husband, be sure to discuss the admissibility of evidence of ***battered woman's syndrome***. Define the syndrome and discuss the rationale for the admission of such evidence. Discuss the requirements for admissibility. Mention the ***different standards*** for admissibility of novel scientific evidence (***Frye***, ***Daubert***).

- ☞ Determine whether the plaintiff is seeking remedies against the ***batterer*** or against a ***governmental entity*** (i.e., for failure to protect battered women). If the latter, examine whether the victim can make a claim of the special relationship requirement (that the police owe victim a duty because a special relationship exists such as caused by their knowledge of a protective order).

- ☞ Be sure to mention the limitation on the special relationship doctrine of ***DeShaney v. Winnebago***.

- ☞ Examine the question for possible ***federal*** issues regarding VAWA or firearms restrictions. If the issue involves VAWA, determine whether the claim involves the VAWA provision regarding the private cause of action for victims of gender-motivated crimes that the Supreme Court declared unconstitutional in ***Morrison***. If the question raises ***firearms restrictions*** on batterers, be sure to discuss the constitutionality of the restriction under *Heller*.

CHAPTER 4

NONTRADITIONAL FAMILIES

ChapterScope

This chapter addresses the legal regulation of nontraditional family forms as well as the changing legal meaning of the term "family." Here are a few of the key principles covered in this chapter:

- **Traditional definition of the family:** The traditional definition of the family was limited to relationships based on a ***ceremonially initiated marriage, consanguinity,*** and/or ***adoption***.
- **Modern definition:** With the decline of the traditional nuclear family, many people now choose ***nontraditional*** family forms, such as ***cohabitation, domestic partnerships, communal arrangements***, and ***extended families***.
- **Extended families:** The Supreme Court has held that the constitutional right to ***family privacy*** applies to extended families (i.e., those based on blood relationships that extend beyond the traditional nuclear family) and enables them to live together.
- **Communal families:** The Supreme Court has held that communal families (of unrelated persons) have ***no fundamental rights to association or privacy***.
- **Unmarried couples:** The traditional legal response to unmarried couples (opposite-sex and same-sex) was ***punitive***, based on the state's desire to uphold moral standards. Today, the Supreme Court has held that the constitutional ***right to privacy*** protects the individual against state interference in private sexual conduct between consenting adults (*Lawrence v. Texas*).
- Moreover, in ***contract*** theory, according to the majority rule, unmarried partners ***may enter into express agreements***. In ***tort law***, however, ***courts are divided*** about permitting cohabitants the same legal rights as traditional family members. In many jurisdictions, cohabitants (opposite-sex and same-sex) also face discrimination in terms of employment, housing, medical care, and inheritance.
- **Same-sex marriage and domestic partnership regulation:** Same-sex marriage is valid in a few jurisdictions (i.e., Connecticut, District of Columbia, Iowa, Massachusetts, New Hampshire, and Vermont). In addition, a few states have domestic partnership legislation that confers on domestic partners varying degrees of benefits that are provided to married couples.

I. INTRODUCTION

A. **Background:** The traditional nuclear family, consisting of a husband and wife and their co-resident children, is on the decline. Currently, only one in four families fits the traditional model. The decline is attributable, in part, to the rising incidence of divorce, a change in sexual mores (i.e., the decreasing stigma of sexual relations outside marriage), and widespread disillusionment with the institutions of marriage and the family.

B. Types of nontraditional families: Many people now reside in nontraditional families. Such families include: quasi-marital relationships (such as opposite-sex cohabitants or same-sex partners), and communal arrangements. Extended families are another family form that varies from the nuclear family.

C. Legal recognition: The law confers legal recognition on some nontraditional families for some purposes. This chapter explores the extent to which the legal system treats members of nontraditional families similarly to, or differently from, members of traditional family units. The chapter, thereby, sheds light on just what is meant, in legal policy, by the term "family."

II. EXTENDED FAMILIES

A. Nature of the constitutional protection for the extended family: To a limited extent, the Constitution protects the freedom of family members to choose to live together as an ***extended family***. An extended family consists of those members who are related to each other more remotely than the parent-child dyad (e.g., grandparents, aunts, and uncles).

Example: Mrs. Moore (Plaintiff) lives with her son (Dale Sr.) and two grandsons (Dale Jr. and John Moore Jr.). The grandsons are cousins rather than brothers (one grandson is Dale Sr.'s child, the other grandson is Plaintiff's son John's child). A city housing ordinance limits occupancy of a dwelling to members of a "single family." As defined, the term fails to include Plaintiff's extended family. Specifically, the ordinance permits a head of household to live with one dependent child and that child's dependent children (i.e., it would have permitted Mrs. Moore to live with Dale Sr. plus Dale Sr.'s child but not with her other grandson). The city sends Plaintiff a notice that she is violating the ordinance and directs her to comply. When she refuses, she is charged with a criminal offense. She argues that the ordinance violates her right to due process. The United States Supreme Court concurs, reasoning that the ordinance fails to serve the stated governmental interests (i.e., prevention of overcrowding, minimizing traffic and parking congestion, and avoiding an undue financial burden on the school system). Reasoning that the tradition of the extended family is rooted in history, the Court concludes that the extended family is equally deserving of constitutional protection as the traditional family. *Moore v. East Cleveland*, 431 U.S. 494 (1977).

B. Scope of the constitutional protection for the extended family: Although the Constitution provides limited protection to the extended family from state interference, it does not require a state to provide certain *governmental benefits* to assist members of extended families to maintain residence together.

Example: Sheri Lipscomb, a disabled child, is removed from her home because of parental abuse and neglect. Her aunt and uncle agree to serve as foster parents. Oregon law provides for foster care for a child who is in the jurisdiction of the juvenile court because of abuse or neglect. However, the state provides foster care benefits only to nonrelative foster parents. Sheri's aunt and uncle, fearing they will have to give up Sheri because of their inability to provide financially for her medical care, challenge the state policy of excluding relatives from foster care payments as a violation of equal protection. The federal appellate court holds that the state policy is constitutional (based on rational basis review) because it promotes the legitimate state purpose of maximizing foster care resources. The court refuses to hold the policy subject to strict scrutiny, declining to recognize close relatives as a suspect class for equal protection analysis (thereby following *Lyng v. Castillo*, 477 U.S. 635 (1986)). The court also reasons that the policy does not impinge on the exercise of the plaintiff's fundamental constitutional right to live with extended family members. The court distinguishes *Moore*, *supra*, by saying that "the existence of a negative right to freedom from governmental interference, however, does not dictate the recognition of an affirmative right on the part of foster children to be placed by the state with relatives." *Lipscomb v. Simmons*, 962 F.2d 1374, 1378 (9th Cir. 1992). (Note that subsequent federal legislation, discussed in Chapter 9 *infra*, has adopted various reforms of kinship foster care.)

III. COMMUNAL FAMILY

A. **Federal protection (or lack thereof) for the communal family:** In contrast to the legal recognition accorded to the extended family for zoning purposes, the Supreme Court refuses to provide similar protection to the communal family.

Example: Six unrelated students at Stony Brook rent a house together in the village of Belle Terre on Long Island. A village ordinance restricts land use to "single family" dwellings and defines single family as "persons related by blood, adoption or marriage, living and cooking together as a single housekeeping unit," and prohibits more than two unrelated persons to reside together. A communal resident challenges the constitutionality of the zoning ordinance as an interference on the right to travel and the freedom of association. The United States Supreme Court upholds the constitutionality of the statute, maintaining that it does not interfere with the right to travel or with any fundamental right. The Court reasons that the statute bears a rational relationship to the permissible state objectives of limiting congestion and noise and promoting family values. *Village of Belle Terre v. Boraas*, 416 U.S. 1 (1974).

B. **State protection for the communal family**

1. **Generally:** Communal families have received more favorable treatment in zoning challenges based on state, rather than federal, constitutional law.

Example: A group of 12 adults rent a ten-bedroom, six-bath house on a one-acre lot in Santa Barbara owned by Ms. Adamson (who also resides in the house). The occupants include a business woman, graduate biochemistry student, real estate broker, lawyer, and others. The city brings an action to enforce a municipal zoning ordinance that restricts the number of unrelated individuals (i.e., unrelated by blood, marriage, or adoption) who may live in single-family zones to "a group . . . not to exceed five (5) persons . . . living together as a single housekeeping unit." The court grants the city a preliminary injunction and restraining order. Three residents of the house appeal, arguing that they regard their group as "a family" and that they consist of "a single housekeeping unit" because they share expenses, rotate chores, and eat evening meals together. The California Supreme Court holds that unrelated persons have a constitutional right (based on the state constitution's right of privacy) to live with others who are not related by blood, marriage, or adoption. The court finds that the city failed to demonstrate that a compelling state interest justifies its restriction on communal living (i.e., reasoning that the assumption that groups of unrelated persons cause an immoral environment for families with children is not legitimate). *City of Santa Barbara v. Adamson*, 610 P.2d 436 (Cal. 1980).

2. **Requirement: Familial-like:** In order to merit legal recognition in some jurisdictions, communal families must evidence certain familial-like criteria. However, courts differ as to the importance they attach to the various criteria that qualify a group as a "single family." This approach leads to inconsistent legal treatment.

   Example: Ten unrelated state college students rent a house together in the Borough of Glassboro. The town's zoning ordinance limits the occupancy of residences to families, defined as: "one or more persons occupying a dwelling unit as a single non-profit housekeeping unit, who are living together as a stable and permanent living unit, being a traditional family unit or the functional equivalency thereof." When the town seeks an injunction against the students' use and occupancy of the house, the students challenge the ordinance. The New Jersey Supreme Court declines to consider the constitutional issues, but affirms the factual finding that the students' occupancy constitutes a single housekeeping unit because they eat together, share household chores, pay expenses from a common fund, and plan to remain together for three years (thereby satisfying the requirement of a "stable and permanent living unit"). The court adds that the purpose of noise regulation and regulation of socially disruptive behavior can be achieved by other means than land use restrictions. *Borough of Glassboro v. Vallorosi*, 568 A.2d 888 (N.J. 1990).

   Example: A nonprofit corporation negotiates the purchase of a house in Brewer, Maine, to serve as a group home for retarded persons and a few employees. The city's zoning ordinance restricts single-family residential uses to "a collective body of persons doing their own cooking and living together . . . as a separate housekeeping unit . . . based upon birth, marriage or other domestic bond as distinguished from a group occupying a boarding house, lodging house, club, fraternity or hotel." The nonprofit corporation appeals the denial of an occupancy permit based on the group's failure to qualify as a single-family use, contending that the purpose of the group home is to create a family environment for the residents. The court holds that the denial of the occupancy permit was appropriate because the group home lacks certain familial-like qualities. Specifically, the facility employs rotating staff, thereby lacking any permanent residential authority figure analogous to a parent or parents. The average stay of residents is short, thereby failing to demonstrate cohesiveness and permanence. Finally, the staff, rather than residents, is responsible for meal preparation and the operation of the household. As a result, the court reasons that the facility is more like a club, boarding house, or fraternity rather than a traditional family. *Penobscot Area Housing Dev. Corp. v. City of Brewer*, 434 A.2d 14 (Me. 1981).

IV. UNMARRIED COHABITANTS (OPPOSITE-SEX AND SAME-SEX COUPLES)

State courts also regulate the relationships between cohabitants, between cohabitants and third parties, and between cohabitants and the state. The legal treatment accorded these family members often depends on the purpose for which, or the context in which, their families are being regulated. In short, the law confers recognition on some nontraditional families but not others, and on these families for some purposes but not others.

A. Criminal sanctions for sexual conduct: Traditional response: Traditionally, the law regarded with disfavor unmarried couples who were living together. The traditional legal response was the imposition of criminal sanctions for such "misconduct" in the form of penalties for fornication, cohabitation, and sodomy.

B. Zoning: Zoning ordinances and the First Amendment: Some state courts extend the Supreme Court's refusal to recognize communal families by the denial of constitutional protection to unmarried couples for zoning purposes.

Example: Joan Horn and E. Terence Jones, an unmarried couple, purchase a seven-bedroom, four-bath home in a single-family residential zone for themselves and the children of their prior marriages. The city zoning ordinance restricts family members to those related by blood, marriage, or adoption. When the city seeks to enjoin the defendants' violation of the zoning ordinance, defendants argue that the ordinance interferes with their freedom of association. They contend that their household is the "functional equivalent" of a traditional family. Relying on *Belle Terre, supra*, the court upholds the zoning ordinance as constitutional because it bears a rational relationship to a permissible governmental purpose of regulating land use for family needs. The court refuses to find that the restriction implicates a fundamental interest or a suspect classification. Further, the court follows other jurisdictions in concluding that such ordinances prevent the erosion of values associated with traditional family life and preserve the governmental interest in marriage and the integrity of the biological family. *City of Ladue v. Horn*, 720 S.W.2d 745 (Mo. Ct. App. 1986). (Note that the case was decided prior to *Lawrence v. Texas* which casts doubt on its holding.)

C. Housing: States have made much progress in terms of remedying housing discrimination against unmarried couples (opposite-sex and same-sex couples).

1. **Occupancy rights to a rent-controlled apartment:** In a landmark decision, New York has recognized the rights of gay partners to be free from housing discrimination. In reaching its holding, the New York court of appeals adopted a broad functional definition of family.

   Example: Miguel Braschi resides with his gay partner, Leslie Blanchard, in a rent-controlled New York City apartment for 11 years. Following Blanchard's death, the building owner notifies Braschi that because Blanchard was the tenant of record, Braschi must vacate the apartment. New York City Rent and Eviction Regulations provide protection from eviction to either the "surviving spouse of the deceased tenant or some other member of the deceased tenant's family." Braschi seeks to enjoin the owner from evicting him. Although the term "family" is not defined by the code, Braschi maintains that he qualifies as a member of Blanchard's family within the meaning of the regulations. The court declares that the term "family," as used in the rent-control laws, should not be limited to marital or adoptive relationships. Legal protection against sudden eviction should "find its foundation in the reality of family life." Courts should determine entitlement based on an examination of the parties' relationship, including (but not limited to):

   - the exclusivity and longevity of that relationship;
   - the level of emotional and financial commitment;
   - the manner in which the parties conduct their lives and hold themselves out; and
   - the reliance the parties place on each other for daily family services.

The court finds that Braschi demonstrated a likelihood of success on the merits because of the parties' lengthy relationship, their being regarded by family and friends as spouses, and their emotional and financial commitment to each other. *Braschi v. Stahl Assocs.*, 543 N.E.2d 49 (N.Y. Ct. App. 1989).

2. **Occupancy rights under state nondiscrimination statutes in the face of a landlord's First Amendment claims:** Landlords sometimes refuse to rent to unmarried couples alleging that such rentals would violate landlords' religious beliefs. Such claims have met with varying success. Although courts occasionally permit landlords to discriminate on religious or moral grounds, many courts refuse to recognize an exemption for landlords from state nondiscrimination statutes on this basis.

   Example: A woman landlord refuses to rent an apartment to an unmarried couple on the basis that she would be committing a sin by renting to persons who would be engaging in nonmarital sex on her property. The state fair housing agency rules that she is discriminating against prospective tenants on the basis of marital status, in violation of state housing law. The landlord appeals. The state supreme court affirms the state agency decision that the landlord's refusal to rent to the unmarried couple violated the state fair housing law and also rules that the federal Religious Freedom Restoration Act does not exempt the landlord from the application of the state anti-discrimination statute. *Smith v. Fair Employment & Hous. Comm'n.,* 913 P.2d 909 (Cal. 1996).

D. **Tort law:** Today, jurisdictions are divided about recognition of the legal rights of cohabitants in the tort context that are available to members of traditional families. Some jurisdictions permit cohabitants to recover in tort for injuries to each other by third parties, whereas other jurisdictions refuse to do so. In the latter jurisdictions, an unmarried partner does not have a claim either for loss of consortium or for negligent infliction of emotional distress arising from an injury by a third party to the other partner.

Example: Catrina Graves has been living with Brett Ennis for seven years. The couple is engaged to marry. One day Brett is riding his motorcycle while Graves is following behind in a car. Defendant Frank Estabrook fails to yield at a stop sign, colliding with Brett's motorcycle. Catrina views the accident and runs to Brett's aid. She stays by his side while he is being treated. Brett dies the next day. Catrina files a complaint for negligent infliction of emotional distress. The New Hampshire Supreme Court holds that her complaint supports such a claim because plaintiff was a bystander who witnessed the accident and also because she was engaged in a stable, enduring, substantial, and mutually supportive relationship with the cohabitant-victim. *Graves v. Estabrook*, 818 A.2d 1255 (N.H. 2003).

Example: David Bozeman dies of lung cancer caused by exposure to silica at his former job. Ruby, his live-in girlfriend, sues his former employer for his injuries and wrongful death. The company argues that Ruby lacks standing because she does not qualify under any of the three categories of standing under the state statute: she is not David's "personal representative," a "listed relative," or an "interested party." The court agrees, finding that Ruby lacks standing because she was not appointed personal representative prior to the commencement of the suit, not a listed relative because cohabitants are not considered "relatives" under the statute, and not an "interested party" because she did not have any legally recognized relationship with David. *Clark Sand Co. v. Kelley*, 2010 WL 653763 (Miss. 2010).

Note that jurisdictions are split regarding whether *same-sex* partners are permitted to sue for wrongful death. Compare *Smith v. Knoller*, No. 319532, Slip Op. (Cal. Super. Ct., Aug. 9, 2001) (later liberalized by statute), with *Charron v. Amaral*, 889 N.E.2d 946 (Mass. 2008).

E. **Contract law: Unmarried couples' rights inter se:** The law regulates and protects marital parties' rights (e.g., support and property rights) upon dissolution. Historically, this legal protection has not been available to members of unmarried couples. This reluctance has been altered somewhat by case law in the last several decades. The current willingness to accord protection to the rights of members of unmarried couples in cases of disputes with each other (i.e., in contract law) stands in stark contrast to the law's reluctance in some jurisdictions to recognize the rights of unmarried couples vis-à-vis third parties (i.e., in tort law).

1. **Traditional rule: Refusal to enforce agreements:** Under the traditional rule, courts refuse to enforce agreements between members of unmarried couples (formerly termed ***meretricious relationships***). Courts hold such agreements are invalid as contrary to public policy (similar to contracts for prostitution). The rationale for the policy was the deterrence of immorality ("living in sin").

   Changing sexual mores (i.e., deceasing stigma of sexual relations outside of marriage) and increasing attention to the rights of women (who appear to be unfairly treated by the traditional rule) have contributed to reform. Currently, jurisdictions adopt one of three approaches to recognition of the rights of unmarried partners:

   - some continue to adhere to the traditional rule and refuse to recognize such claims based on public policy grounds (minority view);
   - others recognize claims if based on an express agreement;
   - still others recognize claims if based on express or implied agreements.

2. **Minority view: Traditional rule:** Some courts continue to adhere to the traditional rule and refuse to recognize the rights of nonmarital parties to enter into contracts with each other about property rights.

   Example: Victoria lives with Robert for 15 years. When Victoria becomes pregnant with their first child, Robert tells her that no formal ceremony is necessary for them to be husband and wife. They notify their relatives that they are married and hold themselves out as spouses. Victoria later alleges that in reliance on Robert's promise to share his property with her, she contributed to his professional education and assisted him in his career of pedodontia. When Robert ends the relationship, Victoria files suit, requesting an equal share of all property accumulated during the relationship. The Illinois Supreme Court holds that contracts between unmarried cohabitants are unenforceable as contrary to public policy. The court reasons that the negative impact of the recognition of such contracts on society and the institution of marriage outweighs the rights of the parties. *Hewitt v. Hewitt*, 394 N.E.2d 1204 (Ill. 1979).

3. **Majority view: Modern judicial approaches**

   a. **Express agreements**

      i. **Statement of the rule:** Unmarried partners may enter into express contracts with each other regarding the ownership of property acquired during their relationship. Under this rule, the contractual rights of nonmarital parties are similar to those of spouses.

ii. Limitation: Illicit consideration: A court will not enforce a contract between nonmarital partners, however, if illicit sexual relations form part of the consideration of the agreement.

Example: Plaintiff and Defendant live together for over 20 years. They have two children. They file joint tax returns. When the relationship ends, the woman seeks $250,000 damages. She alleges, first, the existence of a contract based on her provision of domestic duties and business services at Defendant's request, her expectation of payment, and Defendant's acceptance of her services knowing she expected compensation. Second, she claims that she and Defendant entered into a partnership agreement whereby she agreed to perform domestic and business services and, in return, Defendant agreed to support and maintain her. Affirming the order granting Defendant's motion to dismiss, the New York Court of Appeals holds that Plaintiff failed to show an express contract (reasoning that she performed voluntarily) and finds that an implied contract cannot be implied from this "partnership agreement." Clarifying the law, the court holds that express contracts of unmarried couples are enforceable provided that they are not based on unlawful consideration. However, implied contracts for personal services are not enforceable because such services often are rendered gratuitously in intimate relationships. The court points to policy reasons for its reluctance to recognize implied contracts (fear of fraud inherent in claims for contractual damages) as well as the difficulty of proof. *Morone v. Morone*, 413 N.E.2d 1154 (N.Y. 1980).

iii. Limitation: Cohabitation requirement: Another limitation is that the parties must have actually cohabited, although courts differ as to whether part-time cohabitation suffices.

Example: Attorney Johnnie Cochran begins a relationship with Patricia in 1966, at a time when he is still married to his first wife. The couple has a son, buys a house together and places title in both their names as joint tenants. Johnnie also owns another home. They never live together full-time, but Johnnie stays with Patricia and their son two to four nights per week, keeps clothes there, and eats meals there. Johnnie divorces his wife, but never marries Patricia. Nevertheless, he holds himself out as her husband during some of their 25-year relationship. When Patricia and Johnnie separate, she claims that Johnnie promised to support her for the rest of her life. He contends that because they never cohabited, any alleged agreement would not be subject to *Marvin* (discussed *infra*). The appellate court holds that a triable issue of fact exists as to whether the couple "cohabited," precluding summary judgment, based on their part-time cohabitation over the 17-year period, holding themselves out as husband and wife, and joint ownership of a home where they spent "family time." The court explains that the cohabitation requirement may be satisfied in appropriate cases by living arrangements that are less than full time. *Cochran v. Cochran*, 106 Cal. Rptr. 2d 899 (Ct. App. 2001).

Example: An 85-year-old woman who was involved in a 70-year extramarital affair files suit against her lover (who dies while the suit is pending), claiming that he promised to support her for the rest of her life. The appellate court dismisses, concluding that cohabitation (i.e., setting up a household together) is an indispensable element of a palimony claim. The court finds that the woman failed to establish the requisite cohabitation because, although the couple saw each other regularly, the man stayed overnight at her home only "periodically" and she never moved into the condo that he purchased for them. Moreover, at various times during the affair, each partner was married to another and had children with their respective spouses. *Levine v. Konvitz*, 890 A.2d 354 (N.J. Super. Ct. App. Div. 2006).

b. Express and implied agreements

i. Rule: Some courts recognize ***both*** express and implied agreements between nonmarital cohabitants. Recognition of implied agreements becomes important because nonmarital parties often fail to have express agreements about their support and/or property rights.

Implied contracts may be either implied-in-fact or implied-in-law. In an implied-in-fact agreement, the court infers contractual intent from the parties' conduct. On the other hand, a court imposes implied-in-law remedies to prevent unjust enrichment (i.e., the parties' intent is irrelevant).

ii. *Marvin* case: The landmark case of *Marvin v. Marvin* recognized the rights of nonmarital partners to make express and implied agreements.

Marvin v. Marvin: Michelle Triola Marvin lives with actor Lee Marvin from 1964 until Lee ends the relationship in 1970. (Lee is legally married to another woman for part of that time.) Michelle and Lee never marry, although Michelle changes her surname legally to Marvin. Upon dissolution of the relationship, Plaintiff claims that she and Defendant entered into an oral agreement whereby they agreed to share all earnings and property and to hold themselves out as husband and wife. She further alleges that she agreed to give up her lucrative singing career, and to render services to Defendant as companion, housekeeper, and cook in return for his promise to provide for her financial support for the rest of her life.

Plaintiff asks the court to determine her support rights and rights to the property held in Defendant's name (approximately $1 million in real and personal property, including motion picture rights earned during the relationship), and to impose a constructive trust on half of the accumulated property (i.e., treating her as if she were a legal spouse in a community property jurisdiction).

Defendant raises four arguments:

- the court should not enforce contracts between nonmarital partners because such agreements are contrary to public policy as immoral;
- the alleged contract also violates public policy because it impairs the community property rights of his first wife (from whom he was not yet divorced);
- enforcement of any agreement is barred by the Statute of Frauds requiring contracts for marriage settlements to be in writing; and
- enforcement is barred because the legislature has abolished actions for breach of promise to marry.

The trial court grants Defendant's motion for judgment on the pleadings.

Initially, Plaintiff's complaint asserts only an express contract. She subsequently asks, and receives, permission to amend her complaint to address the issue of her property rights in the absence of an express contract. *Marvin v. Marvin*, 557 P.2d 106 (Cal. 1976) [hereafter *Marvin I*].

The California Supreme Court holds that express agreements between nonmarital partners will be enforced except to the extent that such contracts rest on unlawful consideration. The court, in reversing the trial court, reasons that adult cohabitants are as competent as other persons to contract regarding their property rights. The court noted that changing social mores dictate imposition of a standard that is not based on an abandoned moral code.

Addressing Defendant's arguments (above), the California Supreme Court responds:

- agreements between nonmarital partners fail only to the extent that they rest on illicit sexual services (any severable portion will be enforced);
- the actor's first wife's rights are not impaired because her rights were fixed by her divorce action (in which she had the opportunity to assert her rights);
- the contract at issue is not a contract for a marriage settlement; and
- agreements to pool earnings and to provide support are not barred by abolition of actions for breach of promise to marry.

In the absence of an express agreement, the court holds that implied contracts (both implied-in-fact and implied-in-law) between cohabitants are enforceable to protect the fulfillment of the parties' reasonable expectations. Courts may inquire into the conduct of the parties to fashion relief through a constructive trust, resulting trust, or quantum meruit.

c. Additional equitable remedies

i. Dictum of *Marvin I*: *Marvin I* also states, by way of dictum (see fn. 25 of the opinion), that courts may utilize their broad equitable powers to grant relief to nonmarital partners. Specifically, the court foresaw the possibility of "additional equitable remedies to protect the expectations of the parties . . . in cases in which existing remedies prove inadequate." *Marvin*, 557 P.2d at 122.

ii. *Marvin II*: Taking up the California Supreme Court's invitation (in *Marvin I*) to rely on broad equitable powers to fashion a remedy, the trial court, on remand, awards Michelle Marvin $104,000 as equitable relief. The court makes the award despite finding that: the parties had no express agreement; the Plaintiff suffered no damage from the relationship but, rather, benefited economically and socially therefrom; and the Defendant was not unjustly enriched as a result of the relationship or services performed by the Plaintiff. The monetary award was for the Plaintiff's economic rehabilitation until she could become self-supporting. The court fixed the award at the highest salary she had ever earned ($1,000/week). *Marvin v. Marvin*, 5 Fam. L. Rep. 3077 (1979) [hereafter *Marvin II*].

iii. *Marvin III*: In *Marvin III*, a California court of appeals reverses the trial court's award, on remand, of $104,000 to Michelle Marvin. The appellate court reasons that such an award is not based on traditional notions of equity. (The appellate court states that the trial court reached its award by determining only Plaintiff's need for the award and Defendant's ability to pay.) The appellate court determines, instead, that Defendant was not unjustly enriched nor did he commit any wrongful act. As a result, the award has no basis in law or equity. "A court of equity admittedly has broad powers, but it may not create totally new substantive rights under the guise of doing equity." *Marvin III*, 176 Cal. Rptr. 555, 558 (Ct. App. 1981).

Note: The trial court in *Marvin II* misinterpreted the California Supreme Court's call for the courts to use their broad equitable powers to fashion remedies. That is, *Marvin II* ruled for Plaintiff based on the court's interpretation of "equitable" as "fairness" rather than relying on traditional equitable principles handed down from the English Chancery courts. Specifically, for the remedy of "unjust enrichment," the Defendant must have committed a wrongful act (the "unjust"-ness) and the Defendant must have received a legally cognizable benefit (the "enrichment") that he should be forced to disgorge. Here, it is questionable whether Defendant committed any legally cognizable wrong or whether Defendant received a legally cognizable benefit (because Plaintiff also received benefits that must be offset).

d. Criticism of *Marvin:* Despite *Marvin*'s status as a landmark case recognizing cohabitants' rights, the case does not hold out much hope for relief if the parties are unable to prove an express agreement. (This follows from the holding of *Marvin III*.)

Several courts are critical of *Marvin*. One court points to the difficulty of proof of implied agreements, reasoning that *Marvin*'s rationale regarding such agreements is "conceptually so amorphous as practically to defy equitable enforcement . . . " *Morone*, 413 N.E.2d at 1157. The same court also criticizes *Marvin*'s recognition of implied agreements as being inconsistent with legislative abolition of common-law marriage. *Id.* Still another court rejects *Marvin*, arguing that regulation of the rights of nonmarital parties is better left to the legislature because of its "superior investigative and fact-finding facilities" to determine public policy. *Hewitt*, 394 N.E.2d at 1209.

i. Application of *Marvin* to same-sex couples: Some jurisdictions extend recognition of cohabitation contracts to same-sex partners, either through domestic partnership legislation or under a *Marvin* analysis that applies contractual remedies. In contrast, a few jurisdictions have enacted statutes that void any contracts between members of same-sex couples that relate to the privileges or obligations of marriage.

Example: Two men, residents of New York, enter into a same-sex relationship. During the relationship, Defendant gives Plaintiff expensive gifts, including automobiles and a ski house. The couple goes to Massachusetts to marry and then returns to New York. At that time, however, Massachusetts law permits members of same-sex couples to marry only if both are residents of Massachusetts. The couple later separate and execute a separation agreement (prepared by Defendant's attorney) that provides for the division of their property and also provides for a one-time payment to Plaintiff of $780,000. Following a New York court's decision to uphold the constitutionality of that state ban on same-sex marriage (*Hernandez v. Robles*, 805 N.Y.S.2d 354 (App. Div. 2005)), Defendant seeks a declaration that, as a matter of law, because the parties never validly married, the separation agreement was void and all property transferred thereunder must be returned to Defendant. Although finding the parties' marriage invalid under the laws of either New York or Massachusetts, the court refuses to rescind the separation agreement. The court explains that New York has long recognized the enforceability of express contracts between unmarried cohabitants provided that illegal consideration is not part of the agreement. *Gonzalez v. Green*, 831 N.Y.S.2d 856 (Sup. Ct. 2006).

F. Jurisdiction: Unmarried couples and the domestic relations exception to federal jurisdiction: The increasing frequency of *Marvin*-type "palimony" cases led to litigation concerning whether such cases should be heard in state or federal courts. Federal courts have jurisdiction in cases in which there exists diversity of citizenship (i.e., the parties are domiciliaries of different states) and a requisite amount in controversy.

1. **Traditional rule (pre–*Ankenbrandt v. Richards*):** Prior to *Ankenbrandt v. Richards*, 504 U.S. 689 (1992), federal courts refused to hear disputes such as palimony claims. Under the ***domestic relations exception to federal jurisdiction***, federal courts traditionally refuse to adjudicate family law matters, such as divorce, alimony, or custody, because such matters are more suitable for resolution by state courts.

   Example: Plaintiff institutes an action in state court claiming that Defendant breached his promise to provide her with support for her lifetime in return for her promise to live with him and provide him services. Because diversity of citizenship exists, Defendant removes the case to federal court. The district court, on its own motion, raises the issue whether the case should be remanded to state court based on the domestic relations exception to federal jurisdiction. The court questions whether palimony cases are more closely analogous to contract actions (which are more appropriate for federal jurisdiction) or to spousal property claims (which are more appropriate for resolution based on state law). The court determines that because these cases require judicial investigation into the support needs of the parties, and thereby implicate an important state interest, they are more appropriate for resolution by state, rather than federal, courts. *Anastasi v. Anastasi*, 544 F. Supp. 866 (D.N.J. 1982).

2. **Jurisdiction and unmarried couples' rights (post–*Ankenbrandt v. Richards*):** The Supreme Court narrowed the domestic relations exception to federal jurisdiction in *Ankenbrandt v. Richards*. *Ankenbrandt*, by limiting the domestic relations exception to the issuance of divorce, alimony, or custody decrees, permits federal courts to adjudicate a broader variety of disputes. (See discussion of *Ankenbrandt,* Chapter 5.) Post-*Ankenbrandt*, the assertion of federal court jurisdiction may depend on whether federal courts perceive cohabitants' claims as based more on contract law or domestic relations law. That is, federal courts may still refuse jurisdiction if they perceive cohabitants' disputes as quasi-marital status claims. *See, e.g., Johnson v. Thomas*, 808 F. Supp. 1316 (W.D. Mich. 1992) (holding that palimony-type action falls within the domestic relations exception to diversity jurisdiction because the function of a court is identical to that of a court in granting a divorce).

G. Employment: Unmarried opposite-sex, as well as same-sex, couples encounter discrimination from employers.

1. **Withdrawal of offer of employment or discharge:** In one celebrated case, a lesbian lost an offer of employment because her employer learned of her planned marriage to another woman.

   Example: Defendant-state Attorney General Bowers withdraws his offer of employment after he learns that Plaintiff Shahar plans to marry another woman. Plaintiff alleges violations of her rights to freedom of association, freedom of religion, equal protection, and due process. The Eleventh Circuit Court of Appeals vacates its earlier ruling that Plaintiff's right of association was protected, grants a rehearing en banc, and holds that Shahar's rights were not violated. The court first assumes that Plaintiff's right of intimate association encompasses the right to marry another woman (an assumption on which the court has "considerable doubt"). The court then determines that strict scrutiny is inappropriate and evaluates the Attorney General's decision by resort to the *Pickering* [*Pickering v. Bd. of Ed.*, 391 U.S. 563 (1968)] balancing test (that is applicable to scrutinize a government employer's decision to limit an employee's exercise of her right to free speech). The court considers the Attorney General's claims that Shahar's employment would impugn the credibility of his office, interfere with the ability to handle controversial matters such as enforcing the law against homosexual sodomy, and endanger working relationships within the department. The court concludes that the Attorney General's interests outweigh Shahar's associational rights. 224 F.3d 1097 (11th Cir. 1997), *cert. denied*, 522 U.S. 1049 (1998).

Note: Public employees have also been terminated because of cohabitation with members of the opposite sex. *See, e.g., Kukla v. Village of Antioch*, 647 F. Supp. 799 (N.D. Ill. 1986) (upholding the termination of a male and female police employee who are discharged because of their cohabitation). Note that such case law predates *Lawrence v. Texas*.

2. **Employment-related health benefits:** Increasingly, same-sex couples are seeking rights to employment-related health benefits for their partners. Many private employers voluntarily offer benefits to same-sex partners as part of the employee's health plan. However, some members of same-sex couples have been denied health benefits by public employers in jurisdictions that either do not recognize same-sex marriage or have express prohibitions against it.

   Example: Public employees and their same-sex partners seek a declaratory judgment that the Michigan state DOMA does not prohibit public employers from conferring health benefits on the same-sex partners of employees. The state supreme court finds that the state DOMA, recognizing marriage only between a man and a woman, precludes any state attempt to confer marriage-like benefits, including health benefits, on same-sex partners. *National Pride at Work, Inc. v. Governor of Michigan*, 748 N.W.2d 524 (Mich. 2008).

3. **Unemployment compensation:** Unmarried cohabitants may also be denied unemployment compensation if they leave their employment because of family-related reasons. The outcome may depend on a plaintiff's ability to prove that the relationship resembles a traditional family unit.

   Example: Plaintiff is engaged to, and lives with, the father of her infant. Prior to Plaintiff's scheduled return from a maternity leave, she chooses to leave her employment and relocate to New York in order to care for her partner's ill father. When Plaintiff is unable to find work there, she applies for unemployment insurance benefits. Her claim is denied based upon a determination that she voluntarily quit without "good cause." The court's analysis focuses on the meaning of "good cause." The court holds that Plaintiff has demonstrated good cause based on "compelling family circumstances." The evidence supports a finding that Plaintiff has established a family unit and relocated in order to preserve that unit. The court reasons that the presumption of good cause resulting from a valid marriage is not the exclusive means of demonstrating good cause based on compelling family circumstances. *MacGregor v. Unemployment Ins. Appeals Bd.*, 689 P.2d 453 (Cal. 1984).

Note: Under California's domestic partnership legislation, those persons who register as domestic partners are permitted to relocate without disqualification regarding unemployment benefits (Cal. Unemp. Ins. Code §1030 (1986 & Supp. 2010); §1256 (1986 & Supp. 2010)).

4. **Proposed federal legislation:** The proposed Employment Non-Discrimination Act of 2009 (ENDA), H.R. 3017, 111th Cong. §4(a)(2) (1st Sess. 2009) would extend Title VII of the 1964 Civil Rights Act to ban discrimination on the basis of sexual orientation or gender identity.

5. **Military discharge:** Gays and lesbians who are members of the armed forces have faced discharge if they revealed their sexual orientation. The military policy of "Don't Ask, Don't Tell" (DADT), Pub. L. No. 103-160, 10 U.S.C. §654 (2006), prohibited any person who is not heterosexual from disclosing his or her sexual orientation, or from speaking about any gay and lesbian relationship, while serving in the armed forces. Until recently, federal courts upheld the policy.

   Example: An Air Force reservist nurse who is suspended from duty on account of her sexual relationship with a civilian woman brings an action against the Air Force, Secretary of Defense, and others, challenging the constitutionality of the DADT policy and its application to her. The Ninth Circuit Court of Appeals holds that the military must meet a heightened standard of review based on *Lawrence v. Texas*. The case is remanded for a hearing on whether the nurse's discharge was justified based on an alleged disruption to unit cohesion and discipline. On remand, a federal district court rules that the application of DADT violated the nurse's substantive due process rights because the policy did not significantly further governmental interests in promoting military readiness, unit morale and cohesion (although the court added that the nurse failed to establish a violation of her *procedural* due process rights). *Witt v. U.S. Dept. of the Air Force*, 2010 WL 3732189 (W.D. Wash. 2010).

   Note: Congress voted in December 2010 to repeal the DADT policy.

H. **Inheritance law:** Courts traditionally *refuse* to permit a member of an unmarried couple (opposite-sex or same-sex) to inherit an *intestate share* of the deceased partner's estate. That is, courts refuse to treat unmarried cohabitants as legal spouses. (Intestacy refers to the state of dying without a will.) However, in a few modern jurisdictions, case law and domestic partnership legislation are modifying this result.

   Example: Frank Vasquez was involved in a long-term, stable, cohabiting relationship with the decedent, Robert Schwerzler. The two men acquire property together. At Schwerzler's death, Vasquez files a claim against the decedent's intestate estate, asserting that he is entitled to a share of the couple's community property — by analogy with Washington's law permitting division of community property upon dissolution of cohabitants' relationship. The Washington State Supreme Court holds that a genuine issue of material fact exists as to the type of relationship that existed between the life-partner and decedent and the particular property that was acquired during the course of the relationship which could be subject to equitable division (thereby implying that the court would apply community property laws subject to Vasquez's carrying his burden of proof). *Vasquez v. Hawthorne*, 33 P.3d 735 (Wash. 2001).

I. **Domestic violence:** All states have civil and criminal legislation addressing domestic violence, including provisions for protective orders, as well as orders allowing the victim exclusive possession of the home. Most statutes require that the abuser fall within the designated categories of persons who are either "cohabitants" or "household members" of the victim. However, some state DOMAs prohibit the state from providing marital rights to cohabitants.

Example: Michael Carswell is indicted on one count of domestic violence. He is prosecuted for domestic violence against someone who was "living as a spouse" with him. The alleged victim was a female who cohabited with, but was not married to, Carswell. He challenges the indictment, arguing that recognition of the cohabitation relationship violates the state DOMA that prohibits recognition of relationships of unmarried individuals who are living in situations that approximate marriage. The Ohio Supreme Court rejects his argument, finding that the domestic violence statute was intended to cover a broad class of persons, including cohabitants, and that prosecution for domestic violence does not confer the legal status of marriage on cohabitants. *State v. Carswell*, 871 N.E.2d 547 (Ohio 2007).

J. Modern legislative reform: Domestic partnership legislation: To date, several states and the District of Columbia have enacted a *range* of legal protections for domestic partners. Some states have legislation conferring rights on, specifically, "domestic partners." Other states have legislation protecting "civil unions" or "reciprocal beneficiaries."

Note that the legislation includes a range of protections, ranging from equal treatment as a legal spouse (but without the name "spouse" or "marriage") to more limited protection. Such legislation generally applies only to same-sex couples, although in limited circumstances, legal protections may apply to other relationships. For example, California recognizes as domestic partners those opposite-sex couples over age 62 who are eligible for Social Security benefits. And Hawaii recognizes relationships in which persons are "legally prohibited from marrying one another under state law" — a broad designation that potentially includes such family members as brothers, sisters, a widowed mother, and an unmarried son.

K. ALI *Principles*: Status-based approach to the recognition of cohabitants' rights upon dissolution: The ALI *Principles* adopt a ***status-based*** rather than a ***contractual*** approach to the dissolution of cohabitants' relationships. That is, if cohabitants satisfy the ALI requirements, they will be treated similarly to spouses at dissolution of the relationship in terms of, specifically, property division and "spousal" support (termed "compensatory payments").

According to the ALI provisions, parties who live together with their common child for a statutorily designated period of time (suggested: two years), are deemed domestic partners. Childless cohabitants are presumed to be domestic partners merely if they share a common household for a statutorily designated period of time (suggested: three years). Childless cohabitants who reside together for less than the statutorily designated period may still qualify (based on a rebuttable presumption) if one partner shows that they shared a common household and live together for "a significant period of time."

Note: The ALI equates both opposite-sex and same-sex couples to married couples for the above purposes.

Quiz Yourself on
NONTRADITIONAL FAMILIES

45. Roger lives with his gay partner, Paul, for several years until Paul's death. After Paul's death, Roger files an action against Paul's estate. Roger argues first that he should be treated as a "surviving spouse" in terms of the distribution of Paul's estate, and second, that he has a claim on an express oral agreement in which Roger was to provide services as "lover, companion, homemaker, traveling companion, housekeeper and cook" in exchange for Paul's promise to share their jointly accumulated property. Will Roger's arguments be successful? ____________________

46. Norma resides with her boyfriend Ben in California for several years. Although at one time they planned to marry, they never get around to taking the big step. When Ben decides to move to Washington state, Norma decides to quit her job to accompany him in order to preserve their relationship. When Norma is unable to find work in Washington, she files for unemployment compensation benefits. Her claim is denied on the basis that her leaving her employment to accompany her nonmarital partner does not constitute good cause. Norma appeals the denial of her claim. Will her appeal be successful? ____________________

47. Jonathan and Michael live together in a rent-controlled apartment in Blackacre for ten years until Michael dies of AIDS. Jonathan has been taking care of Michael for the last two years of Michael's illness. Both men's families are aware of their relationship. Because Michael was the named tenant on the lease, the landlord begins procedures to evict Jonathan in order to offer the apartment at a higher rent. Jonathan argues that he is a "family member" for the purpose of protection from eviction. The rent-control statute prohibits eviction following death of a "family member." However, the provision includes a restrictive definition that limits family members to husband, wife, son, daughter, step-relationships, nephew, niece, uncle, aunt, grandparents, grandchildren, and in-law relationships. When Jonathan challenges the eviction, will he be successful? ____________________

48. Lucy lives with Allen for approximately one year. They pool their earnings and expenses. They plan to marry but postpone the wedding date. In expectation of their marriage, they jointly purchase a home, taking title in both names. Again, they set the wedding date. Eight days before the wedding, Allen dies in an airplane crash, allegedly caused by defendant-aircraft company's negligence. Lucy sues the aircraft company to recover for wrongful death under a statute which permits "heirs" to bring the action. The statute defines "heirs" as those entitled to succeed to decedent's property based on the laws of intestacy. Will Lucy be successful? ____________________

49. Mr. and Mrs. Sears are employees of "Abbott House," a private nonprofit agency licensed by the state to care for neglected children. The Searses, their two children, and ten foster children (seven of whom are siblings) lease a home in an area of the city of White Plains. The parents and their children, natural and foster, live together as a family, and cook and eat all meals together. The city restricts land use to "single-family" dwellings, defining family as: "one or more persons limited to the spouse, parents, grandparents, grandchildren, sons, daughters, brothers, or sisters of the owner or the tenant or of the owner's spouse or tenant's spouse living together as a single housekeeping unit with kitchen facilities." The city seeks to enforce its zoning ordinance and to enjoin the Searses' use of their home in this way. When the Sears family challenges the city's actions, will they be successful? ____________________

Answers

45. No. In terms of Roger's claim for an intestate share of Paul's estate, courts traditionally refuse to permit a member of an unmarried couple (either opposite-sex or same-sex) to inherit an intestate share of the deceased partner's estate. However, Roger might be successful if he resides in one of the few modern jurisdictions in which state law modifies this result (via recognition of domestic partnerships). In terms of Roger's contract claim, under the traditional rule, courts refuse to recognize the rights of nonmarital partners to contract with each other about property rights. However, because of changing sexual mores and the increasing acceptance of cohabitation, a majority of courts now permit opposite-sex unmarried partners to enter into agreements. Roger would argue that gay and lesbian partners have the same rights as opposite-sex unmarried partners (under *Marvin, Gonzalez v. Green*, and *Lawrence v. Texas*) to enter into express contracts with each other about the ownership of property acquired during their relationship. Even if the court recognizes this argument, however, Roger would face another hurdle. Courts apply a limitation to the rule that recognizes express agreements between partners: A court will not enforce such a contract if the consideration for the agreement encompasses the provision of sexual services. This limitation stems from the fact that contracts for an illegal act are void. Because the provision of sexual services was inseparably part of the consideration for Roger and Paul's agreement (Roger was to provide services as "lover"), Roger's claim will be denied.

46. No. Norma's claim was properly denied because she left her employment voluntarily and without good cause. The act of leaving employment to accompany a nonmarital partner does not normally constitute legally sufficient good cause (absent statutory authority). The case is distinguishable from *MacGregor* because here the relationship did not manifest sufficient indicia of family-like characteristics, i.e., the couple did not have a child (as in *MacGregor*) nor did they have plans to marry. Also, because Norma and Ben do not qualify as domestic partners, they do not come within statutory protection that would allow them to relocate together without disqualification regarding unemployment benefits.

47. Perhaps. Jonathan should argue that he is protected despite the restrictive definition of family under the Blackacre rent-control provision. He should argue that a functional definition applies because the purpose of the restrictive provision is analogous to the broad rent-control ordinance at issue in *Braschi* — to protect family members from hardship and dislocation following death. Further, the two men's relationship meets the *Braschi* standard: manifesting a long duration, a high level of emotional commitment, care of each other's needs, and an openness about their relationship.

48. No. Because the action is purely statutory, Lucy will not qualify as a lawful spouse in order to bring an action for wrongful death purposes.

49. Probably. The group home manifests permanency and constitutes a single housekeeping unit within the meaning of the ordinance. The group home promotes family values and therefore is analogous to a traditional family unit. Further, case law would support recognition of the group home's claim because the home is more analogous to the extended family of *Moore* (the grandmother's purpose to care for her grandchildren) than to the transient college student commune of *Belle Terre*.

Exam Tips on *NONTRADITIONAL FAMILIES*

The central theoretical question here is the extent to which the legal system treats members of nontraditional families similarly to, or differently from, members of the traditional family. This question necessarily implicates the legal definition of the family.

Extended Families

- The central issue is the nature of the constitutional protection for the extended family.
  - First, examine and explain the ***nature*** of the particular regulation of the extended family that is at issue. For example, does the regulation prevent the family from residing together (as in *Moore*)? Or, does the regulation pertain to the provision of certain benefits that would assist members of extended families to maintain a residence together (as in *Lipscomb*).
  - Another threshold issue involves the determination of ***whether the particular household qualifies*** as an extended family. That is, in order to qualify, the group or household must contain members who are related to each other in some familial relationship. If the members are all unrelated persons, then the group is not an extended family but rather a communal family (see discussion below).
  - Be sure to make clear that the extent of constitutional protection for extended families depends on the nature of the governmental infringement. That is, the Constitution provides protection for family members to choose to ***live together*** as an extended family but ***does not require a state to provide benefits*** to assist that family to remain together.

Communal Families

- Here two issues arise. The first question is the ***constitutional*** protection (or lack thereof) for the communal family. The second question concerns the extent of protection for communal families under ***state law***. The usual context in which these questions arise is ***zoning***.
- Explain that the Supreme Court has ***refused*** to extend constitutional protection to communal families from state regulation for zoning purposes. Point out that such treatment ***differs*** from that accorded to the extended family. Contrast the Supreme Court's treatment of communal families with state treatment of such families. That is, clarify that communal families have received ***more favorable*** treatment in zoning challenges based on state, rather than federal, constitutional law.
- In discussing a regulation of communal families under ***state law***, be sure to highlight the requirement that, in order for such families to merit legal recognition in some jurisdictions, they must evidence ***familial-like criteria***. Be sure to ***analyze which aspects*** of "group living" qualify (financial dependence, emotional dependence, eating together, sharing chores, pooling resources, etc.).
  - Be sure to discuss the possible ramifications for recognition of communal families based on *Lawrence v. Texas* (recognizing the individual's right to enter into sexual relationships between consenting adults in the home).

Unmarried Couples

The two important points to remember here are (1) the law confers recognition on ***some*** but not other nontraditional families, and (2) the law confers recognition on such nontraditional families for some ***purposes*** but not others.

- ☛ First, identify the context of the regulation: sexual conduct, zoning, housing, tort law, contract law, employment, inheritance law. If the issue concerns sexual conduct, explain the traditional legal response (criminal sanctions for nonmarital sexual conduct) versus the modern legal response (based on *Lawrence v. Texas*, recognizing protection of the individual's privacy right to enter into consensual sexual relationships in the home).

- ☛ ***Zoning*** cases necessarily implicate constitutional issues, such as the First Amendment (freedom of association) and Fourteenth Amendment right to familial privacy, as well as state issues of the police power to regulate definitions of the family. Point out that some state courts have extended the United States Supreme Court's refusal to recognize communal families by denying constitutional protection to unmarried couples for zoning purposes. Point out too that *Lawrence* raises doubts as to the constitutionality of such decisions.

- ☛ Issues of ***housing discrimination*** evoke claims under state civil rights statutes. Here, an important issue is the need to balance constitutional rights (i.e., to balance the landlord's First Amendment right to refuse to rent to unmarried couples on religious grounds versus the couple's right to live where they choose free of discrimination).
  - ☞ Explain that landlords' claims have met with varying success under state nondiscrimination statutes because of states' narrow versus broad interpretations of the statutory term "marital status."

- ☛ An exam question may raise ***issues of tort law***. The most likely tort claims are for loss of consortium and/or negligent infliction of emotional distress arising from an injury to a cohabitant. Remember the threshold issue that bystander liability requires the plaintiff cohabitant actually to have been a bystander, i.e., have witnessed the accident to the injured partner.
  - ☞ Mention the split of opinion on recovery. Some jurisdictions permit cohabitants to recover in tort for injuries to each other whereas other jurisdictions reject such claims.
  - ☞ Point out that domestic partnership legislation or same-sex marriage in a few jurisdictions may authorize recovery.

- ☛ ***Contract claims*** may also arise when the unmarried couple terminates their relationship. Usually such claims involve dissolution, but occasionally such claims involve termination of the relationship by death. In dissolution cases, the claim will be "inter se" — one member of the couple suing the other for breach of contract. In cases of death of a partner, the plaintiff generally institutes a contract claim against the deceased partner's estate. Both scenarios require analysis under traditional contract principles. Clarify the nature of the offer, acceptance, and consideration.
  - ☞ Discuss the traditional rule (refusal to enforce agreements) and its rationale (morality, public policy).
  - ☞ Discuss the modern view, based on *Marvin v. Marvin*, that permits express and implied agreements between partners so long as the consideration for the agreement does not include the provision of sexual services.

- Be sure to conclude by discussing the impact of domestic partnership legislation in a few jurisdictions (i.e., legislation that equates the rights of same-sex partners to those of married couples for purposes of dissolution and death), the ALI *Principles* (pertaining to dissolution of such relationships only), and same-sex marriage.

- ***Employment*** issues generally concern (1) employment decision making (i.e., refusals to hire a cohabitant, withdrawal of an offer of employment, or discharge of an employee), (2) the denial of employment-related health benefits, or (3) the denial of unemployment compensation.

  - In the first case, resort to Title VII claims is precluded because Title VII does not protect against discrimination based on marital status or sexual orientation. Plaintiffs, alternatively, may raise constitutional issues, such as violations of the right to freedom of association, due process, and equal protection.

  - In terms of the denial of employment-related health benefits, an issue is whether such decisions constitute permissible marital status discrimination. Point out that many municipalities and private employers are providing such benefits to domestic partners. Of course, domestic partnership legislation in a few jurisdictions also authorizes provision of such benefits to same-sex couples.

  - If the issue concerns unemployment compensation, be sure to explain that the ability of the employee to qualify for unemployment compensation depends on the employee's success in establishing that his or her reason for moving comes within the statutory definition of "good cause." Some courts refuse to consider the desire to follow a partner as good cause unless the plaintiff is able to prove that the relationship resembles a traditional family unit (i.e., involves parenting).

- Whenever you discuss ***domestic partnership*** legislation, always be sure to point out that only a few jurisdictions have enacted such legislation. In addition, be sure to mention that such legislation differs in terms of eligibility requirements and the range of available legal benefits. That is, the legislation generally applies to same-sex couples and, only in limited circumstances, to other relationships. In addition, some domestic partnership legislation treats the partners as legal spouses, but other jurisdictions offer more limited protection.

- Finally, ***inheritance issues*** arise generally when one of the members of an unmarried couple dies. Be sure to identify whether the deceased partner dies intestate (without a will). Intestacy triggers application of state statutes that are generally limited to designated family members ("spouses," "children," etc.). The issue typically is whether the surviving partner qualifies as a "spouse" under the statutory scheme for intestate distribution. Be sure to contrast the traditional versus modern response. Traditionally, courts refuse to permit a member of an unmarried couple (heterosexual or same-sex) to inherit an intestate share of the deceased partner's estate. However, in a few modern jurisdictions, case law and domestic partnership legislation are modifying this result. In the context of death, be on the lookout for cross-over questions that address issues of contract (i.e., *Marvin*-type claims), intestacy (spousal definition), and tort (i.e., loss of consortium, negligent infliction of emotional distress).

CHAPTER 5

DIVORCE

ChapterScope

This chapter explores the traditional fault-based system of divorce and the system of no-fault dissolution that replaced it. Here are a few of the key principles covered in this chapter:

- Historically, courts granted divorces based on ***marital fault***.
- Traditional fault-based ***grounds*** include:
  - adultery,
  - cruelty, and
  - desertion.
- Traditional fault-based ***defenses*** include:
  - recrimination,
  - condonation,
  - connivance, and
  - collusion.
- Some form of ***no-fault dissolution*** is available in every state.
- A ***reform movement*** attempts to re-introduce fault in the dissolution process. ***Covenant marriages*** are a reflection of that movement and permit dissolution only on fault-based grounds.
- Many jurisdictions regulate ***sexual relations*** between an attorney and client.
- ***Subject matter jurisdiction*** is necessary for the plaintiff to secure a divorce.
  - A state has jurisdiction to dissolve a marriage based on plaintiff's ***domicile*** in the forum state.
- ***Personal jurisdiction*** over the defendant is not necessary to dissolve a marriage if the plaintiff is domiciled in the forum state, but ***notice*** to the defendant that complies with due process is required.
- ***The Full Faith and Credit Clause*** of the Constitution requires that a state recognize the decrees of a sister state, provided that the sister state had jurisdiction.
- The ***domestic relations exception*** to federal jurisdiction signifies that federal courts can refuse to hear cases involving divorce, alimony, or child custody.

I. BACKGROUND

American divorce law was more liberal than English ecclesiastic practice. England did not permit judicially granted "absolute divorce" until the Matrimonial Causes Act in 1857. English law distinguished between "absolute divorce" (akin to our modern idea of divorce in which the parties can remarry) and "divorce a mensa et thoro" (i.e., from "bed and board"). The latter is analogous to our concept of a judicial separation — that is, it did not permit the spouses to remarry. Until 1857, the only recourse for English spouses was to seek either an annulment or the rare legislative divorce.

In contrast, by the nineteenth century in America, almost all northern colonies permitted judicial divorce. In the southern colonies during the same period, many legislatures dissolved marriages. Gradually, however, judicial divorce replaced legislative divorce.

Despite increasing demand, divorce was not easily obtainable until the late 1960s or early 1970s. Until that time, states required that a plaintiff establish fault-based grounds for divorce. These grounds varied considerably in the different states.

Furthermore, divorce was awarded only to the innocent party. The innocent party received support, property, and custody. The "guilty" spouse was punished by having to pay (support and/or property) and by the denial of a custody award.

Today, all states have enacted some form of no-fault dissolution (i.e., divorce without proof of fault). Some jurisdictions are pure no-fault, whereas others have engrafted no-fault grounds onto their former fault-based system.

It is important to note that "no fault" does not mean the same thing in all jurisdictions. For example, a few states permit a no-fault divorce only if both parties consent. In contrast, many states permit a "no-fault" divorce if only one party desires it. Further, some states define "no fault" to mean that the parties have "irreconcilable differences"; but other states define "no fault" to signify a marital breakdown that results in the parties physically living apart for a statutorily defined period of time. The various meanings of "no fault" are explored *infra*.

II. FAULT-BASED GROUNDS

All jurisdictions now have some variation of no-fault divorce. However, fault-based grounds still exist in some jurisdictions. The most common fault-based grounds for divorce in the fault era were cruelty and adultery.

A. Cruelty: Cruelty provided a traditional ground for divorce and remains a fault-based ground in some states. Statutes sometimes include the terms of "cruel and inhuman treatment" or "indignities to the person." Cruelty was the most common ground for divorce prior to no-fault (i.e., more frequently pleaded than adultery).

1. Elements: To prove cruelty a plaintiff must show:

- a course of conduct that is so severe as to
- create an adverse effect on plaintiff's physical or mental well-being.

A single act of cruelty does not suffice to satisfy the "course of conduct" requirement unless the act is particularly severe.

2. **Physical versus mental cruelty:** Early American courts required actual or threatened physical violence. Courts gradually permitted mental cruelty to suffice.

   Example: Wife files for divorce, alleging that Husband's demands that she relocate to an Islamic community constitute cruel and inhuman treatment. Wife claims that the community's restrictions and rules (e.g., the requirement that women obtain permission from their husbands before leaving the confines of the community) are oppressive. Although Husband did not physically harm Wife, the court holds that the Husband's conduct constitutes mental cruelty. *Muhammad v. Muhammad*, 622 So.2d 1239 (Miss. 1993).

   Note: Some courts required that the mental cruelty be sufficiently severe as to pose a danger to plaintiff's well-being. The requirement of adverse effect was thought necessary to overcome the judicial concern regarding fraudulent claims.

3. **Short-term versus long-term marriage:** An occasional court has required a higher degree of proof of cruelty for long-term, as opposed to short-term, marriages. The rule developed to avoid the financial hardships suffered by older women (i.e., denial of alimony).

   Example: After a 30-year marriage, Wife petitions for divorce, alleging that Husband's obscenities, inappropriate sexual remarks, and boorish conduct constitute cruelty. The court denies her petition, reasoning that Husband's conduct, when viewed cumulatively, did not sufficiently endanger Wife's physical or mental health. *S.C. v. A.C.*, 798 N.Y.S.2d 348 (Sup. Ct. 2004).

4. **Corroboration:** Traditionally, courts required corroboration of marital misconduct to support a fault-based ground for divorce. Some states continue to adhere to this requirement.

   Example: During their marriage, Husband placed Internet ads seeking sexual partners and, over Wife's objection, allowed a woman he met on the Internet to babysit their child. Wife testified at trial that Husband had engaged in conduct that rendered her condition in life intolerable. The appellate court found that such a conclusory, isolated statement without corroborating evidence was insufficient to support a divorce on the ground of cruelty. *Dee v. Dee*, 258 S.W.3d 405 (Ark. Ct. App. 2007).

B. Adultery

1. **Elements:** To prove adultery a plaintiff must show:

   - opportunity to commit the offense; and
   - disposition to commit it.

   Although courts generally require corroboration for fault-based grounds, they permit circumstantial evidence to prove adultery because the sexual conduct occurs in private.

   Example: Judy and Orville are married for 17 years. Judy works as a secretary, bookkeeper, and office manager for Orville's construction company. Judy becomes suspicious that Orville is having an affair with his new receptionist, Sheila, because the pair spends considerable time together and are absent from work at the same time. In addition, Orville gave Sheila $2,500. Judy fires Sheila, but Orville rehires her and fires his wife. Judy sues for divorce based on adultery. The court finds that there is sufficient testimony that Orville and Sheila had opportunities to conduct their affair and, despite Orville's denials, the facts are sufficient to establish his infatuation. *Lister v. Lister*, 981 So.2d 340 (Miss. Ct. App. 2008).

Although jurisdictions traditionally required acts of sexual intercourse to constitute adultery, modern cases permit a lesser showing of noncoital acts. In New York, adultery was the only ground for divorce until 1967.

2. **Criminal versus civil overlap**

   a. **Definition:** Adultery is a ***crime*** as well as a ***civil*** ground for divorce. At common law, the crime could be committed only with a married woman. For divorce purposes, the definition is broadened to include sexual misconduct with any person other than the defendant's legal spouse.

   b. **Standard of proof:** In contrast to the criminal standard of beyond a reasonable doubt, the majority of states require only a preponderance of the evidence for a divorce based on adultery.

   c. **Double standard:** Historically, a double standard existed regarding proof of adultery. For a wife, a single sexual act might satisfy the requirements, whereas a *course* of adulterous conduct was required for a husband.

3. **Same-sex conduct as adultery?** Traditionally, cases split regarding whether same-sex sexual acts constitute adultery for divorce purposes.

C. **Desertion**

1. **Elements:** Desertion, or abandonment, serves as another traditional ground for divorce. It requires:

   - a voluntary separation;
   - with intent not to resume cohabitation;
   - that is without consent or justification.

   Example: Wife files for divorce and requests permanent alimony. Husband argues that the court should deny her request for permanent alimony because she is not free from fault. Specifically, he alleges that Wife refused to follow Husband when he decided to move for business reasons. The trial court agrees with Husband that Wife's conduct violated a state constitutional provision that requires a wife to follow a husband wherever he chooses to reside. Wife appeals, alleging that the constitutional provision violates equal protection by forcing wives, and not husbands, to comply with a spouse's change of domicile. The appellate court agrees, finding that there is no important governmental objective that is served by the state constitutional provision. *Crosby v. Crosby*, 434 So.2d 162 (La. Ct. App. 1983).

2. **Constructive desertion:** Constructive desertion serves both as an alternative ground for divorce and as a defense. It constitutes conduct that either causes a spouse to leave or justifies the spouse's departure. Thus, a defendant could defend against a plaintiff's claim of desertion by showing that the defendant's departure was justified by plaintiff's acts or behavior.

   Example: Husband seeks a divorce on the basis that Wife deserted him. Wife cross-claims on the grounds of cruelty and constructive desertion. Her claim of constructive desertion alleges that her departure was justified because of Husband's cruelty (cursing, abuse, violent outbursts of temper, physical assaults, destruction of furniture, and indifference). The court determines that Wife was justified in leaving the marital residence because of Husband's conduct (although the court denies the divorce because of a statutory requirement of corroboration). *Graham v. Graham*, 172 S.E.2d 724 (Va. 1970).

Example: Wife files for divorce, claiming constructive desertion. She identifies the following marital problems as justifying her departure, including: (1) Husband's sexual difficulties, (2) his excessive work habits, (3) his failure to assist in rearing their four children, and (4) a general lack of intimacy within the marriage. The court denies Wife's petition, finding that Husband's periodic impotence and long working hours did not justify Wife's departure. Instead, the court holds that, because Wife's response to the marital problems was to terminate marital cohabitation and file for divorce, she committed desertion (and thereby forfeited her right to spousal support). *Reid v. Reid*, 375 S.E.2d 533 (Va. Ct. App. 1989).

D. Other grounds: Other fault-based grounds for divorce include:

- habitual drunkenness or drug addiction;
- incurable impotence;
- failure to support;
- criminal conviction and/or imprisonment; and,
- insanity.

III. FAULT-BASED DEFENSES

Fault-based defenses to divorce include: recrimination, connivance, condonation, and collusion. These defenses largely are irrelevant if the divorce is sought on no-fault grounds.

A. Recrimination:

1. **Rule:** Recrimination is the doctrine that bars divorce in cases in which both spouses are at fault (i.e., both spouses have grounds for divorce).

Example: Michael seeks a divorce from Edith, alleging cruelty and desertion. He contends that Edith called him names, refused to have children, threatened him with a knife, threw hot water on him, tried to strike him with a chair, and removed his bedroom furniture. She testifies that Michael was physically violent, resulting in his arrest on numerous occasions for assault and battery. The court denies the divorce because both spouses are equally at fault. *Rankin v. Rankin*, 124 A.2d 639 (Pa. Super. Ct. 1956).

Example: Wife seeks a divorce for cruel and inhuman treatment and presents evidence showing a pattern of Husband's systematic, continuous abuse that resulted in her hospitalization for anxiety-related disorders. Husband contends that Wife has been guilty of adultery and that the defense of recrimination prohibits the granting to her of a divorce. The court holds that Husband cannot use the defense of recrimination based on Wife's adultery because her misconduct occurred only after the parties' separation (although some jurisdictions do recognize fault-based grounds that occur post-separation). *Parker v. Parker*, 519 So.2d 1232 (Miss. 1988).

2. **Policy rationale:** Policy rationale includes the clean hands doctrine, the idea that divorce should be permitted only for an innocent spouse, preservation of marriage, and the need to provide economic protection to women by denying divorce in order to force husbands to continue to support wives.

3. **Criticism:** Critics charge that the doctrine denies divorces for marriages that genuinely deserve to end.

4. **Limitation:** The harshness of the doctrine led some courts to develop the **doctrine of comparative rectitude** by which a court could determine the degrees of marital fault and award a divorce to the party who was least at fault.

B. **Connivance:** Connivance is participation in, or consent to, the defendant's wrongful conduct. The doctrine was usually limited to suits for adultery.

Example: Suspecting that Wife is fond of their chauffeur, Husband intentionally gives the chauffeur ample opportunity, both day time and at night, to be with Wife. Husband also hires detectives to spy on Wife and inform him of her activities. Husband seeks a divorce on ground of adultery. The court denies the divorce because Husband actively facilitated Wife's commission of adultery and made no effort to warn her or to fire his employee. *Sargent v. Sargent*, 114 A. 428 (N.J. Chancery Div. 1920).

C. **Condonation:** Condonation means that a spouse who has once condoned marital misconduct, such as adultery, is barred from using that misconduct as a grounds for divorce. Condonation exists if the wronged spouse resumes sexual relations with the wrongdoer, following knowledge of the wrongdoer's misconduct. Some courts require both forgiveness and the resumption of sexual intercourse after the misconduct; others hold that either element suffices. The policy rationale is to encourage reconciliation. (Note that some jurisdictions limit the defense of condonation to dissolutions based on adultery.)

Example: Wife petitions for divorce based on abandonment as well as cruel and inhuman treatment, claiming that Husband left the marital home and engaged in adultery (with the adultery serving as the "cruel and inhuman treatment" under New York law). Husband responds by asserting, first, that his departure was justified because Wife admitted her long-term extramarital affair and, second, that his adultery could not constitute cruel and inhuman treatment because it followed on the heels of Wife's revelations. Wife then asserts the defense of condonation, claiming that Husband forgave her infidelity and that the parties attempted to reconcile. The court rules that her defense of condonation fails because that defense is applicable only to a cause of action for adultery (pursuant to New York law) and not to the ground of cruel and inhuman treatment (as here), and also because condonation requires proof of a resumption of marital relations that Wife failed to establish. Instead, the court finds that Husband has proven grounds to divorce Wife because of Wife's extramarital conduct. *P.K. v. R.K.*, 820 N.Y.S.2d 844 (Sup. Ct. 2006).

D. **Collusion**

1. **Rule:** Collusion occurs when the spouses agree (or fabricate evidence) that one partner commits a marital offense to provide grounds for divorce.

Example: Husband seeks, and is granted, a divorce on the ground of adultery. Wife defaults. Wife seeks to set aside the default and defend, alleging that she never committed adultery and only agreed to give plaintiff a divorce because he promised that if she did so, she could have custody of their child. The court grants Wife's motion to set aside the default for the policy reason that courts desire to prevent collusion. *Rankin v. Rankin*, 124 A.2d 639 (Pa. Super. Ct. 1956).

2. **Connivance distinguished:** Connivance includes *consent* by one spouse to the other spouse's marital misconduct, whereas collusion includes a spousal *agreement* to commit a marital wrong.

E. Insanity: Insanity is both a ***ground*** for divorce and a ***defense***. Some courts follow the *McNaghten* test (as formulated in *McNaghten's Case*, 10 Cl. & Fin. 200 (H.L. 1943)), that requires the ability to distinguish right from wrong or to understand the nature and quality of the wrongful act. Other courts follow the *Durham* test (as formulated in *Durham v. United States*, 214 F.2d 862 (D.C. Cir. 1954)) that requires the marital misconduct to be the product of a mental disease or defect.

Quiz Yourself on FAULT-BASED GROUNDS AND DEFENSES

50. Husband files for divorce in a fault-based jurisdiction, alleging that Wife is guilty of cruel and inhuman treatment. Husband alleges that Wife posted YouTube videos to discuss the couple's marital troubles and to humiliate Husband. Husband claims that, in response, he left the marital home, sought medical treatment from his doctor for stress, and obtained psychological counseling. Will Husband be successful? ____________________

51. Husband and Wife are married for 20 years. Several years ago, Wife has an extramarital affair of which Husband was aware. After the Husband's discovery of Wife's affair, the couple continues to live together and have sexual relations. Wife petitions for divorce on the ground of Husband's cruelty in a fault-based jurisdiction. She maintains that he frequently is drunk, vomits throughout the house, provokes arguments, threatens violence, and makes excessive sexual demands. Husband defends by alleging Wife's adultery. Will Wife prevail? ____________________

52. Husband is aware that Wife has had several extramarital affairs during the marriage (as has he). He arranges for a private detective either to engage in an intimate relationship with Wife or to hire persons to do so. Detective employs numerous persons, at least one of whom does engage in sexual conduct with Wife. Husband petitions for divorce on the ground of Wife's adultery. Will Husband's suit for divorce be successful? ____________________

Answers

50. Yes. Wife engaged in a course of conduct that was severe by posting multiple YouTube videos designed to publicly humiliate Husband. Wife's actions prompted Husband to seek medical and psychological treatment, thereby satisfying the "adverse effect" requirement.

51. Yes. The divorce was properly granted on the ground of Husband's cruelty. Under the recrimination doctrine (where both parties are at fault), Wife's adulterous conduct would prevent her from obtaining the divorce she sought. However, here Husband condoned her adultery by continuing to live with Wife and have sexual relations with her, after he had knowledge of her sexual indiscretion.

52. No. Wife's claim of connivance constitutes a defense to Husband's claim of adultery. Husband intentionally provided opportunities for Wife's adultery.

IV. NO-FAULT DIVORCE

A. Early no-fault grounds: Two early no-fault grounds were "living separate and apart" and "incompatibility."

1. Living separate and apart:

a. Elements: Some statutes predated the no-fault revolution by providing for divorce based on the parties' separation for a statutorily designated period of time. This ground eliminated proof of fault.

Today, most states continue to provide for no-fault divorce based on the ground of physical separation. Some states require that marital breakdown be shown by a separation for a statutorily designated period. Other states engraft this ground upon fault-based grounds. That is, these states require that if marital breakdown cannot be proven by physical separation for the statutorily designated period (between six months and two years), the parties may resort to fault-based grounds.

b. Meaning of separate and apart: The term "living separate and apart" may refer to both the physical separation and the intention to dissolve the marriage. Courts differ as to the relevance of, and interpretation of, these two requirements.

c. Physical separation: Some courts hold that the spouses have lived "separate and apart" even though they live in the same house (e.g., in separate bedrooms).

Other courts require that the spouses maintain separate residences (despite the financial burden this imposes). A few courts add the requirement that the couple must hold themselves out to the public as not living together.

Example: When marital difficulties arise, Husband moves out of the marital residence and moves in with his mother. The spouses cease sexual relations and reside apart for 18 months. Despite living with his mother, Husband continues to pretend to neighbors that he is residing with Wife: His mother drives him to his house each morning, he takes his car and goes to work. He returns to the marital home after work where his mother picks him up. On the weekends, he does household chores. He occasionally eats meals with Wife and continues to accompany Wife to social events. Plaintiff seeks a divorce on the ground of separation. The court denies the divorce because Husband's conduct does not constitute living "separate and apart in different habitations" within the meaning of the statute. *Ellam v. Ellam*, 333 A.2d 577 (N.J. Super. Ct. 1975).

d. **Intention:** Some jurisdictions maintain that intention is relevant. That is, some restrictive jurisdictions require that the spouses *voluntarily* (i.e., by mutual consent) live apart for the statutory period. In these jurisdictions, separation by necessity does not give rise to grounds for divorce.

Other jurisdictions require that if only *one* spouse forms an intent to dissolve the marriage, that spouse must clearly manifest this intent to the other partner.

Example: Husband and Wife are married in India. Two years later Husband comes to the United States to pursue graduate work. Wife, who is unable to obtain a visa, remains in India. They correspond regularly. Less than one year after Husband professes his love for Wife in a letter, Husband seeks a divorce. He alleges that the couple has been separated for the requisite three-year statutory period. The divorce is granted; Wife appeals. The appellate court reverses. The court finds that Husband formed his intent to dissolve the marriage only 14 months before filing. Because Husband did not communicate his intent to Wife at the beginning of the three-year period, Husband has not lived separate and apart for the requisite period. *Sinha v. Sinha*, 526 A.2d 765 (Pa. 1987).

2. **Incompatibility:** Incompatibility, adopted by the Virgin Islands, was one of the earliest no-fault grounds. Some courts have held that incompatibility requires more than minor quarrels, i.e., irreconcilable conflict. The standard has not been as widely adopted in no-fault legislation as the marital breakdown standards of either California or UMDA (discussed *infra*).

B. **Modern no-fault legislation:** All states now have enacted some form of no-fault divorce. The no-fault revolution was initiated by ***California*** legislation in 1968. Two years later, the National Conference of Commissioners on Uniform State Laws promulgated the ***Uniform Marriage and Divorce Act*** (UMDA), another approach to no-fault divorce.

The policy underlying no fault is the recognition that divorce is not caused by a party's "fault" (i.e., an act or acts of misconduct). Rather, divorce is caused by a gradual breakdown in the marital relationship. As a result, neither party should be punished in the dissolution process.

1. **Variations in no-fault regimes**

a. **Definitions of no fault:** States define no fault differently. Some states equate no fault with "irreconcilable differences" between the parties. Other states define "no fault" to signify a marital breakdown that results in the parties physically living apart for a statutorily defined period of time.

b. **Pure no-fault v. mixed jurisdictions:** Some states are pure no-fault jurisdictions, i.e., eliminating proof of fault. Other states merely add a no-fault ground (such as "incompatibility," "living separate and apart," or "marital breakdown") to their fault-based grounds.

c. **Unilateral or mutual consent:** Some states (e.g., Mo. Rev. Stat. §452.320 (West 2003)) permit a no-fault divorce only if both parties consent. If mutual consent is lacking, then divorce is available only on fault grounds. In contrast, many states permit a no-fault divorce if only one party desires it. A few states require both mutual consent and a separation agreement to secure a no-fault divorce.

2. **California approach:** California legislation permits divorce on the ground of "irreconcilable differences, which have caused the irremediable breakdown of the marriage." Cal. Fam. Code §2310(a) (West 2004). (California also permits divorce based on "incurable insanity." Cal. Fam. Code §2312 (West 2004)).

   Irreconcilable differences are defined as: "those grounds which are determined by the court to be substantial reasons for not continuing the marriage and which make it appear that the marriage should be dissolved." Cal. Fam. Code §2311 (West 2004).

3. **UMDA approach:** UMDA permits divorce if the marriage is "irretrievably broken." "Irretrievable breakdown" may be established by either: a six-month separation, or a showing of "serious marital discord adversely affecting the attitude of one or both of the parties to the marriage." UMDA §302(a)(2), 9A U.L.A. 181 (1987).

4. **Problems accompanying the trend to no-fault:**

   A number of problems accompanied the shift from fault-based grounds to no fault:

   - some states defined "incompatibility" or "irretrievable breakdown" to require a showing of fault;
   - some confusion existed as to the continued vitality of fault-based defenses in those jurisdictions that were exclusively no-fault, as well as in those jurisdictions that retained some fault grounds. Many states abolished the fault-based defenses when the states embraced no-fault. *See, e.g., Flora v. Flora*, 337 N.E.2d 846 (Ind. Ct. App. 1975) (rejecting fault-based defenses as not compatible with the state's pure no-fault legislation).
   - a few states wrestled with whether a no-fault divorce could be granted in cases of nonconsensual divorces (where only one party desired the divorce).

   A minority of states currently limit the availability of nonconsensual divorces to fault-based actions. The majority, in contrast, will grant a no-fault divorce even if only one spouse contends that the marriage is ended.

5. **New York reform:** New York became the last state to adopt a pure no-fault divorce law in 2010. The new law (following UMDA) permits divorce if a marriage is "irretrievably broken." Prior to the Divorce Reform Act of 1966, the only ground of divorce in New York was adultery. Thereafter, divorce was permitted on several fault-based grounds (i.e., cruelty, abandonment, incarceration, adultery), as well as the no-fault ground of "living separate and apart" for one year based upon either a judicial separation decree or a separation agreement between the parties. If the spouses could not reach an agreement on any marital settlement terms (custody, support, property), they were required to resort to fault grounds. The new law permits unilateral no-fault divorce.

6. **Constitutionality:** No-fault statutes have surmounted constitutional challenges on the grounds of:

   - vagueness,
   - due process, and
   - an impairment of contract rights.

Example: Wife of entertainer Jackie Gleason obtains a legal separation at a time when divorce is available only for adultery. When New York adopts no-fault divorce, Gleason sues for divorce relying on the two-year statutory separation period. Wife opposes the divorce, alleging that the no-fault legislation deprives her of valuable rights without warning her that the separation decree might provide a basis for a subsequent divorce. She claims that the legislation impairs her vested rights (Social Security, pension, inheritance) that are protected by due process. The court holds that the statute does not violate Wife's right to due process. Marital rights are created by the state and can be taken away by legislation before they vest. Nor is marriage a contract within the meaning of the clause of the federal Constitution that prohibits the impairment by states of contractual obligations. *Gleason v. Gleason*, 256 N.E.2d 513 (N.Y. Ct. App. 1970).

7. **Re-emergence of fault: Reform movement:** Despite the widespread adoption of no fault, some states still consider fault to be relevant in the division of marital property and the determination of spousal support.

Note: UMDA precludes consideration of marital misconduct as a factor in property division (§307) or spousal support (§308).

Currently, a reform movement is afoot to increase consideration of fault in dissolution proceedings. Proposed reforms include: (1) the repeal of no fault and the return to fault-based grounds, (2) greater consideration of certain types of marital misconduct (e.g., spousal abuse), (3) higher standards for divorces involving children, and (4) lengthier waiting periods for no-fault divorce. The reform movement already has contributed to some important judicial and legislative changes. For example, many courts now recognize interspousal tort suits for some forms of marital misconduct (e.g., battery, emotional distress). For claims on the basis of intentional infliction of emotional distress (IIED), courts generally require that defendant's conduct be "extreme" and "outrageous." Generally, courts hold that adultery and insults do not meet the requisite standard for IIED. However, other forms of abusive conduct by a spouse may suffice.

Example: Husband and Wife have been married for 20 years. Wife returns to work. Husband suspects Wife of having an affair with her employer. Husband files for divorce on ground of cruelty and adultery. Husband receives confirmation of his suspicions regarding Wife's 11-year affair and adds a claim for IIED to his divorce petition. The court holds that, on policy grounds, interspousal claims for emotional distress should be allowed in divorce actions (even in the absence of physical injury). However, the court concludes that Wife's adultery does not satisfy the "outrageousness" necessary for imposing tort liability. *Ruprecht v. Ruprecht*, 599 A.2d 604 (N.J. Super. Ct. Ch. Div. 1991).

Example: Wife brings a post-divorce action against Husband for intentional infliction of emotional distress, alleging that he physically and mentally abused her during and after their marriage. Husband claims Wife failed to allege facts giving rise to an action for IIED and further that the statute of limitations has run on the alleged misconduct. The Illinois Supreme Court finds the allegations showed a type of domestic violence extreme enough to be actionable and that Wife sufficiently alleged that she suffered severe emotional distress. Further, the court finds that the "continuing tort rule" applies, i.e., the statute of limitations does not bar the action because Husband engaged in tortious behavior as late as the month in which the case was filed. *Feltmeier v. Feltmeier*, 798 N.E.2d 75 (Ill. 2003).

Note that a majority of jurisdictions permit (but do not mandate) joinder of tort claims and divorce claims. *Chen v. Fisher*, 843 N.E.2d 723, 726 (N.Y. 2005).

8. **Covenant marriage:** Beginning in the late 1990s, a reform movement culminated in the adoption of "covenant marriage" laws in some jurisdictions. A few state legislatures (Louisiana in 1997, Arizona in 1998, and Arkansas in 2001) enacted legislation ("covenant marriage" acts) making it more difficult for couples to obtain no-fault divorces. Generally, covenant marriage permits divorce only after a two-year separation or proof of fault (e.g., adultery, commission of a felony or domestic violence, or abandonment). A number of other state legislatures have adopted less stringent variations. Several state legislatures continue to consider, albeit unsuccessfully, measures adopting covenant marriage. For further discussion of the role of fault in alimony and property division, see Chapter 6.

Quiz Yourself on *NO-FAULT DIVORCE*

53. Mary and Larry, a married couple, cease having sexual relations after Mary suffers a stroke rendering her completely paralyzed. Eight years later, because of marital discord, Larry moves out of the house and into a travel van adjacent to the house. He continues to help Mary with household chores. This arrangement continues for several years. When Larry files suit for divorce based on the grounds of living separate and apart for at least two years without cohabitation, will he prevail?

____

54. Gail and Richard have been married for 20 years when Richard moves out of the house and begins engaging in affairs with several women. Three months later, Gail retains legal counsel and files for dissolution. If Gail resides in a jurisdiction that permits divorce on the ground of "irreconcilable differences," will she prevail? ____________________

55. Same basic facts as above. If Gail resides in a jurisdiction that follows the UMDA approach, will she prevail? ____________________

56. After 22 years of marriage, Barbara petitions for divorce and also sues Henry for intentional and negligent infliction of emotional distress. She alleges that Henry was verbally abusive by criticizing and belittling her, being explosive and rageful (i.e., having frequent temper tantrums although he never physically assaulted her), and tightly controlling all finances (i.e., refusing to let her write checks, giving her only $20 at a time for groceries, and insisting on buying all her clothes). Will Barbara be successful on her claims of emotional distress? ____________________

Answers

53. Perhaps. The term "living separate and apart" may require both physical separation and the intention to dissolve the marriage. Some courts require that the spouses maintain separate residences and hold themselves out to the public as not living together. Depending on the jurisdiction, Larry's living in the travel van adjacent to the house may or may not qualify as living separate and apart. Similarly, the fact that the couple continued to hold themselves out as married may militate against a finding that they lived separate and apart. Finally, there was no cessation of marital duties because Larry continued to help with household chores — an additional factor that might militate against a finding that the couple lived separate and apart.

54. Yes. Irreconcilable differences (based on the model California no-fault legislation) are those differences which have caused the irremediable breakdown of the marriage. Gail could successfully argue that Richard's conduct caused the marriage to break down and that such a situation was irremediable.

55. Yes. UMDA permits divorce if the marriage is "irretrievably broken." This divorce ground may be established either by a six-month separation or by a showing of "serious marital discord adversely affecting the attitude of one or both of the parties to the marriage." Although Richard and Gail have only been apart for three months (not the requisite six months), Gail could prove that Richard's extramarital affairs were adversely affecting her attitude toward continuation of the marriage.

56. Perhaps. For claims of infliction of emotional distress, courts generally require that a defendant's conduct be extreme and outrageous. Barbara will prevail if a jury finds that Henry's conduct (verbal abuse, rage, and controlling all finances) was sufficiently outrageous. The policy question is whether the allowance of interspousal claims for emotional distress in divorce actions reintroduces fault into the divorce process.

V. ACCESS TO DIVORCE

A. Religious limitations: The "Get"

1. **Judicial redress for husband's denial of divorce:** Under Orthodox Jewish law, a wife whose husband civilly divorces her without granting her a religious divorce (a "Get") is unable to remarry. If she does remarry, the subsequent marriage is adulterous: any ensuing children are considered illegitimate and are unable to marry another Jew. Some husbands use the threat of denying their wives a "Get" to exact financial concessions from them.

   Women have challenged such denials of divorce on tort and contract principles. Some defendants have raised constitutional challenges, i.e., that judicial enforcement of the "Get" violates the First Amendment's Free Exercise Clause (the husband's right to practice or not practice his religion), as well as the Establishment Clause (prohibiting governmental entanglement in religion).

   Example: Husband and Wife are married in an Orthodox Jewish ceremony. They divorce after 12 years. The parties subsequently reach a settlement before a special referee as to financial matters. Wife seeks damages for intentional infliction of emotional distress and also seeks to have the agreement set aside, alleging that it was brought about by husband's duress: He used knowledge of her desire for a religious divorce to exact extortionate financial demands. The court orders a new trial on the allegations of duress but holds that Wife's counterclaim for intentional infliction of emotional distress was properly dismissed. Tort liability in such cases should not be imposed because it would result in unconstitutional entanglement of courts in the exploration of religious beliefs. *Perl v. Perl*, 512 N.Y.S.2d 372 (App. Div. 1987).

2. **Legislative reform:** The New York legislature enacted a "Get" statute in 1983, providing that no final judgment of divorce may be granted unless both parties have taken all steps within their power to remove all barriers to remarriage. N.Y. Dom. Rel. §253 (McKinney 1999 & Supp. 2009). In addition, a New York equitable distribution statute permits a judge to consider any "barriers to remarriage" in determinations regarding property distribution and spousal support. N.Y. Dom. Rel. Law §236B(5)(h) (McKinney 1999 & Supp. 2009).

   Example: Husband complains that he is prepared to comply with New York's "Get" statute but that Wife refuses to accept the "Get" due to the fact that he obtained an alternative — i.e., a rabbinical court order (a "heter") that permitted him to remarry without giving a "Get." Wife claims that, to obtain the "heter," Husband made allegedly defamatory statements about her fitness as a mother in the rabbinical court and, therefore, the "heter" has the practical effect of preventing her remarriage by tarnishing her reputation. Wife insists that Husband disavow the statements. The appellate court rules that, whereas a court has jurisdiction to require a spouse to remove obstacles to remarriage pursuant to the "Get" statute, the First Amendment entanglement clause proscribes a review of the couple's religious dispute. *Sieger v. Sieger*, 829 N.Y.S.2d 649 (App. Div. 2007).

3. **International perspective:** The Canadian Supreme Court concluded that enforcement of agreements in which the husband promises to give the wife a religious divorce does not violate the husband's freedom of religion. *Bruker v. Marcovitz*, 2007 SCC 54 (Can.).

B. **Financial limitations: Filing fees:** The state cannot require an indigent to pay filing fees and court costs prior to filing for divorce.

Example: Connecticut law requires that litigants pay court fees and costs for service of process in order to bring an action for divorce. Welfare recipients challenge the statute as a violation of their due process rights. The state asserts an interest in prevention of frivolous litigation and the need to use fees and costs to allocate scarce resources, and the striking of a reasonable balance between a defendant's right to notice and the plaintiff's right of access. The U.S. Supreme Court holds that the statutory cost requirement violates due process because the cost forecloses an indigent's right to be heard (when the bona fides of indigence and desire for divorce are undisputed). The Court bases its holding on the position of marriage in society's hierarchy of values as well as the state monopolization of the means for divorce (divorce courts are the only forum available). None of the state's asserted interests are sufficient to override the plaintiff's right to access: No connection exists between assets and seriousness in bringing suit; alternatives exist to fees and cost requirements to deter frivolous litigation (penalties); and alternatives exist to costly personal service of process (mailing). *Boddie v. Connecticut*, 401 U.S. 371 (1971).

Note that some states currently impose fees on divorce filings for the purpose of funding domestic violence centers and/or services.

C. **Right to counsel:** Jurisdictions are divided on whether an indigent parent has a right to counsel in divorce proceedings based on state constitutional or statutory law.

Example: Brenda is the primary caretaker of the couple's three children during a ten-year marriage. At the divorce proceeding, the husband (Michael) is represented by counsel whereas Brenda proceeds pro se. After the trial court awards custody to Michael but visitation to Brenda, Brenda moves for a new trial. When her request for court-appointed counsel is denied, she argues that an indigent parent has a due process right to counsel in dissolution proceedings based on the state constitution. The Washington Supreme Court holds that a parent's due process right of access to the courts, as guaranteed by the state constitution, does not include a right to publicly funded counsel in a dissolution action (and distinguishes the case from parental termination proceedings in which counsel is provided because the latter seek to sever the parent-child relationship permanently). *King v. King*, 174 P.3d 659 (Wash. 2007).

Example: Christine is awarded a divorce from her husband David and all the marital property. David, who is serving a life sentence in state prison, moves for relief from the default judgment and for appointment of court-appointed counsel due to his indigent status. A state statute imposes a mandatory duty on the courts to appoint counsel for civil litigants who meet the statute's requirements. The state supreme court determines that the statute requires appointment of counsel for indigents in civil actions, including divorce, and that such counsel must be compensated. *Sholes v. Sholes*, 760 N.E.2d 156 (Ind. 2001).

D. **Summary dissolution:** A small number of jurisdictions provide for summary dissolutions of marriage. For example, California permits dissolutions without hearings in cases of short marriages (less than five years), for couples with no minor children and no real property, who have agreed to the disposition of marital property, and who waive claims for support. Cal. Fam. Code §2400 (West 2004).

E. **Pro se divorce:** Pro se divorces permit an individual to act as his or her own lawyer, thereby decreasing the costs of divorce. With the rise in no-fault divorces, some entrepreneurs developed "divorce kits" of services to assist divorcing spouses. Bar associations in some jurisdictions have limited spouses' use of these services by means of statutory enforcement of unauthorized practice provisions. Other jurisdictions have allowed lawyers to provide "limited services," such as allowing representation in a child support matter, but not the related custody dispute.

VI. DISCRIMINATION ON THE BASIS OF DIVORCE

One court has held that discrimination on the basis of divorce violates the Constitution.

Example: Linda Littlejohn, an untenured elementary school teacher, receives positive evaluations. Untenured teachers normally are rehired for the following year. Littlejohn and her husband divorce. Despite the principal's recommendation that Linda be rehired, the superintendent decides not to do so, telling the principal that the refusal is based on Linda's divorce. Linda institutes an action in federal district court, contending that the superintendent's action was a violation of her constitutional right to privacy. The school district moves for, and is granted, a directed verdict. The appellate court holds that the district court's grant of a directed verdict for the school district was improper. A denial of employment on the basis of employee's impending divorce is constitutionally impermissible as violative of plaintiff's fundamental right to privacy regarding her marital status. *Littlejohn v. Rose*, 768 F.2d 765 (6th Cir. 1985).

The stigma surrounding divorce affects divorced men as well as women.

Example: A former golf pro sues his employer, alleging marital status discrimination based on his employer's refusal to renew Plaintiff's contract because of Plaintiff's impending divorce. Defendant contends that the employment decision was based, instead, on the husband's engaging in an adulterous affair. However, the evidence reveals Defendant's disapproval of *both* Plaintiff's extramarital affair and the impending divorce. The court of appeals denies Defendant's motion for summary judgment, ruling that the evidence permits an inference that the adverse employment decision was based on Plaintiff's marital status (his impending divorce), and thus was sufficient to avoid summary disposition. *Veenstra v. Washtenaw Country Club*, 2004 WL 895873 (Mich. Ct. App. 2004).

VII. ROLE OF COUNSEL

Several ethical issues arise in the representation of family law clients, including: dual representation and also representation of clients who are involved in different suits over related matters.

A. Dual representation

1. **Different approaches:** Divorcing parties occasionally seek dual representation in order to decrease the costs associated with divorce. Many states regard *dual or multiple representation* (i.e., an attorney represents both spouses) in a divorce action as unethical because it presents an inherent conflict of interest.

   A few states, following the ABA Model Rules of Professional Conduct (promulgated in 1983), permit the practice only if the attorney informs the clients about the risks of dual representation and obtains each client's written consent thereto (Model Rules of Professional Conduct, Rule 1.7). If potential or actual conflicts of interest do arise (e.g., regarding support, property, or custody), the attorney must withdraw or face disciplinary charges. The Model Rules (Rule 2.2) exempt a lawyer-mediator from these restrictions on representation.

   Example: Husband requests Lawyer to represent both spouses in an impending divorce. Husband has been a regular client. Lawyer agrees, provided that the couple mutually agree to all terms and that no disputed issue arises. Later Lawyer represents Wife on a drunk driving charge. Subsequently, Wife is hospitalized for substance abuse. Lawyer files the divorce petition on no-fault grounds. While Wife is hospitalized, Husband brings her an agreement to sign, drafted by Lawyer, that has more favorable provisions to Husband than those to which she agreed. She discharges Lawyer and retains separate counsel. Lawyer, now representing Husband only, amends the complaint to allege cruelty and habitual intoxication, and moves for temporary custody on the ground that Wife is an unfit mother. Lawyer subsequently appeals a finding and sanctions for violations of rules of professional conduct. The appellate court finds that Lawyer's suspension was proper because he violated rules of professional conduct when he undertook and continued dual representation. Specifically, the court finds that he accepted employment that would be likely to involve representation of differing interests; failed to disclose to Wife the nature of the prior relationship which might have led him to prioritize Husband's interests; revealed confidences that he learned while representing Wife and used them to her disadvantage; should have withdrawn if he knew or should have known that his employment was adverse to a former client. *Board of Overseers of the Bar v. Dineen*, 500 A.2d 262 (Me. 1985).

2. **Dispelling the aura of dual representation:** An attorney may not give advice to an unrepresented opposing party. Further, the attorney owes a duty to an unrepresented opposing party not to give the impression that the attorney is representing both parties. ABA Model Rule 4.3 requires a lawyer to refrain from implying that she or he is disinterested and also to correct an unrepresented client's misunderstanding to that effect. An attorney who takes advantage of an opposing client's lack of representation may be disciplined, and any resulting agreement may be set aside on the ground of fraud.

Example: Wife employs Lawyer who contacts and makes an appointment with unrepresented Husband. Lawyer then informs Husband that he and Wife must divide their property and that Husband has to pay Wife spousal support. When Husband inquires whether he needs independent representation, Lawyer replies that Husband should let Lawyer represent both parties for cost reasons. Husband (who has minimal education, has just started a business, and earns considerably less than Wife) agrees to provisions regarding property (i.e., waiving his community property rights) and spousal support that are very favorable to Wife. Lawyer refuses to explain to Husband the terms of the agreement, to give him time to read them, and secures his stipulation as to a default without Husband's knowledge or understanding. Husband subsequently retains separate counsel and seeks to have the agreement set aside. The trial court cancels the marital settlement agreement. The court holds that because the agreement was procured by extrinsic fraud, rescission was proper. Attorney's fraud consisted of omissions and deceptive representations that prevented Husband from acquiring knowledge of his rights. *Adkins v. Adkins*, 186 Cal. Rptr. 818 (Ct. App. 1982).

3. **Confidentiality issues:** One of the dangers of dual representation is that an attorney who previously represented one or both of the spouses may use knowledge that was acquired in the earlier representation adversely to one of the former clients. The ABA Model Rules of Professional Conduct (Rule 1.6) address this problem by requiring that a lawyer not reveal confidential information or use such information to the disadvantage of a client or to the advantage of a third person.

   Example: Husband and Wife meet with Lawyer to discuss their marital problems. Lawyer believes he is "counseling" them in hopes of a reconciliation. Husband and Wife decide to divorce and both retain separate counsel (not Lawyer). Subsequently, Husband meets with Lawyer, discusses the case with him and asks him to represent him. Lawyer defers a decision on representing Husband. A few days later Lawyer agrees to represent Wife. He later withdraws when Husband protests. Husband files a complaint with the bar association against Lawyer. The court holds that Lawyer violated rules of professional conduct and should be reprimanded. Lawyer obtained confidential information when he "counseled" both spouses. Thereafter, he could no longer represent either. It was also improper for Lawyer to agree to represent Wife after Lawyer discussed marital problems with Husband. *In re Braun*, 227 A.2d 506 (N.J. Super. Ct. 1967).

B. **Representation of clients in different suits involving related matters:** Representation of clients involved in different lawsuits that deal with "substantially related" matters may give rise to prohibited conflicts of interest.

Example: Lawyer represents Husband and Wife in their acquisition of a business. Lawyer then represents Husband in the couple's divorce. The conflict of interest arose because the business was an asset of the marital estate, and Counsel would have had to argue on behalf of Husband that he was entitled to a greater share of the business. When Wife later complains, Lawyer fails to show that Wife consented to such a conflict, and it is shown that Lawyer used personal information to the detriment of his former client, the Wife. The Florida Bar determines that Lawyer violated several rules of attorney conduct and recommends that his license be suspended. *Florida Bar v. Dunagan*, 731 So.2d 1237 (Fla. 1999).

Courts often have to determine whether two legal matters are sufficiently "substantially related" to result in disqualification or sanctions of an attorney.

Example: Counsel represents Wife in a personal injury action. Counsel then represents Husband in the couple's divorce action. The court holds that the attorney was properly disqualified from subsequently representing Husband in the divorce because the two matters (personal injury action and the divorce) were "substantially related" given the fact that the attorney had obtained confidential information from Wife in the personal injury action concerning her health, her employment history, and her response to contested litigation that could be used to her detriment in the dissolution action regarding issues of custody, support, and property. *Hurley v. Hurley*, 923 A.2d 908 (Me. 2007).

Example: Counsel represents a man in a bankruptcy proceeding. Counsel then represents the man's former female lover in her defense against a paternity action brought by the bankruptcy client. The court holds that Counsel violated the disciplinary rule prohibiting representation that would conflict with the representation of a former client because Counsel obtained confidences from the first client (in the bankruptcy proceeding) regarding his finances that created a conflict of interest in the attorney's subsequent representation of the second client in the paternity action that would cause injury to the first client regarding custody and support. *In re Conduct of Balocca*, 151 P.3d 154 (Or. 2007).

C. Sexual relations with clients

1. **Different approaches:** An increasing number of states are beginning to regulate attorney-client sexual relationships. These states adopt a variety of approaches.

   - Some states prohibit all sexual relationships between attorneys and clients (this per se prohibition is the strictest approach);
   - Some states ban attorney-client sexual relations but exempt those relationships that predate the representation;
   - New York limits the ban to domestic relations attorneys;
   - Some states prohibit only those attorney-client sexual relationships that adversely affect the practice of law.

   In addition, some states permit the imposition of tort liability and/or sanctions (criminal sanctions or sanctions for violations of state business and professions code).

   Example: Lawyer engages in a sexual relationship with a female client while representing her in a dissolution proceeding. Specifically, he has sex with her on several occasions over a five-month period. The court finds that Lawyer has violated Iowa Code of Professional Responsibility for Lawyers DR 5-101(A) (an absolute prohibition on a lawyer's engaging in sexual relations with a client) and DR 1-102(A)(1) and (6) (providing that a lawyer shall not violate a disciplinary rule or engage in any other conduct that adversely reflects on the fitness to practice law). The court imposes a three-month suspension because Lawyer previously had been admonished for making a sexual advance toward another client only eight months before. *Iowa Supreme Court Attorney Disciplinary Board v. Morrison*, 727 N.W.2d 115 (Iowa 2007).

2. **Background:** California became the first state in 1991 to adopt restrictions on the practice of sexual relations with clients in some situations. California Rule of Professional Conduct 3-120 prohibits an attorney from (1) requiring or demanding sexual relations as a condition of representation, (2) employing coercion, intimidation, or undue influence in entering into sexual

relations with a client, or (3) continuing representation of a client after having sexual relations with that client if the sexual relationship causes the attorney to perform legal services incompetently.

3. **Special case of coercion:** Courts take a particularly dim view of attorneys' misconduct when the sexual relationship is coerced.

   Example: Attorney solicits sex from two former clients in exchange for legal services. The court holds that a three-year suspension from the practice of law was appropriate for the attorney's actions. *Iowa Supreme Court Attorney Disciplinary Bd. v. McGrath*, 713 N.W.2d 682 (Iowa 2006).

   Example: Attorney sexually assaults a female client during an after-hours meeting at his law office. The court holds that disbarment is warranted, despite the fact that the client reported the assault more than 20 years after it occurred. *In re Tenenbaum,* 918 A.2d 1109 (Del. Super. Ct. 2007).

4. **ABA Rule:** ABA Model Rule of Professional Conduct Rule 1.8(j) ("Sexual Relations with Clients") prohibits sexual relations between attorney and client absent a preexisting consensual relationship.

5. **States without specific bans may still find ethical violations:** Even without a specific state prohibition on attorney-client sexual relations, a jurisdiction may nonetheless determine that the attorney's sexual conduct constitutes a violation of *general* conflict-of-interest rules (such as ABA Model Rules of Professional Conduct Rule 1.7: "Conflict of Interest: Current Clients").

   Example: Lawyer engages in a sexual relationship with a client while he is representing her in a dissolution proceeding. He ends the sexual relationship a few weeks later. The client enters psychological treatment as a result of the affair. In a disciplinary hearing, the state supreme court rules that Lawyer's sexual conduct warrants a 30-day suspension, reasoning that the sexual relationship constituted a prohibited conflict of interest even though the relationship was consensual, the client retained Lawyer to represent her in a subsequent action, and there was no evidence of incompetent representation. *In re Tsoutsouris*, 748 N.E.2d 856 (Ind. 2001).

D. **Fees:** Unlike in civil actions where the litigants pay their own attorneys' fees, a court may order one spouse in a divorce proceeding to pay the other's fees. (Although the law is usually gender neutral, the general practice seems to be that the court orders the husband to pay the wife's fees.) Contingent fees in divorce actions are unethical.

Quiz Yourself on *ROLE OF COUNSEL*

57. Husband calls Lawyer, who has previously represented Husband in business dealings, and asks Lawyer to represent Wife and Husband in their divorce. Lawyer agrees and draws up a complaint and property settlement. Lawyer gives documents to Husband who has Wife execute them. Wife later charges Lawyer with malpractice when she discovers that she surrendered her right to an interest in certain community property — the existence of which Husband did not disclose to Lawyer. Will Lawyer incur liability for dual representation? ____________________

58. Atticus Attorney is retained to represent Cleo Client in a domestic relations matter. During Atticus's representation of Cleo, Atticus's wife files for divorce on several grounds, including adultery. During Atticus's representation of Cleo, and while his own divorce action is pending, Atticus is observed leaving Cleo's residence at 3:00 A.M. on a night that Cleo had custody of her minor child. In a disciplinary proceeding, may Atticus be suspended from the practice of law? ____________________

Answers

57. Yes. Many states regard dual representation in a divorce action as unethical because it presents an inherent conflict of interest. In this case, Lawyer in the dual representation situation may be found negligent for breaching his duty of care to Wife. Lawyer should have obtained verification of Husband's financial statement or, at least, informed Wife of the limited representation that she was receiving and pointed out that she might need independent advice.

58. Probably yes. Depending on the jurisdiction, a court might find that suspension is an appropriate disciplinary sanction for an attorney who engages in sexual behavior with a client after the attorney separates from his wife and while representing his client. Here, Atticus failed to inform the client of the possible negative implications of their sexual relationship on the issue of her retention of child custody.

VIII. DIVORCE JURISDICTION

A. Terminology

1. **Jurisdiction in the divorce context:** Jurisdiction refers to *subject matter jurisdiction* that is necessary for the plaintiff to secure a divorce (i.e., durational residency and/or domiciliary requirements) and *personal jurisdiction* over the defendant. (Jurisdictional rules pertaining to personal jurisdiction over the defendant in the divorce context differ from personal jurisdiction rules in other civil contexts, as explained *infra*.)

2. **Definition of domicile:** Domicile includes the twin elements of: physical presence plus intent to remain permanently. Generally, domicile is distinguishable from "residence" because a person may have more than one residence (e.g., a college student) but only one legal domicile. However, some states' "durational residency" requirements for divorce often are construed so as to be indistinguishable from "domicile."

3. **Ex parte versus bilateral divorce:** In an ***ex parte (or unilateral) divorce***, the court has personal jurisdiction over only one spouse. In a ***bilateral divorce***, the court has personal jurisdiction over both spouses. A bilateral divorce, because it is premised on jurisdiction over both parties, cannot be collaterally attacked.

4. **Divisible divorce:** Under this doctrine, a court in an ex parte divorce has jurisdiction *only over the marital status* of the parties. That is, the court can render a divorce decree. *However, the*

court may not determine the support and property rights of the absent spouse. This result follows because the court does not have personal jurisdiction over the "stay-at-home" spouse.

B. Subject matter jurisdiction

1. **Traditional rule: Domiciliary jurisdiction:** A state has jurisdiction to dissolve a marriage based on the petitioner's ***domicile*** in the forum state. Thus, a state's domiciliary requirements, sometimes termed "durational residency requirements" (generally applicable to the divorce petitioner), confer subject matter jurisdiction over the marriage upon a given court. Further, jurisdiction for divorce purposes is "in rem," i.e., over the marital status.

2. **Importance of domiciliary requirement:** The domiciliary requirement assumed considerable importance during the fault era for a spouse who might want to establish domicile elsewhere in order to evade strict fault-based grounds of the marital forum. The importance of the domiciliary requirement diminished with the advent of no fault. It still has relevance, however, for those spouses who relocate to another state at some point during the marital breakup (e.g., for employment or other personal reasons) and who desire to obtain a divorce in the new forum.

3. **Restatement view: Divorce without domicile:** Presence alone, normally, is insufficient to confer jurisdiction for divorce purposes. The Restatement (Second) of Conflict of Laws relaxes the traditional domiciliary requirement. According to the Restatement, a state can dissolve a marriage:

   - if one of the spouses is domiciled in the state (§70); or
   - if both spouses are domiciled there (§71); or
   - if neither spouse is domiciled in the state provided that either spouse has "such a relationship to the state as would make it reasonable for the state to dissolve that marriage" (§72).

   The relaxation of the traditional rule would enable a member of the military or that person's spouse, for example, to obtain a divorce in the jurisdiction where the member of the armed services is stationed. See also UMDA §302(a)(1), 9A U.L.A. 181 (1987) (authorizing divorce for a member of the armed services based on that person's "military presence" in the state).

4. **Durational residency requirements:** Some states impose durational residency requirements instead of a domiciliary requirement or, in addition to that requirement. Durational residency requirements require a petitioner to be a state resident for a period of time, varying from a minimum of six weeks to one year.

   Durational residency requirements may pose a barrier to a divorce petitioner who has recently moved to a state. The U.S. Supreme Court has held that these state requirements are constitutional.

   Example: Wife separates from Husband in New York and then moves with her three children to Iowa. One month later, she petitions an Iowa court for divorce. Husband, who was served with notice during a visit to Iowa to see the children, contests jurisdiction. The Iowa court dismisses Wife's petition on jurisdictional grounds: Husband is not a resident of Iowa, and Wife failed to satisfy the statutory requirement of one year residency preceding her filing of the petition. Wife appeals, contending that Iowa's one-year residency requirement is unconstitutional as a violation of her right to travel. The U.S. Supreme Court holds that Iowa's residency requirement is constitutional because it minimizes the susceptibility of a state's decrees to collateral attack and avoids one state's interference in matters in which another state has an important interest. Further, Iowa's residency requirement does not foreclose a plaintiff's access to the courts but merely delays it. *Sosna v. Iowa*, 419 U.S. 393 (1975).

5. **Full Faith and Credit Clause:** The Full Faith and Credit Clause of the Constitution (Article IV, §1) requires that a state give full faith and credit to the decrees of sister states provided that the sister state had jurisdiction.

   This requirement was interpreted and applied to the divorce context by the U.S. Supreme Court (*Williams I* and *Williams II*, explained *infra*).

   a. **The *Williams* cases:** The doctrine announced by the U.S. Supreme Court in the case of *Williams v. North Carolina* determines whether, and in what circumstances, a divorce decree granted by one state will be recognized by another state under the Full Faith and Credit Clause.

   b. ***Williams I: Whether to give full faith and credit:*** *Williams I* holds that a court in State A must give full faith and credit to the divorce decree of a sister state (State B) when one of the parties is domiciled in that sister state (State B). That is, a state must recognize, under the Full Faith and Credit Clause, a divorce granted to a spouse who is domiciled in a sister state even though the stay-at-home spouse does not appear and is not served with process in the sister state.

      Example: A shopkeeper in a small town in North Carolina elopes with his clerk's wife. The couple goes to Nevada to seek a divorce. After residing there for six weeks, they file for, and are granted, divorces from their respective spouses. They marry and return to their home town in North Carolina. They are tried and convicted of bigamous cohabitation and appeal. The convictions are overturned based on the U.S. Supreme Court's interpretation and application of the Full Faith and Credit Clause. The U.S. Supreme Court holds that a court in North Carolina must give full faith and credit to the divorce decree of Nevada when one of the spouses is domiciled in Nevada. Because the divorce decree states that the husband of one couple and the wife of the other couple were domiciled in Nevada, North Carolina must give full faith and credit to the decree. *Williams v. North Carolina*, 317 U.S. 287 (1942).

   c. ***Williams II:* When to give full faith and credit:** *Williams II* examines the circumstances in which a jurisdictional determination of domicile for divorce may be challenged. In this case, the bona fides of the spouses' domicile in *Williams I* was at issue. Refining the rule of *Williams I*, the Supreme Court holds that one state's determination of a petitioner's domicile is not binding on another state. That is, the decree-granting state's finding of domicile may be reexamined by another state to determine the bona fides of a petitioner's domicile.

      Example: North Carolina retries the shopkeeper and his second wife for bigamous cohabitation. The state asserts that the Nevada decree need not be recognized under Full Faith and Credit because the parties lacked a bona fide domicile in Nevada. The jury instructions charge that the statement in the Nevada decree that the petitioners were domiciled in Nevada is prima facie evidence of domicile. If, however, the jury finds that the petitioners went to Nevada for the sole purpose of obtaining a divorce, then the petitioners never established domicile there and Nevada's assertion of jurisdiction was invalid. The convictions are upheld this time. Although a state has the power to grant a divorce entitled to Full Faith and Credit (*Williams I*), the bona fides of the party's domicile in the decree-granting state may be re-examined. North Carolina may make its own determination of the bona fides of the parties' domicile in Nevada. *Williams v. North Carolina*, 325 U.S. 226 (1945) (*Williams II*).

d. ***Williams'* limitation to the ex parte situation:** The *Williams* rules (permitting judicial reexamination of the findings of jurisdiction by a sister state) operate if the divorce decree was entered in ex parte proceedings. However, the appearance of both parties in a bilateral divorce confers jurisdiction on the court and prevents reexamination of findings of jurisdictional fact.

Example: Margaret and Edward marry and live together in Massachusetts. Following marital strife, Wife takes their two children to Florida, allegedly for a visit. Wife files for divorce in Florida on the ground of cruelty. Husband retains Florida counsel, and enters a general appearance to deny the allegations. The Florida court grants the divorce. Wife remarries. After two months in Florida, the new couple returns to Massachusetts. Former Husband files an action alleging that the Florida decree is invalid and Wife's subsequent marriage is void. The Supreme Court holds that the decree is valid and comports with due process. The Court reasons that, unlike in *Williams*, the finding of jurisdiction was made in a proceeding in which Husband appeared and participated. Full Faith and Credit requires recognition of a decree rendered by a court that has jurisdiction over both parties. *Sherrer v. Sherrer*, 334 U.S. 343 (1948).

Note: A special appearance by a defendant (i.e., defendant's participation in the proceedings for the limited purpose of contesting jurisdiction) will prevent application of the *Sherrer* rule.

C. **Personal jurisdiction over the defendant:** Personal jurisdiction over the defendant is not required to terminate a marriage if the plaintiff is domiciled in the forum state. This special jurisdictional rule, which varies from the usual rule in civil actions requiring personal jurisdiction over the defendant, dates back to *Pennoyer v. Neff*, 95 U.S. 714 (1878). Nonetheless, notice to the defendant in divorce cases that complies with due process is required (to inform the defendant of the pendency of the action).

Furthermore, if personal jurisdiction over the defendant is not obtained, then the court may adjudicate only the issue of marital status (i.e., the termination of the marriage) but not the economic issues (i.e., spousal support, property division). This result follows because depriving the defendant of property rights (i.e., regarding support or property division) without due process would violate the Constitution.

Example: Wife, a citizen of Japan, challenges an Iowa court's jurisdiction to dissolve her marriage on the ground that petitioner-Husband failed to comply with Iowa's residency requirements and that Japan was the more convenient forum. The appellate court finds that (1) the trial court could exercise jurisdiction in the action brought by Husband, a permanent resident alien, without violating the wife's due process right, even though Wife was absent from Iowa, had never been there, and was constructively rather than personally served; (2) Husband established that his domicile was in Iowa for purposes of divorce jurisdiction (he had lived in Iowa for 13 months and had established residence in good faith); and (3) the refusal to dismiss the dissolution proceeding on *forum non conveniens* grounds was not an abuse of discretion because Husband would have been denied protection of Iowa's no-fault divorce law if the proceeding was held in Japan, Wife enjoyed vigorous representation in Iowa, and Iowa's rules on alimony and property division were beneficial to Wife. *In re Marriage of Kimura,* 471 N.W.2d 869 (Iowa 1991).

1. **Proper notice:** Proper notice, to comport with due process, must meet the standards established by the Supreme Court. That is, it must be "notice reasonably calculated under all the circumstances, to apprise interested parties of the pendency of the action and afford them an opportunity [to be heard]," *Mullane v. Central Hanover Bank & Trust Co.*, 339 U.S. 306, 314 (1950). A divorce that does not meet proper notice requirements may be challenged for lack of jurisdiction.

   If the divorce petitioner knows of the defendant's whereabouts, then notice should be either by personal service or mail. However, if the defendant's whereabouts are unknown, notice may be satisfied by constructive service, such as notice by publication or posting.

   Example: Javin files a petition in Coffee County, Tennessee, to divorce his wife Mary. The petition states that Mary is a nonresident who resides in Miami Beach, Florida. He gives Mary notice by publication in a Tennessee county newspaper. After he is awarded a divorce based on Mary's default, he remarries. Shortly thereafter, he dies. Mary files an action to set aside the divorce decree for lack of jurisdiction. The court holds that notice by publication fails to satisfy Wife's due process rights. Wife should have received *Mullane* notice ("notice reasonably calculated under all the circumstances, to apprise interested parties of the pendency of the action and afford them an opportunity [to be heard]" pursuant to *Mullane v. Central Hanover Bank & Trust Co.*, 339 U.S. 306, 314 (1950)). Javin knew or could have ascertained Mary's mailing address. *Baggett v. Baggett*, 541 S.W.2d 407 (Tenn. 1976).

2. **Long-arm statutes:** Although personal jurisdiction over a defendant is not essential for the sole purpose of ending a marriage, the assertion of personal jurisdiction is necessary to resolve the financial incidents of the divorce and also to ensure that a decree is entitled to full faith and credit. Long-arm statutes facilitate the assertion of personal jurisdiction over nonresident defendants.

   According to the traditional rule, personal jurisdiction must accord with the requirements of state long-arm statutes and the Constitution's Due Process Clause. Prior to the 1970s, many states permitted the assertion of jurisdiction over nonresidents in domestic relations cases by expansive readings of their long-arm statutes (e.g., by construing the divorce defendant's actions to be "the conduct of business" or "a tortious act," etc.).

   Beginning in the 1970s, many states substantially increased the scope of jurisdiction over nonresidents in domestic relations cases by revising their long-arm statutes to include specific provisions for the assertion of jurisdiction in claims for spousal support and child support. The U.S. Supreme Court curtailed somewhat this state court expansion of personal jurisdiction over nonresident defendants in *Kulko v. Superior Court*, 436 U.S. 84 (1978), by delineating the scope of due process limitations. Subsequently, in *Burnham v. Superior Court*, 495 U.S. 604 (1990), the Court further clarified the requisites of due process in the divorce context.

   Example: Sharon and Ezra Kulko, domiciliaries of New York, marry in 1959 during a three-day stopover in California en route to Ezra's tour of duty in Korea. They spend the rest of their married life in New York until their separation in 1972. Sharon moves to California. Pursuant to a written agreement (that Sharon flies back to New York to sign), the children are to remain in New York during the school year but spend vacations with their mother in

California. Sharon waives spousal support; Ezra agrees to pay $3,000 in child support for the periods when the children are in their mother's care. Sharon obtains a Haitian divorce that incorporates the terms of the spouses' agreement. She then returns to California. Shortly thereafter, their daughter decides to, and does, come to live with her mother in California. Then, their son decides that he too wants to join her. She sends him a plane ticket, unbeknownst to Ezra. After the son arrives, Sharon commences an action against Ezra in a California court, seeking to establish their Haitian divorce decree as a California judgment, to modify the judgment to give her full custody, and to increase Ezra's support obligation. Ezra appears specially to quash service of the summons, arguing that the state's assertion of personal jurisdiction is improper because he lacks "minimum contacts" with the forum. The United States Supreme Court holds that California's assertion of personal jurisdiction over Ezra is unconstitutional as a violation of the defendant's due process because Ezra lacks minimum contacts with the forum. His marriage in California during a brief stay did not confer jurisdiction. Nor did any of his actions constitute "purposeful act[s]" by which he availed himself of the benefits and protection of California's laws — his acquiescence to his daughter's move to California and purchasing her ticket, or the diminution of his financial obligations because his daughter spent part of the year in California. He has not caused an injury to persons or property in California and could not have foreseen that his actions would subject him to jurisdiction in California. Basic considerations of fairness point to New York as being the proper forum to litigate these issues. (Ezra remained in the state of the marital domicile; therefore, Sharon should bear the expense of litigating in another state.) *Kulko, supra.*

Note: *Kulko* establishes the rule that personal jurisdiction over the respondent that comports with due process/minimum contacts is required for orders determining financial rights and obligations in the divorce context.

3. **Transitory presence:** A state may acquire jurisdiction for divorce purposes over a nonresident defendant who is physically present in the state. Thus, *transitory presence* suffices to satisfy due process requirements even when a defendant has no substantial connection to the forum. This accords with the rule that is applicable to civil actions generally: Personal jurisdiction over the defendant is satisfied by service of process while in the forum state.

   Example: Dennis marries Francie Burnham. They live in New Jersey for ten years. When they agree to separate, Francie moves to California with their children. Before she leaves, they both agree to file for a no-fault divorce. Subsequently, Dennis files in New Jersey for divorce on grounds of desertion, refusing to adhere to their prior agreement. She files suit for divorce in California. When Dennis comes to California on a business trip and to visit his children, he is served with a copy of his wife's divorce petition. He makes a special appearance moving to quash service of process for lack of jurisdiction because he did not have minimum contacts with California. The U.S. Supreme Court holds that the assertion of jurisdiction for divorce purposes over nonresident defendants who are physically present in the state does not violate due process. *Burnham v. Superior Court*, 495 U.S. 604 (1990).

D. Foreign decrees

1. **Comity doctrine: Recognition of divorce decrees rendered by a foreign country:** During the fault era, many Americans sought divorces in other countries (e.g., Mexico, Haiti, or the Dominican Republic) that had more liberal divorce grounds or residency requirements. The ***comity doctrine*** concerns the extent to which American courts recognize the decrees of foreign countries.

The prevailing view, expressed by the Restatement (Second) of Conflict of Laws §98, provides that an American jurisdiction may recognize a judgment of a foreign nation provided that the judgment was rendered after a fair hearing by a court that has personal jurisdiction over one or both of the parties.

Example: Husband and Wife, who are Connecticut domiciliaries, fly to Mexico to obtain a divorce on the ground of incompatibility (not recognized by Connecticut). Their support and property agreement is made a part of that decree. The agreement provides that Husband will pay their children's medical and college expenses. Several years later, Wife alleges that daughter must attend private school, based on doctor's orders, and that, therefore, the "medical" expense should be payable by Husband. She seeks to have the Mexican decree made a decree of the Connecticut court and then enforced. Husband contends that Connecticut cannot enforce the Mexican decree. The court determines that the Mexican divorce decree should be recognized by Connecticut because the Mexican court had jurisdiction over both parties and because recognition would not violate Connecticut's public policy (which subsequently adopted no-fault divorce). *Yoder v. Yoder*, 330 A.2d 825 (Conn. 1974).

a. **Judicial discretion:** A court is not *required* to give the same deference to a divorce decree of a foreign country as to a decree from a sister state (the recognition of the latter is mandated by the Full Faith and Credit Clause). Courts may refuse to apply the comity doctrine to recognize foreign divorces if such recognition would violate public policy.

   Example: After a 17-year marriage, Wife files for divorce in New Hampshire on the basis of irreconcilable differences. Husband moves to dismiss, asserting that the trial court lacks jurisdiction in light of the fact that he had secured a Lebanese divorce, based on Islamic law, by declaring that he divorced Wife three times in her presence and by going to Lebanon to consult an attorney and sign divorce papers. The New Hampshire family court refuses to recognize the Lebanese ex parte divorce. The court reasons that Wife would be forced to bear the burdensome cost of traveling to Lebanon to seek relief from the divorce decree and also that recognition of an ex parte divorce obtained in a foreign nation where neither party is domiciled would frustrate New Hampshire laws regulating divorce. *In re Ramadan*, 891 A.2d 1186 (N.H. 2006).

b. **Rationale:** The rationale supporting recognition of foreign decrees include: vindication of the parties' expectations and achievement of finality.

2. **Full faith and credit distinguished:** Comity is a discretionary doctrine that governs the recognition of decrees rendered by the courts of a foreign country. On the other hand, the Full Faith and Credit Clause of the Constitution mandates judicial recognition of the decrees of sister states (i.e., of the "public acts, records and judicial proceedings" of other states).

   Note: The Full Faith and Credit Clause of the Constitution does not apply to divorces that are granted by foreign nations.

3. **Estoppel:** Many courts in the fault-based era refused to recognize foreign divorces. (The comity doctrine applied only in a minority of states.) Nonetheless, such divorces might be protected by means of the estoppel doctrine. That is, a spouse who obtains a foreign divorce may be estopped from denying its validity subsequently.

   Example: Dr. King and Mrs. Clagett decide to divorce their respective spouses and marry each other. They both obtain Mexican divorces. They marry but the marriage does not work out.

Wife seeks a separation and spousal support. Dr. King counters, seeking an annulment of the marriage on the ground that neither he nor Wife were eligible to marry each other because their divorces from their prior spouses were invalid. The court holds that the Mexican court was without jurisdiction to grant his divorce because the divorcing spouses were domiciliaries of Maryland. However, the husband is barred by estoppel from asserting the invalidity of the Mexican divorce because he sought that divorce. *Clagett v. King*, 308 A.2d 245 (D.C. Ct. App. 1973).

E. Domestic relations exception to federal jurisdiction: *Ankenbrandt v. Richards:* The U.S. Supreme Court narrowed the domestic relations exception to federal jurisdiction in *Ankenbrandt v. Richards*, 504 U.S. 689 (1992). *Ankenbrandt* limits the situations in which federal courts can refuse jurisdiction in those cases in which a party is seeking divorce, alimony, or custody decrees. Thus, *Ankenbrandt* permits federal courts to adjudicate a broader variety of disputes involving the divorcing parties.

Example: Carol Ankenbrandt, a Missouri citizen, files suit against her former husband and his female companion, seeking monetary damages for defendants' sexual and physical abuse of her daughters. Plaintiff alleges diversity jurisdiction. The district court dismisses based on the domestic relations exception to diversity jurisdiction and the abstention doctrine. The abstention doctrine, as announced in *Younger v. Harris*, 401 U.S. 37 (1971), states that federal courts may decline to exercise their jurisdiction in extraordinary circumstances because of federalism concerns (e.g., a reluctance to intervene if the state proceeding involves important state interests). The Fifth Circuit Court of Appeals affirms. Reversing, the U.S. Supreme Court holds that federal subject matter jurisdiction was proper. The Court maintains that the domestic relations exception is still valid only insofar as it divests federal courts of the power to issue divorce, alimony, and child custody decrees. Because plaintiff is not seeking such a decree, federal subject matter jurisdiction exists. The Court adds that application of the abstention doctrine was in error because no state proceeding was pending, nor did Defendant assert that the federal courts should not interfere because important state interests were at stake. *Ankenbrandt v. Richards*, 504 U.S. 689 (1992).

A number of courts have held that intraspousal claims for intentional infliction of emotional distress do not fall within the domestic relations exception.

Example: Woman brings action, based on diversity of citizenship, against her lover following the breakup of their 23-year relationship, alleging that he promised to divorce his wife and marry her, and asserting claims for promissory estoppel and intentional infliction of emotional distress. After his death, his personal representative argues that the case should be dismissed based on the domestic relations exception to diversity jurisdiction. The court of appeals disagrees, stating that this case grew out of the dissolution of an intimate relationship; and the woman's claims do not sound in the specific areas of divorce, alimony, and child custody. *Norton v. McOsker*, 407 F.3d 501 (1st Cir. 2005),

F. Jurisdiction to terminate a same-sex marriage or domestic partnership: Many states are grappling with jurisdictional issues involving the termination of a same-sex marriage or domestic partnership. Currently, same-sex marriage is valid in only a few states (i.e., Connecticut, Iowa, Massachusetts, New Hampshire, Vermont) and the District of Columbia, as well as a number of foreign countries (Belgium, Canada, Netherlands, Norway, South Africa, Spain, and Sweden). A minority of jurisdictions also confer a range of legal protections on same-sex couples based on legislation recognizing domestic partnerships (sometimes also called "civil unions" or "reciprocal beneficiaries"). Jurisdictional issues may arise when the partners move to another jurisdiction and desire to terminate the relationship.

1. **Termination in the original forum:** Problems do *not* arise in terminating the same-sex marriage or domestic partnership in the *original* forum where the union was recognized. Thus, a same-sex marriage validly entered into in Massachusetts by Massachusetts residents may be terminated there on the same basis as a marriage involving opposite-sex partners. Similarly, a domestic partnership validly entered into by residents of one state may be terminated in that particular state.

2. **Termination in another forum:** However, jurisdictions disagree whether a second forum has jurisdiction to dissolve a same-sex relationship that was entered into in another jurisdiction. Note that the federal Defense of Marriage Act (DOMA) permits the second state to refuse to extend recognition (and thereby deprives the courts in that second state of jurisdiction to dissolve the relationship). In addition, the second state may have legislation or a constitutional amendment that might require courts there to deny recognition to the same-sex marriage (and thereby prevent its dissolution).

   Example: Beth R. and Donna M. enter into a lesbian relationship in New York. After Donna gives birth to their daughter, they go to Canada to marry. They return to New York, and have another child before Donna decides to end the marriage two years later. Beth files for divorce and custody in New York. The court rules that it has jurisdiction to dissolve the women's marriage and also to address the custody and child support issues. The court reasons that *Hernandez v. Robles*, 855 N.E.2d 1 (Sup. Ct. 2006) (upholding New York's ban on same-sex marriage) did not address the validity of out-of-state same-sex marriages and adds that such recognition is not against state public policy. *Beth R. v. Donna M.*, 853 N.Y.S.2d 501 (Sup. Ct. 2008).

   Note: In May 2008, New York's Governor David Patterson signed an executive order requiring state agencies to recognize same-sex marriages that were validly performed in other jurisdictions.

   Example: J.B. petitions for a no-fault divorce and division of community property regarding his marriage to his male partner H.B. The two men were married in Massachusetts (where same-sex marriage is valid) and, two years later, moved to Texas (where such marriages are not valid) where they eventually separated. The appellate court rules that the court lacks subject matter jurisdiction because conferring a divorce would require recognition of the underlying validity of the marriage. *In re Marriage of J.B. and H.B.*, 2010 WL 3399074 (Tex. App. 2010).

3. **Jurisdictional prerequisite:** Proper registration of the domestic partnership is a jurisdictional prerequisite to maintaining an action for termination of that domestic partnership.

   Example: Two women register with the city of San Francisco as domestic partners in 1996, when they have a public commitment ceremony, and receive a domestic partnership ceremony certificate. Thereafter, they live together, purchase property together, and commingle their funds. One partner receives health coverage from the other's employer. However, the two women never register as domestic partners with the state after the state legislature enacts domestic partnership legislation. When one partner files to terminate the domestic partnership, the other partner files a motion for dismissal, based upon the ground that the former's claim fails to state facts sufficient to constitute a cause of action. The court of appeals holds that the parties' registration with the city did not confer standing to file a petition for dissolution because formal registration with the *state* is a prerequisite to pursuing dissolution under the Act. *Velez v. Smith*, 48 Cal. Rptr. 3d 642 (Ct. App. 2006).

4. **Jurisdictional limitation:** A civil union must be dissolved in a proceeding specifically for dissolution of a civil union and not in a divorce proceeding.

   Example: B.S. and F.B., two women, enter into a civil union in Vermont. They subsequently move to New York. After they end their relationship, B.S. petitions for a dissolution of the "marriage between the parties" on grounds of cruel and inhuman treatment. A New York trial court rules that, even though the parties' Vermont civil union was valid, New York courts lack the statutory authority to entertain dissolution actions of such civil unions because a civil union is not a "marriage," as required for jurisdictional purpose enabling a New York court to grant a divorce. *B.S. v. F.B.*, 883 N.Y.S.2d 458 (Sup. Ct. 2009).

5. **Alternate approach:** Even if a court in the second forum refuses to terminate the same-sex partners' marriage or domestic partnership, the court may still recognize the parties' contract claims.

   Example: Two male residents of New York enter into a same-sex relationship. During the relationship, Defendant gives Plaintiff expensive gifts, including automobiles and a ski house. The couple goes to Massachusetts to marry and then returns to New York. At that time, however, Massachusetts law permits members of same-sex couples to marry only if both are residents of Massachusetts. The couple separates and executes a separation agreement (prepared by Defendant's attorney) that provides for the division of their property and also provides for a one-time payment to Plaintiff of $780,000. Following *Hernandez v. Robles*, 805 N.Y.S.2d 354 (App. Div. 2005) (upholding the New York ban on same-sex marriage), Defendant seeks a declaration that because the parties never validly married, the separation agreement was void and all property transferred thereunder must be returned to Defendant. Although finding the parties' marriage invalid under the laws of either New York or Massachusetts, the court refuses to rescind the separation agreement. The court explains that New York has long recognized the enforceability of express contracts between unmarried cohabitants provided that illegal consideration is not part of the agreement. *Gonzalez v. Green*, 831 N.Y.S.2d 856 (Sup. Ct. 2006).

IX. ALTERNATIVES TO DIVORCE: ANNULMENTS AND SEPARATIONS

A. **Divorce, annulment, and separation distinguished:** A divorce terminates a valid marriage. An annulment is a judicial declaration that a marriage never took place. A legal separation is a judicial declaration that the parties are separated.

   English ecclesiastic practice distinguished between an *absolute divorce* and *divorce a mensa et thoro* (from bed and board). An absolute divorce permitted the parties to remarry. However, a *divorce a mensa et thoro* decreed that the parties could live separate and apart and might include orders as to temporary support and custody, but did not permit the parties to remarry.

B. Reasons to seek: In the fault era when spouses had difficulty obtaining a divorce in the absence of fault-based grounds, the parties might seek an annulment or legal separation as an alternative. Today, a spouse might seek an annulment for religious reasons (because some religions hold that a divorce bars a party from remarriage), or to reinstate a benefit that was lost upon marriage. Alternatively, a spouse might seek an annulment or legal separation in order to avoid a particular state's lengthy durational residency requirement for divorce.

For further distinctions between divorce and annulments, see Chapter 2.

X. ALTERNATIVE DISPUTE RESOLUTION PROCESSES

Criticisms of fault-based divorce (especially the acrimony and hostility accompanying judicial divorce) contributed to a movement toward alternative dispute resolution. This movement sought new ways to improve divorce procedures and the divorce process. The most common alternatives are arbitration, conciliation, and mediation.

A. Arbitration, conciliation, and mediation distinguished: Arbitration provisions are present in some separation agreements. Such provisions require the parties to submit future disputes (for example, support, property, or custody issues) to an arbitrator prior to initiating court action. Arbitration is an adjudicatory process, an alternative to traditional judicial resolution, by which a neutral third party (an "arbitrator") makes a determination that is binding upon the parties.

Conciliation is marriage counseling with an eye toward reconciliation (thereby avoiding divorce). In the fault era, some states established court-connected conciliation services.

Divorce mediation is a process by which the parties themselves, with the help of a mediator, resolve their disputes. Unlike in arbitration, the parties do not cede their authority to a neutral third party to resolve their dispute. In mediation, the parties themselves make their own agreements with the mediator serving as a facilitator.

Note: Of the three above alternatives, arbitration is most similar to judicial resolution because arbitration is still considered "adversarial." That is, each of the disputing parties, respectively, attempts to convince a third party who acts as decision maker. However, arbitration involves less time, expense, and effort than a full-scale trial.

B. Enforceability of arbitration provisions: Several states enforce agreements to arbitrate disputes in the divorce context. Among these states, however, a few states maintain that arbitration of, specifically, custody and visitation disputes is violative of public policy.

Example: Susan and Roger divorce after 17 years of marriage and 4 children. Prior to their divorce, they execute a marital settlement agreement regarding spousal support, child support, and custody. The agreement requires binding arbitration for any financial disputes between the parties. When Susan claims that Roger is in arrears on support payments and has defaulted on a promissory note regarding property, Roger cross-claims to compel arbitration. The court agrees, and the parties submit to arbitration. After the arbitrator makes an award, Roger argues that arbitration clauses involving domestic disputes should not be permitted as a violation of public policy and also that this award was erroneous. The court disagrees, holding that public policy supports the enforcement of arbitration provisions (by providing an effective alternative to judicial resolution, by reducing court congestion and hostilities, and by providing an opportunity for private resolution of sensitive matters). The court does not reach the question of whether provisions for arbitration of custody and visitation are unenforceable because the issue was not before the court. *Faherty v. Faherty*, 477 A.2d 1257 (N.J. 1984).

C. **Mandatory mediation:** A few states have mandatory mediation for divorcing parties. For example, California requires mediation, prior to judicial action, for couples who have disputes about custody or visitation. Cal. Fam. Code §3173 (West 2004).

For additional material on mediation, see Chapter 7.

D. **Collaborative law procedure:** The term "collaborative law" was coined in the late 1980s by a Minnesota divorce lawyer to signify an agreement by the parties and their attorneys to the use of cooperative techniques without resort to judicial intervention. (If the parties and lawyers are unable to resolve their differences through cooperative techniques, the lawyers must withdraw and cannot serve as counsel.) The collaborative law movement arrived in California in 1993 and spread from there to at least 20 states. In 2001, Texas became the first state, by statute, to recognize collaborative law in divorce proceedings (Tex. Fam. Code §§6.603, 153.0072) (Vernon 2006)).

Note: Collaborative law's requirement that the divorcing parties' lawyers must withdraw if settlement negotiations fail may pose a violation of state rules of professional conduct. *See, e.g.,* Colorado Bar Association, Ethics Opinion 115, Ethical Considerations in the Collaborative and Cooperative Law Contexts (Feb. 24, 2007) (suggesting that such a provision violates state professional conduct rules that bar a lawyer from representing a client if the representation is "materially limited by the lawyer's responsibilities to . . . a third person," because it creates an insurmountable conflict of interest impairing the lawyer's independent judgment about the need for litigation). However, the ABA finds that virtually all other state ethics opinions conclude that collaborative law is consistent with professional conduct rules. ABA Standing Comm. On Ethics and Professional Responsibility, Formal Op. 07-447, 8/9/07.

Quiz Yourself on DIVORCE JURISDICTION

59. Wife obtains a degree of separation in Illinois. Husband, a college teacher, writes to a Nevada attorney inquiring about obtaining a divorce there. He learns that Nevada has a six-week residency requirement. Husband discusses marriage with his new girlfriend. Husband moves to Nevada, telling his employer that he will return to teach in the Fall but retaining saving and checking accounts in Illinois. He obtains an ex parte Nevada divorce. Wife claims that the Nevada decree is not entitled to full faith and credit. Is Husband's divorce decree entitled to full faith and credit? ____________________

60. Husband and Wife reside in Iowa during their marriage. Following a period of marital strife, Wife leaves Husband to live with her parents in Missouri. Husband files a petition for divorce in Iowa based on ground of desertion. He neglects to forward to Wife a notice of the filing of the petition or to serve Wife with a copy of the summons and complaint. He dies shortly after obtaining the divorce. Wife enters a claim for Social Security benefits as his legal wife. Will she prevail? ____________________

61. Husband and Wife lived as a married couple in New York. Wife then moves to Vermont solely to take advantage of its no-fault divorce law. For two years, Wife continues to work in New York, but obtains a Vermont driver's license, votes in Vermont, pays Vermont taxes, and leases property in Vermont. She then files for divorce in Vermont. Does the Vermont court have subject matter jurisdiction over the divorce? ____________________

Answers

59. No. Husband's divorce decree, obtained ex parte, is not entitled to full faith and credit because Husband failed to establish a bona fide domicile in Nevada. Based on the Supreme Court decisions of *Williams I* and *Williams II*, Illinois is entitled to determine for itself the jurisdictional facts upon which the Nevada decree was based. Illinois should determine that the husband was not domiciled in Nevada because he did not intend to abandon his Illinois domicile (as evidenced by his retaining his Nevada job and bank accounts).

60. Yes. Because proper service of process is required for jurisdiction over a defendant, the decree of divorce is invalid. Wife was denied her due process rights because Husband knew her mailing address and should have provided Wife with *Mullane* notice. Therefore, Wife is entitled to Social Security benefits as Husband's legal spouse.

61. Yes. Although Wife's stated intent in moving to Vermont was to take advantage of its more favorable divorce laws, her actions (i.e., obtaining a driver's license voting, paying taxes, and leasing property in Vermont) demonstrate an intent to remain there indefinitely. She thereby satisfied the domicile requirement for subject matter jurisdiction. In addition, because Wife lived in Vermont for at least two years, she met any durational residency requirement imposed by the state.

Exam Tips *on* ***DIVORCE***

☛ Begin the discussion of divorce-related issues by referring to your answer on ***marriage validity***. That is, only if a valid marriage exists do you need to worry about dissolving it. However, do not assume that the invalidity of the marriage obviates the need to discuss divorce. Take care of this problem by saying something like, "Assuming that a valid marriage exists, then the plaintiff must terminate that relationship by divorce." (For annulment, see discussion *infra*.)

☛ Even though all jurisdictions have adopted some form of no-fault dissolution, it is still necessary to determine whether a plaintiff may/must resort to a ***fault-based ground*** or grounds (adultery, cruelty, desertion, etc.). (This is important because some jurisdictions still retain fault-based grounds.)

  ☞ Also determine if the defendant may raise any ***fault-based defenses*** (condonation, collusion, recrimination, connivance). Identify the requisite elements of these grounds and defenses. Remember that ***more than one ground or defense*** may exist.

- Next, explore the applicability of no fault. Determine the ***meaning of no fault*** in the relevant jurisdiction (i.e., "irreconcilable differences," or "living separate and apart"). Do not assume either that a given jurisdiction follows no fault or that the adoption of no-fault dissolution means that fault-based grounds are irrelevant.
  - In discussing no fault, determine if ***both spouses consent*** to a no-fault divorce (see jurisdiction discussion *infra*). In either case (if they both consent or one does not), discuss what difference this might make regarding the application of state statute and/or judicial willingness to grant the divorce.
  - Mention the reemergence of fault (***reform movement***). Determine if the ***covenant marriage*** doctrine is relevant and if so, explain and apply that doctrine.
- Examine the question to see if there are any issues involving ***alternatives*** to divorce (i.e., annulment or separation). Determine if reasons exist (jurisdictional, religious, etc.) for plaintiff to seek separation or annulment rather than divorce.
  - For annulment, explore possible ***grounds*** (i.e., fraud, duress) and the application of the "*relation back*" doctrine.
  - The ***void-voidable*** distinction may be relevant here as well.
- Be on the lookout for possible ***jurisdictional*** issues. Determine if there are issues regarding subject matter jurisdiction (i.e., domicile/durational residency requirements), personal jurisdiction over the defendant, or notice to the defendant.
  - Determine if this is a ***unilateral*** (ex parte) or ***bilateral*** divorce. That is, is only one party before the court or are both spouses present?
  - If the question involves an ex parte divorce, remember that the court in this case is able to grant only the divorce. That is, a court cannot adjudicate the financial aspects of an ex parte divorce because the court lacks jurisdiction over the absent spouse.
  - For issues of ***subject matter jurisdiction***, determine if the plaintiff has established a bona fide domicile. Be sure to check whether personal jurisdiction issues involve cross-over questions with constitutional law. Common issues are due process, and full faith and credit.
  - To establish ***personal jurisdiction*** over the defendant for purposes of support or property, recall that the assertion of jurisdiction must comport with the requirements of state long-arm statutes and the Constitution's Due Process Clause. Be sure to discuss both. For constitutional issues, analyze whether the defendant has sufficient contacts with the forum.
  - Also, make sure that ***notice to the defendant*** complies with the *Mullane* doctrine.
  - If you find a full faith and credit issue, be sure to discuss the *Williams* cases.
  - If a plaintiff seeks a divorce in a foreign country, explore the ***comity doctrine***. Remember that full faith and credit does not apply to divorce decrees issued by a foreign country.
- Before leaving issues of divorce, determine if there are any minor issues involving ***access*** to divorce (e.g., poverty or religious divorce), ***discrimination*** on the basis of divorce (again, a cross-over topic with constitutional law), or ***the role of counsel***. Issues concerning divorce attorneys might involve cross-over issues with ***professional responsibility*** (e.g., dual representation, confidentiality, conflicts of interest, or sexual relations with clients).

☛ Finally, always be alert for possible ***jurisdictional issues***, such as the possible ***applicability of the domestic relations exception to federal jurisdiction***. Normally, federal courts refuse to adjudicate family law matters, such as divorce, alimony, and custody, because such matters are more suitable for resolution by state courts. Any time a plaintiff initiates a lawsuit in federal court, be sure to discuss the domestic relations exception to federal jurisdiction (***define it and discuss its applicability***) and analyze the potential ***impact of Ankenbrandt v. Richards*** (narrowing the domestic relations exception to federal jurisdiction, thereby permitting federal courts to adjudicate a broader variety of disputes) for the particular fact pattern.

CHAPTER 6

FINANCIAL CONSEQUENCES OF DISSOLUTION

ChapterScope

This chapter addresses the financial consequences of dissolution. Specifically, it focuses on the legal rules that courts apply in their allocation of the financial obligations surrounding dissolution (i.e., awards of property, spousal support, and child support). Here are a few of the key principles covered in this chapter:

- Upon divorce, the court divides the spouses' property and may also award spousal support and child support, absent an agreement between the spouses.
- Two marital property regimes exist:
  - *common law*, and
  - *community property*.
- Different ***rationales*** characterize the division of marital ***property*** and the award of ***spousal support***.
  - The traditional rationale underlying both property divisions and awards of spousal support was ***fault***.
  - The ***contribution*** approach has replaced the traditional rationale for ***property*** division.
  - Modern rationales of ***self-sufficiency*** and ***loss compensation*** are replacing the traditional rationale for spousal support.
- ***Statutory guidelines*** have replaced ***discretion*** as the modern method of determining child support.
- Courts generally apply a standard of ***substantial and material change of circumstances*** in order to grant modifications of spousal support or child support.
- To make or modify an award of child support or spousal support, a court must have ***personal jurisdiction*** over the obligor.
- Absent ***merger*** or ***incorporation*** into a judicial decree, a separation agreement is only a contract.

I. STANDARDS FOR THE INITIAL AWARD OF PROPERTY, SPOUSAL SUPPORT, AND CHILD SUPPORT

At divorce, unless the spouses reach their own agreement, the court will divide the property acquired by one or both spouses and may also award spousal support (formerly called "alimony"). In addition, if the couple has minor children, a court will award child support.

A. Division of property

1. **Marital property regimes defined:** Two marital property regimes exist in the United States:

- common law, and
- community property.

Most states follow the common-law approach.

a. **Common law:** At common law, all property belonged to the spouse who acquired it. This included any property derived from that property (rents, profits, etc). Upon divorce, a court awarded property to the spouse who had title. This was called the "title system." Thus, a homemaker, for example, had no right to share in the property acquired by her income-earning husband.

b. **Community property:** Community property is the marital property regime in nine predominantly southern and western states (Arizona, California, Idaho, Louisiana, Nevada, New Mexico, Texas, Washington, and Wisconsin). This system derives largely from Spanish and French influences (except for Wisconsin, which follows a community property system because of its adoption of the Uniform Marital Property Act). The guiding principle of such marital property regimes is that marriage is a partnership.

Note: Statutory variations do exist in community property states. For example, some community property states require an equal division of the community property. However, other community property states adopt equitable distribution (discussed *infra*). Further, even the meaning of equitable distribution varies in community property jurisdictions, especially regarding the treatment of separate property (discussed *infra*).

2. **Equitable distribution generally:** A majority of jurisdictions now adhere to a system of equitable distribution. Equitable distribution has replaced the title system of property ownership. The objective of the equitable distribution system is to order a fair distribution, under all the circumstances, of the spouses' property.

The women's movement, in large part, contributed to the adoption of equitable distribution. Feminists argued that the common-law system failed to reflect and recompense women's contributions to marriage.

a. **Meaning of equitable distribution:** The equitable distribution regime requires courts to take into account a number of statutory factors in determining the most equitable allocation of the property between the spouses. Many states adopted equitable distribution based on the Uniform Marital and Divorce Act (UMDA) as originally formulated in 1970.

Currently, UMDA §307(a) provides four factors that courts may consider in arriving at a "just" division of marital property:

1. the contribution of each spouse to that property (including homemaking services);
2. the value of the property set apart to each spouse;
3. the duration of the marriage; and
4. the economic circumstances of each spouse at the time of dissolution, including the desirability of awarding the family home to the primary custodian of the children.

According to UMDA §307(b), marital property includes property acquired by the parties *subsequent* to the marriage but does *not* include property (1) acquired by gift or inheritance, (2) exchanged for separate property, or (3) subject to a valid agreement of the parties.

Upon divorce, most equitable distribution states follow UMDA and divide only marital property, although some equitable distribution states divide both separate and marital property.

In general, "equitable" (as in "equitable distribution") does not mean the same as "equal." However, in a few jurisdictions, a presumption exists that the most equitable division is an *equal* division, although in these jurisdictions courts are free to deviate from that presumption if it would lead to a more equitable result.

Example: Steve and Alice marry. Both work during the marriage. Fifteen years later, Steve becomes disabled from a job-related accident and receives a Workers' Compensation award. Alice gets laid off, and acquires a business license to sell cars. Steve and Alice purchase a car repair business. Steve is hospitalized for depression. Alice keeps the business going and pays the bills with income from the business. Both spouses acquired several pieces of real property during the marriage. After 22 years of marriage, Alice files for divorce. The trial court awards Alice 60 percent and Steve 40 percent of the marital property. The appellate court reverses, finding a 50-50 split more appropriate. The state supreme court affirms the trial court ruling based on fairness. The state supreme court rejects the view that the long-term nature of the marriage mandates an equal division and explains that the apportionment of marital property is entirely within the discretion of the trial court. *Dawkins v. Dawkins*, 687 S.E.2d 52 (S.C. 2010).

b. Constitutionality of equitable distribution: Courts have rejected constitutional challenges (on grounds of vagueness) to equitable distribution statutes.

c. Treatment of separate property: Separate property merits different treatment under the various property regimes. For example, in some community property jurisdictions (e.g., California), courts divide only the jointly acquired marital property (excluding separate property from the division of assets). In other community property jurisdictions (e.g., Washington and Wisconsin), statutes give courts authority to include separate property in the equitable distribution of assets. Similarly, some non–community property jurisdictions that follow equitable distribution also subject to division both separate and jointly acquired property. The rationale for the inclusion of both separate and jointly acquired property is that courts in equitable distribution jurisdictions are allowed considerable latitude in arriving at a fair division.

Note, however, that gifts and inheritances to one spouse, according to the majority approach (and UMDA), are considered nonmarital property (separate property) and therefore are awarded to the party who received them.

Example: Jane and David marry in 1973 and have three children. In 1992, Jane files for divorce. They cannot agree on an equitable division of their property. The trial court excludes from consideration certain gifts (worth approximately $40,000) made to Jane during the marriage by her family. David argues that these gifts should not be treated as Jane's separate property and that, on this basis, the ensuing property division (of $70,000 to Jane and $15,000 to David) was not equitable. Reversing, the state supreme court determines that under equitable distribution, a trial court must consider all relevant factors. The court concludes that the trial court erred by treating gifts to Jane as separate property rather than as marital property. (This view represents the minority approach.) *Gaulrapp v. Gaulrapp*, 510 N.W.2d 620 (N.D. 1994).

3. **Traditional rationales:** Several different rationales traditionally characterized the distribution of property.

   a. **Fault:** The most longstanding principle of property distribution is fault. That is, a court divides the property so as to punish the spouse who caused the marital breakup. Only innocent spouses traditionally received property (and spousal support) upon divorce.

   b. **Need:** According to the need rationale, a court divides property based on a spouse's need for support. Thus, a nonworking, dependent wife is in "need" of property and spousal support. A determination based on need ignores the duration of the marriage.

   c. **Status:** Based on the status principle, a court divides property based on the status that the parties enjoyed during the marriage. A determination based on status also rejects the duration of the marriage as a factor.

4. **Modern rationale:** A new rationale characterizes the distribution of property.

   a. **Contribution: The partnership model:** A contribution rationale takes into account the contributions of both spouses. The partnership model of marriage is based on this contribution rationale. Under this view, the court divides property based on the view that marriage is an economic partnership. Spousal earnings, as well as assets acquired with those earnings, belong to the partnership and are subject to division upon divorce.

   Note: In accordance with this principle, courts typically refuse to award spousal support because each partner exits with the respective skills brought into, or acquired during, the marriage.

      i. **Valuation of homemaker services:** A problem that arises based on the partnership model is how to calculate the contribution of the spouse who is a homemaker and who contributes services rather than property. The traditional devaluation of housework leads to a low estimate of the value of the stay-at-home spouse's contribution. Judicial and legislative reforms, increasingly, address this problem by providing that homemaker services may be taken into account.

      Example: Wife appeals from a judgment awarding her rehabilitative alimony but no property. The trial court bases its decision on the fact that Wife brought no assets to the marriage and made no monetary contribution to it. The appellate court seeks to determine whether the statute that permits property awards based on a spouse's "contribution" includes nonmonetary as well as monetary contributions. Reversing and remanding, the appellate court holds that, although Wife did not make a monetary contribution to the marriage, she did make a contribution of homemaker services. "A property division ought to accord value to those nonmonetary contributions of one spouse which enable the other spouse to devote substantial effort to paid employment which in turn, enables the family to acquire tangible marital assets." The court adds that legislative history dictates consideration of nonmonetary contributions in the equitable distribution of property at dissolution. *O'Neill v. O'Neill*, 536 A.2d 978, 984 (Conn. App. Ct. 1988).

ii. **Community property and the contribution approach:** The community property regime, based on the idea of marriage as a partnership, reflects the contribution rationale. The partnership concept applies not only at dissolution but during the marriage. That is, a community property regime gives rise to present vested interests in both spouses in all property acquired during the marriage (other than that acquired by gift or inheritance). Management of the community property also is shared.

iii. **ALI innovative approach to contribution:** The American Law Institute (ALI) has formulated *Principles of the Law of Family Dissolution* that reconceptualize some of the financial consequences of dissolution. The objective of the *Principles* is to obtain uniformity among the states and to permit greater predictability of outcomes. One provision (§4.18) recharacterizes separate property as marital property for the dissolution of *long-term marriages* (unless the trial court makes written findings that preservation of the separate character of the property is necessary to avoid substantial injustice). This provision is based on the fulfillment of the reasonable expectations of the parties in long-term marriages.

b. **Limited role for fault as a modern rationale:** Despite the widespread adoption of no-fault, marital fault still plays a limited role in some states' equitable distribution schemes. This occurs, for example, if the fault includes adultery, cruelty, or the waste of marital assets.

Example: Mary has an extramarital affair and her husband John engages in long-standing verbally abusive behavior. A Virginia statute prevents awarding spousal support to a spouse due to her adultery, unless the denial of support would be a manifest injustice based on both the parties' relative degrees of fault and a disparity in their economic circumstances. The appellate court determines that the exception applies because John's 20-year history of profane behavior outweighs Mary's adultery, and also because the parties' economic circumstances were clearly disparate, given John's high-paying job with a family company and Mary's minimal employment. *Congdon v. Congdon*, 578 S.E.2d 833 (Va. Ct. App. 2003).

c. **Reform movement: Reemergence of fault:** Currently, some commentators, as well as legislators, urge that fault should play a more salient role in the determination of the parties' financial rights and responsibilities upon divorce (see discussion in Chapter 5).

Quiz Yourself on *DIVISION OF PROPERTY: RATIONALES*

62. Howard and Lillian are married in a common-law fault-based jurisdiction. Both spouses work during the marriage. They have four children, the youngest of whom is not the biological child of Howard, but rather is the product of Lillian's extramarital affair. Lillian's affair lasted for much of the marriage. Howard petitions for divorce and requests equitable division of the property with the bulk of the property going to him based on Lillian's adultery. Will he succeed? ____________________

63. Laura and Bob have been married for 24 years. They have two teenage children. They live in the jurisdiction of Blackacre. During the marriage, Laura was a traditional homemaker. Bob worked for a local telephone company. All their jointly acquired property is held in Bob's name. Blackacre follows the title theory in the distribution of marital assets. The couple divorces, following a mutually agreed upon separation. When the court awards all the marital property to Bob, Laura appeals. Will she be successful? ____________________

64. Same basic facts as above, except Bob and Laura live in a community property jurisdiction. All the couple's jointly acquired property is held in Bob's name. At the couple's dissolution, the court awards all the community property to Bob. Laura appeals. Will she be successful? ____________________

65. Janet and Peter have been married for ten years. At the beginning of their marriage, Janet received a legacy of $100,000 upon the death of her mother. She purchased stock with the money and titled the stock in her name. When the couple divorces in a jurisdiction that has adopted the Uniform Marriage and Divorce Act, will the court divide the stock between Janet and Paul? ____________________

Answers

62. Perhaps, depending on the jurisdiction. At common law, upon divorce only spouses who were innocent of marital fault were eligible to receive property or spousal support. Lillian was guilty of marital fault because she committed adultery. Therefore, Lillian's fault may bar her claims for an equal division of the property or spousal support. However, today, many fault-based jurisdictions require egregious fault in order to grant an unequal property division. Adultery usually does not meet this standard.

63. No. Under common-law jurisdictions that followed the title theory, each spouse is considered the owner of all property that is titled in his or her name. Therefore, the court was correct in awarding all the marital property to Bob because all property was titled in his name. Today, however, the title theory has been replaced by equitable distribution.

64. Yes. In a community property jurisdiction, each spouse owns a present undivided equal interest in the community ("marital") property. Even though the couple's jointly acquired property is titled in Bob's name, Laura still retains the right to her half of the jointly acquired property based on the jurisdiction's adherence to a community property regime.

65. No. UMDA follows a system of equitable distribution. According to UMDA §307(b), marital property includes property acquired by the parties *subsequent* to the marriage but does *not* include property acquired by gift or inheritance (which is considered each spouse's separate property), or property that is exchanged for separate property. Because Janet purchased the stock with funds that were acquired by virtue of an inheritance from her mother, the stock will be considered Janet's property and not subject to division. Note that separate property merits different treatment under various property regimes. For example, in some community property states, courts exclude separate property (such as inheritances) from the division of assets, whereas other community property jurisdictions permit courts to include separate property in the equitable distribution of assets. Similarly, some non–community property jurisdictions that follow equitable distribution also subject to division both separate and jointly acquired property. UMDA and the majority of jurisdictions exclude gifts and inheritances from the equitable distribution of assets.

---

5. **What is property?**

   a. **Professional licenses and degrees:** During many marriages, one spouse (often the wife) contributes earnings and services while the other spouse may attain a professional license or degree. The supporting spouse does so in the hope that both partners will benefit subsequently from an enhanced standard of living. If the marriage dissolves before that time, the partnership model of marriage dictates that the supporting spouse's contributions be compensated in some manner.

   Increasingly, courts are asked to determine whether the license or degree is an asset subject to distribution upon dissolution. This *characterization* involves a question of statutory interpretation (e.g., is the license or degree "property" within the meaning of an equitable distribution statute).

      i. **Characterization: Majority approach:** Almost all states *refuse* to treat professional licenses and degrees that represent a spouse's enhanced earning capacity as marital property. If a court determines that a license or degree is not property, then the court might find an alternative theory for compensating the supporting spouse. In an effort to achieve a fair result, many jurisdictions, by case law or statute, take licenses and degrees into account in awards of spousal support.

      Example: Leigh Anne marries Matthew. Immediately thereafter, Matthew begins attending law school. Leigh Anne works to support them. Two months before Matthew's graduation, Leigh Anne learns that she is pregnant, and thereafter the couple separates. Matthew takes an associate position with a large law firm in Chicago and files for divorce (after a four-year marriage). The parties have little property. The court determines that Matthew's law degree could not be considered a marital asset. The appellate court agrees but holds that the enhanced earning ability of a degree-earning spouse may be considered in the division of marital assets. The court awards Leigh Anne most of the marital assets. *In re Marriage of Roberts*, 670 N.E.2d 72 (Ind. Ct. App. 1996).

      See also Cal. Fam. Code §2641(b)(1) (West 2004) (providing for reimbursement of the community for contributions to the education or training of a party that substantially increases the earning capacity of that party).

      ii. **Characterization: Minority approach:** Under the minority approach, a few courts characterize a professional license or advanced degree as a marital asset subject to property division and reject the approach that considers enhanced earning capacity as a factor merely in awards of spousal support.

      Example: An accountant marries a nursing student. Wife postpones nursing school to support them while the husband attends law school. She contributes $53,000 while he is in school (he contributes $12,000). Husband finishes school and starts earning

$41,000 at a law firm. Wife returns to nursing school. A few months later, they divorce when Husband meets another woman. The trial court determines that Husband's law degree is a marital asset, awards Wife no alimony, and values the degree at $80,000 (of which $32,000 is awarded to Wife to equalize her share of the marital assets). Both spouses appeal. The appellate court holds that it is equitable that a supporting spouse should be compensated when the supported spouse earns an advanced degree which is the end product of a "concerted family effort." The court rejects the characterization of the degree as alimony, because awards of alimony are discretionary and terminable upon remarriage, and because Wife has demonstrated her ability to support herself and therefore does not "need" alimony. The court advises the trial court, on remand, to focus not on reimbursement for Wife's loss of expectations but rather reimbursement for her sacrifices and contribution toward attainment of the degree in light of the fact that she will not share the fruits of that degree. Among the factors to be considered are: the length of time after attainment of degree that she was able to enjoy the enhanced standard of living (very short here), the vast percentage of financial support that she furnished as well as her nonpecuniary contributions, and the hardships she endured. *Postema v. Postema*, 471 N.W.2d 912 (Mich. Ct. App. 1991).

Note: New York was the first state to treat a professional license (to practice medicine) as a marital asset. *See O'Brien v. O'Brien*, 489 N.E.2d 712 (N.Y. 1985).

iii. **Criticism of minority characterization of licenses and degrees as property:** Most courts have difficulty characterizing professional licenses or degrees as property for the following reasons:

- A degree or license lacks the traditional attributes of property (i.e., it cannot be bought or sold, has no exchange value, is personal to the holder, terminates on the death of the holder and is not inheritable);
- Future earning capacity is too difficult and speculative to value;
- A degree or license is a product of only one spouse's intelligence and skills; and
- Valuation as property would result in indentured servitude forcing one spouse to work to pay the other.

iv. **ALI approach:** The ALI *Principles* adopt the majority rule and refuse to treat earning capacity as divisible property. Instead, the *Principles* provide for "compensatory payments" to reimburse the supporting spouse for the financial contributions made to the other spouse's education or training. ALI *Principles* §§4.07, 5.12. The education must have been completed in less than a specified number of years (set out in a rule of statewide application) before the filing of the dissolution petition. Id. at §5.12.

b. **Goodwill:** Another intangible asset of a marriage is the ***goodwill*** of one spouse's business or professional practice (e.g., law, medicine, accounting). Goodwill is the ***reputation of the business*** that signifies the probability of future earnings. Cases wrestle with whether one spouse has a property interest in the other spouse's business/professional practice or whether the goodwill is personal (i.e., the product of unique skills).

Most courts recognize two types of goodwill in divorce litigation: ***personal goodwill*** and ***enterprise goodwill***. Different approaches exist as to whether personal goodwill and/or enterprise goodwill in a professional practice may be characterized as marital property.

The majority of states, differentiating between "enterprise goodwill" and "personal goodwill," take the position that personal goodwill is not marital property, but that enterprise goodwill is marital property. According to this view, personal goodwill is not marital property because it is intrinsically tied to the attributes and/or skills of a particular individual. However, enterprise goodwill is a business asset that is attributable to the business by virtue of its arrangements with suppliers or customers, and its anticipated future customer base due to factors attributable to the business.

Example: Julie has a successful practice as an oral surgeon, making 90 percent of the marital earnings, while John works as a salaried employee in a separate business. Upon their divorce, the court awards a 50-50 division of the marital property. Julie's expert values her business at $220,000, with $0 for enterprise goodwill, explaining that the success of the business was due to Julie's skills, personality, and work ethic. John's expert values the business at $670,000. The trial court rejects a distinction between personal and enterprise goodwill and awards $222,500 (half of the average between the two values) to John. Julie appeals. The state supreme court grants discretionary review to consider the proper valuation of goodwill. The court holds that there is a distinction between personal and enterprise goodwill, that Julie's practice was attributable to her personal goodwill, and that the trial court erred in awarding John half of the nonmarital personal goodwill, and in choosing an arbitrary number for the value of the business. *Gaskill v. Robbins*, 282 S.W.3d 306 (Ky. 2009).

c. **Other enhanced earning capacity:** Sometimes, during the marriage, one spouse helps the other obtain enhanced earning capacity through some means other than a license or degree. One example is the acquisition of celebrity status. Courts must determine whether such enhanced value of a spouse's career is an asset subject to distribution upon dissolution.

Example: Upon dissolution of a 17-year-marriage, the husband of opera singer Frederica von Stade Elkus argues that her celebrity status constitutes marital property subject to equitable distribution. At the time of the marriage, von Stade was beginning her career (earning $2,250 annually). During the marriage, she became highly successful (earning $600,000 annually). Her husband served as her voice coach and photographer. He claims that he sacrificed his own career to help her and raise their two children. The trial court determines that her celebrity status is not marital property since the husband benefited financially during the marriage and would be compensated adequately by division of their substantial assets. He appeals. Reversing and remanding, the court holds that celebrity status is marital property subject to equitable distribution to the extent that the appreciation in her career is attributable to the husband's efforts and contributions. *Elkus v. Elkus*, 572 N.Y.S.2d 901 (App. Div. 1991).

d. **Pensions and retirement benefits:** Pension benefits may constitute a significant part of the marital property for many couples. Two central issues arise:

- whether pension benefits (vested and nonvested) should be *characterized* as marital property, and
- what is the appropriate method of *valuing* pensions.

i. **Definition:** ***Vested*** pension rights are not subject to forfeiture if the employment terminates (voluntarily or involuntarily) prior to retirement. ***Nonvested*** pensions are subject to such forfeiture.

ii. **Characterization as marital property: Majority and minority views:** Under the majority rule, vested *and* nonvested pensions are marital property subject to equitable distribution. Under the minority rule, vested (but *not* nonvested) pensions are marital property subject to equitable distribution.

Example: Wife files for divorce after a 20-year marriage. Husband was employed as a firefighter for almost the entire duration of the marriage. He is entitled to a pension after 25 years of service. (His pension, therefore, is nonvested.) Husband appeals the trial court decision awarding Wife one-half of his nonvested pension benefits as marital property. Affirming, the state supreme court holds that Husband's nonvested pension benefits are sufficiently concrete, reasonable, and justifiable as to constitute a presently existing property interest for equitable distribution purposes. The court reasons that any uncertainty regarding vesting is more appropriately handled in the valuation and distribution stages, rather than in the classification stage. *Bender v. Bender*, 785 A.2d 197 (Conn. 2001).

iii. **Valuation:** Pension valuation may present complex problems. Jurisdictions choose among different methods of valuation. These include:

- calculating the employee's contributions to the plan, plus interest, and awarding the nonemployed spouse an appropriate share (most useful for pension plans funded by employer contributions rather than those in which the employee only contributes a portion);
- calculating the present value of the prospective benefits when they vest, discounted to present day (based on several speculative possibilities); or
- determining the spousal shares by a formula but retaining jurisdiction until payments actually are received (the reserved jurisdiction approach).

iv. **Federal pension benefits and federalism principles:** The distribution of federal pension benefits may involve a conflict between federal law versus state equitable distribution or community property law. The issue is whether state courts dividing marital property interfere with certain rights guaranteed under federal law. That is, does federal legislation preempt or preclude, under the Supremacy Clause of the Constitution, state statutes that regulate the division of property acquired during the marriage?

(a) **Railroad employees' retirement benefits:** Federal legislation provides for retirement benefits for certain federal employees. Litigation has occurred regarding the rights of a divorced spouse to railroad employees' retirement benefits.

In *Hisquierdo v. Hisquierdo*, 439 U.S. 572 (1979), the California Supreme Court determines that a husband's railroad pension under the Railroad Retirement Act of 1937 (RRA), 45 U.S.C. §§231-231u (2006), is community property because these benefits stem from the husband's employment during the marriage. The U.S. Supreme Court reverses, determining that the anti-alienation provision in the RRA preempts state divorce law. The Court reasons that Congress enacted the RRA to benefit the employee, not the employee's divorced spouse, and that an award to the divorced spouse would frustrate federal policy.

Note: Congress subsequently amends the RRA to extend benefits to those divorced spouses who have been married to the railroad employee for at least ten years. 45 U.S.C. §231a(c)(4)(I-iii) (2006).

Although *Hisquierdo* involved a community property jurisdiction, the decision had applicability to other marital property regimes.

(b) Military retirement benefits: The U.S. Supreme Court again confronts, in the context of military retirement benefits, the issue of federal preemption of state law in terms of state court distribution of federal benefits upon dissolution.

In *McCarty v. McCarty*, 453 U.S. 210 (1981), the U.S. Supreme Court rules that military retirement benefits are the separate property of the retiree. The Court thereby reverses a California Supreme Court decision holding that military retirement pay is community property that is divisible at divorce.

The Court bases its reasoning on the lack of congressional intent. However, the Court goes further than in *Hisquierdo* in its unwillingness to permit state court interference in federal retirement benefit law because the statutory language of the military retirement scheme is far less clear than was the RRA (i.e., the RRA has an anti-assignment provision and provides that spousal benefits terminate upon divorce, whereas the military retirement benefits statute contains neither provision).

Considerable dissatisfaction by women's groups and others led to the enactment of the Uniformed Services Former Spouses Protection Act (USFSPA), 10 U.S.C. §1408 (2006), that overrules *McCarty*. USFSPA permits state courts to apply their own laws in determining the divisibility of military retirement benefits upon divorce. It also facilitates enforcement by permitting payment to be made directly to the former spouse without the need for periodic garnishment actions. Direct payments are subject to the following limitations:

- The ex-spouse must have been married to a service member for at least ten years of the latter's service;
- The ex-spouse's share may not exceed 50 percent of the service member's pension; and
- Payments terminate on the death of either the ex-spouse or the service member (but the ex-spouse retains his or her benefits if he or she remarries).

Because USFSPA permits, but does not require, state courts to divide the federal pension, challenges later arose addressing how state courts (in both community property as well as equitable distribution jurisdictions) would treat the military retirement benefits in certain cases.

Example: Gaye and Gerald Mansell divorce after 23 years of marriage. Gerald then is receiving Air Force retirement pay and disability benefits. (He waives a portion of his military retirement pay in order to receive the disability benefits to obtain more favorable tax treatment.) By contract, Gaye and Gerald agree that she will receive 50 percent of his total military retirement pay and disability benefits. Four years later, after enactment of the federal Former Spouses' Protection Act (USFSPA), Gerald requests modification of that agreement to preclude Gaye from retaining her share of retirement benefits and disability benefits. The trial court denies his request. On appeal, Gerald argues that the USFSPA preempts state community property law, as applied to military retirement pay, so as to preclude treating his waived military retirement pay as community property. The Court of Appeal affirms the denial of his request regarding his retirement pay but does not address his disability benefits. The U.S. Supreme Court holds that, based on congressional intent, the USFSPA precludes states from treating as community property any military retirement pay that the retiree waived to receive disability benefits. According to the Court, the language of the USFSPA grants state courts the authority to treat disposable retired pay as community property but not the portion that the retiree waived in lieu of disability benefits. *Mansell v. Mansell*, 490 U.S. 581 (1989).

(c) **Same-sex couples:** The federal Defense of Marriage Act defines "marriage" and "spouse" to exclude same-sex couples. 1 U.S.C. §7 (2006). Thus, a valid same-sex marriage entered under state law does not qualify a spouse for federal pension benefits. The federal DOMA has similar implications for bankruptcy and federal income tax.

v. **Federal pension benefits regulation: ERISA, REA, and QDROs:** The comprehensive federal pension law, ERISA (the Employee Retirement Income Security Act of 1974), 29 U.S.C §§1000 et seq., originally limited the rights of a nonemployee spouse (e.g., the wife of a covered employee) to share in the employee's pension upon divorce. ERISA's "anti-alienation rule" states that pension plan benefits may not be assigned or alienated.

The purpose of the rule is to ensure that the participant not consume retirement savings prior to retirement. ERISA made no special exceptions for domestic relations claims against an employee's pension plan. In the wake of ERISA, federal and state courts split on whether the anti-alienation rule barred distribution of pension benefits to a nonemployee spouse pursuant to a divorce.

Congress enacted the Retirement Equity Act of 1984 (REA), Pub. L. No. 98-397, 98 Stat. 1426 (codified in scattered sections of 26 and 29 U.S.C.), to remedy this problem that was experienced primarily by ex-wives. REA permits a court to divide pension benefits as a marital asset. REA mandates that the ERISA anti-alienation rule must yield to certain state domestic relations decrees, i.e., those "qualified domestic relations orders" (QDROs).

A QDRO facilitates the enforcement of awards of spousal support and child support by authorizing retirement plan administrators to make payments directly to a former spouse, thereby enabling that spouse not to be dependent on the plan beneficiary to pay the amount awarded by the divorce decree. QDROs apply to both spousal and child support. REA left unresolved some federal-state conflicts about pension rights (such as whether ERISA preempts state succession laws, discussed *infra*).

The federal Pension Protection Act, Pub. L. No. 109-280, 120 Stat. 780 (codified at 29 U.S.C. §1001), amends ERISA and the Internal Revenue Code, inter alia, calling for new regulations on the time and order of the issuance of QDROs and enhancing the protection of former spouses of railroad employees.

vi. **Federal preemption of state succession law: *Boggs* and *Egelhoff*:** The U.S. Supreme Court addressed the issue of federal preemption of state succession law in two cases: *Boggs v. Boggs* and *Egelhoff v. Egelhoff*. *Boggs* involved whether ERISA preempts a state law allowing a nonparticipant spouse to transfer, by testamentary instrument, an interest in undistributed pension plan benefits.

Example: Isaac and Dorothy have three sons. They live together until 1979 when Dorothy dies. Dorothy's will purports to transfer to their sons her community property interest in Isaac's undistributed pension plan benefits. One year after Dorothy's death, Isaac marries Sandra. Isaac and Sandra remain married until Isaac dies in 1989. After Isaac's death, Sandra seeks a survivor's annuity under Isaac's employment plan. Isaac's sons from his prior marriage argue that they have a right to a portion of Sandra's survivor's annuity (based on their mother's testamentary transfer). Sandra seeks a declaratory judgment that ERISA preempts the application of state community property and succession laws that would recognize the sons' interest in the retirement benefits. The district court grants summary judgment against Sandra; the federal circuit court of appeals affirms. Reversing, the U.S. Supreme Court rules that ERISA preempts the state community property and succession laws. The Court determines that Sandra has a surviving spouse's statutory entitlement to the annuity that is not subject to the sons' claims. *Boggs v. Boggs*, 520 U.S. 833 (1997).

The U.S. Supreme Court again held that federal pension regulation (ERISA) preempts state succession law in *Egelhoff v. Egelhoff*.

Example: Husband and Wife divorce shortly before his death. Husband dies without a will, but without having altered the designation of his wife as beneficiary of his life insurance and pension. His children from a prior marriage sue his second wife, claiming entitlement to the life insurance proceeds and pension benefits. A Washington state statute provides for automatic revocation at divorce of any designation of a spouse as a beneficiary in a nonprobate asset. The state statute (favoring the children as recipients of the nonprobate assets) conflicts with ERISA that directs payments according to the plan (favoring the spouse). The United States Supreme Court holds that the Washington automatic revocation statute was preempted, as it applied to ERISA benefit plans (i.e., payments should be made to the wife). *Egelhoff v. Egelhoff*, 532 U.S. 141 (2001). (Note: The holding is not limited to community property states.)

e. **Bankruptcy discharge**

i. **Generally:** Sometimes, certain events occur during or after dissolution that may affect a spouse's ability to pay a property award or spousal support. One such event is bankruptcy. To further the protective policy behind the federal Bankruptcy Code, 11 U.S.C. §541 (2006), a debtor may claim exemption for certain property (e.g., home, car, etc.). The Code also permits a debtor-spouse to be discharged from certain divorce-related obligations.

ii. **Rule: Nondischargeability from support obligations:** The traditional rule is that the obligations attributable to a *property* division upon divorce are dischargeable in bankruptcy. However, *spousal support and child support obligations are not*. This is called "the support-property distinction."

Because of this important difference in treatment, it becomes critical to determine whether an obligation is classified as support or a property division. Such characterization may be difficult because judicial decrees and parties' settlement agreements often blur the distinction between support and property. Therefore, the particular label in the decree or agreement is not determinative. One method to overcome this problem is to rely on the "intent" and "function" of the financial obligation: The court looks behind the label of "property" or "alimony" to find the (court's or spouses') intention in creating the underlying financial obligation and the function of that obligation (i.e., to divide property or furnish support). The trend among courts is to construe "support" broadly. *See In re Busch*, 369 B.R. 614 (10th Cir. BAP 2007) (construing husband's postdissolution obligation to pay off the second mortgage on the family home as nondischargeable support).

iii. **Stay of proceedings:** Federal bankruptcy law provides that the filing of a bankruptcy petition will halt state proceedings (except for paternity actions, and the establishment or modification of spousal support orders). Bankruptcy Code, 11 U.S.C. §362(b)(2) (2006). Further, the bankruptcy court can terminate, modify, annul, or condition a stay "for cause." *Id.* at §362(d)(1). This policy implicates a tension between federal versus state interests.

Example: When Patricia institutes divorce proceedings, the court orders John to make temporary alimony payments of $800 per week. John files for bankruptcy, thereby halting ("staying") the divorce proceedings as provided by federal law. Patricia requests that the bankruptcy court lift the stay so that the state court can proceed to determine the appropriate division of marital assets, arguing that the state court jurisdiction takes precedence because the state action was filed first. The bankruptcy court lifts the stay. John appeals, claiming that federal jurisdiction is exclusive (i.e., it preempts the state action). The federal court of appeals finds no abuse of discretion in the bankruptcy court's decision to defer to the state court to determine the spouse's respective interests in the marital property because this determination is traditionally reserved for state divorce courts. Otherwise, federal bankruptcy law could be used as a weapon in divorce proceedings. *White v. White*, 851 F.2d 170 (6th Cir. 1988).

iv. **Bankruptcy Reform Act (BRA) of 1994:** The Bankruptcy Reform Act, 11 U.S.C. §523(a)(15) (2006), modifies the traditional rule that property obligations are dischargeable. It provides that debtor-spouses may no longer discharge property obligations if the creditor-spouse complies with new filing requirements. To mitigate potential hardship to the debtor-spouse, the Act provides that the debtor-spouse still may discharge property obligations by showing (a) he or she needs these resources for his/her support and that of dependents, or (b) the benefit of the discharge would outweigh the creditor-spouse's detriment.

The Bankruptcy Abuse Prevention and Consumer Protection Act of 2005 (BAPCPA), 11 U.S.C.A., §523(a)(15) (West 2009), further modifies the traditional rule that property obligations are dischargeable. More debts are now *nondischargeable* under Chapter 7.

Property obligations stemming from a dissolution judgment or separation agreement are no longer dischargeable in Chapter 7 bankruptcies. However, the support-property distinction continues to control dischargeability for purposes of Chapter 13 bankruptcies. See 11 U.S.C. §1328(a)(2) (2006) (excepting §523(a)(5) obligations from discharge but not §523(a)(15) obligations). (Chapter 7 provides for a straight bankruptcy liquidation, whereas Chapter 13 involves a repayment plan, usually partial, of debts.) Note that the determination of whether an obligation is nondischargeable is governed by federal, rather than state, law.

v. Dischargeability of liens: One of the common methods for one spouse to secure the payor-spouse's obligation is by the imposition of a lien on the payor-spouse's property. A problem arises if the payor-spouse subsequently declares bankruptcy for the reason that the Bankruptcy Code, 11 U.S.C. §522(f) (2006), permits a debtor to avoid the fixing of a lien in some circumstances.

Example: Jeanne and Gerald divorce after a 20-year marriage. Each receives half of the marital property. Gerald's share gives him title to all real property, including the family home. Thus, although the parties owned the home in joint tenancy during the marriage, after the decree Gerald owns it in fee simple. The court orders him to pay Jeanne her share of $29,000 in two installments. To secure the award, the court orders a lien imposed against Gerald's real property until such time as the total is paid in full. Gerald makes no payments. Instead, he files for bankruptcy, claiming all his real property as exempt. In addition, he seeks to nullify the lien as encumbering his exemption. Jeanne argues that the federal bankruptcy law cannot divest her of her property interest. The bankruptcy court agrees, saying that the lien should not be nullified because it protects Jeanne's preexisting interest. The district court reverses, reasoning that Gerald can avoid the lien because it fixes on Gerald's interest in the property. The Court of Appeals affirms. Reversing, the United States Supreme Court rules in favor of Jeanne based on legislative intent. The Court rules that federal bankruptcy law does not permit a debtor, upon divorce, to avoid a lien and, thereby, to defeat the other spouse's property interest. According to the Court, bankruptcy law permits a debtor to avoid only those liens that fix on a preexisting interest of the *debtor* in property. That is, the debtor can avoid the lien if the following sequence occurs: He possesses a particular property interest and the lien is fixed *subsequently* on that *same* property interest. Because Gerald acquired a new undivided interest in the marital home at the time of the decree (in property formerly held in joint tenancy), the lien did not attach to a preexisting interest of the debtor as §522(f) requires: It attached on his new fee simple interest. (The Court adds, even assuming that no new interest was created and that the decree only reordered preexisting interests, the same result would follow because the decree transferred Jeanne's interest to Gerald and attached to *her* previous interest in the property.) *Farrey v. Sanderfoot*, 500 U.S. 291 (1991).

Note: The Bankruptcy Abuse Prevention and Consumer Protection Act of 2005 provides that a debtor can avoid a lien on exempt property only when the lien does not secure a domestic support obligation. 11 U.S.C.A. §522(f)(1)(A) (West 2009).

f. Personal injury awards: For purposes of equitable distribution, many courts classify personal injury awards depending on the nature of the assets they are intended to replace. That is, many courts hold that the portion of the personal injury award representing compensation for noneconomic losses (i.e., pain, suffering, disability) represents the separate property of the injured spouse. However, the portion of an award representing compensation for economic loss during the marriage (e.g., past wages, medical expenses that diminish the marital estate) is marital property subject to division. *See, e.g., Finkel v. Finkel*, 590 S.E.2d 472 (N.C. App. 2004). Similarly, there is considerable authority for treating as divisible property those personal injury awards designed to compensate for lost future earnings. Note that courts in a majority of states classify disability benefits received *after separation* as separate property.

Quiz Yourself on
WHAT IS PROPERTY?

66. Harry and Wilma are both teachers. When Harry chooses to pursue a medical degree, Wilma continues to teach and contributes all her earnings to their joint support. Harry completes his education and begins employment as a radiologist. A year later, he announces to Wilma that he wants a divorce. At trial, Wilma's expert testifies that the present value of Harry's medical license is $1,000,000 and that the value of Wilma's contribution to Harry's medical education was $200,000. Wilma contends that Harry's medical degree and license are marital property subject to distribution. The jurisdiction follows equitable distribution. Will Wilma prevail? ____________________

67. Jennie and Doug are married. A few months later Doug is hired by the Whiteacre City Fire Department. He immediately begins making contributions from his wages to the state firemen's retirement fund. Jennie and Doug divorce after a 20-year marriage. At that time, Doug has completed 19 years of employment with the city fire department. Under his employer's policy, Doug cannot draw a pension from the retirement fund until he has completed 20 years of service. In the divorce proceedings, the trial court finds that the value of the couple's marital property interest in the firemen's retirement fund consists of Doug's cash contributions to the fund until the date of the divorce (i.e., the cash surrender value of Doug's pension contributions) and awards Jennie half that amount. Jennie appeals, arguing that she has a property right in Doug's nonvested pension benefits. Will she prevail? ____________________

68. Wife and Husband divorce in a common-law jurisdiction after a 30-year marriage. At the time of the divorce, Husband is eligible to receive military retirement benefits based on his service in the marines. Husband argues that his military retirement benefits are exempted from distribution by the divorce court because military retirement benefits are subject to federal law. (At the time, federal law provides that military retirement benefits are the serviceman's separate property.) Wife contends that state courts have the ability to value and distribute military pension rights. Will she prevail? ____________________

Answers

66. Probably not. The court must determine whether Harry's license or degree is "property" within the meaning of the state's equitable distribution statute. If the couple's jurisdiction follows the majority approach, the court will refuse to treat Harry's medical degree and license as marital property. However, even in a jurisdiction that follows the majority approach, Wilma may not be totally out of luck. She may have a claim, depending on case law or statute, that would reimburse her for her contributions and services during the time Harry was in medical school. If Wilma and Harry live in a jurisdiction that follows the ALI *Principles,* Wilma similarly will be unsuccessful in her effort to have Harry's medical license or degree characterized as divisible marital property. The ALI *Principles* adopts the majority rule and refuses to treat earning capacity as divisible property. Instead, the *Principles* provides for "compensatory payments" to reimburse the supporting spouse for the financial contributions made to the other spouse's education or training, provided that the education was completed in less than a specified number of years (set out in a rule of statewide application) before the filing of the dissolution petition. Because Harry completed his training shortly before he sought a divorce, Wilma would probably be successful in her effort to seek "compensatory payments" for reimbursement under the ALI approach.

67. Yes. The traditional rule was that nonvested pension rights were not property, but were a mere expectancy and thus not an asset subject to division upon dissolution of a marriage. However, courts have subsequently ruled that the former rule was inequitable and that the marital community has a property interest subject to division at divorce in the employee spouse's nonvested retirement benefits prior to the time the employee spouse's right to receive the pension becomes vested. Thus, Jennie has a property right in Doug's nonvested pension benefits in the firemen's retirement fund.

68. Yes. The United States Supreme Court held (in *McCarty v. McCarty*) that military retirement benefits are exempted from distribution by state divorce courts on the basis of federal statute. However, subsequently Congress overruled *McCarty* with the enactment of the Uniformed Services Former Spouses' Protection Act. As a result, a state court has the ability to distribute military pension rights. Wife will be able to claim a share of Husband's military pension benefits.

B. Spousal support

1. **Definition:** Spousal support is an award of future payments to one spouse payable from the future earnings of the other spouse. It is also sometimes called maintenance. Formerly, spousal support was termed "alimony." However, the movement toward gender-neutral roles and the desire to remove the stigma from divorce led to a change in nomenclature.

2. **Background:** Our modern law of spousal support derives from English ecclesiastical law and practice. For generations, England permitted only legal separation, not divorce. Neither party was free to remarry. Because societal constraints and marital property law dictated that wives were economically dependent on their husbands, a separated wife needed a means of support. As a result, courts awarded wives alimony (so long as the wife was not "at fault"). Alimony, thus, represented a continuation of the husband's marital duty of support.

   The purpose of spousal support has changed today, influenced by the women's movement and the acceptability of no-fault divorce. In addition, spousal support is no longer a gender-based award.

   Example: After a 36-year marriage, a lawyer-husband and homemaker-wife divorce. An Alabama statute provides that only husbands, not wives, must pay alimony upon divorce.

Husband challenges the constitutionality of the statute as a violation of equal protection. The U.S. Supreme Court holds that the gender-based statute is unconstitutional. The Court reasons that the dual objectives offered by the state (to provide help to needy spouses, using sex as a proxy for need, and to compensate women for past discrimination during marriage) do not justify the statute. Because courts routinely conduct individualized hearings upon divorce, courts have no reason to use sex as a proxy for need. Further, courts may address the compensatory rationale without burdening only husbands. *Orr v. Orr*, 440 U.S. 268 (1979).

3. Rationale for spousal support

a. Traditional theories

i. Need: At common law, the husband had a duty to support his wife. Because women were economically dependent on men, women "needed" support in the event of a marital breakdown.

Courts based awards on the plaintiff's *need* plus the defendant's *ability to pay*. The measure of need was the couple's standard of living during the marriage.

Although most awards of spousal support formerly were granted to needy wives, in appropriate cases spousal support was awarded to needy husbands.

ii. Fault: In a fault-based regime, only the innocent spouse is awarded spousal support. The guilty spouse is "punished" for his/her marital transgressions by denial of awards of spousal support (and property).

Theories of need and fault have been undermined by the spread of no-fault divorce and the transformation of gender roles brought about by the women's movement.

b. Modern rationales

i. Self-sufficiency: Many commentators urge that, because the original purposes of alimony awards (fault/need) are no longer relevant, spousal support should be abolished or else awarded infrequently and for short periods of time.

UMDA was influential in the adoption of self-sufficiency as a rationale for awards of spousal support. For example, UMDA provides for awards of spousal support only for those spouses who do not have sufficient property to provide for their reasonable needs, are unable to support themselves through employment, or have custody of very young children. UMDA §308(a). UMDA aims to provide for a divorced spouse by way of a property settlement rather than spousal support. (The effectiveness of this approach depends, of course, on the existence of property to distribute.)

Example: Michelle divorces John after an 11-year marriage. They have no children. At the time of the dissolution, Michelle is 32 and employed as a bank teller. John is an assistant manager of a grocery store. He makes $2,000/month; she makes $1,000/month. The court determines her needs as $1,550/month. The court divides their property ($27,000) and awards her spousal support of $350/month until her remarriage or death. John appeals. The appellate court holds that the trial court did not abuse its discretion because it carefully analyzed the statutory factors. Reversing, the state supreme court finds that the award of permanent support was not appropriate based on the facts that Wife pursued her career, was young at the time of the dissolution, and the marriage was not long term. The court adds that an award of permanent alimony should be an exceptional situation and is only appropriate in a long-term traditional marriage with an older dependent spouse who has little likelihood of achieving self-sufficiency. *Gales v. Gales*, 553 N.W.2d 416 (Minn. 1996).

ii. **ALI's loss compensation:** The ALI *Principles* propose an innovative rationale of "loss compensation" for spousal support. A spouse would make "compensatory spousal payments" to the other spouse to compensate for certain losses that the second spouse experienced during the marriage. Examples of compensable losses include loss attributable to child care responsibilities and the loss of a standard of living. Thus, for example, a wife who is married to a significantly more wealthy husband would be entitled to compensation upon dissolution for the reduced standard of living she would experience "if the marriage was of sufficient duration that equity requires the loss, or some portion of it, be treated as the spouses' joint responsibility." ALI *Principles* §5.05.

4. **Spousal support and property division distinguished:** Despite the tendency in case and statutory law to blur the distinctions between awards of property and spousal support, important differences exist.

   a. **Modifiability:** Unlike awards of property, spousal support traditionally was *modifiable* upon proof of a subsequent substantial change of circumstances.

   b. **Terminability:** Traditionally, spousal support, unlike payments for purposes of property settlements, was *terminable upon remarriage* of the recipient-spouse or the *death of either* spouse.

   c. **Enforcement by contempt power:** Spousal support obligations, unlike awards of property, are enforceable by means of the contempt power.

   d. **Discharge in bankruptcy:** Traditionally, property awards (but not awards of spousal support) were dischargeable obligations if the payor-spouse declares bankruptcy. Reforms have eroded the "support-property" distinction in some situations.

   e. **Tax consequences:** Finally, different tax consequences (discussed *infra*) flow from the two awards.

5. **Types**

   a. **Temporary:** By statute, either spouse may obtain temporary spousal support (termed "alimony pendente lite") during the pendency of the divorce proceedings.

   b. **Permanent:** Permanent alimony was more commonly awarded during the fault-based era to homemaker spouses in long-term marriages who were free from fault. Permanent alimony is rarely awarded today.

   c. **Modern view:** Two modern forms of alimony are *rehabilitative alimony* and *reimbursement alimony*.

      i. **Rehabilitative alimony:** In accordance with the modern trend to limit awards of spousal support, many courts award "rehabilitative alimony" in lieu of permanent spousal support. This type of support lasts for only a limited period, as determined by the time necessary for the dependent spouse to obtain training or employment and to become self-supporting.

ii. **Reimbursement alimony:** "Reimbursement alimony" refers to spousal support that is awarded in cases in which one spouse has supported the other through a professional program during the marriage. It recompenses the supporting spouse for her contributions (monetary and nonmonetary) to the education and training of the other. Reimbursement alimony represents a compromise by courts and legislatures between adherence to a rule denying relief and the practical difficulties of characterization/valuation of a professional degree or license as property. See also the discussion ("What is Property?"), *supra*, on licenses and degrees.

Quiz Yourself on SPOUSAL SUPPORT

69. Husband and Wife divorce after 38 years of marriage. They both agree to waive spousal support and to award Husband the bulk of the marital property. At the time of divorce, Husband will receive income from a deferred profit-sharing account worth $250,000, whereas Wife has no income and suffers from physical disabilities that prevent her from working. Wife lives on food stamps and cannot afford medical care. Wife subsequently challenges the waiver of spousal support as unconscionable. Will she prevail? ____________________

70. Margaret and Jonathan divorce after a ten-year marriage. Jonathan agrees to pay Margaret $2,500 per month as spousal support for a four-year period. Two years after the divorce, Jonathan is seriously injured in an automobile accident and is unable to return to work while he undergoes extensive physical therapy. He requests a modification of his spousal support to $500 per month — a sum that he can more easily pay from his disability insurance. Will his request be granted? ____________________

Answers

69. Yes. The traditional standard for spousal support is need and ability to pay. Here, Husband has some ability to pay, and Wife has substantial basic needs that she cannot meet on her own. Further, under the modern view, as illustrated by UMDA, spousal support may be awarded to spouses who do not have sufficient property to provide for their needs, who are unable to support themselves through employment, or who have custody of very young children. Because Wife does not have sufficient property or employment to provide for her own needs, her challenge will succeed.

70. Yes. To succeed in his request for modification, Jonathan must show a substantial and material change in circumstances. Given that the automobile accident seriously affected his health and his ability to work, Jonathan's request for a decrease in his spousal support payments should be granted.

C. Child support

1. **Liability of both parents:** At common law, the father was primarily liable for the support of his children. The modern trend is to consider both parents responsible for the support of their children.

2. **Standards**

   a. **Discretion:** Until recently, vague statutory standards permitted courts to use considerable discretion in the award of child support. Criticisms arose regarding arbitrariness, the inadequacy of awards, and the lack of uniformity.

   b. **Guidelines:** A trend has developed to limit judicial discretion by the adoption of more specific standards.

      i. **UMDA:** UMDA began the trend by its provision that a court may order either or both parent(s) to pay child support, without regard to marital fault, after considering all relevant factors, including:

      - the financial resources of the child, the custodial parent, and the noncustodial parent;
      - the family's pre-divorce standard of living; and,
      - the "physical and emotional condition of the child and his educational needs."

      UMDA §309, 9A U.L.A. 400 (1987).

      ii. **Federal law:** The Child Support Enforcement Amendments of 1984, 42 U.S.C. §651 (2006), facilitated the movement to guidelines by requiring states to have guidelines in place or else risk losing a percentage of federal welfare funds. The Family Support Act of 1988 (FSA), 42 U.S.C. §667(a)-(b) (2006), extended the application of the guideline requirement to all cases (not merely to families on welfare), providing that the guidelines should serve as a rebuttable presumption and requiring states regularly to update their guidelines.

3. **Models of determining support:** Because federal law does not recommend any particular set of guidelines, states implemented guidelines based on one of three models:

   - the income shares model;
   - the percentage of income model; and
   - the Melson formula.

   a. **Income shares model:** The income-shares model is the most popular model. It requires that both parents make a monetary contribution to child support. This model is based on a belief that a child should receive the same proportion of parental income as if the parents lived together. First, a court computes the support obligation based on the combined income of the parents in the former intact household. This obligation then is pro-rated in proportion to each parent's income. Finally, the model permits consideration of work-related child care and extraordinary medical expenses.

   b. **Percentage of income:** The percentage of income model, the second most popular model, is the simplest. It allocates child support based on a percentage of the obligor's income and the number of children. For example, in Wisconsin, an obligor must pay 17 percent for one child, 25 percent for two children, 29 percent for three, 31 percent for four, and 34 percent for five or more. The obligor pays the same amount regardless of the custodial parent's income. In many jurisdictions that adhere to this model, provision is made for the obligor's support, child care expenses, or extraordinary medical expenses. However, adjustments may be made for shared physical custody and additional dependents.

c. **Melson formula:** The Melson formula, despite its praise by commentators and courts, has been adopted by only a small number of jurisdictions (including Delaware, where it arose). It involves more complex calculations than the other models. Its fundamental assumption is that the child's needs must be met first before a parent may retain any income beyond that necessary for the parent's basic support needs. That is,

   - parents may keep sufficient income to meet their basic needs but not more than what is required for their own self-support; and
   - children are entitled to share in any additional income so that they can benefit from the absent parent's higher standard of living.

   Statutory factors for determining the amount of support, under this model, include: the health, financial circumstances, and earning capacity of the parties; the parties' subsistence requirements; and the standard of living to which the parties were accustomed prior to the divorce.

4. **Deviation from guidelines:** A court may order a deviation from the statutory guidelines in appropriate cases.

   Example: Michael and Laurie have two children during their ten-year marriage. Upon divorce, the court awards Laurie one extra night of physical custody during a two-week period. The parties share childrearing expenses equally. The marital settlement agreement, which is incorporated into the divorce decree, states that Michael will pay child support of $950 per month. At the time of trial, Michael's combined monthly adjusted gross income is $19,807 while Laurie's is $17,525 (both incomes exceed the uppermost level of the child support guidelines of $15,000). Two years later, Michael requests modification of child support to reflect the substantial increase in Laurie's income since their separation. The court holds that because both parents' incomes exceed the upper level of the guidelines and also because the parents have nearly equal physical time with the children, nearly equal income, and nearly equal expenditures for child-related expenses, the circumstances are of "an extraordinary nature" that render application of the guidelines (requiring Michael to pay $950 per month) as "inappropriate and unjust." The court orders reconsideration of Michael's request on remand according to the standard of a "substantial, material change in circumstances." *Dudgeon v. Dudgeon*, 318 S.W.3d 106 (Ky. Ct. App. 2010).

5. **Liability of stepparents**

   a. **Stepparent liability during marriage to child's parent:** At common law, a stepparent had no legal duty to support a stepchild.

   Some modern statutes, as well as case law, change the common-law rule and impose liability on stepparents. Some of these laws limit liability to co-resident stepchildren or to the duration of the marriage that gave rise to the step-relationship.

   Courts have upheld the constitutionality of stepparent liability statutes.

b. **Stepparent liability upon divorce from child's parent:** At common law, because a stepparent had no legal duty to support a stepchild, courts had no authority to award child support for that stepchild upon termination of the stepparent's marriage to the child's biological parent. In contrast, some modern courts have held that stepparent liability may continue upon the dissolution of the marital relationship that gave rise to the step-relationship.

A few courts impose post-divorce stepparent liability by means of the *equitable estoppel* doctrine. Under this doctrine, a stepparent is estopped, on the basis of that stepparent's conduct (e.g., the stepparent's representations of the child as his for a long period of time), from denying the obligation to support a stepchild upon termination of the stepparent's marriage. *See, e.g., W. v. W.*, 779 A.2d 716 (Conn. 2001).

6. **Post-majority support:** Traditionally, a parent's duty to support a child ceased upon the child reaching the age of majority. Although the age of majority used to be 21, most states now have lowered the age to 18. This has given rise to the issue whether a noncustodial parent is liable for post-majority child support, especially for college expenses.

   a. **Different state approaches:** States adopt different approaches to this issue:

   - Some states rigidly enforce the statutory age limitation (18 years) and refuse to award post-majority support;
   - Other states, by statute or case law, permit support through college through a variety of legal doctrines.

   b. **Constitutional attacks on statutes:** Some courts have upheld the constitutionality of statutes requiring divorced parents to provide post-majority educational support for their children. Other courts hold that post-divorce orders requiring a parent to contribute to college expenses violate equal protection. *See, e.g., Webb v. Sowell,* 692 S.E.2d 543 (S.C. 2010).

   c. **Separation agreements:** Courts have more latitude to permit post-majority support if the parties have provided for that eventuality in a separation agreement.

   d. **ALI proposal:** The ALI *Principles* (§3.16) suggest that post-majority educational support be dependent on a judicial inquiry into parental resources and the likelihood of such support had the parents remained together.

7. **Posthumous support obligation:** According to the traditional view, the obligation to support a child terminates at the obligor's death unless a written agreement binds the obligor's estate.

8. **Support rights of nonmarital children**

   a. **Traditional rule:** Traditionally, nonmarital children had a right to support and inheritance only from their mother, not from their father.

   b. **Modern rule:** According to the modern view, both parents have the duty to support children regardless of the legitimacy of the children.

   c. **Statutes of limitations:** Traditionally, states had short statutes of limitations within which a parent had to bring a paternity action in order to seek support for a nonmarital child. The U.S. Supreme Court invalidated several short statutes of limitations as a denial of equal protection. *See Mills v. Habluetzel*, 456 U.S. 91 (1992) (invalidating a one-year statute of limitations); *Pickett v. Brown*, 462 U.S. 1 (1983) (a two-year statute); and *Clark v. Jeter*, 486 U.S. 456 (1988) (a six-year statute). Afterward, many states lengthened their statutory period for paternity establishment.

d. Federal legislation: Congress lengthened the statutory period for paternity establishment by enacting the Child Support Enforcement Amendments of 1984, 42 U.S.C. §666(a)(5)(A)(ii) (2006). The Amendments provide for extension of the statutory period until 18 years post-birth as a condition of states' receipt of federal funds.

The Family Support Act (FSA) of 1988, 42 U.S.C. §1305 (2006), further strengthens the procedures for paternity establishment. The FSA

- requires states to permit paternity establishment for children whose actions previously were dismissed based on short state statutes of limitations;
- requires states to enact procedures to order all parties to submit to blood tests to determine paternity (subject to a good cause exception);
- makes available to state agencies the Parent Locator Service to facilitate enforcement of child support obligations.

e. Uniform Acts:

i. Paternity: The Uniform Parentage Act (UPA) §4, 9B U.L.A. 287 (1987), facilitated paternity establishment by providing for legal parenthood by fathers who receive a child into their homes and publicly acknowledge the child or acknowledge the child in writing to a court or administrative agency. As amended in 2002, UPA §5 revises the UPA §4(4) presumption that arose by "holding out." Because the original act failed to specify a time frame for the "holding out," uncertainty existed regarding whether the presumption could arise if the receipt of the child into the man's home occurred for a quite limited time or took place long after the child's birth. The 2002 amendments made the "holding out" presumption subject to an express durational requirement that the man reside with the child for the first two years of the child's life.

ii. Inheritance: Uniform Probate Code §2-117 declares that a parent-child relationship exists between a child and the biological parents regardless of the parents' marital status. This provision would enable a nonmarital child to inherit, for example, from a biological father by application of intestate succession law.

f. Discrimination against nonmarital children: Beginning in the 1960s, the U.S. Supreme Court held that some forms of discrimination (specifically, certain statutory benefits schemes) against nonmarital children are unconstitutional. *See, e.g., Weber v. Aetna Casualty and Surety Co.*, 406 U.S. 164 (1972) (state workers' compensation law); *Levy v. Louisiana*, 391 U.S. 68 (1968) (wrongful death). However, the Court was less willing to invalidate some restrictions on nonmarital children's inheritance rights. *Compare Lalli v. Lalli*, 439 U.S. 259 (1978) (upholding a statute that requires judicial establishment of paternity in order for a nonmarital child to inherit from his father), with *Trimble v. Gordon*, 430 U.S. 762 (1977) (holding that a statute permitting nonmarital children to inherit from their fathers only if their fathers marry their mothers post-birth or acknowledge the child violates equal protection). *See also Nguyen v. Immigration and Naturalization Service*, 533 U.S. 53 (2001) (holding that a statute making it more difficult for a nonmarital child born abroad to one U.S. parent to claim citizenship through that parent if the citizen-parent was the father does not violate the equal protection guarantee of the Fifth Amendment).

g. **Standard of proof:** The U.S. Supreme Court holds that the "preponderance of the evidence" standard for paternity establishment does not violate due process. *Rivera v. Minnich*, 483 U.S. 574 (1987).

h. **Indigents' rights to paternity establishment:** The U.S. Supreme Court holds that due process requires that indigent defendants have the right to blood tests to prove (or disprove) paternity. *Little v. Streater*, 452 U.S. 1 (1981).

i. **Voluntary paternity establishment:** Welfare reform legislation strengthens procedures for voluntary paternity establishment. Legislation establishes that voluntary acknowledgments of paternity (subject to a 60-day rescission period) are legal findings and requires states to improve their paternity establishment procedures. Personal Responsibility and Work Opportunity Reconciliation Act of 1996 (PRWORA), 42 U.S.C. §666 (2006).

j. **Multiple parents:** An occasional court has been willing to recognize parental rights of more than two parents for a given child.

Example: Former same-sex partner sues the mother and the sperm donor (of mother's two biological children), seeking full legal and physical custody of the mother's two biological children and two adopted children. The mother sues the former partner for child support for the mother's two biological children. The mother's long-time male friend agreed to be the sperm donor for two of the children and plays an active role in their upbringing. The trial court awards the former partner primary physical custody of one child and partial custody of the other children. The former partner appeals the custody award as well as the trial court's denial of her request to join the sperm donor as an indispensable party. The appellate court affirms the custody award but vacates the award of support, and remands with directions that the sperm donor be joined as an indispensable party for a hearing at which the support obligation of each litigant is to be recalculated. The appellate court reasons that the sperm donor was equitably estopped from avoiding the support obligation, given that the former partner could not avoid the support obligation, and that the father's support obligation was statutorily imposed. *Jacob v. Shultz-Jacob*, 923 A.2d 473 (Pa. Super. Ct. 2007).

9. **Support rights of children of same-sex couples:** Some courts have held that children of same-sex couples have a right to child support from *both* same-sex parents.

Example: Emily is the parent of two-year-old twins who were born to her while she was in a lesbian relationship with Elisa. During the relationship, Elisa gave birth to a child as well, using sperm from the same donor. Each woman was very involved in childrearing of the other woman's child/children. When the women's relationship ended, Elisa eventually stopped providing support for Emily's twins, one of whom had extensive medical problems. The county files an action to establish that Elisa is obliged to pay child support to Emily, who is receiving public assistance. Elisa contends that she is not obligated to pay child support because she is not a legal "parent" of Emily's twins under the California version of the UPA. The state supreme court disagrees, ruling that under the UPA, a child may have two parents, both of whom are women; and also that Elisa is a presumed parent under the UPA because Elisa agreed to raise the children, supported Emily's artificial insemination attempts, and received the resulting twins into her home and held them out as her own. *Elisa B. v. Superior Court*, 117 P.3d 660 (Cal. 2005).

II. MODIFICATION OF SPOUSAL AND CHILD SUPPORT AWARDS

A. Standard

1. **General rule:** The standard for modification of spousal and child support is: a substantial and material change of circumstances since the entry of the decree.

2. **UMDA restrictive rule for modification of spousal support:** UMDA, which adopts a restrictive standard for spousal support generally, also provides for a restrictive standard for *modification of spousal support*. Under UMDA, spousal support may be modified only if a change in circumstances has occurred that is "so substantial and continuing as to make the terms unconscionable" (§316).

B. Relevant factors

Relevant factors: Sometimes, circumstances occur that may affect the support obligation. These circumstances may affect a family member's needs and/or a spouse's ability to pay. Such circumstances or events might include:

- a voluntary change in the payor's occupation;
- the payor's remarriage and resulting increased family responsibilities;
- the payor's increased resources;
- the payor's deteriorating health; and
- the payee's remarriage or cohabitation.

1. **Payor's changed circumstances:** An involuntary change in circumstances results from events beyond a person's control, such as the loss of employment or illness, and may justify a reduction in the support obligation. On the other hand, a *voluntary* change in circumstances generally does not justify a reduction in the support obligation.

   a. **Change of occupation:** When a parent voluntarily changes employment, his or her child support obligation may be reduced only if the voluntary change was reasonable; if the change of occupations was in good faith (not attributable to an attempt to avoid paying support); and if the action will not deprive the child of reasonable financial support. The existence of good faith is a factual determination. If a parent is voluntarily unemployed or underemployed, the child support obligation will be calculated based on *earning capacity*.

   Example: Husband and Wife are both attorneys. Following their divorce, Father petitions to reduce his child support obligation, alleging that his income decreased while he trained for a new career in teaching. The trial court denied his request, finding that Husband was voluntarily underemployed and that he still possessed the same earning capacity. The trial court reasons that, although Husband is free to change careers, his child should not be expected to finance his choice. The Alaska Supreme Court affirms, explaining that even if the career change was undertaken in good faith, Husband's statements that he was a failure at law were undermined by his failure to keep regular office hours and his efforts to reduce his workload. Further, the state supreme court finds that the trial court's conclusion that Husband's earning capacity had not changed was not clearly erroneous because the record showed that Husband previously earned as much or more than Wife as a lawyer and also that his skills continued to allow him to match his prior earnings if he chose to do so. *Olmstead v. Ziegler*, 42 P.3d 1102 (Alaska 2002).

b. **Payor's remarriage and subsequent family obligations:** A court will consider the payor's remarriage if it places increasing demands on his financial resources. However, at the same time, a court may consider the income of the payor's second spouse in the determination of the payor's resources.

Example: When Husband and Wife divorce, they stipulate that Husband is to pay $35/week child support for each of their two children. About a year later, Husband remarries a woman who has a son from a prior marriage. Wife seeks increased child support based on new state child support guidelines. Husband argues that the court should deviate from the guidelines because he has to support his stepson. Although the husband has no legal duty to support his stepson, the trial court holds that a court can exercise its discretion to take that factor into account to order support that deviates from (i.e., is less than) the guidelines. Wife appeals. The state supreme court holds that: (1) a court can consider the expenses of supporting subsequent families in the determination of support, (2) a parent does have a legal duty to support a stepchild that is coextensive with the duty to support a natural child (contrary to the trial court's decision), and (3) the trial court's findings and conclusions were too incomplete to justify the support award (by failing to consider properly the Husband's new spouse's income and the extent to which the Husband voluntarily incurred these new obligations). The court remands for such a determination. *Ainsworth v. Ainsworth*, 574 A.2d 772 (Vt. 1990).

c. **Payor's increased resources:** A significant improvement in the payor's resources may constitute a substantial and material change of circumstances justifying an increase in spousal support. On the other hand, a few courts have held that the recipient spouse should not receive a windfall merely if the payor subsequently experiences success for the reason that the appropriate yardstick for support is the standard of living during the marriage.

Example: Mr. and Mrs. Graham divorce after 20 years of marriage and 3 children. The court orders Mr. Graham to pay $250 a week in alimony and $375 a week in child support, plus half of the mortgage payments and the children's private school tuition. Mr. Graham is earning $100,000 annually. When judgment is entered, Mr. Graham has just signed a new employment contract providing for a salary of $185,000 and increasing to $255,000 in four years. Wife seeks modification of alimony and child support awards based on Husband's salary increases. The trial court rules that an increase in a payor's income is an insufficient basis for modification because the recipient first must demonstrate that her needs and/or those of the children have changed. Wife appeals, arguing that the payor's increased ability to pay, by itself, is a sufficient basis for modification. The appellate court holds that a material change in either (1) the payor's or recipient's resources *or* (2) the needs of the spouse and/or children may be the basis for modification. Thus, a substantial increase, as here, in the payor's salary can be the basis for an increase in support without the recipient's being required to prove increased need for herself or the children. *Graham v. Graham*, 597 A.2d 355 (D.C. 1991).

d. **Payor's deteriorating health:** The payor's health problems sometimes may result in a reduction in payment of spousal support and/or child support. However, the health problems must meet the standard of a substantial change in circumstances.

Example: Husband, a chiropractor, and Wife divorce after 17 years of marriage and 2 children. The court awards Wife $250/month per child, and $600/month spousal support. One year later Husband applies for a reduction in alimony and child support. Reduction of alimony is denied but child support is reduced because the oldest son has married. Two years later (in 1976), Husband again requests termination of alimony and reduction in child support. He claims a change in circumstances brought about by his health problems (carpal tunnel syndrome), and because Wife's income has appreciated. The court reduces alimony to $250/month but maintains child support at $250/month. Husband subsequent asks for yet another reduction in child support and termination of alimony. Husband no longer practices his occupation. The trial court denies his requests because there has been no substantial change in circumstances; Husband appeals. The state supreme court affirms, holding that Husband's health problems have been continuing and, as such, do not constitute a substantial change of circumstances since the most recent (1976) hearing. Moreover, evidence suggests that Husband is considering re-establishing a practice. Wife's property has appreciated but this is the normal result of inflation, which has also increased her child care costs. *Herndon v. Herndon*, 305 N.W.2d 917 (S.D. 1981).

e. **Payor's incarceration:** Some states allow a reduction in child support when the payor is incarcerated and therefore is unable to earn a living.

Example: When Shannon and Shane divorce, Shane is ordered to pay $648 in monthly child support. Shortly after the divorce, Shane is convicted of the attempted first-degree murder of Shannon, and is sentenced to 15 to 20 years in prison. He petitions for a reduction in support based on his reduction in income due to incarceration. The court holds that incarceration is an involuntary reduction in income that constitutes a material change in circumstances justifying a reduction in support. *Hopkins v. Stauffer*, 775 N.W.2d 462 (Neb. Ct. App. 2009).

2. **Recipient's changed circumstances**

a. **Remarriage:** Some jurisdictions follow a rule of automatic termination upon a recipient's remarriage whereas other jurisdictions follow a rule of discretionary termination.

Many state statutes automatically terminate maintenance upon the recipient's remarriage. The reason for terminating maintenance at remarriage is because the former husband's duty of support has been replaced by that of the new husband. In contrast, other states give the courts discretion to decide whether the recipient's remarriage warrants termination.

b. **Cohabitation:** A few states permit modification of spousal support when the recipient cohabits with a member of the opposite sex. "Cohabitation" requires that the parties live together. The policy rationale is that the cohabitation results in a decrease in the need for support.

Example: Husband and Wife's marital settlement agreement provides that spousal support terminates upon Wife's remarriage or her "romantic cohabitation." Wife becomes romantically involved with a man who periodically stays overnight and vacations with her. Husband petitions to terminate Wife's spousal support based on her alleged violation of the marital settlement agreement. Denying his request, the court holds that the term "romantic cohabitation" in the parties' agreement means "living together as a married couple" and does not encompass a sexual relationship with someone who only *occasionally* spends the night. *Chopin v. Chopin*, 232 P.3d 99 (Ariz. Ct. App. 2010).

III. JURISDICTION AND ENFORCEMENT OF CHILD SUPPORT AWARDS

Child support enforcement is difficult when the parties reside in different states. Traditionally, a custodial parent had limited ability to enforce interstate child support obligations for several reasons:

1. the original state lacked personal jurisdiction over the noncustodial parent in the latter's new state;
2. the noncustodial parent's new state could not help because no nexus existed between that state and the custodial parent; and
3. limits were imposed by federalism.

The limits imposed by federalism were that support orders, as continuing obligations, were not enforceable under the Full Faith and Credit Clause, U.S. Const. art. IV, §1, which applies only to final and nonmodifiable child support orders. *Sistare v. Sistare*, 218 U.S. 1 (1920).

To establish or enforce a support order, a custodial parent had to travel to the noncustodial parent's new state and initiate new proceedings there — a costly and burdensome procedure. This problem, to some extent, has been remedied.

A. Jurisdiction generally: To make (or modify) an award of child support or spousal support, a court must have *personal jurisdiction* over the obligor. Although a court may award an ex parte divorce without jurisdiction over one spouse, a court may not resolve the financial incidents of the divorce without personal jurisdiction over both spouses. This is the ***doctrine of divisible divorce*** (affirmed by the U.S. Supreme Court in *Vanderbilt v. Vanderbilt*, 354 U.S. 416 (1957)).

The trend is to expand the traditional methods of acquiring personal jurisdiction over nonresidents for support purposes. The reform results from efforts to address social mobility and the increasing numbers of "deadbeat dads." Indicative of this trend are state and federal reforms and Uniform Acts.

B. State long-arm statutes

1. Types of long-arm statutes: According to the traditional rule, personal jurisdiction must accord with the requirements of state long-arm statutes and the Constitution's Due Process Clause.

Prior to the 1970s, states occasionally permitted the assertion of jurisdiction over nonresidents in domestic relations cases by liberal interpretations of their long-arm statutes (construing the obligor's actions to be "a tortious act," or "the infliction of harm," etc.). Other states (e.g., California) provided similarly broad parameters by permitting the assertion of jurisdiction so long as it met the "constitutional requirements of due process."

In recent years, many states substantially increased the scope of jurisdiction over nonresidents in domestic relations cases by revising their long-arm statutes to includes specific provisions for the assertion of jurisdiction in claims for family obligations (both spousal support and child support). In addition, the U.S. Supreme Court clarified the scope of due process limitations in *Kulko v. Superior Court, infra*, and, subsequently, in *Burnham v. Superior Court, infra*. (See the discussion of these cases in Chapter 5.)

2. **Constitutional limits of long-arm statutes:** The assertion of personal jurisdiction by means of long-arm statutes must comport with the requisites of due process. The U.S. Supreme Court in *Kulko v. Superior Court*, 436 U.S. 84 (1978), delimited those requirements in the child support context.

   Example: Ezra marries Sharon during a three-day stopover in California en route to a tour of duty. Both parties are domiciliaries of New York. They reside together as a family and raise two children in New York City until their separation. Sharon moves to San Francisco. They execute a separation agreement in New York providing that the children will continue to live in New York with their father but spend vacations in California with their mother. Ezra agrees to pay $3,000 annually in child support for the time the children are with Sharon. Sharon obtains a Haitian divorce that incorporates the terms of the agreement. She returns to California and remarries. Soon, the children decide (first the daughter, then later the son) that they want to come to California to live with Sharon. Ezra sends the daughter to California. Sharon, unbeknownst to Ezra, sends the son a ticket. After the son's arrival, Sharon files an action in California to establish the Haitian divorce decree as a California judgment and to modify it to award her custody and increased child support. Ezra appears specially, arguing that the court lacks jurisdiction over him. The California Supreme Court holds that Ezra's "purposeful act" in sending the daughter to live in California warranted the exercise of personal jurisdiction over him. Reversing, the U.S. Supreme Court holds that California's assertion of personal jurisdiction over the defendant violates due process. By Defendant's sending his daughter to California, he did not purposefully avail himself of the benefits of California law or do anything whereby he might have expected to litigate an action in California. Considerations of fairness (i.e., the stay-at-home spouse should not bear the burden of litigating in a new forum) and the fact that the controversy arose in New York militate against California's assertion of jurisdiction. *Kulko v. Superior Court*, 436 U.S. 34 (1978).

C. Interstate enforcement: URESA, RURESA, and UIFSA

1. **General procedure:** The National Conference of Commissioners on Uniform State Laws (NCCUSL) formulated in 1950 the Uniform Reciprocal Enforcement of Support Act (URESA), 9A U.L.A. 747 (1979), and its subsequent 1968 revised version RURESA, 9B U.L.A. 381 (1987 & Supp. 1994), to facilitate interstate enforcement of support orders. The Acts were adopted by all states as the principal means for establishment and enforcement of interstate child support orders.

   The objective of the Acts was to assist custodial parents when a noncustodial parent leaves the state and then refuses to pay support, and also when a custodial parent relocates to another state but wants to enforce a preexisting order.

2. **Continuing problems led to UIFSA:** Although URESA and RURESA significantly increased collections and lightened the burden on the welfare system, problems of a *lack of uniformity* between states and the proliferation of *multiple support orders* remained. In response, the NCCUSL drafted the Uniform Interstate Family Support Act (UIFSA), 9 U.L.A. 121 (Supp. 1994), in 1992 to supersede URESA and RURESA. UIFSA aims to eliminate cases in which

more than one child support order applies to a child (or children) and also to encourage states to apply restraint in the modification of existing child support orders, especially if modification is sought in a state other than the rendering state. UIFSA contains new procedures for *establishing, enforcing, and modifying* support orders.

Note: Welfare reform legislation in 1996 spurred the enactment of UIFSA by requiring states to enact UIFSA in order to qualify for the receipt of federal welfare funds. Personal Responsibility and Work Opportunity Reconciliation Act of 1996, 42 U.S.C. §666(f) (2006).

3. UIFSA

a. **Similarities to URESA and RURESA:** UIFSA retains many of the basic concepts of URESA and RURESA: It has a two-state procedure and a registration process; utilizes some of the same terminology (e.g., responding state, initiating state); and provides that the responding state can establish, modify, and enforce temporary and permanent support orders, and rely on civil and criminal contempt. UIFSA §305(b).

b. **Differences from URESA and RURESA:** Important differences exist, however. UIFSA recognizes the growing role that administrative agencies play in the establishment and enforcement of child support orders, provides for the enforcement of support orders in another state without registration, and does not require reciprocity (that the other state also adopt the legislation) to establish or enforce a support order. And while URESA and RURESA determine that the choice of law is the law of any state where the obligor was present when support was sought, UIFSA applies "the procedural and substantive law, including the rules on choice of law" of the initiating state. UIFSA §303(l).

To eliminate multiple orders, UIFSA provides that only one support order can be in effect at any one time — i.e., the "One-Order-One-Time" rule. UIFSA §205. The court entering the original support order maintains continuing, exclusive jurisdiction until that state ceases to be the residence of the child or a party files consent to another state's jurisdiction. If no state has continuing, exclusive jurisdiction, an order made by the child's home state has priority.

Also, UIFSA, unlike URESA and RURESA, provides for one-state proceedings, as an alternative to the former two-state proceedings. That is, UIFSA §201 provides an expansive long-arm statute that permits the assertion of personal jurisdiction over the obligor by the originating state.

UIFSA has also made changes in the traditional two-state proceedings. Under RURESA, the initiating state determines whether the obligor owes a duty of support. Under UIFSA, the initiating tribunal forwards support documents to the responding tribunal that determines jurisdiction.

UIFSA addresses the modification of support orders as well. Under URESA and RURESA, as explained above, most courts have held that the original state and responding state can modify a support order. Under UIFSA, however, only the state with continuing, exclusive jurisdiction can modify a registered order unless the parties file a written consent to assertion of jurisdiction or the original state is no longer the residence of the child or the parties. UIFSA §205(a).

Example: A custodial mother, who resided out of state with the couple's child, filed a motion for modification of child support. The trial court entered a default judgment against the father, who also lived out of state, and later denied father's motion to set aside the judgment. The father appealed. The appellate court reversed, holding that the trial court that originally entered the child support order at the time of the parents' divorce lost continuing, exclusive subject matter jurisdiction when both parents and subject child moved out of state. *In re Marriage of Myers*, 56 P.3d 128 (Kan. Ct. App. 2002).

D. Federal legislation: Full Faith and Credit for Child Support Orders Act: On the federal level, attempts have been made to encourage widespread adoption of UIFSA. In 1994, Congress enacted the Full Faith and Credit for Child Support Orders Act (FFCCSOA), 28 U.S.C. §1738(B) (2006). The Act requires that states enforce the child support orders of other states. The Act is aimed at eliminating the problem of the multiplicity of support orders under URESA and ensuring that only one child support order at a time will be in effect.

1. UIFSA serves as model: FFCCSOA incorporates many UIFSA concepts. Specifically, FFCCSOA

- requires that a state enforce the child support order made by a court of another state, provided that the court has subject matter jurisdiction and personal jurisdiction over the parties;
- limits modification of child support orders in a manner similar to UIFSA;
- requires that the forum state's law applies in proceedings to establish, enforce, or modify support orders, unless the court is merely interpreting the support order (in which case the law of the originating state applies); and
- provides that the longer of two different statutes of limitations will apply in enforcement actions. 28 U.S.C. §1738B(e) and 28 U.S.C. §1738B(g)(3) (2006).

2. Federal preemption: Courts are split as to whether the Full Faith and Credit for Child Support Orders Act preempts UIFSA.

Example: Husband and Wife marry and have children in Massachusetts. Ten years later, they move to Oregon. Three years later, they obtain a divorce in Oregon. Before judgment is entered, Wife returns with the children to Massachusetts. The Oregon judgment grants shared legal custody with Wife having primary physical custody and Husband receiving reasonable visitation. In addition, Husband must pay $750 a month in child support. Several years later, Wife seeks and obtains and upward modification of the support obligation in Massachusetts. Husband objects, arguing that the court lacks subject matter jurisdiction under UIFSA because Wife was not a nonresident movant. Wife argues, in response, that UIFSA is preempted by FFCCSOA, which provides subject matter jurisdiction in this case. The court agrees that UIFSA's provisions for subject matter jurisdiction are preempted by the comparable provisions in FFCCSOA. *Draper v. Burke*, 881 N.E.2d 122 (Mass. 2008).

E. Enforcement remedies: Studies consistently reveal that a high percentage of noncustodial fathers fail to support their children. Several state and federal remedies address the problem of enforcement of child support obligations.

1. Traditional state remedies: State remedies include: money judgments, criminal nonsupport proceedings, and the contempt power.

a. Money judgments: Most jurisdictions provide for enforcement of child support obligations by money judgments. These include: the imposition of liens, sequestration, attachment of property, and wage garnishment. Resort to these remedies normally requires that the custodial parent obtain personal jurisdiction over the noncustodial parent or over his/her property. Further, such remedies are available only in cases of arrearages (not to collect future payments).

b. **Criminal nonsupport proceedings:** The custodial parent may also institute a criminal proceeding for nonsupport based on state statute. All states have statutes that result in the imposition of criminal sanctions on noncustodial parents who fail to support or abandon their children.

c. **Contempt:** The most common state remedy for nonpayment of child support is contempt. Under its broad equitable power, a court may hold in contempt a noncustodial parent who refuses to pay child support. This results in incarcerating the parent until he or she pays or agrees to pay. To be found in contempt, a court must determine that the obligor first had the ability to pay.

i. **Civil v. criminal nature of contempt:** Contempt may be either civil or criminal in nature, although sometimes it may be difficult to determine which it is. The distinction becomes important because a criminal defendant is entitled to due process protections.

Additional distinctions between criminal and civil contempt include:

- in civil contempt, punishment is remedial (imprisonment only until defendant performs a required act) and for the benefit of the petitioner;
- in criminal contempt, the sanction is punitive (imprisonment for a definite period without the possibility of purging) and to vindicate a court;
- in civil contempt, any fine would be payable to the petitioner;
- in criminal contempt, any fine would be payable to the court.

Example: A court orders Husband to make child support payments. He sporadically complies and then discontinues payment. Wife seeks to enforce his obligation by initiating a contempt proceeding. Husband defends by claiming that he was unable to pay support at the times in question. The court finds the Husband in contempt on several of the counts. He appeals, alleging that his due process rights are violated by the statutory requirement that he must prove his inability to pay (rather than the state's proving his ability to pay), thereby improperly shifted to him the burden of proving an element of the offense. The U.S. Supreme Court holds that the burden shifting violates due process in a criminal proceeding for contempt because it undercuts the requirement that the state prove guilt beyond a reasonable doubt. (It would be permissible in a civil proceeding.) The Court explains that neither the label of the proceedings nor the relief is controlling. Although there were indications that the proceedings were criminal (e.g., his jail sentence for each count and probation for three years), the Court remands for that determination. If Defendant purges his sentence by paying the arrearage, then the proceeding is civil and he has no right to due process protections. *Hicks v. Feiock*, 485 U.S. 624 (1988).

Epilogue: On remand, the court determines that the action was criminal because Defendant's sentence was determinate (a characteristic of criminal proceedings). *In re Feiock*, 263 Cal. Rptr. 437 (Ct. App. 1989).

ii. **Constitutional limitations on contempt power:** Courts permit resort to the contempt power to enforce orders of spousal and child support. However, it is generally thought that imprisonment for failure to pay a property settlement constitutes imprisonment for debt that would violate the Constitution.

iii. **Federalism limits on contempt power:** Federalism concerns may arise if a state court holds a defendant in contempt for failure to pay child support if his payments derive solely from federal benefits.

Example: Husband and Wife divorce after a ten-year marriage and two children. Husband is a totally disabled veteran with no income except for Veterans and Social Security benefits due to a service-related disability during the Vietnam War. The trial court orders him to pay $800/month. He initially makes partial payments. Wife files a petition for contempt. He argues that the state trial court lacks jurisdiction over his federal disability benefits. The State becomes a party, arguing that the statute was constitutional. The court finds Husband in contempt, determines that the statute is constitutional, and the appellate court affirms. Affirming, the U.S. Supreme Court holds that state court jurisdiction (in the form of state contempt proceedings) is not preempted by federal provisions for the payment of veterans benefits. If Congress intended to provide the administrators of the federal benefit agencies with the power to displace a state court's authority over the enforcement of child support orders, it would have been more explicit. *Rose v. Rose*, 481 U.S. 619 (1987).

2. **Modern state remedies: License suspension:** A modern remedy is the *suspension* of licenses of obligors with child support arrearages. Some statutes provide for the suspension of professional, occupational, business, driver's, or recreational licenses. Other states provide for the *denial of a new license or denial of a renewal* of certain licenses for obligors with outstanding child support obligations. Courts have upheld the constitutionality of such statutes.

3. **Federal remedies:** Important federal legislation now provides new tools for the enforcement of child support orders.

   a. **Federal crime:** In 1992 Congress enacted the Child Support Recovery Act (CSRA), 18 U.S.C §228(a) (2006), making it a federal crime to willfully fail to pay a "past due support obligation" for a child who resides in another state. The Act defines a "past due support obligation" as an amount determined by a state court that remains unpaid for longer than one year or exceeds $5,000. The Act provides for incarceration and restitution for the unpaid support. Congress amended and strengthened the CSRA in 1998 with the Deadbeat Parents Punishment Act (codified at 18 U.S.C §228(a) (2006)). The amendment provides that a debt of longer than two years or over $10,000 is punishable by fine or imprisonment of up to 24 months or both. Courts have upheld the constitutionality of the statute. *See, e.g., United States v. Klinzing*, 315 F.3d 803 (7th Cir. 2003) (finding that CSRA is a valid exercise of congressional power under the Commerce Clause).

   b. **Garnishment or income withholding:** Wage garnishment, the most effective weapon in the federal arsenal, permits an employer to pay an employee's child support obligation directly to the other spouse on behalf of a child. The federal Child Support and Establishment of Paternity Act of 1974, 42 U.S.C. §659 (2006), permits the garnishment (or income withholding) of federal wages to facilitate payment of child support to welfare recipients.

Early legislation was so effective that Congress expanded the program by the Child Support Enforcement Amendments of 1984 (CSEA) to require that *all support orders* include a conditional order for wage withholding to begin when payments are one month *in arrears*.

The Family Support Act of 1988 (FSA) goes even further by mandating automatic wage withholding in *all cases, regardless of whether support payments were one month in arrears as formerly*. States must institute wage withholding absent a judicial finding of good cause or a written parental agreement providing otherwise.

Federal welfare reform legislation facilitates collection procedures by providing for a central governmental agency to collect and disburse funds to obligees and also by requiring reporting of newly hired employees to a state agency that forwards this information to the federal government. Personal Responsibility and Work Opportunity Reconciliation Act of 1996 (PRWORA), §§312, 653(a) (2006).

c. **Tax refund intercept:** CSEA also provides for the interception of federal (and state) tax refunds of all obligors. By this means, state or federal tax refunds can be diverted to meet an obligor's unpaid child support obligations. Previously, tax refund intercepts were permitted only for families receiving welfare.

d. **Passport denial:** Federal welfare legislation authorizes the denial, revocation, or nonrenewal of a passport for reason of the nonpayment of support obligations. *See* PRWORA §652 (authorizing revocation of obligor's passport where more than $5,000 is owed and providing for stricter penalties for a debt that remains unpaid for longer than two years). The provision has survived constitutional challenge. *See, e.g., Eunique v. Powell*, 281 F.3d 940 (9th Cir. 2002) (rejecting challenge on right-to-travel ground); *Weinstein v. Albright*, 261 F.3d 127 (2d Cir. 2001) (rejecting challenge on procedural due process and equal protection grounds).

e. **Other mechanisms:** CSEA also mandates that states adopt other collection procedures for enforcing child support orders, including: expedited enforcement (administrative processes for establishing and enforcing support obligations), liens against real and personal property, posting a bond or giving security for overdue support, and disclosure of overdue support to consumer reporting agencies.

Quiz Yourself on CHILD SUPPORT

71. Richard pays $512 each month to his ex-wife for support of their minor child. At the time of their divorce, Richard is an assistant professor of English. Shortly after the divorce, Richard voluntarily resigns his position to attend law school. He petitions the court for a modification in child support based on his reduction in income. Will he succeed? ____________________

72. Mark divorces Sylvia after a five-year marriage in order to marry Glenice. At the time of the divorce, Mark and Sylvia have one daughter, age three. Glenice is a young widow who has been working part-time as a receptionist to take care of her three young children because her husband died from cancer. At the time of the divorce, Mark agreed to pay Sylvia $750 per month as child support. One year later, Mark requests a modification of his support obligation to $500 per month for the reason of his remarriage and additional financial responsibilities to Glenice and her children. This jurisdiction follows the modern (rather than common-law) approach regarding the imposition of stepparent liability. Will Mark prevail? ____________________

73. Jeffrey and Shanon have two nonmarital children. After the parents separate, a court enters an order establishing Jeffrey's paternity and orders him to pay $723 per month for child support. Jeffrey never makes a voluntary payment but has his income withheld for some of the amount he owes. Eventually, he owes more than $52,000 in unpaid support. He tells Shanon that he won't pay because, "They're your girls." He is indicted for willful failure to pay child support. He argues that because he is unable to pay the entire amount of child support, his failure is not "willful." Will he prevail? ____________________

74. Charles and Yetta, both accountants, divorce when their daughter Helen is 15 years old. The court orders Charles to pay $800 a month as child support. Three years later Yetta seeks an increase in child support to pay for costs associated with Helen's college education. Helen is an excellent student and has just been accepted at a private college. Charles contends that an order of child support would unlawfully require him to support Helen past her majority. Will he prevail? ____________________

Answers

71. Perhaps. On the one hand, a voluntary change of occupation that results in the payor's reduced earnings generally does not justify a decreased award of support. Here, Richard gave up a steady salary as a professor to become a law student. However, if Richard chooses to attend law school to seek an improved financial situation and the change was not made simply to reduce his support payments, then a court may grant his request for a reduction.

72. Probably yes. Remarriage is a relevant consideration in the modification of support obligations if the remarriage places increasing demands on a payor's financial resources. Mark's remarriage to a woman with three children has resulted in substantial new financial obligations. Further, although at common law a stepparent had no legal duty to support a stepchild, many modern statutes and some case law impose liability on stepparents for co-resident stepchildren. Thus, because Glenice's three children reside with Mark and Glenice, Mark may have a statutory duty to support his stepchildren. Mark's request for a modification should be granted.

73. No. A parent may be criminally convicted for willful failure to pay child support if he has the ability to pay and refuses to do so. Courts reason that a parent should seek modification of custody if he or she is unable to pay, rather than wait to challenge the child support determination until being incarcerated for nonpayment. Here, a court could reason that Jeffrey has the ability to pay because his income was withheld to pay support in the past, and his words to Shanon clearly indicate an intentional refusal to pay. Therefore, his conviction will be upheld.

74. Perhaps. Traditionally, child support payments could not extend past a child's majority except in extraordinary circumstances (i.e., disability). However, an increasing number of states, by statute or case law, permit child support through college through a variety of legal or equitable doctrines.

Depending on the law in this jurisdiction, it is possible that Yetta may be successful in her claim for Helen's post-majority support for college expenses. Several courts look to the following factors: the child's aptitude, the parents' financial resources, the parents' college background, and the family's expectations had the marriage remained intact. Because of Helen's excellent record and her parents' financial abilities and college backgrounds, it is possible that Charles will have to contribute to Helen's college expenses. However, some courts have ruled that a post-divorce order for a parent to contribute to college expenses violates the Equal Protection Clause.

IV. SEPARATION AGREEMENTS

Separation agreements (sometimes called "marital settlement agreements") are contracts entered into by divorcing spouses that concern the division of property, the support rights of a spouse and children, and sometimes child custody as well.

A. **Premarital agreements distinguished:** Separation agreements are distinguishable from premarital agreements. A separation agreement is entered into by the parties *during* the divorce process. A premarital agreement is entered into *before* the marriage.

B. **Validity:** The validity of a separation agreement is determined by contract law. Such agreements may be set aside for fraud, duress, or overreaching.

C. **Policy:** Formerly, courts regarded separation agreements with suspicion because such agreements were thought to encourage divorce. Courts now favor separation agreements because they reduce the expense, delay, and animosity associated with litigation. The Uniform Marriage and Divorce Act (UMDA) §306 also rejects the traditional policy of disfavor of separation agreements.

D. **Modification:** A court may set aside the provisions of a separation agreement based on the same factors that permit rescission of other contracts (fraud, duress, etc.). However, spousal support provisions in a settlement agreement generally are not modifiable; child support provisions are modifiable if the child's best interests require it.

E. **Enforcement of settlement agreement: Merger:** A settlement agreement may be enforceable by means of the contempt power if the agreement has been **incorporated** and **merged** in the divorce decree. Once an agreement is incorporated into the divorce decree, its provisions become part of the decree and may be enforced by court order, including contempt. On the other hand, if the agreement is incorporated, but is not merged into the decree, it remains a separate enforceable agreement and is not enforceable by contempt.

Example: Joseph and Ida execute a separation agreement providing that Joseph would pay Ida $2,425 a month for spousal support, which may be terminated if Ida remarries or either party dies. The separation agreement also contains a nonmodification agreement, providing that "[t]he terms of this Agreement shall not be subject to modification or change, regardless of the relative circumstances of the parties. . . ." The court finds that the agreement is not unconscionable and incorporates it into the divorce decree. Several years later, Joseph seeks termination of the spousal support, claiming that Ida tried to have him killed. The court refuses because of the nonmodification clause, which (according to the court) was not unconscionable and did not offend public policy, despite the acts of Ida. *Richardson v. Richardson*, 218 S.W.3d 426 (Mo. 2007).

V. TAX CONSIDERATIONS

Tax issues often arise in connection with a dissolution relating to spousal support, property distributions, and child support.

A. Spousal support

1. **Taxable to the recipient:** Spousal support (still termed "alimony" by Internal Revenue Code §71) is taxed differently than child support. The Internal Revenue Service (IRS) treats alimony, similar to salary, as income. Thus, alimony is *taxable* to the recipient (included in gross income).

2. **Deductible by the payor:** In contrast, the IRS permits the payor a deduction for the alimony he pays to the recipient. Thus, alimony is *deductible* by the payor.

   In order to qualify as deductible by the payor, spousal support payments must:

   - be in cash (not property or services);
   - be received by or on behalf of the other spouse according to a divorce decree or written separation agreement; and,
   - terminate upon the recipient's death.

   In addition, to qualify, the parties cannot live together nor file a joint tax return after the payments begin.

3. **Choice of different treatment:** It is important to note that the ex-spouses are not obligated to treat spousal support as the Code dictates. Depending on their respective incomes and tax rates, for example, they may decide that it is more advantageous for them to treat spousal support payments as nontaxable to the recipient and nondeductible by the payor. To do so, they must provide for this in their decree or separation instrument and attach a copy of their agreement to the recipient's tax return for each year for which spousal support is treated as nontaxable to the recipient and nondeductible by the payor (Reg. 1.71-1T(b) Q&A-8).

B. Transfers of property to spouse incident to divorce:

For transfers of property between spouses, including transfers incident to divorce, no gain or loss will be recognized. The property transferred is treated as a gift to the recipient. As a result, any gain or loss inherent in the property is not recognized at the time of the transfer. Further, the recipient takes the donor's basis in the property. This means that the recipient will have the tax burden (or benefit) of any gain (or loss) inherent in the property at the time of transfer.

C. Child support:

Child support payments are *nontaxable* to the recipient and *nondeductible* by the payor. It may be more beneficial to the parties to treat child support payments as alimony, but regulations constrain the parties' ability to do so through a presumption that payments that will be reduced on the happening of a contingency relating to a child (e.g. the child's reaching a certain age) constitute child support (Reg. 1.71-1T(c) Q&A-16, 18).

D. Other tax considerations

1. **Head of household:** A "head of household" obtains preferential treatment under the Code. To utilize this status, the taxpayer must be unmarried on the last day of the taxable year, maintain a household constituting the principal residence for an unmarried descendant or dependent for more than half the year, and pay for over half of the cost of maintaining the household. Thus,

a wife who receives custody of a child or children may file as head of household so long as the child or children live with her for more than half the year and she bears over half the maintenance costs (IRC §2(b)).

2. **Dependency exemption:** In addition to the standard deduction, an ex-spouse may also claim a personal exemption to lower his or her taxable income. IRC §§151 and 152 permit an exemption for any eligible dependents (i.e., defined as those who have a designated relationship to the taxpayer, who have the same principal place of abode as the taxpayer for more than one-half of the taxable year, and who are under 19 years of age or under 24 years for a student at the close of the taxable year). The custodial parent generally has the initial right to claim the exemption, but the parties may agree that a noncustodial parent will claim the exemption instead; to do so, the custodial parent must sign a written declaration, which the noncustodial parent must attach to his or her tax return (IRC §152(e)). A taxpayer may claim the exemption if he or she provides over one-half of the dependent's support.

Quiz Yourself on *SEPARATION AGREEMENTS AND TAX CONSIDERATIONS*

75. Upon their divorce, Husband and Wife enter into a property settlement agreement. The agreement provides that "in consideration of the payment to Wife of $10,000 per year for four years for spousal support, and the conveyance of $20,000 to Wife in personal property, Wife agrees to and does release all rights of inheritance in Husband's estate." The agreement is referred to in the divorce decree and is approved by the court but is not actually made part of the decree. Husband conveys to Wife the $20,000 in personal property in the form of stocks and bonds; however, he fails to make any payments for spousal support. Wife attempts to enforce the agreement by contempt proceedings. Will she prevail? ____________________

76. Martha, a nurse, and George, a lawyer, divorce after 21 years. They have three children. Upon their dissolution, the parties execute a written agreement providing that "Husband will pay Wife $25,000 per year for three years as spousal support, terminable upon Wife's death." George also agrees to pay child support and, in addition, the agreement provides that George is to transfer to Martha the marital residence (which originally cost $100,000 but the current market value is $150,000). Martha and George then seek legal advice as to whether: (a) Martha must pay tax on the spousal support she receives; (b) George will be permitted a deduction for the full amount of alimony he pays Martha; and (c) George will recognize any gain on the transfer to Martha of the home. ____________________

Answers

75. No. A settlement agreement between the spouses may be enforced by contempt if the agreement has been incorporated and merged in the divorce decree. If the agreement is not merged into the decree, it remains a separate enforceable agreement and is enforceable in a separate contract action but not enforceable by contempt. Because Husband and Wife's agreement was referred to in the decree and approved by the court, but not merged into the decree, the marital separation agreement is not enforceable by contempt. Wife will have to sue for breach of contract.

76. (a) The IRS includes Martha's alimony in her gross income. Therefore, Martha must pay tax on the entire amount of alimony she receives, although she may be able to offset her tax liability through the use of various deductions and credits. (b) George will receive a deduction for the full amount of alimony he pays Martha because the agreement contemplates that his payments will be in cash, received by Martha, pursuant to a written separation agreement, the parties do not plan to continue to cohabit nor to file a joint return once payments commence, and George's liability for spousal support is to terminate upon Martha's death. (c) When George transfers the home to Martha, he will not recognize gain, nor will Martha receive income. As for the basis, Martha will take the property at George's basis ($100,000), rather than the fair market value. Thus, if Martha sells the home for $150,000, she must report a taxable gain of $50,000.

Exam Tips on *FINANCIAL CONSEQUENCES OF DISSOLUTION*

General Issues Regarding Support and Property

- Before analyzing support and property issues, be sure to identify various ***threshold issues***.
  - For example, note who is petitioning for divorce in the designated forum. Identify whether one spouse is petitioning or both. Remember that if the facts involve a ***unilateral divorce*** (by one spouse only), the respondent might be able to assert that the court lacks jurisdiction over him or her. (A court lacking jurisdiction over the respondent can only terminate the marriage and cannot adjudicate the financial incidents of the divorce.)
  - Be sure to note also whether the divorce is being sought on ***fault-based grounds or no fault***. If the divorce is sought by a party (or parties) on fault-based grounds, then fault may bar awards of spousal support and property in some jurisdictions.

Property

- For property questions, clarify the ***type of marital property regime*** in the given jurisdiction. If the question states no specific regime, then answer the question as if each of the regimes (common law, community property) would apply. Be sure to explain the rationales of each type of marital property regime (e.g., community property is based on the partnership model, etc.).
  - Mention the shift from the ***traditional*** rationale for *property* division to the ***contribution*** approach.
  - Explain that most states now adhere to ***equitable distribution***. Clarify the meaning of the term "equitable distribution." If the issue involves separate property, be sure to mention the ***lack of uniformity of treatment of separate property*** under the scheme of equitable jurisdiction. (That

is, some equitable distribution jurisdictions treat gifts and inheritances as separate property, whereas others treat those items as marital property.)

- ☛ Be on the lookout for ***frequently tested property issues***. Such issues include: professional licenses and degrees, goodwill, pensions, and bankruptcy. Always specify relevant majority and minority approaches. For example, if the issue involves a professional license or degree, explain the majority rule that most states refuse to treat professional licenses and degrees as marital property. Clarify the reasons underlying that rule. Explain, too, that some jurisdictions find ways to mitigate the harshness of this rule. Be sure to mention the ALI *Principles'* approach here (and wherever relevant).

- ☛ For questions involving pensions, explore whether the problem involves ***vested and/or nonvested pension rights***. Explain the difference between vested and nonvested pension rights. In the determination of whether an employee-spouse's rights have vested, be sure to take note of the numbers of years' service that are necessary for the vesting of pension rights.

  - ☞ Discuss the majority versus minority approach to nonvested pension rights. Remember to clarify that under the majority rule, vested *and* nonvested pension benefits are marital property subject to equitable distribution.

  - ☞ Finally, determine if there are any issues regarding ***federal-state preemption***. Such issues are likely to arise if the pension rights involve federal benefits (military retirement pay, etc.). Discuss the about face in treatment of preemption issues. That is, the U.S. Supreme Court first ruled that certain federal retirement schemes were exempt from application of state marital property rules; however, subsequently Congress overruled that policy by the enactment of federal legislation.

- ☛ For questions involving ***bankruptcy***, explain the protective policy behind the federal bankruptcy legislation.

  - ☞ Discuss the ***"support-property distinction"*** — the traditional rule that obligations attributable to a property division upon divorce are dischargeable in bankruptcy but that support obligations (child support, spousal support) are not dischargeable. Because of this rule, it is necessary to determine whether a particular obligation could be classified as support or property. Recall that the determination is not always crystal clear. In such a case, discuss the implications of a finding that a particular obligation could be classified as either support or property.

  - ☞ Be sure to point out the impact of the Bankruptcy Reform Act that modifies the traditional rule above, providing that property obligations are no longer dischargeable in certain cases.

  - ☞ Be on the alert for enforcement issues. That is, determine if the obligee-spouse has secured the obligor-spouse's obligation by the imposition of a lien on the obligor-spouse's property. If so, be sure to discuss the United States Supreme Court's decision in *Farrey v. Sanderfoot.*

Support

- ☛ When analyzing issues of support, be sure to distinguish if the question is asking about spousal support and/or child support. Different rationale, rules, and policies will apply.

- ☞ Mention that the traditional rationales underlying awards of alimony were ***fault*** and ***need***. However, the modern rationales of ***self-sufficiency*** and ***loss compensation*** (ALI) replace the traditional rationales.
- ☞ Remember that support statutes with ***gender-based*** provisions are unconstitutional (*Orr v. Orr*).
- ☞ Remember, too, that different forms of spousal support are available (***rehabilitative alimony*** and ***reimbursement alimony***). Be sure to explain the meaning of each term and determine whether each form would (or should) be available.

☛ Many questions involve issues of both spousal support and property. In such cases, be sure to remember the ***distinctions*** between the awards. For example, spousal support is ***modifiable***; property awards are not. Spousal support is ***terminable*** upon remarriage; property awards are not. Spousal support awards are enforceable by the ***contempt*** power; property awards are not.

☛ For questions involving spousal support and child support, clarify whether the question involves an ***initial award*** or ***modification***. Always look for cross-over issues between spousal support and property, such as those raised by licenses and degrees.

- ☞ When addressing modification of spousal support, be alert for ***common fact patterns involving changed circumstances*** (especially remarriage, cohabitation, deteriorating health).
- ☞ Remember that a determination of changed circumstances requires that the change be ***substantial*** and ***material*** since the entry of the divorce decree.

Child Support

☛ For child support issues, determine if the jurisdiction is relying on the traditional ***discretionary*** standard or ***guidelines***.

- ☞ If the approach is unspecified, discuss both. If the jurisdiction has adopted guidelines, determine which ***model*** it follows (i.e., income shares model, percentage of income model, or Melson formula) and apply that model to the facts. If no model is specified, discuss all three approaches.

☛ Be alert for ***frequently tested issues***, such as post-majority support, stepparent liability, and support of nonmarital children.

- ☞ For questions involving ***post-majority support***, be sure to mention that states have different approaches to this issue. Be on the lookout for possible issues regarding the constitutionality of a post-majority support statute.
- ☞ For issues of ***stepparent liability***, mention the traditional view (of no duty) and the modern view that imposes liability in some cases.
- ☞ If the question involves ***support of nonmarital children***, be sure to look for constitutional issues of discrimination against nonmarital children (e.g., denial of equal protection), and issues involving statutes of limitations. In the latter case, be sure to mention the influence of federal legislation (Child Support Enforcement Amendments) that extends the statutory period until age 18. Be alert to possible issues regarding the standard of proof, indigents' rights to paternity establishment, and voluntary paternity establishment.

- When addressing ***modification of child support*** (just like modification of spousal support), be alert for ***common fact patterns involving changed circumstances*** (i.e., remarriage, cohabitation, deteriorating health, increased resources, occupational changes).
  - Remember that a determination of changed circumstances requires that the change (since the prior custody order) be both ***substantial*** and ***material***. Discuss the rule and apply it to the given fact pattern.
- Finally, be alert for issues involving ***jurisdiction*** and ***enforcement*** of child support awards.
  - To make or modify an award of child support (or spousal support), a court must have ***personal jurisdiction*** over the obligor.
  - Determine if the obligor is a ***nonresident*** (a frequent fact pattern). If so, note the trend to expand traditional methods of acquiring personal jurisdiction over nonresidents for support purposes. For questions involving personal jurisdiction over a nonresident obligor, remember to discuss both ***state law*** (i.e., the different types of ***long-arm statutes***) and ***constitutional due process***. In discussing the constitutional limits of long-arm statutes, be sure to discuss and apply the United States Supreme Court's decision in *Kulko v. Superior Court*.
- Common fact patterns involving ***interstate enforcement*** issues arise whenever the noncustodial parent leaves the state and refuses to pay support, whenever the custodial parent relocates to another state but wants to enforce a preexisting order, or whenever petitioner seeks modification in a forum that is different than the original forum.
  - If the question involves the possibility (or actuality) of multiple support orders from different jurisdictions, be sure to discuss and apply the Uniform Interstate Family Support Act (UIFSA) which superseded URESA and RURESA. Remember that UIFSA applies to initial awards as well as modifications of support orders.
  - If a petitioner is seeking a modification of support in another state (other than the original forum), be sure to discuss and apply UIFSA's concept of ***continuing, exclusive jurisdiction*** (i.e., the court entering the original support order maintains continuing, exclusive jurisdiction until that state ceases to be the residence of the child or any party, or a party files consent to another state's jurisdiction).
  - For enforcement, discuss both ***state and federal*** remedies.

CHAPTER 7

CHILD CUSTODY

ChapterScope

This chapter examines child custody in the divorce context. Here are a few of the key principles covered in this chapter:

- Historically, courts applied ***presumptions*** to aid the determination of custody disputes.
    - The ***"tender years presumption"*** favored an award of custody to the mother of young children. Courts have held that this presumption violates the Equal Protection Clause.
    - The ***"primary caretaker presumption"*** favors an award of custody to the parent providing primary care. While no state continues to follow this presumption, many states consider it as a factor in custody decision making.
- The modern prevailing standard in custody decision making is ***"the best interests of the child."***
- Certain ***constitutional issues*** may arise in the determination of the best interests of the child.
    - ***Race*** cannot be the determinative factor in custody decisions.
    - The constitutional right to ***freedom of religion*** also restricts consideration of the role of religion in custody decision making.
- Courts also consider other factors regarding ***fitness*** in custody determinations.
    - Under the modern rule, a parent's ***extramarital sexual conduct*** is only relevant if it causes harm to the child.
    - According to the modern trend, a parent's ***sexual orientation*** is relevant only if it has an adverse impact on the child.
    - States now consider ***domestic violence*** as a factor in custody decision making. Some states adopt a rebuttable presumption against custody awards to an abusive spouse.
- Almost all states now permit some form of ***joint custody***. Joint custody grants both parents legal custody, i.e., responsibility for making major childrearing decisions.
- Traditionally, the noncustodial parent received ***visitation rights*** to the child. Courts have discretion to define the scope, time, place, and circumstances of visitation. Courts deny visitation rights reluctantly.
- Custody and visitation are ***not dependent*** variables: failure to support a child may not result in infringement of the parent's visitation rights.
- A ***rebuttable presumption*** favors the biological parent in a custody dispute pitting a ***parent versus a nonparent***.
- All states have ***visitation*** statutes permitting ***third parties*** (such as grandparents) to petition for visitation in certain circumstances.
- Many states consider a ***child's preference*** in making custody decisions.

- ***Representation for a child*** in a custody dispute is ***discretionary***.
- Custody ***modification*** generally requires proof of a ***material or substantial change in circumstances***.
- The ***Uniform Child Custody Jurisdiction and Enforcement Act*** (UCCJEA) governs jurisdiction and enforcement of child custody decision making. It harmonizes differences between the original Uniform Child Custody Jurisdiction Act and the Parental Kidnapping Prevention Act.
- The ***Uniform Child Abduction Prevention Act*** (UCAPA) enables the court to order measures to prevent child abductions.
- Some jurisdictions recommend, or even mandate, ***mediation*** in cases involving custody or visitation disputes.
- **Collaborative law** is the newest form of alternative dispute resolution to help divorcing spouses settle their disputes.

I. INTRODUCTION

This chapter concerns child custody disputes in the context of divorce. In the vast majority of divorces, parents reach private agreements about custodial arrangements. However, contested cases are particularly acrimonious.

A. **Definition of custody:** Custody refers to the right to the care and control of a child, including the ability to make decisions regarding the child's residence, discipline, education, training, medical care, etc.

Traditionally, upon divorce, the court awarded custody to one parent (often the mother) granting that parent broad rights to the care and control of the child. Simultaneously, the court awarded visitation rights to the other parent (usually the father) that encompassed more limited decision making, as well as a duty of support, while the child was temporarily residing with that noncustodial parent. (The concept of joint custody is explained *infra*.)

B. **Functions of custody law:** Custody law has two functions: private dispute settlement and child protection.

C. **Historical background:** Prior to the nineteenth century, a rule of paternal preference prevailed: the father was entitled to custody. Beginning in the mid- to late nineteenth century, feminists advocated for the right to custody and guardianship. Custody law began to reflect a maternal preference for mothers of young children. This maternal preference, which has constitutional shortcomings (explained *infra*), was abrogated in the 1980s.

Fault also played a role, historically, in custody decision making. Upon divorce, custody was awarded to the innocent spouse (i.e., the spouse who was not guilty of a fault-based ground for divorce).

The original version of the Uniform Marriage and Divorce Act (UMDA) rejected fault-based notions in custody determinations. UMDA §402 currently provides: "The court shall not consider conduct of a proposed custodian that does not affect his relationship to the child." Evidence of fault was relevant in early versions of California's no-fault legislation but rejected after 1993.

D. Effects of divorce on children: Divorce has short-term and long-term psychological effects on children. A child's sex, age, and stage of development at the time of the divorce are factors in determining the child's adjustment to divorce.

II. STANDARDS FOR SELECTING THE CUSTODIAL PARENT

A. Presumptions: Some states invoke presumptions to adjudicate child custody disputes.

1. Tender years doctrine (the maternal preference)

a. Definition: The tender years presumption provides that the biological mother of a young child is entitled to custody unless the mother is found to be unfit.

b. Effect: Courts treated the tender years presumption as:

- a rule requiring maternal custody if all other factors are equal,
- a rule placing the burden of persuasion on the father to show that paternal custody is in the best interest of the child, or
- a rule affecting the burden of proof that requires the father to prove maternal unfitness.

c. Ages encompassed: "Tender years" generally was defined to include preschool children. Some courts, however, included children from ages five to ten. A few courts even included older children.

d. Constitutionality: Beginning in the 1980s, several courts invalidated the maternal preference as a violation of equal protection.

Example: A trial court awards a mother custody of two young children, applying the tender years presumption. The father challenges the presumption as a violation of equal protection. Reviewing the historical development of the presumption and its current status, the court holds that the presumption is unconstitutional as a gender-based classification. *Devine v. Devine*, 398 So.2d 686 (Ala. 1981).

e. Modern view: States abolished the tender years presumption in response to constitutional challenges. Courts now assume that both parents are capable of caring for a child. However, courts still may consider the age of a child as a relevant factor in custody decision making.

2. Primary caretaker

a. Definition: One suggestion for the replacement of the maternal preference is the "primary caretaker presumption," by which courts confer a custodial presumption in favor of the parent who has assumed the status of the primary caretaker.

b. Relevant factors: Several factors are relevant to the determination of which parent should be accorded primary caretaker status:

- preparation and planning meals,
- bathing, grooming, and dressing the children,
- purchasing, cleaning, and caring for the clothes,
- obtaining medical care for the child,

- arranging for children's social interactions with peers,
- arranging alternative care,
- putting the children to bed at night and tending to children who awake during the night,
- managing discipline,
- supervising the child's religious, cultural, or social education, and
- teaching elementary skills. *Garska v. McCoy*, 278 S.E.2d 357, 363 (1981).

c. **Modern view:** Despite considerable support by commentators for the primary caretaker presumption, only two states (West Virginia and Minnesota) adopted the presumption. Both states later rejected it. Many states continue to consider primary caretaker status as a relevant factor in custody decision making, although they no longer treat it as a presumption.

d. **ALI "approximation" approach:** When West Virginia rejected the primary caretaker presumption, the state replaced it with the ALI provision. The ALI provides for rules regarding the "allocation of custodial and decisionmaking responsibility" for children. The ALI requires a party seeking custody to submit a "parenting plan" (a written agreement by which parents specify caretaking and decision-making authority and the manner for resolution of future disputes). If the parents agree, the court should enforce that agreement unless it was not voluntary or would be harmful to the child. ALI *Principles* §2.06(1)(a) and (b).

If the parents cannot agree, the court should award custody based on an *approximation standard* that allocates custody based on the amount of responsibility assumed by each parent prior to the separation. ALI *Principles* §2.08(1). The objective is to replicate the division of custodial responsibility that was followed when the family was intact.

3. **Other presumptions:** Several other custody presumptions exist. A common-law presumption holds that custody of a nonmarital child vests in the mother. Some courts have abrogated that presumption on equal protection grounds. Some jurisdictions follow another presumption that separation of siblings is not in their best interests. Still another presumption is the natural-parent presumption favoring custody to a biological parent in custody disputes involving parents and nonparents (discussed *infra* Section IV.A).

B. **Best interests of the child:** Most jurisdictions, rather than adopting a presumption in favor of one parent, follow the "best interests of the child" standard when resolving custody disputes. Despite its widespread adoption, commentators criticize this standard as highly discretionary and imprecise. Several factors are relevant when applying this standard.

1. **Constitutional factors**

a. **Race:** The U.S. Supreme Court determined that race may not serve as the decisive factor in custody decision making.

Example: When Linda and Anthony divorce, Linda is awarded custody of their three-year-old daughter. Subsequently, a court divests Linda of custody because she is living with, and later marries, an African-American. The trial court finds that due to the social stigma accompanying an interracial marriage, the child's best interests will be served by awarding the father custody. The U.S. Supreme Court holds that an award of custody based on race violates the Equal Protection Clause. Race, although it may be a factor in custody decision making, may not be the determinative factor. The effects of racial prejudice cannot justify a racial classification that divests custody from a natural mother who has not been found to be unfit. *Palmore v. Sidoti*, 466 U.S. 429 (1984).

Note: The ALI *Principles* prohibit courts from considering the race or ethnicity of the child, parent, or other member of the household in determining custody. ALI *Principles* §2.12(1)(a).

b. Religion

i. **General rule:** The First Amendment serves as a limitation on judicial consideration of religion as a factor in awarding custody. Under the Free Exercise Clause, a court may not interfere with a parent's right to practice religion. Under the Establishment Clause, a court may not favor one parent's religion or religious observance over another parent's religion or nonobservance.

Example: A Roman Catholic mother with two children from a previous marriage converts to Judaism and marries a man who is Jewish. They have a daughter. Shortly after the child's birth, the mother converts back to Catholicism. At divorce, the court awards custody to the mother and orders the mother to raise the child as a Jew. The mother appeals. The appellate court determines that because of First Amendment concerns, a court may not make a decision favoring a specific religion over the objection of the other parent. *Abbo v. Briskin*, 660 So.2d 1157 (Fla. Ct. App. 1995).

ii. **Limitation:** A court may take into account the *effect* of a parent's religion on the child.

Example: Three years after the parties divorce, conflict develops about the religious upbringing of the parties' young daughter. Husband is Roman Catholic. Wife recently joined the Pentecostal Church, which has several lifestyle restrictions (concerning clothes, make-up, jewelry, sports, dance) that affect daughter. The daughter was baptized a Catholic. Both parents seek sole custody. The trial court awards Husband sole custody. The appellate court holds that Wife's refusal to place child's needs above her religious convictions justified the custody modification in favor of father because the parents' conflict was resulting in the child's confusion, guilt, and fear. However, the court added that any prohibition on Wife's taking the child to her church was unwarranted. *Holder v. Holder*, 872 N.E.2d 1239 (Ohio Ct. App. 2007).

iii. **ALI *Principles*:** The ALI *Principles* prohibit a court from considering the religious practices of either a parent or child in custody decision making except in the following situations: (1) if the religious practices present "severe and almost certain harm" to the child (and then a court may limit the religious practices only to the minimum degree necessary to protect the child) or (2) if necessary to protect the child's ability to practice a religion "that has been a significant part of the child's life." ALI *Principles* §2.12(1)(c).

2. **Fitness factors:** Courts consider a number of factors relevant to the determination of a parent's fitness. These include: sexual conduct, careers, daycare, wealth, domestic violence, and disability.

a. Sexual conduct

i. Generally: Traditionally, a parent's acts of adultery and/or cohabitation resulted in a denial of custody. However, according to the modern view, a parent's sexual conduct is only relevant if it has an ***adverse effect*** on the child. See UMDA §402 ("The court shall not consider conduct of a proposed custodian that does not affect his relationship to the child").

Example: Mother and Father divorce when their son M.J. is two years old. The court awards joint custody but names Mother as primary physical custodian. Father appeals, arguing that Mother's adultery should have resulted in an award of primary physical custody to him. Affirming, the appellate court concludes that the trial court could have been influenced by Mother's testimony that, although she had been in a relationship since separating from Father, her relationship did not have a detrimental impact on her parenting skills or on the child's best interest. *In re M.J.*, 2010 WL 3042438 (Tex. App. 2010).

ii. Same-sex sexual conduct: A parent's same-sex sexual conduct continues to play a role in custody decision making. Courts take three basic approaches:

- same-sex sexual conduct is evidence of parental fitness per se,
- same-sex sexual conduct leads to a presumption of adverse impact that can be rebutted by the parent's showing of absence of harm, or
- custody will be denied only if the parent's sexual orientation has or will have an adverse impact on the child.

This third view, the ***nexus test***, represents the emerging trend (and the view of the ALI *Principles* discussed *infra*).

Example: Beth and Tim divorce on the ground of irreconcilable differences. During the divorce proceedings, Tim testifies that his only concern with leaving their son Zach in Beth's permanent custody was the "homosexual environment" in which Zach would be raised. Tim felt that Beth was qualified in every other way to raise the child. When the trial court awards Tim custody, Beth appeals. The appellate court holds that the trial judge abused his discretion by placing too much weight on the "moral fitness" factor of Beth's homosexuality, that the judge never found the mother unfit to care for the child, and no evidence was presented regarding any detrimental effects the child may have suffered as a result of living with the mother, and that the judge ignored the voluminous evidence presented under the remaining factors supporting Beth as the preferred custodial parent. *Hollon v. Hollon*, 784 So.2d 943 (Miss. 2001).

In an emerging trend, courts are increasingly recognizing the parental rights of the same-sex partner who is not the biological mother or father of the child.

Example: Beth and Donna, a lesbian couple, decide to have a child by artificial insemination. Shortly after Donna gives birth, Beth and Donna marry in Canada, where same-sex marriage is legal. A few years later, Donna has another child by artificial insemination. Donna does not allow Beth to adopt either child, but the children take Beth's last name and call Beth "Mom." Beth adds Donna and the children to her health insurance plan, contributes to their school costs, and in all ways holds out the children as her own. When the older child is three years old, Donna announces that she wants to end the marriage. Beth seeks custody rights, arguing that Donna is equitably estopped from denying that Beth is a parent to the children. Donna seeks dismissal, arguing that Beth has no biological connection to the children. The court holds that it may proceed to determine if the best interests of the children justify granting Beth custodial rights, finding Donna equitably estopped from denying Beth as a parent. The court specifically notes that Donna had treated Beth as the parent of the children, that Donna and Beth were married, and that it may not be in the best interests of the children to suddenly cut out of their lives someone they recognize as their mother. *Beth R. v. Donna M.,* 853 N.Y.S.2d 501 (Sup. Ct. 2008).

iii. *Lawrence v. Texas*: *Lawrence v. Texas* may apply to custody decision making to prohibit judicially imposed conditions based on a parent's sexual conduct. In *Lawrence v. Texas* the United States Supreme Court held that state sodomy laws banning same-sex, but not opposite-sex, sodomy violate the individual's constitutionally protected liberty and that moral disapproval is not a legitimate interest to justify such differential treatment. Courts might hold, however, that a child's best interest is a sufficiently compelling state interest to overcome *Lawrence*'s application to the custody context.

Example: A trial court grants parents joint custody of their children and imposes visitation restrictions that prohibit the father from having his same-sex partner stay overnight during visitation periods, engaging in public displays of affection in the children's presence, leaving the children in his partner's care, and discussing sexuality issues with the children. The father appeals the conditions on custody. The appellate court affirms, stating that, although *Lawrence* "cast serious doubts upon the constitutionality" of state law as it applies to private conduct between consenting adults, nonetheless that "the central holdings" of the court's custody precedents remain the same. The court then affirms the award of joint custody based on evidence showing that the father was discreet about his romantic relationship, the relationship has not had an adverse impact on the children, and the father is a good parent. *A.O.V. v. J.R.V.*, 2007 WL 581871 (Va. Ct. App. 2007).

iv. State DOMAs: State DOMAs may also have an impact on custody decision making.

Example: Therese Fairchild requests visitation rights to a child that she and her partner Denise jointly plan to bear and rear. At the time of the birth, the women voluntarily enter into a court-approved joint custody agreement to ensure that each woman has a legal relationship with the boy. Eight years later when the couple breaks up, Denise attempts to thwart Therese's relationship with their son. Denise argues, inter alia, that Ohio's constitutional amendment banning same-sex marriage invalidates the court-approved shared custody order. The court holds that the custody agreement is valid despite Ohio's constitutional amendment because the constitutional amendment pertains to relationships between two adults—not the relationship between parent and child. *In re Fairchild*, No. 01JU032542 (Ohio Ct. Common Pleas, Jan. 25, 2007) (available at *www.lambdalegal.org/news/pr/ohio-court-says-custody.html*).

v. ALI *Principles*: The ALI *Principles* prohibit a court from considering either the extramarital sexual conduct or the sexual orientation of a parent except upon a showing that such conduct causes harm to the child. ALI *Principles* §2.12(1)(d).

b. Careers: A parent's career may be a factor in the determination of the best interests standard. Gender bias sometimes results in adverse decisions for mothers who work outside the home.

Example: The court awards custody to the father based on the determination that the mother was a "remote-control parent" who left many parenting duties to the father and housekeeper. The mother appeals, alleging that the court failed to apply gender-neutral standards by holding her to a more rigorous standard due to her employment. Reversing, the court determines that mothers with careers should not be penalized because this would impose a higher standard on mothers and force them to choose between a career and parenthood. Also, the court notes that courts and legislatures now encourage divorced women to acquire increased economic independence, and, as a result, it would be incongruous to exact a penalty on custody. *Linda R. v. Richard E.*, 561 N.Y.S.2d 29 (App. Div. 1990).

c. Daycare: The child's daycare arrangements sometimes may be a factor in custody decision making.

Example: Jennifer Ireland and Steven Smith, while they are high school students, have a child, Maranda. Maranda lives with Jennifer and her mother while Steven continues to live with his parents. When Maranda is two, Jennifer petitions for child support and obtains a temporary custody order. Jennifer enrolls and takes up residence at the University of Michigan. She places Maranda in the university daycare center. At a subsequent custody hearing, the court awards custody to Steven. The court is influenced heavily by the child's daycare arrangements, maintaining that Steven's proposal to have his mother (a "blood relative") babysit for Maranda is superior to daycare by strangers that is necessitated by Jennifer's studies. Reversing and remanding, the appellate court finds that the trial court incorrectly focused on the "acceptability" of the custodial arrangement rather than its stability. *Ireland v. Smith*, 547 N.W.2d 686 (Mich. 1996).

d. Wealth: The relative wealth of the parties is not determinative unless one parent is unable to provide adequately for the child.

e. Domestic violence: Increasingly, courts and legislators address the role of domestic violence in custody decision making.

i. Generally: Either by case law or statute, virtually all jurisdictions take into account domestic violence in child custody disputes. Jurisdictions adopt a variety of approaches:

- The majority of states consider domestic violence as a factor in the application of the best interests standard. Legislation also requires courts to consider domestic violence before awarding joint custody.
- A trend is evident in terms of states' adoption of a rebuttable presumption against an award of custody to a parent who has committed domestic violence. Jurisdictions differ in terms of the evidence necessary for the presumption to apply. For example, some states require a severe incident or a pattern of abuse; others require a criminal conviction.
- Some of the rebuttable-presumption states require that the abuse be proximate to the time of the custody proceeding. *See, e.g.*, Cal. Fam. Code §3044 (West 2004)

(requiring, for application of the presumption, that the abuse must have occurred within five years of the custody proceeding).

- Additionally, many states now provide protection for victims of domestic abuse in custody mediation.

ii. Mutual acts of domestic violence: Abusers may contend that the domestic violence was "mutual," i.e., that the victim provoked the abuse. In response, courts must determine whether one or both spouses perpetrated the acts of domestic violence.

Example: Roland and Jenese marry after Jenese became pregnant with their son. One year later, after experiencing several instances of physical abuse by Roland, Jenese files a complaint seeking dissolution of the marriage. The court grants Jenese a divorce on the grounds of adultery, extreme cruelty, and irreconcilable differences. Upon finding Roland had committed domestic violence, the court awards physical custody of their son to Jenese and provides Roland "closely supervised" visitation. Roland appeals, claiming, inter alia, that the trial court erred when it found that he had committed domestic violence and Jenese had not. The North Dakota Supreme Court affirms, holding that although Jenese may have struck, hit, or scratched Roland during their relationship, her actions were largely in self-defense and were far less serious in nature and degree than Roland's domestic violence. *Peters-Riemers v. Riemers*, 644 N.W.2d 197 (N.D. 2002).

According to the ALI *Principles*, acts of self-defense do not constitute abuse. Rather, if one spouse's act is more extreme or dangerous, "it may be appropriate for the court to impose limits on the primary aggressor but not on the primary victim." ALI *Principles* §2.11(c) cmt.

Sometimes, a court will issue mutual orders of protection against both partners. Critics charge that mutual orders of protection are based on misconceptions (the victim must have provoked the abuse), constitute gender bias, serve to blame the victim, fail to give guidance to law enforcement on how to enforce the order, and jeopardize the victim's custody rights because most states favor the nonbattering parent in custody decision making.

iii. Effect of "friendly parent" provisions: Statutes sometimes contain *friendly parent provisions* that require courts, in determining the best interest of the child, to take into consideration which parent is more likely to maintain the child's relationship with the other parent. These provisions may disadvantage battered spouses in custody determinations.

f. Disability: UMDA §402(5) and many state statutes require consideration of the mental and physical health of all individuals when applying the best interests standard.

When the parent is disabled, courts generally focus on the *effect* of the disability on the child.

Example: A husband and wife separate, executing an agreement granting custody of their sons to the father. The father moves to California and begins living with a woman who becomes the sons' stepmother. A few years later, the father becomes a quadriplegic as a result of an accident. During his year-long hospitalization and recuperation, the children visit him several times a week. Five years after the separation, the mother files an action for divorce and modification of custody. The mother has not seen the sons since the separation. The trial court grants a modification of the couple's prior custodial agreement and awards custody to the mother. The court reasons that the father's disability prevents him from establishing a normal relationship with his sons. Reversing, the California Supreme Court holds that a physical handicap affecting the ability to participate in physical activities with children is not a changed circumstance of sufficient relevance and materiality to necessitate a custody change. The court notes that the essence of a child-parent relationship lies in emotional and intellectual guidance. *In re Marriage of Carney*, 598 P.2d 36 (Cal. 1979).

C. **Joint custody (also called "shared custody"):** Beginning in 1979, California initiated the movement toward joint custody. See Cal. Fam. Code §3080 (West 2004). An increasing number of jurisdictions now permit joint custody. This reform was triggered, in large part, by the women's movement with its challenge to gender role stereotypes. The reform also reflects the fact that fathers now take a more active role in childrearing.

1. **Terminology:** Custody involves the twin concepts of legal custody and physical custody. Legal custody confers responsibility for major decision making such as upbringing, health, welfare, and education. Physical custody confers responsibility for day-to-day decisions regarding physical care. Joint custody allows both parents to share legal responsibility for major childrearing decisions regarding upbringing, health, welfare, and education.

   Note: The joint custody labels in decrees and separation agreements may be confusing. For example, an award of "joint legal custody" does not signify that parents have "joint physical custody." Moreover, "the label of joint physical custody often does not reflect the social reality." Eleanor E. Maccoby & Robert H. Mnookin, *Dividing the Child: Social and Legal Dilemmas of Custody* 159 (1992). Joint physical custody may take many different forms (i.e., maternal residence, paternal residence, or dual residence). In about half the cases, a decree of "joint physical custody" actually means that children reside primarily with one parent or the other, stemming from difficulties involved in children's maintaining dual residences (e.g., arranging activities, schools, social networks). *Id.* at 197.

   Note: The ALI uses the term "custodial responsibility" to refer to the concept of physical custody and the term "decisionmaking responsibility" to refer to the concept of legal custody.

2. **Rationale:** Joint custody is based on the rationale that children benefit from continued and frequent contact with both parents and that both mothers and fathers have an important role in childrearing.

3. **Modern trend:** Courts initially were reluctant to order joint custody, fearing the difficulties incumbent upon divorcing parents and also the effects upon the children. However, custody awards of joint custody are now quite common.

4. **Different jurisdictions' approaches:** Most states currently provide for joint custody. States adopt one of the following approaches:

   - Joint custody is a ***presumption***. Some states following this approach require parental agreement.
   - Joint custody is a ***preference***.
   - Joint custody is ***one factor*** in the best interests determination.The third approach is the most common.

5. **"Joint" custody does not mean equal time:** A popular misconception is that joint custody (or joint physical custody) means equal time with each parent. *See, e.g., Birnbaum v. Birnbaum*, 211 Cal. App. 3d 1508, 1515 (Ct. App. 1989) ("Equal division of a child's time between the parents is not the hallmark of joint custody").

6. **Parental agreement and cooperation:** Parental agreement and parental cooperation are not a prerequisite to an award of joint custody. Jurisdictions take different approaches to the factor of the parents' disagreement. Some jurisdictions grant joint custody upon the request of only one party (even if the other parent disagrees). Other jurisdictions require parental agreement. However, severe parental conflict may militate against an award of joint custody.

   Example: Mother and Father are awarded joint legal and physical custody of their infant son, with Mother being named primary physical custodian. Father later requests modification to grant him sole legal custody and primary physical custody on the ground that Mother consistently denied him access. The state supreme court holds that substantial evidence supported the trial court ruling that such a modification was in the child's best interests because Mother made visitation so difficult for Father, and also because her high level of hostility was detrimental to the child and inconsistent with her responsibilities of primary physical custodian. *Doe v. Doe*, 239 P.3d 774 (Idaho 2010).

   Example: The parents share childrearing tasks during the marriage. During their separation, they share alternate physical custody every week; accommodate each other's employment, social, and vacation schedules; and share babysitting expenses. At their divorce proceeding, however, the parents are unable to agree about daycare. The trial court denies an award of joint custody, awards legal and physical custody to the mother, and gives the father visitation rights. The father appeals. Although the appellate court agrees that joint custody generally is inappropriate where parents are unable to cooperate, the court holds that a single conflict over daycare does not warrant a finding of an inability to cooperate. The court is also influenced by the Alaska legislature's express policy favoring awards of joint legal custody. *Bell v. Bell*, 794 P.2d 97 (Alaska 1990).

7. **Parenting plans:** Statutory developments in a number of jurisdictions favor parenting plans—written agreements by which parents specify caretaking and decision-making responsibility authority for their children (and often the manner in which future disputes are to be resolved). The ALI *Principles* reflect this trend by requiring a party seeking custody to submit a parenting plan. ALI *Principles* §2.06(1)(a) & (b). See also discussion *supra* Section II.A.2.d.

Quiz Yourself on STANDARDS FOR SELECTING THE CUSTODIAL PARENT

77. Pauline and Peter's constant bickering leads them to begin discussing divorce. While their discussions are ongoing, Pauline begins a sexual relationship with Sarah, a female co-worker. When Pauline and Peter ultimately decide to seek a divorce, they cannot agree as to custodial arrangements of their two children (ages one and three). Pauline has been doing most of the childcare since the children were born. At a subsequent hearing, Peter asks the court to grant him sole custody. He argues that Pauline's sexual conduct with Sarah renders Pauline an unfit custodian. Pauline asks the court to award sole custody to her based on the tender years presumption. Will Pauline's argument be successful? ____________________

78. Same basic facts as above. Now, Pauline asks the court to award sole custody to her based on the primary caretaker presumption. Will her argument be successful? ____________________

79. Same basic facts as above. Will Peter prevail in his argument that Pauline is an unfit custodian because of her sexual conduct with Sarah? ____________________

80. Meg, a yoga instructor, and Ryan, a financial analyst, divorce. They have a four-year-old daughter Susan. At the time of the divorce, Meg needs hospitalization for an operation. Ryan agrees to care for Susan until Meg recuperates. In the divorce proceeding, Ryan petitions for custody based on Meg's disability. Ryan also argues that he should be awarded custody because he has superior financial resources (i.e., he can provide Susan with her own room, and send her to private schools). Will Ryan's arguments be successful? ____________________

81. Monica and Adiel have a nonmarital son (J.D.). Monica is a Jehovah's Witness, and Adiel is a Muslim. Monica, who has been the primary caretaker of J.D., has raised J.D. as a Jehovah's Witness. When J.D. is four, Monica files an action for paternity establishment and determination of custody. At trial, Adiel argues that Monica should not receive custody because her religion is harmful to J.D. In particular, Adiel argues that Monica proselytizes door-to-door on weekends, has caused J.D. anxiety socially due to her religious beliefs, and teaches J.D. that non–Jehovah's Witnesses will be annihilated, thereby harming J.D. and alienating Adiel. Will Adiel prevail? ____________________

82. Diana, who is Caucasian, marries Livingston, a native of Nigeria and a naturalized U.S. citizen. Six years later when the couple divorces, the court awards custody of their son to Diana and orders Livingston to pay child support. Livingston appeals, arguing that the son's biracial heritage warrants placement with him. He claims that Diana's recent relocation from a Midwestern city with a relatively large African-American population to a smaller town which has no African-American children would be detrimental to his son because the boy would be denied daily contact with any racially diverse individuals. Will Livingston's argument be successful? ____________________

Answers

77. No. In regard to Pauline's request for sole custody, courts no longer apply the tender years presumption (or maternal preference doctrine). That doctrine permitted awards of custody to the mother when the children were "of tender years" (i.e., preschool age). Several courts have declared the doctrine unconstitutional as a violation of the Equal Protection Clause.

78. No. Pauline will not prevail on the basis of the primary caretaker presumption. That presumption would dictate that a court award custody to the parent who was the child's primary caretaker, i.e., the parent who performed such tasks as meal preparation, grooming, discipline, bathing, and putting the children to bed, etc. Even though Pauline might be able to prove that she was the children's primary caretaker, such a showing would be unlikely to result in the application of a presumption in her favor because no jurisdiction currently accords the doctrine presumptive status. Rather, the court would most likely follow the majority of jurisdictions that consider primary caretaker status as one among many factors in the determination of the best interests of the child.

79. Probably not. States are split as to the role of a parent's same-sex sexual conduct in custody determinations. States adhere to different standards: the parent's same-sex sexual conduct is evidence of unfitness per se, presumptively has an adverse impact, or is relevant only if there is proof of adverse impact. Where there is no evidence of adverse effect, Pauline's sexual relationship with Sarah should not result in a custody denial in the majority of jurisdictions.

80. No. The court should accord no weight to Meg's disability. Although many courts and UMDA permit consideration of the parties' mental and physical health, courts generally focus on the effect of a disability on the child. That is, unless a parent's physical disability has harmful effects on a child, it should not be a decisive factor in custody decision making. Ryan has presented no evidence here that Meg's physical condition has resulted in any harm to Susan. In terms of Ryan's argument regarding his superior financial resources, the court should not give any weight to the relative wealth of the parties unless a party's lack of resources inhibits his/her ability to care for the child adequately. Therefore, the court should not take into account Ryan's superior financial resources as a financial analyst compared to Meg's resources as a yoga instructor unless Meg is unable to provide adequately for Susan.

81. No. Monica has had primary responsibility for the child's religious upbringing for the first four years of his life. As a custodial parent, she has the right to determine the child's religion and also to practice her own religion under the First Amendment. In addition, Adiel has failed to show significant actual harm to J.D. resulting from Monica's religious beliefs or religious practices. Therefore, a court will reject his argument and determine custody on nonreligious grounds.

82. No. Livingston is basing his request for custody of his son solely on the argument that he would be a better parent to raise his biracial child, given the fact that his former wife is Caucasian and would raise the child in a Caucasian community. According to the United States Supreme Court's decision in *Palmore*, race cannot be the dominant or controlling factor in a custody decision. That decision would preclude an award of child custody to a fit parent (such as Diana) based on the sole ground of race. Therefore, Livingston's argument will not be successful.

III. STANDARDS FOR SELECTING THE NONCUSTODIAL PARENT: VISITATION

A. Denial of visitation

1. **General rule:** Courts are reluctant to impose a total denial of visitation because the parent-child relationship is constitutionally protected. However, some extreme situations (e.g., severe physical or sexual abuse, substance abuse) may bring about such an outcome.

2. **Visitation and support: Independent variables:** The right to visitation and the duty of support are not interdependent. That is, a parent may not condition visitation upon the other parent's payment of child support. Conversely, if one parent withholds support, the other parent may not deny visitation as retaliation. Some courts make an exception, however, for willful and intentional failure to pay child support that is detrimental to the child.

   Example: A court grants visitation rights to a father and orders him to pay child support. After he is unable to make his support payments and his request for reduction is repeatedly denied, the court finds him in civil contempt and orders him to serve a six-month sentence to be purged upon payment of arrearages (i.e., $40,908.86 past support). The court suspends the father's visitation before his release from jail because he fails to pay the support. He appeals the suspension of his visitation rights. The appellate court holds that the facts do not warrant the suspension of visitation. Child custody and visitation decisions should be guided by the best interests of the child and are not intended to be punitive. The denial of visitation is warranted only when the noncustodial parent is financially able to pay support but refuses to do so. *Turner v. Turner*, 919 S.W.2d 346 (Tenn. Ct. App. 1995).

B. Conditions on visitation: Courts sometimes place conditions on the noncustodial parent's visitation rights or on a parent who has joint custody. Factors that commonly lead to such conditions include: domestic violence, sexual abuse, religious practices or beliefs, and a parent's sexual conduct. Courts also determine the time, place, and circumstances of visitation.

1. **Domestic violence:** Courts occasionally order supervised visitation in cases of domestic violence. Supervised visitation may be conducted by a visitation service or a private individual. Restrictions may encompass extensive or minimal supervision. Visitation may be held either at, or away from, a program center.

2. **Sexual abuse:** In cases of sexual abuse, courts may place conditions on visitation or even terminate visitation.

Example: Mother's ex-husband admits sexual abuse of his 11-year-old stepdaughter that occurred six years earlier. The court orders unsupervised visits with the parties' four-year-old daughter. After a visit, the child complains that her father has inappropriately touched her. A subsequent medical examination determines that abuse is a possibility. The court allows unsupervised visits to continue and even orders overnight visitations. The mother requests review of the court's order granting overnight visitation. Reversing, the appellate court holds that when a parent is justified in believing sexual abuse has occurred, the parent is not required to submit the child for visitation without stringent safeguards. The trial judge should have provided a specific place for the supervised visitation that would have protected the child and should have required supervisors that were satisfactory to both parties. *Hanke v. Hanke*, 615 A.2d 1205 (Md. Ct. Spec. App. 1992).

3. **Religious practices or beliefs:** A parent's exercise of religion sometimes leads to disputes about visitation. However, First Amendment concerns limit a court's power to settle religious disputes. In imposing restrictions on religion, courts sometimes look to the effect of the exposure to the religious practices or beliefs on the children.

Example: Mother is a Catholic, and Father is a Latter Day Saint (LDS). Their children have been raised for ten years in the Catholic faith. Upon Mother and Father's divorce, as part of its determination of custody, the court orders that the children continue to practice their Catholic faith, although the court permits them to attend LDS church with Father if the children wish to do so. A few months later, Mother petitions to modify custody to obtain sole legal custody, arguing, among other things, that Father is violating the order on the children's religion by "forcing" them to attend the LDS church. The trial court awards Mother sole legal custody and orders that the children be raised only as Catholics and prohibits Father from taking them to LDS church. The appellate court affirms, finding the trial court justified in imposing the limitation on Father's visitation where the children needed consistency in their religious upbringing. *Franco v. Franco*, 2008 WL 4814415 (Ariz. Ct. App. 2008).

4. **Sexual conduct:** A parent's sexual behavior may also lead to conditions on visitation.

   a. **Traditional response:** Formerly, courts were especially likely to impose restrictions on visitation when the noncustodial parent was sexually involved in a nonmarital heterosexual relationship.

      Example: The trial court orders that the father not have a female companion stay overnight when the children visit. The father appeals, arguing that the order violates his right to privacy. The mother argues that the moral welfare of her children might be endangered by the presence of an overnight female friend in the father's home. Affirming, the court holds that the mother has an interest in the moral welfare of her children. The court reasons that, although no evidence exists of improper conduct between the father and his companion, there is the possibility of harm to the children's moral welfare. *DeVita v. DeVita*, 366 A.2d 1350 (Super. Ct. N.J. App. Div. 1976).

   b. **Modern view:** Most courts no longer impose restrictions on visitation in the context of opposite-sex relationships. However, some courts continue to impose such restrictions when a noncustodial parent is gay or lesbian.

      Example: Mother and Father have two daughters. Upon their divorce, the court awards shared legal and physical custody. Three years later, Mother seeks primary physical custody and restrictions on Father's visitation. She argues that Father recently began to cohabit with another man and that Father was unwilling to seek professional help to deal with explaining his sexual orientation to the children. The magistrate judge agrees, awarding Mother sole legal and physical custody of the children and prohibiting Father from having overnight visitation in the presence of his partner. The state supreme court affirms, pointing out that under *Lawrence*, a court cannot deprive a parent of custody rights based solely on his sexual orientation, absent a showing of harm to the children. However, the court finds that the restriction on overnight visitation in the presence of Father's partner was appropriate given the hostile relationship between the partner and ex-wife (the partner had tried to make trouble for her at work and with the police). *McGriff v. McGriff*, 99 P.3d 111 (Idaho 2004).

5. **Substance abuse:** A parent's substance abuse might lead to conditions on, or denial of, visitation.

   Example: Wife files for divorce. The trial court awards sole custody of a ten-year-old child to the mother, and denies Husband visitation. Husband appeals. The state supreme court affirms the trial court order, holding that the denial of visitation was not an abuse of discretion because of Husband's chronic use of illegal drugs, inter alia, and not because of his status as an adoptive, rather than a biological, parent. *Taylor v. Taylor*, 646 S.E.2d 238 (Ga. 2007).

C. **Interference with visitation rights:** Noncustodial parents may institute proceedings to enforce their visitation rights. Possible remedies for custodial interference include: civil contempt, a change of custody, tort damages, or makeup parenting time.

1. **Civil contempt:** If a parent refuses to comply with visitation orders, a court may find that parent in contempt. (For further discussion of contempt as a sanction for enforcement of custody decrees, see *infra*.)

   Example: Father files a petition alleging that Mother is in contempt for violating a parenting agreement incorporated into dissolution judgment. The appellate court reverses the trial court decision denying the petition, holding that the evidence was sufficient to establish that Mother should be held in civil contempt for her failure to require the two children to visit Father. The court finds that the children's refusal to visit and their preference for participating in their extracurricular activities did not excuse Mother's noncompliance. *In re Marriage of Charous*, 855 N.E.2d 953 (Ill. App. Ct. 2006).

2. **Change of custody:** The custodial parent has a duty to foster a child's relationship with the noncustodial parent. Interference with that relationship sometimes will be remedied by a change in custody.

   Example: Mother is the children's primary caregiver during and after the marriage. After the divorce, Father petitions for modification of custody. He seeks primary physical custody, after Mother (who lives in Louisiana) refuses to relocate to Utah as required in the original custody order, refuses to acknowledge Father's visitation rights, refuses to help pay the costs of travel so that Father can visit the children, hangs up on Father when the children attempt to talk to him on the phone, makes the children feel guilty about visiting Father, and repeatedly texts and calls the children while they are supposed to have uninterrupted visitation with Father. The court agrees and awards Father primary physical custody, finding that Mother's interference with Father's visitation rights constitutes a material change in circumstances and that the children's best interests are served by having Father as the primary caregiver. *Hanson v. Hanson*, 223 P.3d 456 (Utah Ct. App. 2009).

3. **Tort actions:** A noncustodial parent may seek tort damages for a custodial parent's interference with the former's visitation rights. Some jurisdictions permit recovery by noncustodial parents for the tort of intentional infliction of emotional distress. Far fewer courts are willing to recognize the tort of alienation of affections for visitation interference. Finally, many courts refuse to recognize the tort of custodial interference to permit recovery by noncustodial parents for interference with visitation rights.

   Example: Father and Mother have two nonmarital children. Father sees the children every two weeks. Mother subsequently obtains sole legal and physical custody, moves to New Jersey, changes her telephone number, and blocks all of Father's attempts to contact the children. After Father finds the children through a private investigator and resumes visitation, he contends that Mother's actions have had a negative impact on his relationship with the children. He sues Mother for intentional infliction of emotional distress, arguing that Mother has engaged in extreme and outrageous conduct that has poisoned his relationship with the children. The court dismisses his cause of action as contrary to public policy, finding that such a lawsuit is harmful to the children where neither parent, in bringing or defending the suit, is considering the children's best interests. *Segal v. Lynch*, 993 A.2d 1229 (N.J. Super. Ct. App. Div. 2010).

   Note: Custodial interference is also a crime in some jurisdictions. *See, e.g.*, Wash. Rev. Code §9A.40.060 (2009).

4. **Makeup parenting time:** Some states provide for makeup parenting time in cases of custodial interference, allowing the noncustodial parent to take parenting time (of the same type and duration) at a later date. *See, e.g.*, Mich. Comp. Laws §552.642 (West 2004).

Quiz Yourself on *STANDARDS FOR SELECTING THE NONCUSTODIAL PARENT: VISITATION*

83. Diane and Gary are the divorced parents of 13-year-old Sandra. Prior to the divorce, Gary was charged with sexually molesting Sandra. The charges were dropped when Gary agreed to undergo psychological counseling. During the divorce proceedings, Diane requests that the court deny Gary visitation rights because of the sexual abuse. Will she prevail? ____________________

84. Joan and William are the divorced parents of three-year-old Don. For the past year, William has failed to pay court-ordered child support to Joan. Joan brings an action to hold William in contempt. A court finds William in contempt of court, orders him to pay his child support arrearages, and conditions William's visitation rights on the payment of his past child support. William appeals. Will he prevail?

____

Answers

83. Probably not. Courts are reluctant to impose a complete denial of visitation because the parent-child relationship is constitutionally protected. As a result, the trial court will probably restrict Gary's visitation rights by requiring supervised visitation (specifying the time and place for visitation) in order to protect Sandra.

84. Yes. The appellate court should reverse the trial court decision. According to the general rule, visitation and support are independent variables. That is, visitation should not be conditioned or denied based on payment of support. Thus, although the trial court can hold William in contempt and order him to pay his past-due child support obligations, it should not condition or terminate William's visitation rights based on the fulfillment of his child support obligations.

IV. STANDARDS: PARENT VERSUS NONPARENT DISPUTES

A. Natural parent presumption: A presumption favors biological parents in custody disputes involving parents versus nonparents. That is, courts apply a rebuttable presumption that custody should be awarded to a biological parent absent evidence of parental unfitness, voluntary relinquishment, or other extraordinary circumstances. However, psychological (sometimes called "de facto") parents sometimes may overcome the natural parent presumption.

Example: When a boy's mother and sister are killed in an automobile accident, the father asks the maternal grandparents to care for the child temporarily. A year later the father remarries and wants the return of his son. When the grandparents refuse, the father sues for custody. The court holds that the child's best interests will be served by remaining with the grandparents (thereby refusing to apply the natural parent presumption). The court bases its decision on a comparison of the financial and educational background, and living situations, of the grandparents and parent. Whereas the grandparents are college graduates, have a comfortable home, and are respected in their community, the father never finished college, lives in Berkeley, California, is financially insecure, and aspires to be a freelance writer and photographer. The court also relies on the testimony of a child psychologist to the effect that the child regards the grandparents as parental figures and that removal from their home would be detrimental to the child. *Painter v. Bannister*, 140 N.W.2d 152 (Iowa 1966), *cert. denied*, 385 U.S. 949 (1966).

B. Custody and visitation rights of third parties: Custody disputes sometimes involve such third parties as grandparents, stepparents, or same-sex partners.

1. Grandparents

a. Common-law rule: At common law, grandparents had no right to visitation with grandchildren in the face of parental objection or in the face of death, divorce, or termination of parental rights of the custodial parent(s).

b. Types of statutes: All states now have third-party visitation statutes that permit grandparents (and sometimes other persons) to petition for visitation in certain circumstances.

Grandparent visitation statutes were enacted, relying on different theories:

- statutes conditioned on the related parent's rights ("derivative rights theory"),
- statutes based on nuclear family disruption ("family situation theory"), such as death or divorce,
- statutes based on the best-interests-of-the-child standard, and
- statutes requiring a "substantial relationship" between grandparent and child.

c. Grandparent visitation statutes as a challenge to family autonomy: The United States Supreme Court has held that grandparent visitation constitutes a challenge to family autonomy when a fit custodial parent opposes visitation.

Example: Tommie Granville and Brad Troxel live together for several years and have two daughters out of wedlock. When Tommie and Brad separate, Brad lives with his parents and regularly brings his daughters to his parents' home for weekend visits. Brad commits suicide two years later. A few months later, Tommie informs the grandparents that she wishes to limit their visits to one visit per month. The grandparents petition for visitation rights, requesting two weekends of overnight visitation per month and two weeks of visitation each summer.

The Washington statute provides that any person may petition the court for visitation at any time and that the court may order visitation rights for any person when visitation may serve the best interests of the child. The trial court awards the grandparents visitation; the court of appeals reverses. The United States Supreme Court holds that the state statute, as applied, violated the mother's due process rights because the trial court contravened the traditional presumption that a fit parent will act in his/her child's best interests and gave no special weight to the fit mother's determination of those best interests. The Court reasoned that the state has no right to question the ability of a fit parent to make decisions concerning the rearing of that party's children. *Troxel v. Granville*, 530 U.S. 57 (2000).

In the wake of *Troxel*, state legislatures and courts wrestled with the constitutionality of third-party visitation statutes. Many jurisdictions revised their statutes specifically to limit the number of persons who could seek visitation and to give deference to a fit parent's wishes. In addition, in the case of third parties who are grandparents, some states revised their statutes to require that grandparents demonstrate a significant prior relationship with the child.

States differ on the standard to be applied in grandparent visitation disputes. A majority of states hold that the best interests test applies. However, some jurisdictions have adopted the more stringent harm standard (requiring that a lack of visitation would result in harm or potential harm before a grandparent may be awarded visitation rights).

Example: Maternal grandparents seek visitation rights with their grandchildren after the death of the children's mother from breast cancer and the father's remarriage. The father appeals the order granting the grandparents' petition. The appellate court concludes that the visitation order was reasonable and furthered the children's best interest. The court also holds that due process does not require a showing of harm prior to an award of grandparent visitation, but rather courts must consider a broad array of factors in determining whether visitation with grandparents is in the child's best interests. *Dodd v. Burleson*, 967 So.2d 715 (Ala. Civ. App. 2007).

Example: A grandmother brings an action against the child's father, seeking visitation rights. The appellate court holds that the grandmother's allegations that the father abused the child's mother were sufficient to rebut the presumption of the father's fitness and made the requisite showing that visitation could be necessary to protect the child from significant harm. The court reasons that, although the grandmother was estranged from the child's mother, the grandmother submitted sufficient proof in the form of affidavits from her daughter's employment supervisors that described the mother's abuse by the father as occurring on many occasions prior to the mother's disappearance, allegedly at the hands of the father. *Sher v. Desmond*, 874 N.E.2d 408 (Mass. App. Ct. 2007).

2. **Stepparents:** Case and statutory law sometimes grant visitation rights to former stepparents, especially if they have had a long-term relationship with the child. In addition, some state statutes authorize courts to consider *custody* awards to stepparents as well.

   Example: Katherine gives birth to a daughter, K.A. Shortly thereafter, Katherine marries Robert, and they have twins. K.A. has lived with Katherine and Robert for her entire life, and has had minimal contact with her biological father. Robert has never adopted K.A. When Katherine and Robert divorce, Robert receives visitation rights with K.A. Katherine appeals. The state supreme court finds that because Robert is the only father who K.A. has known and he has cared for K.A. like his biological children, he has established "extraordinary circumstances" justifying a third-party award of visitation rights over the objection of the biological mother. *Edwards v. Edwards*, 777 N.W.2d 606 (N.D. 2010).

3. **Lesbian co-parents:** Traditionally, courts were not receptive to recognition of lesbian co-parenting rights after dissolution of a lesbian relationship. In an emerging trend, some courts are willing to recognize the parental rights (in both custody and visitation disputes) of the "second parent" (i.e., the nonbiological parent) in gay and lesbian families. *See, e.g., Beth R. v. Donna M., supra.*

   Note: Several jurisdictions now permit *adoptions* by "second parents" who are members of same-sex couples. (See Chapter 11.) Also, courts appear to be receptive to recognition of visitation rights to the sperm donors of children born in lesbian relationships. (See "Sperm Donors' Rights," Chapter 8.)

4. **ALI *Principles*:** The ALI *Principles* recognize a category of "de facto" parents. Claims of de facto parenthood (i.e., psychological parent status) are often brought by same-sex partners who have assumed a parental role vis-à-vis a child before the partners separate. Courts are increasingly recognizing visitation rights of de facto parents. To qualify as a de facto parent, the ALI *Principles* require that a person regularly perform an equal or greater share of caretaking as the parent with whom the child primarily lived, lived with the child for a period not less than two years, and acted as a parent for nonfinancial reasons and with the agreement of a legal parent. ALI *Principles* §2.03(1)(c).

Quiz Yourself on *STANDARDS: PARENT VERSUS NONPARENT DISPUTES*

85. Linda and Dustine, two women, have three children by artificial insemination during their relationship. When they break up, Dustine, the biological mother, relocates with the three children. Linda sues for visitation rights, arguing that she has been the primary caretaker of the children since their births and has supported and held out the children as her own. She also argues that Dustine supported the parent-child relationship between Linda and the children and that a shared parenting plan is in the children's best interests. Will she prevail? ____________________

Answer

85. Probably yes. Although, courts traditionally denied parenting rights to a lesbian co-parent who was not the biological parent of the children, courts increasingly use theories of equitable estoppel or "de facto parenthood" to justify awards of custody and/or visitation rights over the objection of the biological parent. Here, because Dustine has allowed Linda to co-parent the children, and because Linda has actively assumed a parenting role in the children's lives, a court can apply both equitable estoppel and de facto parenthood doctrines to allow Linda parenting time.

V. ROLE OF SPECIAL PARTICIPANTS

A. **Child's preference:** Most states, either by statute or case law, require consideration of a child's wishes when making custody determinations.

1. **Different statutory approaches:** Statutes fall into one of four types:

- those which require consideration of the child's wishes (modeled after UMDA §402(2)),
- those which require a consideration of the child's preference after a preliminary finding that the child has sufficient mental capacity,
- those which give controlling weight to the preference of a child of a certain age, or

- those which leave the consideration of a child's preference completely to the court's discretion.

2. **Procedures to obtain child's preference:** States also take different procedural approaches to determine a child's preference. States may:

   - have the child testify in open court,
   - have other witnesses testify in open court concerning the child's preference,
   - have the judge interview the child regarding the parental preference in chambers, either with or without opposing counsel present, and/or
   - require that a record be made of in-chamber interviews.

   A nationwide trend exists in terms of jurisdictions' requiring recordings of in-chamber interviews with children. Some states also require the presence of counsel at such interviews. *Molloy v. Molloy*, 637 N.W.2d 803, 809 (Mich. Ct. App. 2001).

B. Counsel for the child: In most states, appointment of a child's legal representative is within the discretion of the court. The appropriate role of counsel is the subject of debate. Possible roles include:

- advocate,
- neutral factfinder,
- a mouthpiece to bring the child's wishes to the court's attention, and
- investigator.

Example: At the conclusion of the custody hearing in which the parties present their case-in-chief, but prior to any rebuttal testimony, the judge appoints counsel for the children. Ultimately, the court awards custody to the mother. The father appeals, arguing that due process requires that the parties know what the role of the child counsel will be in order to properly prepare for and respond to the evidence the child counsel will present. The appellate court holds that while it would have been preferable for the trial court to enter an order stating the purpose for the appointment, the omission was harmless error. The court also discusses the lack of clarity regarding the role of the attorney for a minor. Relying on a state bar association report, the court identifies possible roles: decision maker, guardian ad litem, and investigator. *Leary v. Leary*, 627 A.2d 30 (Md. Ct. Spec. App. 1993).

The Uniform Representation of Children in Abuse, Neglect and Custody Proceedings Act (adopted in July 2006 to harmonize the different standards of practice for abuse and custody) addresses representation of children in custody-related proceedings (defined to include custody, abuse, neglect, dependency, and termination of parental rights, but not delinquency). The Act defines the roles and responsibilities of children's representatives and provides guidelines concerning the appointment of representatives and the ethical dimensions of the lawyer-client relationship.

C. Expert testimony: Experts frequently are asked to testify in custody determinations. They may conduct evaluations, make recommendations, furnish a second opinion, rebut testimony, or act as mediators in custody disputes. While a judge may base a custody decision on expert opinion, the judge is the ultimate authority.

Example: The trial court awards the mother sole custody, subject to visitation by the father. The mother petitions the court to terminate overnight visitation and to require supervised visitation when she learns that the father is sleeping in the same bed as the child. The father cross-petitions for sole custody. At the hearing, a clinical psychologist who interviewed the mother, father, and child testifies that the child's best interests require the transfer of custody to the father. Another psychologist, a social worker, and the child's legal guardian also recommend a change in custody because the mother tried to exclude the father from the child's life. The mother's expert, who only interviewed the mother, testifies that custody should remain with the mother. The Family Court confirms custody in the mother. The appellate court determines that the trial court erred in rejecting most of the expert testimony. The testimony of the experts favoring custody of the child to the father was convincing and should have been relied upon. *In re Rebecca B.*, 611 N.Y.S.2d (App. Div. 1994), *motion for leave denied*, *Blum v. State*, 645 N.E.2d 1217 (N.Y. 1994).

VI. MODIFICATION

A. **Standard for modification:** Courts have continuing power to modify custody orders. The parent seeking the modification has the burden of proof. The standard for modification is higher than for an initial custody determination.

1. **Rationale for higher standard:** The rationale for the higher modification standard, which favors finality of judgments, is to avoid the disruptive effect of changes in children's lives post-divorce.

2. **Traditional standard:** Courts generally apply one of several standards. The most commonly accepted standard requires the petitioner to show that a *material or substantial change of circumstances* has occurred, after the original decree. Courts differ as to what constitutes a "substantial" change of circumstances. Some courts require very little.

   Example: Custody of the parents' six children is awarded to the mother. The father then petitions for expansion of his visitation rights based on the mother's remarriage. The court grants the father's request for modification. Remarriage of the mother constitutes a material change in circumstances because a second father figure could detrimentally affect the status of the natural father in the eyes of the children. *Selivanoff v. Selivanoff*, 529 P.2d 486 (1974).

   Example: Mother is granted custody of a couple's eight-year-old son. Father requests, and is granted, modification based on the fact that the boy, who is now 12, wants to live with his father in order to engage in hunting, fishing, and hiking. The mother appeals. Affirming, the court holds that a substantial increase in the age of the child during some critical period in his life, standing alone, constitutes a change of circumstances sufficient to warrant a modification. *King v. King*, 333 A.2d 135 (R.I. 1975).

3. **Strictest standard:** Some states follow UMDA and require endangerment. UMDA §409(b) requires serious endangerment (of the child's physical, mental, moral, or emotional health) for nonconsensual changes. Absent serious endangerment, UMDA §409(a) provides for a two-year waiting period following the initial decree.

4. **Most liberal standard:** A few states require only that modification be in the best interests of the child regardless of any change in circumstances.

Example: A father seeks modification of a custody decree that awarded sole custody to the mother. The father alleges that, on a visit to his ex-wife's house, he observes a copy of *Screw* magazine as well as letters in response to an advertisement soliciting responses from other couples or groups "for fun and games." The mother admits placing the ad but establishes that her sex life does not involve or affect the children. The children are well provided for emotionally and physically. The appellate court denies the father's request for modification based on the best interests of the children. The court reasons that both children have resided with the mother since birth and there is no showing that the mother is unfit. A divorced woman's right to engage in private sexual activities that do not affect her children is protected by the constitutional right to privacy. *Feldman v. Feldman*, 358 N.Y.S.2d 507 (App. Div. 1974).

5. **Modification of joint custody:** Some jurisdictions ease the traditional modification rule (from substantial change in circumstances to best interests) when sole custody is modified to joint custody. Similarly, some courts do not require the stricter standard if the requested modification is merely a rearrangement of parenting time in a joint physical custody schedule.

   Example: Mother and Father are awarded joint legal and physical custody of their three-year-old daughter. Father has physical custody each weekend because Mother works on the weekends. Mother subsequently seeks to modify Father's parenting time because she has begun working full time during the week and because the child attends school full time. The trial court changes the parenting schedule, awarding Father physical custody three out of four weekends per month, after finding a change of circumstances so as to make the original physical custody arrangement of the parties not in the child's best interest. Father appeals the decrease of his parenting time, contending that the trial court applied the wrong modification standard. The Missouri Supreme Court affirms the modification based on the best-interests-of the-child standard, explaining that the substantial-change-in-circumstances test is not appropriate for a modification of parenting time in a joint custody award. The court explains the rationale for lowering the standard by saying that the higher standard developed in a different era when gender-based custody preferences and fault-based divorce prevailed. *Russell v. Russell*, 210 S.W.3d 191 (Mo. 2007).

B. Relocation controversies

1. **Generally:** Relocation controversies often arise in the post-decree period when the custodial parent decides to relocate due to reasons of remarriage, employment or educational opportunities, or the promise of moral and economic support from relatives.

   Disputes most often arise in the following contexts:

   - a decree or statute requires the custodial parent to seek permission to leave the jurisdiction,
   - absent a statute, the noncustodial parent petitions to enjoin the move, or
   - faced with an impending move by the custodial parent, a noncustodial parent requests a custody modification.

2. **Standards to resolve disputes:** Courts employ different standards in relocation cases. The strictest standard requires a showing of "exceptional circumstances" before a court will permit the move. Some courts adopt a custodial-parent presumption favoring the custodial parent's right to relocate. Most courts, under the modern trend, adopt the best interest standard that

takes into account all relevant facts, including: reasons for the move, the future quality of life in the new locale, and the feasibility of an alternative visitation schedule for the noncustodial parent.

Example: Mother and Father have joint legal custody of two boys, with Mother having primary physical custody. Mother remarries and has another child. Considerable friction marks the parents' relationship. Mother now seeks to relocate with the children from California to Ohio, where she has relatives and her new husband has a lucrative job offer. Father objects, alleging that Mother has attempted to alienate him from the children and that the move will further impair his parent-child relationship. A custody evaluator reports that the move will negatively impact the children's already-tenuous relationship with Father and speculates that Mother's desire to move stems from an unspoken desire to absent herself from Father. The state supreme court affirms the trial court order that Father should have physical custody if Mother relocates. The supreme court thereby abrogates the prior custodial parent presumption, and adopts a best interests test that considers many factors, including the effect that the proposed move would have on the children's relationship with the noncustodial parent. Specifically, the court explains that the noncustodial parent bears the initial burden of showing that the proposed move would cause detriment and rules that, in the determination of detriment, it is relevant to show the likely impact of the move on the noncustodial parent-child relationship. *In re Marriage of LaMusga*, 88 P.3d 81 (Cal. 2004).

3. **ALI *Principles* standard:** The ALI *Principles* provide that the custodial parent should be permitted to relocate so long as the relocation is "in good faith for a legitimate purpose," to a location that is reasonable in light of that purpose. ALI *Principles* §2.20(4)(a). According to the *Principles*, relocation justifies a change of custody (i.e., constitutes a substantial change in circumstances) only when it "significantly impairs" either parent's ability to exercise responsibilities under a parenting plan. *Id.* at §2.17(1).

4. **Parental motives:** Many courts consider good faith on the part of the custodial parent as a threshold requirement in relocation disputes. Thus, courts may deny relocation requests if the relocation is sought for the sole purpose of restricting the noncustodial parent's visitation rights. Recall the ALI *Principles*' approach (*supra*) that requires that the move be in good faith.

5. **Infringement on the constitutional right to travel:** Feminists criticize relocation restrictions for their disproportionate impact on women (who generally have custody) and the ensuing interference with women's constitutional right to travel. Several courts have held that conditioning a parent's primary custody on remaining in the locale of the noncustodial parent violates the former's right to travel. *See, e.g., Watt v. Watt*, 971 P.2d 608 (Wyo. 1999). *But cf. Mason v. Coleman*, 850 N.E.2d 513 (Mass. 2006) (holding that the child's best interests trumps the parent's constitutional right to travel).

6. **Intercountry moves:** Some courts apply the same rules that govern interstate moves to intercountry moves. In addition, several states have statutes that address international relocations in the context of child abductions. That is, some statutes require courts to consider certain abduction factors in custody decision making, such as whether the other country is a signatory to the Hague Convention (discussed *infra* at Section VIIIC).

7. **Domestic violence:** Relocation restrictions may present significant risks for victims of domestic violence for whom the relocation restrictions constitute obstacles to the victim's efforts to flee from the abuser.

Quiz Yourself on ROLE OF THIRD PARTIES AND MODIFICATION

86. Mary and Frank have been married for six years and are the parents of five-year-old Timmy. They separate because of Frank's violent temper and alcoholism. The trial court awards custody to Mary and provides that Frank would have no visitation rights until a psychiatrist (who had been chosen by the parties) recommends that such visitation should commence and on what terms, guidelines, and locations. The psychiatrist refuses to continue treatment until the father pays the balance of his fees, thereby effectively denying the father visitation. When Frank challenges the court order as an abuse of discretion, will he prevail? ____________________

87. Miriam and Toby divorce. The court awards custody of their two-year-old daughter, Dolly, to Miriam. A few months after the divorce proceeding, Miriam is in a minor automobile accident. Toby agrees to care for Dolly until Miriam recovers. However, when Miriam has recovered, Toby refuses to return Dolly. Toby petitions for a modification of custody. Based on the best interests test, the court modifies custody and awards custody to Toby. Miriam appeals. Will she be successful? ____________________

Answers

86. Yes. The appellate court should invalidate the delegation of authority about visitation (by Frank to Timmy) to the psychiatrist. Jurisdiction over custody and visitation is vested in the court's discretion; no authority exists for the delegation of such jurisdiction to someone outside the court.

87. Yes. Miriam will be successful in seeking a reversing of the custody award to Toby. First, the trial court may have used the wrong standard for modification. The most commonly accepted standard is whether a material or substantial change of circumstances has occurred, after the original decree. Some jurisdictions require an even stricter standard of serious endangerment. Only a few states use the best interests standard for modification, which was the standard used by the court in this case. The rationale for application of a stricter standard for modification (than for initial awards) is in the interests of promoting stability for the child. Here, nothing has occurred that would constitute a material or substantial change of circumstances. Miriam's injuries from a minor auto accident probably will not qualify. Certainly, no endangerment to Dolly has occurred. In the interests of stability, the court should permit Dolly to remain in Miriam's custody.

VII. JURISDICTION AND ENFORCEMENT

A. Jurisdiction

1. **Traditional rule:** According to the traditional rule, a court could assert jurisdiction to adjudicate custody if the child was domiciled in the state. However, courts increasingly rejected the domicile rule, and permitted assertions of jurisdiction if another state had a substantial interest in the child's welfare. This interest might be based on the child's domicile, residence, or temporary presence; or the domicile or residence of one or both parents.

This broad standard frequently led to concurrent assertions of jurisdiction. Two statutes were promulgated to redress problems of custody jurisdiction: the Uniform Child Custody Jurisdiction Act (UCCJA), 9 U.L.A. 115 (1988), and the Parental Kidnapping Prevention Act (PKPA) of 1980, 28 U.S.C. §1738A (2006).

The UCCJA was drafted in 1968 to reduce jurisdictional competition and confusion, as well as to deter parents from forum shopping to relitigate custody. In 1980 Congress enacted the Parental Kidnapping Prevention Act (PKPA), 28 U.S.C. §1738A (2006). Despite its name, the PKPA was also applicable in cases involving jurisdiction over child custody. The PKPA was drafted to provide uniformity in custody decision making. Congress felt that the PKPA was necessary because, at the time of its enactment, it was not clear that all states would enact the UCCJA. Moreover, among those states that had enacted the UCCJA, many legislators had altered the statutory provisions, and some state courts had interpreted the provisions in different ways. The PKPA aimed to ensure that custody decrees issued by states asserting jurisdiction in conformity with the PKPA would receive recognition and enforcement in other states through ***full faith and credit***.

These statutes now have been superseded by the Uniform Child Custody Jurisdiction and Enforcement Act (UCCJEA).

2. **The UCCJEA:** The National Conference of Commissioners on Uniform States Laws revised the UCCJA in 1997 by drafting the Uniform Child Custody Jurisdiction and Enforcement Act (UCCJEA). The new act is intended to harmonize some of the differences between the UCCJA and the PKPA.

   The primary differences among the UCCJEA, the UCCJA, and the PKPA are:

   a. The UCCJEA follows the PKPA in giving priority to home state jurisdiction (i.e., the state in which the child had lived for at least six consecutive months at the time of the commencement of the proceeding) unlike the UCCJA, which did not prioritize among the different bases of jurisdiction;

   b. The UCCJEA eliminates the "best interests" language (that it is in the best interest of the child that a court of the state assume jurisdiction because the child and parents have a significant connection with the state and there is substantial evidence there concerning the child's care);

   c. The UCCJEA severely restricts the use of emergency jurisdiction to the issuance of temporary orders;

   d. The UCCJEA provides strict requirements for modification (restricting the exercise of modification jurisdiction to exclusive continuing jurisdiction, like the PKPA but not the UCCJA);

   e. The UCCJEA clarifies the meaning of "child custody determination" to encompass all custody and visitation decrees (temporary, permanent, initial, and modification); and

   f. The UCCJEA expands the definition of "child custody proceedings" to include those related to divorce, separation, abuse and neglect, dependency, guardianship, paternity, termination of parental rights, and protection from domestic violence.

Virtually all states have enacted the UCCJEA.

3. **Jurisdiction over Native American children: The Indian Child Welfare Act:** The Indian Child Welfare Act (ICWA) of 1978, 25 U.S.C. §§1901-1963 (2006), provides that the Indian tribe has exclusive jurisdiction as against any state concerning a child welfare proceeding involving a Native American child. The term "proceeding" includes foster care placements, adoption, termination of parental rights, and guardianship.

   Note: The ICWA does *not* apply to custody disputes between divorcing parents. (See the discussion of the Indian Child Welfare Act, Chapter 10.)

B. **Enforcement of custody orders:** Civil and criminal remedies to enforce custody determinations include the following: contempt proceedings, writ of habeas corpus, tort recovery, and criminal prosecutions for child abduction.

1. **Contempt:** A parent will be found in contempt of court if that parent could have complied with the custody order, yet willfully failed to do so. Contempt may either be civil (resulting in a fine or a temporary jail sentence until the parent complies with the custody order), or criminal (resulting in a conviction with a fixed sentence). (See the discussion of contempt, Chapter 6.)

2. **Habeas corpus:** A writ of habeas corpus is another custody enforcement mechanism. The remedy was originally used by prisoners claiming illegal arrest or unlawful detention but is being utilized increasingly in custody cases to compel the production of a child who is being wrongfully held or retained. The petitioner must prove both the validity of the custody order and the person who is entitled to custody under that order.

3. **Tort recovery:** Tort recovery is another possible avenue for a custodial parent who has been deprived of a child's custody. Possible tort claims include: intentional infliction of emotional distress and custodial interference.

   Courts generally permit recovery for intentional infliction of emotional distress for child snatching. However, courts are divided about permitting recovery for custodial interference in claims brought by custodial parents. *Compare Silicott v. Oglesby*, 721 S.W.2d 290 (Tex. 1986) (recognizing the tort of custodial interference), with *Larson v. Dunn*, 460 N.W.2d 39 (Minn. 1990) (refusing to recognize custodial interference but permitting claim for intentional infliction of emotional distress). Some courts express the fear that such litigation is not in the best interests of the child by subjecting the child to increased parental hostility.

4. **Criminal sanctions:** Parents who wrongfully remove or retain children may also incur criminal liability for violation of state statutes on child abduction. Some states provide a defense for a parent who acts to protect a child from harm.

VIII. CHILD ABDUCTION

Many child abductions are perpetrated by family members. The traditional approach is to impose criminal liability on the perpetrators. The modern approach is to provide for judicially ordered abduction prevention mechanisms.

A. **Uniform law:** The Uniform Child Abduction Prevention Act (UCAPA), approved in 2006, provides that various parties (including a parent, prosecutor, public attorney or the court on its own motion) may bring an action seeking "abduction prevention measures" after establishing the existence of a credible risk that a child will be abducted. Such measures include: the imposition of travel restrictions, prohibitions on an individual's removing the child from a particular geographic area, or placement of the child's name in the Child Passport Issuance Alert Program. UCAPA also clarifies that one basis for a determination of an "emergency" under the UCCJEA is a credible threat of abduction.

B. Federal law: The International Parental Kidnapping Crime Act (IPKCA), 18 U.S.C. §1204 (2006), enacted in 1993, makes it a federal crime for a parent wrongfully to remove or retain a child outside the United States. The felony is punishable by a fine, imprisonment (for up to three years), or both. Courts have rejected constitutional challenges to the IPKCA.

C. International Treaty on International Child Abduction: The Hague Convention on the Civil Aspects of International Child Abduction is an international treaty that proposes guidelines on international child abduction. The Convention has been adopted by approximately 40 countries, including the United States. It has been implemented in this country via the International Child Abduction Remedies Act (ICARA), 42 U.S.C. §§11601-11611 (2006). The Convention limits the ability of the new haven (to which the child snatcher has fled) to assert jurisdiction by providing for the mandatory return of children under age 16 to their country of habitual residence and for the abstention by the new forum from adjudicating the custody dispute. Criticisms of the treaty include: the one-year statute of limitations is too short and the many nonsignatory nations facilitate evasion of the Convention.

Example: Jacquelyn and Timothy Abbott have one son, A.J.A. They move to Chile where the parents separate. A Chilean court grants Jacquelyn custody and awards visitation rights to Timothy, as well as granting Timothy a *ne exeat* right to consent to a move that takes the boy out of the country. Jacquelyn takes A.J.A. to Texas without permission. Timothy files suit in federal district court, seeking return of his son under the Hague Convention and ICARA. The district court denies relief, holding that the father's *ne exeat* right did not constitute a "right of custody" under the Convention and that the return therefore was not authorized. Reversing, the U.S. Supreme Court holds that the father's *ne exeat* right to consent before removal of the child from Chile was a "right of custody" because the father had direct and regular visitation rights, including the right to determine the child's place of residence, especially in light of the Convention's purpose to prevent harmful removals across international boarders. *Abbott v. Abbott*, 130 S. Ct. 1983 (2010).

IX. PROCESS TO RESOLVE DISPUTES

Most divorcing parents reach private agreements regarding custody. For the small minority of decisions that are contested, several dispute resolution processes are available: the adversary process, custody mediation, and collaborative law.

A. Adversary process: In the adversary process, a court asserts authority over child custody and is the ultimate decision maker. Commentators criticize the adversary process for its hostility, accentuation of differences, high rates of relitigation, and long-term negative psychological effects for the participants.

B. Mediation: Mediation is an alternative to the traditional dispute resolution process. Mediation is a process by which the parties, with the aid of a neutral third party, identify disputed issues, develop and consider options and alternatives, and reach a consensual agreement. Unlike the adversary process in which a judge makes the ultimate decision, mediation respects the parties' autonomy in decision making.

The advantages of mediation are that it is less expensive and less hostile than the adversarial process, gives the parties an active role in decision making, results in increased satisfaction by the parties with the dissolution process, is less likely to result in relitigation, and has better long-term consequences for parents and children.

Among the disadvantages of mediation are the following: concerns about the stronger partner dominating the weaker, reinforcement of gender role stereotypes (i.e., mother as caretaker), and the risk of subjecting battered women to continued abuse by their husbands.

1. **Voluntary vs. mandatory:** Many statutes provide for custody mediation, although a few states mandate it (e.g., Cal. Fam. Code §1830 (West 2004)).

2. **Waiver:** Many states permit mediation to be waived for good cause, or if a party will suffer severe emotional distress. Some states use these waiver provisions to exclude domestic violence cases from mediation. Other states provide for separate mediation sessions in cases of domestic violence or for the abused spouse to bring a support person to the mediation.

3. **Qualifications of a mediator:** Mediation may be provided either by publicly funded court services or by mediators in private practice. Mediators frequently are lawyers or mental health professionals. Statutes generally specify the requisite qualifications for court-connected mediators. However, the lack of regulation for *private* mediators has been a longstanding problem.

   In 1984 the ABA adopted "Standards of Practice for Lawyer Mediators in Family Disputes." Under the Standards a lawyer mediator has six duties:

   a. to define and describe the process and cost before the parties reach an agreement to mediate,

   b. not to voluntarily disclose the information obtained through the mediation process without the prior consent of both participants,

   c. to be impartial,

   d. to assure that the participants make decisions based upon sufficient information and knowledge,

   e. to suspend or terminate mediation whenever continuation of the process would harm one or more of the participants, and

   f. to advise each of the participants to obtain legal review prior to reaching any agreement.

4. **Domestic violence:** Mediation poses special dangers for battered spouses, including the increased risk to victims because the mediation sessions provide more opportunities for abuse. Several schools of thought exist about the wisdom of mediation in domestic violence cases. Some believe that mediation should never be used in cases of domestic violence. Others contend that mediation should be used with adequate safeguards. Still others believe that the choice of mediation should be left to the victim.

5. Ethics

a. **Conflicts of interest and dual representation:** Ethical questions may arise for lawyer mediators. Early concerns focused on whether a lawyer mediator violates the prohibition on representing conflicting or potentially conflicting interests, or the prohibition against dual representation of husband and wife.

State bar ethics committees have ruled that a lawyer mediator can mediate a dispute for the husband and wife so long as the mediator (1) informs the parties that the mediator represents neither of them, (2) will refrain from representing either if the mediation proves unsuccessful, and (3) advises the parties to seek independent legal counsel.

b. **Confidentiality:** Confidentiality is a central part of the mediation process. A controversial issue concerns whether the mediator can make a recommendation to the court if the parties' attempts at mediation prove unsuccessful. In addition to presenting a breach of confidentiality, the practice also raises due process concerns if the mediator is not subject to cross-examination.

Example: A father in a custody dispute moves for a "protective order" that would permit him to cross-examine the mediator (following the mediator's in-court recommendation) if the parties are unable to reach an agreement on custody. California's mandatory mediation statute requires that all mediation proceedings be private, confidential, and privileged. Once a mediator makes a recommendation and is subject to cross-examination, the mediator may have to divulge confidential communications. To address this problem, local court rules require that a mediator not state his/her reasons for a recommendation and therefore denies the parties the right to cross-examination. The court holds that the policy of denying cross-examination is unconstitutional. If local practice permits the mediator to make a recommendation, the court concludes that due process requires that the mediator be subject to cross-examination. *McLaughlin v. Superior Court*, 189 Cal. Rptr. 479 (Ct. App. 1983).

C. **Collaborative law:** Collaborative law is an innovative form of alternative dispute resolution whereby the parties and their attorneys sign a binding agreement in which they agree to use cooperative techniques without resort to judicial intervention except for court approval of the parties' agreement. If the parties are unable to reach an agreement through collaborative law procedures, their attorneys must withdraw from representation. Texas became the first state in 2001 to provide, by statute, for resolution of certain family matters by collaborative law procedures (Tex. Fam. Code Ann. §153.0072 (West 2009)).

The Colorado Bar Association's Ethics Committee (Ethics Opinion No. 115 (Feb. 24, 2007)) declared that collaborative law is per se unethical based on the provision in the attorney-client agreement that if settlement negotiations fail, the lawyers must withdraw from representation. The concern is that this restriction materially limits the lawyer's representation because it creates an insurmountable conflict of interest impairing the lawyer's independent judgment about the need for litigation. However, the ABA and most state bar associations disagree, finding that collaborative law practice is consistent with professional ethics.

Quiz Yourself on ***JURISDICTION AND ENFORCEMENT***

88. Patricia and Kirk's Texas divorce decree incorporates the couple's agreement that Patricia shall have primary custody of the couple's two daughters. Shortly thereafter, Patricia decides that she would like to move to Arizona. She asks Kirk, and he agrees, to take the children for a few months until Patricia finds employment and is able to establish a home for them in Arizona. Kirk then moves with the children to Minnesota with his new fiancée, to be near her extended family. Before Patricia is able to move to Arizona, Kirk files a custody modification motion in Minnesota two months after his arrival there. Does the Minnesota court have jurisdiction to modify the Texas custody decree? ____________________

Answer

88. No. To determine which state (Minnesota or Texas) has jurisdiction for modification purposes, it is necessary to examine the requirements of the UCCJEA. Under the UCCJEA (which superseded the UCCJA and PKPA), a state that has made a prior custody determination has "continuing exclusive jurisdiction" for purposes of modification if the initial court continues to have jurisdiction and the former state is the residence of the child or any contestant. In this case, Texas would be the proper forum under the UCCJEA because Texas rendered the decree and Patricia continues to reside there.

Exam Tips on ***CHILD CUSTODY***

- ***Custody*:** For questions involving child custody, be precise about the facts. Identify important facts such as the age, race, religion, etc. of all children because these facts may be highly relevant subsequently. Clarify whether the request for custody is for sole or joint custody. ***Define relevant terms*** (sole custody, primary custody, joint custody, etc.). Always specify the ***different possible standards***, even if one standard seems to fit the facts best.

- Be on the alert for ***cross-cut issues***. For example, examine facts about the marriage. Was the couple validly married? Or does the question deal with unwed father's rights? If the couple was divorced, were fault-based grounds present? If so, be prepared to discuss the relevance or irrelevance of fault in awards of custody.

- Make sure, also, that you take note of whether the question deals with an ***initial*** award or a ***modification***. If the petitioner requests a modification, specify that ***different standards*** apply for modification than for initial awards. Look for ***common areas of disputes for modifications*** (religious disputes, relocation, etc). Always explore possible ***constitutional*** issues (e.g., First Amendment issues in religious disputes, right to travel issues in relocation disputes).

- ☛ If the question involves an initial grant of custody, then explore the application of the ***relevant standards*** for selection of the ***custodial parent***: presumptions (i.e., tender years presumption, primary caretaker), the best interests of the child, and joint custody. For ***joint custody***, identify whether it operates as a ***presumption***, ***preference,*** or ***option***. Note problems with the application of presumptions: the tender years presumption raises ***constitutional problems*** (equal protection) and the primary caretaker presumption has been abandoned by the two jurisdictions that adopted it originally but still remains a factor in custody decision making in many jurisdictions.

- ☛ Point out that the ***best interests*** of the child is the ***prevailing standard*** for determination of custody disputes. When discussing ***factors*** relevant to the best interests, always be on the lookout for ***constitutional cross-over*** issues (especially those involving race, religion, or gender). Remember that in questions involving race-based discrimination, *Palmore* specified that ***race*** cannot be the ***determining*** factor in custody decision making. For examples of ***gender-based*** discrimination, be sure to specify the different possible ***levels of scrutiny*** (under the Constitution, the test is whether the classification is substantially related to an important governmental objective, but some states apply a strict scrutiny standard).

- ☛ After discussing issues involving the custodial parent, turn to issues involving the ***noncustodial parent***. Such issues generally involve ***visitation*** disputes. Determine if the question involves a ***denial*** of, or ***conditions*** on, visitation. Restrictions on visitation may be a fertile area for a constitutional cross-over question (e.g., First Amendment). Termination of visitation rights (or of custody rights of the custodial parent) may involve cross-over issues with adoption. Determine if the noncustodial parent is experiencing problems with visitation (e.g., ***interference*** with visitation rights). If so, explore possible ***enforcement*** remedies (e.g., contempt, change of custody, tort or criminal liability for custodial interference).

- ☛ Identify and analyze any possible issues regarding ***third-party rights***. Frequently tested issues concern stepparents, grandparents, and same-sex partners. Discuss the natural parent presumption that would apply to favor the biological parent over a third party. If grandparent visitation is involved, discuss the application of the *Troxel* case. If same-sex partners are involved, be sure to discuss whether the partners are legal spouses or domestic partners in a jurisdiction that has domestic partnership laws. (In either case, state law would confer parental rights.) If the same-sex partners are not legal spouses or domestic partners, then discuss the traditional restrictive view and the more liberal modern trend that recognizes the parenting rights of the same-sex partner who is not biologically related to the child. Also, explore whether any other third-party issues exist (e.g., the child's right to representation, experts' role).

- ☛ Always look for issues of ***enforcement*** and ***jurisdiction***. Remember to explore and discuss both civil and criminal remedies for enforcement of custody orders (e.g., contempt proceedings, habeas corpus, tort recovery, and criminal prosecutions for child abduction). Jurisdiction is a frequently tested issue. Recall that the UCCJEA may be applicable in cases of jurisdictional disputes involving initial assertions of jurisdiction or requests for modification.

- ☛ Finally, before finishing your analysis of custody, analyze whether any possible issues of ***alternative dispute resolution process*** (such as custody mediation or collaborative law) are present. For example, if the couple sought custody mediation, determine if ***ethical*** issues (i.e., conflicts of interests, dual representation, confidentiality) or ***constitutional*** problems (i.e., due process) exist.

CHAPTER 8

PROCREATION

ChapterScope

This chapter addresses the legal regulation of reproductive freedom and reproductive control. It examines reproductive rights in the contexts of contraception, abortion, and assisted reproduction. Here are a few of the key principles covered in this chapter:

- The right of ***access to contraception*** does ***not*** depend upon ***marital status***. Both unmarried and married persons have a constitutional right to determine whether or not they wish to bear a child.
- The Constitution protects a woman's ***right to choose*** to have an ***abortion***. The United States Supreme Court extended the right of privacy to encompass the right to an abortion in *Roe v. Wade*.
- Since *Roe v. Wade*, the Supreme Court has limited the scope of that right.
- A state law that imposes an ***undue burden*** (i.e., has the purpose or effect of placing a substantial obstacle) on the woman's decision to have an abortion is unconstitutional.
- A state may ***not*** require ***spousal consent or notification*** prior to an abortion.
- A state ***may*** require ***parental consent and/or notification*** prior to a minor's abortion, provided that the state offers an alternative such as a ***judicial bypass***.
- The traditional legal response toward surrogacy is to regard ***surrogacy contracts as void.*** However, an increasing number of states permit surrogacy, subject to state regulation.
- The ***revised Uniform Parentage Act*** authorizes gestational surrogacy agreements, provided they are validated by a court. Several jurisdictions permit a ***pre-birth determination*** of the ***legal status*** of the intended parents of a child born via surrogacy.

I. CONTRACEPTION

The foundation of a woman's reproductive rights rests on the constitutionally protected right to privacy. The recognition of this right stems from two United States Supreme Court cases, decided in the mid-1960s and early 1970s, dealing with access to contraceptives. In both cases, the Court invalidates state restrictions on contraception. In the first case, the Court enunciates the constitutional right to privacy and, in the second, extends the scope of that right from married people to the individual.

A. **Access to contraception generally:** The right of access to contraception does not depend upon marital status. Both unmarried and married persons have a constitutional right to determine whether or not they wish to bear a child. The Supreme Court enunciates this right for married persons in ***Griswold v. Connecticut***, 381 U.S. 479 (1965) and, subsequently for unmarried persons in ***Eisenstadt v. Baird***, 405 U.S. 438 (1972) (both discussed *infra*).

B. Historical background: Harsh restrictions on contraception date from the 1870s. In 1873, a vice crusader and ex-dry goods salesman, Anthony Comstock, spearheaded passage of federal legislation (known as the "Comstock law") that bans the circulation and importation through the mail of obscene materials (defined to include contraceptives and abortifacients). Many states enacted similar legislation. As a result, physicians were unable to prescribe birth control devices and disseminate information about contraception. Courts upheld the constitutionality of such state legislation as a valid exercise of the police power until the Supreme Court invalidated the Connecticut law in 1965.

C. Married persons' rights to contraception: Married persons have the right to determine matters concerning birth control without interference from the state. This guarantee has its foundation in the constitutional right to privacy.

1. **Case and holding:** A Connecticut statute prohibits any person from using "any drug, medicinal article or instrument for the purpose of preventing conception," or from aiding and abetting another to use contraceptive devices. The statute epitomizes the most stringent of state Comstock laws by prohibiting the "use," rather than merely the distribution, of contraceptives, and by not providing an exclusion for women whose lives would be endangered by a pregnancy. Estelle Griswold (the Executive Director of the Planned Parenthood League of Connecticut which provides information about contraception as well as contraceptives to *married* persons) and the League's medical director are charged with violating the "aiding and abetting" provision of the statute. They argue that the statute violates their married patients' right to privacy under the Fourteenth Amendment. The Supreme Court holds that the restriction is an unconstitutional interference with the right of marital privacy. The case establishes that the right to privacy, although not explicitly mentioned in the Constitution, nonetheless has a constitutional basis.

2. ***Griswold* concurrence:** Justice Goldberg, in a concurring opinion joined by Chief Justice Warren and Justice Brennan, locates the constitutional right to privacy in the Ninth Amendment. He points out that the Ninth Amendment was intended to grant to the people those essential rights that are not specifically enumerated in the Bill of Rights.

3. ***Griswold* dissent:** Justices Black and Stewart, in their dissent, argue that the Court is usurping the power of state legislatures by enabling the judicial invalidation of any "legislative act which the judges find irrational, unreasonable, or offensive" under the relevant constitutional provisions. *Griswold*, 381 U.S. at 511.

4. **Rationale:** The Court invalidates the statute based on the recognition of a constitutional right to privacy. The Court reasons that the statutory prohibition on the *use* of contraceptives (rather than their manufacture or sale) infringes on marital privacy because enforcement would necessitate police searches of the bedroom.

5. **Source of the constitutional right to privacy:** Justice Douglas, author of the majority opinion, reasons that the right of privacy is found in the "penumbras" (*Griswold*, 381 U.S. at 483) "formed by emanations from those guarantees [in the Bill of Rights] that help give them life and substance." Douglas states that these guarantees create "zones of privacy." Among the specific guarantees, he cites: the First Amendment's right of association, the Third Amendment's prohibition against quartering soldiers without the owner's consent during time of

peace, the Fourth Amendment's protection against unreasonable search and seizure, the Fifth Amendment's privilege against self-incrimination, and the Ninth Amendment's identification of unenumerated rights.

Other justices, although concurring that there is a constitutional right to privacy, locate the source of that right in the Ninth Amendment (see "*Griswold* concurrence" *supra*). Neither view of the source of the privacy right is accepted today. Constitutional doctrine since *Griswold* (discussed *infra*) identifies the source of the right to privacy in the Fourteenth Amendment's Due Process Clause ("liberty").

6. **The importance of marriage to *Griswold*'s holding:** Protection of the rights of *married* persons was central to the holding of *Griswold*. The case is clear that the right of privacy inheres in the marital relationship. Both the majority and concurring opinions emphasize the importance of marriage. Justice Douglas speaks of "notions of privacy surrounding the marriage relationship" and the "sacred precincts of *marital* bedrooms" (*Griswold*, 381 U.S. at 485) (emphasis added). Justice Goldberg's concurrence speaks of "the right of marital privacy" (*id.* at 486), "the marital relationship and the marital home" (*id.* at 494), "the intimacy of husband and wife" (*id.* at 498), and "the institution of marriage" (*id.* at 499). Justice Douglas concludes the opinion by stating:

> Marriage is a coming together for better or for worse, hopefully enduring, and intimate to the degree of being sacred. It is an association that promotes a way of life, not causes: a harmony in living, not political faiths; a bilateral loyalty, not commercial or social projects. Yet it is an association for as noble a purpose as any involved in our prior decisions. *Id.* at 486.

7. **Curtailment of police powers:** The United States Supreme Court decides *Griswold* during the civil rights movement. Justice Douglas's opinion reflects an abhorrence of police excesses, particularly regarding governmental invasions into private homes and private matters. Douglas reasons that in order to enforce the prohibition on the use of contraceptives, the police would have to enter and search the home:

> Would we allow the police to search the sacred precincts of marital bedrooms for telltale signs of the use of contraceptives? The very idea is repulsive to the notions of privacy surrounding the marriage relationship. *Id.* at 485.

8. **Fundamental right:** *Griswold* points out that the right to privacy is "fundamental." Constitutional doctrine accords fundamental rights strict scrutiny review (i.e., restrictions on those rights must be *necessary* to a *compelling* state interest).

9. ***Griswold* and the constitutionalization of family law:** Prior to *Griswold*, the United States Supreme Court decided few family law cases. Family law was regarded as a matter of state law. However, *Griswold* heralded the beginning of the "constitutionalization of family law," i.e., the development, application, and extension of constitutional doctrine to family matters.

10. **Subsequent extension of the right to privacy:** The constitutional right to privacy, first recognized in *Griswold* in regard to contraceptives, was extended subsequently to protect the rights of the unmarried to contraception, a woman's rights to abortion (both discussed *infra*), and the right to engage in adult consensual sexual conduct (in *Lawrence v. Texas*, discussed in Chapter 2).

D. Unmarried persons' rights to contraception

1. **Generally:** Unmarried persons have the same constitutional right as married persons to make intimate decisions regarding childbearing. This right was announced by the United States Supreme Court in *Eisenstadt v. Baird* (discussed *infra*).

2. **Background to *Eisenstadt*:** Prior to *Griswold*, some married persons were able to evade statutory bans on the sale and use of contraceptives by seeking the services of private physicians. Such alternatives were not available to the unmarried. Doubt arose after *Griswold* as to how far the Supreme Court might extend *Griswold*'s reasoning with regard to unmarried persons. This doubt stemmed from the Court's emphasis in *Griswold* on a right to *marital* privacy.

3. ***Eisenstadt v. Baird***

   a. **Case and holding:** A Massachusetts statute provides a maximum five-year term for anyone (other than a licensed physician or pharmacist) who "gives away . . . any drug, medicine, instrument or article whatever for the prevention of conception." Mass. Gen. Laws Ann., c. 272. Married persons are permitted to obtain contraceptives, for the purpose of pregnancy prevention, from physicians or pharmacists; single persons are unable to obtain contraceptives from anyone. William Baird, a moral crusader and ex-director of a pharmaceutical company, decides to challenge the Massachusetts ban. In the course of a lecture on contraception that he delivers to Boston University students, he hands a female student a package of vaginal foam. Baird is arrested, charged, and convicted of violating the statute. He challenges the constitutionality of the statute. The United States Supreme Court holds that unmarried persons have a constitutional right of access to contraceptives. *Eisenstadt v. Baird*, 405 U.S. 438 (1972).

   b. **Rationale: Equal protection:** Extending the reasoning of *Griswold*, the Court finds that the statute violates the Equal Protection Clause by providing dissimilar treatment for those persons (married/unmarried) who are similarly situated. The Court states:

      > [W]hatever the rights of the individual to access to contraceptives may be, the rights must be the same for the unmarried and the married alike. *Id.* at 453.

   c. **Rejection of proffered state interests:** The Court rejects both of the proffered state interests (i.e., the deterrence of premarital sex and the promotion of health). The Court reasons that "[i]t would be plainly unreasonable to assume that Massachusetts has prescribed pregnancy and the birth of an unwanted child as punishment for fornication. . . . " *Id.* at 448. The Court rejects the health measure rationale by pointing out that federal and state laws already regulate the distribution of harmful drugs.

   d. **Privacy: Not a marital, but an individual, right:** The Court states that the right of privacy belongs to the individual and not to the marital relationship or to married partners.

      > It is true that in *Griswold* the right of privacy in question inhered in the marital relationship. Yet the marital couple is not an independent entity with a mind and heart of its own, but an association of two individuals each with a separate intellectual and emotional makeup. If the right of privacy means anything, it is the right of the individual, married or single, to be free from unwarranted governmental intrusion into matters so fundamentally affecting a person as the decision whether to bear or beget a child. *Id.* at 452.

e. **Criticism of equal protection approach:** Commentators criticize the doctrinal basis of *Eisenstadt*. They argue that the case should have rested not on equal protection grounds, but rather on substantive due process. That is, the Court should have extended the substantive right to privacy that the Court delineated earlier in *Griswold*.

f. **Significance of *Eisenstadt* for same-sex sexual conduct**

i. **Unanswered question:** An open question after *Eisenstadt* concerned the parameters of the right to privacy, especially in regard to the protection of the sexual conduct. Specifically, did *Eisenstadt* protect, narrowly, procreational freedom (i.e., access to contraceptives) or, more broadly, sexual conduct between consenting adults? The question assumed special importance for gays and lesbians who faced stringent criminal penalties in many jurisdictions for their sexual activity.

ii. ***Bowers v. Hardwick*:** The Court's decision in *Bowers v. Hardwick*, 478 U.S. 186 (1986), first addressed the question left unresolved by *Eisenstadt* concerning same-sex sexual acts. *Bowers* upheld the constitutionality of a Georgia statute criminalizing sodomy that was applied to an adult male committing sexual acts with another adult male in the bedroom of the former's home.

Example: Michael Hardwick is charged with violating a Georgia statute criminalizing sodomy (defined as "any sexual act involving the sex organs of one person and the mouth or anus of another"). He challenges the constitutionality of the statute. The district court grants the state's motion to dismiss for failure to state a claim. The federal court of appeals reverses, finding that the statute violates the defendant's fundamental rights because same-sex sexual activity between consenting adults is protected by the Due Process Clause. The United States Supreme Court reverses and upholds the constitutionality of the statute, maintaining that the Constitution does not confer a fundamental right upon homosexuals to engage in sodomy. The Court bases its holding on the irrelevance of prior privacy cases (dealing with family, marriage, and procreation), the existence of ancient Judeo-Christian proscriptions against homosexual sodomy, and the fact that criminal penalties for sodomy are widespread in other states. The Court also distinguishes *Stanley v. Georgia*, 394 U.S. 557 (1969), which protected possession of pornography in the home (such possession would not have been protected outside the home) by reasoning that illegal conduct is not immunized because it occurs in the home. *Bowers v. Hardwick, supra.*

iii. **Criticism of *Bowers*: Failure to extend the right to privacy:** The *Bowers* dissent (Justice Blackmun, joined by Justices Brennan, Marshall, and Stevens) disagrees that the Georgia statute fails to implicate the constitutionally protected right to privacy. In addition, Justice Blackmun argues that the prohibition involves the privacy interest regarding both intimate decision making and the conduct of private activities in the home.

iv. ***Lawrence v. Texas*:** The United States Supreme Court overturns *Bowers* in *Lawrence v. Texas*, 539 U.S. 558 (2003). *Lawrence* holds unconstitutional a state (Texas) sodomy statute criminalizing same-sex sexual conduct. The United States Supreme Court rules that the state statute violates the defendants' substantive due process rights. The Court chooses a broad due process rationale, protecting the individual's *liberty to engage in intimate personal relationships*, rather than more narrow equal protection grounds. The

Court reasons that moral disapproval cannot justify criminal sanctions for private consensual sexual conduct. (*Lawrence* is discussed further in Chapter 2.)

E. Minors' rights to contraception: A minor has the right of access to contraceptives and to information about contraception. The United States Supreme Court has held that minors have a constitutionally protected right to privacy to obtain contraceptives. (Minors' rights to an abortion are discussed *infra*.)

Some states permit all minors to consent to contraceptive services. However, other states permit only certain minors (e.g., married minors, minors who are parents, minors who are or have been pregnant, mature minors) to consent to contraceptive services.

1. **Access:** The Supreme Court wrestled with minors' reproductive rights in *Carey v. Population Servs. Int'l*, 431 U.S. 678 (1977), which addresses the constitutionality of a restriction on access to contraceptives by minors.

   a. **Case and holding:** *Carey* invalidates a New York statute restricting the distribution of contraceptives to minors under age 16. The Court thereby extends the constitutional right to privacy to minors' contraceptive choices.

      Example: A New York statute makes it a crime (1) for any person to *sell or distribute a contraceptive to a minor* under 16 years of age, (2) for anyone *except a pharmacist* to distribute contraceptives to *persons over 16*, and (3) for anyone, including pharmacists, to *advertise or display* contraceptives. The district court holds unconstitutional the prohibition regarding the distribution of nonprescription contraceptives to minors. The state appeals, arguing that the regulation is constitutionally permissible as a deterrent to sexual promiscuity. The United States Supreme Court holds that the right of privacy protects minors' as well as adults' right of access to contraceptives. *Carey v. Population Servs. Int'l, supra.*

   b. **Rationale: Rejection of proffered state interests:** The *Carey* Court finds no rational basis to uphold the statute. The Court rejects the proffered state interests (deterrence of teenage sexual activity and unwanted pregnancies). The Court doubts whether limiting access to contraception will discourage early sexual behavior.

   c. **Relevance of minors' abortion rights:** The Court bases its protection of minors' right to contraceptives on prior constitutional doctrine regarding abortion. The Court reasons that because the state may not prohibit a minor from terminating her pregnancy (*Planned Parenthood v. Danforth*, 428 U.S. 521 (1976)), the state cannot deny the distribution of contraceptives to minors.

      > The State's interest in protection of the mental and physical health of the pregnant minor, and in protection of potential life are clearly implicated more by the abortion decision than by the decision to use a nonhazardous contraceptive. *Carey*, 431 U.S. at 694.

   d. **Miscellaneous provisions:** The Court also invalidates the requirement that only licensed pharmacists can sell nonmedical contraceptives to adults, finding no compelling state interest (health, morality) to justify it. The Court reasons that the requirement imposes a significant burden on the individual's right to use contraceptives (i.e., limiting accessibility, reducing the opportunity for privacy, and lessening the possibility of price competition). In addition, the Court invalidated the prohibition on contraceptive advertising and displays.

e. **Significance of *Carey* for minors' rights generally:** Although the Court in *Carey* extended the right of privacy to minors' contraceptive decision making, the Court also made clear that the scope of permissible state regulation is broader with respect to minors than adults.

2. **Parental notification for minors' access to contraceptives:** The controversial issue of parental notification of minors' requests for contraceptives has been before the courts on several occasions.

Federally funded providers of family planning services, including contraceptives, under Title X are not required to notify parents or guardians when the providers prescribe contraceptives to minors. In *Planned Parenthood Federation of America v. Heckler*, 712 F.2d 650 (D.C. Cir. 1983), a federal court of appeals invalidates the so-called "squeal rule" that requires parental notification.

Example: Planned Parenthood challenges the validity of regulations issued by the Secretary of the Department of Health and Human Services (DHHS) that require all providers of family planning services receiving federal funding under Title X of the Public Health Services Act, 42 U.S.C. §300-300a-6, to do the following: (1) notify parents or guardians of a minor if the health care providers prescribe contraceptives, (2) comply with state laws requiring parental notice, and (3) consider minors' ability to pay based on their parents' financial resources, rather than their own. The D.C. Court of Appeals invalidates the DHHS regulation, reasoning that the regulation is fundamentally inconsistent with congressional intent in enacting Title X (providing federal funding for family planning services to low-income clients). The court reasons that the regulations contravene congressional intent to "prevent[] unwanted pregnancies among sexually active adolescents." According to the court, Title X intends to encourage, but not require, teens to inform their parents about their sexual activity, and not to delegate federal authority regarding parental notification to state law. Further, the court reasons that a financial eligibility requirement would have the same effect as a parental notification requirement. *Planned Parenthood Federation of America v. Heckler*, 712 F.2d 650 (D.C. Cir. 1983).

Note: The court in *Heckler* does not reach the issue of whether a notification or consent requirement violates a minor's constitutional rights. The United States Supreme Court addresses these issues in subsequent cases (*Bellotti v. Baird*, *Hodgson v. Minnesota*, discussed *infra*).

3. **Constitutionality of condom availability programs for minors:** Courts reject parents' constitutional challenges to condom distribution programs that were formulated as AIDS-awareness policy.

Example: A school district starts a condom availability program that makes free condoms available to junior and high school students. Upon students' request for condoms from the school nurse, students receive counseling and information on sexually transmitted diseases (including AIDS). Parents and students request an injunction against the program unless the district includes a provision for parents to opt out of the program and to notify parents of their children's request. Plaintiffs challenge the policy as a violation of their substantive due process rights to family privacy and to control the education and upbringing of their children, and also their right to free exercise of religion under the federal and state constitutions. The court first explains the requirement that a constitutional violation must consist of state action that is coercive or compulsory (e.g., mandatory and imposes a sanction for failure to participate). Affirming the trial court's grant of summary judgment in favor of the school, the state supreme court rules that the plaintiffs failed to meet the threshold requirement that the program places a coercive burden on their rights. The court reasons that because the program is voluntary (students may choose not to participate, without penalty, and parents may instruct children not to participate), it does not intrude into Plaintiffs' constitutionally protected rights. *Curtis v. Sch. Comm. of Falmouth*, 652 N.E.2d 580 (Mass. 1995).

F. Misrepresentation of contraceptive use: Misrepresentation about contraceptive use generally does not result in tort liability based on public policy considerations (i.e., privacy grounds and the refusal to recognize tort liability for the birth of a healthy child). However, such misrepresentation will not provide a parent with a defense to a claim for child support.

1. **Tort liability:** Although courts are reluctant to grant tort recovery for contraceptive fraud, they have permitted recovery in limited cases in which physical injury results.

   Example: Mother institutes paternity suit against biological father. He concedes paternity but files a cross-claim against the mother for fraud, negligent misrepresentation, and negligence. He alleges that she falsely represented that she was taking birth control pills. The court rejects liability and concludes that, as a matter of public policy, the practice of birth control is best left to the individual without governmental interference. The court rejects the father's contention that he had been deceived by stating that the father, himself, could have taken contraceptive measures. *Stephen K. v. Roni L.*, 164 Cal. Rptr. 618 (Ct. App. 1980).

   Example: A man misrepresents his reproductive capacity to a woman with whom he is having an affair. Before they have intercourse, he states: "I can't possibly get anyone pregnant." She interprets his statement to mean that either he is sterile or has undergone a vasectomy. After she suffers an ectopic pregnancy (a life-threatening condition), she sues for damages. The court holds that the woman may maintain a cause of action for damages that she sustained. The court distinguishes *Stephen K.* because, here, the woman sought damages for bodily injury stemming from the pregnancy, rather than recovery for "wrongful birth." *Barbara A. v. John G.*, 193 Cal. Rptr. 422 (Ct. App. 1983).

2. **Defense to support obligation:** A parent may not avoid child support obligations based on the other parent's misrepresentation that she or he used birth control.

   Example: Peter and Kellie begin an intimate sexual relationship. They agree that Kellie will use birth control pills. Kellie later changes her mind and stops taking the pills but never informs Peter. After Kellie gives birth to a healthy girl, Peter sues Kellie for fraud and breach of contract. He argues that he will suffer substantial economic injury by virtue of having to pay 18 years of child support. Rejecting Peter's claims, the appellate court characterizes his claim as an attempt to circumvent his child support obligation. The court holds that public policy requires the imposition of financial liability on *both* parents. The court similarly rejects Peter's contract claim, explaining that the contract analogy fails because children have a need for support regardless of whether their conception violates a promise between parents. Finally, the court dismisses Peter's tort claims by saying that not all misrepresentations are actionable, by distinguishing the case from lawsuits for wrongful conception against negligent physicians (by saying this is a case of interparental liability), and by noting that, if Peter did not desire children, he was able to practice contraceptive techniques on his own. *Wallis v. Smith*, 22 P.3d 682 (N.M. Ct. App. 2001).

G. Contraceptive equity: After many insurance companies decided to provide health insurance coverage for the male impotence drug Viagra, women's groups began advocating for state legislation providing contraceptive equity. Contraceptive equity is based on the notion that women during their reproductive years spend significantly more than men for health care costs because of the need to purchase prescription contraceptives as well as to cover the costs of unintended pregnancies and neonatal care. Contraceptive equity legislation requires equal health insurance coverage for all FDA-approved contraceptive drugs and devices.

Many state contraceptive equity statutes provide religious exemptions enabling religious employers to refuse coverage for contraceptive methods that are contrary to the employers' religious tenets. Courts have addressed the constitutionality of these exemptions.

Example: A church-affiliated employer challenges the constitutionality (under federal and state Establishment and Free Exercise Clauses) of the state Women's Contraception Equity Act (WCEA), which requires employers who provide group health care and disability insurance prescription coverage to include coverage for prescription contraceptives. The law exempts "religious employers" (who may choose to cover prescription drugs but not "contraceptive methods that are contrary to the religious employer's religious tenets"). However, Plaintiff-corporation does not qualify as a "religious employer" because its purpose is not the inculcation of religious values, it does not primarily hire and serve Catholics, and it does not fall within either of the relevant provisions of the Internal Revenue Code. Based on the reasoning that the government may properly distinguish between secular and religious entities/activities for the purpose of accommodating religious exercise, the California Supreme Court holds that (1) the WCEA provisions do not impermissibly interfere with the employer's religious autonomy; (2) the "religious employers" exemption in WCEA does not offend the First Amendment Establishment (Entanglement) Clause; (3) the challenged WCEA provisions do not violate the state Free Exercise Clause; and (4) a rational basis supports the challenged provisions as the proper standard of review for neutral, generally applicable laws under the state constitution's Free Exercise Clause. *Catholic Charities of Sacramento, Inc. v. Superior Court*, 10 Cal. Rptr. 3d 283 (Cal. 2004).

H. Rights of pharmacists: Women's asserted right of access to birth control (including emergency contraception) conflicts with pharmacists' asserted right to refuse to fill prescriptions that they find morally objectionable. Legislation in many states allows pharmacists to refuse to fill birth control prescriptions or prescriptions for emergency contraceptives that violate their "moral or religious beliefs." In contrast, some states require pharmacists, by statute or case law, to fulfill all prescriptions even if such an act would violate their "moral or religious beliefs."

Example: A pharmacist refuses to fill or transfer a patient's prescription for an oral contraceptive. He appeals the state pharmacy licensing board's reprimand and their condition on his license that he must make his religious objections known to an employer before being hired. He argues that the board's disciplinary actions violate his state constitutional right of conscience. The appellate court holds that the pharmacist engaged in unprofessional conduct by failing to perform in a minimally competent manner, and concludes that his decision resulted in the patient's missing her medication and her suffering emotional harm from worrying about an unplanned pregnancy. According to the court, state licensing statutes are enacted not for the benefit of the individuals licensed, but for the benefit and protection of the public. Finally, the court rules that the pharmacist's rights under the freedom of conscience provision of the state constitution were not violated by the condition on his employment because the pharmacist did not show that he was burdened by the requirement that he make the extent of his religious objections known to an employer. *Noesen v. State Dept. of Regulation & Licensing, Pharmacy Examining Bd.*, 751 N.W.2d 385 (Wis. Ct. App. 2008),

II. ABORTION

A. Generally: The United States Supreme Court extended the right of privacy to encompass the right to an abortion in *Roe v. Wade*, 410 U.S. 113 (1973). Since then, however, the Court significantly limited the scope of that right.

B. Historical background: Early American proscriptions against abortion date from the 1820s. The anti-abortion movement escalated in the second half of the nineteenth century. Approximately 40 states enacted restrictive abortion regulations from 1860 to 1880. Physicians (especially the American Medical Association) spearheaded legislative reform in an effort to end the lucrative abortion practices of nonmedical practitioners. The anti-abortion movement also benefited from the nineteenth century "social purity" campaign supporting the Comstock laws' restriction of access to contraceptives.

Reform began in the 1960s when a number of states adopted the American Law Institute (ALI)'s Model Penal Code abortion provisions liberalizing abortion for pregnancies resulting from rape or incest, those involving a deformed fetus, and those whose continuation would impair the mother's mental or physical health (i.e., "therapeutic abortions"). The women's movement also contributed to abortion reform. Many feminists believed that repeal, rather than reform, was the answer.

C. A woman's right to an abortion: The United States Supreme Court held in *Roe v. Wade, supra*, that a woman has a constitutionally protected right to an abortion. The constitutional source for this protection is the right to privacy.

1. *Roe v. Wade*

a. Case and holding: Jane Roe, an unmarried pregnant woman who desires an abortion, seeks a declaratory judgment that the Texas criminal abortion statute is unconstitutional. The Texas statute makes abortion illegal except for the purpose of saving the life of the mother. Jane Roe is unable to obtain a legal abortion in Texas because her life is not threatened by the continuation of the pregnancy; nor can she afford to travel to another jurisdiction where abortion was legal. The United States Supreme Court invalidates the Texas statute based on the woman's constitutionally protected right to privacy. *Roe v. Wade, supra.*

b. Source of the constitutional right to privacy: The Court finds the right to abortion situated in the Fourteenth Amendment's concept of personal liberty.

c. Abortion as a fundamental right requiring strict scrutiny: *Roe* holds that the right to an abortion is ***fundamental***. The Court, therefore, applies strict scrutiny to the statute. This test requires that the state have a *compelling* interest in restricting abortion and the statute must be *narrowly tailored* to effectuate that interest.

d. The governmental interests in abortion regulation: The state offers three possible government interests for restricting abortion: (1) to discourage illicit sexual conduct, (2) to protect the mother from the hazardous nature of the abortion procedure, and (3) to protect the state's interest in potential life.

The Court dismisses the first governmental interest ("it appears that no court or commentator has taken the argument seriously"). *Id.* at 148. However, the Court accepts the remaining interests (protection of the mother's health and potential life) as compelling. The Court determines that these competing interests must be balanced against the woman's right. Specifically, the woman's right to an abortion is not absolute and must be weighed against the important state interests in regulation.

e. The role of the physician: Justice Blackmun's opinion in *Roe* confers the right to make decisions regarding abortion to the *woman in consultation with her physician*. Blackmun's high regard for the medical profession (he was counsel to the Mayo Clinic) led to his emphasis on the physician's role as well as the appropriation of the trimester framework (the medical approach to pregnancy). Subsequent abortion decisions do not retain this emphasis.

f. Trimester framework: Justice Blackmun, writing for the majority, reaches an accommodation of these competing interests by a trimester framework.

i. First trimester: In the first trimester, the woman has an unqualified right to an abortion that may not be infringed upon by the state. This results from the fact that the stated governmental interests are not sufficiently compelling to justify regulation at this point. Abortion is not a health risk this early in pregnancy; nor does the state have an interest in potential life at this stage, according to the Court. Thus, prior to the end of the first trimester, the Court states that the abortion decision must be left to the woman in conjunction with "the medical judgment of the pregnant woman's attending physician." *Id.* at 163-164.

ii. Second trimester until viability: After the first trimester and until the point of viability, the state may regulate abortion in the interest of maternal health. The state may not place an outright bar on abortions in this period, but it may regulate the abortion procedure for the purpose of protecting the mother's health and safety. For example, the state may regulate the qualifications and licensure of medical personnel who perform abortions, and the conditions and licensure of the facilities in which the procedure is performed. Viability is defined as the point at which a fetus is capable of survival outside the womb.

iii. Third trimester: After viability (loosely defined, at the time of *Roe*, as the beginning of the third trimester), the state's interest in protecting potential life justifies the state in regulating, and even proscribing, abortion except when necessary for the preservation of the life or health of the mother.

g. Criticisms of *Roe*: *Roe* engendered considerable criticism. Critics questioned the Court's enunciation of the right of privacy and the trimester scheme, neither of which is explicit in the Constitution. Criticisms also addressed the Court's emphasis on the importance of viability (as the benchmark in defining the state's interest in prenatal life), in part, because the definition of viability changes as technological advances occur.

Further, some feminists (the most prominent of whom are Catharine MacKinnon and Justice Ruth Bader Ginsburg) argue that the right to abortion should not be based on the amorphous right to privacy. Rather, they contend that restrictions on the right to abortion raise issues of sex discrimination. That is, because only women get pregnant and only women seek abortions, abortion regulations violate women's Fourteenth Amendment right to equal protection.

2. **Constitutional challenges to procedural requirements:** Immediately following *Roe v. Wade*, the federal courts entered an era of evaluation of the constitutionality of state restrictions on abortion procedures that make abortion more difficult to obtain.

   a. **Hospitalization requirements**

      i. ***Doe v. Bolton:*** *Doe v. Bolton*, 410 U.S. 178 (1973), addresses the constitutionality of Georgia abortion legislation. The case challenges an ALI-inspired statute mandating residency and procedural requirements if continued pregnancy would threaten the mother's life or health.

      The Court invalidates the requirements that: (1) the abortion must be performed in an accredited hospital; (2) the woman must secure advance approval by a hospital committee; and (3) the abortion must be justified by at least three physicians.

      When invalidating the above provisions, the Court reasons that: (1) the requirement of accreditation is not legitimately related to the state's objective in protecting the mother's health; (2) the requirement of a committee's advance approval substantially limits women's rights to medical care as prescribed by her physician as well as the physician's right to make medical decisions; and (3) the three-physician requirement is unable to withstand constitutional challenges regarding the patient's needs and the physician's right to practice.

      ii. ***Akron v. Akron Center for Reproductive Health:*** Three abortion clinics and a physician challenge the constitutionality of an Akron city ordinance that requires: (a) the performance of all second-trimester abortions in a hospital; (b) physicians to notify patients of fetal development, physical and emotional complications resulting from an abortion, and the availability of adoption; and (c) a 24-hour waiting period (among other provisions). Reaffirming *Roe v. Wade*, the Court holds the above provisions unconstitutional.

      In invalidating the above provisions, the Court concludes that (1) the hospital requirement does not reasonably further the state's interest in maternal health because it imposes a heavy burden on women's access to a relatively inexpensive and safe medical procedure, (2) the informed consent requirement goes beyond permissible limits in protecting health by attempting to influence the woman's choice of abortion versus childbirth and also intrudes on the physician's discretion, and (3) the waiting period does not further any legitimate state interest because it fails to guarantee the abortion will be performed more safely or to address the concern that the woman's decision be informed. *Akron v. Akron Ctr. for Reprod. Health*, 462 U.S. 416 (1983).

      Note: The case is noteworthy for the dissent's criticisms of *Roe* and its foreshadowing of *Planned Parenthood of Southeastern Pennsylvania v. Casey* (*infra*). Justice O'Connor, in her dissent (joined by Justices White and Rehnquist), sharply criticizes *Roe*'s trimester framework, stating that it is "clearly on a collision course with itself." *Id.* at 458. Also, O'Connor disagrees with the importance of viability as a benchmark, stating that the state's compelling interests in maternal health and potential life "are present throughout pregnancy." *Id.* at 459. She advocates a preference for limiting strict scrutiny review to "unduly burdensome" abortion restrictions. *Id.* at 461.

b. Mandatory viability testing and definition of life: *Webster v. Reproductive Health Services:* The United States Supreme Court examined the constitutionality of a Missouri statute that provides (1) a preamble that declares that life begins at conception, and (2) a viability-testing requirement for a fetus of approximately 20 weeks or more of gestation (as well as prohibitions on performance of abortions by public employees and public facilities, and on abortion counseling and referrals, discussed *infra*).

In regard to the above provisions, the Court (1) dodges the constitutionality of the preamble by concluding that it merely reflects a state's value judgment, and (2) upholds the viability-testing requirement for the reason that it permissibly furthers the state's interest in potential life. *Webster v. Reprod. Health Servs.*, 492 U.S. 490 (1989).

Because the viability-testing requirement is triggered not by viability (the benchmark enunciated in *Roe v. Wade*), but rather by the gestational age of 20 weeks, the Court reexamines *Roe*'s trimester scheme. A plurality prefers to "modify and narrow" (*id.* at 521) *Roe* by describing abortion as a liberty interest under the Due Process Clause and by abandoning reliance on trimesters and viability. Temporarily retreating from her previously expressed dissatisfaction with *Roe*, Justice O'Connor in her concurrence (although labeling the trimester scheme "problematic") sees no reason to reconsider *Roe*. *Id.* at 529.

c. Informed consent and waiting period requirements: *Planned Parenthood of Southeastern Pennsylvania v. Casey:* The Supreme Court retreated significantly from *Roe*'s guarantee of abortion freedom in *Planned Parenthood of Southeastern Pennsylvania v. Casey*, 505 U.S. 833, 846 (1992). *Casey* accords considerably less constitutional protection to the abortion right and, in the process, announces a new standard by which to scrutinize abortion restrictions.

i. Case and holding: The Court examines the constitutionality of a Pennsylvania statute that provides for:

- an informed consent requirement (informing the woman of the nature and health risks of the procedure, alternatives to abortion, fetal age) and a 24-hour waiting period requirement;
- notification of a married woman's husband prior to an abortion;
- a one-parent consent requirement with judicial bypass for pregnant minors;
- a medical emergency exception; and
- reporting requirements for abortion facilities.

The Court upholds all of the Pennsylvania restrictions except the spousal notification requirement. Although reaffirming *Roe v. Wade*, the Court rejects *Roe*'s trimester scheme. The Court concludes that (1) before viability, a woman has a right to an abortion without undue interference from the state; (2) after viability, the state may restrict abortions, provided there are exceptions for therapeutic abortions; and (3) the state has legitimate interests throughout pregnancy in protecting maternal health and potential life. In the Court's view, these principles "do not contradict one another." *Planned Parenthood v. Casey of Southeastern Pennsylvania*, 505 U.S. at 846.

The Court's reasoning is based on the principle of stare decisis. Specifically, the Court points out that in the two decades since *Roe*, women have come to rely upon *Roe*'s constitutional protection to make intimate decisions.

ii. **Fundamental right versus liberty interest:** Rather than continuing to speak of abortion as a fundamental right, the court demotes it to a *liberty interest*. ("The controlling word in the case before us is 'liberty.'") *Id*. Further, all restrictions on abortion no longer are subject to strict scrutiny — only those restrictions that impose an "undue burden."

iii. **Undue burden standard:** *Casey* enunciated a new "undue burden" standard in place of *Roe*'s strict scrutiny for constitutional review of abortion regulations.

> [T]he undue burden standard is the appropriate means of reconciling the State's interest with the woman's constitutionally protected liberty. *Id*. at 876.

Only those regulations that impose an "undue burden" on the woman's abortion decision will be subject to strict scrutiny.

The Court defines undue burden as "the conclusion that a state regulation has the purpose or effect of placing a substantial obstacle in the path of the woman." *Id*. at 877. The Court determines that neither the informed consent requirement nor the 24-hour waiting period creates undue burdens. Here, the Court states that it is departing from prior case law (*Akron*, discussed *supra*) in permitting the state to further its goal of protection of prenatal life by ensuring that the woman's decision be mature and informed.

iv. **Ambiguity regarding viability as the benchmark:** The *Casey* opinion emphasizes the importance of viability, stating that the state may not impose an undue burden on the woman's decision before viability. However, this stance is weakened (perhaps, even contradicted) by the Court's recognition "that there is a substantial state interest in potential life *throughout* pregnancy" (emphasis added). *Id*. at 876. *Casey*'s seeming condonation of state restrictions on abortion "throughout pregnancy" appears to undermine *Roe*'s heightened protection of the right to an abortion during the first trimester.

v. **Concurrence:** The *Casey* Court is remarkably divided. The joint opinion of Justices O'Connor, Kennedy, and Souter upholds the Pennsylvania abortion restrictions. Justices Rehnquist, White, Scalia, and Thomas, although concurring in part, also dissent in part. These justices advocate overturning *Roe*, believing that *Roe* was incorrect in classifying abortion as a fundamental right, and disagreeing that stare decisis compels adherence to *Roe*.

vi. **Dissent:** Justices Stevens and Blackmun vote to reaffirm *Roe* completely. Justice Blackmun would retain the trimester scheme and concludes that the Pennsylvania restrictions violate strict scrutiny. Stevens argues that the 24-hour waiting period is unconstitutional under the "undue burden" standard.

It was not until *Stenberg v. Carhart*, 530 U.S. 914 (2000) (discussed *infra*) that a majority of the Justices embraced the undue burden standard.

d. TRAP laws and informed consent statutes: Some state legislatures have enacted laws that have been called "targeted regulation of abortion providers" or "TRAP" laws. These laws impose requirements on abortion providers that are different and more stringent than regulations applied to comparable medical practices. Such laws mandate, for example, that an abortion provider's facility be licensed as an ambulatory surgical center, be located within 30 miles of a hospital, and adhere to physical plant requirements. In addition, some states have enacted a range of informed consent laws (sometimes termed "Right To Know" laws) that require that a woman seeking an abortion be given factual information by the abortion provider concerning her legal rights, various alternatives to abortion (e.g., adoption), the availability of public and private financial assistance, and certain medical facts, before the abortion is performed. For example, a few states have "fetal pain" legislation requiring that women who seek an abortion after 22 weeks of pregnancy to be informed about the possibility of fetal pain during the procedure. Some states mandate that women be told of the speculative link between breast cancer and abortion.

Example: A South Dakota statute requires doctors to tell women that abortion both increases the risk of suicide and will "terminate the life of a whole, separate, unique living human being." An abortion provider brings an action to enjoin the informed consent law on the ground that it violates physicians' First Amendment right to be free from compelled speech. The Eighth Circuit Court of Appeals disagrees, finding that the statements are permissible because "[w]hile the State cannot compel an individual simply to speak the State's ideological message, it can use its regulatory authority to require a physician to provide truthful, non-misleading information relevant to a patient's decision to have an abortion, even if that information might also encourage the patient to choose childbirth over abortion." *Planned Parenthood of Minnesota, North & South Dakota v. Rounds*, 530 F.3d 724 (8th Cir. 2008).

D. The abortion funding cases: Although the Supreme Court has held that a woman has a constitutionally protected right to an abortion, the Court has also held that the government is under no obligation to provide funds for abortion. This raises the question of how meaningful is a guaranteed right to an abortion without provision of the means to secure that right? A series of abortion funding cases restrict access to abortion by permitting limitations on abortion funding, thereby making it difficult or impossible for indigents to secure an abortion.

1. Background: The abortion funding cases arise in the context of challenges to federal funding of medical care. A federal statute, Title XIX of the Social Security Act, establishes a joint federal-state Medicaid program to assist indigents with medical costs. Prior to 1976, a significant percentage of legal abortions are funded by the Medicaid program. Anti-abortion activists initiate legislative efforts to limit the number of abortions by restricting public abortion funding.

State attempts to limit Medicaid funds for abortion lead to constitutional challenges. In *Beal v. Doe*, 432 U.S. 438 (1977), the United States Supreme Court determines that Title XIX does not require states to fund nontherapeutic (i.e., elective) abortions as a condition of participation in the Medicaid program. *Maher v. Roe*, 432 U.S. 464 (1977), examines whether the funding of only medically necessary abortions violates the Constitution. Holding a Connecticut scheme constitutional, the Court declares that exclusion of elective abortions from Medicaid does not violate the Equal Protection Clause.

2. **Restrictions on funding medically necessary abortions: *Harris v. McRae*:** In another attempt to limit Medicaid funding for abortion, Congress enacted the Hyde Amendment in 1977 to prohibit expenditure of Medicaid funds unless the mother's life is endangered or she is a victim of reported rape or incest. A Medicaid recipient in the first trimester of pregnancy, together with a provider of abortion services, challenged the constitutionality of the Hyde Amendment on due process and equal protection grounds.

   The Supreme Court held that the Hyde Amendment violates neither due process nor equal protection. Rejecting the argument that the Amendment impinges on the liberty interest recognized in *Roe v. Wade*, the Court reasoned that a woman's freedom of choice does not mandate a constitutional entitlement to the financial resources to effectuate that choice. Because the government does not create the obstacle to the woman's abortion (i.e., indigence), the government is not required to remove the obstacle.

   In terms of equal protection analysis, the Court pointed out that the Hyde Amendment does not implicate a suspect classification (poverty). Based on rational basis review, the Court finds that the Hyde Amendment is rationally related to the legitimate government objective of protecting potential life. *Harris v. McRae*, 448 U.S. 297 (1980).

   Congress has renewed the Hyde Amendment since *Harris* with its limitation of Medicaid coverage to those pregnancies caused by rape or incest or to life-saving abortions.

3. **Prohibition on funding abortion counseling: *Rust v. Sullivan:*** Physicians and service providers who are recipients of federal funds for low-income clients challenge Department of Health and Human Services regulations that prohibit clinics that receive federal funds for family planning services (under Title X) from providing *abortion counseling* or *referrals* (i.e., counseling that abortion is a method of family planning and providing referrals for abortion as a method of family planning). The Supreme Court upholds the so-called "gag rule," rejecting claims that the regulations violate the plaintiffs' rights to free speech or a woman's right to choose. The Court reasons that the regulations do not violate free speech "since the Government may make a value judgment favoring childbirth over abortion and implement that judgment by the allocation of public funds" and because "[p]etitioners' view that if the Government chooses to subsidize one protected right, it must subsidize analogous counterpart rights, has been soundly rejected [relying on the abortion funding cases rationale]." *Rust v. Sullivan*, 500 U.S. 173, 192-193 (1991).

   Note: Shortly after taking office, President Bill Clinton rescinds this "gag rule."

4. **Prohibition on use of public hospitals and employees: *Webster v. Reproductive Health Services:*** The United States Supreme Court examined the constitutionality of a Missouri statute in *Webster v. Reproductive Health Services* that prohibits the use of public employees and facilities to perform or assist elective abortions not necessary to save the mother's life (other *Webster* restrictions are discussed *supra*). The Court upholds the prohibition on the performance of such abortions by public employees or in public facilities, relying on the abortion funding cases rationale. The Court reasons that the state's refusal to allow public employees to perform abortions leaves women in no worse position, i.e., women can still have abortions at private facilities performed by private physicians.

5. **Funding restrictions on abortions for military personnel:** Current laws ban funding for abortions for military personnel (i.e., servicewomen as well as female military dependents) while serving in the military. (The women must travel off the base for an elective

abortion — sometimes even to another country.) Also, Defense Department funds may not be used to perform abortions except to save the life of the mother. Moreover, no federal medical facility may be used to perform an abortion except to save the life of the mother or if the pregnancy is the result of rape or incest. 10 U.S.C. §1903(a) & (b) (2006).

6. **Enhanced right to abortion funding under state constitutions:** Indigent plaintiffs are more successful in securing funding for abortion under state constitutions. *See, e.g., Committee to Defend Reproductive Rights v. Myers*, 625 P.2d 779 (Cal. 1981) (holding that the right of privacy explicitly guaranteed by the California constitution mandates public funding of abortions for indigents).

7. **International funding restrictions:** According to a policy adopted by former President George W. Bush, international family planning agencies that accept federal funds (from the U.S. Agency for International Development) are prohibited from advocating, counseling, referring, or offering abortion, even if they use money for those purposes that came from other sources. In 2009, President Barack Obama rescinded this "global gag rule."

E. Clinic access and FACE laws: Access is also a problem for pregnant women who are confronted with anti-abortion activists' tactics at clinics. In response to the murder of abortion providers and harassment of patients at abortion clinics, Congress enacted the Freedom of Access to Clinic Entrances (FACE) Act, 18 U.S.C. §248 (2006), in 1996. FACE provides criminal and civil penalties for the use of "force, threat of force, or physical obstruction" aimed at injuring, intimidating, or interfering with any patients or providers of reproductive health services.

Federal appellate courts have upheld the constitutionality of the Act. *See, e.g., Norton v. Ashcroft*, 298 F.3d 547 (6th Cir. 2002) (holding that the Act does not violate the First Amendment, is not unconstitutionally vague or overbroad, and does not violate the equal protection rights of activists, and that Congress acted validly pursuant to its authority under Commerce Clause); *American Life League v. Reno*, 47 F.3d 642 (4th Cir. 1995) (holding that FACE does not violate the First Amendment, Tenth Amendment, or the Religious Freedom Restoration Act). *But cf. United States v. Bird*, 401 F.3d 633, 634-637 (5th Cir. 2005) (DeMoss, J., dissenting) (concluding FACE exceeds congressional commerce power, as applied to a defendant, who drove a car through a door of a Planned Parenthood facility in Houston).

Example: Planned Parenthood of the Columbia/Willamette, Inc. seeks to enjoin a pro-life activist organization from publishing "wanted posters" featuring photographs and addresses of abortion providers. The posters, circulated in hard copy, also appear on an anti-abortion website called the "Nuremberg Files." Applying FACE, the appellate court upholds the permanent injunction and determines that the posters constitute "true threats" made with the intent to intimidate the providers, given prior incidents, including the murders of some physicians identified on the website. In addition, the court upholds a jury verdict of compensatory damages for the abortion providers, but remands on the issue of punitive damages. *Planned Parenthood of the Columbia/Willamette, Inc. v. American Coalition of Life Activists*, 290 F.3d 1058 (9th Cir. 2002), *cert. denied*, 539 U.S. 958 (2003).

Note: Several states have passed clinic access laws, modeled on the federal legislation, making it a ***state crime*** to obstruct access to clinics.

F. The husband's rights in the abortion context: A husband has *no* constitutional right to influence his spouse's abortion decision making.

1. **Spousal consent:** A state may not require a spouse's *prior written consent* to an abortion.

Example: A Missouri statute requires the prior written consent of the spouse of a woman seeking an abortion during the first 12 weeks of pregnancy unless the abortion is medically necessary to preserve the woman's life. A number of physicians and surgeons challenge this and other provisions of the Missouri statute. The state defends the provision as necessary for the protection of family values in encouraging joint decision making. The United States Supreme Court invalidates the provision, holding that the state may not constitutionally delegate to a spouse that power which the state, itself, is prohibited from exercising during the first trimester by *Roe v. Wade*. *Planned Parenthood v. Danforth*, 428 U.S. 52 (1976).

2. **Spousal notification:** A state may not require spousal *notification* prior to an abortion.

Example: Plaintiffs challenge the constitutionality of a Pennsylvania statute requiring that a married woman cannot receive an abortion without providing her physician with a signed statement certifying that she has notified her husband of her abortion plans. Under the statute, notification is not required if: (1) the husband is not the father, (2) the husband cannot be located, (3) the pregnancy is the result of reported spousal rape, or (4) the woman believes notification will cause her bodily injury. The Supreme Court finds that the spousal notification requirement places a significant obstacle (i.e., an "undue burden") in the path of women's exercise of their right to an abortion. The Court relies on *Danforth* (discussed *supra*), the woman's liberty interest in her body, and empirical evidence suggesting that this provision would prevent many battered wives from securing an abortion. *Planned Parenthood v. Casey of Southeastern Pennsylvania*, 505 U.S. 833 (1992).

G. **Minor's right to an abortion:** A minor's right to an abortion is more limited than an adult's. A number of states mandate parental consent and/or notification when minors seek an abortion.

1. **Parental consent**

a. ***Bellotti v. Baird:*** A Massachusetts statute regulates a minor's right to an abortion by providing (1) an unmarried minor must obtain the consent of both parents, and (2) if one or both parents refuse, the minor may obtain judicial consent upon a showing of good cause. Abortion rights activists and an unmarried minor challenge the constitutionality of the statute as unduly burdening the right to seek an abortion. The United States Supreme Court invalidates and enjoins the statute. Although the Court supports parental involvement, it holds that the statute fails constitutional muster because it permits judicial authorization to be withheld from a mature minor (as determined by a court) and because it imposes a blanket parental consent requirement without providing an alternative procedure. The Court reasons that limitations on the freedom of minors are justified by: (1) children's vulnerability, (2) children's inability to make mature, informed decisions, and (3) the importance of the parental role in childrearing. If a state requires one or both parents' consent, the state must provide an alternative authorization procedure whereby the minor may show that she is either mature enough to make the decision herself, or, if she cannot make such a showing of maturity, that an abortion, nonetheless, would be in her best interests. *Bellotti v. Baird*, 443 U.S. 622 (1979).

Note: Massachusetts subsequently enacted a statute providing for a two-step procedure whereby a judge first makes a determination regarding the minor's maturity and, in cases of determinations of a minor's immaturity, the judge resolves whether the abortion may occur. The First Circuit Court of Appeals determines that the statute satisfies *Bellotti*'s requirements. *Planned Parenthood v. Bellotti*, 641 F.2d 1006 (1st Cir. 1981).

b. Parental consent statutes under state constitutions: Plaintiffs are more successful in securing abortion rights under state constitutions because some state constitutions have broader rights to privacy than the federal right.

Example: A California statute prohibits unemancipated minors from obtaining abortions without either the consent of a parent or judicial authorization. Health care providers challenge the constitutionality of the statute. The state supreme court counters the state attorney general's reliance on United States Supreme Court decisions by pointing to the explicit *state* constitutional guarantee of a right of privacy and prior case law (*Committee to Defend Reproductive Rights v. Myers*, discussed *supra*) based on that right which permits indigents to have public funding for abortion. Although conceding that the asserted state interests (protection of the physical, emotional, and psychological health of minors and promotion of the parent-child relationship) are compelling, the court finds that the statute does not further these interests (i.e., it harms minors' health and is detrimental to the parent-child relationship). Examining the statute under strict scrutiny as required under the state constitutional right of privacy, the court concludes that the statute violates a minor's right to privacy. *Am. Academy of Pediatrics v. Lungren*, 66 Cal. Rptr. 2d 210 (Cal. 1997).

Several ballot measures that would have overturned *American Academy of Pediatrics v. Lungren* and required parental notification of minors' abortions were defeated by voters.

2. **Parental notification:** States also restrict minors' abortion rights by means of parental notification requirements. The Supreme Court has focused on the judicial bypass proceeding in several cases. Although the United States Supreme Court has not explicitly required a judicial bypass proceeding for notification statutes, the Court has held that the presence of such a provision guaranteeing this proceeding renders parental notification statutes constitutional. *See, e.g., Hodgson v. Minnesota*, 497 U.S. 417 (1990) (holding that judicial bypass procedure makes two-parent notification requirement constitutional); *Lambert v. Wiklund*, 520 U.S. 292 (1997) (upholding statute requiring notification of one parent 48 hours before abortion with judicial bypass allowing waiver of notification when notification is not in minor's best interests); *Planned Parenthood of Southeastern Pennsylvania v. Casey*, 505 U.S. 833 (1992) (upholding statute requiring parental notification of one parent plus informed consent requirement with judicial bypass).

   Plaintiffs have been more successful again in challenging parental notification legislation under state constitutions. *See, e.g., Planned Parenthood of Cent. N.J. v. Farmer*, 762 A.2d 620 (N.J. 2000) (parental notification statute violates state equal protection provision); *North Florida Woman's Health and Counseling Servs., Inc. v. State,* 866 So.2d 612 (Fla. 2003) (parental notification provision violates state constitutional right of privacy). Note: Florida's law was overturned in 2005 by means of a state constitutional amendment (Article X, Section 22) that required notification of at least one of a minor's parents before termination of her pregnancy.

3. **Federal parental involvement legislation: Child Custody Protection Act:** Congress has considered legislation that would restrict minors' access to reproductive health care services. For example, the Child Custody Protection Act passed the House of Representatives in 2007 (where it was known as the "Child Interstate Abortion Notification Act," H.R. 1063, 110th Cong. (2007)). The Act would have made it a federal offense for anyone other than a minor's

parents to knowingly transport a minor across a state line, with the intent that she obtain an abortion, in circumvention of a state's parental consent or notification law. The bill died in the Senate.

H. Partial-birth abortion bans: Both state and federal abortion restrictions ban partial-birth abortions. A "partial-birth" abortion involves termination of later-stage pregnancies (those pregnancies in or past the fifth month) by instrumental dismemberment of the fetus as the physician pulls a portion of the fetus through the cervix into the birth canal.

1. **State legislation on partial-birth abortions:** Many state legislatures enacted partial-birth abortion bans. Several federal appellate courts held that such statutes are unconstitutional. *See, e.g., Planned Parenthood of Central New Jersey v. Farmer*, 220 F.3d 127 (3d Cir. 2000) (granting a preliminary injunction to enforcement of New Jersey statute on grounds of vagueness and constituting an undue burden on women's right to an abortion).

2. ***Stenberg v. Carhart:*** Before enactment of the federal partial-birth abortion ban of 2003 (discussed *infra*), the United States Supreme Court held that a Nebraska ban on partial-birth abortions was unconstitutional.

   Example: A physician who performed abortions brought suit on behalf of himself and his patients challenging the constitutionality of the Nebraska statute banning partial-birth abortions unless that procedure is necessary to save the mother's life. "Partial-birth abortion" was defined as: "delivering into the vagina a living unborn child, or a substantial portion thereof, for the purpose of performing a procedure that . . . does kill the unborn child." The United States Supreme Court held that the statute was unconstitutional because it lacked a "health exception" that would have allowed physicians to perform the banned method to protect the mother's health and because the statute imposed an undue burden on a woman's abortion right by restricting the most common and safest dilation and evacuation (D & E) procedure as well as the dilation and extraction (D & X) procedure. *Stenberg v. Carhart*, 530 U.S. 914 (2000).

3. **Federal legislation on partial-birth abortions: *Gonzales v. Carhart:*** In 2003 Congress enacts the Partial-Birth Abortion Ban Act (PBABA), Pub. L. No. 108-105, 117 Stat. 1201, 18 U.S.C. §1531. PBABA bans a form of late-term abortion that pro-life advocates call "partial-birth abortion" (but physicians call "intact dilation and evacuation").

   The PBABA prohibits intact dilation and evacuation (D & E) procedures in abortion (specifically providing that "Any physician who, in or affecting interstate or foreign commerce, knowingly performs a partial-birth abortion and thereby kills a human fetus shall be fined under this title or imprisoned not more than 2 years, or both"). Abortion rights advocates immediately seek to enjoin its enforcement.

   The United States Supreme Court upholds the federal ban on partial-birth abortions in *Gonzales v. Carhart*, 550 U.S. 124 (2007).

   Example: Abortion providers and advocacy organizations challenge the constitutionality of the federal Partial-Birth Abortion Ban Act. Separate district courts (in California, Nebraska, and New York) find the Act unconstitutional and issue permanent injunctions, and the respective courts of appeals affirm. The Supreme Court reverses and upholds the federal ban.

   The Supreme Court holds that the Act's prohibition on intact dilation and evacuation procedure is not void for vagueness on its face, reasoning that the statutory requirement that a living fetus be delivered to one of two anatomical landmarks establishes sufficient guidelines to govern law enforcement, and the scienter requirement ("knowingly performs") limits prosecutorial discretion. The Court also concludes that the most reasonable understanding of the prohibition is that it does not sweep too broadly to include prototypical second trimester D & Es in which the fetus is removed from the uterus in pieces, and thus does not impose an undue burden on second-trimester abortions based on overbreadth.

The Court also finds that the stated congressional purposes of protecting innocent human life from an inhumane procedure and protecting the medical community's ethics and reputation are furthered by the enactment of the ban. Justice Kennedy claims that the ban is also supported by the state's interest in ensuring that the woman's choice is well informed. He suggests that doctors may tend to withhold information from women about the grisly nature of the procedure. The ban thereby prevents women who discover the details of the procedure subsequent to the abortion, he contends, from "struggl[ing] with grief more anguished and sorrow more profound" (*id.* at 159) than those other women who generally "come to regret their choice" of abortion (*id.*).

Finally, the Court addresses the argument that the abortion regulation must have a health exception if substantial medical authority supports the proposition that banning a particular procedure could endanger a woman's health. The Court determines that the Act is not invalid on its face as imposing an undue burden because of the absence of a health exception, reasoning that there is uncertainty in the medical community regarding whether the barred procedure is ever necessary to preserve a woman's health given the availability of other abortion procedures that are considered to be safe alternatives.

Dissent: Justice Ginsburg criticizes the absence of a health exception for the mother. She is also critical of the majority's decision to blur the line between pre-viability and post-viability abortions. In her opinion, the Act is irrational and does not further any governmental interest. Further, she scoffs at Justice Kennedy's suggestion that the ban protects women from subsequent regret about their abortion decision, pointing out that "[e]liminating or reducing women's reproductive choices is manifestly not a means of protecting them" (*id.* at 184 n.9).

The holding results from an ideological shift on the Court (particularly, the appointment of Justice Samuel Alito to replace Justice Sandra Day O'Connor). Critics charge that the case ushers in a new era of state attempts to restrict access to abortion, the Court gives too much deference to congressional fact-finding that was rejected by the appellate courts, and the case signifies the emergence of a new paternalistic governmental interest in regulating abortion (i.e., protecting women from psychological harms associated with the abortion decision).

Note: Notwithstanding *Gonzales,* the undue-burden standard still renders some abortion restrictions unconstitutional. *See Northland Family Planning Clinic, Inc. v. Cox*, 487 F.3d 323 (6th Cir. 2007) (invalidating Michigan statute).

III. RESTRICTIONS ON THE RIGHTS OF PREGNANT WOMEN

A. Generally: States attempt to impose various restrictions on the rights of certain pregnant women, e.g., substance abusers, child abusers, or the terminally ill.

B. Prenatal substance abusers

1. **Imposition of civil and criminal liability:** Courts are divided about the imposition of criminal or civil liability in cases of prenatal substance abuse. Most courts determine that state statutes that impose *criminal liability* for "delivering controlled substances to minors" are inapplicable prenatally. Some courts are more willing to entertain *civil actions* for violations of child abuse or neglect statutes. (A civil action results in the state's taking the child into custody, as opposed to criminal liability that results in the parent's incarceration.)

   Example: The night before she gives birth to a son, Jennifer uses cocaine. Tests of the mother and newborn reveal drug toxicity. A year later, Jennifer becomes pregnant with a daughter. She again uses cocaine during the pregnancy and during labor. Immediately after the daughter's birth, the Department of Health and Rehabilitative Services initiates an investigation for child abuse. The investigation results in the district attorney relying on a novel theory, charging Jennifer with delivery of a controlled substance to a minor, based on the delivery to the children during the birth process of cocaine through the umbilical cord. Jennifer is convicted and appeals. The state supreme court holds that cocaine passing through the umbilical cord after birth, but before cutting of the cord, does not violate the statutory prohibition against delivery of controlled substances to a minor because legislative history does not reveal an intent to use the word "delivery" (of controlled substances) in the birth context. *Johnson v. State*, 602 So.2d 1288 (Fla. 1992).

   Example: Defendant is convicted of homicide by child abuse for giving birth to a stillborn baby girl who had cocaine in her system. Defendant is sentenced to 20 years, suspended upon service of 12 years. She appeals. The South Carolina Supreme Court holds that the issue of whether Defendant had the requisite criminal intent was for the jury; the prosecution did not violate her due process rights because she was on notice that her conduct was proscribed; the prosecution did not violate Defendant's right to privacy; the sentence was not cruel and unusual punishment; and the urine sample taken in a hospital did not violate Defendant's Fourth Amendment rights. *State v. McKnight*, 576 S.E.2d 168 (S.C. 2003).

   Note: *McKnight* characterizes the minority approach.

   Epilogue: After the United States Supreme Court denied certiorari in *McKnight v. South Carolina*, 540 U.S. 819 (2003), Regina McKnight unsuccessfully filed a petition of habeas corpus, arguing that prosecutors did not prove that cocaine use caused her baby to be stillborn. She is currently serving a 12-year sentence.

2. **Constitutionality of testing policy:** The United States Supreme Court invalidated a hospital policy of testing pregnant patients suspected of substance abuse without their knowledge and consent.

   Example: State hospital policy requires testing pregnant patients suspected of drug use. Patients who test positive are arrested. Patients sue hospital, police, and medical personnel alleging violation of the Fourth Amendment. The United States Supreme Court holds that urine tests constitute "searches" within the meaning of Fourth Amendment, and are unreasonable absent consent in view of the policy's law enforcement purpose. *Ferguson v. City of Charleston*, 532 U.S. 67 (2001).

C. State restrictions on the right to procreate for other pregnant offenders: Courts have attempted with mixed results to restrict the right to procreate of persons who have violated certain laws (e.g., nonsupport, child abuse). *Compare State v. Oakley*, 629 N.W.2d 200 (Wis. 2000) (upholding probationary condition of nonprocreation for felon who was convicted of nonsupport of children as encouraging Defendant's rehabilitation to conform to law) *with Trammell v. State*, 751 N.E.2d 283 (Ind. Ct. App. 2001) (invalidating probationary condition of nonprocreation of Defendant who was convicted of neglect, reasoning that condition served no rehabilitative purpose and that less intrusive conditions were available).

D. Pregnant terminally ill patients: A terminally ill pregnant woman has the right to determine the course of her medical treatment, including birth procedures, during pregnancy.

Example: A.C., an adult married woman, has been free of childhood cancer for many years. When she is 26 weeks pregnant, physicians discover that she has terminal lung cancer. Because they determine that the fetus is too small to survive, they decide (with her concurrence) to make her as comfortable as possible until her death. Despite the objections of her family, physicians, and hospital obstetric staff, the court orders a cesarean. The baby dies and two days later, the mother dies. On appeal, a three-judge panel of the District of Columbia Court of Appeals holds that in the constitutional balancing of rights, a terminally ill pregnant woman's rights may be overridden in the interest of the fetus. The D.C. Court of Appeals grants a petition for a rehearing en banc. The court subsequently holds that a terminally ill pregnant woman has the right to determine the course of her medical treatment unless she is incompetent or unable to provide informed consent. In the latter case, the court must ascertain her decision by "substituted judgment" based on a judicial determination of her intent. Her competent choice to refuse invasive medical treatment, such as a cesarean, must be honored even where the choice may be harmful to the fetus. *In re A.C.*, 573 A.2d 1235 (D.C. Ct. App. 1990).

E. Forced cesarean sections: Sometimes pregnant women refuse medical procedures based on religious objections. Historically, courts override pregnant women's free exercise claims and order women to undergo forced cesarean sections when the life of their viable fetus is endangered. *See, e.g., Pemberton v. Tallahassee Regional Med. Ctr.*, 66 F. Supp.2d 1247 (N.D. Fla. 1999). Forced cesarean cases run counter to the general judicial unwillingness to order one person to undergo medical intervention for the benefit of another.

Example: An obstetrician performs tests on Doe, a married woman, that reveal an oxygen deficiency in the placenta of her 35-week viable fetus. He recommends an immediate cesarean section. Because of her religious beliefs, Doe refuses. Two weeks later when the situation worsens, the physician and hospital file a petition with the state attorney to compel Doe to submit to surgery. The court determines that the state failed to demonstrate statutory or case law to support such an intrusive procedure as a cesarean section. Courts should not engage in a balancing of fetal interests against the interest of a competent woman's choice to refuse medical treatment, even in circumstances where the woman's choice may be harmful to her fetus. *In re Baby Boy Doe v. Doe*, 632 N.E.2d 326, 396 (Ill. App. Ct. 1994).

F. Living wills: All states authorize the use of either living wills or powers of attorney (or both) for incompetent patients. However, a majority of states prohibit the withdrawal of life support in cases of pregnancy, thereby elevating the rights of the unborn child above the mother's right to die.

IV. FETAL HOMICIDE LEGISLATION

Federal and state legislatures have enacted legislation criminalizing the killing of a fetus during the commission of a crime.

A. Federal legislation: Congress enacts the Unborn Victims of Violence Act, 18 U.S.C. §1841 (2006) in 2004. The Act is dubbed "Laci and Conner's Law" in memory of a California woman who was murdered when she was eight months pregnant. The Act creates a criminal offense for the killing or injuring of an unborn child (at any period of gestation) during the commission of a federal crime involving a pregnant woman (thus recognizing two victims of the crime). For the first time, the federal government confers legal rights on a fetus — a result that critics claim may have implications narrowing a woman's right to an abortion.

The Unborn Victims of Violence Act applies only to conduct that is charged as a ***federal*** crime.

B. State legislation: A majority of the states currently have fetal homicide laws imposing state criminal liability for harm committed to the fetus as well as the pregnant woman. The laws vary in terms of the degree of protection and the stage of pregnancy at which criminal liability attaches. However, many of these state laws apply to the earliest stages of pregnancy.

Quiz Yourself on *ABORTION*

89. The Blackacre legislature enacts a statute imposing a new restriction on abortion, i.e., a requirement that all second-trimester abortions be performed in a hospital. Physicians who fail to comply with the requirement will be subject to criminal liability. Service providers and physicians bring an action challenging the constitutionality of the abortion restriction. Will Plaintiffs prevail? ____________

____

90. Husband and Wife have been married for five years. They have been trying unsuccessfully to conceive. However, serious marital problems develop and the couple seeks a divorce. Both parties are surprised to learn, during the pendency of the dissolution proceedings, that Wife is a few weeks pregnant. After much soul-searching, Wife decides to have an abortion. She believes that the marriage is dead and that she can better pursue her ambition of becoming a physician if she is unencumbered by a child. When she informs Husband of her decision, he files an action for an injunction seeking to prohibit Wife from terminating her pregnancy. Will he be successful? ____________________

91. Mary Moe, who is 14 years old and in the first trimester of pregnancy, petitions the Superior Court to authorize her abortion. She prefers not to inform her parents that she and her 15-year-old boyfriend have been sexually active. Mary tells the judge that her decision to have an abortion is based on the following considerations: She believes that she is too young to raise a child, she wants to avoid disrupting her education, and her doctor tells her that the medical risks of pregnancy and childbirth for a young teenager far exceed the risks of a first-trimester abortion. The judge determines that Mary is not sufficiently mature to give informed consent to the procedure. He adds that he cannot determine whether an abortion would be in Mary's best interests unless Mary consults at least one of her parents. He therefore denies her petition. Mary appeals. Will she be successful? ____________________

Answers

89. Probably yes. Based on *Roe v. Wade*, Plaintiffs would argue that a woman's right to terminate her pregnancy is encompassed by the right to privacy guaranteed by the federal Constitution. Here, the state would respond that the purpose of the requirement is the protection of maternal health, arguably a compelling state interest. However, the regulation probably would be invalidated as it is not sufficiently narrowly tailored to achieve that objective because second-trimester abortions can be performed safely outside a hospital setting (i.e., in outpatient facilities). Moreover, Plaintiffs could argue that the hospitalization requirement constitutes an "undue burden" under *Casey* in light of the fact that the hospitalization requirement significantly increases the cost of an abortion (thereby creating a "substantial obstacle" in the woman's decision) and also precludes poor women from obtaining an abortion.

90. No. The injunction should not be granted because it would violate Wife's constitutional rights as set forth in *Roe v. Wade* and *Planned Parenthood v. Danforth*. *Roe* guarantees that a woman has a constitutionally protected right to an abortion. *Danforth*, by invalidating a statutory provision requiring the prior written consent of a husband to his wife's abortion, holds that the state may not delegate to a husband that power which the state is prohibited from exercising during the first trimester by *Roe v. Wade*. This latter ruling has been reaffirmed by the United States Supreme Court in *Planned Parenthood v. Casey*, invalidating a spousal notification requirement.

91. Yes. The appellate court should overturn the denial of Mary's petition for judicial authorization of her abortion. The trial court committed judicial error in conditioning its consent on Mary's consultation with at least one parent. The United States Supreme Court has provided for a judicial authorization procedure as an *alternative* to parental consult. Based on *Bellotti v. Baird*, after a judge determines that a minor is not sufficiently mature to make the abortion decision, the judge has to determine whether the abortion would be in the minor's best interests. Here, Mary has demonstrated her thoughtful consideration of several factors involved in the abortion decision. The trial judge should have determined that Mary was sufficiently mature enough to make the abortion decision or, in the alternative, ruled that an abortion would be in her best interests.

V. ALTERNATIVE REPRODUCTIVE TECHNOLOGY

Issues of reproductive freedom and control formerly focused on the means to prevent conception (i.e., access to contraceptives and abortion). In contrast, considerable contemporary concern focuses on the means to facilitate reproduction, i.e., the new reproductive technologies. Primary among these technologies are: in vitro fertilization (IVF), embryo transfers, and surrogate motherhood. Artificial insemination, another reproductive technology, has earlier origins. However, the use of artificial insemination in conjunction with alternative methods of procreation (e.g., surrogacy) also raises some new legal issues. These technologies sometimes are referred to as "assisted conception."

Several social conditions contributed to the development and use of these technologies. These conditions include: an increase in infertility resulting from delayed childbearing, harmful contraceptive methods and pelvic inflammatory disease, and the shortage of infants for adoption.

A. Artificial insemination

1. **Definition:** Artificial insemination is a reproductive technique to combat problems of, primarily, male infertility. In cases when a husband is sterile, has a low sperm count, or carries a genetically transmissible disease, the wife may be inseminated with the sperm of an anonymous third-party semen donor. Technically, this is called heterologous insemination or AID (artificial insemination by donor).

   To correct some types of infertility, the wife may be inseminated with her husband's semen. This is termed homologous insemination or AIH (artificial insemination by husband). Only AID raises legal issues of legitimacy and paternity.

2. **As adultery:** Early cases question whether the use of artificial insemination constitutes adultery for purposes of divorce (i.e., equating the practice with the wife's submission of her reproductive ability to a man who is not her husband). Almost all cases hold that artificial insemination is not adultery for divorce purposes.

3. **Legitimacy of children conceived thereby:** Many statutes on artificial insemination legitimize the resulting offspring as the product of the marriage. Often, these statutes require the woman's husband's written consent as a prerequisite.

   The original version of the Uniform Parentage Act §5a, 9B U.L.A. 301 (1987) (approved in 1973) provides that the husband of a woman who is artificially inseminated is treated, legally, as if he were the natural father (provided that he consents and the procedure is carried out under the supervision of a licensed physician).

4. **Sperm donor's rights:** Many statutes on artificial insemination provide that the sperm donor has no rights or obligations vis-à-vis the child born as a result of the artificial insemination.

   For example, the original version of the UPA §5(b) provides that the sperm donor is not treated legally as the natural father. (See also discussion of surrogacy provisions of revised UPA *infra*.)

   However, occasional cases recognize the *known* sperm donor's parental rights and obligations.

   Example: A woman artificially inseminates herself twice with the sperm of a male friend. Both parties agree (in writing and orally) that the woman will be the primary parent, and the man will serve as sperm donor and male role model but will have no financial obligations toward the child(ren). Both adults comply with the agreement after the birth of the two children. The woman later files a paternity action and seeks child support. The sperm donor objects. The appellate court holds that the man is the natural father who has an obligation to support the children and also that the oral and written agreements purporting to absolve him of financial liability are void. The court imposes financial liability on the man because he is a known sperm donor who has had significant contacts with the children and who held himself out as their father. Further, the court explains that the UPA provision excluding a sperm donor from financial liability is inapplicable because here the defendant supplied the sperm directly to the plaintiff rather than to a licensed physician (as the UPA requires). *Mintz v. Zoernig*, 198 P.3d 861 (N.M. Ct. App. 2008).

5. **Role of consent as giving rise to child support obligation:** A husband's consent to the artificial insemination of his wife gives rise to obligations of financial support for the ensuing child.

Example: After several years of infertility, Husband and Wife consult a fertility specialist for the purposes of artificial insemination. The physician is not aware of the statutory requirement for the husband's written consent. Husband orally consents to the procedure. Wife continues to be artificially inseminated without success and discontinues treatment. She eventually resumes treatment with the same specialist and conceives. Husband, who had no contact with the physician at the time of the successful treatment, is aware of the treatment and does not object. A child is born. When the couple divorces shortly thereafter, Wife sues Husband for child support. He asserts as a defense that he has no duty to support the child because he did not consent to the procedure. The court holds that Husband is estopped from denying that he is the father. Husband's consent to artificial insemination constitutes an implied agreement to support the child and to act as its father. When a husband consents to artificial insemination of his wife, his consent is presumed to continue through the time she becomes pregnant unless he establishes by clear and convincing evidence that he has withdrawn his consent. *R.S. v. R.S.*, 670 P.2d 923 (Kan. Ct. App. 1983).

6. **Status of posthumously conceived children:** Some cases hold that posthumously conceived children are entitled to government benefits (e.g., survivors' benefits from the Social Security Administration for dependents of a deceased insured wage earner). In addition, some state statutes grant inheritance rights to posthumously conceived children provided that the deceased parent gave consent to the insemination (although the scope of the requisite consent varies based on the jurisdiction).

   Example: Widow seeks review of Commissioner of Social Security's denial of claim for survivors' benefits filed on behalf of her twins who were posthumously conceived after Husband's death. Widow appeals the grant of summary judgment for Commissioner. The Ninth Circuit Court of Appeals holds that posthumously conceived children are "children" within the definition of the Social Security Act, and that these children were presumed dependent for purposes of an entitlement to benefits because they were legitimate under applicable state law — stemming from the fact that Husband was their biological father and was married to the mother. *Gillett-Netting v. Barnhart*, 371 F.3d 593 (9th Cir. 2004).

   Revisions to the Uniform Probate Code also address the status of posthumously conceived children. According to UPC §2-120(k) and §2-121(h), if an individual is a parent of a child who is conceived by assisted reproduction after death, that child is treated, for purposes of intestate succession, as being in gestation at the individual's death, provided that the child is either (i) in gestation no later than three years after the individual's death or (ii) born no later than 45 months after the individual's death.

7. **Access by same-sex partners:** Same-sex partners have been discriminated against in the provision of assisted reproductive technology.

   Example: A domestic partner (Guadalupe Benitez) sues medical providers for their refusal to perform intrauterine insemination (IUI) on her, alleging that they violated the state civil rights act that prohibits discrimination based on sexual orientation. Defendants assert their federal and state constitutional right to the free exercise of religion as an affirmative defense (i.e., contending that their religious beliefs prohibited them from performing the insemination). The state supreme court holds that the right to free exercise under the state and federal constitutions does not guarantee physicians the right to deny fertility treatment to lesbian patients under the state civil rights act. However, the court rules that the physicians could present evidence that they denied the fertility treatment due to patient's unmarried status rather than her sexual orientation (in which case the physicians' conduct would not be prohibited under the state civil rights act). *North Coast Women's Care Med. Group, Inc. v. San Diego County Superior Court*, 189 P.3d 959 (Cal. 2008).

8. **Procreative rights of prisoners:** State prisoners do not have the right to procreate by means of artificial insemination.

 Example: Life inmate who is prohibited from conjugal visits requests prison warden to permit him to transport sperm sample outside prison in order to artificially inseminate his wife. When warden denies his request, he brings a §1983 action and state law claims alleging a violation of his constitutional right to procreate. The Ninth Circuit Court of Appeals holds that: prisoner has no federal or state constitutional right to require the prison warden to accommodate his request; right to marry did not require prison to honor his request; and the state's refusal to allow prisoner to provide sperm sample while allowing conjugal visits for some inmates did not violate equal protection or Eighth Amendment prohibition against cruel and unusual punishment. *Gerber v. Hickman*, 291 F.3d 617 (9th Cir. 2002).

B. Surrogacy

1. **Definition:** Surrogacy is a contractual arrangement whereby a woman agrees to be artificially inseminated with the sperm of a man whose wife is unable to conceive or bear a child, and then to surrender the ensuing child to the biological father and his wife. Surrogacy is also being used by gay couples who wish to have children.

2. **Background:** Surrogacy first came to public attention in 1976, when a wife advertised in a newspaper in Berkeley, California, for a woman to carry her husband's child. Since then, surrogacy has been arranged privately and by commercial surrogacy organizations. Early surrogacy arrangements involved surrogate mothers who also were egg donors. Scientific developments have led to increasing use of gestational surrogacy (in which the surrogate mother bears the child but contributes no genetic material).

3. **Traditional view:** According to the traditional view, surrogacy contracts are void. However, an increasing number of states permit such arrangements, subject to state regulation.

 Example: Husband and Wife enter into an agreement with another woman for her to carry their child. Wife donates an egg that is fertilized by Husband's sperm. The zygote is implanted in a surrogate mother (a co-worker of Wife) who agrees to relinquish her parental rights for $10,000. After the birth, the surrogate sues to assert her parental rights. The California Supreme Court holds that where artificial insemination results in a child not genetically related to the birth mother, the birth mother is not the child's mother. The court adopts an *intent-based theory of parenthood*: where a genetic mother and a birth mother both exist, the woman who intends to bring the child into being is the natural mother. The court rejects the birth mother's claim to a liberty interest in the right to care and companionship of her child, reasoning that that right can only be asserted to the detriment of the genetic mother's right. *Johnson v. Calvert*, 19 Cal. Rptr. 2d 494 (Cal. 1993).

 Example: A woman (D.B.) and her husband enter into a gestational surrogacy contract with J.F. (the intended and biological father) and a nonparty egg donor. D.B. agrees to be inseminated with donor eggs and with semen from J.F. The agreement provides that, in return for $20,000 plus expenses, D.B. will terminate her parental rights upon the birth of any child(ren). A custody dispute follows the birth of triplets. J.F. sues D.B. for breach of contract.

The trial court grants summary judgment for D.B. and her husband, concluding that the surrogacy contract violates public policy. The Pennsylvania Supreme Court disagrees, holding that no articulated state public policy bans surrogacy contracts, even when a contractual provision prohibits the gestational surrogate from asserting parental rights regarding children she bears that derive from a donor's artificially inseminated eggs. *J.F. v. D.B.*, 879 N.E.2d 740 (Ohio 2007).

4. **Uniform legislation: The Revised Uniform Parentage Act:** The practice of surrogacy spearheaded considerable legislative activity. In 1988, the National Conference of Commissioners on Uniform State Laws (NCCUSL) approved two alternative proposals to the Uniform Status of Children of Assisted Conception Act (USCACA), §5, 9B U.L.A. 155 (1994) that addressed surrogacy. Unable to agree on a single approach, NCCUSL proposed Alternative A, which regulates surrogacy arrangements through a preconception adoption proceeding, and Alternative B, which makes surrogacy agreements void. Under Alternative A, §5, surrogate contracts are valid provided they are judicially preapproved. However, for those agreements without judicial preapproval, the surrogate is the mother of the child and her husband is the father.

   In 2000, NCCUSL revised the Uniform Parentage Act (UPA) to replace USCACA. These revisions were necessitated by scientific advances in paternity testing and the new reproductive technologies.

   The revised UPA authorizes "gestational agreements," provided they are validated by a court. The Act permits payment to a surrogate mother. Also, it provides that the intended parents may be married or unmarried. In order for a court to validate an agreement: The court must have jurisdiction; the intended mother must be unable to bear a child; a home study must demonstrate that the intended parents are fit; the parties must voluntarily enter into the contract with an understanding as to its consequences; there are no physical or mental health risks to the gestational mother; there are adequate provisions for health care expenses; and the payment for the gestational mother is reasonable. Once a court is satisfied that these requirements are met, the court may issue an order validating the agreement and declare that the intended parents are the parents of the child.

   The new UPA departs from USCACA in several ways:

   - It provides that only validated gestational agreements are enforceable, thereby providing an incentive for the participants to seek judicial approval.
   - It abandons the requirement that at least one of the intended parents be genetically related to the child.
   - It specifies that individuals who enter into nonvalidated gestational agreements and later refuse to adopt the resulting child now may be liable for support.

   Further, revisions to the Uniform Probate Code address surrogacy. UPC §2-121(b) provides that a parent-child relationship regarding a child conceived by means of a surrogacy agreement does not exist unless the parent is so designated by virtue of a court order.

5. **Surrogacy by same-sex partners:** Surrogacy is increasingly being utilized by same-sex partners. In some cases, these partners may be legal spouses or domestic partners. Surrogacy involving same-sex partners raises novel issues. One such issue is: what role should paternity laws (such as the UPA, *supra*) play in the establishment of the rights of children of lesbian couples and the partners' parental obligations?

Example: Emily is the parent of two-year old twins who were born while she was in a lesbian relationship with Elisa. During the relationship, Elisa gave birth to a child as well, using sperm from the same donor. Each woman was very involved in childrearing of the other woman's child/children. When the women's relationship ended, Elisa eventually stopped providing support for Emily's twins, one of whom had extensive medical problems. The county files an action to establish that Elisa is obliged to pay child support to Emily, who is receiving public assistance. Elisa contends that she is not obligated to pay child support because she is not a legal "parent" of Emily's twins under the California version of the UPA. The state supreme court disagrees, ruling that under the UPA, a child may have two parents, both of whom are women; and also that Elisa is a presumed parent under the UPA because she agreed to raise the children, supported Emily's artificial insemination attempts, and received the resulting twins into her home and held them out as her own. *Elisa B. v. Superior Court*, 117 P.3d 660 (Cal. 2005).

Another issue is whether states will permit birth certificates to be issued in the names of two parents of the same sex. The law currently is in a state of flux.

Example: Michael and Keith enter into a gestational surrogacy contract with Michele. Michael is the sperm donor. Before Michele gives birth to twins, Michael and Keith sue the state department of health to compel it to permit them both to be named on the birth certificate as legal parents of the unborn twins. Michele and her husband join with plaintiffs in their request. The trial court refuses their request, ruling that judicial recognition of the concept of intended parenthood violates the public policy recognizing primacy of the "best interests of the child standard" in child custody determinations, and concludes that only Michael, the biological father, and not his same-sex partner (Keith) is entitled under state law to be named the "father" on the birth certificate. *Oleski v. Hynes*, 2008 WL 2930518 (Conn. Super. Ct. 2008).

6. **Foreign legislation:** In 1984, the British Warnock Committee, the most famous foreign commission to address surrogacy, recommended that commercial surrogacy be prohibited. The Surrogacy Arrangements Act, 1985 (C. 49 Eng.) and the later Human Fertilisation and Embryology Act of 2008, ch. 22, §54 (U.K.), codified the committee's recommendation. (However, privately arranged surrogacy, with payment for expenses only, is permissible.)

   In 1996 Israel adopted the Surrogate Motherhood Agreements Act, 1996, S.H. 1577, which is the first comprehensive legislation on surrogacy. The Act permits compensation and commercial surrogacy, and provides for government approval of all surrogacy arrangements.

7. **Public policy concerns:** Opponents contend that surrogacy agreements are invalid as violative of public policy because:

   - surrogacy, premised on contract, violates the best interests standard in custody determinations;
   - the natural father's rights should not prevail over the natural mother's;
   - surrogacy exploits women, especially poor women;
   - surrogacy devalues women by treating them as "baby machines"; and
   - surrogacy commodifies children (i.e., devalues them by treating them as objects).

8. **Statutory violations:** Some courts and commentators contend that surrogacy violates existing statutes on babyselling and on prebirth consent.

   a. **Babyselling statutes:** Every state has legislation criminalizing babyselling that prohibits the payment or acceptance of money or other consideration in regard to the placement of a child for adoption. Courts disagree about whether surrogacy constitutes babyselling.

   Example: The Attorney General of Kentucky seeks to revoke the charter of a commercial surrogacy agency, alleging that it violates the state prohibition on babyselling. The court disagrees, reasoning that fundamental differences exist between surrogacy contracts and babyselling. For example, an agreement to bear the child occurs before conception; therefore, the result focuses on helping the childless couple rather than relieving the financial burdens for parents of an unwanted child. Because the surrogate is free to change her mind, the agreement does not violate public policy. The court refuses to render the contract illegal where the legislature has failed to do so. *Surrogate Parenting Assoc., Inc. v. Commonwealth ex rel. Armstrong*, 704 S.W.2d 209 (Ky. 1986).

   Note: The Kentucky legislature subsequently repealed the babyselling statute (Ky. Rev. Stat. Ann. §199.601). *Compare In re Baby M.* (discussed *infra*) (holding that surrogacy constitutes babyselling).

   b. **Prebirth consent:** All states have statutes prohibiting a mother from granting irrevocable consent to adoption *before* the child's birth. The purpose is to ensure that her consent is knowing and voluntary.

9. **Presumption of legitimacy:** The parties to a surrogacy agreement must overcome the ***presumption of legitimacy*** if the surrogate is married because the surrogate's husband is presumed to be the natural father of any children who are born during the marriage. The typical surrogacy contract, therefore, requires that the surrogate's husband be a party to the agreement and relinquish therein any parental rights he may have.

10. **Constitutional issues**

   a. **Right to procreate:** Proponents of surrogacy argue that restrictions on surrogacy violate the right of privacy (as recognized by *Griswold*, *Eisenstadt,* and *Roe v. Wade*). A famous advocate of this position is law professor John Robertson (author of *Children of Choice* (1994)). Criticisms of this argument include the following:

   - It is a stretch to say that the right includes the right to procreate *noncoitally*;
   - Prior case law involves a different right — the right *not* to procreate; and
   - The right to procreate merely involves the right to conceive the child, not the care and custody of the child.

   b. **Equal protection:** Restrictions on surrogacy may violate the right to equal protection. This argument has several variations:

   - Restrictions on surrogacy treat infertile women differently from infertile men (i.e., surrogacy laws restrict the infertile woman's right, but the law honors an agreement for artificial insemination when the man is infertile); and

- The law grants parental rights to the husband of a woman who conceives a child by means of artificial insemination with another man's sperm but not to the husband of a woman who conceives a child by surrogacy (argument in *Baby M.*, discussed *infra*).

11. **Remedies:** Disputes may occur in the surrogacy context. The most common controversy involves a birth mother who refuses to relinquish the child. On the other hand, the prospective adoptive parents may refuse to fulfill their part of the agreement (if the child is disabled, a product of a multiple birth, the "wrong" gender, or the couple divorces during the process). Although several remedies are possible, each has shortcomings.

   a. **Breach of contract:** If the surrogate mother refuses to relinquish the child, the contracting father and his wife may sue for breach of contract. However, the remedy (damages) does not protect their expectation interest (i.e., a baby).

   b. **Specific performance:** The contracting father and his wife might also sue for specific performance in the event of the surrogate's breach, i.e., to force her to deliver the child to them. (This remedy was sought in *Baby M.*) A possible problem is that courts are reluctant to enforce personal services contracts.

   However, if the prospective adoptive parents are reluctant to fulfill their part of the bargain, a suit for specific performance on the part of the surrogate would not be in the child's best interests.

12. ***Baby M.:*** The most famous surrogacy case, *In re Baby M.*, holds that surrogacy contracts are unenforceable.

   a. **Facts:** Mr. and Mrs. Stern desire a child. Mr. Stern's parents are Holocaust survivors, so he keenly experiences a desire to propagate. Mrs. Stern, who has multiple sclerosis, fears that a pregnancy will worsen her condition. The couple enters into a surrogacy contract, with the help of a surrogacy organization, with Mary Beth Whitehead. Whitehead agrees for $10,000 to bear the child and terminate her parental rights. Whitehead's husband, also a party to the contract, promises to do what is necessary to rebut the presumption of paternity under the state's Parentage Act.

   After the child's birth, Mrs. Whitehead is unable to relinquish the child. Mr. Stern seeks specific enforcement. The court awards temporary custody to the Sterns. When the process server attempts to execute the order, Mr. and Mrs. Whitehead flee to Florida with the child. Mrs. Whitehead telephones Mr. Stern periodically, threatens to kill herself, the child, and falsely to accuse Mr. Stern of sexual molestation. The Sterns discover the location of the Whiteheads and successfully petition for the return of the child.

   The trial court holds that the surrogacy agreement is valid. The court terminates Mrs. Whitehead's parental rights and awards sole custody to Mr. Stern. On appeal, the New Jersey Supreme Court reverses. *In re Baby M.*, 537 A.2d 1227 (N.J. 1988).

   b. **Holding**

      i. **Surrogacy agreement is unenforceable:** The New Jersey Supreme Court rules that the surrogacy contract is unenforceable as violative of the laws and public policy of the state. The court determines that the contract conflicts with prohibitions against babyselling and with public policy.

ii. **Public policy:** The court determines that the agreement violates the policies that children should remain with their natural parents and that the natural parent is the birth mother. The court also concludes that surrogacy is harmful to women and children, and violates the guiding principle of custody determinations (the best interests of the child). The court states: "There are, in a civilized society, some things that money cannot buy." *Id.* at 1249. The court therefore finds that Mrs. Whitehead's consent to the agreement is irrelevant.

iii. **Constitutional issues:** The court disagrees that the prospective adoptive parents have a constitutionally protected right to procreate by means of surrogacy. "The right to procreate very simply is the right to have natural children, whether through sexual intercourse or artificial insemination. It is no more than that." *Id.* at 1253. The court reasons that the right to procreate does not protect the right to the care and custody of any ensuing child. Further, the court states that recognition of Mr. Stern's right of procreation in this context would destroy Mrs. Whitehead's right of procreation. The court also refuses to recognize Mr. Stern's claim that he was denied equal protection. The court says that the claim is really that of Mrs. Stern: that the law recognizes the rights of an infertile husband (by permitting artificial insemination) but not an infertile wife (by permitting surrogacy). The court finds the argument unpersuasive, saying that the situation of a sperm donor is not parallel to that of a surrogate mother.

Finally, the court refuses to reach Mrs. Whitehead's constitutional argument that she has a fundamental interest in the care and custody of her daughter. The court says that its decision, based on statutory law and public policy, obviates the need to resort to the federal or state constitutions.

iv. **Custody:** Despite holding the surrogacy agreement unenforceable, the court grants custody to the Sterns based on the "best interests of the child" standard. The court reasons that the stability of the Whitehead family is doubtful (their home is being foreclosed and Mr. Whitehead is an alcoholic with an unstable employment history). In comparison, the Sterns' household is stable and financially secure. Also, the Sterns have the ability to explain to the child her origins.

The court reverses the trial court's termination of Mary Beth Whitehead's parental rights, finding no statutory basis for the termination (i.e., no abandonment, neglect of parental duties). The court remands for a determination of her right to visitation.

Epilogue: On remand, she is granted liberal visitation rights.

13. **Prebirth determination of parental status:** Several courts have permitted a prebirth determination of the legal status of the intended parents of a child born pursuant to a surrogacy agreement, especially if the surrogate mother is in agreement. *See, e.g., Culliton v. Beth Israel Deaconess Medical Center*, 756 N.E.2d 1133 (Mass. 2001).

However, courts sometimes refuse to permit a prebirth determination of the legal status of intended *same-sex* parents of a child born pursuant to a surrogacy agreement (even if the surrogate is in agreement). *See, e.g., Oleski v. Hynes* (discussed *supra*).

14. **Divorce during surrogacy process:** The intended parents are responsible for the care and support of a child born via surrogacy even if the intended parents separate and divorce during the process.

Example: When Husband and Wife divorce, Wife petitions to establish herself as mother of their child (biologically unrelated to either) who was born by surrogacy. The appellate court holds that the intended parents are treated in law as the natural parents, and the husband is obligated to support the child by causing the child's conception. *In re Marriage of Buzzanca*, 72 Cal. Rptr. 2d 280 (Ct. App. 1998).

15. **Insurance coverage for surrogate mothers:** Some insurance companies exclude maternity services for surrogate mothers. Such exclusions may be invalid.

Example: J.M. and C.S. each agree to serve as a surrogate mother for other couples. The ensuing children are not genetically related to either J.M. or C.S. Both women are insured by Mercy Care Insurance Company and Mercy Care HMO, Inc. During the course of the pregnancies, Mercy Care denies coverage to each woman for the maternity services. Mercy Care contends that their contract does not cover "surrogate mother services." The state Insurance Commissioner concludes that the state statute regulating maternity coverage in group disability insurance policies does not permit an insurer to exclude maternity services for surrogate mothers. Mercy Care seeks judicial review of the Commissioner's conclusions. Agreeing with the Insurance Commissioner, the Wisconsin Supreme Court rules that an insurer may not make routine maternity services that are generally covered under a group disability insurance policy unavailable to a specific subgroup of insureds (such as surrogate mothers) based solely on the insured's reasons for becoming pregnant or the method used to achieve that pregnancy. *Mercy Care Ins. Co. v. Wisconsin Comm'r of Ins.,* 786 N.W.2d 785 (Wis. 2010).

C. In vitro fertilization

1. **Definition:** In vitro fertilization involves the surgical removal of ova that subsequently are placed in a laboratory medium, together with sperm, where fertilization takes place. The resulting embryo is implanted in the uterus of either the ovum donor or another woman.

2. **Early problems of medical ethics:** Early controversy concerns the medical ethics of experimentation with human eggs and sperm.

Example: Husband and Wife begin an in vitro procedure by the surgical removal of the woman's egg and its introduction into the medium with Husband's sperm. The hospital's chief of obstetrics and gynecology destroys the embryo, contending that the procedure constitutes experimentation unapproved by the hospital ethics committee. Husband and Wife sue for damages for loss of property and severe emotional distress. The court upholds the jury's award of $25,000 to Husband and Wife for their emotional distress because of the reckless conduct of the hospital's physician. *Del Zio v. Presbyterian Hosp.*, No. 74 Civ. 3588 (S.D.N.Y. Apr. 12, 1978).

3. **Inheritance issues:** The use of frozen embryos (cryopreservation) in conjunction with in vitro fertilization raises potential inheritance issues. One issue is: whether children who are conceived by in vitro fertilization but who are not in utero at the time of a parent's death (i.e., frozen embryos) should be accorded inheritance rights if a live birth subsequently results. See Section V.A.6 *supra*. Another issue is: whether genetic material constitutes "property." See discussion *infra*.

D. Embryo transfers: Surrogate embryo transfer involves the artificial insemination of an egg, followed by transplantation of the resulting embryo in the uterus of another woman who is to bear the child. This procedure is used when the egg donor is unable to bear the child. Surrogate embryo transfer raises similar legal and social issues to surrogacy (i.e., who is the mother?).

1. **Ownership and custody of reproductive material:** Controversy abounds about issues of ownership of genetic material and custody of an ensuing embryo. That is, is reproductive material "property" or "persons"?

   Ownership issues address the status of the genetic material as property of the ovum donor and/or the sperm donor. Issues of *disposition or custody* arise if the couple subsequently divorces after the wife's eggs have been removed, fertilized, and stored for future insemination attempts.

   a. **Ownership:** The issue of ownership of genetic material has been raised in the context of ethical issues involving a particular hospital's procedures and also testamentary intent.

      Example: Mr. and Mrs. Rios fly to Australia in order to impregnate the wife through in vitro fertilization at one of the first fertility clinics specializing in the procedure. Three eggs are removed and fertilized with the sperm of an anonymous donor. Of the three, one is implanted but does not result in a pregnancy. The other two eggs are frozen. Before another attempt, the Rioses die in an airplane crash in South America, leaving no indication of what should be done with the frozen embryos. Questions arise concerning the fate of the frozen embryos.

      Epilogue: The case was not litigated. The hospital ethics commission recommended destruction of the embryos. The legislature reverses the recommendation. The embryos are implanted unsuccessfully in the wombs of two women.

      Example: William is living with Deborah. William becomes very depressed. Before he commits suicide, he deposits 15 vials of sperm at a sperm bank. His will bequeaths "all right, title, and interest" in the sperm to Deborah. He also leaves instructions in his will and a "donation form" at the sperm bank specifying that the sperm should be given to Deborah if she decides to have a child. His children by a prior marriage file a contest to the will. They argue that it is against public policy to bring a child into the world without a father. Ultimately, they settle with Deborah, permitting her to have 20 percent of the estate assets. When she claims the sperm, the executor asks for instructions from the court. A judge distributes to her 20 percent of the sperm vials (three vials) based on the property settlement agreement. She files a petition seeking release of the remaining vials. William's children appeal. The California court of appeal determines that sperm are "property" and should be distributed to Deborah under the decedent's will based on his testamentary intent. The court does not decide whether any ensuing child would be entitled to inherit as William's heir. *Hecht v. Superior Court*, 59 Cal. Rptr. 2d 222 (Ct. App. 1996).

   b. **Post-dissolution disputes regarding disposition of genetic material:** The dissolution context also involves disputes regarding ownership of genetic material for purposes of disposition of that material. Issues concern:

      - whether the parties' agreement regarding future disposition is enforceable;
      - whether genetic material is "property" (implicating rules regarding the distribution of the marital property) or "persons" (i.e., children) (implicating custody decision making); and

- whether the parent seeking implantation or avoidance of procreation should prevail.

  Example: Scherry and Maharatha Karmasu, a married couple, enter into a cryopreservation agreement with a fertility clinic with regard to their frozen embryos. The agreement provides that in the event of divorce, the fertility clinic shall dispose of the pre-embryos. No children are conceived. At divorce, the husband challenges the trial court's allocation of property that included the disposition of the embryos to the fertility clinic. The appellate court affirms, holding that the trial court did not err in holding that the "custody" of the frozen embryos was controlled by the contract between the parties and the fertility clinic. The court reasons that the trial court had no jurisdiction to interfere in the contract. *Karmasu v. Karmasu*, 2009 WL 3155062 (Ohio Ct. App. 2009).

Quiz Yourself on *ALTERNATIVE REPRODUCTIVE TECHNOLOGY*

92. Sarah, an unmarried woman, decides to use a surrogate to have children after Sarah discovers that she is unable to bear her own. She locates a gestational surrogate (Monica), a sperm donor, and an egg donor. She executes a "Surrogacy Agreement" with Monica. The agreement provides that Sarah is to be the intended mother, Monica will relinquish all rights to the child upon its birth, and all children born as a result of the Surrogacy Agreement will be the children of Sarah. Monica signs the agreement after stating that she sought independent counsel. When the child is born, it has serious medical problems. Sarah gives the child up to the care of a third party. Monica petitions the court to establish maternity and to obtain custody rights. Will she succeed? ____________________

93. Husband and Wife contract with Sally Surrogate for her to be artificially inseminated with Husband's sperm and then to bear and relinquish to them the resulting child. Sally is the married mother of three children. When Sally gives birth to a severely disabled child, Husband and Wife refuse to accept the child. Husband and Wife sue Sally for not producing the "product" (the child) for which they contracted. Will Husband and Wife be successful? ____________________

94. Same basic facts as above. During the litigation, Sally and her husband divorce. Her husband alleges as grounds for the divorce that Sally committed adultery by agreeing to serve as a surrogate. Will he be successful? ____________________

Answers

92. Perhaps. Under the traditional surrogacy rule, Monica can establish the invalidity of the Surrogacy Agreement as being violative of public policy and then establish maternity by showing that she gave birth to the child. Under the revised Uniform Parentage Act (which some courts have held to be applicable to determinations of maternity as well as paternity), Monica can show that a court did not validate the Surrogacy Agreement, thereby making the gestational agreement unenforceable. On the other hand, under general contract principles, Sarah can argue that the gestational agreement consists of an offer, acceptance and consideration, and is not unconscionable or fraudulent. The Surrogacy

Agreement thus constitutes a "declaration of maternity," equivalent to a declaration of paternity, and should be upheld, she would argue. If so, Sarah would have parental rights and could relinquish the child to a third party.

93. No. In Husband's and Wife's suit for specific performance, if the jurisdiction follows the traditional approach, a court will hold the surrogacy agreement void. In that event, the agreement cannot furnish the basis for a breach of contract action. Alternatively, the court might refuse to enforce the surrogacy agreement because it is for personal services.

94. No. Sally's husband will not prevail in his divorce-related claim that Sally's surrogacy constitutes adultery on her part. Virtually all jurisdictions hold that artificial insemination does not constitute adultery for divorce purposes.

Exam Tips on ***PROCREATION***

- ***Abortion*** is a frequently tested family law issue. First, identify and explain the ***nature*** of the abortion restriction. For example, does the restriction pertain to ***abortion procedures*** (i.e., hospitalization, abortion counseling, informed consent, waiting periods, use of public facilities or employees, viability testing)? Or does the restriction pertain to such other issues as abortion ***funding*** or ***clinic access***? Clarify whether the restriction applies to abortions prior to, or after, the point of ***viability*** because different rules may apply given the stage of fetal development (see discussion below).

- Point out whether the restriction is based on ***state or federal law***. Remember that sometimes both may be involved in a given issue (e.g., clinic access is regulated by federal and state law). Note, too, that plaintiffs have been more successful in securing abortion rights under state (as opposed to the federal) constitutions.

- Identify the appropriate ***standard of review*** to use in evaluating the constitutionality of the stated governmental restriction. ***Strict scrutiny*** applies to infringements of fundamental rights, and such rights may be infringed only if the restriction is necessary to achieve a compelling interest. ***Fundamental rights*** include: contraception, abortion (under *Roe v. Wade*, but not under *Casey*), the right to engage in adult consensual sexual conduct (as well as previously studied rights such as the right to marry and to maintain family relationships). On the other hand, if none of these fundamental rights is involved, then the appropriate level of scrutiny is ***rational basis*** (unless gender discrimination is involved which calls for an intermediate level of scrutiny). ***Nonfundamental rights*** may be invalidated under the rational basis test if they bear no rational relationship to a legitimate state interest. Mention the source of the constitutional right to an abortion.

  - Remember that the above analysis requires consideration of both means and ends. That is, be sure to identify the ***end*** (what the restriction is trying to accomplish) and then determine whether the state interest is legitimate or compelling. Then, identify the chosen ***means*** of achieving that objective (how the restriction accomplishes its aim). Is the restriction rationally related to the stated objective? Is it absolutely necessary to the achievement of that objective?

- ☛ Determine also whether the restriction imposes an ***undue burden*** on the woman's decision to have an abortion. According to *Casey*, regulations that impose an "undue burden" on the woman's abortion decision will be subject to ***strict scrutiny***. An undue burden is a ***substantial obstacle***. Because the Supreme Court gave little guidance on what constitutes a substantial obstacle, each case must be determined on its facts. It may be necessary to analogize the stated restriction to the restrictions in *Casey:* The Court held the spousal notification to be a substantial obstacle but not the 24-hour waiting period (because it merely delayed the abortion).

- ☛ Discuss whether the restriction attaches to a particular stage of fetal development. For example, does the restriction apply pre- or post-***viability***? Before viability, *Roe v. Wade* held that women had a fundamental right to an abortion. *Casey* later changed the rule so that only if a state law imposes an ***undue burden***, it will be unconstitutional. ***Post-viability***, the state may ***regulate and even proscribe*** abortion (to promote its interest in human life) except where necessary for the preservation of the mother's life or health (although *Gonzalez v. Carhart* casts doubt on the continued need for a health exception). Recall that *Casey*'s seeming condonation of state restrictions on abortion "throughout pregnancy" undermines *Roe*'s heightened protection of abortion during the first trimester.

  - ☞ Clarify ***whose rights*** are being restricted. Does the restriction infringe upon the ***woman's***, ***husband's***, or ***minor's rights*** regarding abortion? Remember that different rules apply to each participant in the abortion decision. *Roe v. Wade* and *Casey* protected a ***woman's*** right to an abortion. ***Danforth*** provided that the state may not require ***spousal consent*** prior to an abortion. Minors' rights, however, may be curtailed more than adult women's rights (***Bellotti***) because of the minor's vulnerability, inability to make informed decisions, and the importance of the parental role. Thus, a state may require ***parental consent and/or notification*** prior to a minor's abortion, provided that the statute offers an alternative procedure. If a minor does not wish to (or cannot) obtain parental consent or notification, then determine if the statute provides for an alternative such as a judicial bypass proceeding. At that proceeding, the minor may show that she is either mature enough to make the decision herself, or, if she cannot make such a showing of maturity, that an abortion, nonetheless, would be in her best interests. Apply these tests to the minor's case.

- ☛ Issues involving ***contraception*** are less frequently tested. If the constitutionality of a restriction on contraception is at issue, be sure to identify whether the restriction implicates ***due process*** or ***equal protection*** rights. Apply the relevant level of scrutiny. (Review the discussion *supra* about strict scrutiny and rational basis review.) Remember that restrictions on contraception implicate fundamental rights and therefore require strict scrutiny. Identify the source of constitutional protection (e.g., the substantive due process notion of "family privacy" which is encompassed in the liberty aspect of the Fourteenth Amendment). Mention that the right of ***access to contraception*** does ***not*** depend upon ***marital status***. That is, both unmarried and married persons have a constitutional right to determine whether or not they wish to bear a child (based on *Griswold*, *Eisenstadt*).

- ☛ ***Surrogacy contracts*** are another commonly tested area. Determine threshold issues: ***who*** has breached the agreement (i.e., the surrogate or the couple); the ***nature of the breach*** (e.g., the surrogate refuses to relinquish the child, the couple refuses to accept the child); and the ***type of surrogacy*** (i.e., if the surrogate mother is also the egg donor, she may have greater rights). A major issue is the ***validity*** of the contract. Point out the ***different approaches***: the traditional view (by case law or statute) holds that the surrogacy agreements are unenforceable. However, an increasing number of jurisdictions permit surrogacy subject to state regulation. Mention the revised Uniform Parentage Act that authorizes gestational surrogacy agreements subject to court approval.

- ☞ The problem may also raise ***constitutional issues***, such as the right to procreate using assisted reproductive technology. Point out that some commentators believe such a right exists; however, the *Baby M.* court disagreed (confining the constitutionally protected right to procreate to reproduction by means of sexual intercourse or artificial insemination). Still another possible issue concerns the parenthood status of the different mothers (e.g., the birth mother, the egg donor, or the commissioning mother).

- ☞ In terms of validity issues, remember that many courts that have addressed the issue have held that surrogacy contracts are violative of public policy and babyselling statutes. Even if the court rules the contract invalid, however, the court must still decide the ***custody of the child***. Courts often resort to the best-interests-of-the-child standard, which involves a determination of all relevant factors.

- ☞ Be sure to note whether the surrogate is ***married***. Her marital status may raise parentage issues regarding who is the child's legal father. That is, it may be necessary to discuss and apply the presumption of legitimacy: The husband of a married woman is presumed to be the father of her child. To rebut this presumption (in favor of the commissioning father), discuss the theory of "intent-based parenthood" (*Johnson v. Calvert*).

☛ Finally, be sure to discuss and apply ***relevant legislation*** (or if none, then ***model legislation***) on the subject of gestational surrogacy. The revised ***Uniform Parentage Act*** permits gestational surrogacy agreements subject to court approval. Requirements include: infertility of the intended mother, a home study of the intended parents, voluntary execution of the agreement, absence of health risks to the gestational mother, provisions for health care expenses, and "reasonable" compensation.

CHAPTER 9

CHILD ABUSE AND NEGLECT

ChapterScope

This chapter addresses the maltreatment of children by their parents. Here are a few of the key principles covered in this chapter:

- Child abuse forms the basis for state intervention into the family which takes the form of ***civil proceedings*** (e.g., juvenile court dependency hearings) and/or ***criminal proceedings*** (battery, child endangerment, homicide, sexual assault, etc.).
- Juvenile court hearings involving abuse and neglect consist of two stages: a ***jurisdictional hearing*** and a ***dispositional hearing***.
- Parents have a common-law ***privilege to discipline*** their children.
- All states have ***reporting statutes***. Civil and criminal sanctions exist for ***failure to report*** abuse and neglect.
- Defendants' ***right to confrontation*** must be balanced against the ***need to protect*** the child victim as witness.
- For summary seizure and assertions of temporary custody, courts require that the child be subject to ***immediate or threatened harm***.
- For termination of parental rights, courts require that the child must be subject to ***serious physical or emotional harm*** and ***less drastic measures must be unavailing.***
- The state ***does not owe a duty*** under the due process clause for ***failure to protect*** a child from abuse unless the state has taken the child into protective custody (*DeShaney v. Winnebago*).
- ***The Adoption and Safe Families Act*** regulates the state's responsibilities to children in foster care.
- Due process requires ***clear and convincing evidence*** for termination of parental rights but does not require a ***right to counsel*** for indigent parents.

I. HISTORICAL BACKGROUND

Children have been abused and neglected (i.e., beaten, killed, burned, abandoned, sold, and sexually abused) from antiquity. Historically, abuse and neglect were attributable, in part, to the low value placed on children.

Despite its long-standing history, abuse and neglect did not provide a basis for governmental intervention in the family until the sixteenth century in England and the nineteenth century in America.

A. **English legislation:** Parliament in 1601 enacted the Elizabethan Poor Law. This legislation, which inaugurated a social policy linking poverty and child neglect, compelled the poor to work and provided shelter to those persons who were unable to work. Poor children were separated from their families and provided with vocational training.

B. American legal and social policy: American social policy first recognized child abuse with the cause célèbre case of Mary Ellen, an abused child who was removed from the home of her foster mother in New York in 1874. The situation spearheaded the formation of the Society for the Prevention of Cruelty to Children and the first state legislation on child neglect.

Public attention again focused on child abuse and neglect in the 1960s. Concern about child welfare led to the rapid enactment in all states of reporting laws requiring certain professionals to report cases of abuse and neglect (discussed *infra*).

II. THRESHOLD STANDARD FOR INTERVENTION

A. Generally: The state's ability to intervene in the family in cases of abuse and neglect rests on the *parens patriae* power — the historical power of the government to protect children from harm. However, the state must have a compelling justification in order to intervene in the family. This high standard for intervention follows from United States Supreme Court rulings in the early twentieth century (*Meyer v. Nebraska*, 262 U.S. 390 (1923); *Pierce v. Soc'y of Sisters*, 268 U.S. 510 (1925) (both holding that parents have a constitutional right to the care and custody of their children); *Prince v. Massachusetts*, 321 U.S. 158 (1944) (establishing the right of the state to intervene when the child's well-being is at stake)).

In *Meyer v. Nebraska*, a schoolteacher is convicted of violating a state law prohibiting the teaching of foreign languages. Parents (members of a German-speaking religious community) employed the teacher to educate their children in German. The United States Supreme Court concludes that the statute violates the defendant's right to due process (i.e., his liberty to engage in his occupation) and the parents' power to control the upbringing of their children.

In *Pierce v. Society of Sisters*, the Oregon legislature enacts a statute requiring parents to send their children to public schools. Two private schools argue that the statute constitutes a deprivation of their property without due process. The United States Supreme Court agrees and also concludes that the statute unreasonably interferes with the liberty of parents to direct the upbringing of their children.

Although *Meyer* and *Pierce* establish the constitutional doctrine of family privacy, a subsequent case (*Prince v. Massachusetts*, 321 U.S. 158 (1944)) established the principle that the state can infringe family privacy in the interest of child welfare. In *Prince*, a woman is convicted of violating state child labor laws by furnishing her niece with religious magazines to sell on the street at night. The woman contends that the statute violates her freedom of religion and her right to control the upbringing of her child (under *Meyer*, *Pierce*). The United States Supreme Court holds that the freedom of religion claim must yield to the state's interest in children's welfare.

B. Types of intervention

1. **Concurrent jurisdiction:** Governmental intervention in abuse and neglect cases takes the form of civil and criminal proceedings.

2. **Civil proceedings:** Civil proceedings consist of juvenile court hearings.

a. **Stages:** Juvenile court hearings consist of two stages. In the first stage, a *jurisdictional* hearing occurs at which time the state asserts jurisdiction over the child by proving that the child comes within statutory definitions of an abused, neglected, or "dependent" child. Statutory definitions often are vague and tinged with moralistic overtones, leaving considerable latitude for judges' subjective determination of suitable parenting.

Once the state asserts jurisdiction over a child, a *dispositional* hearing occurs at which the state determines a placement for the child. The court may choose among several possible dispositions. A court may remove the child from the home and place the child in foster care or in an institution. A court may allow the child to remain with the parents (sometimes, subject to various conditions, such as counseling). Or a court may terminate parental rights and permit the child to be adopted.

b. **Emergency jurisdiction:** In cases of emergency, a child may be temporarily removed from the home prior to an adversarial hearing. Statutes authorize such "summary seizure." (See also discussion of summary seizure in sections on "Specific standards" and "Intervention," *infra*.)

3. **Criminal proceedings:** Abuse and neglect may also result in criminal sanctions for acts of battery, child endangerment, homicide, sexual assault, etc.

C. **Specific standards**

1. **Vagueness problem:** Typically, state statutes have broad definitions of abuse and neglect. Courts generally reject challenges to such statutes on due process grounds. *But cf. Roe v. Conn*, discussed *infra*.

2. **Standard for summary seizure or temporary custody:** For summary seizure and assertions of temporary custody, courts require that the child be subject to immediate or threatened harm. This high standard is necessary in order to justify infringement on the constitutionally protected right of family privacy.

Example: The Department of Family and Protective Services (DFPS) takes possession of 468 children at the Yearning for Zion Ranch, a polygamous compound, on the basis of a report that a teenager was being physically and sexually abused there. DFPS then files suit, seeking emergency orders removing the children from their parents and limiting the parents' access to the children. The trial court permits temporary custody to DFPS. Mothers of some of the children then seek a writ of mandamus. The state supreme court holds that DFPS's allegations, that the community at the ranch had a culture of polygamy and of directing girls younger than 18 to enter spiritual unions with older men and have children, did not warrant the grant of emergency custody to DFPS as to all 468 children because there was no evidence of imminent danger to the physical health or safety, specifically, of the boys and the prepubescent girls to justify their removal from the Ranch. As a result, DFPS's emergency removal of all the children was invalid. *In re Texas Dept. of Family & Protective Servs.*, 255 S.W.3d 613 (Tex. 2008).

3. **Standard for termination of parental rights:** For termination of parental rights, courts require that the child must be subject to serious physical or emotional harm *and* less drastic measures must be unavailing.

Example: Ms. Wambles lives with Mr. Coppage for five years, during which time they have a son, Richard Roe. Ms. Wambles leaves Mr. Coppage and moves into an African-American neighborhood with an African-American man. Mr. Coppage contacts the Montgomery,

Alabama, police and social services department to report that Richard is neglected. A social service worker advises the police to investigate and to obtain a court order. Despite an absence of evidence of physical abuse or neglect, the police obtain a court order to take Richard into immediate custody (summary seizure). The judge grants the order based on the judge's belief that living in an African-American neighborhood is detrimental to a white child. Ultimately, the court terminates the mother's parental rights. Alabama child neglect law (Ala. Code Tit. 13, §352(4)) permits summary seizure "if it appears that . . . the child is in such condition that its welfare requires that custody be immediately assumed. . . ." Further, the statute permitting termination of parental rights defines a neglected child as one who "has no proper parental care or guardianship or whose home, by reason of neglect, cruelty, or depravity, on the part of his parent or parents . . . is an unfit or improper place . . ." (§350). Ms. Wambles brings a class action challenging the constitutionality of the statute as violative of the fundamental right to family integrity and due process. The appellate court holds that the fundamental right to family integrity requires that the state's actions be subject to strict scrutiny. Because no emergency existed (there was no danger of immediate or threatened harm), the state's interest in child protection is not sufficient to justify summary seizure, i.e., removal prior to notice and a hearing. The court also holds that, regarding *termination of parental rights*, the state's interest in child protection becomes compelling enough to sever a parent's rights only when "the child is subjected to real physical or emotional harm and less drastic measures would be unavailing." The court concludes that Richard was not being harmed and the state offered no assistance to the mother. The court found the statute unconstitutional as violative of the plaintiff's fundamental right to family integrity and void for vagueness (i.e., the terms "unfit" and "improper" are unclear and subjective). *Roe v. Conn*, 417 F. Supp. 769, 799 (D. Ala. 1976).

Example: A mother and her six children live in a small New Haven apartment, supported by welfare payments and state social services. A case worker considers the family situation "marginal," finds no evidence of abuse or neglect, and notes that the children are happy and have a "very warm" relationship with their mother. After the infant dies of unexplained injuries (later determined to be sudden infant death syndrome), the social services division obtains an order permitting summary seizure of the other five children pursuant to statutory authority that permits the assertion of jurisdiction if a child "is in immediate physical danger from his surroundings, and that immediate removal from such surroundings is necessary to insure the child's safety. . . ." Conn. Gen. Stat. §17-38a(e). Two days after the children are taken into custody, the court issues an order granting temporary custody to the Social Services Department based on allegations that the children are neglected because the apartment is dirty and has roaches and beer cans, and the mother drinks beer, occasionally leaves the children alone at night, and sends them to school without breakfast. Temporary custody is authorized pursuant to Conn. Gen. Stat. §46b-129(b), which requires that the child's "condition" or "circumstances surrounding his care require that his custody be immediately assumed to safeguard his welfare." The mother alleges that the statute (Conn. Gen. Stat. §46b-129(b)) permitting assertions of temporary custody violates due process as an infringement on her right to family integrity and is unconstitutionally vague. The court determines that the temporary custody statute (Conn. Gen. Stat. §46b-129(b)) is constitutional based on the court's reasoning that the summary seizure language ("*immediate* danger" and "immediate removal is necessary to insure the child's safety") applies equally to the temporary custody intervention. That is, the state's interest becomes sufficiently compelling to justify temporary removal (either summary seizure or temporary custody) when a child is in immediate danger and immediate removal is necessary to insure the child's safety. After finding the statute constitutional, the court concludes that because the children are not suffering from serious harm, such as illness, injury, or physical danger, it was error to grant temporary custody of the children to the Social Services Department. *In re Juvenile Appeal*, 455 A.2d 1313 (Conn. 1983).

III. DEFINING CHILD ABUSE

Courts examine the nature of parental acts or conduct that constitute abuse. Such acts or conduct include: battering, excessive discipline, religious practices, substance abuse, and potential abuse.

A. Battering: Most victims of physical abuse are very young children. Because physical abuse generally takes place in private settings, direct evidence by witnesses of abuse often is lacking. As a result, successful prosecutions may depend on a court's willingness to admit evidence of "battered child syndrome."

1. Battered child syndrome

a. Generally: Battered child syndrome (BCS) is a term first coined by radiologists who speculated that some unexplained traumatic injuries to children may have been inflicted intentionally by parents. The term has become a widely accepted description in the medical literature as well as case law.

b. Definition: Battered child syndrome signifies a child who manifests multiple injuries in various stages of healing. Parental explanations for the child's injuries are inconsistent with the clinical findings.

c. Effect: Battered child syndrome often involves expert testimony. An expert's testimony that a child is a victim of the battered child syndrome is offered not to furnish an opinion of a particular defendant's culpability, but rather to indicate that the child's injuries were intentionally, rather than accidentally, inflicted.

d. Admissibility: Most jurisdictions admit evidence of the battered child syndrome. The United States Supreme Court has accepted battered child syndrome evidence in criminal cases. *Estelle v. McGuire*, 502 U.S. 62 (1991).

Example: A two-year-old malnourished girl with multiple injuries is pronounced dead on arrival at a hospital. Her parents are tried on charges of involuntary manslaughter and child endangerment. The mother claims that the child bruised easily and that some bruises were caused by the mother's attempt to resuscitate her. A forensic pathologist testifies that the child's injuries are inconsistent with the mother's statements. Following conviction, the parents appeal, arguing that the court erred in admitting testimony on the battered child syndrome (BCS). The appellate court upholds the admissibility of the evidence, maintaining that testimony regarding BCS is admissible when relevant and given by a properly qualified expert witness. The appellate court finds, further, that admission of the evidence by the trial court did not usurp the jury's determination of the ultimate issue. *Commonwealth v. Rodgers*, 528 A.2d 610 (Pa. Super. Ct. 1987).

B. Abusive discipline

1. Common-law parental privilege to discipline

a. Generally: A common-law "parental privilege to discipline" follows from the United States Supreme Court's rulings that parents have a constitutionally protected right to raise their children as they see fit. *See, e.g., Meyer v. Nebraska, supra; Pierce v. Soc'y of Sisters, supra*. However, the privilege is subject to limitations regarding the amount and type of force that may be used (discussed *infra*).

Example: Mother (Jacqueline Newby) repeatedly hits and kicks her six-year-old daughter in a public park. Witnesses call the police. She is convicted pursuant to the assault statute, D.C. Code Ann. §22-404(a), which provides "whoever unlawfully assaults or threatens another in a menacing manner shall be fined not more than $1,000 or be imprisoned not more than 180 days, or both." The statute permits a common-law parental privilege defense. Newby appeals on the ground that the state had to prove malice to overcome her parental discipline defense. She claims she was trying to discipline her child and explains that her daughter had been misbehaving. She insists that she never intended to hurt her daughter, only to discipline her. The appellate court affirms, holding that the government did not have to prove malice and that Newby's constitutional right was sufficiently protected (by requiring the government to overcome the parental discipline defense beyond a reasonable doubt and by requiring that the government prove either that the child's punishment was unreasonable or that it was not genuinely disciplinary). *Newby v. United States*, 797 A.2d 1233 (D.C. Ct. App. 2002).

2. **Case law and statutory formulations:** Various formulations codify the common-law parental privilege to discipline and its limitations. Case law often characterizes the threshold issue as to whether the injury results from abuse or discipline, i.e., what are the parameters of this parental privilege to discipline? If the injury stems from discipline, the force used must be *reasonable* (not excessive) and for purposes of *correction*, i.e., to promote the child's welfare.

   a. **Restatement (Second) of Torts:** According to the Restatement (Second) of Torts §147(1), a parent is privileged to apply such reasonable force or to impose such reasonable confinement as the parent reasonably believes to be necessary for the child's proper control, training, or education.

   Factors in the determination of reasonableness include: age, sex, physical and mental condition of the child; nature of the child's offense and apparent motive; influence of the child's example upon other children of the same family or group; whether the force or confinement is reasonably necessary and appropriate to compel obedience to a proper command, and whether it is disproportionate to the offense, unnecessarily degrading, or likely to cause serious or permanent harm. Restatement (Second) of Torts §150 (1977).

   Example: Mother and her children are playing cards on the porch. Seven year-old B.M. throws popcorn at her 12-year-old sister (J.M.), who retaliates by hitting B.M. in the face. Mother tries to hit J.M. but J.M. swears at Mother, runs inside, and shuts herself in the bathroom. Mother forces her way into the bathroom and punches J.M. on the arm and legs. J.M. runs upstairs to her bedroom. Mother forces her way into the bedroom and continues hitting J.M. about ten times with her hand and belt. J.M. has covered herself with a blanket for protection. Mother takes off the blanket to "get a better shot at her with the belt." J.M. later goes to the home of a friend whose parent reports the incident to the police. Mother claims the parental privilege to discipline. Based on the Restatement standard, the court finds that Mother's degree of force was unreasonable by virtue of her repeated use of a closed fist in both the bathroom and bedroom, and by pursuing her daughter to continue hitting her, and by positioning the daughter to have better access for the beating. *Mathew v. State*, 892 N.E.2d 695 (Ind. Ct. App. 2008).

b. ALI formulation: The ALI Model Penal Code has another test to determine the reasonableness of the discipline. Section 3.08 defines the use of force by a parent as "justifiable" if the force is used to "promot[e] the welfare of the minor, including the prevention or punishment of his misconduct; and, [if] the force . . . is not designed to cause or known to create a substantial risk of causing death, serious bodily harm, disfigurement, extreme pain or mental distress or gross degradation. . . ."

c. Constitutionality: Courts uphold the constitutionality of statutory standards regulating parental punishment.

Example: Defendant leaves work early because he feels ill. He dismisses the babysitter who is caring for his three-year-old stepson and four-month-old daughter. When his attempts to stop the baby's cries are unsuccessful, he slaps her, causing brain damage, blindness, and her eventual death. Two Colorado statutes define the limits of permissible parental chastisement: The felony child abuse statute prohibits intentionally or negligently causing or permitting a child to be "abandoned, tortured, cruelly confined or cruelly punished" and another statute codifies the common-law privilege to discipline as: the use of reasonable and appropriate physical force "reasonably necessary and appropriate to maintain discipline or promote the [child's] welfare." Defendant appeals the jury's verdict of felony child endangerment by arguing that the language "cruelly punished" is unconstitutionally vague. The appellate court agrees. Reversing, the Colorado Supreme Court holds that the language, although in general terms, is intelligible and capable of nonarbitrary enforcement. *People v. Jennings*, 641 P.2d 276 (Colo. 1982).

d. Provocation: In the determination whether a parent had a disciplinary intent, a parent's justifiable anger, provoked by the child's misconduct, may preclude the formation of the requisite state of mind to promote the child's welfare rather than to inflict pain.

Example: A mother is convicted of assault and cruelty to a child after she injures her 11-year-old daughter by hitting her with an unheated curling iron because the obese daughter, who had a history of disruptive and unruly behavior, refuses to stop eating food and get ready for a doctor's appointment. The mother presents the parental discipline defense, which the trial court rejects. The court reasons that the mother did not hit the child for disciplinary purposes. The D.C. Court of Appeals reverses, concluding that the trial court's observation that the mother's anger foreclosed her from acting with the intent of disciplining her child served to unduly restrict the parental discipline defense. The court holds that the privilege of parental discipline is established when the defendant uses reasonable force for the purpose of exercising parental discipline. In addition to noting that anger can coexist with the requisite disciplinary intent, the appellate court finds that the government failed to prove beyond a reasonable doubt that mother's use of the cold curling iron was unreasonable. *Florence v. U.S.*, 906 A.2d 889 (D.C. 2006).

3. Delegable: The privilege to discipline is delegable by the parent, such as to a teacher or to some other person in loco parentis. *See* Restatement (Second) of Torts §147(2); ALI Model Penal Code §3.08(2).

C. Religious and/or cultural practices

1. Abuse or discipline: Cultural defense: Religious and/or cultural practices may dictate the methods parents select to discipline children. In a few cases, parents raise the "cultural defense," arguing that the discipline was reasonable based on their cultural beliefs. Courts, generally, have not been receptive to this defense.

Example: A native of Nigeria resides in New York with his wife and four children, including a seven-year-old son from the father's prior marriage. The son's teacher notifies the father about the boy's misbehavior. In the midst of discussions with the assistant principal, the father strikes the child with his fists and a belt and kicks the youth. The administrator reports the incident. The social services agency petitions the court for temporary removal from the home of three of the children and initiates neglect proceedings. The Family Court Act permits a finding of neglect for "the infliction of excessive corporal punishment." The father argues that he struck his son because this type of punishment, and its immediacy, is appropriate based on Nigerian childrearing practices. Finding that the father's motive is irrelevant, the court determines that the father is guilty of inflicting excessive corporal punishment. The court orders the father to receive counseling. *Dumpson v. Daniel M.*, N.Y.L.J. Oct. 16, 1974, at 17. *Accord In re D.L.W.*, 589 N.E.2d 970, 972 (Ill. App. Ct. 1992) (terminating parental rights and disregarding father's cultural-defense justification for spanking with wooden board and banging son's head against wall).

2. **Dangerous religious practices as abuse:** Religious practices or beliefs may result in injuries that are intentionally inflicted as part of religious rites. In addition, religious practices have been the basis of claims of moral, as opposed to physical, child endangerment. *See, e.g., State in Interest of Black*, 283 P.2d 887 (Utah 1955) (declaring Mormon children neglected and removing them from the home because their polygamous parents were morally neglectful).

   On a parent's religious objections as grounds for state claims of neglect involving withholding medical treatment, see discussion *infra.*

3. **International perspective:** Several countries (including Austria, Croatia, Cyprus, Denmark, Finland, Germany, Iceland, Israel, Italy, Latvia, Norway, and Sweden) currently prohibit corporal punishment by parents.

D. Psychological or emotional abuse: Courts were slow to recognize psychological maltreatment as a form of child abuse. Many statutes now address emotional abuse (influenced by the definition of "abuse" in the Child Abuse Prevention and Treatment Act). Some states, stemming from concerns with problems of proof, require that the emotional abuse must have physical manifestations. Furthermore, abuse and neglect encompass the psychological maltreatment that stems from children's witnessing physical violence between parents.

Emotional abuse is particularly a problem for adolescents. It is a contributing factor to runaway behavior, juvenile prostitution, and adolescent suicide.

E. Sexual abuse

1. **Generally:** Sexual abuse by family members is another form of child maltreatment. Most child molestation is intrafamilial. Legal responses encompass civil as well as criminal proceedings. Civil actions include: proceedings by a juvenile court to assert jurisdiction over a sexually abused child, and civil lawsuits by victims who seek monetary damages against a perpetrator. Criminal sanctions also exist to punish the perpetrator.

2. **Problems of proof:** Like psychological abuse, sexual abuse rarely has physical manifestations. Behavioral indicators are more common. Evidentiary problems abound because of the

lack of physical manifestations, as well as the concern that some children fabricate abuse, the young ages of many victims, and the fact that the sexual acts occur in private.

3. **Sexual abuse allegations in custody disputes:** Sexual abuse allegations sometimes arise in custody proceedings. If proven, sexual abuse allegations may result in the court imposing conditions on a parent's visitation.

4. **Failure to protect:** Many jurisdictions define child abuse to include acts of omission as well as commission. That is, statutes make the parental failure to protect children a form of child endangerment. Some courts subject mothers to liability for failure to protect their children from a father's sexual and/or physical abuse. Sometimes, a parent's failure to protect the child results in termination of that parent's parental rights.

   Example: Mothers and their children bring an §1983 action, challenging the constitutionality of the city's policy of removing children from their mothers' custody solely on the ground that the mothers failed to protect the children from witnessing domestic violence against the mothers. A federal district court certifies a class action and grants a preliminary injunction. The city appeals. The Second Circuit Court of Appeals holds that the city was liable if the city social workers' actions violated the mothers' or children's constitutional rights, and that certification of questions of state law (regarding the scope of the state statutes under which the city had acted) was appropriate. (The Second Circuit Court hesitated to reach the constitutional questions, believing that resolution of uncertain issues of New York statutory law would avoid, or significantly modify, the substantial federal constitutional issues and left the state statutory law issues to New York's highest state court for resolution.) On the certified questions, the New York Court of Appeals holds that evidence that a caretaker allows a child to witness domestic abuse against the caretaker is insufficient, without more, to satisfy the statutory definition of a "neglected child," and also that emotional injury from witnessing domestic violence can rise to the level that justifies removal of child, but witnessing does not, by itself, give rise to any presumption of injury. *Nicholson v. Scoppetta*, 820 N.E.2d 840 (N.Y. 2004).

F. Prenatal abuse: Courts are divided about the imposition of criminal or civil liability on drug abusers for inflicting *prenatal* harm to their children. A civil action results in the state's taking the child into custody as an abused or neglected child, whereas criminal liability results in the parent's incarceration. (Also see discussion of substance abuse in Chapter 8.) Jurisdictions are more reluctant to impose criminal liability on parents for prenatal harm.

Courts do take *newborns* into custody who test positive for drug toxicity. *See, e.g., In re Baby Boy Blackshear*, 736 N.E.2d 462 (Ohio 2000) (finding newborn who tested positive for drugs was per se an "abused child" for purposes of civil child abuse statute and granting temporary custody to county Department of Human Services).

Example: Julie Starks, when seven months pregnant, is arrested for manufacturing and possessing methamphetamine. The court sets bond at $200,000. A few days later, on its own motion, the juvenile court holds an emergency hearing, determines that the fetus is "deprived" (neglected) under the state Children's Code and grants custody of the fetus to the Department of Human Services based upon its belief that the fetus would be harmed if Julie were released. She appeals. The Oklahoma Supreme Court refuses to impose civil liability, holding that a fetus does not come within the definition of "child" under the Children's Code based on either statutory interpretation or legislation intent. *In re Unborn Child of Starks*, 18 P.3d 342 (Okla. 2001). *Accord In the Interest* *of H.*, 74 P.3d 494 (Colo. Ct. App. 2003) (holding that an unborn child does not constitute a "child" for the purpose of child abuse or neglect proceeding). (See also Chapter 8, III.B.)

G. Potential abuse: A court may use its discretion to determine that one child is abused or neglected based on a finding that other children in the same household previously have been abused or neglected.

Example: A mother is charged with abuse and neglect of her infant son based upon the finding of abuse and neglect of an older girl in the same household. The older daughter previously was taken to an emergency room and diagnosed with a fractured skull, black eye, and fractured hand. The mother appeals the finding of abuse and neglect of the infant son. The court holds that the finding of abuse and neglect of the older daughter supported the conclusion that the infant was likely to suffer serious harm in this household despite the lack, as of yet, of any such evidence. *In re Baby Boy Santos*, 336 N.Y.S.2d 817 (Fam. Ct. 1972).

Example: Yolanda has seven children. A juvenile court terminates Yolanda's parental rights to her three older children based on a finding of neglect, but does not make a determination as to the younger children. Yolanda is arrested for slashing her boyfriend's tires. The police find that Yolanda left her four youngest children at home with a knife wedged under the door so they could not escape. The children are removed from the home. A state statute permits termination of parental rights based on the prior neglect of either a child or a sibling of the child at issue. In a dependency hearing, the court finds that Yolanda has unresolved alcohol abuse problems, that the two oldest children have special needs, that Yolanda has neglected her children in the past, and that the latter resulted in the termination of parental rights to her older children. The court then terminates Yolanda's parental rights to the four *younger* children after finding that it is in their best interests. Yolanda appeals, challenging the constitutionality of the statute on due process grounds. The Nebraska Supreme Court upholds the statute provided that a court looks both at prior abuse of siblings *and* the current best interests of the children now being adjudicated dependent. *In re Sir Messiah T.*, 782 N.W.2d 320 (Neb. 2010).

IV. DEFINING CHILD NEGLECT

A. Generally: States also impose criminal and civil liability for a parent's failure to provide adequate care for children. Statutes often include broad definitions of parental acts of misconduct or omission, allowing room for highly subjective determination of proper parenting. Some states have held such statutes unconstitutionally vague. Yet, even redrafted statutes contain broad-based definitions of neglect.

B. Parental acts of omission: A parent has the duty to provide adequate care, including special care if the child's physical or mental condition requires it, even if the parent has limited financial resources. Failure to do so may result in a judicial determination that the child is neglected or abused.

Example: D.H. is a mother of five children between seven months and seven years of age. The Child and Family Services Agency (CFSA) removes the children because of the accumulation of human feces, rotting food, and cockroach infestation throughout the premises. The CFSA charges that the children are without proper parental care and control necessary for their physical, mental, and emotional health, and that the deprivation is not due to D.H.'s lack of financial resources. D.H. claims the evidence of deplorable conditions was insufficient to support the trial judge's findings of neglect. The appellate court disagrees and finds the evidence of deplorably unsanitary and unsafe living conditions credible. The ever-present filth, the lack of heat, refrigeration, and plumbing, the reliance on the oven to warm the apartment, together with the mother's indifferent attitude toward these problems, exposed the children to substantial risks of serious harm. *In re A.H.*, 842 A.2d 674 (D.C. 2004).

Example: Margaret is a single parent of preteen David and teenager Amy. David is frequently truant because he stays home to avoid bullies at school. In the course of an investigation of David's truancy, the Department of Children and Families (DCF) visits the home and finds clothes piled high and completely covering the floors, kitchen surfaces, table tops, and other furniture. The toilet, sink, and bathtub are dirty. A few days after DCF's visit, David commits suicide. DCF charges Margaret with felony child neglect pursuant to the following provisions of the state statute: "Any person who willfully or unlawfully causes or permits any child under the age of sixteen years to be placed in such a situation that the physical or mental health of such child is likely to be injured shall be guilty of felony child neglect." Margaret contends that the statute is unconstitutionally vague as applied to her. The Connecticut Supreme Court agrees, reasoning that the mother had no reason to know that her housekeeping was likely to injure her son's mental health or was otherwise criminal. Moreover, the court points out that the Department of Social Services had concluded that the home did not pose an immediate threat to the son's mental or physical health and also notes that the fact of the boy's suicide did not establish that such harm was foreseeable. *State v. Scruggs*, 905 A.2d 24 (Conn. 2006).

Some modern courts subject mothers to liability for acts of omission (e.g., child neglect) for failure to protect their children from a father's acts of physical or sexual abuse. (See discussion of failure to protect, Section III.E.4 *supra.*)

C. **Religious justification for medical neglect:** Religious practices or beliefs may also result in parents' withholding medical care from children. Several jurisdictions provide that parents who withhold treatment based on religious beliefs (e.g., "faith healing") are exempt from liability for child abuse. However, if a child dies as a result of the parent's religious objections to medical treatment, the parent(s) may be subject to criminal prosecution. Parents' defenses based on the First Amendment have not been successful.

Example: A Christian Scientist mother engages a Christian Scientist practitioner to treat her four-year-old daughter, who is ill with meningitis, with prayer. When the child dies after 17 days without receiving any medical treatment, the mother is charged with involuntary manslaughter and felony child endangerment. A California statute provides that a parent is criminally liable for failure to provide a child with medical or "other remedial care." The mother argues that the prosecution violates her First Amendment rights. Rejecting the mother's defense, the court holds that the prosecution is permitted by statute as well as the free exercise and due process clauses of the state and federal constitutions. The court finds that the imposition of felony liability on the mother for failure to seek medical care for a seriously ill child is justified by a compelling state interest (i.e., child welfare) and represents the least restrictive alternative available to the state. *Walker v. Superior Court*, 763 P.2d 852 (Cal. 1988).

On the "Baby Doe" regulations, see Chapter 10.

D. **Emotional neglect:** Emotional neglect may also be a ground for intervention in the family. One form of such neglect in young children is "failure to thrive," characterized by severe malnutrition and developmental retardation caused by the parent's emotional rejection.

Example: When Donald is scheduled to begin kindergarten, school authorities suggest that he is not physically and mentally ready for school. He is small for his age, walks like a toddler, and is not yet toilet trained. He is hospitalized for observation. A physician determines that the boy has "psychosocial dwarfism," caused by parental neglect, i.e., an absence of physical contact. The court takes jurisdiction over Donald as a neglected child and places him in foster care. The child improves dramatically following removal from his home. The judge terminates the parents' parental rights, reasoning that the child had suffered sufficient damage such that the court could not risk returning him to the home. The parents file for declaratory, injunctive, and monetary relief against the juvenile court judge and state social worker following the termination of their parental rights. The appellate court determines that the parents' claim against the judge is barred by judicial immunity and that their claim against the state Department of Social Services is barred by the Eleventh Amendment. *Castorr v. Brundage*, 674 F.2d 531 (6th Cir. 1982).

Courts and commentators have been slow to recognize emotional maltreatment as child abuse, in part because emotional maltreatment (unlike physical maltreatment) leaves no visible marks. Some courts require physical manifestations of psychological abuse.

Example: A father repeatedly subjects his son, Shane, to verbal abuse directed at his sexual identity. Specifically, he regularly calls him a "fag," "faggot," and "queer." The father also frequently forces Shane to remove his father's shoes and massage his feet. The father has a history of domestic abuse. Shane testifies that he would cry and his stomach would twist when his father verbally abused him. Shane's mother testifies that she was unable to protect Shane from his father's abuse. The court finds that both the mother and the father abused Shane. The mother allowed the abuse to occur and thereby created a substantial risk of protracted impairment to his emotional health. *In re Shane T.*, 453 N.Y.S.2d 590 (Fam. Ct. 1982).

Example: Anthony has physical custody of his daughter Mary. The County Social Services Department files a petition alleging that Mary is a dependent child after they receive a report of suspected child abuse. The petition alleges that Anthony kicked, hit, and pushed Mary, and pulled Mary's hair. He repeatedly calls Mary a whore or slut and tells her that she is taking after her mother, that she would get pregnant, and that she never would amount to much. The court declares Mary a dependent, removes her from his custody, and awards custody to her mother. The father appeals, contending that the evidence was insufficient to support the assumption of dependency jurisdiction and the placement of Mary with the mother. The appellate court affirms, finding that the father's abusive conduct caused Mary emotional damage. *In re Mary D.*, 2006 WL 2513609 (Cal. Ct. App. 2006).

E. Medical neglect: State child protection agencies also may initiate judicial proceedings to address medical neglect.

Example: Phillip, a 12-year-old boy with Down's syndrome, suffers from a congenital heart defect. He has lived in a residential care facility since birth. In a petition filed in the juvenile court, the juvenile probation department alleges that the boy comes within the provisions of California Welfare and Institutions Code §300(b) because he was not provided with the necessities of life. The petition requests that he be declared a dependent child to ensure that he receive cardiac surgery for a congenital defect after his biological parents refuse consent to the surgery. The trial court denies the petition, pointing to medical testimony regarding the risk of cardiac surgery, the higher-than-average risk of postoperative complications for Down's syndrome children, and the presence of pulmonary vascular changes in the boy. The Court of Appeals affirms, finding that the parents' autonomy is constitutionally protected under the Fourteenth Amendment. *In re Phillip B.*, 156 Cal. Rptr. 48 (Ct. App. 1979).

F. **Potential neglect:** Courts sometimes declare children neglected (or abused) even though no parental misconduct or omission has yet occurred.

Example: A 16-year-old unwed mother desires to raise her baby while residing in her parents' home. Her parents, however, are unable to provide financially or emotionally for the infant (her father is an 80-year-old invalid). The young mother previously was placed in a foster home because of her incorrigibility (i.e., sexual promiscuity and disobedience). The social services agency petitions the court to declare the teenager's two-day-old baby a dependent child so that the state may assume guardianship. The mother argues that the state must prove she is unfit before depriving her of custody and that she cannot be found unfit without having the chance to prove that she can care for the child. The court determines that the present situation merits the assertion of dependency jurisdiction and the child's permanent removal from the mother's custody. Although finding the mother unfit based on her emotional instability and financial irresponsibility, the court holds that a finding of unfitness is not an essential prerequisite to a determination that a child falls within the statutory definition of "dependent." Further, the court reasons that a child should not have to endure harm to give the mother an opportunity to prove her fitness. *In re East*, 288 N.E.2d 343 (Ohio Com. Pl. 1972).

Quiz Yourself on DEFINING CHILD ABUSE AND NEGLECT

95. Dawn is born to Loretta and James Smith. Loretta is 17; James is 20. One day when Dawn is four months old, Loretta leaves her in the care of James who has just begun his daily exercise program. When Loretta returns, she notices that the baby is unconscious. Loretta immediately takes the baby to the emergency room where the physician notices severe lacerations on the child's head and buttocks. The baby later dies from a brain hemorrhage. James admits that the baby's crying interrupted his exercise regime. He explains that he got frustrated, so he spanked and shook her. When James is charged with murder, he argues that he acted from a desire to discipline the child. Will his defense be successful? ____________________

96. Sophia is a single mother raising 11-year-old J.J., who has a history of untruthfulness and stealing property. Sophia has tried various forms of discipline, including grounding him, sending him to his room, and withholding privileges. One day J.J.'s teacher sees him giving away a bag of women's clothing. The teacher informs Sophia, who identifies the clothing as hers. When Sophia questions J.J., he denies it. Despite Sophia's warning that his deceit will result in punishment, he maintains his innocence. In response, Sophia strikes him five to seven times on his buttocks with the use of a belt or extension cord. Some of the swats land on his arm and thigh and leave bruises. J.J. shows the bruises to the school nurse who reports Sophia to the police. Sophia contends that her actions were privileged. Will her defense be successful? ____________________

97. Donna and Stephen, the parents of five children, are in poor health. Neighbors report that the children are neglected. The caseworker who investigates discovers that the home is filthy, dirty dishes and garbage are strewn throughout the house, the house reeks of animal fecal matter, the children are dirty, and their bedding is dirty. The children frequently do not attend school, and their medical needs are unattended. The caseworker files a petition with the juvenile court to declare the children neglected. State law permits children to be removed from parental custody if "the home is an unfit place." DSS initiates a petition for termination of parental rights. Will DSS prevail? ____________________

Answers

95. No. Although a parent possesses a common-law right to discipline a child, the punishment must be reasonable and for the purposes of correction. If a parent inflicts excessive or unreasonable corporal punishment, the parent will be subject to criminal liability. Because a four-month-old child is unable to comprehend discipline, James's acts of shaking and spanking the baby were excessive and unreasonable. James will be criminally liable.

96. Probably. Based on the Restatement (Second) of Torts, a court would be likely to hold that Sophia's physical punishment of 11-year-old J.J. by swatting him on buttocks was privileged as "reasonable force" that was "necessary for [his] proper control, training, and education," because J.J. stole from Sophia and lied about it repeatedly, Sophia had tried various and progressive uses of discipline, and the punishment was not particularly degrading and did not result in serious or permanent harm.

97. Perhaps. The parents might argue that the neglect statute is unconstitutional. Statutory definitions of neglect often are vague and highly moralistic, leaving considerable latitude for judges' subjective determinations of suitable parenting. Challenges on grounds of vagueness have met with occasional success. In addition, the parents might attempt to argue that the termination was not justified. The state may terminate the parent-child relationship when the child is subject to real physical or emotional harm and less drastic measures are unavailing (*Roe v. Conn*). The state would argue that the parental neglect of the children's needs and welfare amounts to serious harm. The parents could counter that the dirty state of their home did not result in any serious harm to the children and that less drastic measures (such as the provision of homemaking services) would be successful. The parents' arguments may be successful, depending on the jurisdiction. Some courts have terminated parental rights in such cases.

V. PROCEDURE

A. Reporting laws: All states have reporting laws that require certain designated individuals (generally medical personnel and school officials) to report suspected child abuse and neglect to law enforcement agencies and/or state child welfare authorities.

1. Background: Reporting legislation was enacted rapidly by all states following the discovery of the battered child syndrome by radiologists. Early reporting statutes addressed the problem of identification of *physical* abuse by *medical* personnel. Subsequent amendments broadened the definition of abuse to include other types of abuse (e.g., sexual and emotional), as well as to expand the class of designated reporters.

2. **Civil and criminal sanctions for failure to report:** Many states impose criminal liability for failure to report child abuse. A minority of jurisdictions permit a private right of action against professionals who fail to report abuse or neglect.

   Example: An abused child is brought to a hospital for treatment of fractures and bruises inflicted by the child's mother and the mother's boyfriend. Dr. Flood, the emergency room physician, fails to take full-body X-rays, to diagnose the child as a victim of the battered child syndrome, or to report the abuse to the authorities. As a result, the child is returned to the home. After the child sustains further injuries, she is brought to a different hospital. There, the physician immediately diagnoses the abuse and reports it; the child is taken into protective custody. The mother and her boyfriend are convicted of child abuse. The minor, represented by her guardian ad litem, files a civil action against Flood and the hospital, based on medical malpractice and on the violation of a criminal statute (the reporting law). She alleges that as a proximate result of the medical personnel's negligence, she sustained additional injuries. The court sustains the physician's and hospital's demurrers. Reversing, the California Supreme Court permits a private right of action based on either common-law negligence or a violation of the criminal reporting statute. In regard to the malpractice action, the court determines that the plaintiff is entitled to prove that the standard of care at that time dictated that a reasonably prudent physician would have ordered X-rays and then reported the findings as abuse. The court also determines that the mother's and boyfriend's beating did not constitute an intervening act that would have relieved the physician or hospital of liability because the resumption of abuse was reasonably foreseeable. Finally, the court concludes that for the plaintiff to prove liability based on a violation of the criminal reporting law, she must prove that the physician's failure to comply with the statute was intentional rather than negligent. *Landeros v. Flood*, 551 P.2d 389 (Cal. 1976).

   (For a discussion of agency immunity from liability, see the discussion of *DeShaney v. Winnebago, infra.*)

3. **Immunity from civil liability for false reports:** Statutes often confer immunity on reporters who file reports that are subsequently determined to be erroneous.

4. **Central registry:** Many states incorporate into their reporting laws a requirement that a state agency maintain a register of all reported cases of suspected child abuse. Although the central registry originally was intended to help ascertain the incidence of abuse and to permit professionals to keep track of parents suspected of abuse, it has also been utilized by social services agencies to preclude individuals with abusive propensities from working in the field of child care. Cases sometimes hold that state registries are violative of procedural due process. *See, e.g., Valmonte v. Bane*, 18 F.3d 992 (2d Cir. 1994) (holding unconstitutional New York's statutory procedures).

5. **Clergy:** Many states now mandate reporting of abuse by religious officials.

   Example: Christine G., a 17-year-old student at a private school affiliated with a Pentecostal church, decides to seek help from Pastor Hodges by telling him that her stepfather, a minister in the church, has been molesting her. Appellant assistant pastor is also aware of the allegations, and together with the pastor, tells Christine to return home. Appellants do not report the incident, but decide to address the matter internally within the church. During a subsequent investigation by the police department, Appellant Hodges states he knew that he was a mandated reporter, but that he disciplined the father by having him write a letter of apology to the victim and by having the stepfather confess in front of the entire congregation. Appellants are subsequently convicted of violating the state Child Abuse and Neglect Reporting Act. The appellate court affirms, holding that there was substantial evidence to support the jury's verdict that appellants were requested to report as child care custodians; that the Act was sufficiently specific to defeat a constitutional attack based on vagueness; and that the Act did not violate appellants' rights to free exercise and free speech, or under the Establishment Clause. *People v. Hodges*, 13 Cal. Rptr. 2d 412 (Ct. App. 1992).

B. Evidentiary issues: Evidentiary difficulties arise frequently in child abuse prosecutions for the reasons that: (1) the victims are so young, and (2) the acts of abuse occur in private. The central evidentiary issue concerns how to protect the child victim from the trauma of the judicial process while at the same time safeguarding the defendant's constitutional rights.

1. Competency of child witnesses: Because abuse involves child victims, successful prosecution often requires children to testify. Many states, following Federal Rule of Evidence 601, eliminate distinctions between adult and child witnesses. Such states presume that all persons are competent to testify (thereby shifting the burden of incompetency to the challenging party). Other states require competency hearings before a child may testify. Based on the judge's discretion, even very young children may testify. Competency refers to the child's ability to understand the requirement to tell the truth and to testify accurately.

Example: Five-year-old Barry is brought to an emergency room with second- and third-degree burns. Barry and his older brother testify that their stepfather burned Barry by putting him in hot water. The children also testify that their stepfather beat Barry with a belt and stick. An expert testifies that the injuries are the result of child abuse. The defendant is found guilty of cruelty to a minor. He appeals, arguing that the trial court erred in ruling that the children were competent to testify. The appellate court holds that the trial judge did not abuse his discretion. The trial judge examined the children to determine their understanding. His ruling as to competency is entitled to considerable deference because he had the opportunity to see and hear the children. *State v. Skipper*, 387 So.2d 592 (La. 1980).

Example: The victim of sexual abuse is four years old. The alleged abuse took place when the child was two. The defendant argues that the child was not a competent witness because of her age and the inconsistency of her answers as to whether she knew the meaning of telling the truth. For example, when counsel asked "do you know what it means to tell the truth?" she nods affirmatively at one time but later answers the same question by saying "no." The appellate court examines the record of her testimony (including her answers to questions about telling a "story," the consequences of telling lies, and recognition of certain lies). Based on her testimony and prior case law, the appellate court finds that the trial judge did not abuse his discretion in finding her competent. Any contradictions go to credibility and not to competency. *State v. Ward*, 455 S.E.2d 666 (N.C. Ct. App. 1995).

2. Battered parent profile: Psychologists have developed a "battered parent profile" that reveals certain traits (e.g., impulsiveness, immaturity, low self-esteem) of parents who physically abuse their children. Testimony regarding a defendant's character that is introduced to show that the defendant fits within this profile generally is inadmissible unless the parent puts character at issue.

Example: Mother is charged with, and convicted of, the death of her infant from a severe head injury. The mother says that she may have dropped the baby. Social service workers testify as to the mother's personal history (including the receipt of services by the mother's own family) and the fact that the mother previously sought services. A clinical psychologist testifies about the battered parent profile: The parent is the product of an abusive background, has committed past violent acts, is the victim of chronic stress, has poor judgment, and had a difficult pregnancy. The mother moves for a mistrial, claiming the state impermissibly placed her character at issue. The mother appeals from the denial of her motion. The court holds that the expert's testimony, although not concluding that the defendant fit the battered parent profile, could lead a juror to infer that the state was implying that the parent fit within the syndrome and murdered the infant. Unless a defendant places her character in issue, the state may not introduce character evidence showing a defendant's personal history or personality traits as the foundation for demonstrating the defendant fits the profile. Although conceding that the trial court erred in admitting the testimony, the appellate court determines that the error was harmless because overwhelming evidence establishes the mother's guilt. *Sanders v. State*, 303 S.E.2d 13 (Ga. 1983).

(On the battered child syndrome, see *supra* Section III.A.1.)

3. **Clergy privilege:** Most jurisdictions have a privilege that allows clergy to keep confidential parishioners' communications, such as those involving child abuse. However, in the wake of the clergy sex abuse scandal, a number of state legislatures abrogated or weakened the privilege. In 2002, law enforcement authorities in Boston, Massachusetts, revealed that more than 700 children had been victims of sexual abuse by Catholic priests over the past 60 years. Church officials, although aware of the abuse, chose to keep the matter secret. (Accounts of sexual child abuse by priests also surfaced in other states and countries.)

4. **Child sexual abuse accommodation syndrome:** Psychiatrist Roland Summit discovers the "child sexual abuse accommodation syndrome" (CSAAS) in 1983. This syndrome identifies certain behavioral characteristics of sexually abused children. The majority of jurisdictions admit evidence of CSAAS for rehabilitative purposes to explain commonly misunderstood behavioral patterns of child victims (i.e., recantation, delayed reporting, omission of details). However, courts hold inadmissible such evidence if relied on as proof that sexual abuse occurred in a given case.

   Example: Perez is convicted of sexual offenses with three young girls, ranging in age from five to nine. At trial, one victim gives testimony that is inconsistent with her prior statements about the molestation, and paints Perez in a more forgiving light than did her prior statements. A senior criminal investigator testifies about the pattern of child sexual abuse victims to retract initial allegations of sexual abuse. On appeal, Perez claims that the trial court erred in admitting evidence on CSAAS as unscientific. The appellate court disagrees. The court explains that, although expert testimony on the common reactions of a child molestation victim is not admissible to prove the sex crime charged actually occurred, CSAAS testimony is admissible to rehabilitate the victim's credibility. *People v. Perez*, 105 Cal. Rptr. 3d 749 (Ct. App. 2010).

5. **Statute of limitations and repressed memories:** Children often repress memories of traumatic events. They may only remember the incidents of sexual abuse years after the occurrence, for example, when (as adults) they undergo mental health treatment. By the time the victim remembers the abuse, the running of the statute of limitations may preclude the victim's claim for tort liability. Some jurisdictions address the problem by application of the "delayed discovery rule." This equitable exception to the bar of the statute of limitations tolls the statute until the victim knows, or reasonably could have known, of the injury. Courts

favor application of the rule in cases when the victim has no memory whatsoever of the sexual abuse due to her reliance on repression as a psychological defense mechanism. *See, e.g., Mary D. v. John D.*, 264 Cal. Rptr. 633 (Ct. App. 1989), *reh'g denied*, 800 P.2d 858 (Cal. 1990). On the other hand, if the victim has some memory of the abuse, courts are divided about application of the rule.

The validity of claims of repressed memory is controversial. Critics argue that victims do not actually "recover" repressed memories but rather are susceptible to therapists' suggestions. In some cases, parents have sued therapists for "planting" memories of the abuse.

6. **Anatomically correct dolls:** Children's play with anatomically correct dolls sometimes provides evidence of sexual abuse, especially for very young children who are unable to testify. Although many early cases hold such evidence inadmissible, jurisdictions increasingly permit the admission of such evidence either by statute or case law.

7. **The right to confrontation:** The defendant's right to confrontation implicates problems of special protective testimonial procedures and also the admissibility of hearsay evidence.

   States have enacted special testimonial procedures (e.g., closed circuit television) to protect child victims who are witnesses in child abuse cases. Several cases challenge the constitutionality of such procedures as violative of the defendant's Sixth Amendment right to confrontation.

   The Sixth Amendment provides that an accused shall have the right in criminal prosecutions to confront the witnesses who testify against him.

   a. **Special testimonial procedures: Closed circuit television**

      i. **Face-to-face confrontation sometimes not required by federal constitution:** The United States Supreme Court has held that the Sixth Amendment does not always require *face-to-face* confrontation. Thus, certain testimonial procedures, such as closed circuit television, do not violate the defendant's Sixth Amendment right.

      Example: Sandra Craig, a preschool director, is charged with and convicted of sexual child abuse of a six-year-old schoolchild. A Maryland statute permits the use of one-way closed circuit television to receive the testimony of a child victim-witness. The procedure prevents the child witness from seeing the defendant as she testifies and is cross-examined in the presence of the prosecutor and defense in a separate room. The defendant argues that the procedure violates her right to confrontation. The United States Supreme Court holds that the use of one-way closed circuit television does not violate the Confrontation Clause. The state's interest in protection of child victims is sufficiently important to outweigh, in some cases, the defendant's right to face-to-face confrontation. The Court holds that the state must make an adequate, *case-specific showing of necessity* to overcome the defendant's right to face-to-face confrontation. The Court cautions that the showing must reveal that the child witness not be merely traumatized by the courtroom, but by the *presence of the defendant* and also that the emotional distress must be more than *de minimis*. The Court concludes that the Maryland procedure preserved the requisite safeguards of reliability and adversariness guaranteed by the Sixth Amendment: oath, cross-examination, and observation of the witness' demeanor. The Court remands the case for determination of the requisite case-specific finding of necessity. *Maryland v. Craig*, 497 U.S. 836 (1990).

Epilogue: On remand, the Maryland Supreme Court reversed Craig's conviction, ordering a new trial on the basis that the trial judge should have personally interviewed the child witness before requiring the closed circuit television procedure. 588 A.2d 328 (Md. 1991).

Note: The United States Supreme Court in *Craig* appears to have done an about-face regarding the right to confrontation. In a prior case, *Coy v. Iowa*, 487 U.S. 1012 (1988), the Court held that a statutory procedure permitting the child's testimony from behind a screen violates the right to confrontation because the Confrontation Clause guarantees a face-to-face meeting with witnesses. See also the discussion of the constitutional protection for the right of confrontation regarding a witness's *out-of-court statements* in Sections 6.b and 6.d, *infra*.

ii. **State constitutions may require face-to-face confrontation:** Some states refuse to follow *Craig* based on independent state grounds, finding that a child's testimony outside the defendant's presence violates their state constitutions.

b. **Hearsay:** Hearsay evidence is testimony by a declarant at a hearing regarding a previous out-of-court statement that is offered in evidence to prove the truth of the matter asserted. ("The truth of the matter asserted" might signify, for example, the identity of the perpetrator.) Thus, hearsay is evidence that is not based on the witness's personal experience, but rather on what he or she has heard someone else say.

Hearsay evidence generally is inadmissible unless it falls within one of the recognized exceptions to the hearsay rule. Admission of hearsay evidence raises problems of reliability, memory, etc.

c. **Exceptions to the hearsay rule:** Many states utilize hearsay exceptions to permit a child's previous out-of-court statements about the abuse (such as statements to a parent, relative, friend, therapist, physician) to be admitted into evidence at trial. Moreover, the influential, widely adopted Federal Rules of Evidence also permit admission of children's statements of abuse or neglect in some cases.

States and the Federal Rules of Evidence permit statements to be admitted under traditional exceptions to the hearsay rule. Two traditional exceptions include: *spontaneous declarations* (or excited utterance), and statements made for the purpose of *medical diagnosis and treatment*. The theory for admissibility of these statements is that the manner in which, and the purpose for which, such statements are made serve as guarantees of their reliability and trustworthiness.

i. **Traditional exceptions to the hearsay rule: Spontaneous declarations:** Some states and the Federal Rules of Evidence 803(2) permit the introduction of hearsay statements if the statements are made under the influence of a stressful event. The statement must be made either while perceiving the event or soon thereafter, so long as the declarant is still in an excited condition. The theory is that the spontaneity of the statement and stress of the moment are guarantees of reliability.

ii. **Traditional exceptions to the hearsay rule: Statements for medical diagnosis and treatment:** Some states and the Federal Rules of Evidence 803(4) permit the introduction of statements that are made to medical personnel for the purpose of diagnosis and treatment. The theory is that persons would not lie to a medical provider who is seeking information in order to furnish them with treatment.

The United States Supreme Court decided two cases (*White v. Illinois, Idaho v. Wright*) concerning the admissibility of a child's pretrial out-of-court statements to a physician. The cases were decided under different exceptions to the hearsay rule.

In *White v. Illinois*, 502 U.S. 346 (1992), a four-year-old girl incriminates her abuser by means of statements that she makes to her mother, babysitter, police officer, emergency room nurse, and physician. The defendant appeals his conviction, arguing that the statements are inadmissible hearsay. The girl was unavailable to testify due to emotional difficulties. The United States Supreme Court holds that the statements are admissible because they fall within both "firmly rooted" hearsay exceptions of spontaneous declarations and statements made for the purpose of medical diagnosis and treatment. Additionally, the Court states that the Confrontation Clause does not require that the child appear or be proved unavailable.

In *Idaho v. Wright*, 497 U.S. 805 (1990), a father was convicted on two counts of lewd conduct with a minor under 16 years of age based on one daughter's statements to a pediatrician that incriminated her father as her sister's abuser. After the trial judge determined that the young child was not capable of communicating with the jury, the child's statements were admitted under the state's "residual exception" to the hearsay rule. When the defendant challenged the admission of the child's statements as violative of his right to confrontation, the United States Supreme Court held that the child's hearsay statements lacked the particularized guarantees of trustworthiness required for admission under the Confrontation Clause.

(Note that *Crawford v. Washington*, explained *infra*, casts doubt on *Idaho v. Wright*'s analysis by rejecting the standard under which *Wright* was decided—"residual exception"—and also by *Crawford*'s requirement that a declarant's statement is inadmissible absent the defendant's opportunity for cross-examination.)

d. **Constitutionality of tender years exemption statutes:** The United States Supreme Court held that testimonial evidence (i.e., a witness's out-of-court statements) could be admitted consistent with the Confrontation Clause only if the witness was unavailable and the defendant had a prior opportunity for cross-examination. The decision barred a wife's out-of-court statements to police incriminating her husband because, although she was unavailable due to assertion of spousal privilege, the husband did not have prior opportunity for cross-examination. *Crawford v. Washington*, 541 U.S. 36 (2004). *Crawford* thereby overruled *Ohio v. Roberts*, 448 U.S. 56 (1980), which held that hearsay statements could be admitted if the declarant was unavailable and the evidence bore "particular guarantees of trustworthiness."

The *Crawford* case has major implications for child sexual abuse prosecutions. For example, *Crawford* prohibits the admissibility (as hearsay) of child protective service workers' testimony regarding forensic interviews (or videotapes) with child victims (a procedure that is authorized by some states' tender years exemption statutes) unless the defendant has an opportunity for cross-examination.

Example: Appellant is charged with sexual child abuse for molesting girls aged ten and eight. The trial court admits the hearsay statement of a social worker who interviewed the child victims (after receiving a police report). Maryland's "tender years exemption statute" permits child victims under age 12 not to testify in child sexual abuse cases and authorizes testimony of certain persons in lieu of the child. Appellant complains that the social worker's testimony violates his right to confrontation. The appellate court agrees (citing *Crawford*) and holds that the social worker's testimony about her interviews with the child victims (who did not testify) was hearsay and violated the Confrontation Clause because appellant could not confront his accusers in court. *Snowden v. State*, 846 A.2d 36 (Md. Ct. Spec. App. 2004).

e. **Meaning of testimonial hearsay:** The Supreme Court clarified the meaning of testimonial hearsay in two post-*Crawford* domestic violence cases. In *Davis v. Washington*, 547 U.S. 813 (2006), the Court held that statements to 911 operators are not testimonial and therefore are admissible because they are elicited to resolve an emergency. In contrast, in the consolidated case of *Hammon v. Indiana*, admission of a victim's statement to a responding police officer violates the right to confrontation (absent the opportunity for cross-examination) because the officer was investigating a possible crime.

Several courts have addressed the admissibility of child hearsay in light of *Crawford*, *Davis*, and *Hammon*.

Example: Defendant is convicted of aggravated indecent liberties with a child. He appeals. The Kansas Supreme Court holds that the victim's statements during an interview by a social worker and detective were "testimonial," and therefore inadmissible under the Confrontation Clause in light of the facts that the victim was not available to testify at trial and that the defendant had no prior opportunity to cross-examine the victim. The court adds that the violation of defendant's Sixth Amendment right of confrontation was not harmless and the doctrine of forfeiture by wrongdoing does not apply (i.e., the defendant was not deemed to have forfeited his Sixth Amendment right of confrontation because his actions did not result in victim's unavailability). Nonetheless, the court holds that the evidence is sufficient to support a conviction, because the child was diagnosed with gonorrhea and had been alone with the defendant and because the defendant admitted to a social worker that he had just tested positive for gonorrhea. *State v. Henderson*, 160 P.3d 776 (Kan. 2007).

Example: Vigil and John Kohl are visiting the home of Brett Brown. All the men are drinking. While Brown and Kohl are on the Internet in another room, Vigil plays a game with Brown's seven-year-old son, JW (the victim). The child's father goes to check on Vigil and JW and sees Vigil sexually assaulting the child. JW, who was crying, tells his father that Vigil "stuck his winkie in his butt" and that his "butt hurt." While the father calls 911, Kohl, the father's friend, asks JW if he was hurt. JW repeatedly tells his father's friend that his "butt hurt." Vigil is convicted of sexual assault. The trial court admits statements the child made to his father and his father's friend, statements to the doctor who performed the sexual assault examination, and a videotape of statements the child made during a police interview. The court of appeals reverses Vigil's conviction on the ground that admission of the child's videotaped police interview violated the defendant's constitutional right to confront the witnesses against him and that the erroneous admission was not harmless. The Supreme Court of Colorado reverses, reinstating Vigil's conviction. The state supreme court holds that (1) the victim's statements to the examining physician were not inadmissible under the Sixth Amendment and came within a firmly rooted exception to the hearsay rule as a statement made for purposes of medical diagnosis and treatment; (2) the child's statements to his father were admissible as an excited utterance and were not "testimonial" (because an objectively reasonable witness in the child's position would not have believed the statements would be used at a later trial) and therefore did not violate the federal or state Confrontation Clause; and (3) the admission of the videotaped police interview, although violating the Confrontation Clause, did not constitute plain error because ample other evidence supported the defendant's conviction. *People v. Vigil*, 127 P.3d 916 (Colo. 2006).

8. **Fifth Amendment privilege against self-incrimination:** A parent may not invoke the Fifth Amendment right against self-incrimination to avoid a court order to produce a child.

   Example: Maurice, an abused child, is removed from his mother's care when he is three months old and placed in a shelter. Subsequently, he is returned to the mother's custody. Following a hearing, the juvenile court asserts jurisdiction over the child, but permits the mother to retain custody provided that she agrees to cooperate with the Department of Social Services (DSS). Eight months later, DSS informs the court that the mother has violated almost every provision of the protective order. DSS petitions for removal of the child from the home. The mother refuses to produce the child or reveal his whereabouts. (DSS fears that the child has been killed.) The court orders the mother to be imprisoned until she either produces the child or reveals his whereabouts. The mother invokes her Fifth Amendment right against self-incrimination, contending that producing the child would exhibit her control over, and possession of, the child, which then could assist the state in a subsequent prosecution of her. The United States Supreme Court rules that the mother may not invoke the Fifth Amendment, reasoning that the Fifth Amendment only applies when an accused is compelled to make a *testimonial communication* that is incriminating. A defendant may not invoke the Fifth Amendment when based upon possible incrimination resulting from examination of the *object* produced. Further, the Court reasons that the Fifth Amendment is "not available to resist compliance with a regulatory regime constructed to effect the State's public purposes unrelated to the enforcement of its criminal laws." Because Maurice previously was adjudicated in need of assistance, he was subject to the state's welfare regulatory system. *Baltimore City Dept. of Soc. Servs. v. Bouknight*, 493 U.S. 549, 556 (1990).

Quiz Yourself on ***PROCEDURE***

98. When Christine Jones is 16 years old, she confides in her teacher that her father has been molesting her for many years. The teacher makes an appointment for her to speak with the principal, Mr. Larson. She recounts the abuse to Mr. Larson. That evening Mr. Larson telephones Christine's father and informs him of her allegations. The next day, Mr. Larson calls Christine into his office. He tells her that her father has confessed to everything. Mr. Larson hands Christine a letter of apology from her father. Mr. Larson tells Christine not to tell anyone about what her father has done to her. A few months later after the molestation recurs, Christine runs away from home. When a police officer finds her and asks why she ran away from home, she tells him about the abuse. Mr. Larson is charged with violating the state's reporting statute. Will Mr. Larson be liable? ____________________

99. Ten-year-old Joanna informs her mother that her stepfather Gregory has been touching her pubic area with his penis and that the contact is painful. The mother takes Joanna to the police station where a police officer videotapes an interview with her. The videotape shows Joanna using anatomically correct dolls to describe how Gregory sexually abuses her. Subsequent medical diagnosis confirms repeated sexual penetration. Gregory is charged with the sexual assault of Joanna. The district attorney seeks to introduce the videotape as evidence. Gregory contends that admission of the videotape violates his constitutional rights. Will he prevail? ____________________

Answers

98. Yes. All states have reporting laws that mandate certain professionals to report cases of abuse and neglect. These statutes subject reporters to criminal and, sometimes, civil liability for failure to report. Statutorily designated professionals typically include medical and school personnel. Under the state's reporting statute, Mr. Larson, a school administrator, has a duty to report Christine's sexual abuse to the proper authorities (typically, social welfare personnel or police). Mr. Larson's failure to do so will subject him to liability.

99. Yes. The admission of the videotape violates Gregory's Sixth Amendment right to confrontation. The court should find the videotape to be inadmissible testimonial hearsay under *Crawford*. The videotape of Joanna that was made by the police officer at the police station was intended for the sole purpose of collecting evidence for use at a future criminal proceeding, as opposed to identifying the existence of an emergency to enable medical or law enforcement personnel to respond appropriately. Further, Gregory was not present at that time, and Joanna was not under oath nor was she subject to cross-examination. Thus, Gregory's constitutional challenge should be successful.

VI. INTERVENTION

A. Summary seizure: Statutes permit the summary removal of a child from the home. ("Summary" means ex parte, i.e., without notice to the parent or without the opportunity to be heard.) Such an assertion of jurisdiction is appropriate in a case in which the child is seriously endangered.

Courts generally require that there be *immediate or threatened harm* to the child before a child can be summarily removed from the home.

Example: A state statute authorizes the summary seizure of a child "if it appears that . . . the child is in such condition that its welfare requires." The plaintiff, a white mother, challenges the constitutionality of the statute. The mother's child was summarily seized and the mother's rights subsequently terminated because she was living with an African-American man in an African-American neighborhood. The court holds that the statute is unconstitutionally vague and violates due process. Without immediate or threatened harm to the child, the state's interest in child protection is not sufficient to justify removal of a child prior to notice and a hearing because of the constitutionally protected interest in family integrity. The court reasons that the facts of this case do not justify summary seizure. *Roe v. Conn*, 417 F. Supp. 769 (D. Ala. 1976) (also discussed in Section II.C., *supra*).

The practice of emergency removal of children has come under increasing constitutional attack in recent years as courts struggle to define more precisely the standard to apply. Currently, a majority of the federal courts hold that a state official may remove a child without a warrant based on a "reasonable suspicion that the child has been abused or is in imminent peril of abuse." *Gomes v. Wood*, 451 F.3d 1122 (10th Cir. 2006) (joining the majority approach).

B. Intermediate dispositions

1. Foster care

a. **Generally:** The state places children in foster care either because the children have been adjudicated abused, neglected, or dependent, or because parents voluntarily give the state custody of the children.

b. **Purpose:** The purpose of foster care is to provide the child with a stable environment while preparing the child for eventual return to the biological parents.

Example: Foster parents challenge a decision by the foster care agency, Jewish Child Care Association, to remove a foster child for whom they have cared for four years. Despite the agency's express policy and statements by the natural mother that she would not give up the child for adoption, the foster parents vigorously seek to adopt the child. The agency initiates removal proceedings to prevent any further attachment to the child by the foster parents and to prevent any conflict of loyalty in the child. The New York court of appeals upholds the lower court decision returning custody of the child to the agency with the ultimate goal of returning the child to the natural parent. Removal of custody from the foster parents is proper in light of the goal of foster care to return the child to the natural parent and the natural parent's constitutional right to the care and custody of the child. The dissenting judge argues that the testimony provides clear and convincing evidence that the child's welfare would be served better by continuing placement with the foster parents and that the evidence does not justify return to the natural mother because the mother did not appear able, within a reasonable period of time, to resume custody. *In re Jewish Child Care Assoc.*, 156 N.E.2d 700 (N.Y. 1959).

2. **Foster parents' rights:** Foster parents' claims (on both the federal and state level) that they have a Fourteenth Amendment liberty interest in their relationships with their foster children generally have met with mixed results.

Example: Individual foster parents and an organization of foster parents bring a §1983 action seeking declaratory and injunctive relief. They allege that the procedures governing removal of foster children from foster homes violate due process and equal protection. New York *State's* statutory scheme provides for a "conference" (rather than a preremoval hearing) when a foster child is removed from a foster home. If the child is removed after the conference, the foster parent may request a full adversary administrative hearing. New York *City* regulations provide greater safeguards, permitting a full adversary hearing if the foster child is being transferred to another foster home (but not if the child is returned to his parents). The district court determines that the preremoval procedures constitute a deprivation of due process. The United States Supreme Court reverses, holding that, even assuming foster parents do have a constitutionally protected liberty interest in the relationship with their foster children, the New York state and city hearing procedures adequately protect the parents' due process rights. The Court reasons that the foster parent-child relationship, although it may fulfill psychological needs, has its origins in state law and contract. Further, to recognize a liberty interest in the foster family would infringe upon the liberty interest of those biological parents whose children have been placed in foster care. *Smith v. Organization of Foster Families For Equality and Reform* (OFFER), 431 U.S. 816 (1977).

A few state courts have found that foster parents have a legally protected liberty interest in certain contexts. *See, e.g., Division of Family Serv. v. Harrison*, 741 A.2d 1016 (Del. 1999) (holding that foster parents have standing to petition for guardianship); *Rodriguez v. McLoughlin*, 20 F. Supp.2d 597 (S.D.N.Y. 1998) (holding that a pre-adoptive foster parent has a protected liberty interest in the foster parent-child relationship).

3. **Alternatives to foster care:** A juvenile court may order, as an alternative to foster care, that a child be returned to the custody of the parent if the parent meets various conditions. Some of these conditions (regarding, for example, limitations on reproductive rights or employment) are of questionable constitutionality.

   Example: Jane, a 19-year-old high school dropout, loses custody of her one-year-old son Randy when he is adjudicated neglected. Jane works as a masseuse, giving and receiving massages and masturbating customers. As a result of Jane's substance abuse and employment, Randy is poorly fed, clothed, and supervised. The court directs that DSS retain custody until Jane presents evidence of her fitness. The court requires Jane to obtain psychiatric and group counseling, find a suitable apartment and a competent babysitter, not reside with a male companion who treats Randy badly, and not work as a masseuse. Jane challenges the condition on her employment, arguing that her employment is lawful and does not affect Randy's best interests. On appeal, the court determines that the trial court properly determined that her employment adversely affected the child's health and welfare by having a detrimental effect on her capacity and willingness to provide the child with proper care. The court did not abuse its discretion in requiring that she leave her employment before she could regain custody. *In re Rice*, 236 N.W.2d 40 (Iowa 1975).

C. Sanctions for the state's failure to protect

1. **Duty regarding children not yet removed from the home:** The United States Supreme Court ruled that the state does not owe a duty, based on the Due Process Clause, for failure to protect a child from abuse unless the state has taken the child into protective custody (the "special relationship doctrine") or has created the harm ("the danger creation theory").

   Example: When Joshua is two, his stepmother files a police report that Joshua has been abused by his father. The Department of Social Services investigates but drops the case when the father denies the charges. A physician later notifies DSS of possible abuse. DSS determines there is insufficient evidence of abuse and enters into a voluntary agreement with the father to obtain counseling. After more reports of abuse, a caseworker makes monthly visits. She notes numerous injuries but never removes Joshua from the home. Emergency room personnel again notify DSS of possible abuse. On two visits, the caseworker is told that the child is too ill to see her, but she still takes no action. The father beats four-year-old Joshua so severely that he suffers severe brain damage. Joshua and his mother bring a §1983 action alleging that DSS deprived Joshua of his liberty without due process by failing to protect him from abuse. The United States Supreme Court rules that the state's failure to provide protective services does not constitute a violation of due process unless the state has asserted a *custodial relationship* over the person or *has created the harm.* The Court reasons that the Due Process Clause protects people from the state, not from injuries by private parties. Further, the Court rejects the claim that the state has a duty to protect Joshua arising out of the "special relationship" doctrine. That is, petitioners argue that the state acquires an affirmative duty by undertaking to protect Joshua by the agency's ongoing investigation. Rejecting this argument, the Court reasons that only when the state takes a person into custody and holds him against his will, does the state assume responsibility for a person's well-being. Because no custodial relationship existed, the state owes Joshua no duty. *DeShaney v. Winnebago County Dept. of Social Servs.*, 489 U.S. 189 (1989).

Note: The case left unresolved the question whether the state has a duty to protect children from abuse while they are in foster care. Following *DeShaney*, courts have split on the issue. *Compare T.M. v. Carson*, 93 F. Supp.2d 1179 (D. Wyo. 2000), *with Whitley v. New Mexico Children, Youth & Families Dept.*, 184 F. Supp.2d 1146 (D. N.M. 2001).

Commentators have been especially critical of *DeShaney*'s apparent indifference to the plight of abused children. The countervailing policy argument is that it is inappropriate to expand the liability of social workers who are overworked and underpaid.

2. Duty regarding children placed in foster care

a. Adoption Assistance and Child Welfare Act: Federal legislation (as well as state statutes) delineates the state's responsibilities to children in foster care. In 1980, Congress effectuated major reform with the enactment of the Adoption Assistance and Child Welfare Act (AACWA), 42 U.S.C. §§620-628, 670-679(a) (2006).

The Act provides federal matching funds to states for foster care and adoptive services if states adopt certain standards including:

- the formulation of case plans (*permanency planning*) that are designed to achieve placement in the least possible restrictive setting,
- the conduct of periodic *case reviews*, and
- the state must make *reasonable efforts* to prevent removal of children from the home and to reunify the family following removal.

Congress enacted the AACWA to redress the limbo of foster care by preventing the need for children's removal from the home and facilitating the return of children to their families or placing them for adoption.

b. Adoption and Safe Families Act: In 1997 Congress enacted the Adoption and Safe Families Act (ASFA), 42 U.S.C. §675(5) (2006), to strengthen the requirements of the AACWA. The Act aims to reduce the amount of time that children spend in foster care and to facilitate adoption. The Act does the following:

- *eliminates the "reasonable efforts" requirement* in the AACWA for *aggravated circumstances* (the most severe cases) and if a *parent's rights to a sibling* previously have been terminated;
- requires states to seek termination of parental rights for children who have been in *foster care for 15 of the last 22 months*; and
- *shortens the period triggering permanency hearings* to no later than 12 months after the

child's entry into foster care. Virtually all states have enacted legislation based on ASFA requiring state agencies to make reasonable efforts to preserve or reunify families. Some states have enacted other ASFA provisions as well.

c. **Lawsuits securing compliance with the AACWA:** State compliance with the AACWA varies considerably. Until 1992, several class action lawsuits brought by foster children against state and local agencies were successful in securing foster care reform alleging violations of the AACWA.

Example: Plaintiffs bring a class action on behalf of children in foster care (under the supervision of the District of Columbia DSS) and children who are known to DSS because of reported abuse or neglect. The suit alleges that the District's practices in administering the foster care system violate Plaintiffs' constitutional rights (liberty interest) and federal law (the Adoption Assistance and Child Welfare Act and the Child Abuse Prevention and Treatment Act (CAPTA)) as well as D.C. statutes. Federal and D.C. statutes regulate the investigation of reports of child abuse and the provision of services to children and the parents during foster care. The district court holds Defendants liable for shortcomings in the administration of the child welfare system that deprive foster children of their constitutionally protected liberty interests in violation of §1983. The district court also determines that Defendants violated the AACWA and CAPTA. In particular, the court finds that the District of Columbia failed to (1) initiate and complete investigations promptly, (2) provide services or use "reasonable efforts" to prevent placement in foster care, (3) comply with statutory time limits for voluntary and emergency care, (4) assign appropriate goals to foster placements, (5) prepare written case plans to enable children to realize objectives, (6) provide services to children in foster care, (7) comply with federal and local requirements regarding judicial and administrative review, (8) expedite the progression of children toward permanent placement through adoption, and (9) monitor foster homes and institutions in accordance with local requirements. Distinguishing *DeShaney* by noting that the foster children in *LaShawn* were already in the state's custody, the court concludes that the above-mentioned shortcomings resulted in serious harm to children. *LaShawn A. v. Dixon*, 762 F. Supp. 959 (D.D.C. 1991). (For the epilogue, see "Effect of *Suter*," Section IV.C.4, *infra*.)

d. **Constitutionality of mandatory termination provisions of ASFA:** Several states enacted laws modeled on ASFA mandating termination of parental rights when a child has been in foster care for 15 of the past 22 months. One court invalidated a state presumption that the child's 15-month duration in foster care constituted evidence of parental unfitness. *See In re H.G.*, 757 N.E.2d 864 (Ill. 2001) (holding that the presumption was an unconstitutional violation of parents' liberty interest in the parent-child relationship).

3. ***Suter v. Artist M.*: The end to private enforcement of the AACWA:** The federal courts' willingness to recognize a private right of enforcement of the statutory provisions of the AACWA ended abruptly with the United States Supreme Court's decision in *Suter v. Artist M.*, 503 U.S. 347 (1992). *Suter* halted a promising vehicle for foster care reform.

Example: Children who are beneficiaries of the AACWA file a class action seeking declaratory and injunctive relief under the AACWA. They allege that state social service personnel failed to comply with statutory requirements to make reasonable efforts to prevent removal of children from their homes and to facilitate reunifying children with their families (by, among other acts, failing to assign social workers promptly). The federal court of appeals holds that Plaintiffs can sue to enforce the AACWA and can bring a §1983 action. Reversing, the United States Supreme Court holds that private individuals do not have the right under the AACWA to sue in federal court to enforce state plans under the AACWA. The Court reasons that the "reasonable efforts" language was not intended by Congress to create a private right of action under §1983. *Suter, supra.*

4. **Effect of *Suter:*** Litigants continue to attempt to reform state child protective services. However, to avoid dismissal under *Suter*, litigants can no longer rely on claims under the AACWA but must utilize other constitutional, federal, or state causes of action. *See, e.g., LaShawn v. Barry*, 87 F.3d 1389 (D.C. Cir. 1996) (alleging violations of the Constitution, Child Abuse Prevention and Treatment Act, and local child abuse laws).

D. Permanent dispositions: Termination of parental rights

1. **Termination standard:** The state may terminate the parent-child relationship only when the child is subjected to *real physical or emotional harm* and *less drastic measures are unavailing*. *Roe v. Conn*, 417 F. Supp. 769, 799 (M.D. Ala. 1976).

2. **Standard of proof:** The Supreme Court holds that due process requires that the standard of proof for termination of parental rights proceedings must be, at a minimum, *clear and convincing evidence*.

   Example: Annie and John are the parents of two children. Following reports of neglect, DSS removes one child from the home and, later, removes the other child. When Annie gives birth to a third child, that infant is also removed from the home. Approximately four years later, DSS petitions the family court to terminate the couple's parental rights. The parents challenge the constitutionality of the statutory "fair preponderance of the evidence" standard. The United States Supreme Court holds that the "preponderance of the evidence" standard violates due process in parental rights termination proceedings. Applying the *Mathews v. Eldridge* test (424 U.S. 319, 335 (1976)), the Court reasons that the private interest of the parents in the custody of their children is significant, the risk of error from using the lower preponderance standard is substantial, and the countervailing governmental interest favoring the preponderance standard is slight (i.e., a stricter standard of proof is consistent with the state's interest in child welfare and fiscal burdens). *Santosky v. Kramer*, 455 U.S. 745 (1982).

3. **Constitutionality:** The constitutionality of termination of parental rights statutes has been challenged on grounds of vagueness. Statutory reforms resulted in more precise definitions of acts constituting the requisite level of parental unfitness that is sufficient to lead to the extinguishment of parental rights.

4. **Right to counsel**

   a. **Parent's right to counsel not constitutionally required:** The United States Supreme Court holds that the Due Process Clause does not require that an indigent be afforded counsel prior to the termination of her parental rights.

      Example: William is adjudicated neglected because of a lack of medical care. The court transfers his custody from his mother to the Department of Social Services (DSS). When the mother subsequently is convicted of murder and sentenced to 25 to 40 years in prison, DSS petitions to terminate the mother's parental rights because she has not made any contact with him while he was in foster care. The mother (brought from prison) attends the hearing without the assistance of counsel. The judge asks William's mother whether she should find legal assistance. She fails to assert that she is indigent. The judge does not appoint counsel, reasoning that the mother had ample time to obtain counsel and failed to do so without just cause. During the hearing, the mother calls witnesses, conducts cross-examination of DSS's witnesses, and testifies in her own behalf. The court terminates the mother's parental rights. The mother appeals, arguing that she is indigent and the Due Process Clause entitles her to the assistance of counsel. The United States Supreme Court holds that due process does not require the appointment of counsel in every proceeding to terminate parental rights. The Court balances the private interests at stake, the government's interest (in child welfare and in making a determination as economically as possible), and the risk that the procedures utilized will lead to erroneous decisions. The Court concludes that the trial court did not err in failing to appoint counsel. The weight of the evidence was sufficiently overwhelming that the presence of counsel would not have made a significant difference. *Lassiter v. Dept. of Soc. Servs.*, 452 U.S. 18 (1991).

Note: The case has been criticized for failing to give appropriate weight to the importance of the parent-child bond. Although the Court is not explicit about its reasoning, the Court's failure to recognize a right to counsel in termination proceedings probably stems from fiscal concerns.

b. **Modern view:** Despite the Supreme Court's ruling in *Lassiter*, many jurisdictions hold that an indigent parent has a right to counsel in cases involving termination of parental rights as well as in child abuse, neglect, and dependency proceedings generally.

c. **Child's right to counsel distinguished:** The child has a right to counsel distinct from the parent's right to counsel. Federal legislation spurred the adoption of guardian ad litem (GAL) programs in many states to represent children in child abuse and neglect proceedings. The Child Abuse Prevention and Treatment Act of 1974, 42 U.S.C. §5106a(b)(6) (2006), requires that for states to qualify for federal funds, a guardian ad litem shall be appointed to represent the child "in every case involving an abused or neglected child which results in a judicial proceeding." However, the Act does not require that the GAL be an attorney.

The Uniform Representation of Children in Abuse and Neglect and Custody Proceedings Act (approved by NCCUSL in 2006) addresses representation of children in a variety of legal proceedings (including custody, abuse, neglect, dependency, and termination of parental rights, but not delinquency) by clarifying the roles and responsibilities of children's representatives and by providing guidelines to courts in appointing representatives. It addresses the ethical dimensions of the lawyer-client relationship, discretionary versus mandatory appointment, qualifications and duties of the child's representative, the duration of the appointment, access to the child and to information relating to the child, and the child's claim for damages against the representative. It differentiates between the "child's attorney" (who advocates the child's wishes) and the "best-interests attorney" (who advocates the child's best interests based on an assessment of the evidence and applicable law but is not bound by the child's expressed wishes). It does not recognize the role of the attorney guardian ad litem.

5. **State's failure to provide services as a defense:** Before termination of parental rights, federal legislation (AACWA) mandates that the state make "reasonable efforts" to prevent removal of children from the home and to reunify the family. The AACWA triggered widespread adoption

of similar requirements on the state level. Therefore, a state's failure to provide these mandated support services may constitute a defense to a parent in a termination of parental rights proceeding.

Example: Michelle is a mentally disabled mother of a special needs child. Michelle has low intelligence, manifests psychological problems, and has experienced a history of abusive relationships. Despite her difficulties, Michelle expresses a determination to learn how to be a good parent and undertakes efforts to improve her life and parenting abilities. When her daughter is eight months old, the Department of Social Services files a petition to terminate Michelle's parental rights based on their belief that she was incapable of parenting a special needs child. The court rules that termination of parental rights was improper because the Social Services Department failed to provide any assistance (i.e., educational programs and counseling) to the mother to help her develop the necessary skills to care for her special needs child and where the mother had a clear commitment to be a good parent. *State ex rel. Children's Servs. Division v. Brady*, 899 P.2d 691 (Or. Ct. App. 1995).

6. **Indigent parent's right to record preparation fees:** The United States Supreme Court holds that an indigent parent has the right to record preparation fees in a proceeding for termination of parental rights.

Example: A court terminates M.L.B.'s parental rights to her two children. Because M.L.B. is unable to pay $2,352 for prepayment of record preparation fees (transcripts, binding, mailing, etc.), she is unable to appeal. She challenges the record-preparation prepayment-fee requirement as a violation of her rights to due process and equal protection. The United States Supreme Court holds that the state may not deny appellate review because of a parent's poverty. In balancing the individual versus state interests, the Court concludes that the stakes for the mother are substantial (destruction of the parent-child bond) whereas the countervailing government interest (financial) is small. *M.L.B. v. S.L.J.*, 519 U.S. 102 (1996).

Quiz Yourself on INTERVENTION

100. Carol Cotton is the single mother of Elvira. When four-year-old Elvira steals a neighbor's bicycle, Carol punishes Elvira by making her sit in the front yard for a week wearing a wooden plaque around her neck saying "Thief." Elvira's preschool teacher is horrified when she learns of the punishment. The teacher reports Carol to the child welfare authorities for endangering Elvira's emotional welfare. Sally Social Worker is assigned to the case and requests a family court judge to issue a summary detention order in order for Sally to investigate the allegations of emotional abuse further. The judge issues the order and Elvira is picked up by the police and taken to a detention center. Carol challenges the summary detention order. Will she be successful? ____________________

101. Mandy, a state protective service worker, visits the Smiths' home following an adjudication of the children as neglected. Mrs. Smith has a habit of leaving her small children alone at night, while she is socializing with friends. She also fails to shop for groceries and to feed the children regularly. The court orders Mandy to give the mother training in homemaking services. Mandy visits the Smiths' home only once because Mrs. Smith is not receptive to Mandy's suggestions. Following numerous additional complaints of neglect and without evidence of any improvement, the Department of Social Services (DSS) initiates a petition for termination of parental rights. Will DSS prevail? ____________________

102. Three-year-old Jimmy is removed from the custody of his mother Mary because of her substance abuse. The court awards physical custody of Jimmy to his father. After reports that Jimmy is being abused by his father, the state takes temporary custody again; however, the state fails to file an abuse petition and returns Jimmy to his father's custody. Except for this brief period of state temporary custody, Jimmy remains in his father's legal and physical custody until his father causes Jimmy's death by pouring boiling water on him. Jimmy's estate files a civil rights action under a §1983 claim, alleging that the state deprived Jimmy of his substantive due process right by removing him from his mother's custody and allowing his father to obtain custody. Will Jimmy's estate prevail?

____

Answers

100. Yes. Carol may claim that the summary seizure violates her right to due process. States authorize summary seizure of abused or neglected children, i.e., the temporary removal of a child from the home, in emergency situations. However, absent an emergency, the state must provide notice to the parents and child of the evidence and an opportunity for rebuttal (*Roe v. Conn*). Because no emergency exists here (i.e., the situation presents no danger to Elvira of serious immediate or threatened harm), the state's interest in child protection is not sufficient to justify summary removal of Elvira from the home.

101. Yes. Mrs. Smith would argue that the termination was not justified. The state may terminate the parent-child relationship when the child is subjected to real physical and emotion harm and less drastic measures are unavailing (*Roe v. Conn*). The state would argue that Mrs. Smith's neglect of her children's needs and welfare (leaving them alone at night and failing to feed them regularly) amounts to serious harm and, in addition, that measures to remedy the situation were unsuccessful. Mrs. Smith would counter that the state failed to provide homemaker services. However, her argument will not be successful because, here, the state's failure to provide services resulted from Mrs. Smith's refusal to accept those services.

102. Probably yes. The United States Supreme Court has ruled that the state does not owe a duty, based on the Due Process Clause, for failure to protect a child from abuse. Two exceptions to this doctrine are the special relationship exception (i.e., if the state has taken the child into protective custody) and the danger creation theory (i.e., if the state has created the harm). The special relationship exception does not apply to Jimmy's case because, although the state previously assumed custody of Jimmy, the state had relinquished all right to assert authority over Jimmy at the time of the abuse. However, under the danger creation exception, the state is liable if it has created the danger of maltreatment by a private person, or has rendered a person more vulnerable to such conduct. Under the latter theory, liability would attach if the state caseworkers knowingly placed Jimmy with a dangerous father (with knowledge of the father's propensity toward abuse) after removal of Jimmy from the mother's care. The state had a duty not to consign Jimmy to another dangerous home situation. The case is not necessarily precluded by *DeShaney* because Jimmy was removed from one custody situation and placed with his father by the state (whereas Joshua DeShaney, at the time of his death, was in the same home situation as before the state acted).

Exam Tips on CHILD ABUSE AND NEGLECT

Threshold Standard for Intervention

- Child abuse forms the basis for state intervention into the family and results in considerable limitations on parental autonomy. Threshold issues involve constitutional issues of ***family privacy*** — does the state have a right to intervene in the parent-child relationship? The answer is clear based on the trilogy of Supreme Court cases standing for the proposition that, although parents have the right to the care, custody, and control of their children (*Meyer v. Nebraska, Pierce v. Society of Sisters*), the state may intervene to protect the child's welfare (*Prince v. Massachusetts*).

  - To intervene in the family, the state must prove that a child falls within the ***statutory definition*** of an abused, neglected, or dependent child. Therefore, a given statute must be applied to the specific facts. After determining the ***type of abuse*** (physical, sexual, emotional, potential, etc.), apply the statutory definition. Point out that statutes have been challenged (often unsuccessfully) on constitutional grounds of ***vagueness***. Apply any relevant ***model legislation*** (e.g., Restatement of Torts or Model Penal Code). Make sure that you identify the abuser (i.e., specify whether a family member or some other party).

  - Be sure to note that governmental intervention in abuse and neglect cases takes the form of ***civil and/or criminal proceedings***. Identify whether civil and/or criminal liability is at issue. Note that the involvement of a family member is more likely to evoke both civil (i.e., dependency) and criminal proceedings. Recall the differences between civil and criminal proceedings, i.e., civil proceedings involve deprivations (temporary, permanent) of the child's custody; criminal proceedings result in the application of criminal sanctions to an offender.

  - If the parent (or a person in loco parentis) was the abuser, be sure to discuss and apply the ***common-law privilege to discipline***. The privilege is subject to limitations regarding the amount and type of force that may be used. Here, statutory formulations (Restatement of Torts, Model Penal Code) may be relevant. If a person other than a parent is the abuser, recall that the privilege to discipline may be delegable in some cases (e.g., to a teacher). Explore whether any religious or cultural practices may dictate the parent's choice of discipline and whether the parent is attempting to raise the "cultural defense" (a claim which is generally not successful).

  - If the abuse involves ***prenatal*** acts (substance abuse), be sure to note that courts are divided about the imposition of criminal and civil liability on substance abusers for inflicting prenatal harm to their children. If the acts involve ***medical neglect***, explore whether the parents may resort to a religious justification defense. Some state child abuse statutes exempt those who practice faith healing from liability, although defenses based on the First Amendment are generally not successful.

Procedure

- Commonly tested procedural issues involve ***reporting laws***, ***evidentiary issues*** (competency of child witnesses, admissibility of syndrome evidence), ***statutes of limitations***, and the Sixth Amendment ***right to confrontation***. Remember that reporting statutes may evoke both civil and criminal sanctions. If civil liability is an issue, determine whether the statute confers ***immunity*** on reporters for false reports. If the issue is ***competency*** of child witnesses, remember to mention the different ***federal and state standards***. Remember that most courts hold inadmissible evidence of child sexual abuse accommodation syndrome. Statutes of limitations may bar introduction of evidence of abuse in tort claims, for example, unless jurisdictions have adopted delayed discovery rules.

- If the abuse involves a criminal proceeding, the situation may involve the defendant's Sixth Amendment ***right to confrontation***, especially if the problem addresses a ***special testimonial procedure*** or the ***admissibility of hearsay evidence***. Explain that the United States Supreme Court previously addressed the constitutionality of two special testimonial procedures in sexual child abuse cases (holding that closed circuit television does not violate the defendant's Sixth Amendment right whereas testimony behind a screen does). A question may also involve the admissibility of hearsay (i.e., a declarant's testimony regarding a previous out-of-court statement offered to prove the truth of the matter asserted). Point out that the Court's decision in *Crawford* has implications for sexual abuse prosecutions by limiting admissibility (as hearsay) of social workers' testimony regarding interviews with child victims (a procedure that is authorized by some states' tender years exemption statutes) unless the defendant had the opportunity for prior cross-examination. If the question raises issues of hearsay, determine also if any ***exceptions to the hearsay rule*** apply (e.g., spontaneous declarations or statements for purposes of medical diagnosis and treatment).

Intervention

- Identify the ***type of intervention*** the state is seeking: summary seizure (emergency jurisdiction), temporary custody, permanent custody, termination of parental rights. Recall the different possible ***standards for intervention:*** for ***summary seizure*** and assertions of temporary custody, courts require that the child be subject to immediate or threatened harm. Was the harm immediate? Was it merely threatened? For ***termination of parental rights***, courts require that the child must be subject to serious physical or emotional harm and less drastic measures would be unavailing. Be sure to analyze both prongs of this test for termination purposes. Was the harm sufficiently serious? Were less drastic measures attempted and with what result?

- If the problem raises the issue of ***foster care***, determine if foster ***parents' rights*** are implicated. If so, foster parents may have an argument that the infringement of their rights involves a constitutionally protected liberty interest in their relationships with their foster children. Discuss the issue under federal (*Smith v. OFFER*) and state law. Discuss also whether the state owes a duty to the child for ***failure to protect*** a child from abuse (*DeShaney v. Winnebago*). Note that the general rule of no-duty has two exceptions: the special relationship exception and the creation of danger doctrine. Discuss and apply both exceptions.

☛ Determine if any ***federal legislation*** is relevant to the problem. Discuss the requirements of the Adoption Assistance and Child Welfare Act (AACWA) and the Adoption and Safe Families Act (ASFA). Remember that the objective of both pieces of legislation is to reduce the amount of time that children spend in foster care and to facilitate adoption. A frequently tested issue is the ***reasonable efforts requirement*** in AACWA. Did the state make "reasonable efforts" to prevent removal of the home and to reunify the family following removal (under AACWA)? Did the ASFA eliminate the reasonable efforts requirement in the given case?

☛ If the problem involves termination of parental rights, be sure to explore possible ***constitutional issues*** (e.g., right to counsel, standard of proof, family privacy, vagueness). Determine if the state met the requisite ***standard for termination***.

CHAPTER 10

THE PARENT-CHILD-STATE RELATIONSHIP IN SPECIAL CONTEXTS

ChapterScope

This chapter explores the parent-child-state relationship in special contexts (tort, contract, property, education, and medical care). Here are a few of the key principles covered in this chapter:

- At common law, ***parents*** were ***not liable*** for their children's torts.
- Although ***children are liable*** for their torts, they are subject to a ***different standard of care*** than adults.
- At common law, the contracts of a minor are ***voidable***. If a party tried to enforce a contract against the minor, the minor could ***disaffirm*** the contract (i.e., assert a ***defense of infancy***).
- A parent had a common-law right to a child's ***services and earnings***.
- A child may inherit ***property***, although the court may appoint a guardian to manage that property.
- The ***emancipation doctrine*** permits a child the right to dispose of his or her own earnings.
- The United States Supreme Court has extended significantly the contours of the constitutional ***right of family privacy*** first mentioned in the context of education.
- School students do not possess the same ***First Amendment rights*** as adults.
- School students do not possess the same ***Fourth Amendment rights*** as adults. They may be subject to ***random drug testing*** and searches based on ***reasonable suspicion*** rather than probable cause.
- At common law, only a parent could ***consent to medical treatment*** for a child. Today, some statutes provide that an unemancipated minor may consent to medical treatment.

I. TORTS

A. Children's liability: Traditional rule: Children are liable for their torts—both intentional and negligent torts. At common law, parents were not liable for their children's torts.

1. **Standard of care:** Although children are liable for their torts, they are subject to a different standard of care than for adults. The traditional rule takes into account the minor's *age and experience*. *See, e.g.,* Restatement (Second) Torts §283A (the child's standard of conduct is that of "a reasonable person of like age, intelligence and experience under like circumstances").

2. **Contributory negligence:** Contributory negligence by the plaintiff is normally a bar to recovery despite the defendant's negligence. Jurisdictions adopt different approaches when the contributorily negligent plaintiff is a child.

a. **Majority rule:** The majority rule (sometimes called the "Massachusetts Rule") adopts an age-based standard of care for a child's contributory negligence. Similar to the Restatement Rule on negligence, a child's capacity to be contributorily negligent depends on age, intelligence, and experience in comparison with other children in similar circumstances.

b. **Minority rule:** A minority of jurisdictions adopt a presumption based on age, holding that children below a certain age (e.g., age seven) cannot be held contributorily negligent.

Example: Parents of a 13-year-old boy (Kodi) bring a wrongful-death suit against the school. During basketball practice, Kodi blacks out. His mother later instructs the coach that Kodi should not participate in running or strenuous activity, but that he can "walk through plays." Two days later during practice, the coach requires the players to perform a running drill. During the drill, Kodi collapses and dies. The school district argues that Kodi's own negligence (in running when he had been told not to do so) contributed to his death. Affirming the trial court judgment for the parents, the state supreme court holds that Indiana law recognizes a rebuttable presumption that children between the ages of 7 and 14 are incapable of contributory negligence. *Clay City Consolidated School Corp. v. Timberman*, 918 N.E.2d 292 (Ind. 2009).

B. **Exception to rule of liability: Children's conduct of adult activities:** The modern view abrogates an age-based standard of care when a minor is performing an adult activity (driving a motor vehicle, boat, etc.). In such cases, the adult "reasonable person" standard is applicable.

C. **Parents' liability for children's torts:** Although parents were not vicariously liable at common law for the negligent or intentional torts of their children, they may be liable today for their children's torts by statute. Other exceptions to the general rule include situations in which: (1) a parent is employing his or her child, (2) a parent permits a child to use a dangerous instrumentality (negligent entrustment), or (3) a parent has knowledge of the child's similar acts or disposition and fails to warn a third party.

Example: Christopher P., a 13-year-old boy, shoots his paintball gun from the roof of his garage at a neighbor child, Danielle, while she is in his driveway. A paintball strikes her in the left eye causing injury. Christopher's parents knew that he had a paintball gun and permitted its use. Danielle's parents bring a personal injury action against Christopher's parents. The trial court holds that Christopher's parents are liable for Danielle's injuries under the doctrine of negligent entrustment. The court reasons that a parent owes a duty to protect third parties from harm that is clearly foreseeable from a child's improvident use of a dangerous instrument when the parents are aware of its use. Here the parents knew their son was using a paintball gun which was an illegal act under N.Y. Penal Law (possessing an air gun while being under age 16) and assisted the illegal activity by enabling him to purchase ammunition. *Danielle A. v. Christopher P.*, 776 N.Y.S.2d 446 (Sup. Ct. 2004).

In addition, some jurisdictions have statutes making parents legally responsible for their children's torts, injury to persons, vandalism, or damage to property.

Quiz Yourself on TORTS

103. Andy is the eight-year-old son of divorced parents. Andy has attention-deficit hyperactivity disorder (ADHD) (i.e., he has difficulty sitting still, listening, and paying attention). One day, while playing with a lighter, he starts a fire at his maternal grandfather's house. The garage sustains major property damage. Andy's custodial father was not present at the time of the incident. The maternal grandfather and the grandfather's insurance company file a complaint against Andy's father for negligence. Will Andy's father be liable for property damage caused by Andy? ____________________

104. Same basic facts as above. Andy's grandfather's insurance company now files a complaint against *Andy* for negligence. Will Andy be liable? ____________________

105. Jeannette and her husband Pearce are fishing from their boat on a Minnesota lake. Sam, a 12-year-old boy, is operating a boat with an outboard motor. Because of Sam's inexperience, he crosses too closely behind Jeannette and Pearce's boat. Jeannette feels a jerk on her fishing line. The reel hits the side of the boat, breaks, and a fragment flies into Jeannette's eye. She sues, asserting that Sam was negligent. The trial judge instructs the jury to modify the traditional standard of negligence to take into account Sam's age, intelligence, and experience under the circumstances. Jeannette appeals a jury verdict for the defendant, arguing that the trial court erred in its instruction. Will she prevail? ____________________

Answers

103. No. At common law, parents were not liable for the torts of their child. Parental liability arises, however, if the child's injury is the foreseeable consequence of the parent's negligent act. Because it was not foreseeable that Andy would cause a fire by playing with a lighter (this was the first instance in which his acts caused a fire), the child's father did not owe a duty to the grandfather and his insurer on the claim of negligent parental supervision.

104. No. Children have limited liability for acts of negligence. The traditional rule takes into account the minor's age, intelligence, and experience. Andy, an eight-year-old child who has ADHD, cannot be held to the same standard of care as an average eight-year-old child. The insurance company will not prevail in imputing liability to Andy for negligence in starting the fire at his grandfather's house.

105. Yes. Children have limited liability for acts of negligence. The traditional rule, and that followed by the Restatement (Second) of Torts, dictates that the minor's age and experience should be taken into account in applying the relevant standard of care. Applying this rule might well lead the court to absolve Sam of liability based on the minor's status as a novice. However, the modern view abrogates an age-based standard of care where a minor is performing an adult activity. Because Sam was engaged in an adult activity (driving a motorboat), he should be held to the adult standard of care. His activities exposed others to significant hazard.

II. CONTRACTS

A. **Common-law rule:** At common law, the contracts of a minor are ***voidable***. That is, the minor could enforce his or her contracts against another party. However, if another party attempted to enforce the contract against the minor, the minor could ***disaffirm*** the contract, i.e., assert a ***defense of infancy***. Disaffirmance could occur at any time during minority or even within a reasonable time after the minor reached majority.

B. **Majority rule:** Most jurisdictions still follow the common-law rule permitting minors to disaffirm their contracts.

C. **Policy:** The policy behind permitting minors to disaffirm contracts is to protect minors from overreaching by adults and from their own immaturity.

D. **Modern view:** Some courts and legislatures change the common-law rule in limited situations such as the entertainment industry.

Example: Brooke Shields, a well-known actress, is hired as a ten-year-old model. She is required to pose nude in a bathtub for *Playboy* magazine. The photographs are intended for use in that particular publication. Subsequently, when the plaintiff reaches majority, she learns that several photos appeared in another magazine. She commences an action in contract and tort to prevent the defendant's further use of the photos. A New York statute confers upon a minor's parent or guardian the right to make binding contracts for the minor. The court holds that Ms. Shields may not disaffirm the contract executed by her mother. The court reasons that, although at common law a minor could disaffirm his or her written consent or a contract executed by another on his or her behalf, the state legislature has abrogated the minor's common-law right to disaffirm. The statute is intended to bring certainty to an important industry that employs minors. The dissent argues that the state's interest in child protection should prevail over concerns for commercialism. *Shields v. Gross*, 448 N.E.2d 108 (N.Y. Ct. App. 1983).

Quiz Yourself on CONTRACTS

106. Stephen Barry leaves royal service after serving as Prince Charles's valet for 12 years. Barry desires to publish a book about his experiences with the royal family. He accepts a lucrative book contract even though he signed a pledge of confidentiality at the time he began employment at age 17. When the royal family sues him for breach of contract, he claims that his contract with the royal family is not binding. Will he prevail? ____________________

Answer

106. Yes. At common law, a minor could enforce his or her contracts against another party. However, the minor could disaffirm the contract, i.e., assert a defense of infancy, if the minor was sued by the third party. Because Stephen Barry executed his contract of royal service while he was still a minor (age 17), he should be able to disaffirm the contract.

III. PROPERTY

A. Earnings

1. **Common-law rule:** A parent had a common-law right to a child's services and earnings. Many modern statutes incorporate this common-law rule.

   Example: A creditor obtains a judgment against Claude Kreigh, the father of three daughters. The sheriff seizes and sells 15 sheep in partial satisfaction of the judgment. Before the sale, the plaintiffs/daughters contend that some of the sheep constitute their property (i.e., lambs that were fed and raised by them or, perhaps, even the lambs of those lambs). The plaintiffs sue for conversion. The creditor appeals a judgment for the plaintiffs. Affirming, the court reasons that, according to the common-law rule (announced by Blackstone), only the child's labor or services belong to the parent. Any other property belongs to the child. Thus, the execution of the judgment levied on the sheep did not affect the children's title to the sheep. *Kreigh v. Cogswell*, 21 P.2d 831 (Wyo. 1933).

2. **Emancipation:** ***Emancipation*** is the child's release from parental control. The doctrine permits a child to acquire the right to dispose of his or her own earnings. Emancipation may occur in cases of parental consent, abandonment, the minor's marriage, or service in the armed forces. (For further discussion of emancipation, see *infra*.)

B. Inheritance

1. **Traditional rule:** A child may inherit property (e.g., stocks, bonds, cash, real estate). At common law, if a child inherited property or was given property that required active management, a court appointed a "guardian of the child's estate." Today, many states follow the same rule.

2. **Guardianship and inheritance**

   a. **Definition:** A guardian may be of two types: "a guardian of the person" (who is charged with personal decision making) or "a guardian of the estate or property" (who is charged with asset management). In the event that a child inherits property (e.g., from a grandparent), a court may appoint one of the child's parents as the guardian of the child's estate.

   b. **Problems with guardianship:** Guardianships have several problems. First, a guardianship is expensive to administer because judicial supervision and approval is required for acts of the guardian. Expenses include: court costs, attorneys' fees, the posting of a bond, and annual accountings. Second, the powers of a guardian (e.g., of investment) are limited.

Third, guardianship terminates at the age of majority (typically age 18) which may result in the release of considerable property to an inexperienced youth.

3. Inheritance rights of nonmarital children

a. Traditional rule: Traditionally, both legitimate and illegitimate (nonmarital) children could inherit by intestate succession from their mother. (Intestate succession occurs when a decedent dies without a valid will.) However, only legitimate children could inherit from their father by intestate succession.

b. Modern trend: The modern trend minimizes differences in the treatment of nonmarital versus marital children for succession purposes. The United States Supreme Court liberalized the traditional rule in certain situations.

Example: Gordon dies intestate at age 28 as the result of a homicide. He leaves surviving a nonmarital child, Deta Mona Trimble. Prior to Gordon's death, the child's mother, Jessie Trimble, prevails in a paternity suit and obtains court-ordered child support. Upon Gordon's death, Trimble petitions to administer his estate and to determine the heirs. The court excludes Deta Mona based on a provision of the Illinois Probate Code that provides that a nonmarital child may inherit from her mother but only from her father if two conditions are met: the parents marry (following her birth) and the father acknowledges the child as his. The mother challenges the constitutionality of the statute as a violation of equal protection. The Illinois Supreme Court upholds the statute. Reversing, the United States Supreme Court holds that the statutory provision violates equal protection. The state asserts two objectives: the promotion of legitimate family relationships and the efficient disposition of property at death. The Court determines that the statute has only the "most attenuated relationship" to the first asserted goal. Also, the Court states that, although the second goal is legitimate, the statute is not reasonably related to that objective. That is, the legislature's chosen means of overcoming the problems posed by proof of paternity do not justify the statute. *Trimble v. Gordon,* 430 U.S. 762, 767 (1977).

Example: Robert is the nonmarital child of Mario. Mario openly acknowledges Robert as his son and provides him with a written acknowledgment of paternity by granting him permission to marry when Robert is underage. When Mario dies, Robert attempts to claim a share of Mario's estate. A New York statute requires a judicial order of filiation (paternity establishment) during the putative father's lifetime before a nonmarital child may inherit intestate from his father. The son challenges the constitutionality of the statute. The United States Supreme Court upholds the statute, finding that, unlike the statute in *Trimble, supra,* the New York statute survives rational basis review. The Court distinguishes *Trimble* on two grounds: (1) New York law does not have as its purpose the encouragement of legitimate family relationships and (2) the New York statute is more limited than the Illinois statute (i.e., the Illinois requirement of marriage, in addition to acknowledgment of paternity, was simply too strict). *Lalli v. Lalli,* 439 U.S. 259 (1978).

Note: The real concern of the United States Supreme Court appears to be the problem of proof of paternity. The Court was satisfied with the proof of paternity in *Trimble* (judicial declaration) but not in *Lalli* (informal written acknowledgment).

c. Uniform Parentage Act: Today, states have expanded the inheritance rights of nonmarital children by statute. Many states have done so by adopting the Uniform Parentage Act (UPA). The UPA developed presumptions for identifying the father of a nonmarital child.

One method is by the father's conduct. Specifically, UPA §4(a)(4) (1973) creates a presumption of paternity if "while the child is under the age of minority," the parent "receives the child into his home and openly holds out the child as his natural child." According to 2002 revisions, the "holding out" period must occur for the first two years of the child's life. UPA §204(a)(5).

4. **Capacity to devise property:** Although English law at one time permitted minors to devise real property, almost all states now define certain ages for testamentary capacity (i.e., the power to devise property). Most states set the age at 18.

5. **Gifts:** Children may receive property as inter vivos gifts. However, case law or statute may require the appointment of a guardian of the estate to manage the assets (see *supra*).

6. **Methods of holding property for a minor:** Although property may be held in a child's name, practical problems arise because adults may be reluctant to do business with minors (recall the disaffirmance power, *supra*). As a result, a minor's property typically is held in the name of a guardian (*supra*), or in a trust, or registered in the name of a custodian under the Uniform Transfers to Minors Act.

   a. **Trusts:** A minor may be the beneficiary of a trust in which property is held in trust for the minor by a trustee. The trustee has a fiduciary responsibility to manage, invest, and spend the proceeds for the minor consistent with the terms of the trust instrument. Although an inter vivos trust, unlike a guardianship, does not necessitate the expense and inconvenience of judicial supervision, a trust may involve attorneys' fees to create it.

   b. **Uniform Transfers to Minors Act:** Virtually all states have some form of the Uniform Transfers to Minors Act (UTMA). These statutory provisions permit certain property to be registered in the name of a *custodian* who has broad powers to manage the property without court supervision. Although not as flexible as a trust, gifts based on UTMA are more easily transferred and the assets more easily administered.

Quiz Yourself on ***PROPERTY***

107. Grandma ("Granny") Smith is delighted when her first grandson Max is born. She wants to welcome Max into the world with a substantial gift of $5,000 in shares of a mutual fund to be used for Max's college education. Granny does not want to subject Max's parents to the problems of court supervision relating to the gift, nor does she want to entail the expense of establishing an inter vivos trust with Max as the beneficiary. How would you advise Granny to proceed? ____________________

Answer

107. Granny should be advised to establish a gift for Max under the Uniform Transfers to Minors Act (UTMA). Granny's jurisdiction, similar to most states, probably has enacted a version of UTMA.

This uniform statute would allow Granny to purchase the shares in the mutual fund and to have those shares registered in the name of a qualified custodian (probably Max's mother or father). The custodian then could hold that property until Max reaches age 18 or 21 (as required by state statute) or could expend the property so long as the consumption is for Max's benefit.

IV. EDUCATION

A. **Parents' right to control the upbringing of their children:** In a trilogy of cases, the United States Supreme Court announces a principle of enormous constitutional significance. Parents have a constitutionally protected right to control the upbringing of their children. These cases arose in the context of parents' right to dictate the form of their children's education.

The cases establish the constitutional underpinnings of a right to family privacy (a private realm in which the family is protected from state intervention). For this reason, the cases (discussed below) constitute the origins of the right to privacy subsequently enunciated by the Supreme Court in *Griswold v. Connecticut, supra.* (See Chapter 8.) Subsequently, the Supreme Court extended significantly (to contraception, abortion, etc.) the contours of the constitutional right of privacy first mentioned in the context of education.

Example: A schoolteacher in Zion Parochial School is tried and convicted of violating a Nebraska law that prohibits the teaching of foreign languages in the schools. The teacher teaches reading to the children in German. The children's parents (members of a German-speaking religious community) strongly desire that their children be educated in German. The state argues that the statute (which was enacted during World War I in response to anti-German sentiment) is intended to promote civic development. The state supreme court affirms the conviction. The United States Supreme Court holds that the statute is unconstitutional because it lacks a rational basis. The Court reasons that, although the object of the legislation is legitimate, the means exceed the proper limitations on the power of the state and conflict with the defendant's Fourteenth Amendment rights to due process (i.e., liberty to engage in his occupation) and the parents' rights to control the education of their children. *Meyer v. Nebraska*, 262 U.S. 390 (1923).

Example: An Oregon statute requires parents and guardians of children between the ages of 8 and 16 to send children to public schools or be subject to criminal liability. Two Oregon private schools (the Society of Sisters and the Hill Military Academy) argue that the statute interferes with their ability to engage in their chosen business and constitutes a deprivation of their property without due process in violation of the Fourteenth Amendment. The trial court holds the statute unconstitutional as a deprivation of the schools' property rights and also an infringement on the parents' constitutionally protected "liberty" to direct the education of their children. The United States Supreme Court affirms. Relying on *Meyer v. Nebraska*, the Court concludes that the statute infringes on the defendants' property rights and unreasonably interferes with the liberty of parents and guardians to direct the upbringing and education of children. *Pierce v. Soc'y of Sisters*, 268 U.S. 510 (1925).

Example: Members of the Amish Mennonite Church challenge the constitutionality of Wisconsin's compulsory attendance law that requires them to send their children to school until age 16. Parents of two Amish children, ages 14 and 15, refuse to send their children to public school any longer. The parents' decision is based on their religious beliefs that school attendance will expose their children to negative influences and threaten the survival of the Amish community, and a desire to educate the children by informal vocational training. The parents argue that the compulsory attendance law violates their First and Fourteenth Amendment rights. The parents are tried and convicted of violating the statute, and appeal. The United States Supreme Court holds the statute unconstitutional under the First and Fourteenth Amendments. The Court reasons that the state interest in preparing citizens for a democratic way of life is not sufficient to override the Amish parents' interests in the free exercise of their religion. The Court finds that the additional two years of schooling required by the statute will not advance appreciably the state's interest. *Wisconsin v. Yoder*, 406 U.S. 205 (1972).

B. Minors' First Amendment rights

1. **Political speech:** In the civil rights era of the 1960s, the United States Supreme Court recognizes that students have a right to freedom of expression in the context of political speech. However, students do not possess the same First Amendment rights as adults. Students' exercise of the right to free speech is subject to limitation based on the possibility of disruption of school authority or invasion of the rights of others.

   Example: Three students (a 15-year-old boy, a 16-year-old boy, and a 13-year-old girl) wear arm bands to their respective schools to publicize their objection to the war in Vietnam. The various schools learn of the plan and adopt a policy that students who refuse to remove arm bands will be suspended until the students agree to return without the arm bands. The youths wear the arm bands and are suspended. They petition for an injunction restraining the school officials from disciplining them. The district court upholds the constitutionality of the action as reasonable to promote school discipline. The Court of Appeal for the Eighth Circuit affirms. The United States Supreme Court reverses. The Court holds that students, like teachers, possess First Amendment rights. ("It can hardly be argued that either students or teachers shed their constitutional rights to freedom of speech or expression at the schoolhouse gate.") However, the state has an interest in proscribing misconduct in the schools. In order to justify the prohibition of a particular expression of opinion, the conduct must *materially and substantially interfere with the requirements of appropriate discipline in the operation of the school or invade the rights of others*. Here, the students' wearing of arm bands neither interrupted school activities nor intruded in school affairs. *Tinker v. Des Moines Indep. Community Sch. Dist.,* 393 U.S. 503, 506 (1969).

2. **Free speech in the context of school-sponsored and school-approved activities:** Following *Tinker*, the Court circumscribes students' rights to freedom of expression in other contexts (i.e., school-sponsored newspapers, school-approved rallies for patriotic purposes).

   Example: High school journalism students desire to publish articles in the school newspaper, *Spectrum*, concerning teen pregnancy and the impact of divorce on children. In accordance with school practice, the journalism teacher submits the issue of the newspaper containing the stories to the school principal for prior approval. The principal censors the articles, believing that the content is inappropriate for younger students. The principal then deletes the pages (not just the articles) on which the articles appear. The students contend that the principal's action violates their First Amendment rights. The United States Supreme Court holds that school officials do not violate students' First Amendment rights when school officials exercise control of the content of student speech in *school-sponsored* activities provided that the school officials' actions are reasonably related to legitimate pedagogical goals. Here, the Court reasons that the principal's decision was reasonable in light of his concerns with the protection of privacy of other students. The Court distinguishes *Tinker*, saying that this case concerns whether the school must affirmatively *promote* student speech (i.e., in school-sponsored activities) whereas *Tinker* concerns whether educators must tolerate student speech.

In a strongly worded dissent, Justice Brennan (joined by Justices Marshall and Blackmun) maintains that the principal violated the students' First Amendment rights. Applying *Tinker*, the dissent reasons that the student expression neither disrupted school work nor invaded the rights of others. *Hazelwood Sch. Dist. v. Kuhlmeier*, 484 U.S. 260 (1988).

Example: Joseph Frederick displays a "BONG HITS 4 JESUS" banner during a corporate-sponsored Olympic torch-passing rally occurring across the street from his high school. The student body, teachers, and administrators are dismissed from school to attend the rally. The school principal confiscates the banner. When Frederick is suspended, he alleges a violation of his First Amendment rights. The Ninth Circuit Court of Appeals reverses the district court's grant of summary judgment for the school, holding that the message was a form of protected speech and that it had not given rise to a substantial risk of disruption of the rally. The United States Supreme Court reverses. Because the message advocated illegal drug use and had been disseminated at school, the Court concludes that the school could stifle the message without violating the First Amendment. The Court went on to say that *Tinker*'s "substantial disruption" formula was not the only basis for regulation but that students' First Amendment rights were limited in light of the school's mission of deterring illegal drugs, and that that was a sufficient basis for finding that there had been no violation of the First Amendment. *Morse v. Frederick,* 551 U.S. 393 (2007).

3. **Schools' ability to punish students for their expressive activity:** The United States Supreme Court also addresses the procedural rights of school students in the context of the First Amendment. The Court holds that schools may discipline students for their expressive activity in certain situations without implicating students' First or Fourteenth Amendment rights.

   Example: At a student assembly, Mathew gives a speech nominating a fellow student for student government. The speech contains no patently offensive language but does refer to the candidate in a sexual metaphor. Following the speech, the assistant principal notifies Mathew that he has violated a school disciplinary rule for disruptive conduct, suspends him for three days, and removes his name from the graduation speaker list. Mathew alleges violations of his First Amendment right to freedom of speech and his Fourteenth Amendment right to procedural due process. The district court agrees that Mathew's constitutional rights were violated; the court of appeals affirms. Reversing, the United States Supreme Court refuses to apply the *Tinker* standard. Reasoning that *Tinker* applies only to political speech, the Court applies a balancing test to other forms of student speech. Here, the Court reasons that the school official's interest in inculcating proper values and maintaining a proper educational environment outweighs Mathew's interest in free speech. The Court also rejects Mathew's argument that the discipline violates his right to procedural due process. Because the suspension was so brief, according to the Court, it did not give rise to due process rights. *Bethel v. Fraser*, 478 U.S. 675 (1986).

C. Minors' Fourth Amendment rights

1. **Applicable standard:** The United States Supreme Court holds that the Fourth Amendment's prohibition against unreasonable searches and seizures ***does apply*** to searches of juveniles by

public school officials. However, the standard for searches of juveniles (*reasonable suspicion*) is lower than that for adults (*probable cause*). Thus, the law permits searches of juveniles that would be unconstitutional as applied to adults.

Example: A high school teacher finds two girls smoking in the school bathroom (a violation of school rules). The teacher takes the two girls to Assistant Vice Principal Choplick's office. When Choplick asks the two girls if they were smoking, one girl admits the infraction, but the other (T.L.O.) denies that she had been smoking or that she smokes. Choplick demands to see T.L.O's purse. He opens the purse, finds cigarettes, rolling papers, marijuana, and documents that implicate T.L.O. in dealing marijuana. Choplick gives the evidence to the police. The state brings delinquency charges. T.L.O. moves to suppress the evidence, claiming that the search was unlawful and that the evidence was tainted by the unlawful search. The juvenile court denies the motion to suppress, finds her to be delinquent and sentences her to one year of probation. The United States Supreme Court concludes that the Fourth Amendment applies to school authorities. However, the standard differs in this context (reasonable suspicion) from that applicable to adults. Neither a warrant nor probable cause is required. Rather, the legality of the search depends on "reasonableness under the circumstances." Specifically, the determination of reasonableness requires an exploration of whether the search was justified at its inception and whether it was reasonably related in scope to the circumstances justifying the search. The later inquiry requires balancing the need to search against the invasiveness of the search (in light of the age and sex of the student, and the nature of the infraction). Reasoning that a child has a decreased interest in privacy and the school has a substantial interest in maintaining discipline, the Court concludes that the search was not unreasonable under the Fourth Amendment. *New Jersey v. T.L.O.*, 469 U.S. 325 (1985).

Note: *T.L.O.* did not resolve the issue of the constitutionality of random (suspicionless) searches of juveniles because of the existence of individualized suspicion (i.e., suspicion regarding a particular student in *T.L.O.*). The Supreme Court later addressed the constitutionality of random drug testing in both *Vernonia School District v. Acton* and *Board of Education v. Earls* (discussed *infra*).

2. **Random drug testing:** The Supreme Court subsequently reaffirms that school children's Fourth Amendment rights differ from those of adults. The Court upholds the constitutionality of random drug testing of athletes (*Vernonia*) and of students in all competitive extracurricular activities (*Earls*).

Example: A school district adopts a new drug policy that authorizes random urinalysis testing of students who participate in school athletic programs. The district is motivated by a concern with widespread drug use by students, including student athletes, and the worry that drug use increases the risk of sports-related injury. A seventh-grader, James, is denied participation in the football program when he and his parents refuse to sign the testing consent forms. The student and his parents file suit, seeking declaratory and injunctive relief on the grounds that the policy violates the Fourth and Fourteenth Amendments. The district court denies the claims, but the court of appeals reverses. The United States Supreme Court holds that the policy does not violate the student's constitutional rights. The Court reasons that school children have lesser privacy expectations with regards to medical examinations than the general population, and student athletes have even less expectation of privacy. *Vernonia Sch. Dist. v. Acton*, 515 U.S. 646 (1995).

Example: A high school institutes a policy requiring all students who participate in competitive extracurricular activities to submit to urinalysis drug testing. Students challenge the constitutionality of the school's suspicionless policy. The United States Supreme Court holds that the policy is a reasonable means of furthering the school district's important interest in preventing and deterring drug use among its schoolchildren and therefore does not violate the Fourth Amendment. *Board of Educ. v. Earls*, 536 U.S. 822 (2002).

3. **Canine sniffing:** Courts are divided on the issue of whether "dog sniffing" violates students' Fourth Amendment rights. *Compare B.C. v. Plumas Unified Sch. Dist.*, 192 F.3d 1260 (9th Cir. 1999) (holding that random suspicionless dog sniff of student infringes the reasonable expectation of privacy, and thus constitutes a search for Fourth Amendment purposes), *with Doe v. Renfrow*, 475 F. Supp. 1012 (N.D. Ind. 1979) (holding that dog sniffing is not a search within the meaning of the Fourth Amendment because of students' lessened expectations of privacy).

4. **Locker searches:** Most courts have held that student locker searches are constitutional, relying on the theory that students have no expectation of privacy in their lockers (which are school property) or else that students' expectation of privacy in their lockers is minimal.

   Example: High school students tell a teacher on two separate occasions that one student possesses a "large pot pipe." The teacher informs the assistant principal (without naming the informants) who then searches the accused student's locker. He finds a pot pipe, marijuana, a lighter, and some cash. When the student is charged with delinquency, he moves to suppress the evidence as the product of an unconstitutional search and seizure under *T.L.O.* The state supreme court upholds the search and seizure, finding the information relied on by the assistant principal sufficiently reliable to provide "reasonable grounds" to justify the search, despite the official's ignorance of the names of the informants or the location of the "pot pipe." The court notes that, although the information would likely not support "reasonable suspicion" or "probable cause," these higher standards were inapplicable in the context of a search of a student's locker. *In re Juvenile 2006-406*, 931 A.2d 1229 (N.H. 2007).

5. **Strip searches:** The United States Supreme Court has held that a strip search of a middle school student violates the Fourth Amendment.

   Example: School officials conduct a strip search of a 13-year-old middle school student based on a tip from another student that she possessed over-the-counter pain relief pills (which were prohibited under school rules without advance permission). No pills are found. The student's mother files suit against the school district and school officials alleging that the strip search violated her daughter's Fourth Amendment rights. The U.S. Supreme Court holds that school officials were justified in searching the student's backpack and outer clothing but that the search of her undergarments was unreasonably intrusive. (However, because the Court found that the law regarding student strip searches was not clearly established at the time, the officials were entitled to qualified immunity.) *Safford Unified School Dist. No. 1 v. Redding*, 129 S. Ct. 2633 (2009).

D. **Firearms use by juveniles:** Federal and state legislation restricts juveniles' access to firearms. *See, e.g.,* Violent Crime Control and Law Enforcement Act of 1994, 18 U.S.C. §922(b)(1) (2006) (prohibiting firearms dealers from selling or delivering weapons and ammunition to minors), and 18 U.S.C. §922(x)(1) (2006) (prohibiting any person from selling or delivering a handgun or ammunition to a juvenile). These laws have been upheld against constitutional challenges in the wake of *District of Columbia v. Heller*, 128 S. Ct. 2783 (2008) (invalidating D.C.'s ban on handgun possession in the home as a violation of the Second Amendment). *See, e.g., United States v. Rene E.* (1st Cir. 2009) (upholding 18 U S.C. §922(x)(2) (2006), which prohibits juveniles from owning firearms). In addition, a number of states have child access prevention (CAP) laws that impose criminal penalties for the negligent storage of a firearm if a child uses the weapon to kill or injure himself or another person. The constitutionality of CAP laws after *Heller* has not yet been determined.

Federal law also attempted to establish "gun-free" school zones. In 1990 Congress enacted the Gun-Free School Zones Act, 18 U.S.C. §922 (2006), making it a federal offense for any individual knowingly to possess a firearm in a place that the individual believes or has reasonable cause to believe is a school zone. In *United States v. Lopez*, 514 U.S. 549 (1995), the United States Supreme Court held that Congress exceeded its authority under the Commerce Clause in enacting the provision because possession of a gun in a local school zone is not an economic activity that substantially affects interstate commerce. However, many states have enacted similar statutes.

Quiz Yourself on EDUCATION

108. A high school junior reports to the principal that the sum of $200 from cheerleading candy sales is missing from her unlocked gym locker. The principal orders all the girls in the gym class to place the contents of their pockets on the table. Then, based on the fact that two girls are fidgeting and nervous, the principal requires two eighth-grade students (Amber and Lacy) to submit their backpacks for a search in a private room by a female teacher. No money is found. The girls seek a declaration that the searches are unconstitutional. Will they prevail? ____________________

Answer

108. No. The Fourth Amendment prohibits unreasonable searches and seizures by state officials. *T.L.O.* established that high school students have a Fourth Amendment right to be free from "unreasonable" searches in the school setting, the search must be based on reasonable grounds to suspect that the student has violated the law or school rule, and the search is permissible in scope when the school employee's actions are not excessively intrusive in light of the age and sex of the student and the nature of the infraction. In light of the facts known to the principal at the time (that the girls were "fidgeting"), the girls could argue that the school officials' search of Amber's and Lacy's backpacks for allegedly stealing $200 lacked a reasonable basis from its inception for the officials to believe that the particular students had committed the crime. However, random searches of students have been upheld in some cases (e.g., athletes and student participants in extracurricular competitive activities). But, the girls could argue that these exceptions were not applicable here. In addition, the girls could argue that there was no individualized suspicion as in *T.L.O.* and also that the resulting search was highly intrusive given the age and sex of the students. However, the search was not a strip search (prohibited by *Safford*)—only a search of backpacks and it was conducted in a private room by a female teacher. Thus, Amber and Lacey's Fourth Amendment rights were not violated.

V. MEDICAL CARE

A. **Requirement of parental consent:** At common law, only a parent could give consent to medical treatment for a child. The child lacked capacity to consent. This rule of parental consent accorded with notions of family privacy, parental autonomy, and parental financial responsibility.

B. **Minor's consent:** Some statutes provide that a minor (specifically, an unemancipated minor) may consent to medical treatment.

1. **Limited circumstances:** In many jurisdictions, statutes provide that the minor may consent to medical treatment in cases of venereal disease, alcohol or drug abuse, and pregnancy-related complications (but *not* abortion services).

2. **Emancipated minors' ability to consent distinguished:** An emancipated minor (i.e., a minor who is living apart from parents and managing his or her own financial affairs, or who is married, in the armed services, or has secured a judicial declaration of emancipation) may consent to medical treatment on the same terms as an adult.

3. **Liability for provision of medical care without consent:** If a physician provides medical care to a minor without securing informed consent, the physician may be liable for battery (i.e., a touching without consent).

C. **Exceptions and limitations to parental consent requirements**

1. **Emergency exception:** Under the common-law rule (now codified in many states), physicians may provide medical treatment to a child without parental consent in the event of an *emergency* if a parent is unavailable and delay would endanger the child.

2. **State-imposed health requirements:** The state limits parental prerogatives to consent to their child's medical treatment by certain mandatory health requirements. For example, most states require children to undergo newborn testing and screening, compulsory immunizations prior to school attendance, and school screening procedures (e.g., hearing and eyesight screenings).

3. **Neglect limitation:** Another limitation on the rule of parental consent occurs in the area of child neglect. Based on common law and statute, parents have the duty to provide their child with necessary medical care. If the parents refuse to provide consent to medical treatment, they may be subject to criminal and/or civil liability. Further, under the neglect jurisdiction, a juvenile court may declare the child neglected or dependent and then order the appropriate medical treatment.

   Example: At birth, Mr. and Mrs. B. decide to place their son Phillip, who suffers from Down's syndrome, in a residential care facility. He is diagnosed with a congenital heart defect that requires surgery to avoid damage to his lungs. His biological parents refuse to consent to the surgery. The juvenile probation department files a petition in juvenile court alleging that Phillip is a neglected child and requesting that the court declare him a dependent child for the purpose of ordering the cardiac surgery. The trial court dismisses the petition and the appellate court affirms. The court of appeals notes that, although parental autonomy is not absolute and the state may interfere to safeguard the child, the trial judge found no clear and convincing evidence to support the petition. The appellate court determines that, because the experts disagreed about the likelihood of success of the surgery, the trial court's decision did not constitute error. *In re Phillip B.*, 152 Cal. Rptr. 48 (Ct. App. 1979).

Example: Phillip B. (the child in the preceding case) develops a close relationship with Mrs. H., a volunteer at Phillip's facility. Mrs. H., her husband, and their children help toilet-train Phillip, teach him skills, and educate him. They include him in the foster family's activities and give him his own room in their house. He refers to the foster parents as his "mother" and "father" and refers to their residence as his house. He spends weekends and overnight visits with them until his biological parents forbid this contact. His biological parents continue to be physically and emotionally detached from him. Mr. and Mrs. H. file a petition to be appointed guardians of his person and estate (in part, so that they may order the necessary surgery). The biological parents object. The court of appeal determines that Phillip's best interests will be served by awarding guardianship to his foster parents. Before a court may award custody to a nonparent, it must make a finding that an award of custody to a parent would be detrimental to the child and that the award to the nonparent would serve the best interests of the child. Here, the court reasons that the record is clear that the biological parents' retention of custody would cause Phillip severe harm. *Guardianship of Phillip B.*, 188 Cal. Rptr. 781 (Ct. App. 1983).

Note: The assertion of neglect jurisdiction fails because the court determines that the evidence about the success of the surgery is conflicting. However, the guardianship petition succeeds because the standard is the more subjective "best interests of the child" and because the presumption favoring the biological parents is overcome by the judicial finding that their continuing care is detrimental.

D. Baby Doe cases: A series of cases in the 1980s involving disabled newborns leads to a wave of state and federal legislation and regulations. In 1982 Infant Doe is born in Bloomington, Indiana, with serious birth disabilities (no connection between the esophagus and the stomach and a connection between the trachea and esophagus). Although corrective surgery is possible, the parents refuse consent. The juvenile court rejects the hospital's request to assert jurisdiction to order treatment. *In re Infant Doe*, No. GU 8204-004A (Monroe County Cir. Ct., Apr. 12, 1982). The Indiana Court of Appeals also refuses to order treatment. *State ex rel. Infant Doe v. Baker*, No. 482 S 140 (Ind. May 27, 1982). The infant dies six days later. The United States Supreme Court denies certiorari. *Infant Doe v. Bloomington Hosp.*, 464 U.S. 961 (1983).

In 1982 the Department of Health and Human Services (DHHS) responds to the Infant Doe case by sending notices to health care providers that the providers are discriminating against the handicapped by withholding treatment or nourishment and that the providers should refuse to aid parents who so desire. Shortly afterward, DHHS issues regulations providing that withholding food or medical treatment from disabled infants violates §504 of the Rehabilitation Act of 1973, 29 U.S.C. §794(3) (2006), and requiring hospitals to post notices to that effect that include a hotline number for reports. After challenges by medical providers, a federal court invalidates the regulations on procedural grounds. *Am. Academy of Pediatrics v. Heckler*, 561 F. Supp. 395 (D.D.C. 1983). DHHS adopts new, substantially similar, regulations that encourage hospitals to establish infant care review committees.

Another newborn Baby Doe is born in New York with serious mental and physical disabilities. When DHHS seeks to intervene to obtain release of the child's medical records (over the refusal of the parents and the hospital), a district court determines (and the Second Circuit affirms) that no violation of the Rehabilitation Act occurred. *United States v. University Hosp.*, 729 F.2d 144 (2d Cir. 1984).

Eventually, medical organizations challenge the validity of the DHHS regulations. The United States Supreme Court holds that parental withholding of consent does not constitute discrimination against the disabled and also that the promulgation of the federal regulations exceeded the authority of DHHS. *Bowen v. Am. Hosp. Assn.*, 476 U.S. 610 (1986).

The government counters this defeat by adopting a different strategy based on an approach of child protective services. Congress adds a new provision to the Child Abuse Amendments of 1984, 42 U.S.C. §§5102(3), 5103(b)(2)(k) (2006), providing that the withholding of treatment to disabled newborns constitutes a form of child abuse. 42 U.S.C. §5106 (2006). States must have procedures addressing the withholding of medical care (e.g., appointment of hospital personnel and infant care review committees, child protective service workers who respond to cases as they arise), or face the loss of federal funds for child abuse and neglect.

Commentators doubt that the federal law has much impact on the care of disabled newborns because of the ambiguity of the law and the difficulty of discovering cases of nontreatment.

Quiz Yourself on *MEDICAL CARE*

109. Fifteen-year-old Kevin Sampson suffers from a disease causing a massive deformity of his face and neck. The disease is not life-threatening but results in a grotesque appearance that adversely affects Kevin's self-esteem. Kevin's physicians believe that he should have surgery to correct the condition. His mother, a Jehovah's Witness, is willing for him to have the surgery, but she refuses to consent, on religious grounds, to blood transfusions during the surgery. Can Kevin's physicians proceed without his mother's consent? ____________________

Answer

109. Yes. The physicians may report the case to the county authorities to have them petition the juvenile court to declare Kevin a neglected (i.e., medically neglected) child. Juvenile court statutes typically permit a juvenile court to assert jurisdiction when a parent refuses to provide a child with necessary medical care. If the juvenile court determines that Kevin is neglected, the juvenile court would then order a guardian to consent to the operation with the necessary blood transfusions.

Exam Tips on THE PARENT-CHILD-STATE RELATIONSHIP IN SPECIAL CONTEXTS

Identify the special context that is being tested (tort, contract, property, education, or medical care). Remember that special rules may be applicable to the particular context and that such rules have policy implications concerning the appropriateness of differential treatment of children and adults.

Torts

- If the issue involves ***liability*** for children's tortious acts, explain the different rules for parents and children. That is, at common law, parents were ***not liable*** for their children's torts. Children are liable for their torts — both intentional and negligent torts. However, although children are liable for their torts, they are subject to a ***different subjective standard of care***. Explain the traditional rule that takes into account the minor's age and experience, and then apply that rule to the facts. Determine whether the child may have been contributorily negligent. If so, explain the minority rule presuming that children below a certain age (e.g., age seven) cannot be held contributorily negligent. Determine if the child was performing an adult activity (e.g., driving a car or boat) in which case the adult "reasonable person" standard would apply.

    - Also, be sure to explore whether an exception to the traditional rule of parental nonliability is applicable. That is, is there a special statute that establishes parental liability? Was the parent employing his or her child? Did the parent permit the child to use a dangerous instrumentality such as a weapon? Did the parent have prior knowledge of the child's aggressive acts or disposition and fail to warn the victim?

Contracts

- Determine the nature of the contract at issue. Clarify the offer (especially the terms), acceptance, and consideration. Explore whether the minor would like to ***disaffirm*** (breach the contract), and explain the reason for the breach (i.e., what the minor gains by the breach). Describe the common-law doctrine that a minor's contracts are voidable (i.e., the minor can disaffirm the contract and assert a defense of infancy). Apply the rule to the facts. Mention that this common-law rule is the **majority rule**. Explain also the policy underlying the rule (to protect minors from overreaching by adults and their own immaturity). Explore whether the problem includes one of the **limited situations** (i.e., entertainment contracts) that change the common-law rule.

Property

- Explore whether the problem involves a property-based issue. If so, identify the particular issue. For example, does the problem involve the child's right to services or earnings? Does it involve inheritance? Does it involve a gift?

- Apply the relevant law to the circumstances. Remember that at common law, a parent had the right to a child's services and earnings and that many modern statutes incorporate this common-law rule. If the issue involves inheritance, point out that at common law (and still true today), a court appointed a guardian of the child's estate (i.e., the child's property). Explain the notion of guardianship as involving a guardian of the person and of the estate. Point out the problems with guardianship (i.e., expensive, cumbersome).

☞ For issues involving ***inheritance***, verify whether the child was born during a marriage or outside marriage. Point out the traditional rule of discrimination for nonmarital children—i.e., they could inherit from their mothers who died intestate (if the mother died without a will) but not from their fathers who died intestate. Explain that the modern trend is toward ***minimizing difference in treatment*** of nonmarital versus marital children for succession purposes. Discuss the United States Supreme Court cases in *Trimble v. Gordon* and *Lalli v. Lalli*.

☞ If the issue involves a ***gift to a minor***, clarify the nature of the property that is being given and the donor. Mention the ***different methods of holding property for a minor***. Discuss whether the use of trust or the Uniform Transfers to Minors Act might be appropriate. Be sure to define and explain the features of various options. Mention too the advantages and disadvantages of the use of trusts versus the Uniform Act.

☞ Be sure to identify whether the minor is ***emancipated***. If so, explain the emancipation doctrine and its effect (permitting children to acquire the right to dispose of their earnings). Point out that emancipation is a common-law as well as statutory doctrine. Identify whether common-law grounds (e.g., marriage, service in the armed forces) or particular statutory grounds are relevant.

Education

☛ The most commonly tested issues in the educational context are minors' ***First Amendment*** and ***Fourth Amendment*** rights. First determine the nature of the restriction on minors' rights. Then determine if a state actor or agency is involved. Does the restriction involve a ***prior restraint*** on speech or a ***punishment*** of students for their ***expressive*** activities? Point out that different rules apply to these two types of restrictions.

☛ If the question involves minors' right to freedom of expression, determine the type of speech that is being restricted. For example, does the question involve ***political speech***? Political speech is entitled to the most protection under the Constitution. If political speech is involved, then discuss and apply the rules in *Tinker*. That is, does the conduct ***materially and substantially interfere*** with the requirements of appropriate discipline in the operation of the school or ***invade the rights of others***? Remember that the *Tinker* test has two prongs—the disruptive aspect and the invasion-of-rights aspect.

☞ If the restriction on student speech does not involve political speech, determine if the speech occurred in the context of a ***school-sponsored activity*** (such as a school newspaper). Point out that the Supreme Court circumscribes students' rights to freedom of expression in the context of school-sponsored activities (*Hazelwood*).

☞ If the problem involves ***punishment*** of students for their ***expressive*** activities, then remember to discuss not only students' First Amendment rights but also students' right to procedural ***due process***. That is, the Supreme Court has held that schools may discipline students for their expressive activity in certain situations (*Bethel v. Fraser*). Remember that *Bethel* involved the student's ***brief*** suspension (three days) which the Court held did not give rise to an infringement of the due process right. Therefore, it is important to note the specific nature of the school's punishment. *Bethel* also applied a balancing test to student speech. Discuss and apply that balancing test (i.e., balancing the school official's interest, for example, in inculcating property values and maintaining a proper educational environment against the student's interest in freedom of expression).

☞ Students' ***Fourth Amendment rights*** are also a frequently tested issue. First identify the nature of the search. What was the object of the search (to find drugs, cigarettes, money, firearms, etc.)? Who was conducting the search (a school official and/or police officer)? Recall that the search in *T.L.O.* was conducted only by a school official (but, therefore, a higher standard than reasonable suspicion might be required if a search was conducted in concert with, or at the request of, law enforcement personnel).

☞ Identify the item being searched (i.e., the student's person, locker) because different rules apply to the student's expectation of privacy. For example, a student has a ***lessened expectation of privacy in school property*** (e.g., lockers). Discuss and apply the Supreme Court's holding in *New Jersey v. T.L.O.* Specifically, explain that the Supreme Court held that the Fourth Amendment applies to searches conducted by public school officials, but that a lower standard applies (***reasonable suspicion***) to search of juveniles compared to adults (probable cause). Explain the reasonable suspicion standard—reasonableness under the circumstances—and apply that standard to the circumstances. Specifically, explain whether the search was justified at its inception (i.e., were there reasonable grounds at the time for suspecting that a law or school rule had been violated), and whether the scope of the search was reasonably related to that need. In terms of the latter, it will be necessary to balance the ***need to search*** against the ***invasiveness of the search*** (the invasiveness depends on the age and sex of the student, and the nature of the infraction). In discussing the factor of "invasiveness," mention *Safford v. Redding* (holding that a strip search of a student's undergarments for a prescription drug was not justified by the nature of the circumstances).

☞ Determine whether the search involved ***individualized suspicion*** or a ***random*** suspicionless search. If the latter, then discuss and apply the Supreme Court's holdings in *Vernonia* and *Earls*. Explain the school policy and its object. Explore the facts that motivated the school policy. Determine who is being searched. Remember that the reasoning of *Vernonia* applied to athletes and the reasoning of *Earls* applies to students in competitive extracurricular activities. Analyze the students' expectation of privacy (e.g., are they similar to athletes who have a lessened expectation of privacy), the seriousness of the intrusion on students' privacy (e.g., a urine test is less intrusive than a body search), and the state interest (e.g., protection of students from drug use, promotion of civic values). Be sure to point out that *T.L.O.* left many issues unresolved (i.e., the standard if law enforcement is involved, the constitutionality of various types of searches).

Medical Care

☛ Identify the ***context*** for medical treatment and the ***health care provider*** (physician, hospital, etc.). Clarify the age and sex of the child. Determine the major issues — ***parental consent, minor's consent***. Explain the common-law rule providing that only a parent could consent to medical treatment for a child because the child lacked capacity to consent. Discuss the modern view that many statutes authorize minors to consent themselves for certain types of medical treatment (drug treatment, venereal disease, substance abuse, etc.).

☞ Explore whether there are any ***exceptions and/or limitations*** to parental consent requirements. That is, is this an emergency? Is the parent unavailable? Would delay endanger the child? In such cases, the ***emergency exception*** would enable physicians to provide treatment to a child without parental consent. Is this a situation involving state-imposed health requirements (i.e., newborn screening)? In this case, the law limits parental prerogatives to consent because of the need to promote child welfare by compliance with health requirements.

☞ If the parents refuse their consent, remember to discuss the ***neglect limitation*** on parental consent requirements. That is, although parental consent is generally required, if the parents refuse to give their consent, they may be subject to ***civil and/or criminal liability***. Discuss whether a state actor should resort to the neglect jurisdiction of juvenile court. That is, should a juvenile court declare the child neglected in order to authorize the necessary medical treatment? Be sure to determine if the minor is emancipated. Remember that if the minor is emancipated, he or she may consent to medical treatment on the same terms as an adult (and parental consent is not required).

CHAPTER 11

ADOPTION

ChapterScope

This chapter addresses the adoption process, which creates a new parent-child relationship. Here are a few of the key principles covered in this chapter:

- Adoption was not recognized by the English common law; therefore, American adoption law is entirely ***statutory***.
- The guiding standard in adoption law is the ***best interests of the child***.
- Several factors, including ***race, religion, sexual orientation, and age***, may be relevant in adoption.
- State statutes generally require ***consent of the biological parents*** before an adoption takes place.
- The Supreme Court has held that an ***unmarried father*** is entitled to constitutional protection of his parental rights so long as he manifests certain ***indicia of parenthood.***
- A biological parent may relinquish a child to a public or privately licensed adoption ***agency*** for adoption, or arrange for a ***private*** (i.e., ***independent***) adoption by which a private person/intermediary facilitates the adoption.
- States have ***criminal penalties*** for ***babyselling***.
- An adoption agency may be liable for the tort of ***wrongful adoption*** (i.e., a form of misrepresentation).
- All states provide ***subsidized adoption programs*** to facilitate adoption of those children who are ***difficult to place***.
- Courts generally uphold ***open adoption*** agreements if the agreements are found to be in the best interests of the child.
- Some states now permit adoptees to have ***access to their adoption records***.

I. INTRODUCTION

A. Definition: Adoption is the legal process of creating a parent-child relationship. By adoption, an individual acquires a new parent (or parents). The adoption process terminates the legal rights and responsibilities (e.g., custody and support) of the natural parent(s) and creates new legal rights and responsibilities in the adoptive parent(s).

B. Historical background: Adoption was not recognized by the English common law. This policy stemmed in large part from British emphasis on the importance of the blood line. Therefore, American adoption law and practice is a comparatively modern development and entirely statutory. Massachusetts adopted the first adoption statute in 1851. Model legislation consists of the Uniform Adoption Act, 9 U.L.A. 11 (1971) (adopted by few states) and the revised Uniform Adoption Act, 9 U.L.A. 1 (1996).

C. **Voluntary versus involuntary termination of parental rights:** Adoption results in the termination of the biological parent's rights. This termination may be voluntary or involuntary. On the one hand, a biological parent may choose to relinquish a child for adoption. On the other hand, a biological parent may have his or her parental rights terminated judicially because of some act of parental misconduct (e.g., abuse, neglect, nonsupport, abandonment). The termination of parental rights and the adoption may take place either in the same proceeding or two separate proceedings.

D. **Social reality:** Several factors contributed to a sharp decrease in the number of babies available for adoption. These include: changing sexual mores, the development of oral contraceptives, the legalization of abortion, and the lessened stigma of bearing children out of wedlock and of being illegitimate. The decrease in available infants has led to an increase in ***independent*** (i.e., unlicensed private placement), foreign country, ***open*** (i.e., nonconfidential), and ***transracial*** (formerly "interracial") adoptions. These effects, in turn, produced calls for increased regulation of adoption law and practice.

II. SELECTION STANDARDS FOR ADOPTIVE PARENTS

A. **Generally:** The guiding standard in adoption, as in custody, is the *best interests of the child*. Several factors (discussed *infra*) are relevant in a "best interests" determination.

B. **Relevant factors**

1. **Preference for relatives:** Some statutes incorporate a presumption that adoptive placement with relatives is in the child's best interests, unless good cause to the contrary or detriment to the child can be shown.

   Example: D.L. is born to an African-American mother who is not living with D.L.'s father. The mother's three other children are being cared for by their African-American maternal grandparents. The mother relinquishes D.L. at birth for adoption. D.L. is placed in foster care with Caucasian foster parents. Following termination of the biological mother and father's rights, the foster parents and maternal grandparents all file adoption petitions. The trial court places the child with the grandparents, based on a statutory preference that "the court shall give preference, in the absence of good cause to the contrary, to (a) a relative or relatives of the child, or, . . . (b) a family with the same racial or ethnic heritage as the child." The foster parents appeal, contending that the statute violates equal protection by establishing a family preference only for adoption of minority children. The state supreme court affirms. Without addressing the constitutional issues, the court reasons that adoption law has long favored child placement with family members, regardless of race or ethnic heritage. Further, the possibility of harm caused by separation from the foster parents cannot defeat the family preference. *Matter of Welfare of D.L.*, 486 N.W.2d 375, 377 (Minn. 1992).

2. **Sexual orientation:** States are divided about the issue of whether to permit same-sex partners or unmarried cohabitants to adopt children.

   a. **Restrictive jurisdictions:** A few states prohibit or restrict adoption by same-sex partners or cohabiting couples (whether of the opposite sex or same sex).

Example: Gay and lesbian foster parents and guardians challenge the constitutionality of the Florida prohibition on adoption of children by same-sex partners. The Eleventh Circuit Court of Appeals holds that foster parents and legal guardians have no due-process-protected liberty interest in family integrity, and also that the statute does not violate the Equal Protection Clause because it is rationally related to the legitimate state interest in furthering the best interests of adopted children by placing them with married parents. *Lofton v. Secretary of Dept. of Children and Family Servs.*, 358 F.3d 804 (11th Cir. 2004).

Note: Subsequently, three Florida state courts rule that the prohibition is unconstitutional. *See In re Adoption of Doe*, 34 Fam. L. Rep. 1531 (BNA) (Sept. 30, 2008); *In re Adoption of Doe*, 2008 WL5006172 (Fla. Cir. Ct. 2008); *In re Adoption of Anonymous*, 35 Fam. L. Rep. 1051 (BNA) (Jan. 14, 2010).

b. **Permissive jurisdictions:** Most jurisdictions however, now permit adoption by same-sex couples, called "second parent adoption" (discussed *infra*).

c. **Effect of a second-parent adoption on the first parent's rights:** An issue sometimes arises as to whether adoption by a same-sex partner (i.e., the "second" parent) has the effect of terminating the parental rights of the biological mother. The effect of termination is based on the notion that a child can have only one parent of a given sex.

Example: Susan and Helen are both surgeons who have been companions for ten years. Susan conceives Tammy through artificial insemination with the sperm of Helen's cousin. Tammy is raised by both women and forms psychological bonds with both. Susan and Helen file a joint petition to adopt Tammy. Helen's cousin has no plan to be involved with Tammy except as a distant relative; he supports the adoption. The lower court finds that it would be in the child's best interests to be adopted by both women. The appellate court affirms, finding that Helen's petition to adopt does not result in termination of Susan's legal relationship to Tammy. The appellate court notes that adoption would entitle Tammy to inherit and receive support from both women, to be eligible for insurance coverage and Social Security benefits from each woman, and to preserve ties to both in the event of dissolution of the women's relationship. *Adoption of Tammy*, 619 N.E.2d 315 (Mass. 1993).

d. **Sexual orientation, civil rights statutes, and adoption advertising:** Some states have civil rights statutes that protect against discrimination on the basis of gender, sexual orientation, and marital status. A court has considered whether such statutes apply to prospective adoptive parents' Internet advertisements.

Example: Two California male registered domestic partners, who were approved adoptive parents in that state, unsuccessfully seek to post their profiles on the website of defendants' Arizona-based adoption-related business that allows prospective adoptive parents to post profiles to be considered by birth parents seeking placements. Defendants reject them, based on their policy restricting eligibility to opposite-sex married couples. Plaintiffs then file suit, seeking damages and injunctive relief under California antidiscrimination laws. After ruling that California law was applicable to the action because California had a stronger governmental interest than Arizona, the district court rules that genuine issues of fact exist that preclude summary judgment regarding whether the defendants' policy of not allowing unmarried couples to post profiles on their website amounts to discrimination based on marital status, sexual orientation, or gender discrimination. *Butler v. Adoption Media, LLC*, 486 F. Supp.2d 1022 (N.D. Cal. 2007).

e. **Sexual orientation, adoption, and state paternity laws:** Some states have extended their paternity laws to facilitate parentage determinations to partners in lesbian relationships.

Example: Ingrid and Mona are legally married in the Netherlands. The women desire to raise children together. Mona donates an egg which is fertilized by an anonymous sperm donor whom the women have chosen for his physical similarities to Ingrid. Ingrid subsequently gives birth to Sebastian. The birth certificate names only Ingrid as Sebastian's parent. Mona then seeks a judicial determination of her parentage status (with Ingrid's consent) in order to adopt Sebastian. The trial court explores, as a matter of first impression, whether a lesbian genetic mother of a child born to her partner should be permitted to utilize existing statutory paternity procedures to establish her parentage, rather than the "more expensive, time consuming and intrusive" adoption mechanism. The court reasons that there is no rational reason to discriminate between male and female genetic parents who seek to use state paternity laws to establish parental rights. The court rules that, although adoption currently is the sole means by which a genetic mother could legally establish parentage of a child born to her wife, the state paternity provisions (that are limited to establishing rights of fathers) violate equal protection and should be extended to offer protection to genetic mothers. *In re Adoption of Sebastian*, 879 N.Y.S.2d 677 (Sur. Ct. 2009).

3. **Race**

a. **Generally:** Race may be a relevant, although not determinative, factor in the selection of an adoptive parent.

Example: D. is conceived by unmarried teenage African-American parents. After a few months, D.'s mother relinquishes her parental rights without informing D.'s father. D. is placed with Caucasian foster parents who petition subsequently to adopt her. At the foster parents' request, the Department of Human Resources notifies the biological father of the proposed adoption. He objects. His mother and stepfather then file a petition to adopt D. The District of Columbia adoption statute permits a court to take race into account. The trial court finds that, although both sets of petitioners are suitable, the race of the grandparents tips the balance. The court grants their petition. The foster parents appeal, arguing that the equal protection doctrine prohibits the use of race as a relevant issue in adoption. Reversing, the appellate court rules that race cannot be decisive in adoption placement. The court reasons that, although the statute requires strict scrutiny review, the statute survives that level of scrutiny because advancement of the child's best interest is a compelling governmental interest. The court remands for a determination of all relevant factors. *In re R.M.G.*, 454 A.2d 776 (D.C. Ct. App. 1982).

b. **Effect of *Palmore v. Sidoti:*** A United States Supreme Court case that addresses race in *custody* decision making has implications for the consideration of race in *adoption*. In *Palmore v. Sidoti*, 466 U.S. 429 (1984), a child is removed from his mother's care when the mother marries an African-American (discussed in Chapter 7). The trial court reasons that the child should be protected against the social stigma stemming from the mother's interracial marriage. The Supreme Court reverses, holding that race may not be the sole factor in a custody determination.

The Supreme Court has not yet addressed the issue of race in the adoption context. However, the application of *Palmore* would appear to dictate that race, similarly, may not be determinative for adoption purposes.

c. **Policy debate:** Race-matching policies are the subject of a controversial policy debate. During the civil rights era of the 1960s, transracial adoption was regarded positively. However, in 1972 the National Association of Black Social Workers adopted a resolution at their national convention stating that African-American children should be placed only with African-American families in foster care or adoption. The resolution arose from the fear of cultural genocide.

   Some commentators argue that limits on transracial adoption harm children by restricting the number of possible adoptive homes. In contrast, others argue that transracial adoption results in the loss of children's and the community's racial and cultural heritage.

   Some statutes specify that racial preferences shall be taken into account in adoption placement. *See, e.g.,* Cal. Fam. Code §8708 (West 2004) (if a relative is not available, then placement should be with an adoptive family with the same racial background or ethnic identification).

d. **Multi-Ethnic Placement Act:** In 1994 Congress enacted the Metzenbaum Multi-Ethnic Placement Act (MEPA), 42 U.S.C. §5115a, to address delays caused by racial-matching policies. The Act permitted race to be used as a factor in the agency placement process only if race is relevant to the best interests of the child and is considered in conjunction with other factors. However, an agency that receives federal funds may not "delay or deny" placement of a child "solely" on the basis of the race (or color or national origin) of the adoptive parent or child. The Act was repealed in 1996 and replaced by federal legislation eliminating the word "solely." Race remains a factor in adoption, 42 U.S.C. §1996b (2006).

4. **Religion:** Religion also may be a relevant factor in the selection of adoptive parents. Some states have ***religious-matching provisions*** (i.e., matching the religion of the child and adoptive parent when possible). Courts have rejected constitutional challenges to such provisions.

   Example: The county Department of Social Services denies permission to a prospective adoptive couple on the ground of the couple's lack of religious affiliation. Both the state constitution and adoption statute provide that a child should be placed, when practicable and consistent with the child's best interests, in the custody of a person of the same religious background. The couple appeals the lower court's finding of constitutionality, arguing that the provision violates the First Amendment. The appellate court holds that religious-matching provisions are constitutional because they fulfill a secular legislative purpose, reflect a benevolent neutrality toward religion, and do not foster an excessive government entanglement with church interests. *Dickens v. Ernesto*, 281 N.E.2d 153 (N.Y. Ct. App. 1972), *appeal dismissed*, 407 U.S. 917 (1972).

5. **Age:** Courts may consider the age of a prospective adoptive parent. However, age may not be the sole reason for denying a petition without a determination that such denial would be in the child's best interests.

   Example: A 70-year-old father and 54-year-old mother desire to adopt T. who has lived with them since her birth three years ago. The State Department of Health recommends that their petition be denied because of their ages. The Department argues that older adoptive parents find it difficult to raise a young child, are more likely to contract illnesses, and the child will suffer from teasing by peers. The petitioners have a stable 20-year marriage, are financially secure and in good health. The appellate court holds that the trial court abused its discretion in denying the petition because no evidence supports the finding that petitioners' age is detrimental to the best interest of the child. Relying on principles announced in the classic book by mental health practitioners (Joseph Goldstein, Anna Freud, and Alfred Solnit, *Beyond the Best Interests of the Child* (1973)), the appellate court emphasizes the strength of the psychological parental bonds, the trauma that the child would suffer by leaving her home, and that the success of any alternative placement is speculative. *In re Adoption of Michelle T.*, 117 Cal. Rptr. 856 (Ct. App. 1975).

6. **Divorced co-petitioners:** A court may limit the rights of a parent in post-divorce adoption proceedings.

   Example: A couple has been foster parents to a child for two years. When they divorce, the husband attempts to join his ex-wife in her petition to adopt the child. The lower court holds that the husband cannot be a co-petitioner. The appellate court affirms the trial court ruling based on legislative intent (i.e., the legislature intended to limit adoption to petitioners who would provide a stable household). *In re Jason C.*, 533 A.2d 32 (N.H. 1987).

7. **Preference for infertile:** A few states give explicit preference to couples who are unable to have children. On the other hand, some states merely require prospective adoptive parents to disclose medical information regarding their sterility, implicitly suggesting a preference for the infertile.

8. **Disability of adoptive parent:** Courts may not deny a petition to adopt on the basis of the adoptive parent's disability.

   Example: Husband and Wife, both deaf-mutes, seek to adopt a baby. Husband has steady employment, owns a home, and has modest savings. Both are actively involved in their church. The couple previously raised a small girl for four years who was able to speak with others, communicate in sign language, and got along well with others. The natural mother of the infant chose the couple from among several prospective parents. The judge expresses reservations due to the couple's deafness. Thirteen witnesses support the petition; no testimony is presented in opposition. When the petition is denied, the couple appeals. The appellate court reverses, holding that the denial solely on the ground of disability violates petitioners' rights to due process and equal protection. *In re Adoption of Richardson*, 59 Cal. Rptr. 323 (Ct. App. 1967).

9. **Indian Child Welfare Act (ICWA) of 1978:** Federal legislation dictates that Native-American origins are relevant in adoption. In 1978, Congress enacts the Indian Child Welfare Act (ICWA), 25 U.S.C. §§1901-1963 (2006), stemming from the concern that large numbers of Native-American children are being separated from their families and tribes through adoption or foster care. The Act provides that a Native-American child remain within the Native-American community whenever possible.

   a. **Exclusive jurisdiction and tribal preference:** Two important provisions of the ICWA, §§1911 and 1915, apply to jurisdiction and the establishment of priority in adoption. Section 1911 grants tribal courts *exclusive jurisdiction* over proceedings concerning an Indian child who resides, or is domiciled, on a reservation. Section 1915(a) mandates a *preference for tribal members*. Absent good cause, adoptive placements must be made to members of the child's extended family, other members of the same tribe, or other Indian families.

Example: Nonmarital twins are born to Native-American parents who are members of the same tribe and live on the same reservation. The mother, however, gives birth outside the reservation, and shortly thereafter places the babies for adoption. Both the mother and father sign a consent form. A non-Native-American couple petitions a state court to adopt the children and receives approval. Two months later the tribe moves to vacate the adoption decree on the ground that under the ICWA, the tribal court has exclusive jurisdiction. The lower court denies the motion because the mother intentionally gave birth to the children outside the reservation and the children never resided on the reservation. The state supreme court affirms, holding that the babies are not domiciliaries of the reservation. The tribe appeals, arguing that the state court lacks jurisdiction because the twins were domiciled on the reservation. Reversing, the United States Supreme Court vacates the adoption. The Court reasons that the babies were domiciliaries on the reservation when the adoption proceedings began and, therefore, the tribe possesses exclusive jurisdiction under ICWA. Domicile is defined as physical presence with the intent to remain there. Because most minors are legally incapable of forming the requisite intent, minors take on the domicile of their parents. For a nonmarital child, the domicile is that of the mother. Here, the mother's domicile was that of the reservation; thus, so is the children's. Tribal jurisdiction cannot be defeated by the mother's actions. *Mississippi Band of Choctaw Indians v. Holyfield*, 490 U.S. 30 (1989).

b. "Existing Indian family" (EIF) exception: Some state courts hold that the ICWA does not apply if the Indian child is raised by a non-Indian parent with no tribal contact. This rule is called the "existing Indian family" exception. Other state courts reject this view.

Example: Baby Boy C. is born in California to Rita and her boyfriend, Justin. After the child's birth, Rita and Justin terminate their parental rights, and petitioners (Jeffrey A. and Joshua A.) adopt the child in New York. Included in Rita's consent to terminate her parental rights are representations that she is a member of a federally recognized Indian Tribe, that the child may be an "Indian child" under ICWA, and that she is aware of the ICWA's placement preferences but wants them waived. The Arizona Family Court issues an order terminating Rita's and Justin's parental rights. The adoptive parents take custody of the child, return to New York, and commence adoption proceedings. The Tribe then moves to intervene in the adoption proceeding under ICWA on the ground that this is a "child custody proceeding" involving an "Indian child," and argues that Rita's relinquishment of her parental rights implicates the Tribe's right to protect its relationship with its children. Petitioners contend that ICWA is not applicable because, under the "existing Indian family" exception (EIF), ICWA's purpose of preserving Indian families and tribal culture is not served if Baby Boy C. and his parents do not maintain a relationship with the Tribe. The Family Court denies intervention under ICWA, instead adopting the judicially created EIF. The Supreme Court of New York reverses, holding that the EIF exception is not the applicable law of New York. It grants the Tribe's motion to intervene and remands for further proceedings. *In re Baby Boy C.*, 805 N.Y.S.2d 313 (App. Div. 2005).

Quiz Yourself on
SELECTION STANDARDS FOR ADOPTIVE PARENTS

110. Mr. and Mrs. Allen wish to adopt a child. They file an application with the state social services agency. The application asks them for their religious affiliation. Mrs. Allen is Jewish. Mr. Allen is Catholic. Mr. Allen also has a problem with alcoholism and a history of arrests for drunk driving. The social services agency subsequently refuses to place with them a Catholic infant, explaining that "one of the reasons was your differing religions." The agency has a stated policy to match the baby's birth mother's religion and that of the adoptive parents whenever possible. Mr. and Mrs. Allen challenge the agency policy (i.e., disclosure of their religious affiliation and the denial of their application) as unconstitutional. Will they prevail? ____________________

Answer

110. No. Religious-matching provisions (i.e., matching the baby's religion to that of the prospective adoptive parents) have been upheld as constitutional. Further, religion may be one of several factors taken into consideration when selecting an adoptive parent. Here, the agency could argue that it took into account other factors in denying Mr. and Mrs. Allen's application for adoption. That is, the agency would claim that it would not be in the best interests of the child to be placed in a home where a parent (such as Mr. Allen) has a history of alcoholism.

III. CONSENT

State statutes generally require consent of the biological parents before an adoption may take place. If a child is born in wedlock, consent from both parents is required, absent a showing of abandonment or unfitness. If a child is born out of wedlock, courts sometimes may dispense with the father's consent if he has not indicated sufficient "indicia of parenthood."

A. Consent by the unmarried father

1. **Ramifications of *Stanley v. Illinois:*** The United States Supreme Court has held that a state may not deprive a biological father of custody if he has consistently cared for a child. In *Stanley v. Illinois*, 405 U.S. 645 (1972), the Court addresses the constitutionality of a statute presuming that, on the death of the mother, the father of a nonmarital child born is unfit. In *Stanley*, a mother and father of three children live together for 18 years although they never marry. When the mother dies, the state, pursuant to statute and without a hearing on the father's fitness, declares the children wards of the state. Upon review, the Supreme Court holds that the statute violates the father's procedural due process rights by denying him a preremoval hearing on the issue of fitness.

   Although *Stanley* deals with custody, the case has implications for the rights of unwed fathers in adoption cases. Prior to *Stanley*, many states allowed adoption with the mother's consent alone. In the wake of *Stanley*, many legislatures amended their statutes to confer greater rights on putative fathers. The Supreme Court has addressed the constitutionality of several such statutes.

2. Indicia of parenthood: The Supreme Court holds, in a trilogy of cases, that an unmarried father is entitled to constitutional protection of his parental rights so long as he manifests certain ***indicia of parenthood***. That is, an unwed father does not have an absolute right to notice and an opportunity to be heard before his child may be adopted. Rather, his constitutional rights depend on the degree to which he reveals a ***willingness to assume parental responsibilities*** (i.e., a custodial, personal, or financial relationship). Failure to act in a ***timely*** manner may result in relinquishment of his constitutional rights.

Example: Jessica is born out of wedlock. Her biological father, Jonathan, lives with her mother prior to her birth, and visits the mother in the hospital following her birth. However, he is not listed on the birth certificate, never provides support, does not live with the mother after the birth, and never offers to marry the mother. Shortly after Jessica's birth, her mother marries Richard. Two years later, Richard successfully petitions to adopt Jessica. Jonathan argues that the adoption is invalid because he was not given notice. A New York statute provides that a father must register with the "putative father registry" in order to receive notice of an adoption. Jonathan contends that the statute is unconstitutional as a deprivation of his liberty interest (i.e., his actual or potential relationship with his child) without due process. He argues that he has a constitutional right to notice and a hearing before being deprived of that interest. The United States Supreme Court holds that the rights of only *some* putative fathers merit constitutional protection that requires advance notice and a hearing. Those unwed fathers who demonstrate a full commitment to the responsibilities of parenthood are entitled to due process protection. However, "the mere existence of a biological link does not merit equivalent constitutional protection. . . ." Because Jonathan did not seek any legal recognition of his relationship with Jessica until she was two years old, he relinquished the opportunity to form such a relationship. *Lehr v. Robertson*, 463 U.S. 248, 261 (1983).

Example: Shortly after a mother gives birth to a child, she marries a man who is not the child's father. The biological father (Quilloin) never lives with the mother and/or child and never admits paternity. He makes sporadic support payments and occasionally visits the child. Nine years later, when the mother's husband petitions to adopt the child, the biological father petitions that the adoption be denied. The Georgia statute provides that a mother's consent is sufficient for the adoption of a nonmarital child unless the father legitimates the child by marriage or by court order. Quilloin challenges the constitutionality of the statute, arguing that due process prohibits terminating his parental rights without a finding of unfitness and that the distinction between unmarried and married fathers violates equal protection. The Supreme Court rejects both claims. The Court reasons that due process is not violated (i.e., no showing of unfitness is required) because Quilloin never had nor sought custody. The Court also concludes that Quilloin's interests are distinguishable from those of a married father who has legal responsibility for the rearing of his children. *Quilloin v. Walcott*, 434 U.S. 246 (1978), *reh'g denied*, 435 U.S. 918 (1978).

Example: Abdiel lives with Maria for five years during which time they have two children. When they separate, the mother moves in with another man whom she subsequently marries. Abdiel continues to see the children frequently. At one point, the mother gives him physical custody of them. When Maria and her husband petition to adopt the children, Abdiel and his new wife cross-petition to adopt them. The trial judge approves Maria's petition. Abdiel appeals, alleging that the statute, which provides that a nonmarital child can be adopted with the consent of the mother alone, violates his right to equal protection. The United States Supreme Court holds that the statutory distinction between unwed mothers and fathers violates the Equal Protection Clause because it does not bear a substantial relationship to the state interest in promoting adoption of nonmarital children where (as here) "the father has established a substantial relationship with the child and has admitted his paternity." *Caban v. Mohammed*, 441 U.S. 380, 392 (1979).

In the above cases, the Supreme Court recognizes the rights of only Abdiel Caban who was most involved in his children's lives (saw them frequently and had custody for a period). The other biological fathers (Jonathan Lehr and Quilloin) never sought or had custody, paid little or no support, and did not see their children frequently. Thus, only Caban's parental relationship meets the requisite criteria of "indicia of parenthood."

3. **Consent requirement where father never has opportunity to develop a relationship:** Prior Supreme Court decisions (i.e., the trilogy above) deal with cases in which the biological father has an opportunity to develop a relationship with the child. The most difficult cases occur when a father never has such an opportunity — either because he does not know of the child's birth or because the mother's actions prevent the development of his relationship with the child.

   Note: The dissent in *Lehr* raises this issue (suggesting that the mother prevented the father from establishing a relationship with the child). However, the *Lehr* majority fails to address this issue.

   Example: Marquette is born prematurely. He never lives with his mother. His foster parents, Jeffrey and Karen, have taken care of him since birth and paid for his medical expenses. Seeking to adopt him, they petition to terminate the parental rights of his mother, Denise, and his unknown father. Denise's parental rights are terminated, but she is unable to identify the father of the child. The Child Welfare Bureau locates the father, Bobby, and serves him notice of the pending proceeding to terminate his parental rights. For the first time, Bobby learns that he has a child. Bobby begins to make efforts to contact Marquette and expresses interest in a parent-child relationship. The trial court terminates Bobby's parental rights based on his failure to assume parental responsibilities before he knew of the child's existence, and reasons that his actions after learning of the child are irrelevant. Bobby appeals. The Wisconsin Supreme Court reverses, finding that Bobby's attempts to establish a parent-child relationship with the child are relevant in deciding whether to terminate his parental rights. *In re Marquette S.*, 734 N.W.2d 81 (Wis. 2007).

B. Noncustodial parent's consent in the face of a stepparent adoption: Rising rates of divorce and remarriage result in an increase in reconstituted or blended families. Problems may arise when a stepparent desires to adopt a child from the other spouse's prior marriage, especially if the new spouse's ex-spouse refuses to consent.

Case law and statutory law are becoming more favorable to stepparent adoption. Some jurisdictions now permit stepparent adoptions without the noncustodial parent's consent in some cases (e.g., lack of support, failure to communicate with the child for a designated period of time). Due process generally requires that a divorced noncustodial parent first be given notice and an opportunity to be heard before termination of parental rights.

The Uniform Adoption Act (UAA) facilitates stepparent adoption by making the evaluation of the stepparent's suitability discretionary, preserving the child's inheritance right to the biological parent's intestate estate, and permitting post-adoption visitation by the noncustodial parent (UAA §4-113).

Example: Rusti and John have a nonmarital child, Corbin. They all live together for three years, after which Rusti moves with Corbin without indicating to John where she is going. Rusti later files a petition to establish paternity, custody, and support, identifying John as Corbin's biological father. The court enters a temporary order granting John visitation rights and setting an amount for support. John pays the support but when he attempts to pick up Corbin for visitation, Rusti and Corbin do not show up. The paternity action is subsequently dismissed for lack of prosecution. John claims that he tried to find Rusti and Corbin, but could not locate them. Rusti claims that John did not make any such attempt. Several years later, Rusti's husband wishes to adopt Corbin as his stepchild. John receives a "Notice of Adoption," but does not make a timely response. State law allows a court to dispense with the consent of a putative father if he does not timely object to the notice of a second-parent adoption. The stepparent adoption is granted. John appeals. The Nebraska Supreme Court holds that the statute dispensing with a putative father's consent is unconstitutional as applied to John, because John was the biological father and, in the first three years of Corbin's life, established a parent-child relationship that warranted constitutional protection. Thus, John's consent is required unless he has relinquished his parental rights in writing, abandoned the child, is incapable of consenting, or has been adjudicated unfit. Finding none of these, the court reverses and vacates the adoption. *In re Adoption of Corbin J.*, 775 N.W.2d 404 (Neb. 2009).

Quiz Yourself on *CONSENT*

111. Following a brief sexual relationship with Bill, Stephanie gives birth to a son Michael. Stephanie and Bill never live together. Although Stephanie informs Bill of Michael's birth, Bill never offers support or visits Michael. When Michael is two years old, Bill marries Andrea. After discovering that Andrea is unable to conceive, Bill decides that he would like to obtain custody of Michael or establish visitation rights. Meanwhile, Stephanie, herself, has remarried. Her husband Larry desires to, and does, adopt Michael. When Bill learns of the adoption, he argues that it is invalid because he was not given notice and an opportunity to be heard. Larry argues that Bill's consent was not necessary because he failed to support or to visit the boy. Will Larry prevail? ____________________

Answer

111. Yes. The Supreme Court has held (in *Lehr*, *Caban*, and *Quilloin*) that an unwed father is entitled to constitutional protection of his parental rights so long as he manifests certain "indicia of parenthood." That is, his constitutional rights depend on the degree to which he reveals a willingness to assume a custodial, personal, or financial relationship with the child. Here, Bill has not provided support or visited his son Michael for two years. Bill's failure to assume any parental responsibilities probably will result in relinquishment of his constitutional rights to notice and an opportunity to be heard.

IV. PLACEMENT PROCEDURE

A biological parent (or parents) may relinquish a child to a public or privately licensed adoption agency for adoption. The agency then undertakes to investigate the prospective adoptive parents and to select the adoptive parents. Alternatively, a biological parent (or parents) may arrange for a private (i.e., ***independent***) adoption by which a private person/intermediary facilitates the adoption. A criticism of independent adoption is that this process is largely unregulated by the state.

A. **Agency's role: Disclosure requirements:** An agency that discloses information to prospective adoptive parents about a child's biological parents or medical history has a duty to disclose the information fully so as not to mislead the adoptive parents. If the agency breaches this duty, the agency may be liable for the tort of ***wrongful adoption*** (i.e., a form of misrepresentation). Most courts have not extended an agency's responsibility to include an affirmative duty to *investigate* and discover health information about a child. See also discussion of "wrongful adoption" *infra*.

B. **Independent placement: Intermediary's role:** Parents who wish to place their child for adoption may arrange for a private or independent adoption rather than an agency adoption. Private adoptions are often performed through an intermediary (sometimes called a "baby broker"), such as an attorney or physician. This independent placement is known as "gray market" adoption to distinguish it from "black market" adoption (i.e., solely for profit) (discussed *infra*). The black market is regulated by means of criminal penalties for ***babyselling***.

Some statutes limit or forbid the participation of independent agents in the placement process. Attorneys who act as intermediaries must be careful not to violate conflict of interest rules.

Example: An attorney arranges an adoption for a birth mother who is pregnant with twins, unemployed, and unmarried. He represents both the birth mother and the adopting parents. He charges the adopting parents a $50,000 fee, plus $10,000 in medical expenses, in addition to a nonrefundable $1,500 retainer. Five days after the birth, the attorney files accountings in the probate court because he is required to disclose any and all disbursements of value related to the adoptions. The attorney, who paid the birth mother's living expenses and received over $60,000 from the prospective adoptive parents, represents that no disbursements had been made. The court disbars the attorney, finding that the attorney's deliberate falsification of documents to avoid disclosure of exorbitant fees and dubious payments was contrary to the professional qualities of honesty, justice, and good character. *Stark County Bar Association v. Hare*, 791 N.E.2d 966 (Ohio 2003).

Some rules of professional conduct will allow an attorney to represent multiple clients, but only after full disclosure and consent has been obtained.

Example: Gregory and Barbara (Couple 1) consult an attorney about adopting an infant. The parties agree that if the couple locates a baby for adoption, the attorney would assist them. Later, the couple refers an expectant mother to the attorney. The attorney contacts the couple with regard to adopting the child, and the couple indicates their interest. Shortly thereafter, the attorney recommends that the natural mother place her child with another couple (Couple 2) who also contacted him. When the first couple learns that the child was placed with the other couple, they call the attorney and request that the child be placed with them. The attorney refuses. Gregory institutes a complaint with the state bar, alleging that the attorney violated rules regarding conflicts of interest. The court determines that the attorney should be censured for violating conflict of interest rules by (1) accepting employment from Couple 2, without consent and full disclosure, after having agreed to represent Couple 1; and (2) by continuing multiple employment (of both couples) when such representation would adversely affect the interests of other clients. Censure, rather than suspension, is appropriate because the record does not unequivocally reveal that the attorney knew of the conflict (i.e., he may have been negligent in determining whether the conflict existed). *Matter of Petrie*, 742 P.2d 796 (Ariz. 1987).

Note: The Model Rules of Professional Conduct, addressing the role of attorneys as adoption intermediaries, requires full disclosure of the implications of common representation, client consent thereto, full explanations of each decision to be made, and withdrawal from the matter upon request or dissatisfaction. Further, the attorney must reasonably believe the matter can be resolved impartially and consistent with the clients' best interests. Model Rules Prof'l Conduct R. 2.2 (2004).

V. SUBSIDIZED ADOPTION

A. Definition: All states provide subsidized adoption programs to facilitate adoption of those children who are difficult to place for reasons of age, physical or mental disability, or racial or ethnic background. Specifically, states appropriate funds to social service agencies to provide assistance to adoptive parents who care for these children. The subsidy varies in duration, type (services and funds), and depends on the needs of the child.

B. Federal legislation:

1. **Adoption Assistance and Child Welfare Act:** Although state subsidies first began in 1969 in New York, the federal Adoption Assistance and Child Welfare Act of 1980 (AACWA), 42 U.S.C. §§620-628, §§670-679(a) (2006), encourages the establishment and expansion of such state programs. Hoping to address "foster care drift" (i.e., lengthy stays in foster care), legislators desired especially to provide assistance to those foster parents who would like, but financially were unable, to adopt needy children in their care. The Act provides funds to states who qualify by enacting statutes that authorize subsidies for adoption of children with "special needs."

2. **Adoption and Safe Families Act:** The Adoption and Safe Families Act strengthens the provisions of the AACWA by providing incentives to states to promote the adoption of children with special needs and requiring states to provide for health insurance for such children. 42 U.S.C. §673A (2006) (incentives); §671(a) (2006) (insurance).

VI. INTERNATIONAL ADOPTION

International adoption, the practice by which an American couple adopts a child from a foreign country, has generated considerable controversy. Advocates of the practice argue that international adoptions protect children in third-world countries from institutional care and poverty. Opponents counter that these adoptions deprive children of their cultural heritage.

Different laws apply to international adoption. The prospective adoptive couple must first meet the relinquishment requirements of the foreign country. Then the parents must satisfy federal immigration laws when they bring the child into the United States. Finally, the parents must meet state adoption standards when they petition to adopt the child.

The Hague Convention on Protection of Children and Cooperation in Respect of Intercountry Adoption was adopted in 1993 to facilitate international adoptions by requiring determinations that adoption serves the child's best interests and by establishing supervisory authorities. The United States ratified and enacted implementing legislation for this Hague Convention in 2001. 42 U.S.C. §§14901 to 14954 (2006). The legislation applies only when both countries involved are convention signatories.

Subsequent federal legislation (8 U.S.C. §1101(b)(1)(F) (2006)) made it easier to adopt foreign children by expanding the term "orphan" to include children who were abandoned or whose parent could not provide for them and has irrevocably relinquished them. In addition, many children adopted abroad by U.S. citizens automatically receive U.S. citizenship.

VII. THE LEGAL CONSEQUENCES OF ADOPTION

By its termination of the rights and responsibilities of biological parents and the creation of a new legal relationship with adoptive parents, adoption sometimes results in unique civil consequences.

A. Marriage limitations: Occasionally, persons related by adoption may wish to marry each other. Whether they are able to do so depends on state statute or judicial interpretation.

Example: Martin and Tammy, a brother and sister related by adoption, are denied a license to marry. A statute prohibits marriage between a brother and sister "whether the relationship is by the half or the whole blood or by adoption." Martin's father married Tammy's mother when Martin was 18 and living away from home, while Tammy was 13 and living with her mother. Martin's father adopts Tammy. Martin and Tammy argue that the statutory provision violates the Equal Protection Clause. The court holds that the provision prohibiting marriage between adopted children is unconstitutional because it fails to satisfy the rational basis test. The court reasons that the traditional objections to such marriages (fear of genetic defects in offspring and moral condemnation) are absent. *Israel v. Allen*, 577 P.2d 762, 763 (Colo. 1978).

Note: In *Israel v. Allen*, *supra*, petitioners did not grow up together or live together as a family. Some courts are more reluctant to permit such marriages if the individuals do so.

Example: Tracy and William have a child, D.M.G. When D.M.G. is five, William relinquishes his parental rights to allow Tracy's new husband to adopt the child. When D.M.G. is 16, she attempts to find her biological father, William. Upon meeting D.M.G., William sexually molests her. He is convicted of second-degree incest. He appeals, arguing that because he surrendered all his parental rights to D.M.G., she was no longer his descendant under intestacy laws. Therefore, the incest statute did not apply. The court disagrees, finding that in the incest laws, the biological rather than the legal relationship is significant. The adoption did not negate the biological relationship between William and D.M.G., and therefore, the incest conviction was appropriate. *State v. Hall*, 48 P.3d 350 (Wash. Ct. App. 2002).

B. Inheritance

1. **Intestate succession: By or from the adopted child:** Following a child's adoption by adoptive parents, the child traditionally loses the right to inherit from the biological parents. In particular, an adopted child loses the right to inherit by ***intestate succession*** (i.e., when a biological parent dies without a will). Instead, the adopted child is treated as a member of the adoptive family for purposes of inheritance. Then, the child inherits by intestate succession only from the adoptive parents.

   A corollary is that if the adopted child predeceases a parent, the child's intestate estate passes to the adoptive parent(s) and not to the biological parent(s). This is the rule of inheritance "by or from" the adopted child.

   The situation differs somewhat if the child is adopted by the spouse of a biological parent, as in the stepparent adoption situation (discussed *infra*).

   Note: Of course, if a biological parent leaves a will that specifically names the child as a legatee, then the child will inherit via testate succession.

2. **Inheritance and stepparent adoption:** Problems may arise if a biological parent dies after the child has been adopted by a stepparent. For example, suppose Barbara and Frank marry and have a daughter Allison. Barbara then divorces Frank, and marries Sam. Sam subsequently adopts Allison and becomes Allison's stepfather. Then, Frank dies. May Allison inherit by intestate succession from her biological father Frank? Traditionally, the law had great difficulty accepting the view that a child may have two mothers or two fathers, and thereby, permitting a child to inherit from both a biological father and adoptive father in the situation above. However, this view appears to be changing. Many statutes now provide that an adopted child is still considered a child of a noncustodial biological parent following an adoption by the spouse of that biological parent (as in the remarriage situation above).

3. **Stranger to the adoption rule:** A troublesome question for many courts, following the enactment of adoption statutes, is whether an adopted child takes under the will of a person who is a relative of an adoptive parent (i.e., who is a "stranger" to the adoption). Under the "stranger to the adoption rule," courts refuse to construe class gift language (i.e., language such as "to my nephews," or "to my sister's children") in a will or a trust in such a way as to include adoptees — except in instruments executed by adoptive parents. Application of this rule precludes an adoptee from inheriting ***through*** either the biological parent's or the adoptive parent's family line when a relative of that biological or adoptive parent dies. The rationale for the "stranger to the adoption rule" is a preference for relatives of the blood line.

   Because of the harshness of the doctrine, many jurisdictions carve out exceptions to the rule. A common exception permits an adopted child to take if the child is adopted before (not after) the testator's death (i.e., so that the decedent is aware of the child's adoption and could have altered his or her will to preclude the child if desired).

C. Custody and visitation: Stepparent adoption sometimes gives rise to visitation disputes when a child's grandparents desire to maintain contact with grandchildren in a post-divorce adoption situation. See the discussion of grandparent visitation in Chapter 5.

VIII. OPEN ADOPTION

A. Definition: Traditionally, the severance of the biological parent-child relationship also extinguishes a biological parent's visitation rights. Sometimes, however, the biological parent desires and arranges post-adoption visitation. ***Open adoption*** is a form of adoption that reflects a continuation of contact, following an adoption, between the biological parent and the adopted child.

B. Modern trend: Currently, open adoption is growing in popularity. The modern trend is to recognize open adoption.

C. Best interests standard: Courts, increasingly, are asked to enforce written agreements by adoptive and biological parties that authorize these arrangements. Courts generally uphold such agreements if the agreements are found to be in the best interests of the child.

Example: Debbie gives birth to Laci. Three years later Debbie permits Mr. and Mrs. Clark (a couple with whom she is acquainted) to adopt Laci. Debbie refuses to give her consent to the adoption unless the Clarks permit her to have visitation rights. Both the Clarks and Debbie sign a post-adoption visitation agreement that grants such visitation. The Clarks abide by the agreement for over a year. Subsequently, when Debbie wants to visit Laci on Laci's birthday, the Clarks refuse and tell Debbie that she can no longer visit the child. Debbie requests specific performance of the agreement. The trial court determines that the adoption terminated Debbie's parental rights and holds the visitation agreement unenforceable. The state supreme court concludes that courts should give effect to post-adoption visitation agreements when continued visitation is in the best interests of the child. The court remands for such a determination. *Groves v. Clark*, 920 P.2d 981 (Mont. 1996).

Quiz Yourself on OPEN ADOPTION

112. Samantha, a college student, has just given birth to a daughter, Gail, as the result of a casual relationship. After taking a semester off to care for the child while she works part-time, Samantha decides it would be better to place Gail for adoption. Samantha is convinced that she cannot properly care for Gail at this time because Samantha is not financially independent and also would like to finish her education. Samantha wishes, however, to maintain contact with Gail. With the help of one of her professors, Samantha locates a professional couple, Dr. and Mrs. Jones, who would like to adopt Gail. Dr. and Mrs. Jones agree to sign an agreement that permits Samantha to have visitation rights following the adoption. Following the adoption, Samantha visits Gail every few weeks. Two years later when Gail is going through "the terrible twos," Dr. and Mrs. Jones decide that it might be better for Gail psychologically not to have further contact with Samantha. Samantha sues to enforce the agreement. Will she prevail? ____________________

Answer

112. Yes. A modern court is likely to uphold the agreement (for an "open adoption") if the court finds such an arrangement to be in the best interests of the child. Here, Samantha cared for Gail for several months and continued to visit Gail regularly even after the adoption. Gail and Samantha have formed psychological bonds. A court might well decide that it would be in the child's best interests to enforce the agreement.

IX. EQUITABLE ADOPTION

Equitable adoption is an equitable device whereby courts effectuate an adoption (or effectuate the consequences of an adoption) in cases in which a legal adoption never occurred.

A. Inheritance purposes: The doctrine is most often invoked to permit a child to *inherit from* a foster parent who agreed to, or attempted to, adopt the child but never completed the necessary legal procedure. Occasionally, courts invoke the doctrine to permit a child to *inherit through* a foster parent (i.e., from relatives of the foster parent).

Example: Mr. and Mrs. Daggett desire to adopt a six-year-old girl (Plaintiff) subject to her father's consent. Plaintiff is being raised by her aunt and uncle. The father, upon being informed of the Daggetts' desire, permits the aunt and uncle to deliver Plaintiff to the Daggetts. The Daggetts change the child's name to theirs, baptize her, and raise her as their daughter although they never formally adopt her. When Mr. Daggett dies intestate, Plaintiff seeks to share in his estate as his adopted child. The court decrees an equitable adoption to the extent that Plaintiff becomes an heir of the couple. The court reasons that the remedy is appropriate because the couple took Plaintiff into their home with the understanding that they could adopt her. Although the adoption never occurred, Plaintiff's biological father fully performed his side of the agreement. *Long v. Wiley*, 391 S.W.2d 301 (Miss. 1965).

Example: A child claims an intestate share of his foster father's estate as an equitably adopted son. (The father died without issue or a surviving spouse.) The California Supreme Court holds that, although the evidence revealed a close family relationship (i.e., the child lived with his foster parents from the ages of 2 to 22), there is insufficient proof that the family ever made an attempt to adopt him or stated an intent to do so, as required by statute. *Estate of Ford*, 8 Cal. Rptr. 3d 541 (Cal. 2004).

B. Theories: Courts generally apply equitable adoption by resort to either contract theory or estoppel theory.

1. **Contract theory:** Contract theory envisages specific performance of an adoption agreement when a person has contracted to adopt a child but has failed to fully perform the contract.

2. **Estoppel theory:** Other courts apply estoppel theory to protect the child (who has "relied" on the representation that she is adopted) from the adoptive parents' neglect in order to complete the adoption.

Quiz Yourself on EQUITABLE ADOPTION

113. Mary and John have twin girls. When the twins are only a few months old, Mary is diagnosed with terminal cancer. She dies shortly thereafter. John has extreme difficulty coping with his wife's death and trying to raise the twins. Sally and Tom Lambert, an infertile couple whom John knows, inquire whether John would be willing to let them adopt the girls. John agrees. The Lamberts take the twins into their home and raise them as their own daughters, telling their friends and family that the girls are adopted. In reality, the Lamberts never complete a legal adoption. The Lamberts die intestate, victims of an automobile accident, when the twins are approaching adulthood. The twins petition the probate court to permit them to take a share of the Lamberts' intestate estates. The Lamberts' relatives argue that the twins should not share in the estate because they are not biologically related children. Will the relatives prevail? ____________________

Answer

113. No. Application of the doctrine of equitable adoption would permit the twins to claim their shares in their foster parents' estate. Courts invoke the doctrine as an equitable remedy in cases in which the foster parent(s) promised to adopt a child but never actually does so. Here, the Lamberts agreed with the children's father that the Lamberts would adopt the twins. Under either a theory of specific performance (the Lamberts and the father agreed to the adoption; the father performed his side of the agreement by surrendering the children), or a theory of estoppel (the twins "relied" on the agreement by assuming they were the Lamberts' children so therefore the Lamberts' relatives should be estopped to deny the adoption), a court should equitably decree that the children should share in the Lamberts' estates.

X. ADOPTEE'S RIGHT TO KNOW OF ORIGINS

A. Traditional rule: State adoption statutes traditionally required strict confidentiality. Thus, following an adoption, the original birth certificate and adoption records are sealed so that neither the adopted child nor a biological parent may determine the identity of the other. Historically, courts permitted disclosure only upon "good cause" (e.g., a medical necessity). This traditional rule applied to adoption agencies. However, the agencies often chose to release limited information for genetic or medical purposes.

Example: Roger B. is an adult adoptee who has searched for his biological parents for three years. Roger petitions the court to secure access to his adoption records. He acknowledges that he has no medical or psychiatric need to know. A statute places birth and adoption records under seal and allows their release only for "good cause." Roger argues that the right to know his identity is a constitutionally protected fundamental right based on the right of privacy. The court holds that an adoptee does not have a fundamental right to examine adoption records, reasoning that no fundamental right or right of privacy is implicated. Further, the statute is rationally related to the legitimate purpose of protecting the confidentiality of the adoption process. *In re Roger B.*, 418 N.E.2d 751, *appeal dismissed*, 454 U.S. 306 (Ill. 1981).

B. Modern view: A growing movement allows and facilitates the exchange of information between an adopted child and the natural parents. Some states now permit natural parents to consent to the release of information pertaining to their identity or location. Other states allow those adoptees who have reached the age of majority to have access to their adoption records, to request a state or private agency to investigate the location of a birth parent, or to authorize the agency to release identifying information to family members who may make a similar inquiry.

Quiz Yourself on *ADOPTEE'S RIGHT TO KNOW OF ORIGINS*

114. Timothy, an adoptee, seeks nonidentifying information about the medical history of his biological mother. In his petition to unseal the adoption records, he provides affidavits from his physicians stating that the medical information would be "very helpful" and "should assist" the physicians in better diagnosing and more effectively caring for Timothy and his children. Timothy has no current medical reason for his request. A state statute provides that a court may unseal adoption records for "good cause." Will Timothy succeed? ____________________

Answer

114. No. Although medical necessity traditionally constitutes "good cause" to unseal adoption records, here Timothy has not established a serious health condition necessary to establish a "medical necessity." A court will not unseal an adoption record simply because the knowledge of hereditary information might be useful. Thus, Timothy's request will not succeed.

XI. JURISDICTION

A. Generally: Several jurisdictions hold that some statutes governing multi-jurisdictional custody disputes (such as the Uniform Child Custody Jurisdiction Act (UCCJA) and the Parental Kidnapping Prevention Act (PKPA)) also are controlling in proceedings involving termination of parental rights and adoptions.

Example: Cara (Baby Girl Clausen's mother) and an individual who was erroneously identified as the child's father relinquish their parental rights in Michigan. The prospective adoptive parents (Robert and Jan DeBoer) acquire custody and initiate adoption proceedings in Iowa. Daniel Schmidt, the child's biological father, seeks to intervene in those proceedings. The Iowa court denies the DeBoers' adoption and awards custody to Daniel. The DeBoers then seek, in Michigan, an order rejecting or modifying the Iowa court order that gave Daniel custody. The child's guardian ad litem files a separate suit and asserts that the child had an independent right to a best interests hearing. The appellate court finds: (1) the Michigan courts were required to enforce the Iowa order because the Iowa court made the custody determination in a manner consistent with the PKPA, and the Iowa court had continuing jurisdiction over the matter; (2) neither the PKPA nor the UCCJA require the Iowa court to conduct a best interests hearing; and (3) the child does not have an independent right to seek a best interests hearing under the UCCJA. The Supreme Court of Michigan affirms. *In re Baby Girl Clausen*, 502 N.W.2d 649 (Mich. 1993).

UCCJEA and UAA: The Uniform Child Custody Jurisdiction and Enforcement Act (UCCJEA) explicitly disclaims application to adoption, deferring instead to the Uniform Adoption Act (UAA). The UAA recognizes multiple bases for jurisdiction, including the states having evidence about the care of the child, the state where the child or prospective adoptive parent has lived for the preceding six months, the state where the adoption agency is located, or emergency jurisdiction in the state where the child or a prospective parent is present. UAA §3-101, 9 U.L.A. (pt. IA) 67-68 (1999). In addition, a state must decline jurisdiction if an adoption is pending in another state, or another state has issued a decree and has continuing jurisdiction.

B. Interstate Compact on the Placement of Children (ICPC): The ICPC also governs multistate adoptions. That statute specifies procedural requirements for transferring the custody of a child to adoptive parents from another state but does not establish jurisdiction.

XII. ADULT ADOPTION

A. General rule: Most states allow adoption of an adult. However, some states impose special limitations on adult adoptions.

B. Limitations: Some jurisdictions inquire into the purpose of the adult adoption. Whereas adoptions may not be for fraudulent, illegal, or frivolous purposes, they may effectuate inheritance purposes. Some states allow adult adoptions only when there has been a preexisting parent-child relationship that begins while the adoptee is a minor.

Example: Plaintiff, a 66-year-old man, wants to adopt his 51-year-old male companion in order to recognize the parties' emotional (17-year) commitment and facilitate their estate planning. The adult adoption statute requires only that the adoptee appear in court and consent to the adoption. The lower court denies their petition on the ground that there is no preexisting parental relationship. Reversing, the state supreme court determines that the establishment of inheritance rights is among the permissible purposes for an adult adoption. The court finds that the statute has no qualifying language that requires a parent-child relationship. *Adoption of Swanson*, 623 A.2d 1095 (Del. 1993).

C. Adoption of same-sex partners: Historically, some states refused to permit adult adoption by gays and lesbians. Courts in these jurisdictions reasoned that permitting adoption in contexts other than parent-child would confer legitimacy on same-sex relationships (especially at a time when, and in jurisdictions where, same-sex sexual acts would have subjected the partners to criminal liability).

Example: A 57-year-old male petitions to adopt his 50-year-old male partner. The couple has lived together for 25 years and desires the adoption for social, financial, and emotional reasons. The Family Court denies the petition, reasoning that the adoption would subvert the adoption process for purposes that are more appropriately served by marriage, wills, and business contracts, and also that the couple's relationship is not that of parent and child. The court finds that the legislature could not have intended to permit a lover to adopt the other partner. Because these parties do not intend a parent-child relationship and their relationship reveals no incidents of a parent-child relationship, the statute cannot sanction an adoption that would "distort[] the function of adoption" and be "an unreasonable or absurd result." The court concludes that adoption is not a means of obtaining legal recognition for a nonmarital sexual relationship. *In re Robert Paul P.*, 471 N.E.2d 424, 427 (N.Y. Ct. App. 1984).

The United States Supreme Court's decision in *Lawrence v. Texas* (discussed in Chapter 2) casts doubt on such case law. Furthermore, the advent of domestic partnership legislation and the recognition of same-sex marriage reduce the need for such adoptions by same-sex partners. For a discussion of the role of sexual orientation in the adoption of children, see Section II.B.2, *supra*.

XIII. ADOPTION FAILURE: REVOCATION AND ABROGATION

Adoptions may fail either because of the actions of a biological parent who revokes her or his consent or because of the desires of the adoptive parent(s) to abrogate (vacate) the adoption.

A. Revocation of consent: Statutes confer the right on a biological parent to revoke consent to an adoption in limited circumstances. Traditional grounds include: fraud, duress, and coercion.

Historically, many jurisdictions permitted a birth parent to revoke consent at any time prior to the final decree. Stemming from a concern with certainty and finality, most jurisdictions now ***limit the time period*** during which the birth mother may withdraw consent. The Uniform Adoption Act (UAA) (§§2-408, 2-409) provides that a parent may revoke consent within eight days of the child's birth (absent fraud or duress). Consent given before a judge (rather than to an agency) is immediately effective. (Such rules apply to post-birth consent — many states invalidate *pre-birth consent*.)

Example: A Colombian woman conceives a child out of wedlock. Fearing shame to herself and her family, she moves to New York to have the child. She relinquishes the four-day-old infant to an adoption agency. Ten days later, the agency places the infant with a couple for adoption. Five days later, the mother changes her mind. After learning that her wealthy parents will assist her to raise the child, she requests that the child be returned to her. When the agency refuses, she files a habeas corpus proceeding seeking return of the child. The relevant statute permits a birth mother to revoke consent unless she is proven unfit. After the court refuses to allow the prospective adoptive parents to intervene, the prospective adoptive parents argue that the court's refusal deprives them of due process. The court holds that the best interests of the child dictate that the child should be returned to her natural mother whose relinquishment decision was improvident and motivated by concern for the child. The court reasons that the mother has not been proven unfit, and is educated, financially secure, and in a position to assume the child's care. The trial court's refusal to permit the adoptive parents to intervene did not violate due process because the prospective adoptive parents do not have legal custody (i.e., the agency does). *Scarpetta v. Spence-Chapin Adoption Serv.*, 269 N.E.2d 787 (N.Y. Ct. App. 1971).

Epilogue: The prospective adoptive parents flee to Florida with the child before the New York court's decision. When the mother files a habeas corpus petition in Florida, the prospective adoptive parents argue that they are not bound by the New York decision because they were not parties to the litigation (i.e., the court did not permit them to intervene). A Florida court subsequently holds that, based on the best interests of the child, the baby should remain with the adoptive parents. The New York legislature subsequently overruled *Scarpetta* by statute (N.Y. Dom. Rel. §115-b(6)(d)(v) (McKinney Supp. 2005)) to make it more difficult for the birth mother to revoke her consent.

Note: Many jurisdictions require a high standard for duress. That is, courts have held that parental persuasion by the birth mother's family to give the child up for adoption is insufficient duress to support her revocation of consent. *See, e.g., In re Baby Boy L.*, 534 N.Y.S.2d 706 (App. Div. 1988), *appeal dismissed without opinion*, 541 N.E.2d 427 (N.Y. 1989).

B. Abrogation

1. **Definition:** Abrogation is the annulment of an adoption by the adoptive parents. Most states allow abrogation in some circumstances.

2. **Traditional view:** Traditionally, states permitted abrogation of an adoption for an undiscovered illness or disability.

3. **Modern view:** Under the modern view, courts are less willing to permit abrogation. Their concern is whether abrogation serves the best interests of the child. Some states allow abrogation only if there is evidence of fraud or misrepresentation on the part of the agency or a procedural defect in the adoption.

4. **Wrongful adoption:** Some states that refuse to permit abrogation may permit *damages* in a tort suit against the agency for "wrongful adoption" (i.e., negligent or intentional misrepresentation).

   Example: Richard and Charlene adopt a baby from the Children's Home Society (CHS) and name him Jordan. They are told by the agency that the child has no medical history of substance abuse. Several months later Charlene becomes curious about Jordan's unusual facial features and contacts a CHS caseworker to ask if Jordan's birth mother used alcohol during pregnancy. The caseworker assures Charlene that, to the best of her knowledge, his birth mother did not consume alcohol during her pregnancy, and that his unusual facial features are merely a "familial look." Later, Charlene requests information on the reason for Jordan's developmental delays, and CHS again assures her that fetal alcohol syndrome was not involved. In fact, agency records reveal that the birth mother admitted that she was an alcoholic and that she frequently got drunk during the pregnancy. Charlene and Richard file suit against CHS, alleging intentional and negligent misrepresentation and breach of contract. The court holds that the adoptive parents stated an actionable claim against the adoption agency for its intentional and negligent misrepresentation of facts regarding alcohol abuse by the child's birth mother. *Wolford v. Children's Home Soc'y of W. Va.*, 17 F. Supp.2d 577 (S.D. W.Va. 1998).

Quiz Yourself on *ABROGATION*

115. Mr. and Mrs. Xavier file an application with the ABC Adoption Agency to adopt a child. The agency informs Mr. and Mrs. Xavier that a baby is available. The agency also tells them that the child's paternal grandmother died of a genetic disease, Huntington's disease. The agency also informs Mr. and Mrs. Xavier that, because the child's father tested negative for the disease, the child is not at risk. In fact, no such test existed. The child is diagnosed with the disease four years later. The adoptive parents sue the agency for "wrongful adoption" (negligent misrepresentation). Will they prevail? ____________________

Answer

115. Yes. The agency assumed the duty of informing the adoptive parents, the Xaviers, about the child's medical background (i.e., the family history of Huntington's disease and about the child's chances of developing the disease). Having done so, the agency breached their duty by informing the Xaviers that the child's biological father tested negative for the disease when no such test existed.

Exam Tips on ADOPTION

- ***Commonly tested issues*** in the area of adoption include: selection standards for adoptive parents; consent; placement procedures; various types of adoption (open adoption, equitable adoption, adult adoption); the adoptee's right to know of origins; and adoption failure.

- First, discuss the ***effect of adoption*** (i.e., the creation of a new parent-child relationship and termination of the legal rights and responsibilities of the biological parents). Determine whether there are any initial issues regarding the validity of the termination of the biological parents' rights (e.g., cross-over issues with the child abuse context such as whether the court had jurisdiction and whether the parents' due process rights were safeguarded). Explain the guiding ***standard*** in adoption law (***the best interests of the child***). Then, explore whether there are issues of ***selection standards*** for the adoptive parents. Look for frequently tested standards involving ***religion, race,*** and ***sexual orientation***. Discuss the traditional rules on the relevance of each factor (i.e., religious matching, race matching). Discuss possible ***constitutional issues*** (First and Fourteenth Amendments) if public adoption agencies are involved. Then, apply the best-interests-of-the-child test to the particular facts.

  - If the question involves the issue of ***sexual orientation***, discuss the ***different views*** that restrict or permit such adoptions. Discuss also the traditional and modern views on the effect of a second-parent adoption on the first parent's rights, i.e., whether adoption by a same-sex partner has the effect of ***terminating the parental rights of the biological parent***.

  - Remember that if the question involves placement of a Native-American child, federal legislation (the ***Indian Child Welfare Act***) is relevant. That Act mandates a preference for tribal members, absent good cause.

- Another commonly tested issue is ***consent***. Consent issues may arise concerning the ***biological mother or biological father***. For example, was the mother's consent valid, or subject to ***fraud or duress***? Consent issues also may concern the ***biological father***. Determine if the child's parents were married or unmarried. If the question involves an ***unmarried father***, determine how his rights may have been infringed. What relief is he seeking? Is he seeking notice of the adoption proceedings and an opportunity to be heard? Is his objection to the adoption timely? Has he registered in the paternity register in the requisite jurisdiction?

  - If the unmarried father is alleging that his procedural ***due process*** rights have been infringed (i.e., his right to notice and an opportunity to be heard), be sure to discuss and apply United States Supreme Court rulings in *Stanley v. Illinois*, *Quilloin v. Walcott*, *Caban v. Mohammed*, and *Lehr v. Robertson*. Explain and apply the rule that an unmarried father is entitled to constitutional protection of his parental rights so long as he manifests certain ***indicia of parenthood.*** Application of the rule requires an exploration of the father's actions vis-à-vis the mother and the child: Did the father pay for the mother's medical expenses (and support) prior to, and/or after, the child's birth? Did the father attend birthing classes with the mother? Did the parents live together before and/or after the birth? Is the father named on the birth certificate? Did the father provide support for the child after the birth? Did the father communicate and/or visit with the child after the birth? If the father has not manifested the requisite indicia of parenthood, explore the reason why. For example, did the birth mother thwart his efforts? If so, did he act in a timely manner once he learned of the child's birth or location and manifest his willingness to assume parental responsibilities? Discuss the relevance of model legislation (the new Uniform Adoption Act) which permits termination of a father's parental rights over his objection in some circumstances.

- Keep in mind whether this is an ***agency adoption*** or an ***independent adoption***. If the former, did the agency follow the ***proper procedures*** (regarding consent and disclosure)? If the latter, make sure that no criminal statutes for ***babyselling*** are implicated. Point out that some states limit or prohibit participation of independent agents in the adoption process. If the intermediary is an attorney, check whether there is a violation of any rules of professional conduct (e.g., conflicts of interest).

- Explore whether various forms of adoption might be relevant — open adoption, equitable adoption, and/or adult adoption. For ***open adoption***, discuss the ***traditional view*** of confidentiality and the ***modern view*** that favors open adoption. Explain and apply the rule that courts generally uphold open adoption agreements if found to be in the child's best interests. Remember that the ***equitable adoption*** doctrine is used to permit a child to ***inherit*** from a foster parent. Discuss and apply the various theories (contract theory, estoppel theory) that courts utilize in equitable adoption cases. For adult adoption, discuss the ***general rule*** (permitting adults to adopt other adults) and the various ***limitations*** (e.g., the requirement of a preexisting parent-child relationship beginning during the adoptee's minority).

- Determine whether an adoptee is seeking ***access to his or her birth records***. If so, discuss the ***traditional view*** of confidentiality (permitting release of medical records for good cause) and the ***modern trend*** permitting broader access.

- Explore whether ***adoption failure*** is an issue. If so, explore which aspect of adoption failure is involved: a biological parent who revokes consent and/or an adoptive parent who seeks to vacate the adoption. In the former case, specify the traditional rule that permits revocation of consent in limited circumstances. Explore whether those circumstances (fraud, duress) exist.

☞ If abrogation is involved, determine whether the biological parent revoked his or her consent in a ***timely*** manner. Explain the ***modern trend*** that state statutes and model legislation now limit the time period within which a birth parent may revoke consent and the policy underlying that trend (to ensure stability for the child). If an agency is involved, explore whether the adoptive parents might have an action for ***wrongful adoption***. Mention that some jurisdictions permit such tort claims against adoption agencies. Then, explore whether the requisite elements of the tort claim are present. For example, was there an intentional or negligent misrepresentation (or failure to disclose) on the part of the agency? What was the nature of that misrepresentation (or failure to disclose)? And finally, did the adoptive parents rely on that misrepresentation when they adopted the child?

Essay Exam Questions

QUESTION 1: Rachel and Samuel Martin have been married for eight years and reside in the jurisdiction of Blackacre. Samuel is 32 years old; Rachel is 30 years old. Both are in good health. They are the parents of four children, ranging in age from seven years to one month.

Rachel works as a teacher in a local preschool. She is able to bring her infant son with her to work where he is cared for by her co-workers at the preschool. Rachel currently earns $50,000 a year. Throughout the marriage, Samuel, a scholar of linguistics, has been unemployed. When they married, Rachel agreed to support the family while Samuel devoted himself to the study of ancient languages and the completion of his Ph.D. The couple manages financially with Rachel's salary plus approximately $15,000 annually in gifts to Samuel from Samuel's parents. Samuel uses all of his parents' financial gifts in furtherance of his scholarly work, which includes drafting a treatise explaining biblical texts.

Serious marital difficulties have arisen. Six months ago, Rachel moved out of the marital bedroom and into quarters in the basement. She recently filed for divorce. Samuel continues to refuse, as he has throughout the marriage, to provide financially for Rachel and the children. Samuel argues that he is not purposely seeking to avoid his support duties. Rather, he points out that his life's work as a linguistics scholar prevents him from acquiring an income-producing vocation.

Before the couple's marital difficulties force Rachel to move into the basement, she approaches Attorney Aaron Atwood. She requests Atwood's advice as to how she might force Samuel to provide for her and the children—now and in the future, in the event of a divorce. Rachel wonders on what grounds she should petition for divorce. If a divorce should occur, she informs Atwood that she is thinking of leaving Blackacre to reside with her parents (who live in another jurisdiction). She would like to refuse to allow Samuel to see the children unless he provides support.

Rachel tells Attorney Atwood that she has been the sole provider for the family during the marriage. As a result, she believes that she should be entitled to all of the marital property, which includes the equity in the family residence as well as the funds in a savings account in Samuel's name (approximately $50,000) that were derived solely from gifts from Samuel's parents. She also wonders whether she has a claim for repayment of any funds derived from her employment that Samuel spent in furtherance of his Ph.D. studies during the marriage.

Further, Rachel wonders if she has any right to any of the royalties from a linguistic treatise that Samuel just published. The treatise is being hailed as a major achievement and has led to national recognition of Samuel as a linguist of extraordinary ability. Royalties on the treatise are expected to be approximately $25,000 a year.

What advice should Attorney Atwood provide to Rachel about child support and spousal support (now and in the future), possible grounds for divorce, and the division of the couple's property?

QUESTION 2: Ellen meets Trenton Smith while she is employed as a computer programmer in Trenton's business. Soon after, they move in together, and Ellen gives birth to a daughter Katie. Ellen and Trenton live together with their daughter in the jurisdiction of Greenacre for four years. Their friends and acquaintances believe that they are married, although they have never undergone a marriage ceremony. Ellen uses the name "Smith" for all purposes. The names "Mr. and Mrs. Smith" appear on their mailbox. Ellen and Trenton travel together frequently for purposes of Trenton's business, especially to the jurisdiction of Redacre where Ellen's parents reside and where Trenton has a business supplier. On numerous occasions, they stay in Redacre hotels for business, for periods ranging from three days to three weeks. Unlike Greenacre, Redacre recognizes common-law marriages.

Ellen's and Trenton's relationship begins to be stormy. They have frequent fights about money and about Trenton's indulgent childrearing practices. On one occasion while they are visiting Redacre, Ellen threatens to leave Trenton. Trenton tells her that she cannot leave, because "you are my wife in the eyes of God." She agrees to patch up the quarrel, responding, "I'm as married to you as I ever could be."

Several months after their return to Greenacre, Trenton announces that now he wants to separate. Ellen agrees to move out. She and Trenton enter into a joint custody agreement whereby they agree that Katie will remain in Ellen's physical custody but Trenton will have liberal visitation rights. Ellen and Katie subsequently move to Redacre where Ellen's parents reside and where Ellen has employment.

After Ellen and Katie have been in Redacre for eight months, Trenton files a petition in Redacre for modification to sole custody in his favor. Trenton is angry that Ellen has decided to move in with her new partner, Linda. Katie has written to Trenton that Katie does not like life in Redacre and that she particularly does not like her mother's new girlfriend. Katie is depressed because she misses her best friend from Greenacre. Although Katie is doing well in school and likes her new school, she has not yet made friends there and is sometimes teased about her mother's same-sex relationship. Ellen believes that Trenton's request for custody modification is not justified.

While the custody battle is in progress, Trenton dies intestate, i.e. without a will. Discuss Ellen's claims in the custody dispute and Ellen's claim to Trenton's estate as Trenton's common-law wife.

QUESTION 3: Carl Brady is arrested and charged with armed robbery. Pending his trial, he marries Diana Simpson, a woman he has known for several years. He is convicted and receives a seven-year sentence. At his sentencing, Carl is assigned to Blackacre State Prison, a maximum security facility. When Carl arrives at the prison, he receives a "Resident's Handbook" that explains the procedures and operations of the facility. Among these procedures, the handbook explains the prison's visiting policy:

> Visiting is conducted on Tuesday and Thursday between the hours of 6 P.M. and 9:30 P.M. and on Saturday and Sunday between 8 P.M. and 11 P.M. All residents are permitted 15 hours of visiting each month. A visiting room is provided for inmates and their guests. Limited physical contact is acceptable, subject to supervision by correctional officers in order to ensure the safety and security of the prison. Conjugal visits are not permitted. The introduction of contraband will result in permanent expulsion of a visitor.

Carl presently is 45; Diana is 39. Carl and Diana have often discussed the possibility of having children. However, they are worried about Diana's advancing age, which decreases the likelihood of conception and increases the likelihood of birth defects. They would like to have the opportunity to conceive a child before Carl is released from prison. Carl decides to join a number of other prisoners to challenge the no-conjugal-visit policy.

In the event such a challenge is unsuccessful, Carl and Diana decide to consider the possibility of artificial insemination. He and Diana both agree that Diana will attempt artificial insemination with a third-party donor. Diana consults a gynecologist who agrees to perform the procedure. Carl signs a written consent form. Diana undergoes the insemination, conceives, and gives birth to a little girl, Samantha. She raises the child herself for several years until Carl is released from prison.

Upon his release, Carl takes up residence with Diana and Samantha. Unfortunately, Carl has employment-related difficulties, and he and Diana have difficulty readjusting to each other. Also, Diana learns from Carl's probation officer that Carl was not incarcerated for armed robbery, as he told her. In fact, he was convicted of a felony murder—murder of a policeman during the robbery. Diana is so fed up with Carl generally and so incensed at Carl's deception that she decides to end their relationship. Because of her religious beliefs, she desires to secure an annulment rather than a divorce.

When Diana informs Carl that she has decided to end the marriage, he is furious. He tells her that he "won't give her or Samantha a dime!" Diana has no desire for spousal support for herself, but she does think that Carl should have to support Samantha. When she petitions for divorce and requests child support, Carl counters with the claim that Samantha is not his child, so he does not have to pay child support.

Part A. What constitutional arguments should Carl and the other prisoners raise about the prison's conjugal visiting policy?

Part B. What arguments should Diana raise in her attempt to annul her marriage to Carl?

Part C. What is the basis of Carl's claim refusing to support Samantha? What is the likelihood of his success?

Essay Exam Answers

SAMPLE ANSWER TO QUESTION 1:

Support during the marriage

First, Rachel inquires how she may require Samuel to provide support for her and the children at the present time (in the midst of the marital difficulties). Attorney Atwood should advise Rachel about the jurisdiction's rules on the duty of support. At common law, the husband had a duty to provide support for his dependents, i.e., his wife and children. The husband was required to furnish "necessaries" such as food, clothing, and shelter. In the event that the husband refused to pay, the law permitted indirect enforcement of the husband's duty by enabling a creditor to sue the husband for the costs of these items.

However, because a gender-based duty of support violates equal protection, jurisdictions have changed the common law. Rachel's likelihood of success depends on whether Blackacre follows the common law, has abolished the doctrine, extends liability to both spouses, or imposes primary liability on the serviced spouse. If the jurisdiction follows the common law, Samuel will incur liability for support of his dependents. If the jurisdiction extends liability to both spouses or imposes primary liability on the serviced spouse, Rachel, herself, will incur financial liability for the family expenses.

Rachel faces another problem with efforts to force Samuel to provide for her and the children in the midst of marital difficulties. She may be precluded from obtaining support by the doctrine of nonintervention. This doctrine, enunciated in *McGuire v. McGuire*, holds that a court will not interfere in an ongoing marriage. The doctrine is intended to promote family harmony, and to avoid adjudication of *de minimis* (trivial) issues. At the time Rachel first consults Attorney Atwood, her marriage is still intact, as she has not yet moved into the basement quarters. Thus, the court may refuse to adjudicate the matter.

Rachel can also attempt to obtain support from Samuel for herself and the children by means of civil and criminal actions for nonsupport. Criminal remedies for nonsupport now exist by statute in all states with respect to children, and in many states with respect to spouses as well. However, Rachel faces an additional problem. Statutory remedies for spousal support dictate that relief is available only if the marital parties live apart. Because Rachel is still living with Samuel, she may not be able to benefit from these statutory remedies for her nonsupport.

Support upon divorce

Rachel will also attempt to obtain spousal support and child support from Samuel in the event she decides to seek divorce. At common law, a husband's duty to support his dependents extended to the duty to provide alimony in the event of a divorce. Spousal support was available to the party who was without fault. At common law, then, Samuel would have had a duty to pay Rachel alimony, especially since she had not committed any fault-based act (unless a court interpreted her acts as desertion, see discussion *infra*).

However, *Orr v. Orr* declared that gender-based support requirements upon divorce are unconstitutional. In response to women's liberation and changing gender roles, modern courts take a much more restrictive approach than did the common law to spousal support following divorce. If Blackacre follows the Uniform Marriage and Divorce Act, for example, Rachel will probably be out of luck. UMDA provides that a spouse should receive maintenance only if that spouse lacks sufficient means to support himself or herself "through employment or because of child care responsibilities." Based on this provision, a court is unlikely to award Rachel spousal support because she is currently employed, has been the sole provider for the family for the last eight years, and is in good health. Her only hope would be to argue that she is unable to work because of her child care responsibilities to her infant son. This argument probably will fail because there is no evidence to support it. The infant is cared for at Rachel's place of employment.

Further, it is even possible, based on *Orr*'s invalidation of gender-based duties of support, that Rachel may have to pay Samuel spousal support in the event that they divorce. But, again, if Blackacre follows the UMDA approach, a court may decide against such an award to Samuel because he is able physically to support himself through employment (i.e., he could go out and get a job).

Rachel also desires child support from Samuel, in the event of divorce, for the couple's four children. At common law, the father was primarily liable for the support of his children. However, the modern trend is to consider both parents responsible for the support of their children. Courts, traditionally, based the standard for child support on the needs of the children and the parents' ability to pay. Applying this standard, it seems likely that the court will order Samuel to provide support for his children based on his ability to pay (i.e. he is capable of gainful employment). Perhaps he could pay his support obligations from his book royalties, or else, he would have to find employment.

Rachel's request for child support also depends on Blackacre's guidelines on child support. Federal legislation spearheaded the movement from discretion to guidelines. According to the Child Support Enforcement Amendments of 1984, the Family Support Act of 1988, and subsequent welfare reform legislation (Personal Responsibility and Work Opportunity Act), every state must establish guidelines for child support awards. Application of such guidelines by Blackacre would also support the imposition of liability on Samuel for child support. Because the federal law does not recommend any particular set of guidelines, the actual support ordered under Blackacre's guidelines will depend on which of the three models the jurisdiction has adopted: the income shares model (the most popular), the percentage of income model, or the Melson formula. Under any of these models, it is likely that Rachel will have to pay more toward support of the children than will Samuel, unless his income increases.

Attorney Atwood should also advise Rachel against any attempt by her to condition Samuel's visitation rights on his payment of child support. Most jurisdictions hold that a parent's right to visitation is not dependent on the duty to pay child support. Thus, Rachel may not withhold from Samuel the right to visit the children if Samuel does not pay child support. Atwood should advise Rachel that there are other methods available for the establishment and enforcement of child support awards, even in the event that she leaves Blackacre to reside with her parents. For example, legislation exists to establish child support obligations and to facilitate interstate enforcement of those obligations. All jurisdictions now have adopted the Uniform Interstate Family Support Act (UIFSA) to replace the Uniform Reciprocal Enforcement of Support Act (URESA) and the Revised Uniform Reciprocal Enforcement of Support Act (RURESA). In addition, once Rachel secures a support order, she may be able to resort to various enforcement remedies, such as contempt, income withholding, liens against Samuel's property, suspension of his driver's license. Given that Samuel has little property, the most effective remedy might be to hold him in contempt (if he refuses to pay child support).

Grounds for divorce

Rachel also requests Attorney Atwood's advice about possible grounds for divorce. Rachel might face difficulties if she were seeking a divorce during the fault-based era or if Blackacre's statute specifies that a petitioner must resort to fault-based grounds in some situations, such as in case of a nonconsensual no-fault divorce or covenant marriage. Proof of the traditional grounds for divorce (i.e., adultery, cruelty, and desertion) presents problems for Rachel. Samuel has not committed adultery. Although mental as well as physical acts qualify as cruelty, it is questionable whether Samuel's refusal of support rises to the requisite level of cruelty (i.e., a course of conduct with adverse physical effects). And Samuel has not deserted Rachel. In some jurisdictions, Rachel might be able to rely on nonsupport as one of the miscellaneous fault-based grounds. In fact, Attorney Atwood should advise Rachel (if the jurisdiction retains fault-based grounds) that Samuel might secure a divorce based on Rachel's desertion (i.e., her moving into the basement, without justification, with the intent not to resume cohabitation).

Atwood should advise Rachel that all states today have some form of "no-fault divorce." Although no-fault is interpreted differently in different states, Rachel may not need to establish that Samuel has been guilty of a fault-based ground (unless, as discussed above, the jurisdiction requires fault-based grounds for nonconsensual no-fault divorces or covenant marriage). Instead, depending on Blackacre law, Rachel may be able to petition for divorce on the ground of "irreconcilable differences." Alternatively, depending on the jurisdiction, she may have to show that she and Samuel have been living "separate and apart" for a statutorily designated period of time. In the later event, a question may arise as to whether Rachel's residence in the basement for the past six months constitutes sufficient "living separate and apart."

Rachel's chances of success depend on the jurisdiction's requirements for "living separate and apart." Her six months' residence in the basement may satisfy the requisite time period (which tends to vary in different jurisdictions from six months to two years). More importantly, the term "living separate and apart" refers to both the act of physical separation and the intention to dissolve the marriage. Courts differ as to the relevance of, and interpretation of, these two requirements. Some jurisdictions hold that the spouses have lived "separate and apart" even though they live in the same house (e.g., as did Rachel and Samuel in separate bedrooms). Other jurisdictions require that the spouses maintain separate residences. In terms of intention to dissolve the marriage, some restrictive jurisdictions require that the spouses live apart by mutual consent. Other jurisdictions require that if only *one* spouse forms an intent to dissolve the marriage, that spouse must clearly manifest this intent to the other. If Blackacre is one of these latter jurisdictions and if Rachel and Samuel are not in agreement about living separate and apart, Rachel would have to show that she communicated her intention to terminate the marriage to Samuel in order for the statutory period to begin to run.

Division of property

Attorney Atwood's advice to Rachel about the division of property will depend on which marital property regime Blackacre follows. At common law, jurisdictions traditionally followed the title method, according to which property belonged to the party who has title. If Blackacre follows this approach (which is unlikely because all jurisdictions now have abandoned this approach), the family residence would belong to the spouse(s) whose name(s) appears on the deed. For example, the funds in the bank account, held in Samuel's name, would belong to Samuel.

More likely, the court will divide Rachel and Samuel's property based on equitable distribution principles. The most common marital property regime today is equitable distribution. The objective of this system is a fair distribution, under all the circumstances, of the spouses' property. Under this approach, a court considers a number of relevant statutory factors, such as the duration of the marriage, the age, health, employment of the parties, etc. Although in some jurisdictions, a presumption exists that the most equitable division is an equal division, courts are free to deviate from that presumption if it would lead to a more equitable result.

Alternatively, Blackacre may be a community property jurisdiction. This system, in a minority of states, considers marriage as a partnership to which both parties have contributed equally. Even if Blackacre has adopted this approach, some statutory variations do exist in community property states. For example, whereas a few community property states require an equal division of the community property, others follow a regime of equitable distribution.

Depending on the applicable marital property regime, Rachel may or may not have a claim to certain assets in the division of property. Under equitable distribution, after taking into account the statutory factors (such as Rachel's major financial contributions to the family and Samuel's history of nonsupport), a court might decide to award Rachel a substantial fraction of the marital property. In contrast, in a community property state, based on partnership principles, Samuel might well have an equal right to the marital property. Depending on the jurisdiction, Rachel faces an additional problem in regard to Samuel's bank account: some jurisdictions regard property that was acquired by gift as the separate property of the recipient spouse.

Rachel also may have a claim to Samuel's "enhanced earning capacity" (i.e., profits he derives from his work as a linguistic scholar) to the extent that that earning capacity is attributable to her efforts. During marriage, one spouse may help the other obtain a license, degree, or some other means of enhanced earning capacity (e.g., the acquisition of celebrity status). Courts sometimes must determine whether the enhanced value of a spouse's career is an asset subject to distribution upon dissolution. In one case involving opera singer Frederica von Stade Elkus, the court determined that celebrity status constituted marital property subject to equitable distribution. However, the *Elkus* case is distinguishable because the opera singer's husband's contributions appear to have been greater than Rachel's here: He served as voice coach and photographer, sacrificing his own career to advance hers. Rachel's best argument is that Samuel's new-found status is attributable to her efforts and contributions (financial and otherwise) in maintaining the household and rearing the children so that Samuel could devote his full-time effort to the project. Rachel faces the obstacle that a court might find that Samuel's enhanced earning capacity was personal to Samuel, i.e., attributable to his unique skill and efforts.

Rachel also might have a claim for reimbursement of her efforts involved in "putting hubby through" the Ph.D. program in linguistics. Unfortunately, if Blackacre follows the majority approach, Rachel's claim would not be successful. The majority of jurisdictions refuse to treat professional degrees that represent a spouse's enhanced earning capacity as marital property. If this is the case, Rachel's only hope is that Blackacre is one of the jurisdictions which, instead, attempt to achieve a fair result by taking the degree into account in an award of spousal support. Some courts award "reimbursement alimony" in cases in which one spouse has supported the other through a professional program during the marriage to recompense the supporting spouse for her contributions (monetary and nonmonetary) to the education and training of the other. Reimbursement alimony represents a compromise by courts and legislatures to the harshness of denying relief versus the difficulties of characterization and valuation of a professional degree or license as property.

Rachel might also hope that Blackacre follows the ALI *Principles'* innovative rationale of "loss compensation" for spousal support. Under that approach, a recipient spouse would have to make "compensatory spousal payments" to the donor spouse to compensate for certain losses that the donor spouse experienced during the marriage. Examples of compensable losses include loss of a standard of living. Thus, for example, Rachel might be entitled to compensation upon dissolution for the reduced standard of living she experienced based on her sacrifices to put Samuel through the Ph.D. program in linguistics.

SAMPLE ANSWER TO QUESTION 2:

Ellen's claims in the custody dispute

Ellen and Trenton entered into an agreement to share joint legal custody of Katie. They also agreed that Ellen would have physical custody of the girl. Trenton appears to be basing his claim for modification of the custody agreement on the ground that Ellen's cohabitation with Linda renders Ellen an unfit mother. Traditionally, a parent's cohabitation resulted in a denial of custody. However, according to the modern view, a parent's same-sex sexual conduct is only relevant if it has an adverse effect on the child. To succeed, Trenton must show that Ellen's cohabitation with Linda is having an adverse effect on Katie. Trenton may point to Katie being teased at school as harmful, but absent additional facts, it does not appear that this teasing meets the burden of the necessary degree of harm. Katie's present unhappiness with her life in Redacre is attributable primarily to the move. Being the subject of teasing as a new student is not sufficiently unusual or harmful for children that it would constitute an "adverse effect."

Ellen would also argue that Trenton is unable to meet the requisite standard for a custody modification. The parent seeking modification has the burden of proof. The standard for modification generally is higher than for an initial custody determination because of a judicial concern with avoiding the disruptive effect of changes in children's lives post-divorce. Different jurisdictions apply one of several standards for modification. Depending on Redacre's approach, Trenton may have to establish a material and/or substantial change of circumstances; to show that the "best interests of the child" dictate a modification; or that the modification is necessary because of the presence of serious endangerment of a child's physical, mental, moral, or emotional health. In the last case, if the jurisdiction follows UMDA ("serious endangerment") and Trenton cannot show endangerment, he would have to fulfill a two-year waiting period following the initial decree before he could petition for modification.

Trenton would argue that Ellen's cohabitation with Linda constitutes a "material and/or substantial" change of circumstance because now Ellen has less attention for Katie. Ellen would argue that Katie's life with her mother continues largely as before (i.e., when they left Trenton). She would argue that she still spends considerable time with Katie and does the same caretaking tasks for her as before.

Trenton could argue also that Katie is being seriously endangered, physically and emotionally, because of Linda's living with them. He might charge that the endangerment is moral because Ellen and Linda are lesbians living together without being married. Ellen would counter that no endangerment exists. She might even point to the benefits that have accrued to Katie from Linda's interest in the child. Ellen might also argue that, under *Lawrence v. Texas*, it is unconstitutional to deprive her of custody based on her same-sex relationship with Linda. In *Lawrence*, the Supreme Court held that state sodomy laws banning same-sex, but not opposite-sex, sodomy violate the individual's constitutionally protected liberty and that moral disapproval is not a legitimate interest to justify such differential treatment. However, Trenton might argue that Katie's best interest is a sufficiently compelling state interest to overcome *Lawrence*'s application to the custody context.

Trenton's best hope is that the jurisdiction follows the lowest standard for modification—merely that modification be in the best interests of the child regardless of any change in circumstances. Even so, Trenton would have difficulty meeting this standard because Katie appears to be adjusting to her new life in Redacre. She has been with her mother in Redacre for eight months. She is doing well in school and likes her new school. Modification, which would entail uprooting her at this time, would not be in her best interests.

Trenton might also argue that Ellen's relocation to Redacre where her parents reside and where she has employment constitutes grounds for modification. Jurisdictions employ different standards in relocation cases. According to the strictest standard, Ellen would have to show "exceptional circumstances" that justify the move. She probably would not be able to satisfy this burden unless she can show that she could not find employment in computer programming anywhere else. Ellen would have an easier time establishing the most liberal standard because that standard incorporates a presumption favoring the custodial parent's decision that relocation is in the child's best interests. However, most courts adopt the third approach, i.e., a balancing test that takes into account all relevant factors. If the court follows this approach, Ellen might have a difficult time because the relocation might affect negatively Trenton's ability to visit Katie. Thus, Ellen's claims for custody would depend on Redacre's standard for modification.

Ellen's claim as Trenton's common-law wife

Ellen's claim to share in Trenton's estate as his legal spouse rests on the argument that Ellen was Trenton's common-law wife. A common-law marriage, which is recognized by about a dozen states, requires no marriage ceremony. For a valid common-law marriage, the parties must presently *agree* to enter into a legal marital relationship, *cohabit*, and *hold themselves out* as husband and wife in the community.

To establish that she and Trenton had a valid common-law marriage, Ellen first must establish that she and Trenton agreed to enter into a marital relationship. Although no specific words are required, the couple's words must indicate a present agreement. Ellen would argue that Trenton's statement that she is "[his] wife in the eyes of God" and her response, "I'm as married to you as I ever could be," constitute the present agreement to marry.

Second, Ellen would argue that she and Trenton satisfied the cohabitation requirement. That is, she could show that they lived together in Redacre, a jurisdiction that recognizes common-law marriage. Statutory and case law fail to require a specific period of cohabitation. Ellen and Trenton's short visits to Redacre for purposes of Trenton's business and to visit her parents probably would suffice to establish this element.

Third, Ellen must show that she and Trenton held themselves out as husband and wife. Their conduct probably would satisfy this element. Their friends believed that they are married. And Ellen used Trenton's surname for all purposes. Having met the requisite elements to establish a common-law marriage, Ellen should be entitled to inheritance rights as Trenton's common-law spouse. Alternatively, Ellen might argue that she is justified in a share of Trenton's intestate estate because she was Trenton's "putative spouse." However, this argument would fail. A putative spouse is a marital partner who has a good-faith belief in the validity of the marriage. But, Ellen knew that she was not validly married to Trenton because they had never undergone a marriage ceremony. Therefore, Ellen does not qualify as a putative spouse.

SAMPLE ANSWER TO QUESTION 3:

Part A.

Prisoners' arguments regarding prison's conjugal visiting policy

Carl and the other prisoners would argue, first, that Blackacre State Prison's policy of refusing the inmates conjugal visits violates their constitutional rights. First, the prisoners would argue that the policy infringes their *right to marry* because the right to marry includes a right to engage in sexual intercourse with one's spouse. The United States Supreme Court in *Loving v. Virginia*, *Zablocki v. Redhail*, and *Turner v. Safley* recognized the constitutional right to marry. Those cases declared that the right to marry is a fundamental right. As such, it is subject to strict scrutiny. That is, to survive constitutional challenge, the restriction must be necessary to a compelling state interest (discussed *infra*).

Second, the prisoners would argue that the prison's restriction on conjugal visitation infringes on the *right to privacy*. The Supreme Court in *Griswold v. Connecticut* enunciated the constitutional right of privacy. In invalidating a Connecticut statute prohibiting the use of contraceptives by married couples, the Court held that the right to privacy protected intimate decision making by marital partners. Carl and the other prisoners would argue that the prison policy interferes with this right to privacy, i.e., by infringing on his right to marital intimacy with his wife. The prisoners would argue that this infringement, similar to the infringement on the right to marry, should call for strict scrutiny review (discussed *infra*). They would argue that the Supreme Court in *Griswold*, *Eisenstadt* (both regarding contraceptives), and *Roe v. Wade* and *Planned Parenthood v. Casey* (both regarding abortion), as broadly interpreted, guaranteed a right to procreational freedom. The prisoners would argue that the right to procreation is meaningless if the prison bars access to the means to effectuate that right by banning conjugal visits.

The prisoners' first argument, based on the constitutional protection for the right to marry, would not prevail. The cited cases (*Loving*, *Zablocki*, and *Turner*) did, indeed, establish constitutional protection for the right to marry. However, those precedents concerned the right to *enter into* the marital state. The prison prohibition on conjugal visits does not interfere with a prisoner's right to marry. It prohibits, instead, sexual intimacy with one's spouse.

The prisoners' second argument, based on the alleged infringement with the right of privacy, would also be unsuccessful. The prison would argue that *Griswold* is distinguishable from the present situation. *Griswold* involved the right to make intimate decision making, specifically, regarding contraception. The prison might argue that the prison policy does not interfere with couples' decision making regarding the use of contraceptives. Rather, the policy pertains, instead, to overnight spousal visitation, which implicates security concerns (discussed *infra*).

The prisoners' third argument is that the policy infringes on their privacy rights in terms of their interest in procreation, based on *Griswold*, *Eisenstadt*, *Roe v. Wade*, and *Casey*. Even if the prison were to agree that the ban on conjugal visitation violates the prisoners' procreational freedom, the prison would probably be able to justify the policy by showing that the ban survived constitutional scrutiny. *Roe v. Wade* held that an infringement on the individual's right to procreational freedom (technically, abortion) called for strict scrutiny. Yet, *Casey* held that not all restrictions on abortion call for strict scrutiny—only those that create an undue burden. Applying the *Casey* standard, the prison would argue that the prohibition on visitation does not create an undue burden. That is, the ban does not create a legal obstacle to a prisoner's procreational rights. Rather, the prison would argue that it only creates a delay, i.e., the prisoner may procreate upon release from prison. In other situations, the Supreme Court has upheld the constitutionality of restrictions which merely delay the exercise of constitutional rights (e.g., the waiting period in *Casey*, durational residency periods in *Sosna v. Iowa*). If the policy does not constitute an undue burden, then the prison need only justify the policy by showing that it is rationally related to a legitimate governmental interest.

The prison would have little difficulty meeting this standard. The prison would argue that the ban on conjugal visitation is justified by the legitimate governmental interest in maintaining internal security of the facility. That is, permitting spouses to stay overnight in private visits in the prison entails the serious risk that such persons would bring in weapons or drugs. A ban on conjugal visits serves to minimize this risk. Given that prisoners' rights are considerably circumscribed during incarceration (*Turner*), it is likely that this argument would succeed.

Finally, the prison would have a countervailing argument to the prisoners' argument that the right to procreation is meaningless if the prison bars access to the means to effectuate that right. The prison would find support for their counterargument in an analogy to the abortion funding cases. In *Harris v. McRae*, the Supreme Court held that, although the individual has a constitutional right to an abortion, the state does not have the responsibility to fund that right by the provision of federal Medicaid funds. By extension, the prison would argue that although the individual has a constitutionally protected right to procreate, the state does not have the responsibility of facilitating the exercise of that right. Thus, the prisoners would not prevail in their efforts to invalidate the ban on conjugal visits.

Part B.

Diana's request for an annulment on grounds of fraud

Diana wonders if she might be able to secure an annulment from Carl on the ground of fraud. Carl informed her that he was being imprisoned for armed bank robbery. Instead, she learns from the probation officer that his crime was more serious—felony murder. Diana would argue that Carl's misrepresentation gives her the requisite ground for an annulment of the marriage.

Most states provide that fraud furnishes grounds to annul a marriage. The existence of fraud vitiates the party's consent and makes the marriage voidable at the request of the injured party. Diana faces several problems in her efforts to have the marriage annulled. First, Diana would have to find out which test is used in her jurisdiction to establish fraud. If the jurisdiction relies on the strictest test, the fraud must go to the "essentials" of the marriage, especially if the marriage has been consummated. Other jurisdictions adopt a "material" or "but for" test (similar to the materiality standard for ordinary contracts), requiring that the plaintiff would not have married had she or he known of the misrepresentation.

Diana will have a tough time trying to satisfy either of these two tests. First, Carl's fraud does not appear to go to the "essentials" of the marriage. Case law has interpreted that requirement as referring to sexual intercourse or procreation. Carl's misrepresentation only referred to the nature of his offense, not his ability to have sexual relations or to procreate. In addition, Diana may not be able to meet a "materiality" standard. It is not clear that Carl's statement induced the marriage or that she would have refrained from marrying Carl had she known of the true basis for his criminal conviction. Finally, Diana faces an added problem: misrepresentations of health, wealth, and status, generally, are not legally sufficient bases for annulment. A court might find that Carl's misrepresentation is analogous to a fraudulent representation about social standing. These types of statements are not sufficient to justify annulment of marriage.

Part C.

Carl's refusal to pay child support for Samantha

Carl will not be successful in his efforts to refuse child support for Samantha, the child conceived by Diana by means of artificial insemination with a third-party donor. A husband's consent to the artificial insemination of his wife gives rise to obligations of support for the ensuing child. Carl gave his consent to the insemination while he was in prison. By his consent, he impliedly agreed to support any ensuing child and to assume paternal obligations. Therefore, Carl may not assert Samantha's parentage as a defense to Diana's claim for child support.

Glossary of Terms

This glossary gives definitions for key terms and concepts used in this Outline.

Abortifacient: This herb, product, or implement is used to induce an abortion.

Abrogation: This procedure is the annulment of an adoption by adoptive parents. Despite a concern with the negative impact on the adoptee, courts permit abrogation in some cases (e.g., when the adoptive parents are victims of fraud, such as on the part of an agency).

Absolute divorce: English law, historically, distinguished between "absolute divorce" (our modern idea of divorce) and "divorce a mensa et thoro" (i.e., a legal separation which did not permit the parties to remarry). Absolute divorce was not granted in England until 1857. In contrast, by the nineteenth century in America, all the northern colonies granted judicial divorces.

Adoption: In this legal process, the adoptive parent(s) assume(s) all legal rights and obligations in relation to an adoptee and, thereby, terminates all rights and obligations of the biological parents. The process may also be used in many jurisdictions to adopt an adult (e.g., for inheritance purposes).

Adultery: Adultery, i.e., the act of engaging in sexual relations with someone other than one's legal spouse, is both a criminal act and a fault-based ground for divorce.

Affinity: Affinity (to be distinguished from "consanguinity," which refers to relationships by blood) involves a relationship created by law (e.g., step-relationships, in-law relationships). A marriage between persons who are related by affinity may be invalid depending on the jurisdiction. *See also consanguinity.*

Alienation of affections: This tort claim is based on a third party's intentional interference with the marital relationship. It was only available to husbands at common law.

Alimony: Alimony was the term formerly used to signify payments from one spouse (traditionally the husband) to the other for support either pending the divorce litigation ("alimony pendente lite") or following the divorce. Modern usage has replaced the term with the gender-neutral "spousal support" and "maintenance." Gender-based statutes prescribing that husbands shall pay wives alimony violate equal protection.

Annulment: This judicial declaration specifies that no marriage occurred because of the existence of some impediment. An annulment declares a marriage void ab initio, unlike a divorce which terminates a valid marriage. Annulments were more common during the fault-based era when divorce was difficult to obtain.

Antenuptial agreement: *See premarital agreement.*

Anti-heartbalm legislation: These state statutes (sometimes confusingly called "heart balm acts") abolished claims, such as breach of promise and alienation of affections, because of their sexist, outdated, and extortionate nature.

Anti-miscegenation statutes: These laws, which were declared unconstitutional in *Loving v. Virginia*, prohibited interracial marriages.

Antinepotism policies: These policies, which were originally enacted to prevent public officials from conferring employment on unqualified relatives, prevent a spouse's employer from employing the other spouse (hence, sometimes called "no-spousal employment" policies).

Arbitration: This dispute resolution process (commonly used in the labor context) is sometimes resorted to by marital parties to permit a third party, chosen by the parties, to serve as a decision maker.

Artificial insemination: This reproductive technique, originally used in humans to combat male infertility, results in the introduction of a man's sperm into a woman's uterus.

Assisted conception: This contemporary term refers to methods of new reproductive technology to combat infertility, such as in vitro fertilization, embryo transplants, and surrogacy.

Babyselling: This criminal offense punishes the payment or acceptance of money or other consideration in exchange for the adoption of a child. Some courts and commentators analogize surrogacy to this practice.

Battered child syndrome: This medical condition, discovered by radiologists in the 1960s, refers to injuries to children which are in various stages of healing and inflicted by parents who provide inconsistent causal explanations.

Battered parent profile: This syndrome, which is not widely accepted in evidence by courts, describes the factors (abusive background, chronic stress, past violent actions, etc.) that might explain why a parent is likely to be abusive to children.

Battered woman's syndrome: This syndrome, discovered by psychologist Lenore Walker, describes the nature of the abuse suffered by long-term victims of battering. The modern trend is the acceptance of the admissibility of this evidence to establish a defense in intimate partner violence.

Best interests of the child: These criteria, based on a concern with child welfare, shape the subjective standard for custody and adoption decisions. Many factors (race, religion, sexual orientation, domestic violence, disability) enter into the determination of the child's best interests.

Bigamy: This criminal offense involves being married to more than one spouse at one time, i.e., contracting a second marriage without having terminated legally the prior marriage.

Bilateral divorce: This type of divorce proceeding, in which personal jurisdiction exists over *both* spouses, permits a court to settle property issues incident to the divorce (not just the marriage termination).

Breach of promise to marry: This cause of action, now abolished by many states, permits the imposition of tort liability for the violation of a promise by one person to marry the other.

Capacity: A marriage may be annulled for lack of capacity, i.e., the ability to understand and fulfill a marriage contract. Statutory requirements for capacity include: the parties must be of opposite sexes; married to only one spouse at a time; not related; and above the statutorily defined age. These requirements are distinguished from "state of mind" restrictions, which require that the parties marry voluntarily, without fraud or duress.

Central registry: This database of reported cases of suspected child abuse, established by many states, was intended originally to ascertain the incidence and nature of abuse, to assist professionals to determine whether a child has been previously abused, and to keep track of persons suspected of abuse. Social services agencies also use these registries to preclude individuals with abusive propensities from working in child care.

Civil union: A civil union is a form of domestic partnership that recognizes a legal relationship between same-sex partners. Civil union legislation grants same-sex partners all the same legal rights and obligations as opposite-sex spouses except for the designations "marriage" and "spouse."

Cohabitation: Cohabitation is the state of living together without being formally married, and is generally thought to include sexual intercourse. It is one of several requisite elements of a common-law marriage. (See *infra.*)

Collaborative law: Collaborative law involves an alternative dispute resolution process in divorce by which the parties and their respective lawyers agree to negotiate a settlement without judicial intervention. If either party decides to litigate subsequently, he or she must retain different counsel.

Collusion: The presence of this defense, i.e., a spousal agreement to perpetrate a marital offense (feigned or actual) for the sole purpose of divorce, serves to preclude the plaintiff from securing a divorce.

Comity doctrine: Under this doctrine, an American court may exercise its discretion to recognize a judgment granted by a foreign nation, provided that that judgment was obtained after a fair hearing by a court with jurisdiction over one or both parties. Comity, often relied on to recognize foreign divorces, is distinct from the constitutional requirement of "full faith and credit." (See *infra.*)

Common-law marriage: This form of marriage, followed by approximately a dozen states, requires opposite-sex couples to enter into a present agreement to be married, to cohabit for a period of time in a jurisdiction that recognizes common-law marriages (although the time may be quite brief), and to hold themselves out as husband and wife. Common-law marriage, since it is a valid marriage, must be dissolved by death or divorce before the parties may enter into a subsequent marriage with other parties.

Communal family: This family unit is a group of unrelated people who live together, often forming a single housekeeping unit, who may or may not be regarded as a "single family" for zoning purposes (depending on the jurisdiction). The Supreme Court, in *Boraas v. Belle Terre*, refused to accord this family unit constitutional protection.

Community property: Under this marital property regime based on a partnership model, a husband and wife who reside in a community property jurisdiction are regarded (as of the date of the marriage) as the respective owners of an undivided one-half interest in all property which is acquired following the marriage. Community property is distinct from "separate property." (*See separate property.*) Whereas a few community property states require an equal division of the community property, others follow a regime of equitable distribution. Further, statutes in some community property jurisdictions give their courts authority to include separate property in equitable distribution, whereas other community property states exclude separate property.

Comstock laws: These state and federal laws banned the circulation and importation of "obscene" materials through the national mail at the end of the nineteenth century. "Obscene" materials were defined to include articles for prevention of conception, producing abortion, or other immoral purposes.

Conciliation: This form of alternative dispute resolution consists of marital counseling that is entered into with the object of reconciliation. In the fault era some states established court-connected conciliation services, which now provide mediation services.

Conditional gift: This present, often an engagement ring, is given by a donor on the condition that the donee will perform a future act (such as undergo a marriage). The theory underlying a conditional gift is that if the act upon which the gift is conditioned does not occur, then the donee must return the gift.

Condonation: According to this fault-based defense to divorce, the act of forgiveness by an innocent spouse for the guilty party's commission of a fault-based ground (such as by the resumption of sexual relations following infidelity) precludes the plaintiff from obtaining a divorce.

Confidential marriage: This procedural variation, permitted in some jurisdictions, similar to proxy or common-law marriage, permits a marriage to be entered into without the necessity of fulfilling all the usual requirements (e.g., dispensing with blood tests).

Connivance: This doctrine in the era of fault-based divorce (specifically a fault-based defense) bars a divorce when a spouse participates in or consents to the other's wrongful conduct.

Consanguinity: This term denotes a blood relationship between two persons, such as parent-child, brother-sister, uncle-niece, etc. It is distinguishable from affinity relationships (relations created by law). Almost all jurisdictions have incest statutes that provide criminal sanctions for marriage or sexual intercourse between persons related by consanguinity. In addition, civil restrictions prevent persons thus related from obtaining a marriage license.

Consortium: The cause of action for "loss of consortium" consists of a tortious interference by a third party with a spouse's rights to the services, companionship, affection, and sexual relations of the other spouse. The action was available first only to husbands, but later extended to wives.

Constitutionalization of family law: By this process the United States Supreme Court has applied constitutional doctrine to many areas of family law that were formerly the subject only of state regulation.

Constructive desertion: This fault-based ground for divorce (which is also a fault-based defense) consists of a "guilty" spouse's conduct which, without justification on the part of the "innocent" spouse, causes the innocent spouse to leave or justifies the innocent spouse's departure. Frequently, one spouse's charge of desertion is countered by the other's charge of constructive desertion (i.e., to show that the defendant's departure was justified by the plaintiff's behavior).

Consummation: This term signifies the act of sexual intercourse following a marriage. Consummation became significant in the fault-based era because a higher standard for fraud was required if consummation had occurred in order to annul a marriage (for the reason that the woman had been "sullied").

Covenant marriage: This type of marriage, recognized by statute in a small number of states, makes divorce more difficult to obtain by permitting the spouses to divorce only after a two-year separation or proof of fault. Covenant marriages stem from a reform movement aimed at countering the rising number of divorces and the negative effects of divorce on children.

Coverture: Under this common-law term (from the Norman French), the husband and wife became one legal entity upon marriage. The doctrine is also referred to as the "fiction of marital unity" or "merger." Coverture resulted in significant common-law disabilities for married women (regarding property, contracts, etc.), which were largely eliminated by the nineteenth century Married Women's Property Acts.

Criminal conversation: Under this common-law tort, a husband might seek damages against another man for the latter's interference with the marital relationship. Unlike the tort of alienation of affections, criminal conversation required proof of the tortfeasor's sexual intercourse with the wife.

Cruelty: This fault-based ground for divorce consists of a course of conduct that is so severe as to create an adverse effect on a plaintiff's physical or mental well-being. Although early courts required actual or threatened physical violence, courts subsequently permitted mental cruelty to suffice.

Cryopreservation: This mode of assisted conception, which involves the preservation of embryos by the freezing process, poses issues about the property rights which attach to genetic material.

Defense of Marriage Act (DOMA): This federal law defines marriage as occurring only between a man and a woman, and permits states to exercise discretion to refuse to recognize state marriages. The federal DOMA has encouraged states to adopt their own constitutional or statutory laws, called "baby DOMAs," that refuse to recognize same-sex marriages.

Degenderization of family law: This process, triggered by the women's movement, entails a shift away from traditional gender-specific family roles that characterized the woman as the caretaker of the home and children, and the father as the financial provider. The movement has influenced significantly the substance and terminology of family law.

Desertion: This fault-based ground for divorce consists of conduct on the part of the defendant, which is without consent or justification by the plaintiff, by which the defendant voluntarily departs from the plaintiff or the marital abode with intent not to resume cohabitation. *See also constructive desertion.*

Disability, common law: This signified married women's civil disabilities (or legal inabilities) to work in certain professions, sue or be sued without their husband's consent, execute a contract, make a will, etc. *See also coverture.*

Dispositional hearing: This second stage of a juvenile court proceeding, such as for abuse or neglect (following the first adjudicatory stage), determines the appropriate placement for the child (i.e., with a relative, foster care, return to the home).

Dissolution: The word "divorce," with its gender-based stereotypes and stigma, has been replaced with this more modern usage.

Divorce a mensa et thoro: *See absolute divorce.*

Domestic partnership legislation: This legislation, which has been enacted in a few jurisdictions, extends various degrees of legal protection to same-sex couples, and, occasionally, to some opposite-sex couples as well. It requires public registration of the partnership and formal dissolution of the partnership.

Domestic relations: The older terminology for the substantive field of family law.

Domicile: This legal concept is a prerequisite for the assertion of jurisdiction in many family law matters, such as marriage, divorce, custody, and adoption. At common law, a married woman acquired the domicile of her husband. Domicile includes physical presence plus intent to remain permanently. Although the term generally is distinguishable from "residence" (since a person has only one domicile but may have many temporary residences), some states' durational residency requirements for divorce often are construed so as to be indistinguishable from "domicile." *See also durational residency requirements.*

Dual representation: Commentators and courts criticize this practice of having one attorney represent both spouses in a divorce proceeding as resulting in an inherent conflict of interest. The practice is also referred to as "multiple representation."

Due process, procedural: According to this constitutional guarantee (under the Fourteenth Amendment), the government may infringe life, liberty, or property only if it does so by a procedure that provides adequate notice and an opportunity to be heard before the decision is rendered.

Due process, substantive: According to this constitutional guarantee (under the Fourteenth Amendment), the government may infringe certain fundamental rights (those rights inherent in the concept of "liberty") based only upon a strong justification that survives strict scrutiny.

Durational residency requirements: Durational residency requirements require a divorce petitioner to be a state resident for a specific period of time, varying from a minimum of six weeks to one year. Some states impose durational residency requirements either instead of, or in addition to, a domiciliary requirement. The Supreme Court in *Sosna v. Iowa* held that these state requirements are constitutional.

Ecclesiastical courts: These English courts, historically, asserted jurisdiction over church-related activities and rituals, including marriage and divorce. In the American colonies, marriage and divorce were regarded as secular matters.

Emancipation: This procedure releases a minor from parental care and control. Thus, it enables a child to acquire, for example, the right to retain earnings and to make decisions regarding medical care. Emancipation may occur expressly, such as by parental consent, or implicitly, such as by acts of parental abandonment. At common law, marriage or service in the armed forces resulted in emancipation. A minor may also secure emancipation judicially.

Embryo transplant: In this method of assisted conception, a fertilized embryo is implanted in the uterus of a woman who will bear the child.

Enoch Arden statutes: Named after the protagonist in a Tennyson poem, these statutes constitute a defense to a charge of bigamy. The statutes permit a spouse, who entertains a good-faith belief that her former spouse is dead, to remarry after a statutorily designated period (often five years).

Equal protection: This guarantee, under the Fourteenth Amendment, prohibits the government from denying equal protection under the law. This requirement has been interpreted as meaning that the government must treat alike those persons who are similarly situated.

Equal treatment/special treatment: These two theoretical approaches provide opposing rationales for maternity leave policies. The equal treatment approach signifies that women should be treated equally with men (which would result in "parental" leaves rather than "maternity" leaves, as exemplified in the Family and Medical Leave Act). The special treatment approach signifies that women should receive special protections.

Equitable adoption: By resort to this equitable remedy, courts effectuate an adoption (or effectuate the consequences of an adoption) in cases in which a legal adoption never occurred. The process is sometimes referred to as "virtual adoption." Many cases arise when a foster parent dies and the foster child seeks a determination of inheritance rights. Courts generally apply equitable adoption by resort to either contract theory or estoppel theory.

Estoppel: This doctrine was relevant in the fault-based era when many courts refused to recognize foreign divorces. Such divorces might be protected by means of the estoppel doctrine. That is, a spouse who goes to a foreign country and secures a foreign divorce could be estopped from denying its validity subsequently.

Ex parte divorce: In an ex parte or unilateral divorce, a court has jurisdiction over only one spouse. This enables the court to terminate the marriage but not to adjudicate the financial incidents of the marriage (i.e., property, spousal support).

Failure to thrive: This medical condition, which usually occurs during the first few years of a child's life, is characterized by retarded mental and physical development. It is attributable to physical and/or emotional neglect.

Family and Medical Leave Act (FMLA): Congress enacted this legislation in order to provide employees with gender-neutral leave for reasons of childbirth, adoption, or illness. It provides for three months of unpaid leave to care for infants or seriously ill family members and applies to employers of over 50 employees.

Fault-based divorce: This doctrine permitted divorce to the "innocent" spouse, thereby placing blame for the marital breakdown on the "guilty" spouse who had committed a marital wrong. Traditional fault-based grounds for divorce included: cruelty, adultery, and desertion. Traditional fault-based defenses include: recrimination, connivance, and condonation. Prior to the late 1960s when the movement for no-fault divorce emerged, fault-based divorce was the only type of divorce permitted in the United States.

Federalization of family law: This movement signifies the increasing importance of congressional legislation in matters of family law, such as child support, child custody, child abuse and neglect, paternity establishment, etc.

Fetal Protection Policies: These employment policies, which prohibit women from certain types of employment because of the potential harm that might ensue to the fetus, were declared a violation of Title VII by the Supreme Court in *International Union, UAW v. Johnson Controls.*

Freedom of Access to Clinic Entrances (FACE) Act: Congress enacted this legislation in 1994 to penalize the use of force, threat of force, or physical obstruction to the entrance of abortion clinics. The legislation was enacted in response to violent protests at abortion clinics which reduced women's access to abortion.

Forum shopping: This practice (sometimes referred to as "migratory divorce"), by which a spouse sought to secure a divorce by establishing temporary residence in a jurisdiction with liberal divorce laws, was common during the fault-based era. The practice was also resorted to prior to legalization of abortion and by parents involved in custody disputes.

Free exercise clause: This First Amendment provision prohibits government from interfering with the individual's exercise of his or her religion (religious beliefs or religious conduct).

Full Faith and Credit Clause: This constitutional provision (Article IV, §1) provides that a state shall give full faith and credit to "the public acts, records and judicial proceedings" of other states. The doctrine was especially important, in the fault-based era, to give effect to divorce decrees granted by other states which had jurisdiction over, at least, one of the marital parties. The Clause is also important today in terms of the controversial issue of same-sex marriage: The Clause would appear to dictate that a state must recognize same-sex marriage if validly contracted in another state, but DOMA dictates otherwise.

Fundamental right: For equal protection purposes, fundamental rights are rights that are either explicitly or implicitly guaranteed by the Constitution. For substantive due process purposes, fundamental rights are those rights that are "deeply rooted in our history and traditions" (according to *Griswold v. Connecticut*), and may or may not be explicitly enumerated. They are subject to strict scrutiny review.

Gestational surrogacy (also called "surrogate parenting"): This method of assisted conception consists of a contractual agreement that specifies that a woman agrees to be artificially inseminated with the semen of a man who is not her husband (or fertilized with an egg that is not her own), to carry the fetus to term, and to surrender the child at birth to the contracting party. Some jurisdictions have held such agreements to violate public policy, although courts are increasingly recognizing them as valid under the revised Uniform Parentage Act.

Get: This religious divorce follows Orthodox Jewish practices. The "Get" has been used as a type of spousal blackmail since, without a Get, a marital partner is stigmatized and unable to remarry another Jew, and future children are bastardized.

Goodwill: This constitutes the reputation of a business or profession which predictably will result in future earnings. Similar to other intangible marital assets, it is difficult to divide upon dissolution. Cases wrestle with how to characterize it as a property interest or as personal (i.e., the product of unique skills). Although a division of authority exists, the modern trend is to hold that goodwill constitutes a marital asset subject to distribution.

Guardian ad litem: This individual, who may or may not be an attorney (depending on the jurisdiction), represents a child who is the subject of a child abuse and neglect proceeding or custody dispute.

Hague Convention on Protection of Children and Co-operation in Respect of Intercountry Adoption: This Hague Convention is an international convention dealing with international adoption that attempts to secure the recognition in a member nation of adoptions made in accordance with the Convention.

Hague Convention on the Civil Aspects of International Child Abduction: This Hague Convention is an international treaty that proposes guidelines on international child abduction and attempts to ensure the prompt return of children who have been abducted from their country of habitual residence or wrongfully retained in a contracting nation that is not their country of habitual residence.

Heartbalm acts: *See anti-heartbalm legislation.*

Heartbalm suit: These causes of action provide tort liability for such claims as breach of promise to marry and alienation of affections. Many states have abolished or circumscribed recovery for these actions. *See anti-heartbalm legislation.*

Illegitimate: This term for a child who is born out of wedlock, i.e., to parents who are not married, has been replaced by the less stigmatizing term "nonmarital child."

Incest: Incest signifies marriage or sexual relations between persons who are related by consanguinity or affinity. Incest constitutes both a criminal offense and a civil restriction on marriage.

Incompatibility: This early no-fault ground for divorce eliminated proof of fault.

Independent adoption: This form of adoption is the placement of children with adoptive parents by private (i.e., not state) persons or agencies. Because of the unlicensed nature of the practice, it is the subject of public policy concerns.

Indian Child Welfare Act (ICWA): This federal legislation applies to Native American children in adoption, custody, and child placement proceedings. It mandates a preference for placement of the child with tribal members, absent good cause.

Intermediate scrutiny: This middle-tier test is used by courts to review possibly unconstitutional legislative classifications. The test is used by the United States Supreme Court for gender-based classifications (among others), although some states use strict scrutiny for gender-based classifications.

Interspousal immunity: This common-law doctrine precluded one marital partner from recovering in tort from the other. The preclusion was based on the rationale that the partners constituted one legal entity and that judicial intervention would disturb marital harmony. The majority of courts have abolished the doctrine for intentional and negligent torts.

Interspousal wiretapping: This practice involves electronic surveillance by one spouse of the other within the marital home. Most federal courts hold that liability attaches for interspousal wiretapping under Title III of the Omnibus Crime Control Act.

Intestate succession: An "intestate" is a person who dies without a will. Adopted children generally lose the right to inherit from a biological parent who dies intestate because the adoption terminates the child's former relationship with the biological parent(s). In addition, inheritance law, traditionally, also precluded nonmarital children from inheriting from their father (but not their mother) by intestate succession. The Supreme Court has declared this policy a violation of equal protection in some situations (e.g., *Trimble v. Gordon*).

In vitro fertilization (IVF): In this method of assisted conception, an ovum is removed surgically from a woman and subsequently placed in a laboratory medium with sperm. The resultant embryo is then implanted either in the ovum donor or another woman.

Irreconcilable differences: This no-fault ground for divorce (sometimes termed "irretrievable breakdown") specifies that the marriage is broken but does not place blame on either party.

Joint custody: Joint custody (technically joint legal custody) is a custody arrangement, based on the rationale that children need frequent and continuing contact with both parents following divorce, which confers legal responsibility upon both parents for major childrearing decisions regarding the child's upbringing, health, welfare, and education. "Joint legal custody" is distinguishable from "joint physical custody." That is, parents may share joint legal custody, although the children may reside primarily with one parent.

Learned helplessness: This aspect of the battered women's syndrome is characterized by a depression which affects the victim such that she loses the ability to respond to the physical abuse. It is used to explain to juries why victims do not leave their abusers.

Level of scrutiny: This term refers to the appropriate test that courts use to evaluate laws or legislative classifications that burden constitutional rights. The three tests include: minimal scrutiny (the rational basis test), intermediate scrutiny (substantially related to an important governmental objective), or strict scrutiny (necessary to a compelling interest).

Lex loci: The rule of lex loci (Latin for "law of the place") holds that a marriage which is valid in the place where it was performed is valid everywhere. The major exception to the rule is when a marriage is contrary to public policy.

Licensure: Licensure is one of the formalities states require for entry into marriage. Specifically, states require that parties who desire to marry procure a marriage license, often by applying to a county clerk. The clerk may refuse to issue the license if the information provided by the parties reveals that they are ineligible to marry. *See also solemnization.*

Living separate and apart: This no-fault ground for divorce refers to a physical separation or intention to dissolve a marriage. Courts do not always require that the spouses actually reside in separate homes.

Long-arm statutes: These statutes confer personal jurisdiction over nonresidents who have contacts with the forum which are sufficient to meet the requisites of due process. Prior to the 1970s, many states permitted the assertion of jurisdiction over nonresidents in domestic relations cases by liberal interpretations of their long-arm statutes. Now, many states have revised their long-arm statutes to include specific provisions for the assertion of jurisdiction in claims for spousal support and child support. The United States Supreme Court delineated the scope of due process limitations in *Kulko v. Superior Court* and *Burnham v. Superior Court.*

Maiden name: This term describes a woman's surname at birth. Traditionally, by custom, a woman gave up her maiden name upon marriage and adopted her husband's surname. Modern social mores have resulted in more women retaining their maiden (or "birth") names.

Maintenance: This modern term, used to describe the financial support given by one spouse to the other following divorce, has replaced the former term "alimony."

Marital rape: This act, which was not recognized as a criminal offense until recently by several states, consists of a husband forcing his wife to have sexual intercourse with him against her will.

Marital unity: *See coverture.*

Marriage for a limited purpose: *See sham marriage.*

Married Women's Property Acts: This legislation, enacted in many jurisdictions in the mid- to late nineteenth century, eliminated many of the disabilities which women faced at common law.

Maternity leave: This policy provides women with a temporary leave from employment for the purposes of pregnancy or childbirth. *See equal treatment/special treatment; Family and Medical Leave Act; Pregnancy Discrimination Act.*

Matrimonial Causes Act: England did not permit judicial divorce until this legislation in 1857.

Mediation: Divorce mediation is a process by which the parties themselves, with the help of a third-party mediator, resolve their disputes. Unlike in arbitration, the parties do not cede their authority to a neutral third party to resolve their dispute, but rather make their own agreements with the mediator serving as a facilitator. Some jurisdictions make mediation mandatory (e.g., California for custody and visitation disputes).

Meretricious relationship: This form of relationship (signifying a "sham" marriage) often refers to unmarried opposite-sex couples living together.

Minimal scrutiny: This test is the lowest level of scrutiny that is used by courts to review legislative classifications. It requires only that the challenger prove that the classification is not rationally related to any permissible governmental purpose. Almost any classification can survive minimal scrutiny on the theory that a legislature must have had a sound reason to enact a given law.

Miscegenation: This term refers to the "mixing" of blood of persons of different races. Prior to 1968 when the Supreme Court declared a state anti-miscegenation law unconstitutional, many states had statutes proscribing marriage or sexual intercourse between persons of different races. *See anti-miscegenation statutes.*

Necessaries: These items (e.g., food, shelter, medical care) are deemed by courts to be necessary for basic sustenance. At common law, a husband was responsible for the necessaries of his wife and children and could be charged for payment of necessaries even without the husband's consent.

Ne exeat: This equity writ restrains a person from leaving or removing property from the jurisdiction; it is often used to restrain a parent from removing a child from the jurisdiction.

No-fault divorce: This form of divorce largely eliminates the importance of finding one spouse at fault for the breakdown of the marriage. After first being enacted in California in 1968, it has now been adopted, in one form or another, by all jurisdictions. However, no-fault divorce does not have the same meaning in all jurisdictions: some states permit no-fault divorce only if both parties consent, whereas other states permit it even if only one party desires it. Further, some states define "no fault" to mean that the parties have "irreconcilable differences," but other states define it to signify a marital breakdown that results in the parties' physically living apart for a statutorily defined period of time.

Nonintervention, doctrine of: According to this doctrine, the courts should not interfere in an ongoing marriage to settle disputes between the marital parties. This doctrine, based on a desire to preserve family privacy and marital harmony, has come under severe criticism by law reformers in the context of domestic violence.

Nonmarital child: This modern term is used to describe a child whose parents are not married to each other. The term eliminates the stigma of such traditional terms as "illegitimate" or "out-of-wedlock."

No-spousal employment policies: *See antinepotism policies.*

Nuclear family: This traditional family was composed of husband and wife and their co-resident children. It is now decreasing in importance with the rising incidence of divorce and the growth of alternative family forms.

Open adoption: In this modern form of adoption, the biological parents of a child who is placed for adoption are aware of the identity of the adoptive parents. Similarly, the adopted child is aware of the identity of the biological parents. Occasionally, the biological and adoptive parents may enter into an agreement regarding the adoption such that the biological parent(s) continues to play some role (e.g., visitation) in the child's life.

Out-of-wedlock: *See illegitimate; nonmarital child.*

Palimony: This term refers to a lawsuit, award, or agreement by a member of an unmarried couple who seeks "quasi-spousal support," similar to alimony (hence the name "palimony"). Such claims became popular in the wake of *Marvin v. Marvin,* which held that unmarried couples may enter into express contracts (unless the consideration for these contracts rests on the exchange of sexual services) and implied contracts as well.

Parens patriae: This Latin term (literally "parent of the country") signifies that the state is responsible for the welfare of its vulnerable citizens (such as children). The concept is often invoked when courts assert jurisdiction over abused and neglected children.

Parental privilege to discipline: This right, based on constitutional principles derived from *Meyer v. Nebraska* and *Pierce v. Society of Sisters*, permits parents to discipline their children as part of their protected Fourteenth Amendment "liberty interest" in raising their children as they see fit. However, by statute in many jurisdictions, the force used to administer discipline must be reasonable and for purposes of correction.

Partial-birth abortion: This type of abortion occurs in the late stage of pregnancy (in or after the fifth month). Many states enacted prohibitions on partial-birth abortions. Congress successfully enacted a federal prohibition.

Polygamy: This criminal offense involves having *more than two* spouses at one time, and is distinct from "bigamy," which means having two spouses at one time, and "monogamy," which means having only one spouse. Civil restrictions prevent an individual who is validly married from obtaining a license to marry (again) without terminating the prior marriage.

Post-majority support: This form of child support, after a child reaches the age of majority (18 in most jurisdictions), may be ordered by a court, for example, to require a noncustodial parent to pay for the child's college expenses.

Preemption: This doctrine holds that federal statutes preclude operation of state law on a given subject according to congressional intent.

Pregnancy Discrimination Act: This amendment to Title VII of the Civil Rights Act of 1964 was enacted by Congress in 1978 to address employment discrimination against pregnant employees. The act analogizes pregnancy to a disability by mandating that an employer shall provide the same benefits for pregnant employees as the employer provides to disabled employees. Feminists have criticized the act for its outmoded treatment of pregnancy as a disability.

Premarital agreement: This contract (also called an "antenuptial" agreement), which is executed by prospective spouses, establishes the parties' property rights in the event of death or dissolution.

Presumption of legitimacy: Courts often apply this presumption, which holds that the husband of a married woman is the natural father of any child to whom she gives birth at any time during the marriage. The presumption is based on a desire not to interfere with family harmony. The presumption raises potential problems in the surrogacy situation because the surrogate's husband may thereby acquire parental rights to the child; surrogacy agreements must overcome this presumption.

Primary caretaker presumption: This presumption would accord custody to the parent who has been the child's "primary caretaker" (i.e., performed the majority of caretaking tasks). Although it no longer operates as a presumption, many jurisdictions take primary caretaker status into account in the determination of the best interests of the child.

Private ordering: This principle signifies the ability of the divorcing parties to resolve matters of property and support themselves without judicial intervention. The practice has been on the increase since the 1960s and was triggered by considerable dissatisfaction with traditional dispute resolution processes.

Pro se divorce: In this process, an individual represents himself or herself in a divorce proceeding. Although it makes divorce easier and less expensive, some legal commentators argue that it precludes the divorcing parties from obtaining adequate representation.

Proxy marriage: This procedural variation of the traditional marriage ceremony permits a third party to substitute for the bride or groom. The practice often is permitted in time of war or other conflict, especially to legitimize children.

Putative spouse doctrine: This doctrine protects the property rights upon death or dissolution of an "innocent" spouse by upholding the validity of a marriage provided that that spouse has a good-faith belief in the validity of the marriage. The doctrine is distinguishable from common-law marriage because, in the putative spouse situation, the parties have undergone a marriage ceremony which at least one spouse believes has resulted in a valid marriage.

Recordation: This aspect of the process of getting married follows the solemnization of the marriage. The person who officiates at the wedding signs the marriage certificate and submits it to the county clerk. Recordation occurs when the county clerk registers the marriage so that it becomes part of the public record.

Recrimination: This defense to fault-based divorce barred a divorce when both spouses were found to be at fault. Rationales included: the clean hands doctrine; the availability of divorce only for an innocent spouse; preservation of marriage; and the need to provide economic protection to women by denying divorce so that husbands will continue to provide support. Commentators criticized the doctrine because it denies divorce in cases of marriages which merit termination.

Rehabilitation: Under this modern principle of dissolution, a spouse is awarded only enough spousal support to permit her to become self-supporting. Thus, a court may award a dependent wife enough funds to enable her to obtain education or training to begin a new career or take up a career that she abandoned upon the marriage.

Relation back doctrine: This doctrine has the effect of rendering a marriage that has been nullified judicially to be considered void from inception. As a result, the doctrine may result in reinstatement of a benefit, for example, that was lost because of the relationship.

Religious- (or racial-) matching provisions: These provisions, applicable to adoption, provide that the religion (or race) of the adoptive parents shall match that of the adopted child, whenever possible. The constitutionality of these provisions has been upheld.

Separate property: This term, as used in community property jurisdictions, signifies property that is acquired by a spouse prior to the marriage *and* property acquired after the marriage, by either spouse, by gift, devise, or bequest. Statutes in some community property jurisdictions give courts authority to include separate property in equitable distribution, whereas other community property jurisdictions exclude separate property. *See also community property.*

Separation agreement: This agreement, which is entered into by spouses who have decided to separate (and, usually, to terminate their marriage as well), addresses the financial incidents of the divorce (property, spousal support, etc). It is sometimes referred to as a "settlement agreement."

Settlement agreement: *See separation agreement.*

Solemnization: This is one of the formalities that states require for entry into marriage. All states require solemnization of marriage by an authorized person before witnesses (subject to some exceptions), although no specific form of ceremony is prescribed. *See also licensure.*

Sham marriage: This form of marriage is entered into solely for the convenience of the parties (i.e., not because of genuine affection between them). Cases of immigration fraud are sometimes considered "sham marriages" or "marriages for a limited purpose." That is, one person gives consent to marry the other for a limited purpose (e.g., to enable the other person to qualify for immigration entry status). Congressional legislation addresses such cases of immigration fraud.

Special relationship doctrine: Some courts recognized a federal civil rights cause of action (based on 42 U.S.C. §1983 that imposes liability on governmental officials for deprivation of a constitutional right under color of law) against law enforcement or municipalities for the failure to protect battered women. A cause of action will not arise for failure to provide a specific individual with police protection unless a "special relationship" exists between the governmental agency and the individual, such that the governmental agency assumes an affirmative duty to act on behalf of the injured party, has knowledge of the consequences of inaction, and incurs the injured party's justifiable reliance on the municipality's affirmative undertaking. The Supreme Court limited application of this doctrine in *DeShaney v. Winnebago*.

Spousal support: This modern term is used to describe the financial support provided by one spouse to the other following the termination of a marriage. Traditionally, it was referred to as "alimony."

Strict scrutiny: This level of scrutiny is the highest level of judicial examination that is used to determine the constitutionality of a regulation or act. The test requires that the regulation or act must be necessary to a compelling state interest in order to be upheld. This level of scrutiny is applied to racial qualifications and also to determine whether a fundamental constitutional right has been violated. The Supreme Court has not applied strict scrutiny to sex-based discrimination, although some state courts do so.

Subsidized adoption: This policy provides state funds in order to facilitate the placement of children with special needs, i.e., those children who are hard to place owing to their age, race, or background.

Substantially related to an important governmental interest: This phrase describes the intermediate level of scrutiny, which the Supreme Court has determined (in *Craig v. Boren*) is applicable to review sex-based discrimination. Although higher than the rational basis test, this test is not as rigorous as the strict scrutiny test.

Summary dissolution: This divorce procedure, authorized by statute in many jurisdictions, permits termination of marriage in a relatively short period of time. It often obviates the need for an appearance. Some states provide for the procedure if both parties consent, have no children, have no real property, and have few debts and the marriage is of short duration.

Summary seizure: This disposition, which is sometimes ordered by courts in child abuse and neglect cases, provides for the removal of a child from an abusive home without notice to a parent or parents. Removal of the child, prior to a full hearing, is permitted based on the state's concern that the child is being endangered by immediate or threatened harm. Courts and commentators have expressed constitutional concerns about vagueness of applicable statutes and the arbitrary nature of the practice.

Surrogate motherhood: This method of assisted conception consists of a contractual agreement that specifies that a woman agrees to be artificially inseminated with the semen of a man who is not her husband (or fertilized with an egg that is not her own), to carry the ensuing fetus to term, and to surrender the child at birth to the intended parent(s). Many jurisdictions have held such agreements to be violative of public policy. The most famous surrogacy case is *In re Baby M*. *See also gestational surrogacy*.

Tender years presumption: According to this presumption which came into effect in the mid- to late nineteenth century, courts presume that a child of "tender years" (defined differently in various jurisdictions but generally includes preschool children) should be in the custody of the mother. Modern courts have held that the presumption violates equal protection.

Therapeutic abortion: This type of abortion is undertaken in order to safeguard the mother's mental or physical health. The liberalization of state abortion restrictions began in the 1960s when many jurisdictions adopted the American Law Institute (ALI)'s Model Penal Code abortion provisions liberalizing abortion for pregnancies resulting from rape or incest, for those involving a deformed fetus, and when necessary to safeguard the mother's health.

Transracial adoption: This type of adoption, formerly known as "interracial adoption," refers to an adoption of a child by parents of a different race. Today, it is a highly controversial practice.

Trimester framework: These guidelines for abortion were established in *Roe v. Wade*. The Supreme Court held that, due to the constitutionally protected right to an abortion, the state may not interfere with the abortion decision during the first trimester. However, during the second trimester, the state may regulate abortion in the interest of maternal health. And, after viability, the state may regulate, and even proscribe, abortion in the interests of the protection of potential life. The trimester scheme was subsequently abandoned by the Court.

Undue burden: This standard, by which to evaluate state abortion restrictions, was announced by the United States Supreme Court in *Planned Parenthood v. Casey*. Only those regulations that impose an "undue burden" on the woman's abortion decision will be subject to strict scrutiny. The Court defines undue burden as the placement of a substantial obstacle in woman's path. The *Casey* Court determines that neither the informed consent requirement nor the 24-hour waiting period creates undue burdens, although spousal notification policies do.

Unilateral divorce: *See ex parte divorce.*

Vagueness: This shortcoming renders a classification unconstitutional because the classification fails to alert people as to the specific conduct that is prohibited. That is, it constitutes a violation of due process under the Fourteenth Amendment.

Void marriage: States have substantive requirements regarding capacity which determine marriage validity (restrictions about incest, bigamy, same-sex marriages, etc.). The presence of any of these substantive defects renders a marriage "void," i.e., invalid from its inception.

Voidable marriage: In addition to states' substantive restrictions regarding capacity, jurisdictions also have state of mind requirements for entry into a valid marriage. Unlike substantive defects, which render a marriage void, a defect concerning state of mind renders a marriage "voidable." For example, the existence of fraud or duress vitiates consent and makes the marriage voidable at the request of the injured party.

Waiting period: Many states impose a waiting period (often three to five days) between the time the applicants apply for the license and its issuance in order to deter hasty marriages.

Warnock Committee: This British commission studied the issue of surrogacy and recommended legislation. Their recommendations, which included the prohibition of commercial surrogacy, were codified by Parliament in 1985 as the Surrogacy Arrangement Act.

Wrongful adoption: This doctrine enables an adoptive parent to recover tort damages (similar to an action for misrepresentation) from an adoption agency that fails to disclose fully information about a child's biological parents or prior history.

Table of Cases

References are to pages.

Table of Statutes

Federal Rules of Evidence

Uniform Acts

State Statutes

Subject Matter Index